Donated by
Ian Thomson

Not for loan

OXFORD MONOGRAPHS ON LABOUR LAW

*General Editors*: PAUL DAVIES, KEITH EWING, MARK FREEDLAND

# The European Employment Strategy

## *Labour Market Regulation and New Governance*

*Oxford Monographs on Labour Law*



This series is the first new development in the literature dealing with labour law for many years. The series recognizes the arrival not only of a renewed interest in labour law generally, but also the need for a fresh approach to the study of labour law following a decade of momentous change in the UK and Europe. The series is concerned with all aspects of labour law, including traditional subjects of study such as industrial relations law and individual employment law, but it will also include books which examine the law and economics of the labour market and the impact of social security law upon patterns of employment and the employment contract.

**Titles already published in this series**

*The Right to Strike*
K. D. EWING

*Legislating for Conflict*
SIMON AUERBACH

*Justice in Dismissal*
HUGH COLLINS

*Pensions, Employment, and the Law*
RICHARD NOBLES

*Just Wages for Women*
AILEEN MCCOLGAN

*Women and the Law*
SANDRA FREDMAN

*Freedom of Speech and Employment*
LUCY VICKERS

*International and European Protection of the Right to Strike*
TONIA NOVITZ

*The Law of the Labour Market*
SIMON DEAKIN AND FRANK WILKINSON

# The European Employment Strategy

*Labour Market Regulation and New Governance*

DIAMOND ASHIAGBOR

OXFORD
UNIVERSITY PRESS

OXFORD
UNIVERSITY PRESS

Great Clarendon Street, Oxford OX2 6DP

Oxford University Press is a department of the University of Oxford.
It furthers the University's objective of excellence in research, scholarship,
and education by publishing worldwide in

Oxford New York

Auckland Cape Town Dar es Salaam Hong Kong Karachi
Kuala Lumpur Madrid Melbourne Mexico City Nairobi
New Delhi Shanghai Taipei Toronto

With offices in

Argentina Austria Brazil Chile Czech Republic France Greece
Guatemala Hungary Italy Japan Poland Portugal Singapore
South Korea Switzerland Thailand Turkey Ukraine Vietnam

Oxford is a registered trade mark of Oxford University Press
in the UK and in certain other countries

Published in the United States
by Oxford University Press Inc., New York



First published 2005



British Library Cataloguing in Publication Data
Data available

Library of Congress Cataloging in Publication Data

Ashiagbor, Diamond.
The European employment strategy : labour market regulation and new
governance / Diamond Ashiagbor.
p. cm.
Includes index.
ISBN 0–19–927964–0 (hardback : alk. paper) 1. Unemployed—Legal status, laws,
etc.—European Union countries. 2. Manpower policy—European Union countries. I. Title.
KJE3195.A97 2005
344.2401′137—dc22 2005024547

Typeset by Newgen Imaging Systems (P) Ltd., Chennai, India
Printed in Great Britain
on acid-free paper by
Biddles Ltd., King's Lynn

ISBN 0–19–927964–0 978–0–19–927964–7

1 3 5 7 9 10 8 6 4 2

to my parents, Edward Ashiagbor and
Patience Ashiagbor (née Dosoo): Papa kple Dada,
akpe manyagblor-aɖe nami; miawoe wɔ dɔ, Diamond

# *General Editors' Preface*

The aim of our series of labour law monographs has been to publish works which are, on the one hand, of the highest quality of scholarship, and which are, on the other hand, innovative or experimental, serving to expand the boundaries of the subject or to throw bright new light upon established areas of discussion. We feel quite sure that the present work fully maintains that by now established tradition. It also continues the progressive extension of the series from British to transnational labour law, and from labour law, as previously understood, towards a larger notion of regulation of the labour market.

The particular territory, that of the European Employment Strategy, which Diamond Ashiagbor has chosen for the pursuit of these interests, could scarcely be a more fertile one. In the brief period between Diamond's completion of her book and the writing of this preface, the debate about the role and functioning of the 'European social model' has moved to the centre of the European political stage: and Diamond rightly perceived some time ago that the evolution of the European Employment Strategy is one of the key focal points of that debate.

However, Diamond does not content herself, as all too many of the political actors on this particular stage seem to do, with mere contrasts between 'social' and 'economic' policies. She moves beyond that simplistic analysis in certain key respects. Firstly, she shows, more fully than has previously been achieved, how the displacement of social policy by economically oriented employment policy has occurred in a crucial conjunction with a shift from legislative harmonization to the use of 'soft law' methods of governance.

Secondly, and perhaps even more originally, she shows how, in her own words, 'the main interest, for lawyers, in examining the EU's employment policy . . . is to illuminate the process by which particular conceptions of the way in which the economy functions can lead to certain policy recommendations, goals, or "guidelines" which in turn have implications for law in its regulatory role'.

This is a perfect exposition of the set of issues which labour lawyers need to confront in the increasingly neoliberal political environments in which our discipline is called upon to function and develop. We feel confident that that this book will make a specific and valuable contribution to helping us to do so.

Paul Davies, Keith Ewing, and Mark Freedland
July 2005

# *Preface*

Labour law and social policy have long provided an arena within which key debates over the depth and pace of European integration have taken place. Increasingly, as the European Union's employment policy has matured, employment and economic policy discourses have come to displace discourses around social policy and social law, a displacement which has occurred in tandem with a shift from legislative harmonization to the use of 'soft law' and governance by means of guidelines.

This book charts the evolution of the European Employment Strategy and the new forms of governance to which it has given rise, in particular the 'open method of coordination'. It offers an interdisciplinary exploration of European social law and employment policy, scrutinizing the law and economics of labour market regulation in the European context and responding to the economic critique of traditional notions of social protection. Through a detailed examination of the legal and economic underpinnings of the European Employment Strategy, the book outlines the implications of this strategy for labour law, social protection and industrial relations within the EU.

Using the open method of coordination in the European Employment Strategy as a case study, the book also provides a timely contribution to the growing literature on 'new governance' in the EU. This innovative form of governance has the potential to forge a middle course through the regulatory choices facing the EU: the choice over the appropriate level of regulation in the EU, whether national or supranational; that over the legitimate role for the state in regulating or deregulating the labour market; and ultimately, the choice between centralized harmonization and regulatory competition.

Originally the subject of a PhD thesis, a great many people have helped me in the course of researching and writing this book. I would like to thank my doctoral supervisors, Silvana Sciarra and Karl Klare for their guidance, their insights, their encouragement, and for helping me to clarify what it was I really wanted to say. I am also very grateful for the support received from the editors of the Oxford Monographs on Labour Law series, Paul Davies, Keith Ewing and Mark Freedland; and to Gwen Booth, John Louth and Rebecca Smith at OUP for their support for this project.

Parts of this book and many of the ideas which inform the whole have benefited enormously from conversations with friends and colleagues and discussions with fellow participants in various seminars, workshops and conferences. I received support and encouragement from colleagues at the institutions where I researched and worked during the writing of this book. At the European University Institute in Florence where I undertook my doctorate, I would like to thank Christian Joerges, Bo Stråth and all those who contributed to their lively seminars in the Law Department, as well as fellow members of two EUI discussion groups, on Legal Theory, and Markets and Social Law, for providing a stimulating environment in which to explore my ideas. Thanks must also go to Simon Deakin, for introducing me to the annual 'Pontignano' seminars on comparative labour law, which first gave me the idea of studying law in Tuscany, and for his encouragement since. At the University of Oxford, I am grateful to Jenny Dix, Mark Freedland, Stephen Weatherill and Katja Ziegler at the Institute of European and Comparative Law; and to my colleagues at Worcester College for being so welcoming. At University College London, I have benefited from the help and encouragement of Lizzie Barmes, Lucinda Miller, Jane Holder, Ingrid Boccardi and Jessica Hughes.

During my research I was fortunate to be a visiting scholar at Columbia Law School, with support from the EUI and the Fulbright Commission, which provided a valuable insight into US debates on labour market regulation. I am grateful to my hosts at the Law School's European Legal Center for helping to make my stay in New York both productive and enjoyable. Colleagues at the *Arbetslivsinstitutet* (the Swedish National Institute for Working Life) provided helpful feedback and ideas on the role of Member States in the Employment Strategy.

I also wish to extend my warmest thanks to those friends and family not already mentioned above, for their emotional and intellectual support during this period. Particular thanks must go to Kara Preedy, Caroline Ellis, Gideon Amos, Claire Kilpatrick, Emma Jones, Felicity Spector, Chara Bakalis, Matthew Martin, Patrick Glencross, Danny and Anna Nutakor, Tony and Lizzie Kugbega and Dani Jacobs. Finally, my largest debt is to my family, my parents, Patience and Eddie, and my brother and sister, Richard and Lucy, for their continuing love, support and encouragement.

Diamond Ashiagbor
May Day/Festa del Lavoro, 2005

# *Acknowledgements*

I am very grateful to the following copyright holders for permission to reproduce extracts from previously published material:

D. Ashiagbor, 'Economic and Social Rights in the European Charter of Fundamental Rights' (2004) 1 *European Human Rights Law Review*, at 62–72; published by Sweet & Maxwell/Thomson Publishing Services

D. Ashiagbor, 'The European Employment Strategy and the Regulation of Part-Time Work' in Paul Davies, Mark Freedland and Silvana Sciarra (eds.), *Employment Policy and the Regulation of Part-Time Work in the European Union: A Comparative Analysis* (Cambridge: Cambridge University Press, 2004) at 35–62

D. Ashiagbor, 'Soft Harmonisation: The "Open Method of Coordination" in the European Employment Strategy' (2004) 10:2 *European Public Law*, at 305–32; published by Kluwer Law International

D. Ashiagbor, 'EMU and the Shift from a Social Policy Agenda to an Employment Policy Agenda in European Labour Law' in Lars Magnusson and Bo Stråth (eds.), *From the Werner Plan to the EMU: In Search of a Political Economy for Europe* (Brussels: PIE–Peter Lang, 2001) at 301–25

# *Contents*

# *List of Figures and Tables*

## Figures



## Tables

# *List of Abbreviations*

| | |
|---|---|
| ALMP | active labour market policy |
| BEPG | Broad Economic Policy Guideline |
| BJS | US Bureau of Justice Statistics |
| BLS | US Bureau of Labor Statistics |
| CEC | Commission of the European Communities |
| CEEP | Centre européen des enterprises à participation publique et des enterprises d'intérêt économique général (European association representing public sector employers and employers' organizations) |
| EC | European Community Treaty, 1957 (formerly the Treaty of Rome) |
| ECB | European Central Bank |
| ECJ | European Court of Justice |
| ECOFIN | Economic and Financial Affairs Council of the Council of Ministers |
| ECU | European Currency Unit (now obsolete) |
| EDP | Excessive Deficit Procedure under Stability and Growth Pact |
| EDRC | Economic and Development Review Committee of OECD |
| EEA | European Economic Area |
| EES | European Employment Strategy |
| EFTA | European Free Trade Association (precursor to EEA) |
| EMU | Economic and Monetary Union |
| EPL | employment protection legislation |
| ERDF | European Regional Development Fund |
| ERT | European Round Table of Industrialists |
| ESF | European Social Fund (an ERDF) |
| ETUC | European Trades Union Confederation |
| EU15 | Austria, Belgium, Denmark, Finland, France, Germany, Greece, Ireland, Italy, Luxembourg, the Netherlands, Portugal, Spain, Sweden and the United Kingdom |
| EU25 | As above, plus Cyprus, Czech Republic, Estonia, Hungary, Latvia, Lithuania, Malta, Poland, Slovakia and Slovenia |
| FTE | full-time equivalent (wage, etc) |
| ICT | information and communication technology |
| IGC | Intergovernmental Conference |

| | |
|---|---|
| JIR | Joint Report on Social Inclusion |
| LDC | less-developed country |
| LTU | long-term unemployment |
| MPC | Monetary Policy Committee of the Bank of England |
| NAIRU | non-accelerating inflation rate of unemployment |
| NAP | National Action Plan(s)—from . . . , National Reform Programme(s) |
| NAP/Incl | National Action Plan(s) on Social Inclusion |
| OCA | optimum currency area |
| OECD | Organisation for Economic Cooperation and Development |
| OMC | open method of coordination |
| OOPEC | Office for Official Publications of the European Communities |
| SME | small and medium-sized enterprise |
| TEU | Treaty on European Union |
| TUAC | Trade Union Advisory Committee to OECD |
| UEAPME | Union européenne de l'artisanat et des petites et moyennes enterprises (the employers' organization representing the interests of European crafts, trades and SMEs at EU level) |
| UNICE | Union des Industries des pays de la Communauté européenne (European association representing private sector employers and employers' organizations) |

# *Table of Cases*

## European Court of Justice (chronological)

# *Table of EU Material*

Unless otherwise stated, all documents are published by the Office for Official Publications of the European Communities, Luxembourg

## Treaties

European Community Treaty, 1957 (EC) (formerly the Treaty of Rome)
Treaty on European Union, 1992 (TEU) [incorporating the Social Policy Protocol]
Treaty of Amsterdam, 1997
Treaty of Nice, 2001
Treaty establishing a Constitution for Europe, OJ C 310/1, 16.12.2004

## Commission Communications

*Action for Employment in Europe: A Confidence Pact*, CSE (96) 1 final, 5 June 1996
Commission Communication: *Modernising and Improving Social Protection in the European Union*, COM (97) 102
Commission Communication: *Proposal for Guidelines for Member States' Employment Policies* 1998, COM (97) 497
Commission Communication: *From Guidelines to Action: The National Action Plans for Employment*, COM (98) 316
Communication from the Commission, *Framework on Training Aid* OJ C 343, 11.11.98
Communication from the Commission to the Council, the European Parliament, the Committee of the Regions and the Economic and Social Committee: *The Competitiveness of European Enterprises in the Face of Globalisation—How It Can Be Encouraged*, COM (98) 718 final, Brussels, 20.01.1999
Commission Recommendation for Council Recommendations on the implementation of Member States' Employment Policies, COM (99) 445, Brussels, 8.9.1999
Communication from the Commission to the Council, the European Parliament, the Economic and Social Committee and the Committee of the Regions: *Social Policy Agenda*, COM (2000) 379 final, Brussels, 28.6.2000
Communication from the Commission on the Legal Nature of the Charter of Fundamental Rights of the European Union, COM (2000) 644 final, Brussels, 11.10.2000
Communication on European Social Fund Support for the European Employment Strategy, COM (2001) 16 final/2, Brussels, 23.01.2001
Communication from the Commission to the Council, the European Parliament, the Economic and Social Committee and the Committee of the Regions: *Employment and Social Policies: A Framework for Investing in Quality*, COM (2001) 313 final, Brussels, 20.6.2001
Communication from the Commission to the Council and the European Parliament on an *Open Method Of Coordination for the Community Immigration Policy*, COM (2001) 387 final, Brussels, 11.7.2001
Communication from the Commission to the Spring European Council in Barcelona (Synthesis Report) *The Lisbon Strategy: Making Change Happen*, COM (2002)14 final, Brussels, 15.1.2002

Communication from the Commission to the Council, the European Parliament, the Economic and Social Committee and the Committee of the Regions: *Commission's Action Plan for skills and mobility*, COM (2002) 72 final, Brussels, 13.2.2002

Communication from the Commission: *Taking Stock of Five Years of the European Employment Strategy*, COM (2002) 416 final, Brussels, 17.07.2002

Communication from the Commission: *Streamlining the Annual Economic and Employment Policy Co-ordination Cycles*, COM (2002) 487 final, 3.9.2002

Communication from the Commission: *The Future of the European Employment Strategy (EES): A Strategy for Full Employment and Better Jobs for All*, COM (2003) 6 final, Brussels, 14.1.2003

Communication from the Commission: *Improving Quality in Work: A Review of Recent Progress*, COM (2003) 728 final, Brussels, 26.11.2003

Communication from Commission: *The Implementation of the 2003–05 Broad Economic Policy Guidelines*, COM (2004) 20 final, Brussels, 21.1.2004

Communication from the Commission: *Joint Report on Social Protection and Social Inclusion*, COM (2005) 14 final, Brussels, 27.01.2005

Communication to the Spring European Council, *Working together for growth and jobs: A new start for the Lisbon Strategy*, COM (2005) 24, Brussels, 02.02.2005

Communication from the Commission on the Social Agenda, COM (2005) 33 final, Brussels, 9.2.2005

Commission Communication: *Recommendation/Proposal for Integrated Guidelines for Growth and Jobs* (2005–2008) COM (2005) 141 final, Brussels, 12.4.2005

## Commission Reports

*Follow-up to the Essen European Council on Employment*, COM (95) 74 final

*Employment in Europe 1997, including An Employment Agenda for the Year 2000*, COM (97) 479 final, 01.10.1997

*The Amsterdam Treaty: A Comprehensive Guide* (1998)

*Growth and Employment in the Stability-Oriented Framework of EMU: Economic Policy Reflections in View of the Forthcoming 1998 Broad Guidelines*, II/33/98-EN

*Employment Rates Report 1998: Employment Performance in the Member States*, COM (98) 572 final

*1999 Annual Economic Report. The EU Economy at the Arrival of the Euro: Promoting Growth, Employment and Stability*, COM (1999) 7 final, 20.01.1999

*A Concerted Strategy for Modernising Social Protection*, document drawn up on the basis of COM (99) 347 final

*Commission Report on the Application of the 1995 Guidelines on Aid to Employment*, adopted by the Commission on 21.12.2000

*Report on the Implementation of the 2001 Broad Economic Policy Guidelines*, Brussels, 21.02.2002, ECFIN/16/02-EN

## Economic and Employment Reports

*Employment in Europe 1997, including An Employment Agenda for the Year 2000*, COM (97) 479 final

*Employment in Europe 2001: Recent Trends and Prospects*

*Employment in Europe 2001: Autumn Update 2001*

*Employment in Europe 2002: Recent Trends and Prospects*

*Employment in Europe 2003: Recent Trends and Prospects*
*Employment in Europe 2004: Recent Trends and Prospects*
*European Economy 2004*

## Joint Reports

Commission Draft for the *Joint Employment Report 1997*
*Employment Policies in the EU and in the Member States: Joint Report 1998*
*Joint Employment Report 1999*
*Joint Employment Report 2000*
*Joint Employment Report 2001*, COM (2001) 438 final, 12.9.2001
*Joint Employment Report 2002*
*Joint Employment Report 2003–4*, COM (2004) 24 final
*Joint Employment Report 2004–5*
*Draft Joint Report an Social Inclusion*, Brussels, 12 December 2001, 15223/01
*Joint Report on Social Inclusion 2004*

## Green and White Papers

White Paper on *Completing the Internal Market*, COM (85) 310 final
White Paper on *Growth, Competitiveness, Employment: The Challenges and Ways forward into the 21st Century*, COM (93) 700 final
Green Paper on *European Social Policy: Options for the Union*, COM (93) 551, Brussels, 17.11.1993
White Paper on *European Social Policy: A Way Forward for the Union*, COM (94) 333 final of 27 July 1994
Green Paper: *Partnership for a New Organisation of Work* COM (97) 128 final
*European Governance: A White Paper*, COM (2001) 428, Brussels, 27.7.2001

## Commission: Other

Guidelines on State Aid for Employment, OJ C 334, 12.12.1995
*The European Jobs Summit* available at *http://europa.eu.int/comm/employments_social/elm/summit/en/what/what.htm* [accessed April 2005]
'Introduction to the EES: The Added Value of an Open Method of Co-ordination' available on the Europa website, at *http://europa.eu.int/comm/employment_social/employment_strategy/index_en.htm* [accessed 10 April 2005]
Commission Decision of 11 May 1999 concerning aid granted by Italy to promote employment (2000/128/IC) OJ L 42, 15.02.2000
*Joint Employment Report 2004–5: Background document, Commission Staff Working Paper revised following bilateral and EMCO meetings*
'ESF 2000–2006' available at *http://europa.eu.int/comm/employment_social/esf2000/introduction_en.htm* [accessed 10 April 2005]
*Commission Staff Working Document in support of the report from the Commission to the Spring European Council, 22–23 March 2005, on the Lisbon Strategy of economic, social and environmental renewal*, SEC (2005) 160, Brussels, 28.1.2005

## Regulations

Council Regulation (EC) No 1466/97 of 7 July 1997 on the strengthening of the surveillance of budgetary positions and the surveillance and co-ordination of economic policies, OJ L 209, 2.08.1997

Council Regulation (EC) No 1467/97 of 7 July 1997 on speeding up and clarifying the implementation of the Excessive Deficit Procedure, OJ L 209, 2.08.1997

Regulation (EC) No 1784/1999 of the European Parliament and of the Council of 12 July 1999 on the European Social Fund, OJ L 213, 13.08.1999

Commission Regulation (EC) No 68/2001 of 12 January 2001 on the application of Articles 87 and 88 of the EC Treaty to training aid, OJ L 10/20, 13.1.2001

Commission Regulation (EC) No 69/2001 of 12 January 2001 on the application of Articles 87 and 88 of the EC Treaty to *de minimis* aid, OJ L 10/30, 13.1.2001

Commission Regulation (EC) No 70/2001 of 12 January 2001 on the application of Articles 87 and 88 of the EC Treaty to State aid to small and medium-sized enterprises, OJ L 10/33, 13.1.2001

Commission Regulation (EC) No 363/2004 of 25 February 2004, on the application of Articles 87 and 88 of the EC Treaty to training aid, OJ L 63, 28.02.2004

## Directives

Directive 76/207/EEC on the implementation of the principle of equal treatment for men and women as regards access to employment, vocational training and promotion, and working conditions, OJ L 39, 14.02.1976

Council Directive 93/104/EC of 23 November 1993 concerning certain aspects of the organization of working time, OJ L 307, 13.12.1993

Council Directive 96/34/EC of 3 June 1996 on the framework agreement on parental leave concluded by UNICE, CEEP and the ETUC, OJ L 145, 19.06.96

Council Directive 97/75/EC of 15 December 1997 amending the above, OJ L 10, 16.01.1998

Council Directive 97/81/EC of 15 December 1997 concerning the framework agreement on part-time working concluded by UNICE, CEEP and the ETUC, OJ L 14, 20.01.98

Council Directive 98/23/EC of 7 April 1998 amending the above, OJ L 131, 05.05.98

Council Directive 99/70/EC of 28 June 1999 concerning the framework agreement on fixed-term work concluded by UNICE, CEEP and the ETUC, OJ L 175, 10.07.1999

Council Directive 2000/43/EC of 29 June 2000 implementing the principle of equal treatment between persons irrespective of racial or ethnic origin, OJ L 180/22, 19.7.2000

Council Directive 2000/78/EC of 27 November 2000, establishing a general framework for equal treatment in employment and occupation, OJ L 303/16, 2.12.2000

Directive 2002/14/EC of 11 March 2002 establishing a general framework for informing and consulting employees in the European Community, OJ L 80/29, 23.3.2002

Directive 2002/73/EC of 23 September 2002 amending Council Directive 76/207/EEC on the implementation of the principle of equal treatment for men and women as regards access to employment, vocational training and promotion, and working conditions, OJ L 269/15, 5.10.2002

Directive 2003/10/EC of 6 February 2003 on the minimum health and safety requirements regarding the exposure of workers to the risks arising from physical agents (noise) (Seventeenth individual Directive within the meaning of Article 16(1) of Directive 89/391/EEC) OJ L 42/38, 15.2.2003

## Council Resolutions

Council Resolution of 16 June 1997 on Growth and Employment, OJ C 236, 2.08.1997
Council Resolution of 17 June 1997 on the Stability and Growth Pact, OJ C 236/1, 2.08.1997
Council Resolution of 15 December 1997 on the 1998 Employment Guidelines, OJ C 30/98, 28.01.1998
Council Resolution of 22 February 1999 on the 1999 Employment Guidelines, OJ C 69, 12.03.1999

## Council Decisions

Council Decision of 24 January 2000 establishing the Employment Committee (2000/98/EC), OJ L 29/21, 4.02.2000
Council Decision of 13 March 2000 on guidelines for Member States' employment policies for the year 2000 (2000/228/EC), OJ L 72/15, 21.03.2000
Council Decision of 19 January 2001 on guidelines for Member States' employment policies for the year 2001 (2001/63/EC), OJ L 22/18, 24.1.2001
Council Decision of 18 February 2002 on guidelines for Member States' employment policies for the year 2002 (2002/177/EC), OJ L 60/60, 1.3.2002
Council Decision of 22 July 2003 on guidelines for the employment policies of the Member States (2003/578/EC) OJ L 197/13, 5.8.2003
Council Decision of 4 October 2004 on guidelines for the employment policies of the Member States (2004/740/EC) OJ L 326/45, 29.10.2004

## Council Recommendations

Council Recommendation of 7 July 1997 on the broad guidelines of the economic policies of the Member States and of the Community (97/479/EC) OJ L 209, 2.08.97
Council Recommendation of 6 July 1998 on the broad guidelines of the economic policies of the Member States and of the Community (98/454/EC) OJ L 200/34, 16.7.98
Council Recommendation of 12 July 1999 on the broad guidelines of the economic policies of the Member States and of the Community (1999/570/EC) OJ L 217, 17.8.1999
Council Recommendation of 14 February 2000 on the implementation of Member States' employment policies (2000/164/EC) OJ L 52/32, 25.2.2000
Council Recommendation of 19 June 2000 on the broad guidelines of the economic policies of the Member States and the Community (2000/517/EC) OJ L 210, 21.08.2000
Council Recommendation of 19 January 2001 on the implementation of Member States' employment policies (2001/64/EC) OJ L 22/27, 24.1.2001
Council Recommendation of 15 June 2001 on the broad guidelines of the economic policies of the Member States and the Community (2001/483/EC) OJ L 179/1, 2.7.2001
Council Recommendation of 18 February 2002 on the implementation of Member States' employment policies (2002/178/EC) OJ L 60/70, 1.3.2002

Council Recommendation of 21 June 2002 on the broad guidelines of the economic policies of the Member States and the Community (2002/549/EC) OJ L 182/1, 11.7.2002

Council Recommendation of the 26 June 2003 on the Broad Guidelines of the Economic Policies of the Member States and the Community for the period 2003–2005 (2003/555/EC) OJ L 195, 01.08.2003

Council Recommendation of 22 July 2003 on the implementation of Member States' employment policies (2003/579/EC) OJ L 197/22, 5.8.2003

Council Recommendation of 5 July 2004 on the 2004 update of the broad guidelines of the economic policies of the Member States and the Community (for the 2003–05 period), in CEC, *European Economy No 4/2004*

Council Recommendation of 14 October 2004 on the implementation of Member States' employment policies (2004/741/EC), OJ L 326/47, 29.10.2004

## Council of Ministers: Meetings

2357th Council Meeting, Employment and Social Affairs Ministers, Luxembourg, 11 June 2001, Press Release No. 9397/01

2407th Council Meeting, Economic and Finance Ministers, Brussels, 12 February 2002, Press Release DN: PRES/02/28

2546th Council Meeting, Economic and Finance Ministers, Brussels, 25 November 2003, Press Release No. 14492/03

## European Council: Presidency Conclusions

Presidency Conclusions, Edinburgh European Council, 11 and 12 December 1992, Bulletin of the EC-12/1992

Presidency Conclusions, Essen European Council, 9 and 10 December 1994, Bulletin of the EU-12/1994

Presidency Conclusions, Turin European Council, 29 March 1996, Bull EU-3/1996, 1–8.

Presidency Conclusions, Florence European Council, 21 June 1996, Bull EU-6/1996, 1–23

Presidency Conclusions, Dublin European Council, 13 and 14 December 1996, Bull EU-12/1996, 1–38

Presidency Conclusions, Amsterdam European Council, 16 and 17 June 1997, Bull EU 6/1997, 1–31

Presidency Conclusions, Extraordinary European Council Meeting on Employment, Luxembourg, 20 and 21 November 1997, Bull EU-11/1997, 7–13

Presidency Conclusions, Cardiff European Council, 15 and 16 June 1998, Bull EU-6/1998, 1–35

Presidency Conclusions, Vienna European Council, 11 and 12 December 1998, Bull EU-12/1998, 1–56

Presidency Conclusions, Cologne European Council, 3 and 4 June 1999, Bull EU-6/1999, 7–37

Presidency Conclusions, Tampere European Council, 15 and 16 October 1999, Bull EU-10/1999, 1–16

Presidency Conclusions, Lisbon European Council, 23 and 24 March 2000, Bull EU-3/2000, 7–17

Presidency Conclusions, Santa Maria de Fiera European Council, 19 and 20 June 2000, Bull EU-6/2000, 1–58

Presidency Conclusions, Nice European Council, 7–9 December 2000, Bull EU 12/2000, 1–37

Presidency Conclusions, Stockholm European Council, 23 and 24 March 2001, Bull EU-3/2001, 1–40

Presidency Conclusions, Göteborg European Council, 15 and 16 June 2001, Bull EU-6/2001, 1–43

Presidency Conclusions, Laeken European Council, 14 and 15 December 2001, Bull EU-12/2001, 1–26

Presidency Conclusions, Barcelona European Council, 15 and 16 March 2002, Bull EU 3/2002, 1–56

Presidency Conclusions, Brussels European Council, 20 and 21 March 2003, Bull EU 3/2003, 1–49

Presidency Conclusions, Brussels European Council, 25 and 26 March 2004, Bull EU 3/2004, 1–50

Presidency Conclusions, Brussels European Council, 22 and 23 March 2005, Bull EU 3/2005, 1–39

## European Council: Other

The Reflection Group on the 1996 Intergovernmental Conference, *Reflection Group's Report, Messina 2nd June 1995*

Conference of the Representatives of the Governments of the Member States, Note No 6, CONF/3806/96, 2 April 1996

Conference of the Representatives of the Governments of the Member States, *Report from the Presidency to the European Council*, CONF 3860/1/96, Brussels, 17 June 1996

Conference of the Representatives of the Governments of the Member States, *The European Union Today and Tomorrow: Adapting the European Union for the Benefit of its Peoples and Preparing it for the Future*. A General Outline for a Draft Revision of the Treaties, Brussels, 5 December 1996

Dutch Presidency Conference (1997) *Social Policy and Economic Performance: Employment, Activating the Welfare State and Economic Competitiveness*, Amsterdam 23–25 January 1997

Resolution of the Amsterdam European Council on Growth and Employment, 16 June 1997, OJ C 236, 2.8.1997

Charter of Fundamental Rights of the European Union, adopted by a 'Solemn Proclamation' of the European Parliament, Council and Commission at the Nice European Council in December 2000, OJ C 364/01, 18.12.2000

## European Parliament

European Parliament, IGC Briefing No 37 *Employment and the* IGC (First update: 2nd April 1997)

European Parliament, Intergovernmental Conference Task Force, *White Paper on the 1996 Intergovernmental Conference, Volume II: Summary of Positions of the Member States of the European Union with a view to the 1996 Intergovernmental Conference*

European Parliament, Intergovernmental Conference Task Force, 18 December 1996

European Parliament Directorate-General for Committees and Delegations, Committee on Institutional Affairs, *Initial Analysis of the Treaty of Amsterdam, Based* on a *Provisional Version of the Treaty*, Conf 4001/97 of 19 June 1997

Letter from Elisabeth Gogou and Elmar Brok to Noel Dorr, President of the Conference of the Representatives of the Governments of the Member States, 24 July 1996, CONF 3891/96

European Parliament General Secretariat Working Party, Task Force on the Intergovernmental Conference, *Note on the European Parliament's Priorities for the IGC and the new Amsterdam Treaty: Report and Initial Evaluation of the Results*, 15 July 1997

European Parliament, 'Parliament and EMU', 27 April 1998

European Parliament, *Report on the Commission's Social Policy Agenda*, A5-0291 2000 final, 16 October 2000

European Parliament, Fact Sheets, No 4.8.2. *The European Social Fund*, 1.12.2000

European Parliament, Fact Sheets, No 4.8.3. *Employment Policy*, 23.10.2000

## European Parliament: Resolutions

European Parliament, Resolution on the Dublin European Council of 13 and 14 December 1996, OJ C 33/63, 03.02.1997

European Parliament, Resolution on the application of the open method of coordination, 5 June 2003, OJ C 68 E/604, 18.3.2004

## Proposals

Proposal for a Council Directive establishing a general framework for informing and consulting employees in the European Community, COM (1998) 612 final, Brussels, 17.11.1998

Proposal for a Council Decision on Guidelines for Member States' employment policies for the year 2002, COM (2001) 511 final, Brussels, 12.9.2001

Proposal for a Directive of the European Parliament and the Council on working conditions for temporary workers, COM (2002) 149 final, Brussels, 20.3.2002

Amended proposal for a directive on working conditions for temporary workers, COM (2002) 701 final, Brussels, 28.11.2002

Proposal for a Council Decision on Guidelines for the Employment Policies of the Member States' COM (2003) 176 final, Brussels, 8.4.2003

Proposal for a Regulation of the European Parliament and of the Council on the European Social Fund, COM (2004) 493 final, Brussels, 14.7.2004

## Press Releases

Parliament-Council Conciliation Committee, Press Release, 'Agreement paves the way for the establishment of information and consultation of employees': Brussels, 17 December 2001, 15424/01 (Presse 479)

CEC, 'Pedro Solbes, Member of the European Commission responsible for Economic and Monetary Affairs, Press conference on stability and convergence programmes, Brussels', 30 January 2002 Press Release, SPEECH/02/3330

CEC, Commission assesses the implementation of the 2001 Broad Economic Policy Guidelines, Press Release, IP/02/282, Brussels, 21 February 2002

CEC, 'New streamlined funding for European Social Fund and social policy', Press Release, IP/04/928, Brussels, 15 July 2004

CEC, 'Kok report calls for more determined political action to revitalise Lisbon strategy' Press Release, Brussels, 3 November 2004

CEC, Speech of Vice-President Franco Frattini, Commissioner for Justice, Freedom and Security, SPEECH/05/34, 25 January 2005

CEC, 'Commission launches ambitious Growth and Jobs strategy for the EU', Press Release, IP/05/130, Brussels, 2 February 2005

CEC, 'Question & Answer: A new start for the Lisbon Strategy' MEMO/05/34, Brussels, 2 February 2005

CEC, 'The new Integrated economic and employment guidelines' MEMO/05/123, Brussels, 12 April 2005

CEC, 'President Barroso proposes a new framework to "lock-in" a culture of fundamental rights in EU legislation', Press Release, IP/05/494, Brussels, 27 April 2005

## Eurostat: Statistical Office of the European Communities in Luxembourg

News Release No 78/99, 10 August 1999
News Release No 127/2000, 7 November 2000
News Release No 47/2001, 3 May 2001
News Release No 61/2001, 6 June 2001
News Release No 82/2001, 1 August 2001
News Release No 90/2001, 4 September 2001
News Release No 114/2001, 6 November 2001
News Release No 125/2001, 4 December 2001
News Release No 1/2002, 4 January 2002
News Release No 19/2002, 5 February 2002
News Release No 27/2002, 5 March 2002
News Release No 40/2002, 3 April 2002
News Release No 44/2005, 1 April 2005

## Miscellaneous

Social Protection Committee and the Economic Policy Committee, *Joint report on objectives and working methods in the area of pensions: Applying the open method of coordination*, Report submitted to the Council of the European Union, SOC 469/ECOFIN 334, Brussels, 23 November 2001

Employment Committee, *Making work pay: Facts, figures and policy options*, EMCO/21/091003/EN, 1 October 2003

## National Action Plans

Netherlands: National Employment Action Plan 1998
UK: Employment Action Plan 1998
Netherlands: National Employment action Plan 1999
UK: Employment Action Plan 1999
Netherlands: National Action Plan for Employment 2000
UK: Employment Action Plan for 2000

Belgium: National Action Plan for Employment 2001
France: National Action Plan for Employment 2001
Netherlands: National Action Plan for Employment 2001
UK: Employment Action Plan for 2001
Dutch National Actin Plan: Against Poverty and Social Exclusion, 1 June 2001
France: National Plan for Employment 2002
Netherland: National Action Plan for Employment 2003
UK: National Action Plan for Employment 2003
Belgium: National Action Plan for Employment 2004
Netherland: National Action Plan for Employment 2004
Portugal: National Action Plan for Employment 2004
UK: National Action Plan for Employment 2004

# Introduction

The European Commission's White Paper *Growth, Competitiveness and Employment* of 1993 marked a watershed in the gradual emergence at European Union (EU) level of a policy, or strategy, to tackle the perceived unemployment crisis in the Member States. The high levels of unemployment within (most) EU Member States were seen as creating a problem for the Union as a whole, not only because such levels of unemployment suggest human suffering on a wide scale, lead to a waste of human resources, and threaten the Union's declared aim of social cohesion, but also because high unemployment undermines the Union's core goal of developing and maintaining a competitive market economy.[1] Indeed, the Treaty on European Union (TEU) commits the Union to the promotion of economic and social progress and a high level of employment, whilst the objectives of the Community, as stated in the amended European Community (EC) Treaty, now include the promotion of a high level of employment, a high degree of competitiveness and convergence of economic performance, as well as economic and social cohesion among Member States.[2]

This drive for 'convergence' and 'cohesion', and the process of European integration more generally, have to varying degrees been driven by two—internally contested and overlapping—types of discourse: an economic policy discourse, which has lent support to EC economic regulation, and a social policy discourse which supported EC social regulation.[3] That these two discourses are interlinked owes much to the fact that, since the inception of the European Community, European social policy has been subject to the dictates of the Community's market integrationist rationale, and thus developments in social

[1] 'The economic and social costs of this unemployment are enormous. They include not only the direct expenditure on providing social security support for the unemployed, but also the loss of tax revenue which the unemployed would pay out of income if they were working; the increased burden on social services; rising poverty, crime and ill-health; and the increasing levels of educational under-achievement.' Commission of the European Communities (hereinafter, CEC) White Paper, *Growth, Competitiveness and Employment: The Challenges and Ways Forward into the 21st Century*, COM (93) 700 final (Luxembourg: Office for Official Publications of the European Community (hereinafter OOPEC) 1993) at 127.

[2] Article 2, Treaty on European Union; Article 2, Consolidated Version of the Treaty Establishing the European Community, as amended by the Treaty of Amsterdam.

[3] Mark Freedland, 'Employment Policy' in Paul Davies, Antoine Lyon-Caen, Silvana Sciarra and Spiros Simitis (eds.), *European Community Labour Law: Principles and Perspectives* (Oxford: Clarendon Press, 1996) at 286.

policy have long been justified by reference to the economic goal of market integration.[4] From this interaction between economic and social policy has emerged an employment policy discourse which combines (aspects of) each: the EU's employment policy discourse is concerned not only with labour market efficiency, job creation and the perceived need for labour market flexibility, but also with the citizenship- and rights-based concerns and the desire for social cohesion which have been the hallmark of social policy.

The advent of a discourse around employment policy has, though, had the effect of displacing social policy discourse (albeit the evolving European social policy was mostly employment-related) at a time when social policy had only recently acquired a firmer legal basis in the EC Treaty. This displacement of discourses around social policy by those concerned with employment, can be seen in the Treaty of Amsterdam, in the way in which debates around employment policy dominated the Intergovernmental Conference (IGC) which led to the new Treaty, and also dominated the final text of the amended EC Treaty: the new Title VII on Employment, followed immediately after and was expressly linked to the Title on Economic and Monetary Policy, whereas the Social Policy Title stood somewhat isolated from questions of employment creation or macroeconomic policy. Furthermore, although a change of government in the UK had enabled the then fifteen Member States to agree to the incorporation of the Maastricht Agreement on Social Policy into the body of the EC Treaty,[5] this was 'largely symbolic' since the Social Policy Title contained no new initiatives.[6]

It can thus be said that European employment policy came of age at Amsterdam; informed by social policy as well as by economic policy, but ultimately owing more to the latter. It is against such a backdrop that this book aims to provide a better understanding of the development of, and competing rationales for, the European Employment Strategy. This book is a study of the elaboration of the European Union's strategy to combat unemployment, and how this strategy connects with discourses around the legitimacy and content of EU social policy, as well as discourses around EU economic policy and the wider 'labour market flexibility' debate on the role of labour law in job creation. Drawing upon economic theory and socio-legal methodologies, the book uncovers the legal and economic underpinnings of the European Employment Strategy in order to make explicit the assumptions on which the EU is building

[4] Paul Davies, 'The Emergence of European Labour Law' in William McCarthy (ed.), *Legal Intervention in Industrial Relations: Gains and Losses* (Oxford: Blackwell, 1992), 313–59; Simon Deakin, 'Labour Law as Market Regulation: The Economic Foundations of European Social Policy' in Paul Davies *et al.* (eds), 163–93.

[5] Title XI (formerly Title VIII) Social Policy, Education, Vocational Training and Youth; the Social Policy Agreement is now contained in Articles 136–145 of this Title.

[6] Simon Deakin and Hannah Reed, 'The Contested Meaning of Labour Market Flexibility: Economic Theory and the Discourse of European Integration' in Jo Shaw (ed.), *Social Law and Policy in an Evolving European Union* (Oxford: Hart Publishing, 2000) at 88.

its strategy and to discern what the implications of these assumptions will be for labour law, social protection and industrial relations. The main interest for lawyers in examining the EU's employment policy in the light of its economic and social policy, is to illuminate the processes by which particular conceptions of the way in which the economy functions can lead to certain policy recommendations, goals or 'guidelines', which in turn have implications for law in its regulatory role.

## Approach and structure

The approach adopted by this book involves a synthesis of detailed policy analysis with an interpretative study of the ideological setting in which such policy is developed. A purely doctrinal approach would have been inappropriate to capture the dynamic, multifaceted nature of EU law- and policy-making in the area of employment, and this work accordingly undertakes a *contextual* study of the law and regulatory policy. Such a socio-legal approach has been particularly pertinent to the examination of how economic theory has construed legal regulation of the labour market. In particular, the book draws on theories and methods developed in a number of social science disciplines, primarily from economics, but also makes use of traditional legal analysis. In the context of a study of EU law- and policy-making, this approach has necessitated the application of socio-legal techniques to the law and institutions of the EU in order to uncover the ideological foundations of legal rules, and to explore the role of law in European integration.[7]

Within this overarching approach, the primary method adopted has been a critical re-evaluation of existing data, focusing in particular on the official documentation of the EU institutions, whilst drawing comparisons where appropriate with the documentation of international organizations such as the Organisation for Economic Cooperation and Development (OECD). Of the EU institutions, particular attention has been paid to the Presidency Conclusions of the European Council; Green and White Papers, Communications, Reports and other policy documents of the European Commission; Decisions, Recommendations and Resolutions of the Council of Ministers and of the European Parliament. As the Employment Strategy evolves and matures, the need for legal analysis of its role in European integration becomes ever more apparent. The close scrutiny and interpretation undertaken in this book of the official documentation of the EU and its Member States has therefore made possible new insights into the development of employment policy and its contribution to European integration and polity-building.

[7] Jo Shaw, 'Socio-Legal Studies and the European Union' in Philip A. Thomas (ed.), *Socio-Legal Studies* (Aldershot: Dartmouth, 1997); Donald Harris, 'The Development of Socio-Legal Studies in the United Kingdom' (1983) 2 LS, 315–33.

As mentioned, the process of European integration has drawn from a number of competing and interlinked policy discourses, which I have identified as the economic policy, social policy and employment policy discourses. The theme of this book is the displacement of the 'social' by the 'employment' discourse which has occurred in tandem with the displacement of 'hard' law by 'soft' law. The focus is: *first*, on the economics of labour market regulation and the emphasis given, in the EU discourse, to the link between labour market 'rigidities' and unemployment; *second*, on how European policy-makers have conceptualized the unemployment problem and developed a 'European' employment strategy; and *third*, on the extent to which national labour law systems can be said to be converging or deregulating in their response to the 'labour market flexibility' debate.

This exploration of the development of the EU's employment policy raises a number of questions as to the legitimacy and direction of EU regulation of the labour market; in particular, the tension between state action (intergovernmentalism) and Community competence (supranationalism), and that between regulation and deregulation. First, the question of the choice between national and supranational levels of governance and law-making: there exists a tension between the gradual 'Europeanization' of labour law and employment policy, and the reluctance of Member States to cede sovereignty over an area where the competence or legitimacy of the Community to regulate is far from clear. Second, the choice between regulation and deregulation: are Member States and the Community committed to the idea of a European social model, and if so, to what extent does the path taken by the employment policy agenda in fact necessitate a degree of deregulation in the name of labour market flexibility?

Both themes inform the analysis contained in the substantive chapters. Chapters 1 and 2, in exploring economic arguments for and against labour market regulation, uncover the economic assumptions on which the Employment Strategy is based, and provide a framework of analysis through which to assess the subsequent interaction between EU employment, social and economic policy. Chapters 3 and 4 explore how the Member States' unwillingness to confer competence over employment policy to the EU—in particular, their reluctance to sanction an expansionary fiscal policy and large-scale infrastructure and public works programmes as the route to job creation—resulted in an Employment Strategy which took a particular form and content, resorting to 'soft' rather than 'hard' law mechanisms. Chapters 5 and 6, moreover, shed new light on this tension between levels of governance: the Employment Strategy is examined in terms of the co-existence of several forms of governance, in particular the 'open method of coordination', which serve to blur the sharp distinction between intergovernmentalism and supranationalism.

Finally, the concluding chapter brings these two themes—national versus supranational and state versus market—together, and shows how the Employment Strategy, in giving rise to innovative forms of governance such as the 'open method of coordination', has the potential to forge a middle course through the regulatory choices facing the EU: between full harmonization, on the one hand, and mutual recognition or regulatory competition, on the other.

In detail, the structure of the book is as follows. In order to understand better the theories of unemployment and regulation behind the EU policy on combating unemployment and creating employment, Chapters 1 and 2 undertake a critical analysis of neoclassical economic accounts of the market, which have been opposed to labour market regulation and, drawing upon new institutionalist perspectives, assert the constitutive role of law in (labour) markets. Thus, the question of 'where the boundary line should be drawn' between government regulation and market action, becomes rather an appreciation of the role of 'law' in constructing the 'market'. The deregulatory impetus of the EU's strategy is questioned, in light of the efficiency reasons for labour market regulation offered by new institutional and related perspectives on regulation. Ultimately, however, whilst recognizing the overlap between equity and efficiency reasons for labour market regulation, the book proceeds to a normative argument for labour market institutions and regulation, based on the goals of social justice.

Chapter 3 examines the conceptualization of European unemployment, by means of a comparison between the OECD *Jobs Study*[8] and the Commission's White Paper *Growth, Competitiveness and Employment.* The emergence of a European employment policy is examined in terms of a shift from a 'social policy' agenda to an 'employment policy' agenda, arising out of the interaction between economic and social policy, but owing more to the former, in particular with regard to the perspective adopted on the role of labour market 'rigidities' in unemployment.

Chapter 4 focuses more precisely on the Employment Strategy proper, and in particular on the economic context of the Employment Title. The finding is that the influence of economic policy in the form of the Broad Economic Policy Guidelines and the Stability and Growth Pact; the three-pillar approach of the European Employment Pact, placing economic reform (the Cardiff process) and macro-economic dialogue (the Cologne process) alongside the coordinated employment strategy (the Luxembourg process); and the link between employment and competitiveness—are all factors which strongly suggest a deregulatory agenda for the Employment Strategy. Such emphasis on economic cohesion and convergence, at the expense of social policy and social protection, was thrown into sharp relief following the landmark European Council meeting in Lisbon in 2000,[9] where for the first time since the introduction of the Employment Title, an explicit attempt was made to fully integrate policies on employment, economic reform and social cohesion. Chapter 4, however,

[8] Organisation for Economic Cooperation and Development, *The OECD Jobs Study: Evidence and Explanations* and *Facts, Analysis, Strategies* (Paris: OECD, 1994).

[9] Presidency Conclusions, Lisbon European Council, 23 and 24 March 2000, Bulletin of the EU 3/2000, 7–17.

proceeds to examine the implications of the attempt, post-Lisbon, to reconcile economic with social policy objectives: in the course of integrating economic, employment and social policy, the real significance of Lisbon may well be to signal a *continuation* of hard-headed economic policies (restrictive fiscal policy and liberalization of markets), alongside an acceptance of the importance of social cohesion and social policy, but a version of social policy which is predicated on equalizing the marketability and employability of individuals in the market, rather than protecting them from the market.

Adopting a critical perspective on the new 'open method of coordination', Chapter 5 argues that, through its creative use of soft law mechanisms, the evolving Employment Strategy has the *potential* to fashion a middle course through the regulatory choices facing the EU, between full harmonization, on the one hand, and mutual recognition or regulatory competition, on the other. But difficulties and tensions remain within this approach: I argue that the 'soft' coordination of the open method does in fact have quite a 'hard' impact, placing powerful political pressure on Member States to comply with centrally designed policies, and constraining their policy choices. Further, I question whether—in the context of an explicitly 'hard' economic policy coordination backed by sanctions—a form of governance which eschews centralized social policy norms can adequately ensure a core of social rights, below which no Member State can fall. In other words: how can soft law steer this middle course without resort to hard law mechanisms establishing the normative framework?

Chapter 6 assesses the extent to which the Employment Strategy has 'Europeanized' national policy, through four levels of analysis: *first*, an analysis of the legal significance of the National Action Plans for Employment (NAPs); *second*, an examination of the extent to which the interaction between the Employment Strategy and EMU has given rise to new forms of corporatism in national wage and collective bargaining; *third*, an overview of Member States' NAPs since 1998, concentrating on the extent to which national labour law systems can be said to be converging in their response to the 'labour market flexibility' debate; and *fourth*, a review of the impact of EU internal market law on national employment and social policy. Chapter 6 also focuses on the impact of the Employment Strategy in two Member States, the Netherlands and the UK, or rather, on the interaction between the objectives of EU policy and domestic political agendas for reform of welfare states and labour markets. This involves an assessment of the influence of 'Third Way' thinking on the labour market policy of these two Member States, and a critique of the supply-side agenda which characterizes the 'Third Way', shedding light on how the 'full employment' policies and 'active' welfare state advocated by the EU post-Lisbon may evolve in other Member States.

By way of conclusion, Chapter 7 draws together the main arguments of the book, and refocuses on two sets of issues which highlight the competing approaches to European integration: the tension between intergovernmentalism and supranationalism, and that between regulation and deregulation. Noting the importance of national institutional diversity, I argue that the competition between regimes which such diversity permits requires a sufficiently robust framework of social rights at European level if a form of the European social model is to be preserved.

# 1

# The economics of labour market regulation

## 1. Introduction

The aim of this and the following chapter is to explore legal and economic debates on labour market regulation and the proper role for the law in governing markets, in particular, focusing on the question 'where the boundary line should be drawn' between government regulation and market action. These two chapters serve as a backdrop to the examination, in Chapters 3–6, of the substantive questions with which this book is concerned: the evolution and development of the European Employment Strategy. Accordingly, they will examine how economic theory has construed legal regulation of the labour market, since an understanding of the competing (economic) theories on unemployment in general and the role of labour market institutions in particular, is a necessary preliminary to the discussion of how the *European* unemployment problem has been conceptualized by EU policy-makers.

Whilst much of what follows in this chapter is micro-analytical in nature, this analysis has important implications for the macro-economic questions about the role of the state in regulating the economy at the heart of this book: a review of the economic literature is thus useful in order to understand not only theories as to the regulation of the employment relationship, and the regulation of the wider labour market, but also theories on the regulation of competition between (labour) markets, which will be the subject of the concluding chapter of this book.

The use of new institutionalist economic analysis to critique neoclassical perspectives on regulation is central to this project. Whilst recognizing the limitations of the new institutionalist approach, the chapter uses new institutionalist analysis as a means to evaluate the traditional economic suspicion of labour market regulation, which equates labour market institutions with high unemployment. This critique is fundamental to the discussion of theories of unemployment and the philosophies behind the European Union policy on combating unemployment and creating employment.

Essentially, my engagement with the regulation debate has a normative agenda: whilst it is important to highlight the efficiency-enhancing attributes of certain institutions in the context of the ongoing discourse on labour market deregulation, I conclude that reasons of political economy and the desire to retain social cohesion will mean that efficiency cannot be the only goal.

## 1.1 Law and economics

This discussion of economic theories of labour market regulation will necessitate an exploration of the interaction between the law and the economy. *First*, because the role of regulation in general and law in particular in ordering the economy has been questioned with increasing vigour since the 1970s. This idea has been expressed in a number of ways, but its main manifestation is a radical re-evaluation and ultimate rejection of a role for the state in governing economic activity.[1] *Second*, because I believe there is a connection between those macroeconomic models which see labour market regulation as a cause of unemployment, and a more general critique of labour law (in particular, from within the 'law and economics' tradition) which considers regulation to be an exogenous interference in the workings of the labour market.[2]

I use the phrase 'law and economics' to refer to modern American economic analysis of law, which continues to be dominated by the neoclassical Chicago-school strand. For me, the relevance of a 'law and economics' approach to European law- and policy-making is the way it connects to the paradigm shift which has occurred since the 1970s and 1980s, towards a belief in the efficacy of self-adjusting market mechanisms;[3] in other words, that markets are the most efficient means of coordinating economic activity, without the need for what is considered to be 'damaging' public intervention.[4]

In order to move beyond the Chicago-school dominance of law and economics scholarship, I therefore contrast neoliberal with institutionalist approaches to the debate on regulation, competitiveness and economic performance. One of the insights central to the new institutionalist approach, which I use to challenge the neoliberal perspective on regulation, is the rejection of (some of) the assumptions of a self-regulating market economy, and the acknowledgement that markets are not natural or autonomous phenomena,[5] but are embedded in

[1] See David Campbell and Sol Picciotto, 'Exploring the Interaction Between Law and Economics: The Limits of Formalism' (1998) 18 LS 249–78, at 256; see also, Lars Magnusson and Bo Stråth, 'Introduction' in Lars Magnusson and Bo Stråth (eds.), *From the Werner Plan to the EMU: In Search of a Political Economy for Europe* (Brussels: PIE-Peter Lang, 2001).

[2] Simon Deakin and Frank Wilkinson, 'Labour Law and Economic Theory: A Reappraisal' in Hugh Collins, Paul Davies and Roger Rideout (eds.), *Legal Regulation of the Employment Relation*, WG Hart Legal Workshop Series (London/The Hague: Kluwer, 2000) at 29.

[3] J. Rogers Hollingsworth and Robert Boyer, 'Coordination of Economic Actors and Social Systems of Production' in J. Rogers Hollingsworth and Robert Boyer (eds.), *Contemporary Capitalism: The Embeddedness of Institutions* (Cambridge: CUP, 1997) at 1.

[4] Robert Boyer, 'The Variety and Unequal Performance of Really Existing Markets: Farewell to Doctor Pangloss?' in Hollingsworth and Boyer, n. 3 above, at 56.

[5] William M. Dugger, 'Williamson, Oliver E.' in Geoffrey M. Hodgson, Warren J. Samuels and Marc R. Tool (eds.), *The Elgar Companion to Institutional and Evolutionary Economics: L–Z* (Aldershot: Edward Elgar, 1994) at 380.

social relations.[6] I therefore analyse EU policy with sensitivity to the use of the language of deregulation, where it equates employment protection and labour market institutions with 'rigidities'.

### 1.2 Theories of unemployment and the labour market flexibility debate

European employment and labour market policy provide an important context in which to explore the choice between centralized harmonization and the adoption of minimal standards, a debate which has been conducted since the founding of the European (Economic) Community,[7] a context which will be explored further in Chapter 2. The debate about comparative advantage is a debate not only about the appropriate *forum* for regulation (the state or the supranational level) but the *content* of such regulation (whether it should be minimalist or comprehensive). A significant component of this tension between harmonization and regulatory competition is the labour market flexibility debate. There has existed a very powerful flexibility discourse amongst labour economists, policy-makers and legislators concerned about high unemployment in Europe, who looked with envy—in particular during the 1980s and 1990s—at the achievements of the comparatively unregulated US labour market. The central assumption here is that institutions and legislative interventions impede the ability of the labour market to clear, and that market equilibrium in Europe can be restored through deregulation. The analysis in this chapter of the role of the state in regulating (labour) markets will accordingly be applied in Chapter 2 in order to provide a critique of the labour market flexibility debate.

## 2. The interaction between the law and the economy: neoclassical versus new institutionalist perspectives on regulation

To gain a better understanding of economic theories of unemployment and the effects of labour market regulation, it will be useful to explore the terrain where these two disciplines meet. The 'law and economics' literature is a useful lens through which to view the debates on the role of regulation in ordering the economy, and the specific debate on labour market regulation.

As mentioned in the Introduction, the phrase 'law and economics' is used within this book to encompass the modern American economic analysis of law.

[6] Mark Granovetter, 'Economic Action and Social Structure: A Theory of Embeddedness' (1985) 91 *American Journal of Sociology*, 481–510.

[7] Comité Intergouvernemental Créé par la Conférence de Messine, *Rapport des Chefs de Délégation aux Minstres des Affaires Etrangères* (Brussels, 1956), the 'Spaak Report', summarized in English in 'Political and Economic Planning', *Planning* No 405 (1956).

However, a number of dualities will be employed; in particular, I contrast neoclassical/neoliberal 'law and economics' with an economic analysis of law which owes much to 'new institutionalist' thinking. I propose to draw upon some of the observations of new institutional economics as well as the insights of economic sociology as a means to critique the neoliberal perspective. Rather than rejecting *all* law and economics outright for being too right wing (which, according to David Campbell, is the general response of the socio-legal approach[8]) I will, where appropriate, consider the subject of labour market regulation through the *lens* of economic analysis, albeit with a new institutionalist or sociological emphasis, in order to understand the thinking and motivations of policy-makers who have to an increasing extent internalized the basic tenets of the economic approach.

## 2.1 Classical economics, neoclassical economics and the paradigm shift towards neoliberalism

The old orthodoxy of the mid-twentieth century,[9] which legitimized the belief that economies could be politically governed,[10] seems to have been definitively rejected by economists, and increasingly also by governments, during the course of the 1970s and 1980s. There then followed a paradigm shift towards a neoliberal orthodoxy that economic forces should be given free rein. The experience of political planning and governance of the economy acquired during the two world wars[11] had lent support to (Keynesian) economic theory of the 1950s and 1960s, that public regulation and fine tuning of monetary and fiscal policies could promote 'quasi-full' employment, along a steady growth path.[12] However, such ideas progressively lost credibility in the wake of accelerating unemployment, growing public budget deficits and increasing inflation.[13]

[8] David Campbell, 'The Relational Constitution of Contract and the Limits of "Economics": Kenneth Arrow on the Social Background of Markets' in Simon Deakin and Jonathan Michie (eds.), *Contracts, Co-operation and Competition: Studies in Economics, Management and Law* (Oxford: OUP, 1997) at 308.

[9] 'During the "golden age", Keynes's policy legacy seemed both substantial and secure. Nearly all economists accepted some version of Keynesian macroeconomics and believed that they could model the economy, diagnose its condition and devise appropriate fiscal or monetary interventions.', David Purdy, 'Economic Theory and Policy from the Keynesian Revolution to the Third Way' in Magnusson and Stråth (eds.), n. 1 above, at 114.

[10] Lars Magnusson and Bo Stråth, 'Introduction: From the Werner Plan to EMU: In Search of a European Political Economy. Historical Perspectives and Future Prospects' in Magnusson and Stråth (eds.), n. 1 above, at 27.

[11] Bo Stråth, 'After Full Employment and the Breakdown of Conventions of Social Responsibility' in Bo Stråth (ed.), *After Full Employment: European Discourses on Work and Flexibility* (Brussels: PIE-Peter Lang, 2000) at 13–14.

[12] Robert Boyer, 'The Variety and Unequal Performance of Really Existing Markets: Farewell to Doctor Pangloss?' in Hollingsworth and Boyer (eds.), n. 3 above, at 55.

[13] Stråth, n. 11 above, at 14.

The relevance of this resulting paradigm shift to the debate on labour market regulation and the proper role of law in markets is the extremely sceptical view which neoliberal theory has of legislative or other state 'interference' in markets. These ideas are not entirely new; they derive from the classical economic liberalism of the nineteenth century which 'proclaimed "the market" as the proper guiding instrument by which people should organize their economic lives',[14] and which, in turn, owed a great deal to Adam Smith.[15] Whether expressed in terms of the operation of the 'invisible hand' (Adam Smith), a 'spontaneous order' (Hayek) or a 'self-organizing system' (Paul Krugman),[16] the guiding idea in classical and neoclassical economics is that of a 'free' market: a decentralized market economy coordinated by a price mechanism.

What classical and neoclassical economics share is a belief in individual freedom and market order. Such individual liberty naturally includes economic freedom or *laissez faire*, 'out of which spontaneously emerges a vast and intricate system of cooperation in exchanging goods and services'.[17] It is important to stress the connection between individualism and the invisible hand *laissez faire* assumption:[18] the self-interested activity of individuals, free from artificial constraints and within the framework of the law leads, by a process of 'sifting and winnowing' (as Hayek describes it), to the evolution of a highly differentiated spontaneous exchange order of the market.[19] Also the spontaneous order which results is much more likely to be consistent with productivity than any order which was centrally planned or controlled.[20] To this, Hayek further elaborates the idea of the market as the ideal 'discovery procedure',[21] considering the market as the most efficient mechanism capable of processing the huge amount of disparate information necessary to coordinate the plans of individual economic agents.[22]

What *neoclassical* economics adds to this picture is an assumption of general market clearing.[23] In other words, that a perfectly competitive free market

[14] Arthur MacEwan, *Neo-liberalism or Democracy? Economic Strategy, Markets, and Alternatives for the 21st Century* (London/New York: Zed Books, 1999) at 4.

[15] George J. Stigler, 'The Economist and the State' Presidential Address delivered at the Seventy-Seventh Annual Meeting of the American Economic Association, Chicago, 29 December 1964; reprinted in George J. Stigler, *The Citizen and the State: Essays on Regulation* (Chicago: University of Chicago Press, 1975).

[16] Razeen Sally, *Classical Liberalism and International Economic Order: Studies in Theory and Intellectual History* (London: Routledge, 1998) at 1 and accompanying references.

[17] Sally, n. 16 above, at 17.

[18] Andrew Schotter, *Free Market Economics: A Critical Appraisal* (New York: St Martin's Press, 1985), at 6, discussing Hayek's *Law, Legislation and Liberty* (Chicago: University of Chicago Press, 1976).

[19] Sally, n. 16 above, at 21–3.

[20] Schotter, n. 18 above, at 12.

[21] Friedrich A. Hayek, 'Competition as a Discovery Procedure' in F. A. Hayek, *New Studies in Philosophy, Politics, Economics and the History of Ideas* (Chicago: University of Chicago Press, 1978).

[22] Schotter, n. 18 above, at 39–40.

[23] 'Although the British classical economists saw the removal of mercantilist controls and the establishment of general contract and property rights as providing the basis for the increase in

economy, satisfying certain assumptions, will lead to a competitive equilibrium outcome that is Pareto-optimal,[24] namely where there can be no further change without making some member of society worse off.[25] What this means is that for all commodities, including capital and labour, supply and demand are perfectly balanced by changes in prices: '[t]he result of the millions of transactions mediated by the price mechanism is a general economic equilibrium in which all resources are utilized in the most efficient way possible'.[26] The idea of general economic equilibrium also presupposes other givens, namely, perfect knowledge, stable preferences and rationality on the part of the market participants.[27] In particular, the Chicago-school version of neoclassical economics is based on the assumption that individuals act efficiently in their own interests and that their tastes neither change capriciously nor differ importantly between people. Hence, all differences between, and changes in behaviour of, individuals are assumed to be determined by objective constraints such as prices, costs and income.[28]

The core belief in the rationality of economic self-interest can be found in the works of Adam Smith, but it is debatable whether the classical liberal tradition goes so far as to assume that individuals are entirely rational utility maximizers with perfect knowledge.[29] Adam Smith's analyses of society, economy and polity were extremely complex and subtle, and are thus open to a number of differing

productive capacity... recent research has shown that they made no assumption of general market clearing', Simon Deakin, 'Law and Economics' in Philip A. Thomas (ed.), *Legal Frontiers* (Aldershot: Dartmouth, 1996) at 68.

[24] Schotter, n. 18 above, at 12.

[25] An exchange or situation is Pareto-efficient if it is impossible to change it so as to make at least one person better off (in his own estimation) without making another person worse off (again, in his own estimation). Kaldor–Hicks efficiency (also known as a potential Pareto improvement), on the other hand, holds that an exchange is efficient if it makes one person better off, and that person is capable of compensating the disadvantaged. For a potential Pareto improvement, compensation does not actually have to be made, but it must be possible in principle: see Robert Cooter and Thomas Ulen, *Law and Economics* (Reading, MA: Addison-Wesley, 2000) at 12, 43–4. 'Wealth-maximisation, for Posner, is to be equated with Kaldor–Hicks efficiency': Neil Duxbury, *Patterns of American Jurisprudence* (Oxford: OUP, 1995) at 401.

[26] Fred Block, *Postindustrial Possibilities: A Critique of Economic Discourse* (Berkeley: University of California Press, 1990) at 47.

[27] 'It is also a critical assumption that the preferences of the market participants are stable and formed outside of the transactions. Equilibration requires some fixedness in preferences; were individual preferences to jump around, there is no reason supply and demand should balance.' Block, n. 26 above, at 49.

[28] Anthony I. Ogus and Cento G. Veljanovski, 'Notes' in Anthony I. Ogus and Cento G. Veljanovski (eds.), *Readings in the Economics of Law and Regulation* (Oxford: Clarendon Press, 1984) at 11–12.

[29] Sally, n. 16 above, at 18. It is beyond the scope of this chapter, and of this book, to elaborate further on the argument that classical and neoclassical economics, whilst exhibiting an equally strong preference for a 'spontaneous' market order over a 'constructed' one, nevertheless differ in the divergent emphasis placed on the psychological portrayal of individual behaviour, and notions of rationality and utility. One interpretation of the classical tradition is that, rather than viewing human beings as rational utility-maximizers with perfect knowledge, it 'has a complex and realistic model of man in mind, emphatically not the fantastically unreal postulates of *homo oeconomicus*': ibid.

interpretations.[30] Chicago neoclassical economists, for example, view Smith as a mentor, but one whose starting points require further elaboration.[31] Other contemporary neoclassical economists adopt a less absolutist, or more 'bounded', view of human nature.[32]

Furthermore, Smith's view of the 'invisible hand' which serves to coordinate the activities of individuals, is usually equated with non-interventionism. However a better reading is that he was not advocating unmitigated *laissez faire*,[33] but that '[w]here the individual does not know, or does not have the power to advance, his own interests, Smith feels remarkably free to have the state intervene'.[34] Nonetheless, the paradigm shift to 'radically classical'[35] or neoliberal economics has meant an increased faith in *laissez faire* and, arguably, has also strengthened neoclassical economists' belief in the optimality of markets, and thus the above premise of 'general equilibrium' has become the platform to urge that 'markets become purer and that more realms of society become markets'.[36]

The importance of these distinctions (between the classical liberal tradition and modern Chicago-inspired interpretations of it), lies in the starting point they give to (new) institutional economics (which is, after all, also based on the classical tradition) to offer alternatives to the neoclassical/neoliberal perspective, especially when applied to law. This is of particular importance since the Chicago version of neoclassicalism is arguably 'market-favoring in the extreme',[37] and relies 'somewhat uncritically' on general equilibrium analyses of the market process.[38] Thus, a central insight of the new institutionalist approach, which is used to challenge the neoliberal perspective on regulation, is the rejection of (some of) the assumptions of a self-regulating market. In view of the subtleties in the work of Adam Smith and his contemporaries, this insight can even be traced to classical liberalism:

'the classical liberal case centrally rests on an institutional foundation of law and appropriate public policy at different levels of governance, displaying much greater

[30] Warren J. Samuels, 'Smith, Adam' in Hodgson, Samuels and Tool n. 5 above, at 288.

[31] 'Modern Chicago neo-classical economists endeavoured, among other things, to fill in the gaps which they believed had been left open by Adam Smith. This demanded, most importantly of all, that they explain more precisely than had Smith the rationality of economic self-interest; for, without such an explanation, the conclusion that the public regulation of private economic affairs ought to be kept to a bare minimum would seem inevitably, to those not naturally inclined to such a conclusion, to lack foundation'. Duxbury, n. 25 above, at 367–8.

[32] 'Economists have . . . frequently employed models based on bounded rationality—the limited human capacity to formulate and solve complex problems—and game theory—strategies engaged in by individuals with imperfect information—which do not necessarily generate utility maximizing solutions.' Ogus and Veljanovski, n. 28 above, at 11.

[33] Samuels, n. 30 above, at 290.

[34] Stigler, 'The Economist and the State' n. 15 above, at 40.

[35] Robert Kuttner, *Everything for Sale: The Virtues and Limits of Markets* (New York: Alfred A. Knopf, 1997) at 5.

[36] Kuttner, n. 35 above, at 5.

[37] Oliver E. Williamson, 'Transaction Cost Economics Meets Posnerian Law and Economics' (1993) 149:1 *Journal of Institutional and Theoretical Economics*, 99–118, at 113.

[38] Deakin and Wilkinson, n. 2 above, at 61.

sensitivity to real-life institutional constraints and policy choice than the neoclassical tradition.'[39]

## 2.2 The resurgence of the market: Friedman, Epstein, Posner and Chicago-school law and economics

The Chicago-school variant of neoclassical economic theory, which dominates much law and economics scholarship, is well summed up by Milton Friedman:

'In discussions of economic policy, "Chicago" stands for belief in the efficacy of the free market as a means of organizing resources, for scepticism about government intervention into economic affairs, and for emphasis on the quantity of money as a key factor in producing inflation.'[40]

Specifically, Friedman argues that the scope of government should be limited and its power dispersed.[41] In keeping with the basic premise of Chicago neoclassical economics that the most efficient method of organizing economic activity is through voluntary exchange, the role of government should therefore be confined to maintaining law and order so as to prevent coercion, enforcing contracts voluntarily entered into, defining and enforcing property rights, and the provision of a monetary framework.[42] George Stigler further argues that: 'markets are normally best left to their own devices because neo-classical theory leads us to predict that any attempt at economic regulation is likely to yield unintended and unwelcome consequences'.[43]

Following on from this, Chicago-inspired law and economics therefore has a distinct preference for private ordering over public regulation, and for common law over statute law as a system for the ordering of private affairs.[44] For example, Richard Epstein argues, in terms very similar to those of Milton Friedman, that

'the defense of a common law system is not an assertion that "the market" can handle every social problem. The law of property and the law of torts are strictly required in order to establish the framework of original rights in which voluntary transactions can take place. Nonetheless, the reference to common law solutions throughout this article does reflect a basic intellectual orientation in favor of limited government and the maximization of private autonomy.'[45]

[39] Sally, n. 16 above, at 5.
[40] Milton Friedman, 'Schools at Chicago', *University of Chicago Magazine*, Autumn 1974, 11–16, at 11; quoted in Duxbury, n. 25 above, at 366.
[41] Milton Friedman, *Capitalism and Freedom* (Chicago: University of Chicago Press, 1962) at 2–3.
[42] Friedman, n. 41 above, at 27.
[43] Duxbury, n. 25 above, at 374. See Stigler, 'The Economist and the State', n. 15 above, at 39, 50, 52, 55–7.
[44] Duxbury, n. 25 above, at 312 and 414.
[45] Richard Epstein, 'A Common Law for Labor Relations: A Critique of the New Deal Labor Legislation', (1983) 92 *Yale Law Journal* 1357–1408, at 1359.

The assumption of a self-regulating market economy is implicit in this very strong defence of private autonomy:

'The creation of voluntary arrangements is . . . never an occasion for increased state regulation of private transactions apart from the faithful enforcement of their agreement, be it in employment relations or anything else.'[46]

So-called 'inequality of bargaining power' between employer and employee does not justify a limitation on the parties' freedom of contract through intervention into a contract voluntarily entered into.[47] The case for protecting such freedom of contract rests on the belief in mutual gains through trade or exchange, so that only when bargaining takes place in circumstances where mutual gain is not the probable outcome (such as fraud, misrepresentation and duress—but not economic duress) does Epstein consider it permissible for the law to step in to set that transaction aside.[48] Freedom of contract is essential not only for advancing individual autonomy, but also for promoting the efficient operation of (labour) markets.[49]

In addition to contractual freedom, Epstein also holds private property as sacrosanct. In reviewing the New Deal industrial relations legislation, he roundly attacks decisions under Section 8(1) of the original National Labour Relations Act, which attempted to balance employees' statutory rights to conduct union activity on employers' property, with competing interests of employers: '[a]ny balancing under the Act, however reasonable, quite clearly cuts back on the absolute power to exclude that is the hallmark of any system of private property'.[50] As is apparent, Epstein's 'simple rules for a complex world' consist almost entirely of private law; no explicit system of public law is envisaged, as this would amount to an interference with individual freedom.

Richard Posner's approach, on the other hand, in making greater use of price theory, 'is essentially law seen through the eyes of the Chicago neo-classical economist'.[51] Posner begins from the core neoclassical assumption that

[46] Epstein, n. 45 above, at 1366. [47] Ibid., at 1371–2.

[48] Richard Epstein, *Simple Rules for a Complex World* (Cambridge, MA: Harvard University Press, 1995) at 80–81. See also Epstein, 'The Optimal Complexity of Legal Rules' University of Chicago, John M. Olin Law & Economics Working Paper No. 210 (2nd Series), April 2004, especially at 7–8.

[49] Richard Epstein, 'In Defense of the Contract at Will' (1984) 51 *Chicago Law Review*, 947–82, at 951. Epstein also notes that one way to argue for the contract at will is to insist on the importance of freedom of contract as an end in itself (at 953). However, this is generally *not* what Chicago (lawyer) economists argue, since their starting point is efficiency. As Cass Sunstein points out, '[t]he classical liberal position is based on a conception of private entitlement, not on a desire to promote aggregate economic welfare. Under this approach, if a system based on entitlements promotes "efficiency", that is a fortunate coincidence, but it is not the motivating force behind the system.' Cass Sunstein, 'Rights, Minimal Terms, and Solidarity: A Comment' (1984) 51 *Chicago Law Review*, 1041, at footnote 12.

[50] Epstein, n. 45 above, at 1389. For a critique of the NLRA's treatment of employers' property rights as 'natural' rather than 'conventional' (ie a creation of law), see Karl E. Klare, 'Workplace Democracy and Market Reconstruction: An Agenda For Legal Reform' (1988) 38:1 *Catholic University Law Review*, 1–49, at 45–9. [51] Duxbury, n. 25 above, at 397.

individuals are rational maximizers,[52] an assumption which leads him systematically to the conclusion that the quest for economic efficiency, or wealth maximization as he calls it, constitutes the underlying logic of a substantial range of legal activity.[53]

'Wealth maximisation, as defined, is achieved when goods and other resources are in the hands of those who value them most, and someone values a good more only if he is both willing and able to pay more in money (or in the equivalent of money) to have it.'[54]

The notion of efficiency bound up in the concept of wealth maximization,[55] provides Posner with a 'powerful analytical tool' for deriving a system of optimal government.[56] Posner is an 'economic libertarian'[57] in that he uses economic theory to identify what he considers to be the appropriate boundaries of the state: namely a minimum state, with the role of government limited to intervening to correct 'serious market failures'.[58] The next section will consider what the implications of this view of an essentially self-regulating market economy are for the role of law, in those limited cases where the market can be said to have 'failed'.

## 2.3 The Coase Theorem: regulatory and deregulatory implications

A common source of both neoclassical law and economics, and new institutional economics, is the Coase Theorem.[59] I wish in this section not merely to analyse the implications of the Theorem for the development of law and economics scholarship,[60] but also to elaborate on how the dominant strand (and even the

[52] '[M]an is a rational maximiser of his ends in life': Richard Posner, *Economic Analysis of Law* (Boston: Little, Brown & Co., 1973) at 1.

[53] William Scheurman, 'Free Market Anti-Formalism: The Case of Richard Posner' (1999) 12:1 *Ratio Juris*, 80–95, at 83.

[54] Ronald Dworkin, 'Is Wealth a Value?' (1980) 9:2 *Journal of Legal Studies*, 191–226, at 191. Dworkin's article is extremely critical of wealth maximization, nevertheless his definition of the term is endorsed by Richard Posner in 'The Value of Wealth: A Comment on Dworkin and Kronman' (1980) 9:2 *Journal of Legal Studies*, 243–52, at 243.

[55] That is, the Kaldor-Hicks standard of efficiency, rather than Pareto efficiency: 'Under the Kaldor-Hicks definition of efficiency . . . a reallocation of a resource is efficient if it enables the gainers to compensate the losers, whether or not they actually do so. This is equivalent to wealth maximization.' Posner, n. 54 above, at 244.

[56] Francesco Parisi, 'Introduction: The Legacy of Richard A. Posner and the Methodology of Law and Economics' in Francesco Parisi (ed.), *The Economic Structure of the Law: The Collected Economic Essays of Richard A. Posner* (Cheltenham: Edward Elgar, 2000) at xvi.

[57] Richard A. Posner, 'Law and Economics *is* Moral' (1990) 24:2 *Valparaiso University Law Review*, 163–73, at 165.

[58] Posner, n. 57 above, at 166.

[59] Simon Deakin and Jonathan Michie, 'The Theory and Practice of Contracting' in Simon Deakin and Jonathan Michie (eds), *Contracts, Co-operation and Competition: Studies in Economics, Management and Law* (Oxford: OUP, 1997) at 3.

[60] Of perhaps equal importance—in particular for the development of new institutional economics—is Coase's earlier work 'The Nature of the Firm' (1937) 4 *Economica* (NS), 386–405; reprinted in Coase, *The Firm, the Market and the Law* (Chicago: University of Chicago Press, 1988) at ch. 2. Subsequent references are to the 1988 version.

new institutionalist perspective) within law and economics is inextricably linked to the debate during the last quarter of the twentieth century and the early twenty-first over the proper role for the state in regulating markets.[61]

The Coase Theorem[62] challenges the Pigovian assumption[63] that government intervention (by means of taxation or regulation) is desirable when 'externalities' occur.[64] An 'externality' is defined as the (negative or positive) effect of one person's decision on someone who is not a party to that decision.[65] The traditional Pigovian approach was to say that where such 'harmful effects'[66] or 'uncompensated dis-services'[67] are caused to third parties who are not parties to a transaction, then the costs of remedying them should be 'internalized', namely, borne by those who incur them. Rejecting the argument that the presence of externalities constitutes a *prima facie* case for governmental intervention in a market economy, Coase instead argued that this problem may be better solved by the market or the firm.[68] This is because the initial (mis)allocation of resources, including 'harmful effects', can be fully cured in the market through bargaining:[69]

'It is always possible to modify by transactions on the market the initial legal delimitation of rights. And, of course, if such market transactions are costless, such a rearrangement of rights will always take place if it would lead to an increase in the value of production.'[70]

In other words, 'the law which assigns property rights and liability does not matter as long as transaction costs are nil; bargaining will result in an efficient outcome no matter who bears the burden of liability'.[71] This would seem to suggest suspicion of government intervention or regulation to deal with the problem of externalities, and as Deakin and Wilkinson point out, one (widely adopted) interpretation of the Coase Theorem is that 'since efficiency depends

[61] As Simon Deakin puts it, '[t]he revival and growth of interest in economic theories of law is closely bound up with contemporary policy debates over regulation versus deregulation, the process of privatisation and the appropriate role of the state in ensuring the efficient delivery of public services.' Deakin, 'Law and Economics', n. 23 above, at 66. See also Campbell and Picciotto, n. 1 above, at 256.

[62] Coase's conclusions were formalized by George Stigler, who coined this phrase, in *The Theory of Price*, 3rd edition (New York: Macmillan, 1966) at 113: 'The Coase theorem . . . asserts that under perfect competition private and social costs will be equal'.

[63] A.C. Pigou, *The Economics of Welfare* (London: Macmillan, 1932); discussed in R.H. Coase, 'The Firm, the Market and the Law' 20 ff; and 'The Nature of Social Cost' 133 ff., both in Coase, *The Firm, the Market and the Law* (Chicago: University of Chicago Press, 1988).

[64] Coase, 'The Firm, the Market and the Law', n. 63 above, at 24. [65] Ibid.

[66] Coase prefers this term to 'externalities'; Coase, n. 63 above, at 27.

[67] Coase, 'Notes on the Problem of Social Cost' in Coase, n. 63 above, at 179.

[68] Coase, 'The Problem of Social Cost' in Coase, n. 63 above, at 118.

[69] 'If one assumes rationality, no transaction costs, and no legal impediments to bargaining, *all* misallocation of resources would be fully cured in the market by bargains.' Guido Calabresi, 'Transaction Costs, Resource Allocation, and Liability Rules—A Comment' (1968) 11 *Journal of Law and Economics*, 67–73.

[70] Coase, 'The Problem of Social Cost' in Coase, n. 63 above, at 114.

[71] Robert Cooter, 'The Cost of Coase' (1982) 11 *Journal of Legal Studies*, 1–33, at 14.

above all on the capacity of agents to contract at low cost, the law should seek to reduce barriers to exchange and to give as wide an ambit as possible to unqualified property rights and to freedom of contract'.[72] However, the analysis contained in 'The Problem of Social Cost' is not as straightforward as this, as Coase himself has subsequently clarified, in two important respects. First, the Coase Theorem does not *inherently* suggest a 'deep skepticism as to the desirability of government intervention'.[73] To say as much would be a 'misleading statement' of Coase's views.[74] Indeed, 'The Problem of Social Cost' argues that

'[d]irect governmental regulations will not necessarily give better results than leaving the problem to be solved by the market or the firm. *But equally*, there is no reason why, on occasion, such governmental administrative regulation should not lead to an improvement in economic efficiency.'[75]

It is arguable, as the new institutionalist economists have shown, that what the Coase Theorem does is not so much to advocate a particular policy, but rather to suggest a method of determining policy.[76] Instead of dictating 'where the boundary line should be drawn'[77] between governmental regulation and market action, the Coase Theorem is perhaps better understood as suggesting 'what the economic approach to the problem should be'.[78]

Second, and more crucial, is the treatment of transaction costs within the Coase Theorem. In the above quotation, Coase explains how any misallocation can be cured in the market through bargaining '*if such market transactions are costless*' (emphasis added) but goes on to recognize that the world of zero transaction costs is 'a very unrealistic assumption'.[79] Transaction costs, '[n]arrowly conceived, . . . refer to the costs of making, monitoring, and enforcing contracts . . . but, more broadly, they can be thought of as including any kind of barrier to efficient, decentralized exchange'.[80]

What are the implications of the Coase Theorem for the development of law and economics scholarship? A core paradox in Coase's work is that, whilst accepting that the world of zero transaction costs is an unobtainable goal, the

72 Deakin and Wilkinson, n. 2 above, at 36.

73 This was the interpretation of Coase's writings offered by A. W. Brian Simpson in 'Coase v. Pigou Reexamined' (1996) 25 *Journal of Legal Studies*, 53–97, at 58.

74 Ronald Coase, 'Law, Economics and A. W. Brian Simpson' (1996) 25 *Journal of Legal Studies*, 103–9, at 106.

75 Coase, 'The Problem of Social Cost' in Coase, n. 63 above, at 118; emphasis added.

76 Michael Swygert and Katherine Earle Yanes, 'A Primer on the Coase Theorem: Making Law in a World of Zero Transaction Costs' (1998) 11 *DePaul Business Law Journal*, 1–42, at 26.

77 Coase, 'The Problem of Social Cost' in Coase, n. 63 above, at 119.

78 Ibid. See also Deakin and Wilkinson, n. 2 above, at 38: 'A better view is that the Coase theorem does not dictate any particular position with regard to the efficiency of labour law regulation. It certainly does not point with any clarity to deregulation as the preferred option'.

79 Coase, 'The Problem of Social Cost' in Coase, n. 63 above, at 114.

80 Deakin and Michie, n. 59 above, at 5, references omitted. See also Robert Ellickson's taxonomy of transaction costs in 'The Case for Coase and Against "Coaseanism"' (1989) 99 *Yale Law Journal*, 611–29, at 614–15.

theory *first* accepts the traditional methodology of neoclassical economics based on the assumption of zero transaction costs, and *then*, leads to the inescapable conclusion that the design of social institutions should be aimed at the reduction of transaction costs.[81] As a result, although Coase has taken pains to point out that transaction costs do matter,[82] nevertheless, the Coase Theorem has become a starting point for (lawyer) economists who have been reluctant to move beyond the 'zero transaction costs postulate',[83] and thus assume that empirical markets will tend to be markets at zero transaction costs.[84] Alternatively, since perfectly efficient markets are markets which have zero transaction costs, namely, where the information gathering, communication and negotiation necessary for a market transaction are costless, the challenge, in real life, is to reduce such costs, ideally to zero, without reducing the value of the goods produced or exchanged. The role of the law thus becomes to analyse each legal situation in order to effect the maximum reduction in these costs.[85] And from this position, we arrive at the scepticism towards government intervention which Coase denied was implicit in the Coase Theorem: if the role of law is defined as seeking to reduce barriers to exchange—the view of the majority of law and economics scholars—this would imply 'a legal regime of minimal regulation, since any constraint on freedom of disposition and freedom of contract can be read as reducing competitive intensity and introducing market distortions'.[86]

### *2.3.1 Chicago-school economics and the Coase Theorem*

Perhaps unsurprisingly, the Chicago-school interpretation of the Coase Theorem uses it to justify a regime of minimal regulation. The position is well summed up by Richard Posner: '[h]ostility to public intervention in markets beyond what is defensible in strict wealth-maximisation terms is . . . a leitmotif of Coase's work'.[87] Posner argues that, '[w]hen the costs of private coordination are prohibitive, the law may step in by specifying property rights or imposing liability'.[88] But by this he means common law, not statute or other forms of state regulation, since the common law not only should, but actually does, support efficient markets, thus precluding the need for state intervention: 'common law judges have tried, whether consciously or not, to assign property rights and fashion liability rules in such a way as to prevent or at least minimize misallocations

[81] Campbell and Picciotto, n. 1 above, at 253.

[82] Coase, 'The Firm, the Market and the Law' in Coase, n. 63 above, at 26.

[83] Campbell and Picciotto, n. 1 above, at 262

[84] See Ellickson's critique of the tendency of law and economics scholars to downplay 'transactional frictions': Ellickson, n. 80 above, at fn 21 and related text.

[85] Coase, 'The Problem of Social Cost', n. 63 above, at 114–8; see also Ian Ward, *An Introduction to Critical Legal Theory* (London: Cavendish Publishing, 1998) at 128.

[86] Deakin and Michie, n. 59 above, at 6.

[87] Richard Posner, 'Ronald Coase and Methodology' (1993) 7:4 *Journal of Economic Perspectives*, 195–210, at 201. But compare Ronald Coase, 'Coase on Posner on Coase' (1993) 149:1 *Journal of Institutional and Theoretical Economics*, 96–8, at 97: 'I regard the concept of "rational utility maximization" as meaningless'.

[88] Posner, n. 87 above, at 202.

due to the presence of prohibitive transaction costs'.[89] Thus, (common law) legal rules should be used to ensure that the costs of a transaction are apportioned so as to 'mimic' as closely as possible what would have occurred in a hypothetical perfect market: 'in short, interventionism is to be used for the sake of *laissez faire*'.[90] The idea that the common law should 'mimic' what the market would have done, but for high transaction costs, leads Posner to conclude that legal rights ought to be conferred on the party who values them the most, that is, on the highest bidder.[91]

At the risk of contributing to a possibly fruitless quarrel over which school (Chicago or new institutionalist) is the true heir to Coase, it is nevertheless useful to explore alternative interpretations of what the Coase Theorem means for the state's proper role in regulating markets. Although he has expressed dissatisfaction with some of the ways in which his theories have been (mis)applied or misunderstood by successive economists,[92] it is not entirely clear that Coase wishes to be 'rescued' from Chicago. As David Campbell puts it, 'Coase's institutionalism *saves* neo-classical assumptions'; it 'permits lengthy discussion of the conditions for the plausibility of those assumptions, without, crucially, ever questioning them!'[93] Whilst Coase was undoubtedly working within the paradigm of neoclassical economics,[94] his work does nevertheless provide a basis from which to abandon or modify some of its basic tenets, as the new institutionalist economists have done. In particular, Coase is anxious to avoid some of the 'hyperreality'[95] which so often characterizes neoclassical economics:

'The world of zero transaction costs has often been described as a Coasian world. Nothing could be further from the truth. It is the world of modern economic theory, one which I was hoping to persuade economists to leave.'[96]

[89] Ibid., at 201. Elsewhere, Posner argues: '[i]n settings in which the cost of voluntary transactions is low, common law doctrines create incentives for people to channel their transactions through the market.... In settings in which the cost of allocating resources by voluntary transactions is prohibitively high, making the market an unfeasible method of allocating resources, the common law prices behaviour in such a way as to mimic the market'. Richard Posner, *Economic Analysis of Law*, 4th edn (Boston: Little, Brown & Co, 1992) at 252.

[90] Neil Duxbury, 'Is There a Dissenting Tradition in Law and Economics?' (1991) 54: 2 MLR, 300–11, at 310.

[91] Posner, n. 52 above, at 18. See also Duxbury, n. 25 above, at 390.

[92] 'My point of view has not in general commanded assent, not has my argument, for the most part, been understood.' Coase, 'The Firm, the Market and the Law' in Coase, n. 63 above, at 1.

[93] David Campbell, 'Ayres v Coase: An Attempt to Recover the Issue of Equality in Law and Economics' (1994) 21 *Journal of Law and Society*, 434–63, at 438, emphasis in the original.

[94] Campbell and Picciotto, n. 1 above, at 257: 'The limits of formal neo-classical analysis were... well-known to Coase, although he did not go so far as to displace its epistemological assumptions in any radical way'. See also Deakin, n. 23 above, at 75.

[95] Coase, n. 87 above, at 97.

[96] Ronald Coase, 'Notes on the Problem of Social Cost' in Coase, n. 63 above, at 174. See also Robert Ellickson, n. 80 above, at 611, references omitted: 'Coase's name is consistently attached to propositions that he himself has explicitly repudiated. Predictions identified as "Coasean" are predictions that Coase would never make. The "Coasean world" is not only not Coase's but, ironically, is more like the world of the economic theorists that Coase has attacked'.

On the contrary, as Calabresi has pointed out, '[m]any economists mistook the article ['The Problem of Social Cost'] to be a justification of the primacy of markets and for the absence of any need for law or command. As such, it did not seem to require hard work in comparative institutions, but only more, and more elegant, tinkering with market processes'.[97] However, by stressing the importance of transaction costs, Coase's work set the stage for other economists to engage in an exploration of 'institutional responses to market failure',[98] and provides scope for recognizing that markets are not always the most efficient institutional form for economic coordination.[99] Together with his earlier article 'The Nature of the Firm', Coase's work can be seen as 'laying the basis for a fundamental modification of the neoclassical approach'.[100]

### *2.3.2 New institutional (and related) perspectives on regulation*

In stark contrast to the Chicago-school, market-preferring, interpretation of Coase's work, an alternative, equally plausible, reading of the Coase Theorem leads to a recognition of the importance of institutions. Rather than drawing on the original, 'old' institutionalism, which 'emerged largely out of a critique of orthodox assumptions,'[101] 'new' institutional economics 'is substantially conducted within the research programme, or paradigm, of neoclassical economics'.[102] Nevertheless, new institutional economics treats the zero transaction costs postulate as an 'analytical device'[103] to assist in the study of the world of *positive* transaction costs. The alternative understanding of the Coase Theorem, as Deakin and Michie explain, argues that

> '[u]nregulated markets are necessarily characterized by high transaction costs, arising from limits on the availability of information and other barriers to exchange; in these cases, the role of law is not to promote market competition *as such,* but instead to underpin non-market institutions . . . in order to ensure the more effective co-ordination of economic resources.'[104]

The argument that regulation is made necessary by certain forms of market failure sees economic institutions as a potential response to the high transaction costs inherent in a system of decentralized exchange. This was the central message of Coase's paper 'The Nature of the Firm'. It argued that since there were costs of

[97] Guido Calabresi, 'The Pointlessness of Pareto: Carrying Coase Further' (1991) 100 *Yale Law Journal*, 1211–37, at 1213, references omitted.

[98] Deakin and Michie, n. 59 above, at 5.

[99] Hollingsworth and Boyer, n. 3 above, at 7.

[100] Deakin, n. 23 above, at 75.

[101] Geoffrey M. Hodgson, 'Institutionalism, "Old" and "New"' in Geoffrey M. Hodgson, Warren J. Samuels and Marc R. Tool (eds.), *The Elgar Companion to Institutional and Evolutionary Economics: A–K* (Aldershot: Edward Elgar, 1994) at 397.

[102] Warren J. Samuels, ' Law and Economics' in Geoffrey M. Hodgson, Warren J. Samuels and Marc R. Tool (eds.), *The Elgar Companion to Institutional and Evolutionary Economics: L–Z* (Aldershot: Edward Elgar, 1994) at 8.

[103] Williamson, n. 37 above, at 101.

[104] Deakin and Michie, n. 59 above, at 6, emphasis in the original.

using the price mechanism,[105] non-market institutions such as firms would emerge, as contract costs would thereby be 'greatly reduced' (although not eliminated).[106] Together, these two papers by Coase form the basis of the new institutional approach. Following on from Coase's assertion that 'the distinguishing mark of the firm is the supersession of the price mechanism',[107] Oliver Williamson has argued that institutions such as the firm 'have the main purpose and effect of economizing on transaction costs'.[108]

In what way can such new institutionalist analysis aid our understanding of the workings of the (labour) market and the question of optimal regulation? William Dugger suggests that several important implications for the role of the state in the economy flow from transaction cost economics, the 'main plank'[109] of new institutional economics.[110] Namely, that the state plays a determining role in institutionalizing exchange transactions, adjudicating disputes and providing public goods.[111] But the observation that 'markets would not even exist without the property rights that are defined and protected by the state'[112] does not take us a great deal further than Richard Epstein's assertion that private law is necessary to establish the framework of rights within which voluntary transactions can take place.[113] What is possibly more helpful within new institutional thinking is the recognition that non-market institutions 'arise because they are less costly than continuous recourse to the market or exchange'.[114] This is linked to the nature of exchange relations, as highlighted by Karl Klare:

> 'Some economists imagine that a labour market resembles a daily bazaar bringing together sellers and purchasers (technically, lessors and lessees) of commodified labour power. This may be a passable description of what happens in a few labour markets, but most labour economists, students of industrial relations, and labour lawyers take a more institutional view that sees employment as an on-going relationship'[115]

The same could be said of exchange relations more generally: the fact that contracts (employment contracts, in particular) extend over periods of varying or

[105] 'The most obvious cost of "organizing" production through the price mechanism is that of discovering what the relevant prices are.... The costs of negotiating and concluding a separate contract for each exchange transaction which takes place on a market must be taken into account.' Coase, 'The Nature of the Firm', n. 60 above, at 38–9.

[106] Ibid., at 39.

[107] Ibid., at 36.

[108] Oliver E. Williamson, *The Economic Institutions of Capitalism: Firms, Markets and Relational Contracting* (London: Macmillan, 1985) at 1.

[109] Deakin and Michie, n. 59 above, at 10. See also Oliver E. Williamson, *The Mechanisms of Governance* (Oxford: OUP, 1996) at ix.

[110] William M. Dugger, 'Transaction Cost Economics and the State' in Christos Pitelis (ed.), *Transaction Costs, Markets and Hierarchies* (Oxford: Blackwell, 1993) at 188.

[111] Dugger, n. 110 above, at 188–9.

[112] Ibid., at 213.

[113] Epstein, n. 45 above, at 1359.

[114] Geoffrey M. Hodgson, 'Transaction Cost Economics and the Evolution of the Firm' in Christos Pitelis (ed.), n. 110 above, at 79.

[115] Karl Klare, 'The Horizons of Transformative Labour and Employment Law' in Joanne Conaghan, Karl Klare and Richard Michael Fischl (eds.), *Labour Law in an Era of Globalization: Transformative Practices and Possibilities* (Oxford: OUP, 2002) at 12.

indefinite duration means that 'relational' contracts will tend to replace 'spot' contracting.[116]

In a similar vein, Williamson elaborates three key concepts which suggest efficiency reasons for non-market institutions: the fact that human actors have limited cognitive competence such that contracting parties have an imperfect ability to predict the future ('bounded rationality'[117]); the risk that one party will engage in self-seeking behaviour ('opportunism'[118]); and the fact that the parties make mutual investments which can only be realized within that specific relationship[119] ('asset specificity') all point to the need for governance structures to ensure the contract is effectively and efficiently carried out.

For example, in the context of the employment contract, the ongoing relationship means that both parties make relationship-specific investments against a backdrop of uncertainty, which gives rise to a situation of *mutual dependence*.[120] The length of the contract is often uncertain, as is the exact content and intensity of the work; the employee may acquire firm-specific skills and expertise which are likely to be of limited value elsewhere; whilst the employer cannot effectively 'screen' potential employees for their skills and aptitude prior to the contract, and cannot fully monitor performance during it.[121] Contracts of employment are necessarily 'incomplete' due to such uncertainties over future performance, yet there are limits to the employer's power to direct the pace and organization of the employee's work. This would seem to suggest the need for the parties to renegotiate the contract or to have frequent recourse to the market prior to every unforeseen change. Such (costly and cumbersome) renegotiation is obviated, however, if the employee cooperates in areas not covered by explicit or implicit agreement.[122] To ensure optimal contractual performance in such circumstances therefore requires a specialized governance structure,[123] in order to elicit cooperation over the long term, create trust and internalize the work obligation.[124] Such cooperation is generally granted by the employee in response to 'credible

[116] Deakin, n. 23 above, at 89; discussing Ian Macneil 'The Many Futures of Contracts' (1974) 47 *Southern California Law Review*, 691–816.

[117] Oliver E. Williamson, 'The New Institutional Economics: Taking Stock, Looking Ahead' (2000) 38 *Journal of Economic Literature*, 595–613, at 600–1. The term originates with Herbert Simon, who defined bounded rationality as behaviour that is '*intendedly* rational, but only *limitedly* so': Herbert Simon, *Models of Man* (New York: John Wiley & Sons, 1957) at xxiv, quoted in Williamson.

[118] Dugger, n. 5 above, at 379.

[119] Deakin, n. 23 above, at 89.

[120] Ulrich Mückenberger and Simon Deakin, 'From Deregulation to a European Floor of Rights: Labour Law, Flexibilisation and the European Single Market' (1989) 3 *Zeitschrift für ausländisches und internationales Arbeits- und Sozialrecht*, 153–207, at 187–90.

[121] Deakin and Wilkinson, n. 2 above, at 43.

[122] Simon Deakin and Frank Wilkinson, 'Contracts, Co-operation and Trust: The Role of the Institutional Framework' in David Campbell and Peter Vincent Jones (eds.), *Contract and Economic Organisation: Socio-Legal Initiatives* (Aldershot: Dartmouth, 1996) at 105–6.

[123] Deakin and Wilkinson, n. 2 above, at 44.

[124] Mückenberger and Deakin, n. 120 above, at 189.

commitments'[125] offered by the employer, such as promises in respect of pay, seniority rights and pension entitlements.[126] To the extent that private law (contractual) mechanisms may be insufficient to protect employee interests and generate the requisite trust, the normative framework may be supplemented or supplied by labour law or the wage system.[127]

Accordingly, an efficiency argument is made for legal regulation—for example, in the form of implied contractual terms or mandated benefits—since such forms of intervention 'play an important role in protecting *implicit* elements of contractual governance'.[128] Thus, in answer to the question of how transaction cost/ new institutional analysis can further our understanding of the labour market, Williamson *et al.*[129] show that this approach can offer a persuasive explanation for the rise of vertical integration, internal labour markets and collective bargaining, institutions which can be viewed as governance mechanisms designed to enhance efficiency and facilitate high levels of cooperation on the part of employees, leading to 'consummate' as opposed to merely 'perfunctory' cooperation.[130]

Thus, whilst there may be limitations to the new institutional approach (for example, new institutional economics retains enough of neoclassical orthodoxy to aim for efficiency, and does not fully accept the implications of the embeddedness of markets (see below); nevertheless, this approach does provide an important starting point for a critique of the traditional economic suspicion of labour market regulation, which equates labour market institutions with high unemployment. This critique is fundamental to my discussion, in Chapter 2, of theories of unemployment and the philosophies behind European Union policies on combating unemployment and creating employment. A crucial observation is that

'[i]n neglecting the efficiency and performance-related effects on production induced by the wage structure and by legal incentives, neoclassical writers have failed to grasp the point that regulation actually creates and secures employment.'[131]

Deakin and Wilkinson make a similar point:

'certain characteristic features of labour law (as found in virtually all systems other than those of the United States), which include the legal imposition of mandatory minimum labour standards, statutory support for collective workplace representation, and a high level of standardisation of terms and conditions of employment, can be seen as performing an important economic role'[132]

[125] Oliver E. Williamson, 'Credible Commitments: Using Hostages to Support Exchange' (1983) 73 *American Economic Review*, 519–40.

[126] Deakin and Wilkinson, n.2 above, at 44–5. [127] Ibid., at 46. [128] Ibid., at 45.

[129] Oliver E. Williamson, Michael L. Wachter and Jeffrey E. Harris, 'Understanding the Employment Relation: The Analysis of Idiosyncratic Exchange' (1975) 6:1 *Bell Journal of Economics and Management Science*, 250–78.

[130] Ibid., at 270. See also Simon Deakin, 'The Many Futures of the Contract of Employment' in Conaghan, Klare and Fischl, n. 115 above.

[131] Mückenberger and Deakin, n. 120 above, at 190.

[132] Deakin and Wilkinson, n. 2 above, at 49.

Both Macneil's 'relational' contracts theory and the transaction costs approach illustrate how long-term contracts may require to be embedded within some form of governance structure. In addition to and following on from these two perspectives, a third, related, justification for regulation, is that offered by game theory. Game theory involves the study of the 'strategic' behaviour of economic agents in response to the anticipated moves of others.[133] Traditional neoclassical analyses argue that free exchange based on self-interest by rational actors leads to efficient outcomes. However, as illustrated by the prisoners' dilemma game,[134] 'rational transactors may fail to reach welfare-maximizing solutions'.[135] This is because, in a 'non-cooperative game' such as the prisoners' dilemma, none of the parties will cooperate unless they rationally see this as being in their self-interest, even if they would be collectively better off if they cooperated.[136] The (contractual) autonomy of the parties can thus result in them choosing a strategy with sub-optimal results, such that 'legal limits on contractual freedom may in some circumstances mitigate the strategic inefficiencies'.[137] Whilst repeated exchange may lead to a situation where cooperation emerges spontaneously,[138] nevertheless the conditions under which agreements can become 'self-enforcing' are rare. Thus,

'[g]ame-theoretical reasoning can be deployed... to show that, in the absence of institutional regulation, private ordering can lead to sub-optimal outcomes in bargaining relationships, in particular where the relationship is affected by asymmetric information.... One implication of these models, then, is that unfettered competition may not

[133] Deakin and Michie, n. 59 above, at 8.

[134] In brief: 'two prisoners accused of criminal conduct are placed in separate rooms and asked simultaneously either to "confess" to the crime or to "remain silent". Although remaining silent would secure the best joint payoff for the parties combined, the payoffs of the game are structured so that each player individually does better by confessing than by remaining silent, no matter what the other player is doing': Eric Talley 'Interdisciplinary Gap Filling: Game Theory and the Law' (1997) 22 *Law and Social Inquiry*, 1055–86, at fn. 5. If both prisoners confess ('defection'), both receive a sentence of ten years' imprisonment; if both stay silent ('cooperation'), both receive only two years; if one confesses and the other stays silent, the defector will go free, whilst the other will receive a twenty-year sentence. 'So each prisoner feels that no matter what the other does it is always better for him to confess. So both of them confess guided by rational self-interest and each goes to prison for ten years. If, however, neither had confessed, both would have been in prison for only two years each. *Rational choice would seem to cost each person eight additional years in prison*'. Catherine Barnard, 'Regulating Competitive Federalism in the European Union? The Case of EU Social Policy' in Jo Shaw (ed.), *Social Law and Policy in an Evolving European Union* (Oxford: Hart Publishing, 2000) at 58–9, emphasis added.

[135] Barnard, ibid., at 57.

[136] Simon Deakin, 'Two Types of Regulatory Competition: Competitive Federalism versus Reflexive Harmonisation. A Law and Economics Perspective on *Centros*' (1999) 2 *Cambridge Yearbook of European Legal Studies*, 231–60, at 237.

[137] Ian Ayres and Robert Gertner, 'Strategic Contractual Inefficiency and the Optimal Choice of Legal Rules' (1992) 101 *Yale Law Journal*, 729–73, at 743. See also the discussion in Klare, n. 50 above, at 31–5: 'the value of efficiency does not *a priori* rule out, and may actually be served by, substantive restrictions on freedom of contract'.

[138] Because 'each party now calculates that the costs of defection include the prospect of retaliation by the other party in future rounds of bargaining'. Deakin and Michie, n. 59 above, at 9.

be welfare-maximizing, and that regulatory interventions may increase economic welfare.'[139]

This finding has implications not just with regard to regulation of the employment relationship, but also in the context of regulation of the wider labour market and competition between labour markets (to which I will return in the concluding chapter of this book):

'In short, game theoretical analysis does not give clear guidance on the optimal level of regulation. Nevertheless, it offers valuable insights into the nature of the strategic action problems which arise in the context of decentralised rule-making. The question which faces those responsible for the design of federal institutions can be rephrased as follows: what kind of institutions are needed to alter the legal environment in such a way as to induce the cooperation which is needed for regulatory competition to function effectively?'[140]

As far as the regulation of the wider (labour) market is concerned, it is possible to identify real-life examples, arising from the variety of existing forms of capitalism, which suggest that states may well choose to order national political economies with greater or lesser amounts of institutional regulation, whilst being equally 'efficient'. In contrasting 'liberal market economies' with 'coordinated market economies', Hall and Soskice illustrate how firms in liberal market economies tend to coordinate their activities primarily through hierarchies and competitive market arrangements, whilst firms in coordinated market economies are *in addition* able to draw upon organizations and institutions to resolve the sort of coordination problems which occur within capitalism—and that such recourse to institutions may on occasion provide comparative economic advantage.[141]

In conclusion, one can point to a set of important observations to be drawn from new institutional perspectives on regulation—and related perspectives, such as those of game theory and 'relational' contracts theory—which can illuminate the discussion of unemployment and the labour market flexibility debate: essentially, that an efficiency argument can be made for legal regulation of the labour market. *First*, that wholly private ordering may lead to sub-optimal outcomes, and *second*, that labour market institutions can be viewed as governance mechanisms designed to enhance efficiency. If we accept that employment is an ongoing relationship, to the extent that private law mechanisms may be insufficient to generate the requisite trust, regulation by means of labour law and/or the wage system may actually help create and secure employment. This applies not only to regulation of the individual employment relationship, but also to regulation of the labour market as a whole, through the imposition of mandatory

[139] Deakin and Michie, n. 59 above, at 9–10. [140] Deakin, n. 136 above, at 239.

[141] Peter A. Hall and David Soskice, 'An Introduction to Varieties of Capitalism' in Peter A. Hall and David Soskice (eds.), *Varieties of Capitalism: The Institutional Foundations of Comparative Advantage* (Oxford: OUP, 2001) especially at 8–9, 21–33, 36–44.

minimum labour standards and statutory support for institutions of collective workplace representation, and the regulation of competition between firms.

## 3. State and market

### 3.1 Efficiency versus equity? The limits of the new institutional approach

The main purpose of the comparison between neoclassical and new institutional perspectives on regulation has been to provide a critique of orthodox economic perspectives on regulation, *from within that paradigm*, and to begin to illustrate some of the weaknesses of the argument (applied with such vigour to the discourse on combating unemployment) that labour market institutions are a cause of inefficiencies. Whilst recognizing that 'the boundary between efficiency arguments and equity arguments is often blurred',[142] nevertheless, this book ultimately proceeds to a normative argument for labour market institutions and regulation, based on the goals of social justice, rather than seeking to justify such regulation *solely* by virtue of its functional role in achieving efficiency.

As mentioned earlier, my argument is that, whilst it is important to highlight the efficiency-enhancing attributes of certain institutions in the context of the ongoing critique of labour market regulation, reasons of political economy and the desire to retain social cohesion will mean that efficiency cannot be the only goal. It is in this respect that the new institutional approach is found to have serious limitations. New institutional economics (or at least the transaction costs economics which is part of it) continues to privilege private ordering over public regulation.[143] More crucially, although new institutionalist scholars recognize that markets are not always the most efficient institutional form for economic coordination, nevertheless, new institutionalism remains sufficiently within the neoclassical paradigm to consider the attainment of 'efficiency' as the central goal. As Simon Deakin argues in the context of the emergence of the contract of employment, the new institutional approach is 'explicitly functionalist' in the sense that it explains the emergence and persistence of institutions in terms of their efficiency, or 'adaptiveness' to particular conditions.[144] For example, in an early essay, Williamson *et al.* attribute an efficiency rationale to the evolution of internal labour markets, which serve to 'economize on bounded rationality and attenuate opportunism'.[145]

[142] Klare, n. 50 above, at 34.

[143] '[T]ransaction cost economics maintains that *the governance of contractual relations is primarily effected through the institutions of private ordering rather than through legal centralism*'. Williamson, n. 108 above, at xii, emphasis in the original.

[144] Deakin, n. 130 above, at 6.

[145] Williamson, Wachter and Harris, n. 129 above, at 275.

Thus, new institutionalism retains some of the basic weaknesses of traditional neoclassical analysis in that it is ahistorical.[146] Whilst rejecting (some of) the assumptions of a self-regulating market economy, and accepting that markets are not autonomous phenomena but are embedded in social relations, much new institutionalist thinking nevertheless operates on the basis that markets emerged 'naturally'. The assumption is of an initial, institution-free 'state of nature'.[147] As Williamson puts it, 'in the beginning, there were markets'.[148] This 'market primacy assumption' views state intervention, or the rise of institutions, as 'man-made substitutes which emerged only after the defects in the market . . . became unbearable'.[149] Furthermore, related to the market primacy assumption, is that new institutionalism is unwilling to accept 'limits' to economic reasoning. As David Campbell observes: 'at the basis of exchange lie fundamentally co-operative social relations which are necessary for, and cannot be explained by, as they ontologically precede, exchange relationships'.[150]

So, as a preliminary conclusion, having utilized new institutionalist thinking as a platform from which to critique orthodox economic perspectives on regulation, and made an efficiency argument for labour market regulation, it is now important to move *beyond efficiency*.

## 3.2 Regulation and deregulation: a critique of the idea of the 'free' market

The above discussion of neoliberal and new institutional contributions to the debate on (labour market) regulation is, for the most part, premised on an opposition between 'market' and 'regulation' or 'market' and 'state'. Neoliberal ideology, in particular, is founded on a belief in the legitimacy of markets, and '[t]o establish this legitimacy, neo-liberals treat markets, usually without explicit acknowledgement, as existing outside society and outside history. "The market" is simply there'.[151] As Mark Granovetter shows, even the new institutionalist version of neoclassical economics 'deflect[s] the analysis of institutions from sociological, historical, and legal argumentation and show[s] instead that they arise as the efficient solution to economic problems'.[152] If one accepts the thesis that the market 'emerged naturally', then state action is seen as an added extra—in neoliberal theory such action is an exogenous interference in the workings of

[146] See the critique of Oliver Williamson's 'markets and hierarchies' research programme by Mark Granovetter, n. 6 above.

[147] Geoffrey M. Hodgson, 'Frontiers of Institutional Economics' (2001) 6:2 *New Political Economy*, 245–53, at 247.

[148] Oliver E. Williamson, *Markets and Hierarchies* (New York: The Free Press, 1975) at 20.

[149] Ha-Joon Chang, 'An Institutionalist Perspective on the Role of the State: Towards an Institutionalist Political Economy' in Leonardo Burlamaqui, Ana Célia Castro and Ha-Joon Chang (eds.), *Institutions and the Role of the State* (Cheltenham: Edward Elgar, 2000) at 14.

[150] Campbell, n. 8 above, at 318.

[151] MacEwan, n. 14 above, at 11.

[152] Granovetter, n. 6 above, at 505.

the market; in new institutional theory, such 'man-made substitutes' may emerge to cure market failure.

However, it is important not to overstate this supposed dichotomy between 'regulation' and 'market', and this section will, accordingly, elaborate the implications for labour market regulation which follow from the recognition that markets do not exist in a 'state of nature'. A stronger justification for 'regulation' may emerge if one recognizes that 'regulation' is indeed constitutive of markets in the first place.

Drawing upon the work of Karl Polanyi,[153] the tradition of economic sociology challenges the idea that markets are a separate realm, instead arguing that they are embedded in social relations.[154] Similarly, from a socio-legal perspective, I would argue that rather than being natural phenomena, markets are social constructs, constituted by law and social norms. There is no such thing as a *pre-legal* market order, since 'all markets are based on and constituted by a structure of legal rules'.[155] Even neoclassical lawyer-economists, such as Epstein, recognize that *private* law is necessary to establish the framework of rights within which voluntary transactions can take place.[156] But why stop there, with property law and the law of tort, and say that any more is illegitimate 'regulation'? The background rules (of property and tort) are taken for granted in the notion of the 'unregulated market', whilst public law is considered as an interference with individual freedom. That this is a rather artificial distinction between 'free market' and 'state intervention' can be illustrated by the example of child labour in developed and developing economies, as discussed by Ha-Joon Chang, in a passage worth quoting at length:

> 'Few people in the OECD countries at present would consider the ban on child labour as state intervention "artificially" restricting entry into the labour market, whereas many Third World capitalists (and indeed the capitalists in the now-OECD economies in the late 19th and the early 20th centuries) regard it as just that. In developed countries the rights of children not to toil but to be educated are totally accepted and have been incorporated into the structure of (property and other) rights and obligations underlying the labour market... they are *not* a matter of policy debate (i.e. there is no debate on whether the ban on child labour is "efficient" in some sense). In contrast, in the developing countries (of today and yesterday), such rights of children are not so totally accepted, and therefore state action regarding child labour is considered an "intervention", whose impact on "efficiency" is still a *legitimate* subject of policy debate.'[157]

Regulation, therefore, is not something separate from markets,[158] but is essential for the very existence of markets. For example, in a common law system, 'deregulation' by way of the removal of statutory employment protection rules, is

[153] In particular, *The Great Transformation* (Boston: Beacon Press) 1944.
[154] Block, n. 26 above, at 23. [155] Klare, n. 50 above, at 17.
[156] Epstein, n. 45 above, at 1359. For a critique of this version of the 'market paradigm', see Mückenberger and Deakin, n. 120 above, at 179–83.
[157] Chang, n. 149 above, at 8; emphasis in the original. [158] Klare, n. 50 above, at 17.

likely to result in the *restoration* of a different type of regulation, such as contract law or the law of tort.[159] What will have changed is the nature and content of the regulation, not its existence. Further, it is also clear that deregulation does not necessarily mean a reduced role for the state. In fact, one can envisage an increase in the volume of statutory intervention in the implementation of a 'deregulatory' policy. As Spiros Simitis argues, 'contrary to all appearances, the "activist" state is by no means dismissed... far from simply rejecting all interference, the state is assigned the task of setting the elementary conditions for a functioning market'.[160] For example, in the UK the aim of 'deregulating' collective bargaining and weakening trade union power led to increased regulation since 1979, by way of statutory intervention in the internal organization of trade unions and in the ability of trade unions and their members to organize and conduct industrial action.[161]

Markets can only be brought into existence or constructed on the basis of socially agreed 'rules of the game'. Furthermore, in terms of their historical development, Karl Polanyi has shown how '[t]he road to the free market was opened and kept open by an enormous increase in continuous centrally organized and controlled interventionism'.[162] Why, then do markets appear to be 'natural' or self-regulating? In their critique of the notion that the labour market, like other markets, is a spontaneous order or self-organizing system, Deakin and Wilkinson contend that

> 'the role of self-enforcing norms and conventions cannot be separated from that of more formal mechanisms of legal regulation and intervention (judicial decisions, legislation, collective self-regulation). These formal mechanisms can operate to change the 'architecture' or parameters within which the conventions of the market evolve, and in so doing can influence the path of social and economic development.'[163]

## 4. Conclusion

In conclusion, conceptualizing the market as an institution which has been constructed just as other institutions, and not as a natural phenomenon which

[159] See Brian Towers, 'Employee Protection Policy, the Labor Market, and Employment: The UK Experience' in Christoph F. Büchtemann (ed.), *Employment Security and Labor Market Behavior: Interdisciplinary Approaches and International Evidence* (Ithaca, NY: ILR Press, 1993) at 338; and Simon Deakin and Gillian Morris, *Labour Law* 3rd edn. (London: Butterworths, 2001) at 57–62, 237 ff. and Chapter 11.

[160] Spiros Simitis, 'Juridification of Labor Relations' in Gunther Teubner (ed.), *Juridification of Social Spheres* (Berlin: Walter de Gruyter, 1987) at 128.

[161] For example, through the Trade Union and Labour Relations (Consolidation) Act 1992, as amended by the Trade Union Reform and Employment Rights Act 1993; see Sandra Fredman 'The New Rights: Labour Law and Ideology in the Thatcher Years' (1992) 12:1 OJLS, 24–44; Deakin and Morris, n. 159 above, Chapters 10 and 11.

[162] Polanyi, n. 153 above, at 140.

[163] Simon Deakin and Frank Wilkinson, 'Capabilities, Spontaneous Order and Social Rights' (2000) ESRC Centre for Business Research, University of Cambridge, Working Paper No 174, at 2.

somehow precedes state action, helps one to see the interaction between 'market' and 'state' as the interaction between different sets of institutions. In other words, if we accept that public power does indeed structure bargaining relationships, the governance of firms and the labour market itself,[164] then the only question which remains is how or where this balance should be drawn. Also, as Chapter 2 will elaborate, the question of which regulatory choices should be made in structuring markets cannot be answered solely by reference to efficiency criteria.

See also Boyer and Drache, who suggest that '[i]f specific markets give the impression of being self-equilibrating mechanisms, this is the result of their adherence to sophisticated regulations concerning the quality of the goods exchanged, the inner organization of transactions, the legal penalty for non-compliance, etc. In the absence of such surveillance mechanisms, private sector opportunism and corporate self-interest would severely distort the alleged smooth adjustment process of supply and demand': Robert Boyer and Daniel Drache, 'Introduction' in Robert Boyer and Daniel Drache (eds.), *States Against Markets: The Limits of Globalization* (London: Routledge, 1996) at 6.

[164] Klare, n. 50 above, at 18–19.

# 2

# Theories of unemployment and the labour market flexibility debate

## 1. Introduction

As will be elaborated in Chapters 3 to 6, within the EU discourse on unemployment, a clear link is made between flexibility and adaptability of labour markets, and jobs growth; in particular, the Employment Title of the EC Treaty now commits Members States and the Community to the promotion of 'a skilled, trained and adaptable workforce and labour markets responsive to economic change'.

That this analysis of flexibility and employment at times adopts a deregulatory stance, reveals the pervasiveness of the powerful flexibility discourse amongst labour economists, policy-makers and legislators concerned about high unemployment in Europe who have, over the latter decades of the twentieth century, looked with envy at the achievements of the comparatively unregulated US labour market.[1] The central argument here has been that the institutions and legislative interventions which figure so prominently in European economies impede the ability of the labour market to clear, and that market equilibrium in Europe can be restored through deregulation. However, the effect of institutions and regulations on labour markets and unemployment is enormously difficult to measure or predict. This chapter will therefore survey theories of unemployment and explore the main tenets of the labour market flexibility debate in order to assess in subsequent chapters both the extent to which this orthodoxy has been internalized within the EU discourse on unemployment and the policy implications for the EU.

[1] Much of what follows in this chapter, and in the book as a whole, is premised on (sometimes contested) comparisons of the employment performance of the US, Japan on occasion, and the EU. Throughout this book, emphasis will be placed *primarily* on the employment situation of the EU15 (Belgium, Denmark, Germany, Greece, Spain, France, Ireland, Italy, Luxembourg, the Netherlands, Austria, Portugal, Finland, Sweden and the UK) and *secondarily* on the enlarged EU25 (EU15 + Czech Republic, Estonia, Cyprus, Latvia, Lithuania, Hungary, Malta, Poland, Slovenia and Slovakia) for the purposes of comparison with the US, since the stylized comparisons from the 1970s onwards (the contrast between 'Eurosclerosis' and the US 'employment miracle') have been essentially based on distinctions between the competing models of the US and 'old', 'social democratic', pre-enlargement Europe.

## 1.1 Theories of unemployment

'There was a time when broad agreement prevailed on what caused unemployment, and what governments should do about it. Since then we have awoken from this comforting dream and have come to recognise that unemployment can have a wide variety of potential causes, matched by a similar variety of policy responses. The trouble is that, in practice, the causes are difficult to identify and the policies difficult to evaluate.' (Snower and de la Dehesa, 1997)[2]

'There are many models of unemployment in the literature. Since no model has been entirely successful in explaining the rise in unemployment, different authors often use different models on the basis of beliefs about the economy rather than hard evidence.' (Pissarides, 1999)[3]

These two quotes neatly illustrate the difficulty of identifying any one theory to explain the increase in the European unemployment rate since the 1970s. The standard macro-economic paradigm to explain unemployment is that there is a relatively constant 'natural rate' of unemployment,[4] but that demand (or supply) shocks lead to temporary deviations from that natural rate.[5] On the basis that the labour market functions not unlike commodity markets, neoclassical theory assumes a downward-sloping demand curve for labour: as the real wage (the 'price' of labour) falls, the demand for labour rises (and the supply of labour to the economy is assumed to increase as the real wage rises), so that for employment to increase, wages must fall.[6] Unemployment thus occurs when the labour market fails to clear.

'The intersection of the aggregate demand and supply curves of labour determines the wage which firms can afford to pay *and* which clears the market of all workers willing to work and capable of working for that wage. Unemployment is then taken as evidence of

[2] Dennis J. Snower and Guillermo de la Dehesa, 'Preface' in Dennis J. Snower and Guillermo de la Dehesa (eds.), *Unemployment Policy: Government Options for the Labour Market* (Cambridge: CUP, 1997) at xxi.

[3] Christopher A. Pissarides, 'Policy Influences on Unemployment: The European Experience' (1999) 46:4 *Scottish Journal of Political Economy*, 389–418, at 391–2.

[4] The 'natural rate of unemployment' or 'non-accelerating inflation rate of unemployment' (NAIRU) is the term used to describe the minimum unemployment rate which puts no upward pressure on inflation. NAIRU has dominated macro-economic thinking for decades, since it was coined by Milton Friedman and Edmund Phelps in the late 1960s: see James K. Galbraith, 'Time to Ditch the NAIRU' (1997) 11:1 *Journal of Economic Perspectives*, 93–108, and references therein. Galbraith is extremely critical of NAIRU, arguing that the theoretical case for a 'natural rate' is not compelling, and the policy implications unappealing: 'speaking politically, the natural rate hypothesis has served a conservative cause. Since Friedman's speech, orthodox macroeconomics has virtually always leaned against policies to support full employment. In spite of stagnant real wages, it has virtually never leaned the other way'; ibid., at 102.

[5] Charles R. Bean, 'European Unemployment: A Survey' (1994) 32 *Journal of Economic Literature*, 573–619, at 615.

[6] Frank Wilkinson, 'Inflation and Employment: Is There a Third Way?' (2000) 24 *Cambridge Journal of Economics*, 643–70, at 644; and John F. Brothwell, 'Unemployment' in Geoffrey M. Hodgson, Warren J. Samuels and Marc R. Tool (eds.), *The Elgar Companion to Institutional and Evolutionary Economics: L–Z* (Aldershot: Edward Elgar, 1994) at 357–8.

a lack of appropriate skill on the part of [the] jobless, an unwillingness to work at the going rate, imperfections in the labour market which prevent wages falling to their equilibrium level, or any combination of these.'[7]

In such an equilibrium, according to neoclassical theory, unemployment is 'voluntary', save for some 'frictional' unemployment as labour moves between firms in search of better conditions, and 'structural' unemployment, as the changing output mix of the economy requires labour to be reallocated across industries.[8]

However, the natural rate theory did not fully explain the sharp rise in European unemployment from the 1970s,[9] and there remains a lack of consensus on the relative importance of the various underlying causes of the trend increase.

As Alicia Adserà and Charles Boix point out, two main sets of theories have been developed to explain the divergence between unemployment rates in the EU and the US: structural theories, which explain differences in employment trends as a result of exogenous shocks to the developed economies, and institutional accounts, which refer to the role of domestic institutional frameworks, such as labour laws or patterns of collective bargaining, to explain national variations in unemployment.[10] Of the institutional theories, a highly influential work is that of Layard, Jackman and Nickell,[11] who attribute high European unemployment to imperfectly competitive wage-setting institutions and the generosity of social insurance, which leads to a high 'reservation wage' (the level of pay for which workers are prepared to accept a job) and makes the decision to work unattractive.[12] Whilst subsequently being careful to distinguish between 'which labour market institutions really are bad for unemployment and growth, and which are not',[13] nevertheless, Layard *et al.* argue (using 'cross-country regression analysis' to support their hypothesis) that higher levels of trade union density are associated with higher levels of unemployment. Similar conclusions

[7] Wilkinson, n. 6 above, at 644, emphasis in the original.

[8] Brothwell, n. 6 above, at 358.

[9] 'In the 1960s the trend unemployment rate in the United States, at around 5 per cent, was significantly higher than elsewhere. It then moved up only modestly in the 1970s and was around 6 to 8 per cent in the 1980s, though with large cyclical fluctuations around the trend rate. In contrast, Europe, which had had a trend rate of unemployment of only 2 to 3 per cent in the 1960s, significantly less than in the United States, saw unemployment move to around 8 to 9 per cent by the end of the 1980s with, in general, less cyclical volatility of actual unemployment.' Organisation for Economic Cooperation and Development, *The OECD Jobs Study: Evidence and Explanations. Part I—Labour Market Trends and Underlying Forces of Change* (Paris: OECD, 1994) at 69.

[10] Alicia Adserà and Charles Boix, 'Must We Choose? European Unemployment, American Inequality and the Impact of Education and Labor Market Institutions' (2000) 16 *European Journal of Political Economy*, 611–38, at 612–14.

[11] Richard Layard, Stephen Nickell, and Richard Jackman, *Unemployment: Macroeconomic Performance and the Labour Market* (Oxford: OUP, 1991).

[12] For a critique, see Peter G. Gahan, 'European Unemployment: The Role of Labor Market Regulation? A Review Essay' (1998) 19 *Comparative Labor Law and Policy Journal*, 455–72.

[13] Stephen Nickell and Richard Layard, 'Labour Market Institutions and Economic Performance', Centre for Economic Performance, London School of Economics, Discussion Paper No 407, September 1998, at 1.

are reached by 'insider–outsider' models of the labour market,[14] which argue that labour market imperfections allow 'insiders' undue market power over wage levels, dismissal protection and other employment regulations, and thus act as an obstacle to recruitment.[15]

Adserà and Boix suggest a combination of both approaches (structural and institutional); in other words, that an exogenous shock (or set of exogenous shocks) has altered the supply conditions of all advanced nations, but the resulting unemployment rate has been determined by the nature of a particular country's labour force and institutional and legal settings.[16] This, in essence, is the view of the OECD and the IMF. Both organizations identify the interaction of the two oil price shocks of the 1970s and the inability of many labour markets to adjust to rapid change as key causal factors of high unemployment, especially European unemployment.

'Both these elements [labour market rigidities and adverse shocks] are essential to a satisfactory explanation of the current predicament: structural rigidities alone fail to explain developments in Europe, since by most standards these rigidities were already largely in place during the 1960s, when the European unemployment rate was significantly lower than that of the United States. And the negative shocks hitting the European economies in the 1970s do not by themselves provide a satisfactory explanation of the persistent deterioration in Europe's labor market performance, since similar shocks hit other advanced economies (the United States and Japan) without causing comparable trend increases in unemployment rates.'[17]

The recommendations of the OECD's *Jobs Study* and their impact or otherwise on the development of the EU Employment Strategy will be examined in more detail in Chapter 3 but, in summary, the OECD advised that all member countries, not just those in Europe, should concentrate on creating a stable macro-economic environment, and increasing the adaptability of their labour markets. In particular, European states were advised to enact measures which avoid sudden increases in unemployment, as well as reforms of the structures and mechanisms that tend to prolong it.[18] According to Assar Lindbeck, this involves tackling mechanisms of unemployment persistence in particular. For example: liberalization of job security legislation and other measures to reduce the market power of 'insiders' and trade unions; less generous and more strictly administered

[14] Assar Lindbeck and Dennis J. Snower, *The Insider–Outsider Theory of Employment and Unemployment* (Cambridge, MA: The MIT Press, 1988).

[15] For applications of the 'insider–outsider' theory, see OECD, *The OECD Jobs Study: Implementing the Strategy* (Paris: OECD, 1995) at 18–23; and Commission of the European Communities (hereinafter, CEC), White Paper *Growth, Competitiveness and Employment: The Challenges and Ways Forward into the 21st Century*, COM (93) 700 final (Luxembourg: OOPEC, 1993) at 124.

[16] Adserà and Boix, n. 10 above, at 3–4; see also Pissarides, n. 3 above, at 390.

[17] International Monetary Fund, *World Economic Outlook* (Washington, DC: IMF, 1999), Chapter IV Chronic Unemployment in the Euro Area: Causes and Cures, at 92; see also, OECD, *The OECD Jobs Study: Facts, Analysis, Strategies* (Paris: OECD, 1994) at 30.

[18] Assar Lindbeck, 'The West European Employment Problem', University of Stockholm, Institute for International Economic Studies, Seminar Paper No 616, 13 August 1996, at 3.

unemployment benefits (in response to the weakening of the work ethic which occurs when major macro-economic shocks hit societies with generous benefit systems); and investment in human capital, to reduce 'mismatches' between demand and supply and raise the productivity of workers.

This latter point has been a particular concern of the European Central Bank (ECB), which has generally adopted a very similar perspective to that of the international organizations on the causes of high European unemployment. One ECB report on the labour market matching process[19] (that is, the ability of the labour market to match labour supply and demand and thus to create employment by bringing the non-employed into employment and by filling vacancies) quotes with approval a study by Blanchard and Wolfers, which found that the interaction of some labour market institutions with cyclical and structural shocks contributes to explaining the increase in European unemployment over time as well as the heterogeneity in unemployment developments across EU countries.[20] The ECB thus considers wage systems and labour market institutions as crucial to the adjustment process in the labour market. The former should be sufficiently flexible to translate fluctuations in the business cycle, changes in the production structure of the economy as well as changes in the characteristics of the labour force into adequately differentiated wage adjustments; the latter, if too rigid, may increase labour market imbalances—for example, overly generous unemployment benefits relative to wage incomes may reduce incentives to search for job opportunities.[21] The ECB's conclusions are therefore that improved job mediation, more flexible wages and increased wage differentiation, improved education, training and lifelong learning, reforms of tax and benefit systems, less restrictive employment protection regulation, working-time flexibility and measures to increase labour mobility are all necessary to help make the matching process more efficient and labour markets more flexible.[22]

It is against this backdrop that the strategy to reduce unemployment across EU Member States (now supplemented by a commitment to raise employment rates) must be analysed. I contend in Chapter 3 that the shift from a social policy agenda to an employment policy agenda is best viewed as a collective response by the EU and its Member States to the growing acceptance of the above economic orthodoxy—reinforced by the demands of Economic and Monetary Union—that greater 'flexibility' in labour markets is the key to solving Europe's unemployment ills, along with macro-economic stability, restrictive fiscal policy and wage restraint. Alongside this engagement with the labour market flexibility debate, another important facet of the above theories of unemployment which has influenced the EU's discourse on unemployment is the emphasis on

[19] European Central Bank, *Labour Market Mismatches in Euro Area Countries* (Frankfurt am Main: ECB, 2002).

[20] Oliver J. Blanchard and Jan Wolfers, 'The Role of Shocks and Institutions in the Rise of European Unemployment: The Aggregate Evidence' (2000) 110 *Economic Journal*, C1–C33.

[21] ECB, n. 19 above, at 8. [22] Ibid., at 28.

'employability', and its interaction with flexibility of labour markets.[23] Active labour market policies (ALMPs), which stress 'employability', are a logical complement to flexible labour markets,[24] based as they are on the assumption that the problem is not so much *unemployment* as *unemployability*.[25] Thus, tackling 'rigidities' (which, for example, prevent wages falling to their equilibrium level) goes hand-in-hand with ALMPs and training, so as to remedy the lack of appropriate skill on the part of jobseekers. Both strategies seek to bring the labour market into equilibrium.

The importance of the interaction between 'adaptability' and 'employability' will be seen in particular in the shift to a more supply-side orientated policy following the Lisbon European Council meeting in 2000 (discussed in Chapter 4), a sharper version of which is evident in the employment policy of the New Labour government in the UK (explored, alongside the policies of the Dutch government, in Chapter 6). 'Skilled, trained and adaptable' workers and labour markets 'responsive to economic change' strongly imply that, rather than protecting jobseekers or workers *against* the market (through social transfers or employment protection legislation), the aim of European employment policy becomes to equip them (through skills and training) to survive *within* the market, to attain security by virtue of being *employable*.[26]

## 1.2 The basic tenets of the labour market flexibility debate

Orthodox economic thinking has long held that the systems of labour market regulation which exist in most EU Member States are the major cause of their high unemployment, and that the EU would therefore do best to adopt the more flexible wage systems, employment practices and labour laws of the United States. Such 'labour market rigidities' are routinely blamed for high European unemployment, and this was certainly the conclusion of the OECD *Jobs Study*,[27] which Robert Solow dryly suggests is more appropriately described as the *assumption* of the OECD *Jobs Study*.[28]

Since, it is argued, only free, unrestricted operation of market forces produces optimal results—in labour markets, as in commodity markets—state intervention

[23] As will be seen in Chapter 4, two of the four 'pillars' of the EU Employment Strategy as originally structured were Adaptability and Employability, in addition to Entrepreneurship and Equal Opportunities.

[24] Jamie Peck and Nikolas Theodore, 'Beyond "Employability"' (2000) 24 *Cambridge Journal of Economics*, 729–49, at 731.

[25] Wilkinson, n. 6 above, at 665.

[26] This approach is explored further, as a form of 'supply-side egalitarianism', in Chapters 4 and 6; see Raymond Plant, 'The Third Way', Friedrich-Ebert-Stiftung, Working Papers 5/98; and Wolfgang Streeck, 'Competitive Solidarity: Rethinking the "European Social Model"' Max Planck Institute for the Study of Societies (MPIFG) Working Paper 99/8.

[27] OECD, *The OECD Jobs Study: Evidence and Explanations* and *Facts, Analysis, Strategies* (Paris: OECD, 1994); see discussion in Chapter 3.

[28] Robert M. Solow, 'What is Labour-Market Flexibility? What is it Good For?' (Keynes Lecture in Economics) (1998) 97 *Proceedings of the British Academy*, 189–211.

through regulation serves to distort labour supply and demand, restrict job creation and increase unemployment.[29] So, with regard to the labour market rules or institutions which are the subject of the EU's scrutiny in its discourse on unemployment, the orthodox neoclassical view would have it that by limiting freedom of contract, such labour standards erect barriers to market entry and prevent labour markets from achieving their allocative function.[30] Thus the solution proposed, that of deregulation, would return the labour market to its original 'state of nature', the traditional ordering of rights based on the common law of the contract of employment.[31]

This deregulatory solution to high European unemployment cannot be emphasized enough. According to Alogoskoufis *et al.*, 'a quarter of the 59 policy recommendations in the OECD *Jobs Study* relate more or less directly to the removal of restrictions on the terms of employment'.[32]

However, despite the extensive literature on the subject, there remains a lack of consensus as to what exactly are to be included within the definition of labour market 'institutions' or 'rigidities' for the purposes of measuring the effect on employment or unemployment.[33] For example, Buchele and Christiansen[34] in their comparison of US and EU unemployment, consider the impact of three different kinds of labour market institutions: employment protection laws; wage-setting institutions; and unemployment insurance and other income support programmes. Nickell and Layard,[35] however, examine five institutional differences which might explain differences in unemployment and growth: the levels of labour taxation; the systems of employment protection; trade union activity and minimum wages; income support for the unemployed and active labour market policy; and education and skill formation. Siebert, on the other hand,[36] distinguishes four different institutional layers affecting the labour market: 'the market process, rules affecting the wage formation process, the legal system and the system of nonemployment income'. Which institutions are studied can have an important effect on the conclusions, since certain 'rigidities'

[29] Nick Adnett, *European Labour Markets: Analysis and Policy* (London: Longman, 1996) at 278.

[30] Simon Deakin and Frank Wilkinson 'Rights vs Efficiency? The Economic Case for Transnational Labour Standards' (1994) 23:4 ILJ, 289–310, at 293.

[31] Richard Epstein, 'A Common Law for Labor Relations: A Critique of the New Deal Labor Legislation' (1983) 92 *Yale Law Journal* 1357–1408 and 'In Defense of the Contract at Will' (1984) 51 *Chicago Law Review*, 947–82. See Chapter 1, Section 3.2 for a critique of this supposed distinction between a 'free' or 'unregulated' market and state intervention.

[32] George Alogoskoufis, Charles Bean, Giuseppe Bertola, Daniel Cohen, Juan Dolado and Gilles Saint-Paul, *Unemployment: Choices for Europe* (London: CEPR, 1995) at 71.

[33] 'It is difficult to define precisely what we mean by labour market institutions, so we simply provide a list of those features of the labour market which we will consider. The boundaries of this list are somewhat arbitrary': Nickell and Layard, n. 13 above, at 7.

[34] Robert Buchele and Jens Christiansen, 'Do Employment and Income Security Cause Unemployment? A Comparative Study of the US and the E-4' (1998) 22 *Cambridge Journal of Economics*, 117–36, at 123.

[35] Nickell and Layard, n. 13 above.

[36] Horst Siebert 'Labor Market Rigidities: At the Root of Unemployment in Europe' (1997) 11:3 *Journal of Economic Perspectives*, 37–54, at 39.

may not in fact have the effect of increasing unemployment,[37] and others still may actually enhance labour market 'efficiency'.[38]

There is, of course, some overlap in the types of institutions studied, and these are usefully divided by Esping-Andersen into three broad regulatory categories:[39] the welfare state, wage-setting mechanisms and employment protection. To turn from the descriptive to the normative, an important synthesis of the economic orthodoxy is provided by the OECD, which has identified four main causes of persistent and rising unemployment within western Europe.[40] *First*, overly restrictive employment and labour protection legislation, which discourages recruitment; *second*, existing collective bargaining practice, which prevents the 'adjustment' of income levels to productivity and individual performance; *third*, high statutory minimum wages; and *fourth*, non-wage labour costs. The strategy recommended by the OECD to overcome this unemployment problem was thus to combine macro-economic policies to keep inflation and budget deficits under control, specific measures to improve targeting and design of labour market policies (to introduce ALMPs) with the introduction of downward flexibility in wage levels, the decentralization of collective bargaining to enterprise level and the relaxing of restrictions on employment contracts and on working time.[41]

Here are some of the most frequently repeated assertions of the labour market flexibility debate, organized around the broad regulatory categories suggested by Esping-Andersen.[42] *First*, the institutions of the welfare state are said to distort the labour supply. Generous social insurance and unemployment benefit levels in European countries mean that workers are under less pressure to seek jobs. The expansion of the European welfare state in the 1970s has led to unemployment and other benefits (such as those for incapacity or disability) which not only grant high net replacement rates, but are also of long duration. Together with lax eligibility criteria (for example, where there is no obligation on unemployed

[37] See below, Section 2; see also Stephen Nickell, 'Unemployment and Labor Market Rigidities: Europe versus North America' (1997) 11:3 *Journal of Economic Perspectives*, 55–74, at 72.

[38] See Chapter 1, Section 2.3.2 on new institutional (and related) perspectives on regulation.

[39] Gøsta Esping-Andersen, 'Who is Harmed By Labour Market Regulations? Quantitative Evidence' in Gøsta Esping-Andersen and Marino Regini (eds.), *Why Deregulate Labour Markets* (Oxford: OUP, 1999) at 73.

[40] OECD, *Labour Market Flexibility: Report of A High-Level Group of Experts to the Secretary-General* (Paris: OECD, 1986); *The OECD Jobs Study: Implementing the Strategy* (Paris: OECD, 1995), at 18–23; see also *OECD Employment Outlook 2004* (Paris: OECD, 2004) in particular, the Editorial, 'Reassessing the OECD Jobs Strategy'.

[41] For further analysis of the OECD's *Jobs Study*, see Chapter 3; see also the discussion of the OECD's recommendations by Hedva Sarfati, 'Negotiating Trade-offs Between Jobs and Labour Market Flexibility in the European Union' (1998) 14:4 *The International Journal of Comparative Labour Law and Industrial Relations*, 307–24.

[42] Some of these arguments for labour market deregulation will doubtless seem familiar from the discussion of theories of unemployment, since much of the economic analysis of unemployment proceeds from an implicit belief in the link between joblessness and labour law; see Gahan, n. 12 above, at 457.

persons to be 'actively seeking employment') such generosity makes the decision to work less attractive, as the 'reservation wage' is high. The unemployed are 'trapped' in unemployment,[43] since they lose the incentive to work, and also 'price' themselves out of the labour market.[44] The suggested solution, according to the OECD, is as follows:

'There is considerable evidence that benefits affect unemployment rates. Countries which currently have high unemployment and significantly reduce benefit disincentives may experience a considerable improvement in their unemployment situation within a few years . . . in the long term, if unemployment is to be kept low, it is vital to limit entitlements to benefit and refuse benefit to people who are not available for work.'[45]

*Second*, the wage structure: labour market institutions, such as collective bargaining (and employment protection legislation, see below) are also said to impair the equilibrating function of the market mechanism, for example by influencing bargaining behaviour.[46] Whereas 'wage formation in the United States comes close to being a market process',[47] the opposite is true in most European countries. Wage formation in the US is decentralized, with low unionization and low coordination of wage changes across the economy, as a result of which wages are flexible downwards; in Europe, however, high unionization rates and/or high coverage rates[48] mean that there is less wage differentiation between regions, age groups or productivity levels. The OECD's response to European wage rigidity is that these countries should instead be making wage and price formation more flexible, so as to make them more responsive to market conditions, since greater wage and price flexibility will increase the demand for labour, by lowering the relatively high tax and legislated (or collectively bargained) costs of employing a worker.[49] So, for example, the minimum wage is said to increase unemployment by 'destroying jobs for unskilled workers whose marginal product, in equilibrium, would be below the minimum wage'.[50] The ideal wage formation system is thus one which provides both aggregate and relative wage flexibility.[51]

[43] Siebert, n. 36 above, at 51.

[44] Esping-Andersen, n. 39 above, at 73–7, in particular for a critique of the importance of the reservation wage.

[45] OECD, *The OECD Jobs Study: Evidence and Explanations. Part II: The Adjustment Potential of the Labour Market* (Paris: OECD, 1994) at 213.

[46] Siebert, n. 36 above, at 43.

[47] Ibid., at 46.

[48] Union density is low in France, at about 10%, but there is wide extension of collective agreements, so that approximately 90% of workers are covered by collective agreements.

[49] OECD, *The OECD Jobs Study: Implementing the Strategy* (Paris: OECD, 1995), at 18. However, see the discussion in Section 2.1 below on the Calmfors–Driffill model and the comparison between 'centralized' and 'decentralized' wage formation systems.

[50] Gilles Saint-Paul, 'Labour Rigidities and the Performance of the French Economy' in Horst Siebert (ed.), *Structural Change and Labor Market Flexibility: Experience in Selected OECD Countries* Institut für Weltwirtschaft an der Universität Kiel (Tübingen: Mohr/Paul Siebeck, 1997), at 33.

[51] OECD, n. 49 above, at 20: 'aggregate wage flexibility, ensuring that real wages are sufficiently sensitive to changes in the unemployment rate, and relative wage flexibility, ensuring that wages appropriately reflect underlying productivity'.

For example, changes in markets since the 1970s have led to a fall in demand for unskilled workers. In the US, the wages of unskilled workers have fallen dramatically, in real terms, because there is wage flexibility; so unskilled workers in the US are employed, but at the cost of massive increases in inequality.[52] In Europe, so the argument goes, coordinated wage determination and the Welfare State have meant that wage levels are 'sticky': they remain high and as a result unskilled workers are left jobless. As Bertola and Ichino explain:

'[The] evidence suggests that whatever caused wage dispersion in the U.S. did hit continental Europe too, but for institutional reasons, affected employment rather than wages.... [M]inimum-wage regulations and other wage rigidities may have prevented European labor markets from reacting to skill-biased technological progress and to increased exposure to LDC [less developed country] imports by reducing low-end wages. In this view, aggregate shocks are accommodated in the U.S. by lower real wages and in Europe by higher unemployment; at a more disaggregated level, structural shocks which lead to wider age differentials in the American labor market cause more dispersion of European unemployment rates.'[53]

*Third*, there is the critique of employment protection legislation (EPL). Such institutional arrangements allegedly weaken the demand for labour, making it less attractive to hire workers.[54] For example, layoff restraints and the obligation on employers to grant severance pay make it costly for employers to dismiss workers, so they will be reluctant to hire them in the first place. Legal regulation is also said to affect the capacity of firms to adopt flexible patterns of labour management: laws and collective agreements limit firms' ability to respond to changes in the external market by, amongst other things, hiring and firing labour at will, setting variable wage rates, varying working time schedules, using fixed term contracts or independent contractors.[55]

However, in spite of the 'extensive public debate and much economic research' on the links between EPL and labour market performance, even the OECD admits that 'empirical research to date has not provided a clear-cut answer to this question'.[56] With regard to unemployment, the OECD cites a number of studies which show that the effect of EPL on overall unemployment *levels* is inconclusive, although the existence of strict EPL may affect the *dynamics* and *composition* of unemployment—where EPL restricts dismissals

[52] 'Between the late 1970s and the early 1990s... the real wages of low-ranked workers like janitors fell 15 per cent or more, while the real earnings of high-end occupations like doctors and corporate executives rose 50 per cent or more'. Paul Krugman, 'Europe Jobless, America Penniless?' (1995) *Foreign Policy*, 19–24, at 23.

[53] Giuseppe Bertola and Andrea Ichino, 'Wage Inequality and Unemployment: US vs Europe', Centre for Economic Policy Research, CEPR Discussion Paper No 1186, May 1995, at 6; references omitted.

[54] Siebert, n. 36 above, at 43.

[55] Simon Deakin and Ulrich Mückenberger, 'Deregulation and European Labour Markets' in Alberto Castro, Philippe Méhaut and Jill Rubery (eds.), *International Integration and Labour Market Organisation* (London: Academic Press, 1992) at 136.

[56] OECD, *OECD Employment Outlook, June 1999* (Paris: OECD, 1999) at 47 and 68.

and discourages hirings, the unemployment pool becomes more stagnant due to lower inflows and outflows, and longer durations.[57] The OECD's 1999 *Employment Outlook* thus concurred with earlier empirical studies that 'EPL strictness has little or no effect on overall unemployment'.[58] This conclusion has been to some extent confirmed in subsequent research, in the plethora of economic studies on the impact of labour market institutions on the economic performance of OECD countries.[59] However, lest the statement in the OECD's 1999 *Employment Outlook* be misunderstood as a rejection of economic orthodoxy, or of the deregulatory conclusions of the 1994 *Jobs Study*, the OECD took great care to clarify its position and to reaffirm the recommendations of the Jobs Strategy[60] in favour of increased flexibility in national labour markets in a number of areas, including working time, wage and labour costs, and legislation designed to protect employment.[61] Furthermore, the OECD stressed that 'countries with relatively strict EPL which have a serious problem of long-term unemployment and/or relatively low overall employment rates, should consider relaxing their employment protection as part of a comprehensive policy to improve labour market outcomes'.[62] However, as part of the process of re-assessment of the 1994 *Jobs Study*, by 2004, the OECD had reached a more nuanced position on the effect of employment protection legislation on employment. This more balanced approach recognized that some EPL could be welfare-improving, by protecting workers over a limited period of time against labour market uncertainties and causing firms to internalize some of the social costs of their dismissal decisions.[63] Nevertheless, on balance, the OECD position remains committed to the critique of EPL as hampering labour market dynamics and employment flows, and in particular the employment rates of certain groups in the labour market, such as new entrants,[64] whilst acknowledging that active labour market policies may well counteract the negative effects of EPL.[65]

[57] Ibid., at 69–70. [58] Ibid., at 88.

[59] For example: Luca Nunziata, 'Labour market institutions and the cyclical dynamics of employment' (2003) 10:1 *Labour Economics*, 31–53; Michèle Belot and Jan C. van Ours, 'Does the recent success of some OECD countries in lowering their unemployment rates lie in the clever design of their labor market reforms?' (2004) 56:4 *Oxford Economic Papers*, 621–42.

[60] See Chapter 3, Section 2.1.1.

[61] OECD, 'OECD's View on Employment Protection Legislation' *OECD News Release*, 13 July 1999, at para 1; available at: *http://www1.oecd.org/media/release/nw99-76a.htm* [accessed on 10 April 2005]. [62] Ibid., at para 4.

[63] See *OECD Employment Outlook 2004*, n. 40 above, Chapter 2, in particular at 63: 'EPL may foster long-term employment relationships, thus promoting workers' effort, co-operation and willingness to be trained, which is positive for aggregate employment and economic efficiency.' See also Trade Union Advisory Committee to the OECD (TUAC) *OECD Employment Outlook July 2004: TUAC Evaluation*, (Paris: TUAC–OECD, 2004).

[64] *OECD Employment Outlook 2004*, n. 40 above, at 76–89.

[65] Ibid., at 63–4 and 95–6. See the discussion in Chapter 4 of the post-Lisbon phase of the European Employment Strategy for a similar, concurrent, shift to focus on active labour market policies equipping jobseekers to be self-sufficient, to survive *within* the market, and to attain security by virtue of being *employable* rather than by means of EPL.

## 2. Moving beyond the rhetoric: a critique of the labour market flexibility debate

How valid or compelling is the stylized critique of labour market institutions which is increasingly informing the EU discourse on employment? In particular, to what extent is it possible to draw a causal link between labour market institutions and unemployment? Gøsta Esping-Andersen suggests that the deregulatory message is only tenuously anchored to economic theory and empirical research.[66] Three main arguments, which are central to my critique of the deregulation discourse, follow from the recognition of the weak link between labour market institutions and unemployment. First is the observation that different labour market institutions have different effects on (un)employment. As Stephen Nickell points out,[67] it is important to disaggregate the effects of labour market institutions: their impact may not all be one way.

Second, drawing on the insights of new institutionalism, it is arguable that some labour market institutions actually enhance efficiency: Mückenberger and Deakin make the point that '[i]n neglecting the efficiency and performance-related effects on production induced by the wage structure and by legal incentives, neoclassical writers have failed to grasp the point that regulation actually creates and secures employment'.[68] Third is the argument which goes 'beyond efficiency' to adopt a normative argument for labour market institutions and regulation, based on the goals of social justice.

As will become apparent, rather than attempting to 'prove' or 'disprove' the causal link, the following sections will offer alternative perspectives on the labour market flexibility debate, which argue for the merits of labour market institutions—ultimately from a normative viewpoint.

### 2.1 The variable effects of labour market institutions

'Concentrating on the impact on unemployment, evidence suggests that some institutions tend to raise the equilibrium rate of unemployment, such as weakly policed, generous unemployment benefits of long duration. Others, predominantly affect the composition of equilibrium unemployment, such as employment protection measures.... Still other labour market institutions may have little effect on unemployment or participation, instead affecting wages.... Finally, some institutional forces affect unemployment and participation rates in different ways depending on other characteristics of labour market behaviour.' (Adnett, 2001)[69]

[66] Esping-Andersen, n. 39 above, at 66.

[67] Nickell, n. 37 above; see also Nickell and Layard, n. 13 above.

[68] Ulrich Mückenberger and Simon Deakin, 'From Deregulation to a European Floor of Rights: Labour Law, Flexibilisation and the European Single Market' (1989) 3 *Zeitschrift für ausländisches und internationales Arbeits- und Sozialrecht*, 153–207, at 190.

[69] Nick Adnett, 'Modernizing the European Social Model: Developing the Guidelines' (2001) 39:2 *Journal of Common Market Studies*, 353–64, at 356–7.

With regard to the effect of 'generous' welfare provisions on unemployment, even those analysts who reject the unreflective assertion that inflexible labour markets cause unemployment nevertheless regard generous unemployment benefits as leading to high unemployment, in particular if they are allowed to run on indefinitely, with little or no pressure on the unemployed to work.[70] There are, however, some dissenting studies, which conclude that the impact of social protection on unemployment is, at best, marginal: first, that the negative incentive effect of benefits is important only at the margins, and may even have a positive effect if workers remain on unemployment benefits longer than necessary, but in so doing, improve the job-matching process.[71] Second, a point which even Nickell and Layard concede, is that while high benefits may lead to high unemployment, they also lead to high participation—employment insurance induces people to take up employment so as to qualify for higher benefits.[72] However, for a stronger critique of the commonly held view that generous unemployment benefits will inevitably increase unemployment, one has to abandon the *a priori* belief that the labour market essentially follows a competitive model. Paul Gregg and Alan Manning show how the basic assumption of most economists that regulation moves the market even further from market clearing, means that the link between benefits and unemployment becomes a matter of faith.[73]

As far as the impact of wage-setting mechanisms on employment is concerned, again, the effect of high levels of unionization and collective bargaining coverage is not clear-cut. The assumption is that trade unions tend to raise wages, and in so doing raise unemployment: in line with the orthodox neoclassical theory, unions are 'imperfections' in the market which prevent wages falling to their equilibrium level, and if they succeed in pushing up the real wage (the 'price' of labour) the demand for labour will fall. However, even allowing for this assumption, it is not necessarily the case that unemployment will rise: 'if unions and firms can coordinate their wage bargaining activities, they can overcome some of the externalities generated by decentralized collective bargaining, moderate wage pressure and, thereby, reduce the unemployment consequences of trade union wage bargaining'.[74]

A related, and highly influential, theory of institutions and wage formation *within* the context of neoliberal thinking, is that of Calmfors and Driffill, whose model suggests that wage bargaining institutions will not necessarily lead to unemployment.[75] The authors posit a hump-shaped relationship between

[70] Nickell, n. 37 above, at 72–3; Nickell also argues, writing with Layard, that '[l]ong-term benefits generate long-term unemployment': Nickell and Layard, n. 13 above, at 56.

[71] Esping-Andersen, n. 39 above, at 75.

[72] Nickell and Layard, n. 13 above, at 57; Esping-Andersen, n. 39 above, at 75.

[73] Paul Gregg and Alan Manning, 'Labour Market Regulation and Unemployment' in Snower and de la Dehesa (eds.), n. 2 above, at 410 ff.

[74] Nickell and Layard, n. 13 above, at 52.

[75] Lars Calmfors and John Driffill, 'Bargaining Structure, Corporatism and Macroeconomic Performance' (1988) 6 *Economic Policy*, 14–61.

centralization[76] and unemployment: either end of the curve can be associated with containment of real wages. So, extreme decentralization with 'free', self-clearing labour markets, *or* extreme centralization, where centralized organizations of capital and labour are able to fix wage levels in an non-inflationary way, can be compatible with low unemployment.[77] Thus, weak trade union power, as in the US, or broad consensual corporatism, as in Sweden, helps explain these two countries' (erstwhile) ability to contain unemployment.[78]

Furthermore, with regard to the minimum wage, in its 1998 *Employment Outlook*, the OECD acknowledged that neither economic theory nor econometric calculations had been able to assess the exact impact of minimum wages on employment.[79] The consensus emerging from more recent literature is that high minimum wages and egalitarian wage structures have 'little or no effect on unemployment as such', although they do affect job opportunities for young and low-skilled workers.[80] Thus, it was recognized by the OECD that any negative impact on employment could be limited, for example, by fixing lower minima for young workers and trainees.[81] Having said this and conceding the advantages of wage minima—countries with relatively high minimum wages have narrower wage disparities and comparatively few low-paid jobs—nevertheless, the OECD remains committed to the greater flexibility of wages.[82]

However, even here—an issue on which neoclassical theory appears most self-assured—some micro-economic studies in the US and the UK have found zero or positive effects of minimum wages on employment.[83] Card and Krueger (in a

[76] Critics of this model have indicated that wage bargaining systems need not necessarily be centralized in order to achieve wage restraint—highly coordinated systems can achieve the same result: David Soskice, 'Wage Determination: The Changing Role of Institutions in Advanced Industrialized Countries' (1990) 6 *Oxford Review of Economic Policy*, 31–61.

[77] Colin Crouch, 'National Wage Determination and European Monetary Union' in Colin Crouch (ed.), *After the Euro: Shaping Institutions for Governance in the Wake of European Monetary Union* (Oxford: OUP, 2000) at 204–6.

[78] The fact that Swedish unemployment levels have risen dramatically since the 1980s moreover lends support to the theory, since Sweden witnessed a marked decentralization of wage bargaining during the 1980s: Esping-Andersen, n. 39 above, at 82. For an alternative view, rejecting the hump-shape hypothesis, see Traxler, who disputes that there is any 'systematic or robust impact' of bargaining centralization on aggregate wage increases, inflation or unemployment: Franz Traxler, 'Bargaining (De)centralization, Macroeconomic Performance and Control over the Employment Relationship', (2003) 41:1 *British Journal of Industrial Relations*, 1–27, especially at 3–4.

[79] OECD, *OECD Employment Outlook, June 1998* (Paris: OECD, 1998) at 31 and 42–5. See also the discussion in Hedva Sarfati, 'Labour Market Flexibility vs. Jobs: A Challenge for Social Dialogue in Europe', IAE de Paris, Université Paris 1, Panthéon-Sorbonne, GREGOR Working Paper 1999–07, at 5–6.

[80] See Esping-Andersen, n. 39 above, at 82, and references within.

[81] OECD, n. 79 above. See also David Neumark and William L. Wascher, 'Minimum Wages, Labor Market Institutions, and Youth Employment: A Cross-National Analysis' (2004) 57 *Industrial and Labor Relations Review*, 223–48, who argue that disemployment effects of minimum wages appear to be smaller in countries that have 'subminimum wage provisions' for young workers.

[82] See, for example, OECD, 'Key Employment Policy Challenges Faced By OECD Countries', Labour Market and Social Policy Occasional Papers No 31, OECD Submission to the G8 *Growth, Employability and Inclusion* Conference, London, 21–22 February 1998 (Paris: OECD, 1998).

[83] Gregg and Manning n. 73 above, at 409, and references within.

study of the fast food industry) go so far as to argue that higher minimum wages actually *encourage* job growth,[84] which could be due to the fact that more workers are attracted into the labour market because it is offering better opportunities.[85]

Finally, turning to employment protection legislation, as mentioned earlier, the OECD admits that 'empirical research to date has not provided a clear-cut answer' to the assumed link between EPL and unemployment. It is in the case of EPL that one can most clearly see the importance of disaggregating the effects of labour market institutions. Nickell and Layard bluntly state that: 'time spent worrying about strict labour market regulations, employment protection and minimum wages is probably time largely wasted'.[86] Indeed, the study by Edward Lazear is so often quoted in the literature because it is one of the very few empirical studies to conclude that employment security provisions have had a strongly and clearly adverse impact on employment;[87] in fact most other studies using aggregate data have failed to establish such an immediate relationship.[88] The 'common sense' view (within a neoclassical framework) is as follows:

'If regulations make it difficult to dissolve existing employment relationships then, other things being equal, large and sudden declines in employment (and therefore sharply rising unemployment) should indeed be less likely. On the other hand, however, there will also be less job creation: hence the individuals who do find themselves unemployed at any moment (including new entrants to the labour market) are less likely to exit into employment and are more likely to experience long-term unemployment.'[89]

The *overall impact* on employment is likely to be rather small, since the reduction in short-term unemployment and the rise in long-term unemployment tend to cancel each other out.[90] Thus, as recognized in the OECD's comprehensive survey of the empirical literature on the subject, EPL appears to have little impact on the *levels* of unemployment, but more on its *composition*.[91]

In conclusion, what this means in policy terms is that the EU discourse on unemployment is required to be more nuanced, and to distinguish between those

[84] David Card and Alan Krueger, 'Minimum Wages and Employment: A Case Study of the Fast Food Industry in New Jersey and Pennsylvania' (1994) 84 *American Economic Review*, 772–93; and *Myth and Measurement: The New Economics of the Minimum Wage* (Princeton, NJ: Princeton University Press, 1995).

[85] Gregg and Manning n. 73 above, at 409.

[86] Nickell and Layard, n. 13 above, at 70–1. They consider trade unions and social security systems to be greater causes for concern.

[87] Edward P. Lazear, 'Job Security Provisions and Unemployment' (1990) 105:3 *The Quarterly Journal of Economics*, 699–726.

[88] Christoph F. Büchtemann, 'Introduction: Employment Security and Labor Markets' in Christoph F. Büchtemann (ed.), *Employment Security and Labor Market Behavior: Interdisciplinary Approaches and International Evidence* (Ithaca, NY: ILR Press, 1993) at 33.

[89] Alogoskoufis *et al.*, n. 32 above, at 65.

[90] Nickell, n. 37 above, at 66.

[91] OECD, n. 56 above, at 69–70; see also Esping-Andersen, n. 39 above, at 67 and Nickell, n. 37 above.

'rigidities' which are 'dynamically harmful' to labour market performance, and those which may be benign in the face of other causes of unemployment, such as product and labour market failures.[92]

## 2.2 The efficiency-enhancing effect of labour market institutions

Drawing on the insights of new institutionalism, it is arguable that some labour market institutions ('rigidities' even) may well be beneficial to labour market performance, for reasons of efficiency or social cohesion[93] and should not all be 'deregulated' out of existence.

As seen above, labour markets do not conform to the ideal of classical 'spot' markets: labour market transactions tend to result in open-ended relationships, characterized by a high degree of uncertainty, informational asymmetries and sunk costs.[94] The resulting mutual dependence of the parties to the ongoing employment relationship necessitates either (costly and cumbersome) renegotiation of the necessarily incomplete employment contract, or recourse to specialized governance structures in order to generate trust and cooperation over the long term. Hence, the explanation offered by transaction cost/new institutionalist analysis for the rise of labour market institutions: vertical integration, internal labour markets, and collective bargaining are all governance mechanisms which supplement private law mechanisms, in order to internalize the work obligation and facilitate cooperation on the part of employees, by granting 'credible commitments' and 'efficiency wages'.[95] In other words, the normative framework supplied by labour law not only reduces transaction costs, but also provides stability in long-term relationships, which facilitates a higher degree of internal (namely, functional) flexibility and acceptance of technological change, incentives for investment in human capital by firms, and skill formation—thus improving productivity and competitiveness.[96]

This latter point, that labour market institutions can enhance efficiency by encouraging internal flexibility, is illustrated by the following example; the example also demonstrates how studies which narrowly focus on legal dismissal restraints (or only single components of them) and ignore their wider institutional settings are likely to come to misleading conclusions about the overall impact of employment protection policies.[97]

[92] See Adnett, n. 69 above, at 361. See also Krueger and Pischke, who argue that '[a]n alternative view is that labor market inflexibility is not the source of employment problems, but inflexibility elsewhere in the economy manifests itself in slower job growth. For example, restrictions on bringing new products to market or on starting new enterprises could reduce job growth', Alan Krueger and Jörn-Steffen Pischke, *Observations and Conjectures on the US Employment Miracle*, National Bureau of Economic Research Working Paper 6146 (Cambridge, MA: NBER, 1997).

[93] See Section 2.3 below.

[94] Deakin and Wilkinson, n. 30 above, at 293; Büchtemann, n. 88 above, at 51.

[95] See Chapter 1, Section 2.3.2 and references quoted therein.

[96] Büchtemann, n. 88 above, at 13. [97] Ibid., at 23–4.

Horst Seibert argues that, in the UK, '[s]everal laws contributing to rigid labor markets were passed in the 1960s and 1970s',[98] naming, amongst others, the Redundancy Payments Act 1965 and the 'Unfair Dismissal Law' of 1971.[99] However, a very convincing argument can be made that the Redundancy Payments Act, at least, which had the stated goal of promoting labour mobility and flexibility, in fact had some success in achieving this aim.[100] Although the liability to pay dismissed workers a fixed cash sum clearly increases employers' labour costs, in the industrial relations context of the time, the Act can be said to have greatly weakened resistance to change on the part of the workforce, and to have made economic dismissals more acceptable to employees and their trade unions,[101] thus facilitating the structural changes required by new technology, changing methods of production and changes in demand.[102] Although this is a weaker point, the unfair dismissal legislation can also be argued to enhance efficiency, on the basis, first, that secure workers are less likely to resist technological change and work reorganization,[103] and second, that the absence of appropriate dispute settlement procedures undermined cooperation and trust. Indeed, a particular concern of the UK government at the time of the enactment of the unfair dismissal provisions was the desire to reduce disruption to production due to industrial action, in great part in response to what were considered to be arbitrary dismissals by employers.[104]

Accordingly, it is important not to consider labour market institutions in isolation: employment protection legislation, for example, may well be contained within a wider institutional framework which provides incentives to stabilize employment, and a supporting infrastructure that enables firms to benefit from the efficiency advantages of internal labour markets and relational contacts.[105]

[98] Siebert, n. 36 above, at 41.

[99] Provisions introducing the right against unfair dismissal were in fact contained in the Conservative government's Industrial Relations Act 1971, ss 22–32, 106, 118–19; see Paul Davies and Mark Freedland' *Labour Legislation and Public Policy: A Contemporary History* (Oxford: OUP, 1993) at Chapter 5.

[100] Davies and Freedland, n. 99 above, at 142–64; Hugh Collins, *Justice in Dismissal: The Law of Termination of Employment* (Oxford: Clarendon Press, 1992) at 164–5.

[101] As Davies and Freedland explain, the government's view of the nature of the prevailing resistance to redundancy was that there was not simply resistance at the point when redundancies were proposed, but also a general unwillingness to accept efficient methods of working, coupled with a *collective* resistance to change: Davies and Freedland, n. 99 above, at 156–8.

[102] Evidence from a study of the operation of the redundancy payments legislation reports some success in achieving these goals: S. R. Parker, C. G. Thomas, N. D. Ellis and W. E. J. McCarthy, *Effects of the Redundancy Payments Act* (London: HMSO, 1971); quoted in Collins, n. 100 above.

[103] Esping-Andersen, n. 39 above, at 71.

[104] See Collins, n. 100 above, at 23–9, in particular his discussion of the Royal Commission on industrial relations which preceded the legislation: Royal Commission on Trade Unions and Employers' Associations (the 'Donovan Commission') Cmnd 3623 (London: HMSO, 1965–8).

[105] See Büchtemann, n. 88 above, at 65.

## 2.3 Beyond efficiency

'The main object of labour law has always been, and we venture to say will always be, to be a countervailing force to counteract the inequality of bargaining power which is inherent and must be inherent in the employment relationship.' (Kahn-Freund, 1977)[106]

The previous sections have explored the argument that *certain* labour market institutions have a benign or even positive effect on labour market performance, as well as the stronger claim that there are efficiency arguments for labour market regulation *as a whole*. These two sets of arguments for labour market institutions provide an important and useful counterpoint to the ongoing critique of labour market regulation from within neoclassical economic theory, the promulgation of a deregulatory agenda by the various international organizations,[107] and the increasing adoption of this agenda within the discourse of the EU institutions.

Why, then, is it necessary to go 'beyond efficiency' if an efficiency argument can be made for regulation? As both Hugh Collins and Karl Klare point out, efficiency arguments and equity arguments for labour market regulation can in fact overlap; equity concerns do not inherently conflict with other values: '[i]n particular, egalitarian redistribution does not intrinsically conflict with allocative efficiency'.[108]

Ultimately, however, the regulatory choices which have to be made in the structuring of markets, are choices which call for democratic decision; and in their analysis of such choices, a normative perspective is required from labour lawyers, without which 'Labour Law will lose its critical edge, and . . . may dissolve into simply another economistic exercise of evaluation of the efficiency of market regulation'.[109] The normative perspective provided by Kahn-Freund, as seen in the above quote, locates the justification for labour market regulation in the subordination of labour.[110] Whether one situates the origins of this subordination in the intrinsic inequality of bargaining power, the institution of wage labour, or the bureaucratic power exercised by hierarchies, labour market

106 Otto Kahn-Freund, *Labour and the Law* (London: Stevens, 1977) at 6.

107 This is examined again, in Chapter 3, in the context of the OECD's recommendations for European countries.

108 Karl Klare, 'Countervailing Workers' Power as a Regulatory Strategy' in Hugh Collins, Paul Davies and Roger Rideout (eds.), *Legal Regulation of the Employment Relation*, WG Hart Legal Workshop Series (London/The Hague: Kluwer, 2000) at 71. Hugh Collins proposes two sets of justifications for extensive regulation of the employment relation: market failure and distributive concerns, with some of the most persuasive justifications being 'mixed' ones: Hugh Collins, 'Justifications and Techniques of Legal Regulation of the Employment Relation' in Collins, Davies and Rideout (eds.).

109 Hugh Collins 'Labour Law as a Vocation' (1989) 105 LQR, 468–84, at 482.

110 Hugh Collins contrasts Kahn-Freund's conception of labour law, which considered the subordination of labour to be grounded in the intrinsic inequality of bargaining power, to alternative sources of subordination in (a) the institution of wage labour and (b) the bureaucratic power exercised by hierarchies: n. 109 above.

regulation is necessary to redress this imbalance. Since for most workers, the employment relation is their principal source of income, reasons of social justice necessitate labour standards so as to grant workers some security against being arbitrarily deprived of their subsistence, to give workers some countervailing power against employers in decision-making which affects their livelihood, and to provide some measure of redistribution.

To this conception of labour law, I would also add the importance of recognizing, and harnessing, the (macro-)economic goals to which labour law has been, and will be, directed.[111] Together, these two conceptions of labour law inform this book, in recognition of the fact that modern labour law serves a number of differing regulatory objectives: Karl Klare, for example, lists efficiency, macro-economic management, rights and redistribution.[112] Perhaps most importantly, the role of labour law is to provide a site for the reassessment and balancing of these competing narratives, but with the overriding mission of ensuring equity. Deakin and Wilkinson's view of this balancing is as follows:

> 'The case for fundamental employment rights must rest, in the final analysis, on factors which lie beyond any purely economic calculus; but it is equally clear that an assessment of the economic consequences of social legislation, whether at national or transnational level, should form a part of the process of social policy making.'[113]

It is against this backdrop, therefore, that the regulatory choices facing the EU are to be considered: that, whilst regulation may pursue differing regulatory objectives simultaneously, when it comes to the perceived 'trade-off' between social equity and economic efficiency, the requirements of redistribution, social justice and social cohesion should prevail over efficiency concerns.

## 3. Comparisons of labour market regulation in the EU and the US

Unfavourable comparisons with the relative successes of the US economy in creating employment have become a key feature of the debate within and between the EU institutions: the starting point for many discussions becomes the 'presumably drastic difference' between the US and continental European countries in labour market performance.[114] An example of this can be seen in the

[111] See Collins n. 109 above.

[112] Klare, n. 108 above, at 68–9. A valuable review of the competing functions of labour law is contained in the debate across the pages of the *Industrial Law Journal:* see Keith Ewing, 'Democratic Socialism and Labour Law' (1995) 24:2 ILJ, 103–32; Bob Hepple, 'The Future of Labour Law' (1995) 24:4 ILJ, 303–22; Hugh Collins, 'The Productive Disintegration of Labour Law' (1997) 26:4 ILJ, 295–309 and 'Regulating the employment relation for competitiveness' (2001) 30:1 ILJ, 17–48; Claire Kilpatrick, 'Has New Labour Reconfigured Employment Legislation?' (2003) 32:3 ILJ, 135–63.

[113] Deakin and Wilkinson, n. 30 above, at 310.

[114] Heiner Ganssmann, 'Labor Market Flexibility, Social Protection and Unemployment' (2000) 2:3 *European Societies*, 243–69, at 244.

policy pronouncements of Directorate-General II of the European Commission (Economic and Financial Affairs), for example in the contention that

'[i]f one looks at the overall performances of the European Union in terms of productivity and external equilibrium, the picture is satisfactory. . . . However, as regards the labour market, the most dominant feature of the EU is *the mediocrity of its employment growth and level* with respect not only to what the Union was able to sustain during the 1960s but also compared to the United States and Japan.'[115]

There are two underlying premises here: first, that the reason the US economy is better at promoting employment growth, or at transforming population growth into employment, or at employing more of its workforce (that is, the higher US employment rate, in addition to its lower unemployment rate) is that it has a more flexible labour market; that the 'more flexible wages, employment practices, and laws in the US better conduce toward job generation than do the more rigid practices and laws in Europe'.[116] Second, that US-style labour market flexibility is therefore the answer to Europe's unemployment ills.

The first premise has been unpacked in the above sections on the basic tenets of the labour market flexibility debate, and the critique of this debate. As for the second, Chapters 3 and 4 will argue that the preparedness to adopt the US model of labour market regulation is a relatively recent development in the EU's discourse; that a change in emphasis is detectable, between the way in which the unemployment problem was diagnosed within EU debates of the early 1990s, as exemplified by the Commission White Paper of 1993,[117] and the way in which the problem is currently being discussed in the post-Amsterdam, post-Lisbon era. The questions for this section are whether it really is the case that a 'flexible' labour market is the main cause of the US 'employment miracle', and whether policy-makers in the EU and its Member States should continue to place so much emphasis on the US–EU comparison.

## 3.1 The US 'employment miracle'

'Many European analysts and policymakers view the US labor market as a paradise of neoclassical flexibility. Wages respond rapidly to changes in supply and demand in local labor markets with little institutional intervention. Jobs are readily created for those who seek them. Firms hire and fire at will, with little government or union restrictions. Spells of unemployment are short in duration, and unemployment benefits modest. As a result, so the story goes, the United States has avoided the long extensive joblessness that has characterized Europe since the early 1980s. . . .

[115] CEC, *Growth and Employment in the Stability-Oriented Framework of EMU: Economic Policy Reflections in View of the Forthcoming 1998 Broad Guidelines* (Luxembourg: OOPEC, 1998) II/33/98-EN, at 5–6; emphasis in the original.

[116] Editorial Comment, 'The US "Employment Miracle": Employment Protection and Job Generation' (1998) 19 *Comparative Labor Law and Policy Journal*, 279.

[117] CEC, White Paper *Growth, Competitiveness and Employment*, n. 15 above.

'Many American analysts and policymakers, however, view the US job market differently. Wage inequality grew in the 1980s. The real earnings of the less-skilled plummeted, to the point where workers in the lower parts of the earnings distribution have living standards below those of comparatively situated workers in Europe.' (Freeman, 1996)[118]

During the 1980s, employment grew rapidly in the US, prompting many commentators to label the US economy the 'great American job machine' or to call this the phenomenon the 'US employment miracle'.[119] As can be seen from Figure 2.1 and Figure 2.2, since the early 1980s the standardized[120] rates of unemployment in the US have been consistently lower than those in the EC/EU—for over a decade, the US unemployment rate was roughly 3 percentage points below that in Europe.[121] US unemployment fell during the 1980s when that in the EC was rising and was again in abeyance for most of the 1990s,[122] lending support to the labour market flexibility hypothesis.

There is a similar picture with regard to employment rates and jobs growth. In 1974, the ratio of employment to the population aged 15–64 was the same in the US and in OECD–Europe, ie 64.8 per cent. However, by 1992 the employment rate was 71.1 per cent in the US and 60.1 per cent in OECD–Europe.[123] One of the main explanations for this fall in labour market participation across many European countries was the rise in 'non-employment', namely increased resort to early retirement, and the rise in the number of people on incapacity or disability benefits, in part as a response to mass unemployment.[124] As for employment growth, with the exception of Ireland, the US has clearly outperformed the EU Member States in terms of average net employment growth over the past two decades, as shown by Figure 2.3. The strength of the US economy in generating

[118] Richard Freeman 'Doing It Right? The US Labor Market Response to the 1980s–1990s' in Herbert Giersch (ed.), *Fighting Europe's Unemployment in the 1990s* (Berlin/New York: Springer, 1996) at 23; reference omitted.

[119] See the special issue of *Comparative Labor Law and Policy Journal* (1998) Vol 19; see also Susan N. Houseman, 'Job Growth and the Quality of Jobs in the US Economy' *Labour: Review of Labour Economics and Industrial Relations* 1995 (IIRA) S93–S124, at S93.

[120] See Section 3.2.1 below for the significance of this term in the context of unemployment statistics.

[121] Freeman, n. 118 above, at 33.

[122] With the exception of the early 1990s, when the US economy fell into recession, but then 'rebounded with the longest running expansion in the Nation's history': Julie Hatch and Angela Clinton, 'Job Growth in the 1990s: A Retrospect' (2000) 123:12 *Monthly Labor Review*, 3–18, at 3. For the statistics, see US Department of Labor, Bureau of Labor Statistics, *Labor Force Statistics from the Current Population Survey*, available at *http://www.bls.gov/cps/*, data extracted on 10 April 2005.

[123] Freeman, n. 118 above, at 33.

[124] See Chapters 4 and 6. The shift from state-sanctioned early retirement and other labour shedding strategies, towards an increased emphasis within the EU on greater labour market participation, especially by women and older workers, was crystallized in the goal of 'full employment' articulated at the Lisbon European Council, and reinforced at the Stockholm European Council the subsequent year. Thus, Member States committed themselves to raising the overall employment rate to as close as possible to 70% by 2010, and the female employment rate to more than 60% (Presidency Conclusions, Lisbon European Council, 23 and 24 March 2000, Bull EU 3/2000, 7–17, at para 30) as well as to increasing the average employment rate amongst older workers (55 to 64) to 50% by 2010 (Presidency Conclusions, Stockholm European Council, 23 and 24 March 2001, Bull EU-3/2001, 1–40, at para 9).

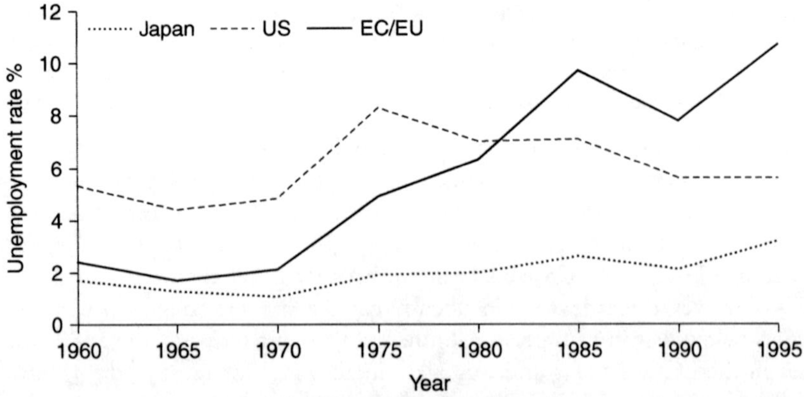


**Figure 2.1** The evolution of unemployment rates 1960–1995

*Sources:* OECD standardized unemployment rates (as a percentage of the total labour force), 1960–2001 (see Note).

*Note:* This chart has been created using OECD standardized unemployment rates, taken from Richard Layard, Stephen Nickell and Richard Jackman, *Unemployment: Macroeconomic Performance and the Labour Market* (Oxford: OUP, 1991) at Annex 1.6, Table A.3.

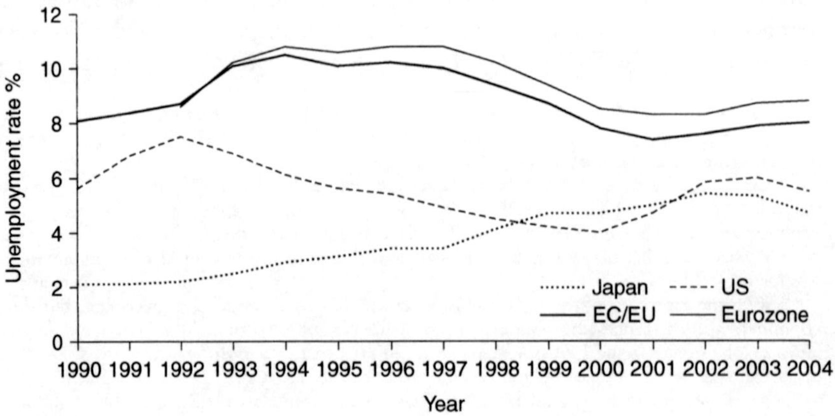


**Figure 2.2** The evolution of unemployment rates 1990–2004

*Sources:* OECD standardized unemployment rates (as a percentage of the total labour force), 1990–2004 (see Note).

*Note:* This chart has been created using OECD standardized unemployment rates, taken form *OECD Economic Outlook No 73*, June 2003, Statistical Annex (Paris: OECD, 2003) Table 15; *OECD Economic Outlook No 75* June 2004, Statistical Annex (Paris: OECD, 2004) Table 14; *OECD Main Economic Indicators, April 2004* (Paris: OECD, 2005) at 16.

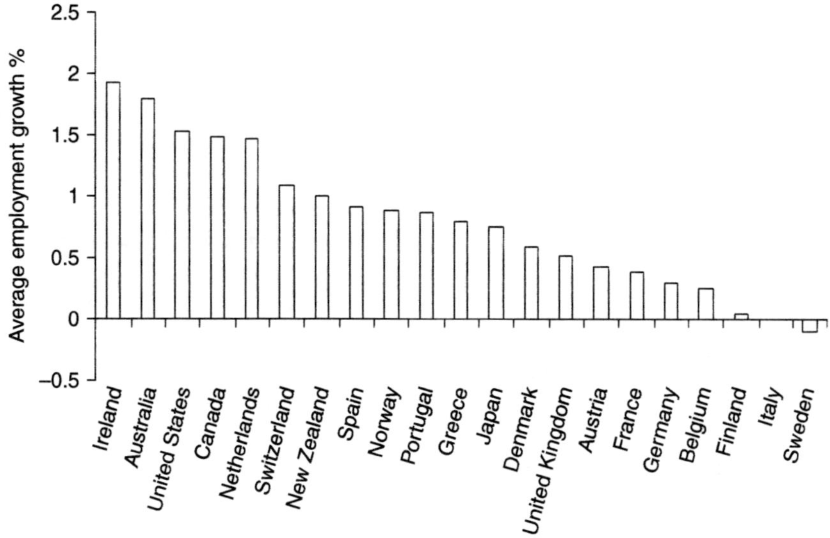


**Figure 2.3** Net employment growth in selected OECD countries, 1980–2000

*Sources:* Pietro Garibaldi and Paolo Mauro, 'Anatomy of Employment Growth' (2002) *Economic Policy*, 67–173, at 78.

new jobs is further highlighted by the IMF: in a comparison between the US and the Euro area,[125] the IMF reports that

'The underlying weakness in the labor market performance of the euro area is even more striking when comparing private sector employment growth, although this partly reflects differences in growth of the labor force: nongovernment employment in the United States increased by 70 percent between 1970 and 1998, while the increase was well below 5 percent in the euro area over the same period.'[126]

Since the credit for this employment miracle is so regularly attributed to the deregulated regime of the US labour market, it is worthwhile to review briefly the key features which differentiate this system from labour market regulation in most EU Member States. The three broad regulatory categories used above (social protection/welfare state provision, wage-setting mechanisms and employment protection legislation) will again be adopted.

Starting with EPL, with regard to protection of workers against (individual) dismissal, the OECD in 1999 and again in 2004 ranked member countries'

[125] Namely, the EU15 minus Denmark, Sweden and the UK; although the Euro area did not come into being until 1 January 1999, the term is used by the IMF to refer to the group of countries that now form the area, before as well as after the area's inception.

[126] IMF, n. 17 above, at 88.

dismissal protection on the basis of the procedural inconveniences an employer faces when trying to dismiss, notice and severance pay conditions, and prevailing standards of and penalties for unfair dismissal.[127] Not unexpectedly, the US was ranked as the least restrictive overall on both occasions (with the UK and Canada joint second both times). Within OECD–Europe, the Netherlands, Sweden, Portugal and Italy were amongst the most restrictive in 1999, with Spain and Greece replacing the Netherlands and Sweden by 2004.[128] Historically, employment relationships in the US have been governed by the common law doctrine of employment at will. Under this rule, either party can, in the absence of an express term, unilaterally terminate the contract at any time, meaning that employees can be dismissed without notice or compensation. This doctrine has of course been challenged in state courts and numerous decisions have recognized 'exceptions' to employment at will.[129] In addition, some states have passed laws requiring 'just cause' for dismissals,[130] and federal law prevents discrimination, including discriminatory dismissal, for engaging in lawful trade union activities, or on grounds of race, sex, age and disability.[131] The employment at will doctrine has thus been significantly eroded by statutory and common law protections against wrongful discharge. Nevertheless, regulation is still very minimal in comparison with EU Member States, and to the extent that there *are* restrictions on managerial prerogative, it is possible to avoid the effect by increased resort to temporary and other contingent labour, which is for the most part un- or lightly regulated.[132] There are no restrictions on the use of fixed-term contracts, or limits on the number of times such contracts can be renewed, or on the type of work for which temporary work agencies can be used.[133]

[127] *OECD Employment Outlook, June 1999*, n. 56 above, at 54; OECD, *OECD Employment Outlook 2004*, n. 40 above, at 112.

[128] *OECD Employment Outlook, June 1999*, n. 56 above, at 57, table 2.2–Indicators of the strictness of employment protection for regular employment; *OECD Employment Outlook 2004*, n. 40 above, at 112.

[129] Of the three major exceptions to employment at will developed at common law (the public policy exception, the implied contract exception and the 'covenant of good faith and fair dealing') 43 of the 50 states recognize the first, 38 the second, and 11 recognize the third: Charles J. Muhl, 'The Employment-at-Will Doctrine: Three Major Exceptions' (2001) 124:1 *Monthly Labor Review*, 3–11, at 4.

[130] See Thomas J. Miles, 'Common Law Exceptions to Employment at Will and US Labor Markets' (2000) 16:1 *Journal of Law, Economics and Organization*, 74–101.

[131] Namely, the National Labor Relations Act 1935, the Civil Rights Act 1964, the Age Discrimination in Employment Act 1967, and the Americans with Disabilities Act 1990.

[132] 'Employment in the temporary help services industry is observed to grow by about a statistically significant 15% in the presence of an employment at will exception': Miles, n. 130 above, at 98.

[133] In 1999, the US (jointly with Canada and the UK) came out at the bottom of the OECD's ranking for overall strictness of regulation of temporary employment, with France, Italy and Portugal at the top of the ranking: *OECD Employment Outlook, June 1999*, n. 56 above, at 63, table 2.3–Regulation of temporary employment. By 2004, the UK regulation was considered to be marginally stricter: *OECD Employment Outlook 2004*, n. 40 above, at 115. Since 1999, however, the UK as an EU Member State has become subject to the EC directive on fixed-term workers, and will in time become subject to the EC directive on temporary workers, the intended aim of which is to strike a balance between flexibility and job security for this group of non-standard

As for collective dismissals, Canada, the UK and the US occupy a middle position in the country rankings for overall strictness, due to the fact that each country has 'considerable' waiting periods and notification requirements in the event of collective dismissals, which have been imposed by legislation.[134] In the case of the US, the federal Worker Adjustment and Retraining Notification Act (WARN) of 1988 requires firms to which the Act applies to provide employees with 60 days' advance notice of plant closures and large-scale layoffs. However, there is strong evidence that compliance with the Act has not been effectively enforced at state level.[135] Problems with compliance and enforcement are not, of course, unique to US labour law,[136] but a particular difficulty, connected to the decline in trade union density, is that resources for organization and staff to enforce legal rights have not increased: 'given limited regulatory staff and absent works councils or other local groups of employees to work with management to monitor local work conditions, American workers have flooded agencies and courts with suits on employment issues'.[137]

Another key facet of labour market regulation in the US which differs so sharply from that found in the EU relates to wage-setting institutions. In most EU Member States, with the exception of the UK, trade unions play a very significant role in wage determination.[138] However, in the US union density fell dramatically from the 1960s onwards, and by 2000 stood at 13.6 per cent,[139] compared with union density rates of 39 per cent for Italy and the UK, and 33 per cent for Germany.[140] So, although the 1935 National Labor Relations Act gives workers the nominal right to self representation,[141] the long-standing

workers: Council Directive 99/70/EC of 28 June 1999 concerning the framework agreement on fixed-term work concluded by UNICE, CEEP and the ETUC, OJ L 175, 10.07.1999; CEC, Amended proposal for a directive on working conditions for temporary workers, COM (2002) 701 final, Brussels, 28.11.2002.

134 OECD, *OECD Employment Outlook, June 1999*, n. 56 above, at 64.

135 Buchele and Christiansen, n. 34 above, at 124.

136 A difficulty with which lawyers have long been familiar, and of which economists are now becoming increasingly aware (see Bertola, Boeri and Cazes, n. 176 below) is that any claims as to the effect of the law on the statute books must somehow take account of the fallibility of enforcement mechanisms. However, the point I am making here is simply that the formal regime at federal level in the US is one of minimal regulation of the employment relation in comparison with most EU Member States.

137 Freeman, n. 118 above, at 40.

138 Nickell, n. 37 above, at 62.

139 Barry T. Hirsch, David A. Macpherson and Wayne G. Vroman, 'Estimates of union density by State' (2001) 124:7 *Monthly Labor Review*, 51–5.

140 See Nickell, n. 37 above, at 63, drawing upon OECD figures for the mid-1990s. As previously noted, union density is low in France, at about 10%, but there is wide extension of collective agreements, so that approximately 90% of workers are covered by collective agreements. Multi-employer bargaining with arrangements for extending the scope of bargains to all firms in either a sector or the whole country exists in nearly all EU countries, with the exception of the UK and Ireland: Crouch, n. 77 above, at 212–13.

141 (The Wagner Act) Ch 372, 49 Stat. 449 (1935); now at 29 USC para 151–68 (1970). For the view that federal labour law generally fails to protect even the nominal rights of workers, see Karl Klare, 'Judicial Deradicalization of the Wagner Act and the Origins of Modern Legal Consciousness' (1978)

weakness of US trade unions has meant that wage formation is highly decentralized, both across industries and even within individual firms.[142] As a result, wages are extremely flexible downwards: the severe fall in union density and the related drop in collective bargaining coverage occurred in parallel with the stagnation of median wages, the decline in lower-paid workers' wages and the increased inequality of wage distribution.[143]

Finally, with regard to welfare provision, in particular income support for the unemployed, the unemployment benefit replacement rate, at 50 per cent of the mean wage, is described as 'fairly generous by US standards'[144] but this is offset by the fact that its duration is limited to six months, and eligibility for benefits is much lower in the US than in most EU countries.[145] Furthermore, this initial net replacement rate becomes markedly less generous once the replacement ratio is averaged over various family types and benefit duration periods.[146] On the basis of this assessment, the US is shown to provide the least generous level of support for the unemployed, as compared with the EU, Norway and Switzerland.[147]

This, in brief, is the model of labour market flexibility which the EU has sought, or been recommended, to emulate. By the early 1980s, the OECD and others were becoming concerned that regulations and welfare provision in European countries were seriously reducing labour market flexibility and increasing unemployment. Additionally, US policy-makers have sought to export this model: in the 1980s the US government developed guidelines which emphasized the need for OECD countries to remove barriers to efficient resource allocation. For labour markets, this meant eliminating rigidities which interfere with the efficient operation of the labour market, such as overly generous unemployment compensation and welfare payments, high non-wage labour costs for employers, state or centralized determination of wages, restrictions on hiring or firing, and high minimum wages.[148]

62 *Minnesota Law Review*, 265–339; and Joel Rogers, 'Divide and Conquer: Further Reflections on the Distinctive Character of American Labor Laws' (1990) *Wisconsin Law Review*, 1–147.

[142] IMF, n. 17 above, at 95.

[143] Buchele and Christiansen, n. 34 above, at 131. The writers also note a similar pattern in the UK, where the earnings distribution became more sharply unequal as union density and collective bargaining coverage also declined, although median earnings did in fact rise strongly. See also Gosling and Lemieux, who argue that the extent and pattern of wage inequality became increasingly similar in the UK and the US between 1979 and 1998, a convergence which they attribute to 'US style' reforms in the UK labour market: Amanda Gosling and Thomas Lemieux, 'Labour Market Reforms and Changes in Wage Inequality in the United Kingdom and the United States' in David Card, Richard Blundell and Richard Freeman (eds.), *Seeking a Premier Economy: The Economic Effects of British Economic Reforms, 1980–2000* (Chicago: University of Chicago Press, National Bureau of Economic Research Comparative Labour Market Series, 2004).

[144] Nickell, n. 37 above, at 61. [145] Esping-Andersen, n. 39 above, at 75.

[146] In its *World Economic Outlook*, the IMF created a synthetic 'generosity indicator', in an attempt to compare levels of income support for the unemployed, which took account of two income levels, three duration categories and three types of family situation: IMF, n. 17 above, at 103–4. [147] Ibid.

[148] US Department of State, 'US Government Approach to Structural Adjustment' (unpublished manuscript) Washington: Department of State, 1984; quoted in Melvin M. Brodsky, 'Labor Market Flexibility: A Changing International Perspective' (1994) 117:11 *Monthly Labor Review*, 53–60.

## 3.2 Is the US an appropriate model?

'The currently popular contrast between sclerotic Europe and dynamic America is no doubt simplistic but, worse, it is also poor analytical practice. Does it make sense to compare 16-odd European nations with one single alternative, the United States?' (Esping-Andersen, 1999)[149]

The following is not intended to dispute the fact of the impressive employment growth which has occurred in the US, but rather to suggest that the 'miraculous' nature of this employment growth has been overstated, and that such growth has not been without a cost, namely, that of increased inequality. Thus, the question as to whether the US is an appropriate model for the EU to follow requires a consideration, first, of whether the US is a suitable *comparator* for the EU; and second, of whether the deregulated labour market in the US was really the cause of its 'employment miracle' (bearing in mind the analysis above, casting doubt on the link between labour market institutions and unemployment).

### *3.2.1 Problems of cross-country comparisons*

With regard to the first set of issues, there exist numerous difficulties with making cross-country comparisons of labour market performance.[150] One important obstacle to accurate comparison is the definition of unemployment used in the comparative statistics. Standardized unemployment rates, as used by Eurostat, the OECD, the US Bureau of Labor Statistics (BLS) and the ILO, are based on the definition of unemployment adopted by the 13th Conference of Labour Statisticians (the ILO Guidelines). According to these guidelines, a person is recorded as unemployed if she or he is currently not engaged in paid work, is available to start work within the next two weeks, and has actively sought employment within the previous four weeks. However, different countries have chosen to implement these latter two criteria differently, which causes certain incompatibilities in the measurement of unemployment internationally.[151]

As Ganssmann points out, many unemployed persons are unlikely to fulfil the third of the ILO criteria, actively searching for a job, for example, because they live in a high unemployment area with few job openings, in which search efforts seem futile.[152] Such passive jobseekers are, however, included in the numbers of unemployed in Canada and by Eurostat for the EU, but excluded from the US figures.[153] An unpublished Bureau of Labor Statistics analysis (based on 1997 data) indicates that if passive jobseekers who were without work and available for work had been included in the unemployed, they would have composed about 3.4 per cent of total US unemployment. Their inclusion would have increased

[149] Gøsta Esping-Andersen, *Social Foundations of Postindustrial Economies* (Oxford: OUP, 1999) at 99.
[150] See Constance Sorrentino, 'International Unemployment Rates: How Comparable Are They?' (2000) 123:6 *Monthly Labour Review*, 3–20.
[151] Ibid., at 4.
[152] Ganssmann, n. 114 above, at 254.
[153] Sorrentino, n. 150 above, at 8 ff.

the unemployment rate only marginally, by about 0.15 percentage point.[154] However, it is important to bear in mind that there are also differences in concepts which cause the US unemployment rate to be *overstated*.[155] Accordingly, adjustments are made for comparability by the ILO, OECD, Eurostat and the BLS. Nevertheless, many important differences—such as the lower age limit—remain unadjusted,[156] leaving incompatibilities in the statistics and other variables which undermine the accuracy of cross-national comparisons.

Furthermore, differences in eligibility for unemployment benefit also contribute to divergent classification of passive jobseekers or the 'nonemployed'. For example, reforms in the UK in 1996 replaced unemployment benefits with a 'jobseekers allowance' combined with tighter eligibility and mandatory periodic review of applicants' search efforts.[157] Layard *et al.* suggest that the earlier fall in British unemployment had been related to the introduction of stricter eligibility rules.[158] However, similarly strict eligibility criteria, *where combined with relative generosity* with regard to the amount and duration of benefit, can lead to more people being classed as unemployed, as more will wish to qualify for benefits.[159] Jobseekers in the US, however active, who have been unemployed for more than six months (the cut-off point for receipt of unemployment benefit) are less likely to remain on the lists of the unemployed. Such differences in unemployment insurance coverage contribute to the non-employed being counted as unemployed in countries which either do not impose strict eligibility criteria, or in which such restrictions are tempered by generous benefits of long duration; indeed Card and Riddell have attributed a large share of the difference in the overall unemployment rates between the US and Canada to such effects.[160]

### *3.2.2 Differences between EU Member States*

The quotation from Gøsta Esping-Andersen that introduces Section 3.2 above alludes to the danger of overstating the similarities between (un)employment

[154] Phil Rones, 'Comparison of the Labor Market Outcomes of Active and Passive Job Search', paper presented at the 6–7 July 1998 meeting of the Paris Group, London; quoted in Sorrentino, above n. 150.

[155] For example, in contrast to the EU, in the US students who are available for work and who are seeking a job are classified as unemployed, as are all persons on temporary layoff, with no requirement to conduct a job search: Sorrentino, n. 150 above, at 8.

[156] The US lower age limit is 16 years. Canada and Eurostat use a lower limit of 15 years. Youths aged 15 tend to have higher-than-average unemployment rates: Sorrentino, n. 150 above.

[157] See Peck and Theodore, n. 24 above, at 735; and the discussion in Chapter 6.

[158] 'There is evidence of increasing lenience of administration in Britain for the mid-1960s through the 1970s.... Since 1986 conditions have been substantially tightened, with marked apparent effects on outflow rates': Richard Layard, Stephen Nickell and Richard Jackman, *Unemployment: Macroeconomic Performance and the Labour Market* (Oxford: OUP, 1991) at 258.

[159] Ganssmann, n. 114 above, at 254.

[160] David Card and W. Craig Riddell, 'A Comparative Analysis of Unemployment in Canada and the United States' in David Card and Richard Freeman (eds.), *Small Differences that Matter: Labor Markets and Income Maintenance in Canada and the United States* (Chicago: University of Chicago Press, 1993).

trends in EU Member States in order to provide a suitable contrast with the US 'employment miracle'. As Stephen Nickell cautions, 'labor markets in Europe exhibit enormous diversity; in fact, differences within Europe are much greater than are the differences between the European average and North America.[161] And indeed, the figures for February 2005 indicate a wide variation in levels of *unemployment* across EU Member States: from 4.3 and 4.6 per cent in Ireland and Austria, to 16.2 and 18.1 per cent in Slovakia and Poland.[162] The *employment* rate also varies enormously around the average of 64.3 per cent for the EU15 (62.9 per cent for the EU25), from 51.2 per cent in Poland, to 75.1 per cent in Denmark,[163] in comparison with the US rate of 65.6 per cent in March 2005.[164]

Dutch unemployment rates have been lower than those in the US since 1998,[165] and the country's employment rate has also been consistently higher, currently at 73.5 per cent.[166] Furthermore, whilst the Dutch Welfare State has shrunk to some degree, it is still one of the most generous and comprehensive social security systems in the world, with some of the lowest poverty rates.[167] So why should the rest of the EU not be encouraged to adopt the Dutch model, to emulate the Dutch 'employment miracle'?[168] Another possible model for

[161] Nickell, n. 37 above, at 55. For an attempt to explain such diversity, see Gilles Saint-Paul, 'Why are European Countries Diverging in their Unemployment Experience?' (2004) 18:4 *Journal of Economic Perspectives*, 49–68.

[162] Eurostat: Statistical Office of the European Communities in Luxembourg, Euro-indicators News Release No 44/2005, 1 April 2005. As could be expected, the statistical range has widened considerably since the EU's enlargement to 25 Member States in May 2004; nevertheless, even in the EU of 15, there was still significant divergence in the experience of unemployment and employment. For example, the figures for January 2002 ranged from 2.3 and 2.6 per cent in the Netherlands and Luxembourg, to 9.0 and 12.9 per cent in Italy and Spain: Eurostat, Euro-indicators News Release No 27/2002, 5 March 2002 and No 40/2002, 3 April 2002.

[163] These figures from 2003, the last year for which statistics are available for EU countries, are taken from CEC, *Joint Employment Report 2004–5: Background document, Commission Staff Working Paper revised following bilateral and EMCO meetings*, (Luxembourg: CEC, 2005) and CEC, *Employment in Europe 2004: Recent Trends and Prospects* (Luxembourg: CEC, 2004). Prior to enlargement in 2004, Italy and Greece had been the outliers, with employment rates some 15–20 percentage points behind those in Sweden, Denmark and the UK.

[164] US Department of Labor, Bureau of Labor Statistics, *News–The Employment Situation: March 2005* (Washington, DC: BLS, 2005). The 2005 figures are mostly unchanged from the rate of 66% in 2003.

[165] OECD, *Quarterly Labour Force Statistics, 2004/4* (Paris: OECD, 2004) at 153.

[166] CEC, *Employment in Europe 2004: Recent Trends and Prospects* (Luxembourg: CEC, 2004), at 255.

[167] Uwe Becker, 'A "Dutch Model": Employment Growth by Corporatist Consensus and Wage Restraint? A Critical Account of an Idyllic View' (2001) 6:1 *New Political Economy*, 19–43, at 33–5. See also Jan C. van Ours, 'Has the Dutch Miracle Come to an End?' CESifo (Munich Society for the Promotion of Economic Research) Working Paper No 917 Category 4: Labour Markets, April 2003.

[168] For a rather sanguine assessment of just why the Dutch model is not an appropriate one for the rest of the EU, see Becker n. 167 above, who points to the size of the country (16 million people) and the uniqueness of its (wage formation) systems, making international translation difficult. See also the discussion of the 'Dutch miracle' in Chapter 6.

other EU countries is Denmark. The *Joint Employment Report 2001* pointed out that

'The Danish economy continues to perform strongly, with economic growth at 2.9% in 2000. Although there was only a small rise in the overall employment rate to 76.3%, it is still the highest in the EU, both for men (80.8%) and women (71.6%). Unemployment has further decreased to 4.7%, particularly for women, youth unemployment has gone down to 5.3%, and long-term unemployment is 1%.'[169]

As Jane Lewis reminds us, Scandinavian countries have adopted an adult worker model, just as developed as in the US, which assumes that all citizens will be in the labour market. The difference is in the level of welfare state provision: for example, care work in the US is entirely unsupported, while in the Scandinavian countries it is supported in a variety of ways, by services and by generous leave entitlements with wage replacement.[170] Denmark, for example, has pursued active labour market policies which place pressure on the unemployed to participate in employment or training programmes, but this has been underpinned by high levels of social security, and a coordinated and mostly consensual system of industrial relations with high union density.[171] The result has been high rates of employment and low unemployment combined with one of the most generous welfare systems and highest rates of equality in the OECD world.

However, there are a number of reasons why the Dutch or Danish systems are not so frequently cited as possible models for the rest of the EU to emulate. The employment successes are still fairly recent, and may yet turn out to be mostly cyclical.[172] Furthermore, particularly in the case of Denmark, a relatively small and homogenous country can take measures which larger countries cannot, and achieve a greater degree of consensus. But it is arguable that the most important reason the US model continues to be held up as the example for others to follow is that the paths taken by the Netherlands and Denmark do not quite conform to the route foreseen within the 'standard neoclassical policy blueprint'[173] of a deregulated economy. My argument, elaborated in greater detail in Chapter 3, is that the framing of the EU discourse around unemployment, welfare and labour market policies and reform of labour market intuitions, owes much to the discourse of the international financial institutions, in particular that of the OECD, as articulated

[169] CEC, *Joint Employment Report 2001*. 163, at 43. Following a seven-year period of strong economic growth, resulting in a 25-year low in employment in 2002, Denmark experienced economic slowdown in 2002–3, but was set to recover in 2004–5: CEC, *Joint Employment Report 2004–5: Addendum I (Country Reports)* (Luxembourg: CEC, 2005) at 13–14.

[170] Jane Lewis, 'Social Insurance and Future Work' in David Marsden and Hugh Stephenson (eds.), *Labour Law and Social Insurance in the New Economy: A Debate on the Supiot Report* (London: Centre for Economic Performance, LSE, 2001) at 52.

[171] Christoffer Green-Pedersen, Kees van Kersbergen and Anton Hemerijck, 'Neo-liberalism, the "Third Way" or What? Recent Social Democratic Welfare Policies in Denmark and the Netherlands' (2001) 8:2 *Journal of European Public Policy*, 307–25, at 314–19. See also Christoffer Green-Pedersen, 'Small States, Big Success. Party Politics and Governing the Economy in Denmark and the Netherlands from 1973 to 2000' (2003) 1:3 *Socio-Economic Review*, 411–37.

[172] Ganssmann, n. 114 above, at 265. [173] Ibid., at 263.

in the 1994 *Jobs Study* and reiterated in the 2004 reassessment of the *Jobs Study*.[174] As far as regional models or exemplars are concerned, on international rankings, the EPL of both countries (especially that of the Netherlands) is still considered 'strict'. Both the Netherlands and Denmark have in recent years engaged in differing versions of labour market flexibility, but within limits: for example, the Netherlands is noted for flexibility in the organization of working time, although wage flexibility remains limited.[175]

This brings me to the question of the measurement of the strictness of EPL, as distinct from arguments as to its effect on labour market performance. Traditionally, as we have seen, economists have tended to attribute the poor employment performance of European labour markets in comparison to the US to the strictness of their employment protection legislation. However, Bertola, Boeri and Cazes argue that although the effects of EPL are fairly clear from a *theoretical* standpoint, they are difficult to study *in practice*. The empirical work provides mixed results in the evaluation of the influence of labour market regulation on labour market adjustment: '[s]tudies using "rigidity rankings" as indicators of EPL [do] not give clear-cut results. This may be due to the elusive and complex nature of available information, and of the EPL concept itself'.[176]

In other words, the role played by EPL in labour market outcomes is mostly an empirical matter, but the empirical research on the macro-economic effects of EPL has had to rely on 'highly imperfect' measures of the strictness of these regulations. Recent reforms to EPL in most countries, and the expansion of non-standard forms of employment have rendered the existing information obsolete and called into question the methodological basis for such empirical exercises.[177] As for the implications for policy, Bertola, Boeri and Cazes therefore suggest that

'policy recommendation should be formulated with caution, and should not be based on the largely unsatisfactory information available to date. In particular, available rankings of employment protection cannot be used for the purpose of surveillance of structural reforms in the labour market area, as envisaged in the European context of the Luxembourg process. A broad conclusion of the report is that simplification of rules in this area is needed for Governments to regain control over the enforcement of EPL.'[178]

174 See Chapter 3; see also Jörg Michael Dostal, 'Campaigning on expertise: how the OECD framed EU welfare and labour market policies—and why success could trigger failure' (2004) 11:3 *Journal of European Public Policy*, 440–60.

175 See Chapter 6 for an assessment of the Dutch policy of 'flexicurity'.

176 Giuseppe Bertola, Tito Boeri and Sandrine Cazes, 'Employment Protection and Labour Market Adjustment in OECD Countries: Evolving Institutions and Variable Enforcement', International Labour Organization, Employment and Training Papers No 48, 1999.

177 Gek-Boo Ng, 'Foreword' in Bertola, Boeri and Cazes, n. 176 above.

178 Bertola, Boeri and Cazes, n. 176 above. See also: Giuseppe Bertola, Tito Boeri and Sandrine Cazes, 'Employment protection in industrialized countries: The case for new indicators' (2000) 139:1 *International Labour Review*, 57–72; and OECD, *Policy Brief—Employment Protection: The Costs and Benefits of Greater Job Security*, September 2004 (Paris: OECD, 2004).

What this means for analyses which present the US as a model for others to copy is that not only can their assumptions as to the causal link between EPL and unemployment be doubted (as above) but also their empirical assumptions as to the greater strictness of EPL in most European countries.

### *3.2.3 Alternative explanations for high US jobs growth and its low rates of unemployment*

Those who have deconstructed the US 'employment miracle' argue that the US provides a flawed model for the EU because a large percentage of its faster jobs growth can be attributed to its faster population growth, rather than the more flexible labour market operating in the US. Todd Godbout, for example, attributes about three-quarters of the employment growth between 1970 and 1990 to the growth in the population of working age, and one-quarter to the increase in workforce participation.[179] Other estimates vary between 60 and 70 per cent.[180] Ganssmann suggests that the significant population growth in the US—a stark contrast to most European countries—leads 'quasi-automatically to employment growth since the economy can expand by simply doing more of the same'.[181] However, at least some credit is due to the US economy, in that it was necessary for the rise in the population—the increased supply of labour—to be accompanied by a rise in labour force participation, and here it does seem clear that the US was better at transforming population growth into employment: 'the US has managed to absorb added workers—especially female workers—into employment at a greater rate than most countries'.[182]

A second alternative explanation for US jobs growth is that there have been low wage increases, which have encouraged the hiring of more workers; in effect leading to a form of job-sharing amongst low-waged workers.[183] Bertola *et al.* offer a more nuanced view of the correlation between the low relative unemployment rate in the US and the slower growth of real wages since the 1970.[184] They document the familiar claim that high wage inequality and low wage levels are associated with low unemployment, noting for example that '[b]etween 1979–81 and 1994–98, median real weekly earnings of male full-time workers in the United States fell by 5.5%, while across six major OECD countries (Australia, Austria, Canada, West Germany, Sweden and the UK), they rose by 22.6%.'[185]

[179] Todd Godbout, 'Employment Change and Sectoral Distribution in 10 Countries, 1970–1990' (1993) 116:10 *Monthly Labor Review*, 3–20.

[180] Houseman, n. 119 above, at S96: 'In the United States over 70 percent of the growth in employment may be attributed to the growth in the working age population over the 1979–89 period'; Krueger and Pischke, n. 92 above, at 4: 'about 60 percent of the faster US employment growth can be accounted for by faster population growth in the US'.

[181] Ganssmann, n. 114 above, at 260.

[182] Krueger and Pischke, n. 92 above, at 2.

[183] Brodsky, n. 148 above, at 58.

[184] Giuseppe Bertola, Francine D. Blau and Lawrence M. Kahn, 'Comparative Analysis of Labor Market Outcomes: Lessons for the US from International Long-Run Evidence', in Alan Krueger and Robert Solow (eds.), *The Roaring Nineties: Can Full Employment Be Sustained?* (New York: Russell Sage Foundation, 2002) 159–218.

[185] Ibid., at 161.

A third explanation for high US jobs growth is the expansionary fiscal policy which was pursued from the late 1970s: 'even during *the* supply side era, that of the Reagan administration, considerable fiscal expansion and an "invisible" industrial policy under the guise of defence spending gave an extraordinary boost to the American economy'.[186] Thus, the US may have spent its way out of unemployment, in particular by means of the huge defence spending during the Reagan era which helped create employment in industries (such as aircraft and shipbuilding) which make products primarily or predominantly for military use, and related industries (such as transport and communications).[187] Henry and Oliver estimated that from 1980 to 1985, total defence jobs increased by almost 22 per cent, whilst private sector jobs attributable to defence purchases increased by 45 per cent.[188] The observation here is that as well as fewer external constraints brought about by its hegemonic global position, the relatively deregulated labour market allowed the US to pursue an expansionary fiscal policy without the risk of inflation.[189]

Fourth, a potentially important factor which helps explain the low rates of unemployment, especially amongst 'prime-age' males, is the US policy of incarceration.[190] Bruce Western and Katherine Beckett argue that 'US incarceration lowers conventional measures of unemployment in the short run by concealing joblessness among able-bodied, working-age men, but it raises unemployment in the long run by damaging the job prospects of ex-convicts after release'.[191] The implication is that sustained low unemployment in the future will depend in great part on the continuing expansion of the penal system. The number of people

[186] Francesca Bettio and Samuel Rosenberg, 'Labour Markets and Flexibility in the 1990s: the Europe–USA Opposition Revisited' (1999) 13:3 *International Review of Applied Economics*, 269–79, at 272; emphasis in the original.

[187] David K. Henry and Richard P. Oliver, 'The Defense Buildup, 1977–85: Effects on Production and Employment' (1987) 110:8 *Monthly Labor Review*, 3–11.

[188] Ibid., at 7.

[189] See Constance Sorrentino and Joyanna Moy, 'U.S. Labor Market Performance in International Perspective' (2002) *Monthly Labor Review*, 15–35, at 33; see also Simonazzi, who points out that: 'In the US, a less binding external constraint has favored the sustainability of expansion. The degrees of freedom and the privileges still enjoyed as the hegemonic country enabled the US to manage its domestic demand with no direct consideration of the external constraint. In the 1970s, attack on the labor market institutions . . . was accompanied by expansionary fiscal and monetary policies, and the pressure of increasing external deficits on the exchange rate was dealt with by letting the dollar fall (the policy of "benign neglect"). In the following two expansions, in the first half of the '80s and in the '90s, the piling up of external deficits was not considered a sufficient reason for curbing domestic growth. Only when domestic expansion threatened the stability and the international hegemony of the US financial system was monetary policy tuned to its defense, with scant consideration of the effects this might exert on the rest of the world.' Annamaria Simonazzi, 'Innovation and growth: supply and demand factors in the US expansion' Università degli Studi di Roma 'La Sapienza' Dipartimento di Economia Pubblica, Working Paper No 53, October 2002, at 5.

[190] My thanks to Karl Klare for first alerting me to this unusual phenomenon.

[191] Bruce Western and Katherine Beckett' 'How Unregulated is the US Labor Market? The Penal System as a Labour Market Institution' (1999) 104:4 *American Journal of Sociology*, 1030–60, at 1031. See also Bruce Western, Meredith Kleykamp and Jake Rosenfeld, 'Did Falling Wages and Employment Increase U.S. Imprisonment?' Russell Sage Foundation Working Paper Series (New York: RSF, 2005).

imprisoned in the US grew by 300 per cent between 1980 and 1996; incarceration was unevenly spread across the adult population, concentrated amongst the young, the less educated and African-Americans.[192] In 1993, approximately 2 per cent of all men of working age were incarcerated, including 9 per cent of all black men of working age, and 13 per cent of black men aged 18–34.[193] Ten years later, the statistics had changed only to the extent that the prison population as a proportion of the working age population as a whole had increased, and the proportion of black men subject to incarceration in comparison with white and Hispanic men had also increased—in 2003, an estimated 12 per cent of black males, 3.7 per cent of Hispanic males, and 1.6 per cent of white males in their twenties were in prison or jail.[194] In other words, incarceration removes from the US labour market precisely those groups whose market power is weak—who represent a 'high unemployment risk'[195]—and who constitute the numbers of the (long-term) unemployed in European countries.[196] The conclusion reached by Western and Beckett is that, despite the strong economic growth and job creation in the US, adjusting the figures to include the prison population as unemployed would mean that the US labour market had performed worse than the European average for most of the period between 1976 and 1994.[197] Adjusting the unemployment rates to take account of the prison and jail population seriously undermines the more strident claims of those urging increased deregulation on European markets. In particular, the much-vaunted low rates of long-term unemployment in the US appear less impressive: an estimated two-thirds of the difference between US and European male long-term unemployment rates is eliminated if discouraged and incarcerated males are included in the figures.[198]

[192] Western and Beckett, n. 191 above, at 1034–5.

[193] Freeman, n. 118 above, at 39. See also Steven Raphael, 'The Socioeconomic Status of Black Males: The Increasing Importance of Incarceration' unpublished paper (Berkeley, CA, 2004) available at: *http://ist-socrates.berkeley.edu/~raphael/* [accessed on 10 April 2005].

[194] Paige M. Harrison and Jennifer C. Karberg, 'Prison and Jail Inmates at Midyear 2003' *Bureau of Justice Statistics Bulletin* (Washington: BJS, 2004), at 11; see also Thomas P. Bonczar, 'Prevalence of Imprisonment in the U.S. Population, 1974–2001' Bureau of Justice Statistics Special Report (Washington: BJS, 2003).

[195] Western and Beckett, n. 191 above, at 1038.

[196] For example, ethnic minority workers experience disproportionately high unemployment across many EU countries. In the UK, in comparison with the unemployment rate of 5.7 per cent for white men and women, the rate was 14.6 per cent for black workers, 9.1 per cent for Indian workers, and 20.4 per cent for Pakistani/Bangladeshi workers: Richard Dickens, Paul Gregg and Jonathan Wadsworth, 'New Labour and the Labour Market' (2000) 16:1 *Oxford Review of Economic Policy*, 95–113, at 97. In the Netherlands, unemployment amongst Islamic men from Turkey and Morocco is six times as high as that of the indigenous population, and amongst men from Surinam and the Dutch Antilles four times higher: Becker, n. 167 above, at 25.

[197] Western and Beckett, n. 191 above, at 1044.

[198] Buchele and Christiansen, n. 34 above, at 123. For a contrary view, see Elwert, who attempts to show empirically that the causal effect of incarceration on unemployment is considerably smaller than previously reported, not large enough to impact noticeably on US–European performance differentials, and potentially increasing, rather than decreasing, the official US unemployment rate: Felix Elwert, 'Incarceration, Unemployment, and "Eurosclerosis"', unpublished paper (Cambridge, MA, 2002) available at: *http://www.wjh.harvard.edu~winship/cfa_papers/ElwertIncarceration.pdf* [accessed on 10 April 2005].

Finally, alternative explanations for sluggish employment growth in the EU in comparison with the US suggest that the latter's greater entrepreneurial climate and more liberal product market regime, as opposed to its more flexible labour market, may be stronger reasons for its jobs growth. Krueger and Pischke argue that

'labor market inflexibility is *not* the source of employment problems, but inflexibility elsewhere in the economy manifests itself in slower job growth. For example, restrictions on bringing new products to market or on starting new enterprises could reduce job growth.'[199]

Whilst the impact (or otherwise) of labour market institutions on unemployment has been well documented, much less has been written about the potential impact on unemployment of deregulation or liberalization of product markets. Thus, wage flexibility could be of decidedly secondary importance for employment creation, compared with the removal of (non-labour) demand-side constraints in European markets.[200] The argument here is that competitive product markets create incentives to use labour efficiently; the opposite (namely, restrictions on entrepreneurs and high company start-up costs) can affect employment patterns by influencing the creation of new firms and therefore total job creation.[201] Gersbach places a slightly different emphasis from Krueger and Pischke on the importance of product market reforms, namely that they are necessary, but not sufficient, to reduce structural unemployment in Europe; labour market reforms would, in his view, remain necessary.[202]

### *3.2.4 The costs of the US model*

Related to the argument that the success of the deregulated labour market of the US in creating employment/reducing unemployment has been overstated, is the argument that the *costs* of this model have been underestimated. That the US has paid a high price for its superior labour market 'flexibility' is becoming an increasingly familiar argument.[203] Friedman and Weller, for example, argue that the US model of a minimally regulated labour market, despite delivering better job growth than the European model, does so only at enormous social and economic cost, with the greater downward wage flexibility in the US contributing to sharply higher poverty rates, particularly amongst young families with

[199] Krueger and Pischke, n. 92 above, at 7; emphasis added.

[200] John T. Addison, 'The US Employment Miracle in Comparative Perspective' (1998) 19 *Comparative Labor and Policy Journal*, 283–300, at 292.

[201] HM Treasury, *EMU and Labour Market Flexibility* (London: HMSO, 2003) at paras 4.55–4.58, and references therein.

[202] Hans Gersbach, 'Promoting Product Market Competition to Reduce Unemployment in Europe: An Alternative Approach?' (2000) 53:2 *Kyklos*, 117–34, at 129–130.

[203] John Schmitt, Lawrence Mishel and Jared Bernstein, 'Dangers for European Workers in the US Economic Model' (1998) *WorkingUSA*, May/June 1998, 73–85; Chris Tilly, 'Arresting the Decline of Good Jobs in the USA?' (1997) 28:4 *Industrial Relations Journal*, 269–74.

children.[204] Furthermore, as Houseman points out, 'although job growth in the US economy has been generally strong over the last decade, many have argued that the "quality" of the jobs being generated is low',[205] where quality refers to things like pay, benefits and job security.

If one accepts the commonly held view that there has been a major fall in demand for unskilled workers,[206] this would explain the dramatic fall in wages of lower-skilled workers in the US, whereas their counterparts in EU economies which lack wage flexibility would, according to this theory, be unemployed. Whatever the causes, it is certainly the case that there has been a decline in real wages for less skilled/educated workers in the US: during the 1980s, real hourly wages for workers at the bottom of the wage distribution (the 10th percentile) fell by over 13 per cent, whilst real hourly wages for workers at the top (the 90th percentile) rose slightly.[207] More recently, in 2003, wages were essentially stagnant or falling for low-, middle- and high-wage earners amongst both men and women, with only very high earners enjoying real wage growth.[208] Thus, not only did real wages fall or stagnate for many workers, but furthermore, the pay gap between the highest- and the lowest-earning workers widened, leading to the most unequal earnings distribution amongst developed countries.[209] Amanda Gosling and Thomas Lemieux report similar findings in the UK, where the adoption of US-style reforms have resulted in a convergence in the extent and pattern of wage inequality between the UK and the US.[210] Some observers of the US labour market go further, contending that the institutional context faced by low-wage workers in the US has become increasingly punitive, and not merely deregulated.[211]

Increased wage inequality is related to the wider observation about the *quality* of the jobs created by the US 'job machine', with even the OECD taking

[204] Sheldon Friedman and Christian Weller, 'One More Time: Labor Market Flexibility, Aggregate Demand, and Comparative Employment Growth in the US and Europe' (1998) 19 *Comparative Labor Law and Policy Journal*, 307–319, at 308–9.

[205] Houseman, n. 119 above, at S100.

[206] Nickell, n. 37 above, at 71, for an alternative view: he argues that there is no evidence that skill shifts have made a substantial contribution to the rise in European unemployment.

[207] Houseman, n. 119 above, at S107–S108; see also Michael C. Wolfson and Brian B. Murphy, 'New Views on Inequality Trends in Canada and the United States' (1998) 121:4 *Monthly Labour Review*, 3–23.

[208] Lawrence Mishel, Jared Bernstein, and Sylvia Allegretto, *The State of Working America* (Ithaca, NY: Economic Policy Institute/Cornell University Press, 2005) at 26. As far as the poorest workers were concerned, in 2003, the minimum wage was worth just 34 per cent of what an average worker earned per hour, the lowest point for this ratio in 40 years. This ratio was about 50 per cent in the late 1960s, about 45 per cent in the mid-1970s and about 40 per cent in the early 1990s: *The State of Working America: Fact Sheet on Wages* (Washington, DC: Economic Policy Institute, 2005).

[209] Freeman, n. 118 above, at 32, drawing upon OECD statistics.

[210] Gosling and Lemieux, n. 143 above.

[211] Bruce Western and Josh Guetzkow, 'Punitive Policy and Neoliberalism in the U.S. Labor Market', unpublished paper, prepared for the American Sociological Association, Chicago, August 2002, available at *http://www.princeton.edu/~western/* [accessed 10 April 2005].

note of the 'poor quality' of some of the jobs.[212] 'Quality' in jobs can be difficult to measure, as evidenced by the EU's difficulties since the Lisbon and Stockholm European Councils, in realizing the goal of 'better' jobs or 'quality' in employment.[213] In the absence of an adequate single summary measure, Chris Tilly has made use of partial measures—including wages, fringe benefits, due process in discipline, hours' flexibility, permanence, upward mobility and control over the work process—and finds on all counts that jobs in the US have unambiguously become worse over the past two or three decades.[214] Susan Houseman reaches a more cautious verdict, arguing that moderate growth in the share of employment in part-time and temporary jobs (which are characterized by low wages, few benefits and little job security) provides some evidence of deteriorating job quality.[215] Whether this same accusation as to deteriorating job quality could be levelled at policy trends within the EU, in particular following the post-Lisbon emphasis on 'full employment' will be explored in Chapter 4.

In conclusion, with regard to the question whether the US is an appropriate model for the EU to follow, we have seen that some doubt can be cast on the robustness of historical comparisons of EU and US labour market performance: there *has* been impressive job growth in the US, but the above analysis suggests that the disparities between the US and the EU are not as great as traditionally conceived. Moreover, the extent to which the more flexible labour market in the US has indeed been the cause of this jobs growth is also questionable. Individual EU countries have experienced recent labour market successes (albeit, possibly fragile or cyclical improvements) with a limited form of flexibility—such as 'flexicurity' or negotiated flexibility—and without completely abandoning the strong welfare states and commitment to equality which are so central to the ideal of the 'European social model'. Ultimately, the adoption of US-style reforms or convergence towards the US model of labour market regulation, comes down to a matter of political economy: if there *is* a trade-off between social cohesion and equity on the one hand, and employment creation on the other, it would appear that individual EU Member States have, for the time being, chosen the former.

## 4. Conclusions: which type of flexibility for the EU?

This overview of the central tenets of the labour market flexibility debate has focused on the use of the flexibility concept in the context of systems of labour market regulation, in which 'flexibility' almost becomes a synonym for labour market deregulation. The conceptualization of unemployment in the EU, and the development of the European Employment Strategy, initially balanced

212 OECD, *The OECD Jobs Study: Facts, Analysis, Strategies*, n. 17 above, at 30.
213 See Chapter 4, Sections 4.3–4.5.
214 Tilly, n. 203 above, at 271 and 273.
215 Houseman, n. 119 above, at S103 and S107.

this emphasis on the *external* flexibility of labour market systems, with a focus on questions of *internal*, ie functional, flexibility within the firm.[216] The Commission's 1993 White Paper *Growth, Competitiveness and Employment*, had stressed the importance of both types of flexibility: '[t]he question of labour flexibility needs to be examined from two angles: that of the external labour market, where supply meets demand, and that of the market internal to each business, ie the human resources at its disposal which it adjusts according to its needs'.[217] It remains the case that the European Employment Strategy continues to urge Member States to make work patterns more flexible, since promoting 'atypical' or non-standard work is seen as a way of increasing the level of employment as well as improving competitiveness and productivity.[218] However, as Chapters 3 and 4 will show, the interaction between the Employment Guidelines on the one hand, and the Union's annual Broad Economic Policy Guidelines and Stability and Growth Pact on the other, has led the EU discourse on flexibility more clearly towards a perspective on labour market flexibility which is more accepting of the aforesaid orthodoxy, and more focussed on a need to tackle 'rigidities' in the external labour market. The European Central Bank, for one, as illustrated by its report on labour market mismatches in Euro area countries, sees ample scope for a continued policy of reform to make the labour market more efficient and flexible.[219]

The approach currently advocated at EU level therefore involves a focus on structural reform of labour markets and flexibility; but also on employability, requiring reform of tax, benefit and training systems, as part of a wider project of promoting active labour market policies. This is a theme which has recurred increasingly in the EU discourse on employment in the wake of the Lisbon summit in March 2000, which committed the Union and its Member States to the pursuit of 'full employment'. The flexibility and employability discourses are closely connected: if, as I argue in subsequent chapters, it is the case that Member States remain reluctant to make employment protection legislation fully flexible and to permit wider wage differentiation, this is counteracted by their greater apparent openness to reform welfare states. This is the sort of labour market flexibility which Stephen Nickell and Richard Layard[220] would encourage

> 'the key labour market institutions on which policy should be focussed are unions and social security systems.... For social security, the key policies are benefit reform linked to active labour market policies to move people from welfare to work. By comparison, time

[216] See in particular, the Commission's 1997 Green Paper: CEC, *Green Paper: Partnership for a New Organisation of Work* COM (97) 128 final (Luxembourg: OOPEC, 1997).

[217] CEC, White Paper *Growth, Competitiveness and Employment*, n. 15 above, at 17.

[218] See Chapter 4, Section 4.2.

[219] ECB, n. 19 above.

[220] Both are advisers to the UK government: Stephen Nickell is a member of the Monetary Policy Committee (MPC) of the Bank of England (until May 2006); the MPC is responsible for setting UK interest rates to meet the government's 2.5 per cent inflation target; Richard Layard has been an adviser to the Department for Education and Employment (now renamed the Department for Education and Skills) on the New Deal, and is a Labour member of the House of Lords.

spent worrying about strict labour market regulations, employment protection and minimum wages is probably time largely wasted.'[221]

As will be seen in Chapters 4 to 6, such a perspective on labour market reform has gradually infiltrated the EU discourse. It would seem that an emerging, EU-specific, answer to the debate on labour market flexibility has been to reach a compromise, to focus on certain labour market institutions more than others in the attempt to tackle unemployment. Thus, the post-Lisbon Employment Strategy, renewed and relaunched in 2005,[222] is revealed as strongly supply-side oriented, for example, placing emphasis on an 'active and dynamic welfare state', active rather than passive labour market policies, and modernized systems of social protection. The Lisbon version of full employment essentially requires a shift from comprehensive employment protection and social benefits, towards a greater investment in human capital, thus equalizing the marketability and employability of individuals, rather than protecting them from the market.

[221] Nickell and Layard, n. 13 above, at 70–1.

[222] Presidency Conclusions, Lisbon European Council, n. 124 above, at para 24 ff; Presidency Conclusions, Brussels European Council, 22 and 23 March 2005, Bull EU 3/2005, 1–39.

# 3

# Conceptualizing European unemployment: the emergence of a European employment policy

## 1. Introduction: conceptualizing the problem of unemployment

This chapter will examine how the employment problem within EU Member States has been conceptualized by the EU institutions. It will also explore the emergence of employment policy at EU level, in response to the perceived need for action by the European Union as a whole to tackle the problem of high unemployment within its Member States. Shifts in the development of policy will be explored, for the light they cast on the ability, legitimacy and competence of the EU to regulate this area. In particular, this chapter will focus on the change in emphasis from the development of a social policy for the EU, to the development of an employment strategy; the reluctance of (most) Member States to hand over their regulatory competence in this area to the EU, and how this has resulted in the Employment Strategy taking a particular form—for example, using 'soft' rather than 'hard' law mechanisms. The chapter will also consider how the Employment Strategy connects with Economic and Monetary Union (EMU), and how this link (essentially bringing employment within the criteria for monetary union) has placed employment policy within a particular discourse, one which takes a distinctive perspective on the role of labour market institutions, or 'rigidities', in creating or perpetuating unemployment.

In analysing the EU's discourse on labour market regulation, it is arguable that a shift has occurred in the EU's position on the 'labour market flexibility' debate: that the EU institutions are more readily accepting of the orthodoxy that labour market regulation and labour market institutions are a major cause of unemployment within EU countries and that a deregulatory approach, which emphasizes greater 'flexibility' in labour markets, is the key to solving Europe's unemployment ills, along with macro-economic stability, restrictive fiscal policy and wage restraint. As the EU's Employment Strategy has matured, this increased emphasis on employment policy has come to displace discourses around social policy. Such a change in emphasis has important implications for EMU since it signals a reorientation from an approach to labour market regulation which had as its core a strong concept of employment *protection* and high labour standards, to an approach which prioritises employment *creation*, and minimizes the role of social policy, since social policy is seen as potentially increasing the regulatory burden.

Chapter 2 explored the growing orthodoxy which explained differences in postwar unemployment levels between developed countries, in part, as a result of differences in labour market regulation. The focus will now be on how the unemployment problem has been conceptualized in relation to EU economies, and has come to be perceived as a *European* problem. The two are, arguably, linked: the particular perspective that the EU institutions came to adopt on the underlying causes of high unemployment in the various EU Member States may have led inexorably to the conclusion that there were factors common to all or most of these systems, which in turn required a concerted, centrally determined, *European* solution. The similarities in systems of labour market regulation adopted in the EU Member States, as distinct from the more 'deregulated' Anglo-American model, might lead to the conclusion that one of the solutions to European unemployment was a reform of the systems of labour market regulation which dominated these economies.

The OECD *Jobs Study*,[1] which will be discussed in greater detail below, provided detailed empirical and analytical support for the thesis that, whilst there was 'no single recipe for full-employment',[2] nevertheless, Europe's unemployment problem should be addressed by a combination of structural reforms and judicious[3] macro-economic management. It will be of interest to note the extent to which the discourse of the EU institutions on unemployment differed at this time from the approach advocated by the OECD. In particular, comparisons will be drawn with the EU's approach to combating unemployment as evidenced in the Commission's White Paper *Growth, Competitiveness and Employment*,[4] which was published at the same time as the OECD *Jobs Study*. Questions to be considered here are: was there a shift in later years from the approach to unemployment of the White Paper, in the Union's subsequent policy pronouncements on unemployment? Did the EU institutions begin to echo more closely the discourse of the OECD and other international financial institutions in the course of developing a European employment strategy?

[1] Organisation for Economic Cooperation and Development (OECD), *The OECD Jobs Study: Evidence and Explanations* and *Facts, Analysis, Strategies* (Paris: OECD, 1994); see also *OECD Employment Outlook 2004* (Paris: OECD, 2004) and International Monetary Fund (IMF), *World Economic Outlook* (Washington, DC: IMF, 1999); Chapter IV Chronic Unemployment in the Euro Area: Causes and Cures.

[2] OECD, *The OECD Jobs Study: Facts, Analysis, Strategies*, n. 1 above, at 41.

[3] IMF, n. 1 above, at 109.

[4] Commission of the European Communities (hereinafter CEC) White Paper *Growth, Competitiveness and Employment: The Challenges and Ways Forward into the 21st Century*, COM (93) 700 final (Luxembourg: Office for Official Publications of the EC, 1993).

## 2. Perspectives on European unemployment

### 2.1 The OECD *Jobs Study*

The Organisation for Economic Cooperation and Development's *Jobs Study* was the end result of a project undertaken pursuant to the mandate of the OECD Ministers in 1992, that the Organisation should analyse the causes and consequences of high and persistent unemployment and propose effective remedies to tackle the problem.[5] A similar mandate was issued by the meeting of OECD Employment and Labour Ministers in September 2003, calling on the OECD to reassess the *Jobs Study* of 1994 and the Jobs Strategy to which it gave birth.[6] There are some similarities in methodology between the initial *Jobs Study* and the later EU Employment Strategy, in that the OECD made detailed policy recommendations, and then proceeded to monitor the progress made by each country in implementing these recommendations, and the impact of these recommendations on labour market performance. The study was published in two parts: the first, *Facts, Analysis, Strategies*, described the incidence of unemployment in OECD countries, analysed the key factors producing it, and put forward a menu of detailed policy measures to help create jobs and prepare people to fill them.[7] The second, *Evidence and Explanations*, presented the analytical background, detailing labour market trends and the adjustment potential of the labour market.

#### *2.1.1 How the OECD conceptualized European unemployment*

As far as the main causes of high unemployment were concerned, especially European unemployment, the OECD identified the interaction of the two oil price shocks of the 1970s and the inability of many labour markets to adjust to rapid change as key causal factors:

'in the midst of this tumultuous period when so many forces were testing the flexibility of economies, policies to achieve social objectives were extended, with the unintended side-effect of making markets, including labour markets, more rigid. This erosion of the ability to adapt to change was probably most pronounced in continental Europe and in Oceania.'[8]

The roots of the problem however, were, laid in the late 1960s. The OECD's diagnosis was as follows: after a period of (admittedly historically unique) of nearly 5 per cent annual growth in the OECD area from 1950 to the first oil shock of

[5] OECD, n. 1 above, at 3; see also Jørgen Elmeskov, John P. Martin and Stefano Scarpetta, 'Key Lessons for Labour Market Reforms: Evidence from the OECD Countries' Experiences' Centro Interdipartimentale di Studi Internazionali sull'Economia e lo Sviluppo (CEIS) Working Paper No 62, Università degli Studi di Roma 'Tor Vergata', 1998.

[6] OECD, Meeting of Employment and Labour Ministers, Paris, 29–30 September 2003, *Communiqué: Towards More and Better Jobs* (Paris: OECD, 2003); 'Spotlight on Employment', in *OECD Observer* No 239, September 2003; *OECD Observer* No 240/241, December 2003.

[7] OECD, n. 1 above, at 7–8, Introdcution.

[8] OECD, n. 1 above, at 30.

1973, economic performance was constrained by inflationary pressures brought to bear, in part, by the inability of collective bargaining to keep wage increases in line with the economies' capacities to pay.[9] Labour market institutions further hindered adjustment in many countries, although here one can see the distinctions already being drawn between European and North American labour markets:

'In North America, real wages rose very little and increases in unemployment were quickly reversed through substantial employment growth. . . . The effect of wage developments on employment was particularly marked in Europe, especially in contrast to the United States. . . . As real wage growth outstripped productivity, employment suffered.'[10]

Further, in the EC/EU

'following the oil price hike in 1974, there was a continuous and rapid rise in unemployment in the EC area and by the mid-1980s the European Community had overtaken North America as being a high-unemployment region. . . . The EFTA countries were more successful in containing rises in unemployment following each of the oil price hikes but their success ended with the recession of the early 1990s when unemployment rates rose substantially.'[11]

The growing gap between unemployment rates in Europe and those in the US—reversing the statistics of the 1960s, in which US unemployment had been much higher—was one of the strongest factors in the shift to a new orthodoxy in economic thinking: that the less regulated labour market of the US was more conducive to employment growth, and that the 'rigidities' of European markets needed to be tackled in a strategy to create jobs:

'The contrast between Europe and the United States is instructive. In the 1960s the trend unemployment rate in the United States, at around 5 per cent, was significantly higher than elsewhere. It then moved up only modestly in the 1970s and was around 6 to 8 per cent in the 1980s, though with large cyclical fluctuations around the trend rate. In contrast, Europe, which had had a trend rate of unemployment of only 2 to 3 per cent in the 1960s, significantly less than in the United States, saw unemployment move to around 8 to 9 per cent by the end of the 1980s with, in general, less cyclical volatility of actual unemployment. It was in part this contrast between the two sides of the Atlantic, as well as the much greater job growth in the United States, that gave rise to the hypothesis of much greater labour market flexibility there and to a search for improvements in such flexibility in Europe.'[12]

The OECD, whose pronouncements are strongly supportive of the labour market flexibility hypothesis, therefore set out a broad programme of action designed to tackle the problem of unemployment across OECD countries in

[9] OECD, *The OECD Jobs Study: Evidence and Explanations. Part I—Labour Market Trends and Underlying Forces of Change* (Paris: OECD, 1994) at 63.

[10] Ibid.

[11] Ibid., at 38. EFTA (European Free Trade Association) became the European Economic Area (EEA) in 1994 when the agreement establishing the EEA came into force, and by 1995, three former EFTA countries (Sweden, Finland and Austria) had become part of the EU.

[12] Ibid., at 69.

general by (a) improving the ability of economies and of societies to adjust and adapt to changing economic conditions and (b) increasing their capacity to create knowledge and to innovate.[13] With regard to improving the capacity of economies to create jobs, the OECD placed emphasis on facilitating the development and use of new technology, working-time flexibility, encouraging entrepreneurship, and a review of policies which might be impeding job creation.[14] Such structural reforms were seen as particularly important in Europe, since 'there is much evidence in OECD countries, particularly in Europe, of a major structural element in unemployment which requires changes in labour and product markets'.[15] Whilst recognizing that there was no clear-cut distinction between cyclical and structural unemployment, the OECD nevertheless argued that country-specific structural reforms were necessary so as to avoid rigidities preventing resources from moving to their most profitable uses: '[m]aximising the productive potential of the economy will be jeopardized if governments allow industrial, regional, labour market and other microeconomic policies to preserve inefficient economic structures'.[16] In particular, attention had to be paid to increasing wage flexibility, reducing barriers to labour mobility and improving competition.[17] These prescriptions find strong echoes in the European Employment Strategy's four-pillar approach to combating unemployment; in particular, there are similarities between the first limb of the jobs strategy ('improving the ability of economies and of societies to adjust and adapt to changing economic conditions') and Article 125 of the EC Treaty, as amended by the Treaty of Amsterdam, which now commits the EC to 'a skilled, trained and adaptable workforce and labour markets responsive to economic change'.

The main planks of the Jobs Strategy for the whole OECD area, not just Europe, expand on the two-pronged approach of creating a stable macroeconomic environment, and of adaptability. The OECD's nine policy guidelines were as follows:

### The nine policy guidelines of the OECD Jobs Strategy[18]

1. Set macro-economic policy so that it will both encourage growth and, in conjunction with good structural policies, make it sustainable, ie non-inflationary.
2. Enhance the creation and diffusion of technological know-how by improving frameworks for its development.
3. Increase the flexibility of working time (both short-term and lifetime) voluntarily sought by both workers and employers.

[13] OECD, n. 1 above, at 43 and *The OECD Jobs Study: Implementing the Strategy* (Paris: OECD, 1995) at 14.
[14] OECD, n. 1 above, at 33–6.
[15] OECD, n. 9 above, at 73.
[16] Ibid.
[17] Ibid.
[18] OECD, n. 1 above, at 44.

4. Nurture an entrepreneurial climate by eliminating impediments to, and restrictions on, the creation and expansion of enterprises.
5. Make wages and labour costs more flexible by removing restrictions that prevent wages from reflecting local conditions and individual skill levels, in particular of younger workers.
6. Reform employment security provisions that inhibit the expansion of employment in the private sector.
7. Strengthen the emphasis on active labour market policies and reinforce their effectiveness.
8. Improve labour force skills and competences through wide-ranging education and training systems.
9. Reform unemployment and related benefits—and their interaction with the tax system—so that societies' fundamental equity goals are achieved in ways that impinge far less on the efficient functioning of the labour markets.

With regard to the recommendations concerned with 'adaptability' (particularly 3, 4, 5, 6, 7 and 9), these can be further broken down: (1) dismantling barriers in labour and product markets to job creation, (2) increasing the flexibility of working time, (3) reforming the tax and benefit system and (4) active labour market policies.[19] The *Jobs Study* itself and the follow-up report on implementation of the Jobs Strategy,[20] both placed emphasis on how these two sets of structural reforms, revolving around adaptability on the one hand, and creativity on the other, are premised on the existence of a stable macro-economic environment, since

> 'Structural policies must operate in tandem with macroeconomic policy in any effective strategy to enhance growth and employment. Structural reforms will bear fruit only in a stable macroeconomic environment in which private sector participants can be more confident about medium-term prospects and can thereby adjust more easily to changing circumstances. . . . And macroeconomic policy has more chance of succeeding in supporting the desired level of demand if the structural conditions and policies prevent rigidities and allow resources to move to their most profitable uses. *The less rigid the economy, the more scope there is to translate macroeconomic stimulus into faster growth rather than accelerating inflation.*'[21]

Thus, fiscal consolidation or restraint, rather than fiscal expansion, was emphasized by the OECD, requiring limitations or reductions in public expenditure and the control of inflation on the part of member countries.[22] The OECD briefly considered, but ultimately rejected, the use of more expansionary policies to accelerate the recovery of output and employment, this rejection due in part to fears that such policies would compromise the goals of long-term growth and keeping inflation in check.[23] The macro-economic policy being

[19] OECD, *The OECD Jobs Study: Implementing the Strategy*, n. 13 above, at 5. [20] Ibid.
[21] OECD, n. 1 above, at 32; emphasis added. [22] OECD, n. 13 above, at 16–17.
[23] OECD, n. 9 above, at 59; See also n. 13 above, at 16–18.

recommended by the European Union (or, at least, by the European Commission) at this time, however, seemed to veer in the opposite direction, advocating a more expansionary fiscal policy and large-scale infrastructure and public works programmes as the route to job creation.[24]

By the time of the report *Implementing the Strategy*, one year after the *Jobs Study*, the OECD was able to report back on some examples of best practice under the rubric of the nine policy proposals. Not surprisingly, the examples all seem to point in one direction, towards greater labour market flexibility in the following five areas: non-wage labour costs, minimum wages, wage formation systems, employment security provisions and product market competition.[25] The focus in this section of the report, on measures taken to dismantle barriers in labour and product markets, was on shifting the balance from protection of 'insiders' towards greater access to employment of 'outsiders', in the effort to create jobs. The overall goal which the OECD considers member countries should be working towards is to make wage and price formation more responsive to market conditions, as greater wage and price flexibility will increase the demand for labour, by lowering the relatively high tax and legislated (or collectively bargained) costs of employing a worker.[26] So, countries which have managed to reduce non-wage labour costs, such as employer social security contributions, even if only for selected groups of workers, are singled out for praise. Similarly with minimum wages, which are seen as pricing some potential workers out of the market, countries such as Canada, Mexico and the US (which do not automatically index minimum wages to prices) are congratulated since such a policy keeps down the level of minimum wages and total labour costs.[27] Further, a 'successful' wage formation system is described as one which provides both aggregate and relative wage flexibility.[28] Finally, on the question of where to draw the appropriate balance between flexibility and employment security, whilst recognizing that employment security can lead to higher levels of productivity by fostering a long-term employment relationship, the OECD is nevertheless cautious about the effects of employment protection on job creation, since over-strict rules protecting insiders will make employers cautious in hiring, to the detriment of 'outsiders'.[29] The OECD Secretariat identified nine countries (all but one of which are EU Member States)[30] as having problems with respect to the strictness of their employment protection legislation.[31]

[24] CEC, White Paper *Growth, Competitiveness, Employment*. The contrast between the views of the European Commission and the OECD are explored further in Section 3.2; see also, Valerie Symes, *Unemployment in Europe: Problems and Policies* (London: Routledge, 1995) at 191–2.

[25] OECD, *The OECD Jobs Study: Implementing the Strategy*, n. 13 above, at 18–23.

[26] Ibid., at 18. [27] Ibid., at 19. [28] Ibid., at 20.

[29] As discussed in Chapter 2, the OECD's reassessment of the *Jobs Study* in 2004 further underlined this recognition that some EPL could be welfare- and efficiency-enhancing, by promoting greater effort and cooperation on the part of workers in response to employers' 'credible commitments': *OECD Employment Outlook 2004*, n. 1 above.

[30] Belgium, France, Greece, Italy, the Netherlands, Norway, Portugal, Sweden and Spain.

[31] OECD, *The OECD Jobs Study: Implementing the Strategy*, n. 13 above, at 20.

A second element in enhancing the ability of economies to adjust and adapt, beyond dismantling barriers in labour and product markets, is the recommendation that member countries should increase the flexibility of working time. This is connected with the wider proposal on greater flexibility of employment protection legislation, since many of the existing measures designed to provide security for workers impose restrictions on the use of fixed-term contracts, temporary work arranged through private sector agencies, and other forms of flexible work arrangements. The *Jobs Study* concluded that

'traditional working-time arrangements, which have been enshrined in legislation or collective agreements, may hinder labour market flexibility and, indirectly, job creation. Firms' labour requirements vary over time and across sectors.... A single set of rules for all firms or sectors constrains both workers and firms, leading to reduced output and employment.'[32]

The argument here is that making it easier for firms to hire workers on more fluid contracts enhances job creation, since firms can be more responsive to changes in production, seasonal and cyclical changes, and can reduce overtime costs. A relevant comparison here would be with the European Commission's 1997 Green Paper *Partnership for a New Organisation of Work*, which focused on improving employment and competitiveness through a better (ie more flexible) organization of work at the workplace.[33] However, the proposal from the Commission and the OECD is emphatically not the same as arguing that there is a finite amount of work to be done in the economy, and that a solution to the problem of unemployment is to divide this 'lump of labour' between a greater number of workers, by encouraging or compelling part-time, short-term or casual employment.[34] The OECD is quite clearly dismissive of the idea that 'job sharing' is a practical solution to unemployment:

'It is important to distinguish between voluntary work-sharing programmes, often at the enterprise level, which enable workers to reduce their hours worked (with commensurate

[32] Ibid., at 23.

[33] CEC, *Green Paper: Partnership for a New Organisation of Work*, COM (97) 128 final (Luxembourg: OOPEC, 1997).

[34] It is difficult to overstate just how dismissive most (orthodox) economists are of the notion that an economy supports a fixed level of employment and that this lump of employment can be apportioned so that, whether there are fewer workers working more hours or more workers working fewer hours, output remains constant. This 'lump of labour' fallacy is one of *The Economist's* favourite *bêtes noire*, rebutted by the argument that (a) technology creates new demand, either by increasing productivity and hence real incomes, or by creating new goods, and (b) the demand for labour depends upon labour costs and productivity, which are affected by the hours each employee works. See: 'Short measure', *The Economist*, 31 January 1998, Vol. 346, Issue 8053, at 79; 'One lump or two?' *The Economist*, 25 October 1997, Vol. 345, Issue 8040, at 17. However, the French economy created 500,000 new jobs in 2000, and supporters argued that 280,000 of those were due to the 35-hour maximum working week, introduced under the Aubry law designed to create employment by redistributing work. Nevertheless, the evidence linking the 35-hour week to job creation is mixed. For a discussion of the French 35-hour week, see Chapter 6, Section 2.2; see also Sylvaine Laulom, 'France: Part-Time Work—No Longer an Employment Policy Tool' in Silvana

reductions in pay) and programmes where job-sharing is imposed.... [S]tate funded early-retirement programmes and across-the-board work-sharing initiatives, such as legislated reductions in the work week that are not accompanied by adjustment of remuneration to productivity changes, *are not viable long-term solutions to the unemployment problem.*'[35]

This emphasis on 'enhancing the ability of economies to adjust and adapt' can be summed up in one oft-used term, 'flexibility'. However, as with the EU discourse on flexibility in the context of the European Employment Strategy, there is no clear definition of the term within the OECD discourse, beyond its use in specific circumstances, whether to refer to flexibility in working-time arrangements, in employment protection legislation, or wage flexibility. What does seem clear, though, is the centrality of flexibility to the sort of reconstructed system of labour market regulation which is deemed essential to enhance labour market efficiency and tackle unemployment. However, as examined in Chapter 2, some doubt did creep in with the OECD's *Employment Outlook* of June 1999,[36] which *appeared* to suggest and was interpreted as suggesting that evidence of links between employment protection legislation (EPL) and overall employment and unemployment was not particularly strong: 'EPL strictness has little or no effect on overall unemployment'.[37] However, the OECD took pains to point out that its view remained that EPL *does* affect the structure of employment and unemployment:[38] for example, that although job tenure is higher in countries with stricter EPL, stricter EPL is associated with larger flows into and out of unemployment and longer durations of unemployment.[39] The OECD thus reaffirmed the approach recommended in the Jobs Strategy, that

'countries with relatively strict EPL which have a serious problem of long-term unemployment and/or low overall employment rates, should consider relaxing their employment protection as part of a comprehensive policy to improve labour market outcomes.'[40]

### *2.1.2 The* Jobs Study: *aftermath and analysis*

In the years following publication of the *Jobs Study*, the OECD monitored the progress of member countries towards reducing unemployment in two ways: first, a series of thematic reviews by the OECD Secretariat explored appropriate policy orientations in specific fields;[41] second, the Economic and Development

Sciarra, Paul Davies, and Mark Freedland (eds.), *Employment Policy and the Regulation of Part-Time Work in the European Union: A Comparative Analysis* (Cambridge: CUP, 2004).

[35] OECD, *The OECD Jobs Study: Implementing the Strategy*, n. 13 above, at 24; emphasis added.

[36] OECD, *OECD Employment Outlook June 1999* (Paris: OECD, 1999).

[37] Ibid., at 88.

[38] OECD, 'OECD's View on Employment Protection Legislation' *OECD News Release*, 13 July 1999 (Paris: OECD) at para 1; available at: *http://www1.oecd.org/media/release/nw99-76a.htm* [accessed on 10 April 2005].

[39] OECD, n. 36 above, at 82.

[40] Ibid.

[41] The Secretariat's reports on four thematic reviews were presented to Ministers in May 1996 and were summarized in the Secretary-General's report to Ministers (OECD, *Pushing Ahead with the Strategy* (Paris: OECD, 1996)). The four areas were: (1) enhancing the effectiveness of active

Review Committee (EDRC) was mandated by OECD Ministers to examine implementation of the *Jobs Study* recommendations in individual member countries. The results of this work, undertaken for each of the 25 countries which were OECD Members when the *Jobs Study* was presented to Ministers in 1994, were published as separate chapters in OECD Country Surveys on the theme 'Implementing the Jobs Strategy'. This analysis of labour market developments focused on the role that economic policies played in shaping these developments. The 1997 overview, based on the EDRC review process but drawing also on thematic reviews and recent work by the Secretariat, drew six key lessons from this detailed country-by-country review, which will be summarized below.[42] As will become apparent from the study in Chapters 4 and 5 of the evolution of the EU's Employment Strategy, there is a strong correspondence between the OECD's Strategy and that of the EU, not only with regard to the substance of the policy prescriptions and the nature of the discourse, but also in respect of the methodology adopted, namely mutual learning, the dissemination of best practice, and the use of 'peer review'.[43]

**i. High and persistent unemployment has been the result of both conjunctural and structural forces, and it can be durably reduced**

The OECD identified 'success stories' which illustrate this argument, namely Ireland, the Netherlands, New Zealand and the UK, where the structural unemployment rate has decreased significantly. The point being made here is that there is evidence to challenge the prevailing pessimism about tackling high and persistent unemployment.

**ii. Most countries have taken some steps to reduce unemployment but only the 'successful' countries did so on a sufficient scale. Elsewhere, progress was uneven both between countries and between different areas of policy**

Within the 'success stories', it is noteworthy that the OECD seeks to highlight what it considers to be important common features in the reform process, namely: (a) the use of stability-oriented macro-economic policy frameworks which focused on reducing public sector deficits and debt and controlling

labour market policies; (2) making work pay: a thematic review of taxes, benefits, employment and unemployment; (3) interactions between structural reform, macro-economic policy and economic performance; and (4) technology, productivity and job creation. A fifth thematic review concerned policies to enhance entrepreneurship: OECD, *Implementing the OECD Jobs Strategy: Lessons from Member Countries' Experience* (Paris: OECD, 1997) at 1.

[42] The following is taken from OECD: *Implementing the OECD Jobs Strategy*, n. 41 above; and OECD, 'Key Employment Policy Challenges Faced by OECD Countries', Labour Market and Social Policy Occasional Papers No 31, OECD Submission to the G8 Growth, Employability and Inclusion Conference, London, 21–22 February 1998.

[43] See Chapter 5, Section 2; see also OECD, *Policy Brief, Peer Review: A Tool for Co-operation and Change*, December 2003 (Paris: OECD, 2003) and Bernard Casey, 'The OECD Jobs Strategy and the European Employment Strategy: Two Views of the Labour Market and of the Welfare State' (2004) 10 *European Journal of Industrial Relations*, 329–52.

inflation; (b) the implementation of a broad range of structural reforms in labour and product markets; and (c) a preparedness to undertake reforms that moderated the bargaining power of labour market insiders.

All three features, the first two in particular, will be explored later in Chapter 4 as key facets of the OECD's Strategy which find especially strong echoes in the European Union's Employment Strategy.

### iii. The central issue dividing the more comprehensive reformers from the less comprehensive is differences in judgement about potential conflicts between better labour market performance and concerns for equity and social cohesion

This is a matter of particular resonance for the EU, in two ways: *first*, the EU as a whole has committed itself to growth and economic development which respects social cohesion—a strategy which, arguably, means that some sort of *balance* must be found between employment promotion and social protection.[44] *Second*, to varying degrees, the individual Member States have reached the sort of domestic political settlement wherein certain 'trade-offs' have been entrenched economically. As Alogoskoufis *et al.* put it, talking of labour market regulation and generous welfare state provisions in many European states: 'European governments have predominantly chosen to maintain social cohesion by retaining, or even strengthening, the existing structure'.[45] They also argue that European society 'as a whole simply does not appear to be ready to sacrifice the advantages of high wages, benefits and job protection in order to fight high unemployment'.[46] The OECD goes so far as to recognize this as an issue of concern to some member countries: that implementation of the Jobs Strategy recommendations may be delayed or partial due to the belief that some of these recommendations would conflict with existing policy on equality and social cohesion: '[t]his concern usually centres around the series of OECD recommendations designed to achieve greater flexibility in labour and product markets'.[47]

However, in the view of the OECD, and in particular, its Economic and Development Review Committee, there was no conclusive evidence as to the nature and magnitude of any potential trade-off. On the contrary, the EDRC observed that it may be that these two objectives (of social cohesion and greater employment) may not necessarily be in conflict in that increased employment is likely offset, at least partly, by the impact of greater wage dispersal and reduced social transfers/welfare provision.[48] Another, related argument designed to appease concerns that the OECD Strategy would lead to greater inequalities is that some low-paid employment may be a stepping-stone to better pay. However, in spite of these reassurances from the OECD, it nevertheless remains the

[44] See Article 2 TEU and Article 2 EC.

[45] George Alogoskoufis, Charles Bean, Giuseppe Bertola, Daniel Cohen, Juan Dolado and Gilles Saint-Paul, *Unemployment: Choices for Europe* (London: CEPR, 1995) at 1.

[46] Ibid., at 2.

[47] OECD, 'Key Employment Policy Challenges', n. 42 above, at 9.

[48] OECD, *Implementing the OECD Jobs Strategy* n. 41 above, section III.

case that there continues to be a deep divide between OECD countries as to the importance of this trade-off between horizontal equity and employment objectives:

'for two very different sets of reasons, representatives from [a number of] countries rejected the notion of a trade-off. Thus, representatives from some English-speaking countries saw low unemployment as an essential condition for, or element of, horizontal equity. And those from some continental European countries saw equity as a more fundamental goal than low unemployment.'[49]

**iv. There are significant synergies between structural reforms in different fields**

The EDRC review process confirmed the importance of one of the *Jobs Study* conclusions, that broad-based reform is likely to be more effective than reform focused on particular areas. For example, the OECD views product market reform and labour market reform not only as complementary, but in fact as barely effective in isolation. On the one hand, product market reform is necessary to ensure that labour demand will react swiftly and strongly to changes in wages; on the other, it is necessary to reform regulations governing industrial relations, minimum wages and employment protection so as to ensure the rapid reallocation of labour freed as a result of product market competition.[50]

**v. Macro-economic conditions and their interactions with structural forces are important for labour market outcomes**

One of the main themes of the *Jobs Study*, that of combining fiscal restraint, low inflation and macro-economic stability, is once again emphasized. The argument is that, by ensuring macro-economic stability, governments can minimize *fluctuations* in unemployment, which in turn curtails the overall increase in unemployment.

**vi. Overall, the Jobs Strategy remains an effective response to labour market problems in member countries, and the EDRC has encouraged countries to press on with its implementation**

The OECD is cheerfully confident as to the merits of its approach to combating unemployment:

'Improved labour market outcomes in the countries that have gone the furthest in implementing the Jobs Strategy, including the United Kingdom, the Netherlands, New Zealand, and, to some extent, Ireland, and deteriorating conditions in some of those that have not, is an indication that the Strategy works.'[51]

The prescription for OECD countries as a whole has been discussed, but for high-unemployment continental European countries in particular, the EDRC individual country reviews put even greater weight on measures to increase

[49] Ibid. [50] Ibid.; see also OECD, 'Key Employment Policy Challenges', n. 42 above, at 9–10.

[51] OECD, *Implementing the OECD Jobs Strategy*, n. 41 above, section VI.

labour and product market flexibility so as to enhance the ability of the economies to adjust and adapt.[52] In comments which seem to be speaking directly to European economies the OECD warns that, whilst there has been resistance to implementing the recommendations of its Jobs Strategy, especially in respect of the trade-offs at the margin between efficiency and equity,[53] the concerns are misplaced. Whilest, it is argued, a trade-off might exist in the short run, this is compensated for by the fact that '[a]ccess to a job is just as much an equity issue as relative income levels, and . . . participation in paid employment, even a low paid job, helps to improve lifetime incomes and consequently reduces income inequality over time'.[54]

However, subsequent reviews in 1999 and 2004, whilst continuing to accentuate the policy prescriptions of the Jobs Strategy, drew attention to the varying degrees to which member countries had successfully 'internalized' the message of the *Jobs Study*. The 1999 review found that unemployment within OECD member countries remained 'high and persistent', drawing a tentative correlation between implementation of the Jobs Strategy and labour market performance in member countries:

> 'evidence . . . suggests that the Jobs Strategy works. Countries that have progressed the most along its lines have often experienced significant improvements in labour market conditions. . . . The successful countries have adopted different approaches to implementing reform in their labour and product markets, depending on their social, cultural and institutional characteristics, but in all cases reforms have followed the main thrusts of the Jobs Strategy.'[55]

The response has been to repeat earlier claims that reluctant modernizers would do better to emulate the more 'comprehensive reformers' such as the Netherlands and Ireland—countries seemingly less concerned about the perceived trade-off between equity and efficiency. By the time of the 2004 review, however, the OECD approach had become more nuanced, recognizing, *first*, the importance in combating unemployment and increasing employment, of achieving a balance between the different policy planks (such as EPL, unemployment benefits and active labour market policies)[56] but *second*, also acknowledging the need to combine the pursuit of 'more and better jobs' with other social objectives, in particular adequate social protection, a better reconciliation of work and family life, and equity outcomes in line with national preferences.[57] Whilst this approach has led some observers to suggest that the OECD is

[52] OECD, *Implementing the OECD Jobs Strategy*, n. 41 above, section VI.

[53] OECD, *Pushing Ahead with the Strategy*, n. 41 above, at 20.

[54] Ibid. The OECD returns to the debate over the apparent trade-off between a strong employment performance and a more equal distribution of earnings in its *Employment Outlook 2004*, above, n. 1, in particular in Chapter 3 'Wage-setting Institutions and Outcomes'.

[55] OECD, *Implementing the OECD Jobs Strategy: Assessing Performance and Policy* (Paris: OECD, 1999) at 41.

[56] *OECD Employment Outlook* 2004, n. 1 above, at 64, 76–89.

[57] Ibid., at 12.

softening its line on labour market reform,[58] it is notable for the purposes of comparison with the EU that the policy discourse within both institutional contexts is increasingly shifting to a greater focus on active labour market policies, 'employability' of job seekers, and the synergies between such policies and traditional concerns over labour market regulation.

## 2.2 A 'European' problem

To what extent has the European Employment Strategy followed the lead of the OECD Jobs Strategy, in terms of its conceptualization of, and solutions to, high European unemployment? Even if it is possible to identify a clear link between the prescriptions offered by the OECD and EU policy, to what extent has the EU as a whole been able to reach a consensus on the path to be taken; and if such a consensus has been reached to pursue the OECD path to employment generation, to what extent have individual Member States pursued such policies in the national sphere?[59]

High unemployment in (some) EU Member States is seen as creating a problem for the EU as a whole, since high levels of employment, competitiveness and social cohesion are all key goals of the Union;[60] goals which would be threatened by mass unemployment. Nevertheless, it has taken some time for Member States to agree to transfer competence over employment policy to the EU institutions, instead preferring national solutions. Even then, the actual competence of the central EU institutions over employment policy is limited to a monitoring or 'benchmarking' capacity, rather than a more proactive role in implementing a centralized labour market policy, or attempting to generate employment through Europe-wide programmes of expenditure. How, then, did (un)employment come to be seen as a problem for which a European-level solution was most appropriate?[61] After all, was it correct, in the 1990s, to talk of

[58] 'Economics Focus: A Gentler Touch', *The Economist*, 8 July 2004.

[59] This latter point will be addressed more fully in Chapter 6, on the influence of the Employment Strategy on Member States' employment policies, regulatory strategies and labour law.

[60] Article 2 of the TEU reads: 'The Union shall set itself the following objectives—to promote economic and social progress and a high level of employment and to achieve balanced and sustainable development, in particular through the creation of an area without internal frontiers, through the strengthening of economic and monetary cohesion and through the establishment of economic and monetary union'.

In addition, Article 2 of the EC Treaty reads: 'The Community shall have as its task... to promote throughout the Community a harmonious, balanced and sustainable development of economic activities, a high level of employment and of social protection, equality between men and women, sustainable and non-inflationary growth, a high degree of competitiveness and convergence of economic performance, a high level of protection and improvement of the quality of the environment, the raising of the standard of living and quality of life, and economic and social cohesion and solidarity among Member States'.

[61] For early discussions on a possible European level employment policy, see the Cecchini Report of 1988, on the completion of the internal market: Paolo Cecchini, *The European Challenge 1992: The Benefits of a Single Market* (Aldershot: Gower, 1988).

such a phenomenon as an EU unemployment problem, in view of the fact that 'the variation in unemployment in 1996 between the highest, Spain, and the lowest, Luxembourg, was 19 per cent, and the average rate of difference between the three countries with the highest and the lowest unemployment was around 12 per cent'.[62] The diversity in levels and in the duration of unemployment is often downplayed or ignored in the desire to present unemployment across EU countries as a problem with a common cause (over-regulation, leading to rigid labour markets) and thus a common solution (deregulation and labour market flexibility). Stephen Nickell cautions against overstating the similarities between (un)employment trends in EU Member States in order to provide a suitable contrast with the US 'employment miracle'.[63] As observed in Chapter 2, there was no consensus over the relative importance of the various underlying causes for the trend increase in the European unemployment rate from the 1970s onwards, but it is true to say that 'the most prevalent or "dominant" view is that the current unsatisfactory situation in European labour markets is a result of the interaction of labour market rigidities and a series of adverse shocks since the early 1970s.'[64]

The comparisons between overall unemployment rates in the EU and those in the US (and also Japan) are striking (see Figure 2.1 and Figure 2.2 on page 54).

The standardized or 'harmonized' unemployment rate for the 15 EU Member States was 8.1 per cent in February 2005, in comparison with a figure of 5.4 per cent for the US.[65] This gap has only recently narrowed—EU unemployment has been falling, whilst that in the US rising, from rates of 10.5 per cent (EU) and 4.5 per cent (US) in 1998[66]—and it was only in late 1998 that the level of unemployment across the EU fell below 10 per cent of the civilian labour force for the first time since 1992.[67] In addition to the unfavourable *unemployment* rate, there has been a growing divergence between the overall *employment* rate[68] within EU Member States and that of the US over the past 20 years, from a

[62] Valerie Symes, *Unemployment and Employment Policies in the EU* (London: Kogan Page, 1998) at 6. By 2005, the variation between the highest and lowest of the EU25 had narrowed to 13.8 per cent: in February 2005, unemployment was 4.3 per cent in Ireland, and 18.1 per cent in Poland. However, the variation as between the EU15 had narrowed further, to 6.2 per cent, with an unemployment rate of 10.5 per cent in Greece. Eurostat: Statistical Office of the European Communities in Luxembourg, Euro-indicators News Release No 44/2005, 1 April 2005.

[63] Stephen Nickell, 'Unemployment and Labor Market Rigidities: Europe versus North America' (1997) 11:3 *Journal of Economic Perspectives*, 55–74, at 55.

[64] International Monetary Fund, n. 1 above, at 91–2.

[65] Eurostat, n. 62 above.

[66] OECD, n. 36 above, at 19.

[67] CEC, *1999 Annual Employment Report. The EU Economy at the Arrival of the Euro: Promoting Growth, Employment, Stability*, COM (1999) 7 final, Brussels, 20.01.1999, at 39.

[68] The number of employed persons relative to the population of working age: 'The employment rate is an effective measure of the performance of an economy in the sense that it measures how the economy is able to provide jobs for all those who are able to work. It focuses attention both on employment, and on the employment potential of the non-employed, including both "economically inactive" people and the unemployed'. CEC, *Employment Rates Report 1998: Employment Performance in the Member States*, COM (98) 572 (Luxembourg: OOPEC, 1998).

position of relative comparability to one in which the EU employment rate trailed the US by some 14 percentage points.[69]

As Pierson *et al.* point out, the view of unemployment which informed the European Commission's 1993 White Paper is that, 'although it spreads across the continent, European unemployment is not one discrete challenge, but many separate and simultaneous ones'.[70] However, it is also clear that the dominant perspective amongst commentators is that there is a peculiarly *European* problem, which demands a *European Union* solution; a problem possibly related to that feared disease of 'Eurosclerosis',[71] with its particular 'take' on the role of labour market 'rigidities' in creating unemployment. If one accepts the argument that labour market rigidities are at the root of unemployment,[72] then it would certainly make sense to consider European countries as having a common problem, arising from the similarity in the patterns of labour market regulation and institutions, at least as compared with the more lightly regulated US market. Furthermore, as Richard Jackman argues, it may be that the creation of the EC in itself contributed to the growth of unemployment in the Member States.[73]

The European Commission's 1993 White Paper, however, evidenced doubts that the high levels of unemployment could be categorized as a peculiarly European phenomenon:

'The difference between the unemployment rates currently experienced in the major economic areas in the world—11% of the civilian labour force in the Community against rates of about 7% and 2.5% in the United States and Japan respectively—has given rise to questions about the existence of a *specific European unemployment problem*.'[74]

But this is countered by the observation that:

'An examination of the Community's past performance and a comparison with the other major areas, however, suggest that no hasty negative conclusions should be drawn.'[75]

So, *on the one hand*, there was concern not to overplay the view of unemployment as a peculiarly 'European' problem, as this might appear to endorse the view that 'rigidities' lay at the heart of unemployment in EU countries which had

[69] Ibid.

[70] Christopher Pierson, Anthony Forster and Erik Jones, 'The Politics of Europe: (Un)employment Ambivalence' in Brian Towers and Michael Terry (eds.), *Industrial Relations Journal: European Annual Review 1998* (Oxford: Blackwell, 1998) at 5. Also, see Jørgen Elmeskov, 'The Unemployment Problem in Europe: Lessons From Implementing the OECD Jobs Strategy', EUI Working Paper RSC No 98/24: 'There may not be much which is particularly European about the unemployment problem in Europe'.

[71] Herbert Giersch, 'Eurosclerosis', Kiel Discussion Paper No 112 (Kiel: Institute for World Economics, 1985).

[72] Horst Siebert, 'Labor Market Rigidities: At the Root of Unemployment in Europe' (1997) 11:3 *Journal of Economic Perspectives*, 37–54.

[73] Richard Jackman, 'The Impact of the European Union on Unemployment and Unemployment Policy' in David Hine and Hussein Kassim (eds.), *Beyond the Market: The EU and National Social Policy* (London: Routledge, 1998) at 60.

[74] CEC, White Paper *Growth*, n. 4 above, at 40; emphasis added. [75] Ibid.

pursued what might be called the 'European social model':

'[The White Paper] recognises the need for more efficient labour market and associated policies. It also recognises that the market alone cannot solve the employment, unemployment and associated social problems faced by the Community.... This means significant changes, but it does not simply mean a deregulation of Europe's labour markets. Rather, it implies an updated, rational and simplified system of regulation and incentives which will promote employment creation, without putting the burden of change on those already in a weak position in the labour market.'[76]

*On the other hand*, political expediency required *some* common effort to combat unemployment if greater market integration was to occur. In particular, although Member States had failed to include employment within the convergence criteria for monetary union, it was inescapable that if they did not individually take action at the national level to combat such high levels of unemployment, they would face difficulty meeting criteria such as public expenditure targets. As markets of all types converge within the EU, it becomes clear that huge disparities in labour market performance across Member States are incompatible with increased integration, both economically and politically, since the need to 'create more jobs for our citizens'[77] is almost as important as 'strengthening the Union's democratic legitimacy'[78] in the push to make the Union more acceptable to its citizens.

How did the EU institutions view the problem of high European unemployment? At one level, if there was scope to improve the employment-intensiveness[79] of growth through a more centralized coordination of macro-economic policies, it would make sense to seize this opportunity, rather than blaming common systems of labour market regulation for European unemployment. However, one must not underestimate the role played by the EU institutions, and by the Commission in particular, in extending the competence of the EU by creating an impetus for European solutions. The conceptualization of European unemployment in such a way that a 'European' solution was deemed necessary may owe much to the Commission's strategic attempts to expand its own role.[80] Majone has argued that the Commission is best understood as an institution which seeks to maximize its influence within the EU system,[81] and there is much evidence, in the social policy area, of strategic use of policy instruments and initiatives to increase the EU's competence, and thus the influence of the Commission.[82]

[76] CEC, White Paper *Growth*, n. 4 above, at 123.

[77] Presidency Conclusions, Essen European Council, 9 and 10 December 1994, Bulletin of the EU-12/1994. [78] Ibid.

[79] 'The **employment intensity** is the relationship between the rate of growth of an economy and its rate of employment creation': CEC, n. 4 above, at 43; emphasis in the original.

[80] Bryan Wendon, 'The Commission as Image-Venue Entrepreneur in EU Social Policy' (1998) 5:2 *Journal of European Public Policy*, 339–53.

[81] Giandomenico Majone, *Regulating Europe* (London: Routledge, 1996).

[82] Laura Cram, 'Calling the Tune Without Paying the Piper? Social Policy Regulation: The Role of the Commission in European Community Social Policy' (1993) 21 *Policy and Politics*, 135–46

In addition, the absence of any reference to employment in the Treaty on European Union (TEU) was criticized during the national debates in the run-up to its ratification.[83] It appeared as though the EU, as a polity, cared little about unemployment at a time of high unemployment and fiscal rectitude. However, this is not to say that the convergence criteria which were eventually agreed upon did not, in actual fact, have a profound effect on Member States' employment and social policies.[84] Certainly, many EU countries were experiencing increased unemployment, as governments sought to meet the monetary and fiscal criteria for monetary union, placing further constraints on public expenditure.[85] The importance of such domestic political pressures in the development of an overarching EU employment strategy is not to be underestimated. Pierson *et al.*, for example, argue that '[i]n such a context, whether these two processes—unemployment and convergence—were causally related became less important than whether they were linked in public perceptions'.[86] High European unemployment became an important political issue partly *because* it came to be linked with popular support for monetary integration.

## 3. The shift from a 'social policy' agenda to an 'employment policy' agenda

Social policy at EU level has always been underdeveloped, in particular, lacking a clear Treaty basis. The fragmented nature of the legal base, or competence, for social policy law led to years of stagnation in this area. At the time of the original Treaties, however, the prevailing wisdom was that the goal of market integration did not require harmonization of Member States' social policy. According to the report produced by the International Labour Organization's Committee of Experts in 1956 (the Ohlin Report),[87] it was not necessary, in creating a single market, for national systems of labour and social law to be harmonized. The theory of comparative advantage which underpinned the Report held that differences in levels of social protection or labour law or wage costs between states

and *Policy Making in the EU: Conceptual Lenses and the Integration Process* (London: Routledge, 1997).

[83] Finn Laursen and Sophie Vanhoonacker (eds.), *The Ratification of the Maastricht Treaty: Issues, Debates and Future Implications* (Maastricht: Martinus Nijhoff, 1994).

[84] Ray Barrell, Julian Morgan and Nigel Pain, 'The Impact of the Maastricht Fiscal Criteria on Employment in Europe' EUI Working Paper RSC No 96/61 (fiscal impact); Paul Teague, *Economic Citizenship in the European Union: Employment Relations in the New Europe* (London: Routledge, 1999) Chapter 7 (social consequences).

[85] Paul Teague, n. 84 above, at 167.

[86] Pierson, Forster and Jones, n. 70 above, at 7.

[87] International Labour Organization, *Social Aspects of Economic Co-operation: Report of a Group of Experts*, Studies and Reports, New Series, No 46 (Geneva: ILO, 1956) (the Ohlin Report; summarized as International Labour Office, 'Social Aspects of Economic Co-operation' (1956) 74 *International Labour Review* 99).

engaged in international trade did not, in themselves, pose a serious obstacle to competition or efficiency because these differences broadly reflected differences in productivity.[88] The conclusions of the Ohlin Report, which had been commissioned by the prospective Member States,[89] were substantially adopted by the intergovernmental Spaak Report of 1956,[90] on which the Treaty of Rome was based. The goal of economic liberalization at the centre of the putative Community was thus founded on the idea that

'competition does not necessarily require a complete harmonisation of the different elements in costs; indeed, it is only on the basis of certain differences—such as wage differences due to differences in productivity—that trade and competition can develop. . . . In addition, wage and interest rates tend to level up in a common market—a process which is hastened by the free circulation of the factors of production. This is a consequence rather than a condition of the common market's operation.'[91]

The social policy which *did* develop was one which was, on the whole, justified on market integrationist grounds: the incremental development of a framework of basic minimum standards was justified as a protection against destructive downwards competition, to provide 'a bulwark against using low social standards as an instrument of unfair competition, and protection against reducing social standards to gain competitiveness'.[92] Legislative activity in the area of social policy developed at a faster pace in the early 1990s, given impetus by the availability of qualified majority voting under Article 118a of the EC Treaty (now renumbered as Article 137), and inspired in 1989 by the acceptance by eleven of the then twelve Member States of the Charter of Fundamental Rights for Workers.[93] Whilst the EU's competence in the area of *social* policy has undoubtedly grown from what was envisaged by the Treaty of Rome, *employment* policy remained the preserve of Member States, with the exception of small areas such as vocational training.[94] This reluctance to hand over competence in employment matters was exemplified by the negotiations in the Intergovernmental Conference prior to the 1992 Treaty on European Union. Subsequently, in particular since the Essen European Council in 1994, there has been a shift

[88] Simon Deakin 'Labour Law as Market Regulation: The Economic Foundations of European Social Policy' in Paul Davies, Antoine Lyon-Caen, Silvana Sciarra and Spiros Simitis (eds.), *European Community Labour Law: Principles and Perspectives* (Oxford: Clarendon, 1996) at 66.

[89] Paul Davies, 'The Emergence of European Labour Law' in William McCarthy (ed.), *Legal Intervention in Industrial Relations: Gains and Losses* (Oxford: Blackwell, 1992) at 318–19.

[90] Comité Intergouvernemental Créé par la Conférence de Messine, *Rapport des Chefs de Délégation aux Minstres des Affaires Etrangères*, Brussels, 1956 (the Spaak Report), summarized in English in 'Political and Economic Planning', *Planning* No 405 (1956).

[91] Ibid., at 233.

[92] CEC, White Paper, *European Social Policy: A Way Forward for the Union* COM (94) 333 final (Luxembourg: OOPEC, 1994) at 5.

[93] Erika Szyszczak, 'Future Directions in European Union Social Policy Law' (1995) 24:1 ILJ, 19–32.

[94] Mark Freedland, 'Vocational Training in EC Law and Policy—Education, Employment or Welfare? (1996) 25 ILJ, 110–20.

from an emphasis on social policy to employment policy,[95] albeit the social policy which had existed was mostly an employment-related social policy.[96]

We have witnessed a move away from legislative proposals on social law, first towards coordination of Member States' social policy, and more recently towards coordination of Member States' employment policies. Having gained a clear competence to legislate on social policy following the TEU through the inclusion of the Protocol and Agreement on Social Policy in the Maastricht Treaty (a competence which was further confirmed through the introduction of a new Title on Social Policy by the Treaty of Amsterdam), the EU institutions, and in particular the Commission, then appeared to shy away from making new social policy proposals which would, it was feared, increase the regulatory burden. For example, the Commission's 1994 White Paper *European Social Policy* stated:

> 'Given that the solid base of European social legislation has already been achieved, the Commission considers that there is not a need for a wide-ranging programme of new legislative proposals in the coming period.'[97]

Further, in the 1997 Green Paper *Partnership for a New Organisation of Work*,[98] the Commission envisaged the need to move 'from rigid and compulsory systems of statutory regulations to more open and flexible legal frameworks'.[99] The preference seems to be to leave regulation of the social field to agreements between the social partners, which are seen as being somehow less interventionist.

One very useful framework of analysis which can help one understand the origins (and possible future direction) of the EU Employment Strategy, is that offered by Mark Freedland.[100] He posits a distinction between EC economic regulation supported by an economic policy discourse and EC social regulation supported by a social policy discourse,[101] although 'EC employment policy measures are informed by economic policy as well as by social policy'.[102] Freedland argues that the White Paper *Growth, Competitiveness and Employment* and the Green Paper *Social Policy*[103] 'conform very exactly to [this] dichotomy between economic and social policy'.[104] The subsequent European Employment Strategy can be seen as an arena within which these tensions are being debated. The question becomes whether this economic efficiency/employment policy

[95] Catherine Barnard and Simon Deakin, 'A year of living dangerously? EC social rights, employment policy, and EMU' (1999) 30:4 *Industrial Relations Journal: European Annual Review 1998*, 355–72.

[96] Mark Freedland, 'Employment Policy' in Paul Davies *et al.*, n. 88 above, at 277.

[97] CEC, n. 92 above, at 5.

[98] CEC, *Green Paper: Partnership for a New Organisation of Work*, COM (97) 128 final (Luxembourg: OOPEC, 1997).

[99] Ibid., para 44.

[100] Unpublished paper given at a conference at the European University Institute, Florence, 11–12 February 2000; see also, Freedland, n. 96 above.

[101] Freedland, n. 96 above, at 286.

[102] Ibid., at 291.

[103] CEC, Green Paper *European Social Policy: Options for the Union*, COM (93) 551 (Luxembourg: OOPEC, 1993).

[104] Freedland, n. 96 above, at 297.

discourse can be reconciled with the social justice/social policy discourse. One argument runs that the Union 'should set itself the purely economic goal of market liberalization, and that social policy, in so far as it is incompatible with this approach, should be marginalized'.[105]

Freedland identifies three discourses or policy agendas currently competing for dominance of the EU labour law agenda:

1. a social policy agenda which provides a continuation of the policy discourse of the 1970s and 1980s, stressing social dialogue, the role of the social partners, and ideas in respect of representation at the workplace;
2. an employment policy agenda which redefines priorities as the creation and maintenance of high levels of employment; this agenda reorientates the discourse towards macro-economic ideas of competitiveness; and
3. a human and equality rights agenda, focusing on rights, for example as encapsulated in the EU Charter of Fundamental Rights.[106] This agenda provides one possible way to recapture the ground lost in the move to the employment policy agenda.

Freedland is right to note that 'social policy' as it was conceived consisted almost entirely of employment issues; but I would argue that it is still useful to think in terms of a decided shift towards a more specific 'employment policy', because what we are observing is a move away from social *law* and *legislative* initiatives, towards *soft law*, or rather *policies* aimed at employment creation, which for the most part eschew legislation. Perhaps it would be simpler and more accurate to talk of a move from employment law to employment policy. In this context, the second of the above agendas seems to be in the ascendancy in the policy discourse of the EU institutions, connecting employment policy with EMU, and thus having a knock-on effect on the direction of future labour market regulation.

## 3.1 The Green and White Papers on social policy

The 1993 Green Paper defines social policy as including the 'the full range of policies in the social sphere including labour market policies'.[107] However, it seems true to say that Community social policy has almost always been an *employment-related* social policy. When describing the width of coverage of Community social policy, the Commission in fact reveals that it is quite narrowly focused on employment-related issues:

'Community social policy has covered a wide range of areas, these include equality of opportunity, health and safety matters, employment and labour law matters, issues of

[105] Barnard and Deakin, n. 95 above, at 359.

[106] Charter of Fundamental Rights of the European Union, adopted by a Solemn Proclamation of the European Parliament, Council and Commission at the Nice European Council in December 2000, OJ C 364/01, 18.12.2000.

[107] CEC, n. 92 above, at 6.

social protection and social security, as well as action focused on specific points such as poverty and the role of the disabled.'[108]

This list of issues considered central to the Union's fledgling social policy reveals a *protectionist* bias; with the exception of a separate sub-discourse on poverty and social exclusion, the emphasis seems squarely on protecting those in employment rather than employment-generation. A major step towards the realization of a European employment policy came in 1993: first with the Commission's Employment Framework Initiative, which set out the basis of a concerted strategy for employment; and second, with the *Growth* White Paper,[109] which developed that employment strategy in the wider economic, industrial and social context of the Union. This strategy was then endorsed by the Brussels European Council in December 1993.[110] As a precursor to the Essen criteria, the Brussels European Council identified seven areas for action by Member States, in response to the suggestions for combating unemployment and improving employment contained in the *Growth* White Paper:

1. improving education and training systems, especially continuing training;
2. improving flexibility within enterprises and within the labour market;
3. the reorganization of work at enterprise level;
4. targeted reductions in the indirect costs of labour (statutory contributions), particularly of less skilled work;
5. better use of public funds set aside for combating unemployment;
6. specific measures concerning young people without adequate training;
7. developing employment in connection with new requirements.[111]

However, by the time of the Essen Council, two (related) events had occurred: the White Paper *Social Policy* had appeared, wholeheartedly adopting the 'employment policy' agenda of the *Growth* White Paper—and its concomitant downplaying of a Community legislative agenda. Secondly, the Commission's strategy to create 15 million jobs in five years, at a cost of ECU 600 billion[112] had failed to gain acceptance by Member States:

'member state Finance Ministers resisted those measures which required substantial expenditure . . . and the Council itself rejected the idea of an ambitious and costly initiative. Hence the measures agreed at the Essen summit were far more modest.'[113]

Could one describe this expansionist agenda (ultimately thwarted) as an example of the Commission's 'Keynesian' aspirations, which were reined in by

108 Ibid., at 9.

109 For the sake of brevity, the 1993 White Paper (n. 4 above) will be referred to as such, but this is not to understate the importance of the other goals of 'competitiveness' and 'employment'.

110 CEC, n. 92 above, 9.

111 Ibid.

112 The European Currency Unit; the ECU rate was determined against a basket of currencies of the Member States.

113 Janine Goetschy, 'The European Employment Strategy: Genesis and Development' (1999) 5:2 *European Journal of Industrial Relations*, 117–37.

the Essen Council? I would argue that the Growth Initiative can be read as one of the Commission's 'Keynesian' solutions which was loathed, and ultimately quashed, by Member States reluctant to hand over significant budgetary independence to the EU institutions to tackle unemployment from the centre:

'There can be no doubt that the causes and consequences of high and rising unemployment in Europe represent the single most serious challenge facing Member States today.... There is general agreement that the main solution to the problem will come from increased growth. In this regard, a number of measures are already in hand, including in particular, the Growth Initiative agreed at the Edinburgh European Council and reinforced at the Copenhagen Council. However, there is also a growing recognition that growth alone will not be enough.... *It is clear that many of the policy levers which will have to be pulled are, and will continue to be, a matter of exclusive Member State competence.*'[114]

This sentiment was reiterated—and in fact strengthened—at a later date: as Commission President Jacques Santer pointed out at the time of the Stability and Growth Pact at the Amsterdam European Council in 1997:[115] 'our generation will neither see economic government nor political government in Europe'.[116] Furthermore, he added: 'We do not wish to have a Keynesian policy and to launch major programmes'.[117]

## 3.2 The White Paper *Growth, Competitiveness and Employment*: comparisons with the OECD *Jobs Study*

Although the Green Paper was ostensibly about *social* policy, an important by-product of it was the Community-wide Framework for Employment, proposed by the Commission in May 1993, and adopted by the Social Affairs Council of June 1993. Further evidence of 'employment policy' displacing 'social policy' came with the *Growth* White Paper, which placed employment policy firmly within the context of wider economic integration and monetary union: 'We must... place our thinking within a macroeconomic reference framework for both economic and monetary convergence which will increase the opportunities available to our economies'.[118]

[114] CEC, n. 98 above, at 40–1; emphasis added.

[115] Resolution of the European Council on the Stability and Growth Pact; Amsterdam, 17 June 1997, OJ C 236/1, 2.8.97, p 1; Council Regulation (EC) No 1466/97 of 7 July 1997 on the strengthening of the surveillance of budgetary positions and the surveillance and co-ordination of economic policies, OJ L 209, 2.8.97, at 1. After years of debate over the need to reform the Stability and Growth Pact, these two Regulations are now due to be reformed: the meeting of Member States' Finance Ministers (ECOFIN) in March 2005 produced a report, *Improving the Implementation of the Stability and Growth Pact*, which was endorsed by the European Council meeting in March 2005 and is currently the subject of Commission proposals to amend the Regulations; see discussion in Chapter 4, Section 2.2.

[116] *Agence Europe*, No 6993 (n.s.) Thursday, 12 June 1997, at 2.

[117] Ibid., at 6.

[118] CEC, n. 4 above, at 12.

By the time of the *Growth* White Paper, the emphasis had very much switched to employment-generation. As with the OECD's diagnosis, the explanations for European unemployment put forward by the White Paper were that Member States were gravely affected by the oil price shocks of the 1970s,[119] resulting in a fall in investment and a rapid growth of inflation. In particular, 'inflation had arisen largely because of rising wages, hence encouraging the introduction of labour saving technology, which resulted in fewer jobs being generated from economic growth'.[120] The White Paper did not advocate a 'quick fix' to the EU's unemployment problems, but rather a combination of macro-economic and structural measures.[121] Of the latter, three main areas for action were identified: first, greater flexibility in the economy as a whole, and in the regulatory framework in particular, which should become more 'enterprise-friendly'; second, the creation of an efficient labour market able to respond to new competitive situations; and third, an open international environment.[122] So far, so similar to the prescriptions of the OECD's *Jobs Study*. However, the issue of flexibility and deregulation of labour markets provides a major area of divergence between the *Jobs Study* and the White Paper.

Although 'labour market flexibility' has become an increasingly dominant chord in the EU discourse on unemployment as this discourse has matured, it seems that the White Paper adopted a more nuanced view of the causes of unemployment, including an acceptance of the role played by social factors, such as demographic changes.[123] The White Paper proposed 'necessary structural measures', amongst which were greater flexibility within the economy in general, and within the regulatory framework in particular, as well as strategies to create an efficient labour market able to respond to new competitive situations.[124] Arguably, however, this emphasis on labour market efficiency and flexibility did not necessarily signal a deregulatory agenda.

This approach was spelt out more clearly in the section of the White Paper entitled 'Turning Growth into Jobs'.[125] Given the need for both sustained economic growth and a more employment-intensive pattern of growth, the White Paper recognized 'the need for more efficient labour markets', whilst also noting that '*the market alone cannot solve unemployment*'.[126] The strategies suggested to boost the employment-intensiveness of growth involved measures to make labour markets more flexible, to tackle such problems as the inadequate

[119] Ibid., at 40–3; see also Symes, n. 62 above, at 30. [120] Symes, n. 62 above, at 30.
[121] CEC, n. 4 above, at 48. [122] Ibid., at 50.
[123] For example: 'Community unemployment has increased steadily since the beginning of the 1970s with the exception of the second half of the 1980s, when nine million jobs were created through a combination of appropriate national policies, a favourable external environment and the dynamism resulting from the prospect of the single market. *Overall, however, since the early 1970s demographic factors have led to an increase in the number of people seeking jobs, while the number of jobs available stagnated or increased only modestly*. Other developed economies have been patently more successful in responding to the challenge of boosting job creation'. CEC, n. 4 above, at 39; emphasis added. [124] CEC, n. 4 above, at 50.
[125] Ibid., at Chapter 8, 123–35. [126] Ibid., at 123; emphasis added.

match of labour supply to the needs of the market (what could be labelled 'mismatch unemployment') and those caused by overprotection of 'insiders' at the expense of 'outsiders',[127] for example, social protection schemes which protect those already in work, acting as an obstacle to recruitment.[128] However, it is clear that, for the Commission at least, increased flexibility was not to be seen as synonymous with deregulation.[129]

The White Paper rejected 'wholesale labour market deregulation' especially of employment protection legislation and wage determination, as 'the only way of bringing its labour markets into equilibrium',[130] but instead promoted a vision of greater labour market flexibility without a consequential reduction in levels of job protection,[131] especially as the Community 'cannot hope to address the consequences of the international relocation of jobs through wage–price competition'.[132] It would seem, in this period at least, that the EU institutions were firmly at odds with the OECD over how to deal with the 'trade-off' between horizontal equity and employment objectives: as far as the Commission was concerned, the trade-off exists, but is generally unacceptable. Indeed, it would perhaps be unrealistic to expect individual Member States to adopt, *at this stage in European integration*, the sort of wholesale deregulation advocated by the OECD. The OECD's finding that some continental European countries considered equity as a more fundamental goal than low unemployment has already been noted.[133] This much can also be seen from the reluctance of most Member States to engage in modernization of their regulatory regimes as demanded by the Employment Guidelines as evidenced, for example, in their 'National Action Plans' for the year 2000, although the thrust of the Guidelines, whilst pushing flexibility, is by no means *automatically* deregulatory.[134]

In order to create more jobs, the White Paper therefore recommended an expansionary policy, which would involve investing at least ECU 400 billion in large-scale transport, telecommunications and environmental projects. It is interesting to note the explicitness with which such job creation schemes were advocated; the White Paper contains clear commitments—targets, even—which do not appear in subsequent policy pronouncements and certainly do not form part of the Luxembourg Process.[135] For example,

'The European Union should set itself the target of creating 15 million jobs by the end of the century.'[136]

'For all the countries of the Union, it is essential to reduce the cost of unskilled and semi-skilled labour by an amount equivalent to 1 or 2 points of GNP by the year 2000.'[137]

[127] Assar Lindbeck and Dennis Snower, *The Insider–Outsider Theory of Employment and Unemployment* (Cambridge, MA: MIT Press, 1989). [128] CEC, n. 4 above, at 124.
[129] Ibid., at 123. [130] Ibid., at 128. [131] Ibid., at 129. [132] Ibid.
[133] OECD, n. 41 above. [134] This point is further elaborated in Chapter 6.
[135] One of the very few real 'targets' which survived the process from the *Growth* White Paper to the Amsterdam Treaty is that in respect of youth unemployment; the other relates to the numbers of unemployed who are offered training or similar 'active' measures.
[136] CEC, n. 4 above, at 11; further elaborated at 43. [137] Ibid., at 18.

Areas in which the White Paper envisaged such job creation occurring included employment in what would become a new (or revitalized) 'social economy'.[138] Further hopes were pinned on the above-mentioned 'trans-European networks'[139] which cover developments in information technology, transport and energy. With regard to transport, the White Paper leant very heavily on Article 129b EC (now Article 154 EC)[140] to advocate renewed infrastructural investment, argued as necessary in itself, and also for its job-creation potential. Following on from the Commission White Paper, the 1994 European Council in Essen launched an 'integrated employment strategy',[141] which adopted, for the first time at European level, short- and medium-term policy on employment, in addition to initiating an annual process of Commission monitoring of Member States' employment policies which was to be codified at Amsterdam. The Essen Council identified five 'priority areas' for action by Member States:

1. promoting investment in vocational training;
2. increasing employment through periods of growth (an attempt to end to the peculiar European phenomenon of 'jobless growth');
3. reducing non-wage labour costs;
4. improving the effectiveness of labour market policy; and
5. improving measures to help groups at risk of exclusion from the labour market.

A particularly important initiative of the Essen Council was the adoption of a multilateral employment monitoring procedure along lines similar to the economic monitoring procedure introduced by the Maastricht Treaty, although without the sanctions for non-compliance.[142] Member States were urged to act on the above recommendations in their national policies, and submit annual reports on their progress, to improve efficiency by exposing national policies to scrutiny, and to learn from examples of 'best practice'. Whilst this procedure

[138] Ibid., at 19–20; suggested sources of new jobs in the social economy include improvements in the quality of life, such as the renovation of old housing, and local services such as home help for the elderly and disabled.

[139] Ibid., at Chapter 3.

[140] Article 154(1): 'To help achieve the objectives referred to in Articles 14 and 158 [respectively: the completion of the internal market as an area without frontiers by 1993; and economic and social cohesion] and to enable citizens of the Union, economic operators and regional and local communities to derive full benefit from the setting-up of an area without internal frontiers, the Community shall contribute to the establishment of trans-European networks in the areas of transport, telecommunications and energy infrastructures'.

[141] Presidency Conclusions, Essen European Council, n. 77 above.

[142] Article 103 EC Treaty (now Article 99, after the Amsterdam renumbering) provides for the Council to adopt 'broad guidelines of the economic policies of the Member States and of the Community'. It also establishes a 'multilateral surveillance procedure' under which Member States must monitor their policies and report back. These 'Broad Economic Policy Guidelines' are the 'main instrument of collective control in the framework of the national [economic] stability plans': Erika Szyszczak, 'The Evolving European Employment Strategy' in Jo Shaw (ed.), *Social Law and Policy in an Evolving European Union* (Oxford: Hart Publishing, 2000) at 212.

represented the softest of 'soft law', it was nevertheless important in prefiguring the Employment Strategy initiated by the Amsterdam Treaty, in particular, the so-called 'Luxembourg process'.[143]

Further stimulus to the employment creation agenda was given by the Florence European Council in June 1996, which, in accordance with the Confidence Pact for Employment[144] proposed by the Commission, exhorted Member States to adopt a series of initiatives to improve job generation programmes. Whilst not legally binding, the Confidence Pact anticipated the Amsterdam employment guidelines as an instance of the use of 'soft law' measures, which nevertheless placed informal pressure on Member States to coordinate their employment policies. There then followed the Dublin European Council of 13–14 December 1996, which further endorsed the proposal in the Confidence Pact for a commitment by all the social and economic 'agents' to play their full part in employment matters, and urged swift action on the projects for territorial employment pacts.

Ultimately, however, the Commission's proposals for infrastructure and public works programmes were blocked by Member States (in particular, by finance ministers) who refused to sanction the necessary centralization of expenditure and competence for employment policy which this would have necessitated.[145] The European Council meeting at Essen failed to reach agreement to endorse this proposed expansion of public investment to increase jobs. Why? One possible explanation:

> In contrast to the macroeconomic policy recommended in the Delors report [the *Growth* White Paper], the OECD [the OECD *Jobs Study* of 1994] sees a stable macroeconomic framework, with control of inflation as its central aim, and a reduction in public sector deficits, again in order to establish low inflation, as the primary requisite in the European economy. Expansionary fiscal policy is viewed as unacceptable since it could increase inflation and damage the growth confidence within the private sector. Wage flexibility is viewed as essential for competitive advantage, and minimum wages are considered to be a form of social policy which, in most circumstances, results in decreases in employment.[146]

In order to achieve the target (set by the Commission), of creating at least 15 million jobs by the year 2000, it would prove vital to tackle the employment intensity of growth. Although there had been some (albeit modest) growth in EU economies the poor job content of such growth was a problem which was much lamented in the literature.

Although the two texts (the Commission's White Paper and the OECD's *Jobs Study*) do not directly 'speak' to each other, one can see a number of interactions

[143] See Chapter 4, Section 3.1.

[144] CEC, *Action for Employment in Europe: A Confidence Pact*, CSE (96) 1 final (Luxembourg: OOPEC, 1996).

[145] 'In total some ECU 400 billion of investments in the transport and energy trans-European networks will be required in the next 15 years, of which some ECU 220 billion by 1999': CEC, n. 4 above, at 32.

[146] Symes, n. 24 above, at 191–2.

and parallels between the two. The White Paper, followed almost immediately by the Essen European Council which was to lead eventually to the Luxembourg Process with its annual guidelines and monitoring of national employment policy, finds echoes with the OECD Jobs Strategy, which also led to its own 'active, detailed and multilateral monitoring'[147] of proposed reforms, and 'peer review', namely, multilateral surveillance of countries by one another.[148]

However, what is more fundamental is the differing policy choices which these two papers represented. The OECD *Jobs Study* route to combating unemployment was through increasing the employment intensity of growth, via structural reform and the pursuit of stringent macro-economic framework. The Delors route, on the other hand, would have necessitated an expansionary fiscal policy, and whilst acknowledging the necessity of structural reform, was loath to equate such reform with outright deregulation, if by that was meant an abandonment of traditional social settlements which valued a high level of social transfers and social inclusion. Both papers acknowledged the importance of tackling the employment intensiveness of growth: in particular, this would be essential in order to achieve the Commission's target of creating at least 15 million jobs by the year 2000.

Ultimately, in refusing to endorse the Commission's more expansionary vision, Member States would appear to be preferring the OECD's more restrictive view of macro-economic policy. However, I would contend that Member States were, at the time of the Essen European Council in 1994, acting more to reject the expansionary fiscal policy of the Delors White Paper, and its concomitant increase in competence for the central EU institutions in the area of macro-economic policy, than to endorse the sort of thinking which was behind the parts of the *Jobs Study* which advocated greatly increased wage flexibility and diminished social policy interventions. One could argue that the approach of the Member States at this time was to steer a middle route (not to be confused with a 'Third Way') between the austerity of the OECD's approach and the ambitions of a Delors Commission which, unlike its successor, *could* envisage a form of 'economic government'. As Barnard and Deakin put it:

> 'For a while in the mid-1990s there was an active debate about whether to use centralised expenditure to stimulate demand through investments in infrastructure and public works. This received some impetus from the publication of the 1993 White Paper, *Growth, Competitiveness and Employment*, but the member states refused to countenance a significant increase in the Commission's budget and the idea faded away.'[149]

The form which the later EU Employment Strategy took was, in part, dictated by Member States' reactions to the expansionary proposals of the White Paper. Member States' rejection of the supply-side measures advocated by the White

[147] OECD, n. 13 above, at 3. [148] Ibid., at 4.
[149] Barnard and Deakin, n. 95 above, at 356.

Paper led, ultimately, to a policy based on centralized coordination of employment policies, rather than a more distinctly European employment policy.[150]

## 3.3 The White Paper and deregulation: the US as a comparator

'[T]he Community's economy, with the exception of the period 1986–90, has always been characterized by low employment creation . . . and the origin of its problems go back to the beginning of the 1970s, when it proved unable to increase its rate of job creation to match the increase in the number of people seeking employment. By contrast, the USA has been able to respond to an even larger increase in the number of people looking for jobs with a strong increase in employment creation.' (European Commission, 1993)[151]

The comparison between increasing unemployment in EU countries and the US 'employment miracle' has often proved irresistible.[152] However, what is very clear from an examination of the institutional discourse in respect of the US 'employment miracle' is that there is some caution expressed, certainly in the early 1990s, over following the American model too closely, at least with regard to measures to increase the employment intensity of growth. The path to higher employment creation should not, it would seem, be at the cost of increasing wage inequality or major downward wage mobility, beyond what would be acceptable to European 'civil society' in terms of political economy. It is worth noting the following:

'An increase in the employment intensity of Community growth to match the US performance would require the implementation, on a large scale, of measures increasing the willingness of employers to hire workers and in particular:

(i) a considerable downward widening of the scale of wage costs in order to reintegrate those market activities which at present are priced out of it;

(ii) a reduction in all other costs associated with taking on or maintaining labour, e.g. social security rules.'[153]

Instead of this path of modest growth and very high employment intensity, an alternative, that of a more modest increase in the employment intensity of growth with a stronger rate of growth is seen as preferable:

'An increase in the employment intensity of growth of the order of magnitude of the one envisaged in this second scenario, while not being easy to achieve, would not require the drastic measures needed to reach the performance of the USA. *In addition it could be achieved with the consensus of most of those concerned*'.[154]

[150] Barnard and Deakin, n. 95 above, at 356. '[A]ny programme with even a whiff of Keynesian expansion [was] immediately shot down': Paul Teague, 'Reshaping Employment Regimes in Europe: Policy Shifts Alongside Boundary Change' (1999) 19:1 *Journal of Public Policy*, 33–62, at 37.

[151] CEC, n. 4 above, at 41–2.

[152] See the discussion in Chapter 2, especially Section 3.

[153] CEC, n. 4 above, at 45.

[154] Ibid., at 46; emphasis added.

This is just one example of the unwillingness, at that moment in time, of the EU institutions to advocate adoption of the US model of labour market regulation. Matching US performance was to be achieved though methods other than those used in the US, for reasons of political economy and out of respect for the desire which existed in most Member States to protect social solidarity and avoid increased inequality. Flexibility, according to the Commission, requires a 'remodelled, rational and simplified system of regulation, not simply deregulation of Europe's labour markets'.[155]

If one compares the approach adopted by the White Paper in particular, and the Commission in general, it is quite different from the solution to the EU's unemployment ills proposed by international organizations such as the OECD. It was perhaps unrealistic to expect individual Member States to adopt the sort of wholesale deregulation advocated by the OECD:

> 'The desire to maintain gains in social welfare through wage rates and working conditions, which have been made in Europe in the last fifty years, are not easily abandoned. Throughout most of Europe deregulation of the labour market is socially and politically unacceptable. . . . To ignore the strong commitment of most European countries to the protection of workers' rights and social equity within the labour market is unrealistic'.[156]

This question will be addressed in greater detail in Chapters 4 and 6: on the one hand, the discourse at EU level has in recent years moved closer to the economic orthodoxy, advocating greater wage flexibility, reductions in non-wage labour costs and stronger 'incentives' on the unemployed to take up work; in particular a 'disincentive' discourse is now prevalent within the EU's economic policy guidelines. On the other hand, there is a continued reluctance within several Member States to engage in large-scale modernization of their regulatory regimes as envisioned by the Employment Guidelines.

## 4. The Maastricht IGC and competence over employment policy

> 'Most European countries are currently entering a recession, yet they have signed up to the Maastricht Treaty which requires a degree of fiscal contraction.' (Barrell *et al.* 1994)[157]

As mentioned, the Treaty on European Union (the Maastricht Treaty) dealt extensively with social policy, in giving it a firm treaty base for the first time. A great deal has been written about these developments,[158] but what is more

[155] Ibid., at 123. [156] Symes, n. 24 above, at 192.

[157] Ray Barrell, Guglielmo Maria Caporale and James Sefton, 'Prospects for European Unemployment' in Jonathan Michie and John Grieve Smith (eds.), *Unemployment in Europe* (London: Academic Press, 1994) at 39–40.

[158] See, for example, Brian Bercusson, 'Maastricht: A Fundamental Change in European Labour Law' (1992) 23 *Industrial Relations Journal*, 177–90 and 'The Dynamic of European Labour Law

pertinent in this context is how social law and social policy and employment issues were kept so clearly separate from the debate on monetary union, and ultimately excluded from the convergence criteria for monetary union.

Following the ratification of the TEU, combating unemployment and encouraging non-inflationary growth became central aims of the newly formed European Union.[159] Nevertheless, a moot point during the Intergovernmental Conference leading up to the TEU had been whether or not to include employment *targets* within the convergence criteria which Member States had to respect if they wanted to participate in Economic and Monetary Union.[160] Ultimately, however, the anxiety of most Member States to retain their competence in the area of employment policy led to the exclusion of this policy area from the convergence criteria.[161] The Delors Committee Report,[162] which was responsible for determining much of the future content of EMU,[163] had envisaged EMU as a three-part process, involving (a) closer coordination of Member States' economic and monetary policies, (b) the establishment of a European Central Bank, and (c) the replacement of national currencies by a single European currency.[164] Furthermore, as Francis Snyder points out, the thinking at the time was that wage flexibility and labour mobility were essential to avoid differences in competitiveness between different regions and countries.[165] This perspective is interesting in being so very much at odds with the 'comparative advantage' approach, which had dominated the Treaty of Rome, tolerating the absence of a 'level playing field' in labour costs between Member States.[166] Now it appeared that the reality of a common currency required Common Market countries to behave more like an entity with a common labour market, if EMU was to work.

After Maastricht' (1994) 23 *Industrial Law Journal*, 1–31; Barry Fitzpatrick, 'Community Social Law After Maastricht' (1992) 21:3 *Industrial Law Journal*, 199–213; Erika Szyszczak, n. 93 above.

[159] The Treaty of Amsterdam subsequently amended Article 2 EC again, but following the TEU, it stated that the Union's tasks included promotion of 'sustainable and non-inflationary growth respecting a high level of employment and social protection'. See also Catherine Barnard, *EC Employment Law* (Chichester: Wiley, 1995) at 65.

[160] To ensure that the sustainable convergence required for the achievement of EMU came about, the TEU set five convergence criteria which needed to be met by each Member State before it could take part in the third stage of EMU. Checks on whether the criteria were being met were to be carried out on the basis of reports by the Commission and the European Monetary Institute.

[161] The convergence criteria are referred to in Article 121 of the EC Treaty and set out in Protocol 21 annexed to the Treaty.

[162] Committee for the Study of Economic and Monetary Union (the Delors Committee), *Report on Economic and Monetary Union in the Community* (Luxembourg: OOPEC, 1989) Annex I, 39. Much of the discussion of the Report is taken from Francis Snyder, 'EMU Revisited: Are We Making a Constitution? What Constitution Are We Making?' in Paul Craig and Gráinne de Búrca (eds.), *The Evolution of EU Law* (Oxford: OUP, 1999).

[163] The recommendations of the Delors Committee formed the basis for the EMU provisions of the TEU, inserted into the EC Treaty as Articles 2, 4, 8 EC and Title VII EC (formerly Articles 2, 3a(2), 4a and Title VI, prior to the Treaty of Amsterdam).

[164] Snyder, n. 162 above, at 431.

[165] Ibid., at 432.

[166] International Labour Office, n. 87 above; see also Deakin, n. 88 above.

Given the TEU's explicit goal of combating unemployment, plus the new commitment to monetary union, the reluctance to transfer competence over employment policy to the EU level requires some explanation. Clearly the path taken by national employment policies was not insignificant to the success of EMU, especially in view of the need for coordinated Europe-wide macro-economic policy and fiscal policies. Why were Member States not willing to surrender control over employment policy even though employment policy is, arguably, such a fundamental part of macro-economic policy?

One explanation for the absence of social, employment or industrial policy issues from the EMU negotiating agenda, and ultimately from the EMU convergence criteria, is the way in which the institutional characteristics of the EMU negotiations narrowed down the agenda. The EMU negotiations have been described as a 'core executive' activity,[167] involving almost exclusively Member States' finance and foreign ministries, heads of state or government, central bank officials and the EC Monetary Committee. Even the Commission was displaced from its normal central role in agenda-shaping,[168] and furthermore,

> '[s]ectoral interests were very much excluded from the EMU negotiations. Employers' organizations, trade unions, and industrial and banking associations were not incorporated in the process, either at national or EC levels.'[169]

The convergence criteria were thus restricted to the more 'technocratic' issues, on which it was, apparently, easier to reach consensus. As Dyson and Featherstone point out: 'The EMU negotiations were concluded successfully precisely because certain highly contentious issues, which were rooted in conflicts of basic political belief, were factored out of the bargaining'.[170]

A further explanation for the absence of social and employment issues from the Maastricht agenda is that this was an(other) example of what Robert Salais labels 'social nationalism'.[171] Member States were reluctant to cede sovereignty over an area, employment policy, which was so closely tied to national economic performance, and hence, national identity. It was not until 1993 and 1994, following the European Council meetings in Brussels and Essen respectively, and the Commission's Green and White Papers on Social Policy, that the Union seemed prepared or able to stake a claim for a more clearly *European* employment policy—or at least the coordination of *national* employment policy at European level.

Although, as discussed above, the European Council meeting at Essen failed to sanction the Commission's proposed expansion of public investment to increase

[167] Kenneth Dyson and Kevin Featherstone, *The Road to Maastricht: Negotiating Economic and Monetary Union* (Oxford: OUP, 1999) at 13–15 and 754–6. [168] Ibid., at 755.

[169] Ibid., at 14. [170] Ibid., at 756.

[171] Robert Salais, 'Filling the Gap Between Macroeconomic Policy and Situated Approaches to Employment: A Hidden Agenda for Europe' in Lars Magnusson and Bo Stråth (eds.), *From the Werner Plan to the EMU: In Search of a Political Economy for Europe* (Brussels: PIE–Peter Lang, 2001).

jobs, it nevertheless marked a significant juncture in the development of EU employment policy.[172] The Essen Council endorsed the employment policy agenda of the *Growth* White Paper; what it did not do, however, was to consent to a major allocation of competence over employment policy to the Commission. Instead, it could be argued that having 'discovered' employment policy as a matter of concern for the EU as a whole, the Essen Council marked the beginning of a process whereby political initiative was shifted from the Community institutions to the Member States, acting within the parameters set by the European Council.[173] As the Presidency Conclusions stated:

> 'The European Council urges the Member States to transpose these recommendations[174] in their individual policies into a multiannual programme having regard to the specific features of their economic and social situation.'[175]

These policy recommendations, or guidelines, on employment were to be part of an annual process of Commission monitoring of Member States' employment policies. With this came a concomitant change of emphasis from legislative harmonization to the use of 'soft law'; the emphasis was now to be on coordination rather than harmonization, through the use of guidelines rather than legislative instruments.

Employment policy and economic policy were to become more closely coordinated through early, rather vague and non-binding, initiatives such as the Confidence Pact for Employment,[176] leading eventually to the sort of 'Reinforced Economic Policy Co-operation' which placed employment at the heart of a successful monetary union, with the Resolution on growth and employment,[177] and the Employment Title itself.

## 5. The emergence of a fully fledged employment policy

By way of conclusion, is it possible to say—following the insertion of a Title on employment into the EC Treaty by the Treaty of Amsterdam—that the EU now has a 'fully fledged' employment policy, which is not parasitical on its social

[172] Silvana Sciarra, 'The Employment Title in the Amsterdam Treaty: A Multi-Language Legal Discourse' in David O'Keefe and Patrick Twomey (eds.), *Legal Issues of the Amsterdam Treaty* (Oxford: Hart Publishing, 1999).

[173] Jeff Kenner, 'The EC Employment Title and the "Third Way": Making Soft Law Work?' (1999) 15:1 *International Journal of Comparative Labour Law and Industrial Relations*, 33–60, at 34.

[174] The Essen recommendations/criteria were (1) promoting investment in vocational training; (2) increasing employment through periods of growth; (3) reducing non-wage labour costs; (4) improving the effectiveness of labour market policy; and (5) improving measures to help groups at risk of exclusion from the labour market.

[175] Presidency Conclusions, Essen European Council, n. 77 above.

[176] CEC, n. 144 above.

[177] Resolution of the European Council on Growth and Employment, Amsterdam, 16 June 1997, OJ C 236, 2.8.97, at 3.

policy? Subsequent chapters will consider the implications of the relaunching of the Employment Strategy, first at Lisbon in 2000, and subsequently, the 'new start' for the Lisbon Strategy in the spring of 2005. But for now, there are two preliminary observations to make. *First*, the Member States' rejection of the Commission's proposed supply-side measures, in the years leading up to the Treaty of Amsterdam, proved to be a major obstacle to the full realization of a specifically *European* employment policy. Instead, the process begun at Essen led to a Luxembourg process based on centralized coordination of *national* employment policies.[178] As a result, I would argue, the Union's employment policy is still (after two relaunches) very much a circumscribed policy; a core element of employment policy still remains largely national, and as Barnard and Deakin describe, facilitative rather than prescriptive.[179]

*Second*, the need to find an effective employment strategy to reduce unemployment and to offset the potentially adverse effects of EMU on jobs has been hindered, it seems, by unresolved tensions, by 'the continuing differences between those pressing for greater labour market deregulation and those advocating an increase in expansionist macro-level intervention'.[180] The possibility of reconciling existing or restructured models of social protection with employment growth is a difficult question which was, to some extent, avoided in policy discourse in the years following the Amsterdam Treaty, until the Lisbon European Council took up the issue of social protection and brought it into the foreground of debates on employment.[181]

In considering the status of EU employment policy, it is important to remember that the employment policy measures put in place by the Treaty of Amsterdam almost entirely take the form of 'soft law'.[182] The Amsterdam Treaty introduced a new Title on Employment (Title VIII) into the EC Treaty, together with the Title on Economic and Monetary Policy (Title VII), the combined effect of which is a strategy to promote employment based on the coordination of Member States' macro-economic policies and structural reforms. The core of the new Employment Strategy remains unchanged throughout the successive relaunches, which have rather ushered in procedural tweakings and strengthened the interaction between different policy strands (employment, economic and social policy). As set out in Articles 125 to 130 EC, the Employment Strategy introduced by Amsterdam is centred on a new power vested in the Union,

[178] Barnard and Deakin, n. 95 above, at 356; and Paul Teague, 'Reshaping Employment Regimes in Europe: Policy Shifts Alongside Boundary Change' (1999) 19:1 *Journal of Public Policy*, 33–62, at 37.

[179] Barnard and Deakin, n. 95 above, at 358.

[180] Towers and Terry, n. 70 above, at 274.

[181] Presidency Conclusions, Lisbon European Council, 23 and 24 March 2000, Bull EU-3/2000, 7–17; see also Presidency Conclusions, Santa Maria de Fiera European Council, 19 and 20 June 2000, Bull EU-6/2000, 1–58.

[182] For an analysis of the constitutional and institutional implications of this recourse to 'soft law', see Chapter 5; see also Silvana Sciarra, 'Integration Through Coordination: The Employment Title in the Amsterdam Treaty' (2000) 6:2 *Columbia Journal of European Law*, 209–29.

*supplementary* to that of the Member States, to promulgate common guidelines similar to those adopted at the Essen Council. The annual procedure for the creation of employment guidelines begins with the adoption by the European Council of conclusions on the employment situation in the Union, on the basis of a joint annual report prepared by the Council and the Commission (Article 128); these conclusions enable the Commission to propose employment policy guidelines, which must be consistent with the economic guidelines established under Article 99(2) for monetary union. The Council then adopts these employment guidelines by qualified majority after consulting the European Parliament, the Economic and Social Committee, the Committee of the Regions and the Employment Committee (Article 128(2)). The second strand of the employment strategy involves action by Member States, which are obliged to report annually, in National Action Plans for Employment, on measures taken to implement employment policy in accordance with the Broad Economic Policy Guidelines (Article 128(3)).[183]

This procedure, for the production of annual employment guidelines, is modelled closely on the convergence arrangements for national economic policies, with two exceptions: first, the common employment guidelines do not advocate measures to harmonize national provisions, although they do have an indirect impact on Member States' policy. Second, in contrast to the provisions on EMU, Title VIII does not prescribe any macro-economic objectives to be achieved, along the lines of the economic convergence criteria.[184]

The first set of Employment Guidelines, formally adopted by a resolution of the Council in December 1997,[185] centred around four 'pillars'—improving employability, developing entrepreneurship, encouraging adaptability in businesses and their employees, and strengthening the policies for equal opportunities—which were further elaborated through nineteen Guidelines.[186] Although the 'pillars' and guidelines have a clear Treaty basis, in Title VIII and Article 128, they can be seen as examples of 'soft law' in that they are not produced in the form of legally binding instruments, such as directives or regulations, which the EU institutions have at their disposal. Nevertheless, these guidelines have important implications for policy and law-making within Member States.

[183] The annual policy cycle was simplified from 2003, so that the Employment Guidelines, the BEPGs and the Employment Recommendations now cover a three-year period and will only be reviewed fully every three years. In addition, the Spring European Council in March 2005 approved a simplified governance arrangement, with one set of 'Integrated Guidelines' dealing with macro-economic, micro-economic and employment issues: see discussion in Chapter 4.

[184] Brian Towers and Michael Terry, 'Editorial: Unemployment and Social Dialogue' (1999) 30:4 *Industrial Relations Journal, European Annual Review 1998*, 272–6, at 274.

[185] Council Resolution of 15 December 1997 on the 1998 Employment Guidelines, OJ C 30/98, 28.01.1998.

[186] The 'pillar' structure has subsequently been modified and replaced by three 'overarching objectives' for the Employment Strategy, of full employment, quality and productivity at work, and cohesion and an inclusive labour market.

The EC Treaty is careful to spell out that legislation and regulation is still a matter for Member States. Article 127 EC states that the Community shall encourage cooperation and complement Member State action to promote employment, but nevertheless, Member States' competences must be respected. In addition, Article 129 EC states that measures taken by the Council to promote employment 'shall not include harmonization of the laws and regulations of the Member States'. Further, in contrast to the situation where a Member State acts inconsistently with the economic policy guidelines, there are no real sanctions which can be imposed on a Member State which fails to comply with the employment guidelines.

Thus, in place of the sort of harmonizing legislation which was the hallmark of the Union's increased competence in the area of social policy, the new Employment Strategy is marked by coordination rather than convergence,[187] with use made of 'benchmarking',[188] rather than targets as such. The legal obligations to which the Employment Title may give rise are still far from clear. As Silvana Sciarra observes:

> '"Employability" has no precise legal standing as a word, but is the policy side of a new and peculiar legal command addressed to Member States. So are "entrepreneurship, adaptability and equal opportunities"—all difficult criteria to be translated into binding norms and yet the essence of a "co-ordinated strategy for employment".'[189]

This increased use of 'soft law' and governance by means of guidelines has run parallel to what I have argued has been a more general shift from social law to employment policy. There have, of course, been exceptions, in that the focus on a discourse of employment creation has not entirely silenced social policy/social law discourse. One important exception, illustrating Mark Freedland's analysis of the co-existence of competing policy agendas, is the social dialogue process which, in the period since the Treaty of Amsterdam, has produced three directives, on parental leave,[190] part-time work[191] and fixed-term work.[192]

Furthermore, one should not underestimate the impact which such 'soft law' measures are having on Member States' employment strategies and regulatory policies towards the labour market. For example, benchmarking of employment

[187] Marco Biagi, 'The Implementation of the Amsterdam Treaty with Regard to Employment: Co-ordination or Convergence?' (1998) 14:4 *International Journal of Comparative Labour Law and Industrial Relations*, 325–36.

[188] Leonello Tronti, 'Benchmarking Employment Performance and Labour Market Policies: The Results of the Research Project' (1999) 4 *Transfer: European Review of Labour and Research*, 542–62.

[189] Sciarra, n. 172 above, at 165.

[190] Council Directive 967/34/EC of 3 June 1996 on the framework agreement on parental leave concluded by UNICE, CEEP and the ETUC, amended by Council Directive 97/75/EC of 15 December 1997, OJ L 145, 19.06.96 and OJ L 10, 16.01.1998.

[191] Council Directive 97/81/EC of 15 December 1997 concerning the framework agreement on part-time working concluded by UNICE, CEEP and the ETUC, amended by Council Directive 98/23/EC of 7 April 1998, OJ L 14, 20.01.98 and OJ L 131, 05.05.98.

[192] Council Directive 99/70/EC of 28 June 1999 concerning the framework agreement on fixed-term work concluded by UNICE, CEEP and the ETUC, OJ L 175, 10.07.1999.

policies may be useful not only as a procedure by which Member States can measure and compare the operation of their labour markets, but also as a means by which the worse-performing countries can improve their employment performance, in part through adopting examples of best practice.[193] In addition, although the Employment Strategy in general, and in particular the annual guidelines and Commission monitoring of Member States' employment policies, do not *directly* affect Member States' regulatory systems, nevertheless, there has been indirect pressure for change.[194]

Nevertheless, 'soft law' has its limitations. The *de facto* bringing of employment questions into EMU has occurred in a rather narrow manner; narrow because it has been almost entirely divorced from the traditional social policy concerns which used to dominate this policy area before the shift to a focus on employment creation. Thus, for example, whilst at a purely formal level—in the amended EC Treaty—there is a clear connection between Title VII on Economic and Monetary Policy and Title VIII on Employment, there is no interaction between economic and employment policy, and Title XI on Social Policy, Education, Vocational Training and Youth. The provisions of the Social Policy Title on, for example, social security and social protection of workers, or social dialogue between management and labour, are presented almost in a vacuum, unrelated to questions of employment creation or macro-economic policy. In this context, therefore, the importance of the Lisbon Strategy and its 2005 relaunch cannot be overstated. The key achievement of the Lisbon meeting was to integrate all the various 'processes'[195] arising out of the Employment Strategy, and to provide, for the first time since Amsterdam, a positive and unambiguous link between social, employment and economic issues.[196] Lisbon differed from other post-Amsterdam summits, in placing the renewal of the 'European social model' at the heart of an integrated economic and employment strategy. The language used, that of 'full employment' (in contrast to the reference to 'high levels of employment' in the Treaty of Amsterdam) and 'modernizing and improving social protection', indicates a political willingness once again to prioritize social policy. The extent to which this renewed emphasis on social policy since Lisbon has resulted in a renewal of the European social model, with or without recourse to 'hard law' mechanisms, will be explored in Chapters 4 and 5.

[193] Tronti, n. 188 above.

[194] See Chapter 6 for an analysis of the impact of such 'soft law' mechanisms on Member States' employment policies and regulatory strategies. See also Manfred Weiss, 'The Future Role of the European Union in Social Policy' in Chris Engels and Manfred Weiss (eds.), *Labour Law and Industrial Relations at the Turn of the Century: Liber Amicorum in Honour of Roger Blainpain* (The Hague: Kluwer Law International, 1998).

[195] Previous European Council meetings at Luxembourg (20–21 November 1997), Cardiff (15–16 June 1998) and Cologne (3–4 June 1999) had each spawned a new 'process' to describe the implementation of the employment strategy, and its relation to structural reform and economic policy.

[196] See the follow-up Commission document: *Communication from the Commission to the Council, the European Parliament, the Economic and Social Committee and the Committee of the Regions: Social Policy Agenda*, Brussels, 28.6.2000, COM (2000) 379 final.

# 4

# The evolution of the European Employment Strategy: towards full employment

## 1. Introduction

In light of the emergence of a European Union employment *policy*, as discussed in Chapter 3, this chapter will focus more specifically on the development of the European Employment *Strategy* since the Treaty of Amsterdam: examining the employment guidelines, the institutional framework for employment policy generation, and the implications of the attempt to integrate economic, employment and social policies.

The development of the Employment Strategy is traced through policy documents of the EU institutions, in particular, the European Commission and the European Council. It is through the European Council Presidency Conclusions that one can discern most clearly the shifts in the dominant EU discourse on employment. A central argument of this chapter, building on the premise of Chapter 3, is that the principal benchmark by which to evaluate progress in employment policy and labour market reform has been an economic one, which has left unanswered the question of how to reconcile existing or restructured models of social protection with employment growth. This is borne out by an exploration of the economic context of the Employment Title, of the 'economic governance' of the three processes (Luxembourg, Cardiff and Cologne) which it has generated, and of the 'Lisbon Strategy', centred around the goal for the EU to become 'the most competitive and dynamic knowledge-based economy in the world capable of sustainable economic growth with more and better jobs and greater social cohesion.'

Since Lisbon, not only has there been a *substantive* change in EU policy, with a positive and unambiguous link made between social, employment and economic policies, but also the European Council has introduced a related *procedural* innovation, giving formal recognition to new regulatory techniques—governance by means of guidelines, peer review, and benchmarking—which have crystallized in the 'open method of coordination'.[1] With regard to the substantive policy

[1] See Chapter 5 for a critical analysis of the procedural innovations of the Employment Strategy. The 'open method of coordination' is the label given by the European Council to the methodology

post-Lisbon, this chapter will posit the Employment Strategy, and its rapid absorption into the wider 'Lisbon Strategy', as representing an ambitious attempt to realize a quantum shift within the EU economy, centring on the goal of full employment, whilst remaining committed to the traditional values of the European 'social model'. That the European 'social model' might, to the contrary, be at risk from such economic integration and modernization is a view which has become increasingly widespread, as evidenced by the mood of the French electorate in that country's referendum in May 2005 on ratification of the Treaty Establishing a Constitution for Europe.[2] Ultimately, however, the main contention is that the objectives underlying the Employment and Lisbon Strategies do indeed risk relegating social and employment policy to the role of mere adjuncts of economic integration.

## 2. The Treaty of Amsterdam

The economic and employment context for the introduction of the Employment Title by the Treaty of Amsterdam has already been discussed in Chapter 3, but bears repeating, to remind one of the sense of crisis pervading the Union in the mid-1990s. Unemployment remained 'stubbornly high', at a rate of 10.8 per cent in mid-1997,[3] more than double the US rate of 5.0 per cent.[4] It was in response to this sense of urgency that the Luxembourg European Council[5] called for the immediate implementation of the relevant provisions of the new Employment Title in the amended EC Treaty, prior to the Treaty's ratification.[6] The emphasis at the time of the signing of the Amsterdam Treaty was very much on the 'fit' between employment policy and macro-economic policy. The presumption was that EMU was an unalterable feature of the Union's landscape—a presumption formalized by Articles 126 and 128 of the EC Treaty as amended by Amsterdam[7]—and

which had evolved for the elaboration and implementation of employment policy, revolving around the setting of guidelines, benchmarks and indicators at EU level, their translation into national policies and the periodic monitoring of such implementation: Presidency Conclusions, Lisbon European Council, 23 and 24 March 2000, Bull EU 3/2000, 7–17, at para 37.

[2] Wolfgang Munchau, 'EU's misjudged No votes', *Financial Times*, 5 June 2005: ' [Those voting No] were opposed to a constitution they regard as focused too much on market deregulation, free trade and economic reform. What they want is protection against globalisation and more "social Europe", whatever that may mean'.

[3] CEC, *Employment in Europe 1997*, COM (97) 479 final, 1 (Luxembourg: OOPEC, 1997).

[4] Eurostat: Statistical Office of the European Communities in Luxembourg, News Release 78/99, 10 August 1999.

[5] Presidency Conclusions, Extraordinary European Council Meeting on Employment, Luxembourg, 20 and 21 November 1997, Bull EU-11/1997, 7–13.

[6] Ibid., paragraphs 3 and 20: 'In order to harness all resources available to combat unemployment, the European Council has decided to apply straight away in practice and by consensus the method provided for in the future Article 128, as adopted in Amsterdam'.

[7] Article 126 (1) EC states that 'Member States, through their employment policies, shall contribute to the achievement of the objectives referred to in Article 125 in a way consistent with the

employment policy was thus to be subservient to the dictates of economic policy. This point is made clear in Kerstin Ahlberg's examination of the Member States' negotiations on what became the Employment Title, in the Intergovernmental Conference leading up to Amsterdam.[8] A central point on which agreement was reached at an early stage in negotiations was that employment measures envisaged at Union level should 'under no circumstances influence or reopen the timetable or the criteria for EMU or have any consequences that would be incompatible with budgetary discipline'.[9] Thus, whilst high levels of employment are seen as a good in themselves, rather instrumentally, high employment is also a prerequisite for the sort of competitive economy necessary to ensure the success of EMU:

> 'The European employment strategy is of fundamental importance in tackling the employment problem, and will be even more important when Economic and Monetary Union is implemented. While high employment and well functioning labour markets are priority objectives in their own rights, *high employment is the best way to make EMU successful.*'[10]

Eventually, we can observe the shift in thinking epitomized by the Lisbon European Council, when the EU institutions once again began to draw a clear link between economic, employment and social policy, indicating a political willingness to prioritize the 'European social model', by means of 'activating' the welfare state and modernizing social protection. But this only came after several years of insistence on the link between employment and economic policy, and a near-silence on social policy objectives.

## 2.1 The Amsterdam Intergovernmental Conference

This section will examine the negotiations and debates leading to the conclusion of the new Employment Title in the Treaty of Amsterdam, and how the tensions between a more interventionist/supranational approach and a more deregulatory/national approach were played out. It is important to unpack this particular dichotomy: what we are dealing with is two sets of arguments which interact—on the one hand, the conflict between state action (intergovernmentalism) and Community competence (supranationalism), and on the other, the conflict between regulation and deregulation, state and market.

As became apparent during the course of the Intergovernmental Conference (IGC) launched in 1996[11] and culminating with the Amsterdam European

broad outlines of the economic policies of the Member States and the Community adopted pursuant to Article 99(2)'; Article 128 EC further provides that the Employment Guidelines adopted annually by the Council must also be consistent with the broad economic policy guidelines of Article 99(2).

[8] Kerstin Ahlberg, 'The Making of the Employment Title', unpublished manuscript on file with the author (Stockholm: National Institute for Working Life, 2002).

[9] Ahlberg, n. 8 above; referring to the Conference of the Representatives of the Governments of the Member States, 'Report from the Presidency to the European Council', Brussels, 17 June 1996, CONF 3860/1/96, Rev 1.

[10] CEC, n. 3 above, at 4; emphasis added.

[11] Presidency Conclusions, Turin European Council, 29 March 1996, Bull EU-3/1996, 1–8.

Council in June 1997, the Member States most opposed to any extension of the Community's competence in the field of employment or the introduction of new provisions on employment were the UK, France and Germany.[12] However, is it fair to describe this divergence between Member States as assuming that those arguing for more labour market intervention also advocated a centralized approach to combating unemployment, and concomitantly, that those urging deregulation favoured the retention of undiminished national sovereignty over employment policy? This is certainly true if one looks at the position of the UK, but not so in the case of France. It is arguable that the French opposition to the introduction of specific new Treaty provisions[13] was based more on the arguments which had been rejected at Essen, namely that employment growth was best pursued by means of the Commission's proposed supply-side measures and centralized expenditure on large infrastructural projects.[14] Furthermore, the desire to retain high levels of labour standards and social protection may exist in conjunction with a reluctance to transfer competence to the European level, due not only to concerns over the lack of democratic legitimation at supranational level for such redistributive polices,[15] but also to fear of a dilution of such high standards.[16] In the case of employment policy, however, it might still be seen as desirable to allow for a supranational 'floor of rights', so as to prevent a 'race to

[12] The UK government's rather critical submission to the IGC had been published by the Foreign and Commonwealth Office on 12 March 1996 (*A Partnership of Nations: The British Approach to the European Union IGC*, Cm 3181 (London: HMSO, 1996)). However, there was a change of government in May 1997, from Conservative to Labour who, when in opposition, had given their support to a chapter on employment in the new Treaty: see Karl Magnus Johansson, 'Tracing the Employment Title in the Amsterdam Treaty: Uncovering Transnational Coalitions' (1999) 6:2 *Journal of European Public Policy*, 85–101, at 98.

[13] See 'Les orientations de la France pour la Conférence Intergouvernementale de 1996', published in *Le Figaro*, 20 February 1996; document summarized in *White Paper on the 1996 Intergovernmental Conference, Volume II: Summary of Positions of the Member States of the European Union with a view to the 1996 Intergovernmental Conference*, European Parliament, Intergovernmental Conference Task Force, 18 December 1996; available from Online Archive of the European Parliament, *http://www.europarl.eu.int/igc1996/pos-toc_en.htm* [accessed on 10 April 2005]. See also the 1996 Intergovernmental Conference Retrospective Database of the European Parliament, available at: *http://europa.eu.int/en/agenda/igc-home/index.html* [accessed on 10 April 2005]; and Ahlberg, n. 8 above.

[14] See Chapter 3, Sections 3.1 and 3.2. In the words of French President Jacques Chirac, in order to combat social exclusion and high unemployment, it was necessary to redefine the European social model ('il est temps de définir un véritable modèle social européen') and to implement the policies agreed at Essen ('Ces objectifs sont bons, mais où sont les réalisations?'). In particular, this was to be done by resurrecting the dormant plans for large trans-European networks, which would stimulate hiring, especially in the public sector. Further, he advocated increased use of the Community's annual budget, as a 'formidable instrument' for employment. 'Pour un modèle social européen' opinion by Jacques Chirac published in *Libération*, 25 March 1996.

[15] Wolfgang Streeck, 'Public Power Beyond the Nation-State: The Case of the European Community' in Robert Boyer and Daniel Drache (eds.), *States Against Markets: The Limits of Globalization* (London: Routledge, 1996) at 306.

[16] See, for example, Wolfgang Streeck's discussion of the apparent paradox of the French position, historically favouring supranational state-building, whilst also concerned with the preservation of French national sovereignty: ibid., at 301.

the bottom' which would undermine even the strongest regimes of social and employment protection.

Nevertheless, it has generally been the case that (social) nationalism has most strongly been linked with neoliberalism—Streeck talks of an 'elective affinity' between nationalism and a neoliberal programme of deregulatory market expansion based in decision rules of intergovernmental diplomacy.[17] Also, as pointed out in the Spanish submission to the 1996 IGC,[18] it is useful to conceive of the debate on employment policy as prefiguring and belonging to this more general tension between two approaches to European integration—where the two arguments, mentioned above, come together. On the one hand, a continuation of integration on the basis of exclusively free-market and largely intergovernmental criteria, with minimal cost to the budget, a wide margin of national autonomy and subsidiarity as the golden rule (an approach the Spanish document attributed to the UK, France and Germany); on the other hand, a centralization of authority, thus ensuring the operation of generously financed common policies and greater political neutrality in approaches to policy and decision-making (a supranational choice attributed to Spain, Belgium, Luxembourg and—up to that point in time—Italy). To what extent were the original drafts of the Employment Title amended or weakened during the course of the IGC and, if so, was this linked to the unwillingness to pursue what could be seen as centralized regulation (supranational *and* anti-market), or the wider reluctance of Member States, as evidenced at Essen, to sanction centralized expenditure to stimulate demand?[19]

The Reflection Group on the 1996 Intergovernmental Conference was the body responsible for preparing the agenda and draft texts for the IGC, and worked for six months on the European Council mandate to 'pave the way for the revision of the Treaty . . . and any other improvements in the Union's operation'.[20] The Reflection Group was established by the Corfu European Council of 24–25 June 1994, and composed of representatives of the Foreign Affairs Ministers of the fifteen Member States, of the President of the Commission and two representatives of the European Parliament. Its initial offering on employment policy was a frank recognition of the existing tensions and differences in approach. Whilst there was consensus over the challenge of job creation, the need to promote employment as part of making the Union more relevant to its citizens, and the continued role of the institutions (the

[17] Ibid., at 305.

[18] 'Elementos para una posicion española en la conferencia intergubernamental de 1996' ('The 1996 Intergovernmental Conference: Starting Points for a Discussion') 2 March 1995; document summarized in *White Paper on the 1996 Intergovernmental Conference*, n. 13 above.

[19] Catherine Barnard and Simon Deakin, 'A year of living dangerously? EC social rights, employment policy, and EMU' (1999) 30:4 *Industrial Relations Journal: European Annual Review 1998*, 355–72, at 356.

[20] The Reflection Group on the 1996 Intergovernmental Conference, *Reflection Group's Report, Messina 2nd June 1995* (Brussels: OOPEC, 1995).

Commission, the Economic and Financial Affairs Council and the Social Affairs Council) in monitoring, coordinating and reporting back on national employment policy, the Group was not initially in agreement over strengthening the objective of job creation in the legal bases of economic and other policies.[21] Furthermore, the proposal to include a specific chapter on employment policy (to be inserted into the Treaty on European Union) was originally a minority position: this proposal came from the Swedish representative in the Reflection Group, supported by the European Parliament representatives, and went so far as to argue for an 'employment union' in parallel with economic union.[22] Other members of the Reflection Group were clearly opposed, arguing that introducing new employment policy provisions into the Treaty was not necessary, nor would it help to improve competitiveness or job creation:

> 'they underline that job creation is the result of greater competitiveness, flexibility of the economy and reducing bureaucratic burdens. They further believe that employment policy is a matter for Member States to decide in the light of their individual circumstances. In this view, at the Union's level, job creation should be a matter for practical improvements of the ways and means to coordinate national policies'[23]

Two key principles on which it was possible to reach agreement were that the primary responsibility for employment lay with the Member States, and that the provisions on the single currency agreed at Maastricht and subsequently ratified by Member State parliaments must remain unchanged.[24] However, even whilst reiterating such sentiments, some of the Member States' proposals on employment policy were sufficiently far-reaching that they would in fact 'entail a shift in the balance of power between the Member States and the EU or modify the direction of EMU'.[25] For example, the Portuguese submission to the IGC considered that 'economic and monetary progress should be accompanied by a series of pro-employment instruments applying throughout the Union, rather than conjuncturally as has hitherto has been the case'.[26] Here, in other words, was a very similar suggestion to that of the European Parliament, that employment be placed 'at the heart' of all economic policies, including EMU,[27] so that

[21] The Reflection Group on the 1996 Intergovernmental Conference, *Reflection Group's Report, Messina 2nd June 1995* (Brussels: OOPEC, 1995), at para 58.

[22] 'Note of July 1995 on the fundamental interests of Sweden with a view to the 1996 Intergovernmental Conference' summarized in *White Paper on the 1996 Intergovernmental Conference*, n. 13 above. See also, Johansson, n. 12 above, at 91 and 97. Johansson also traces the origins of the Employment Title proposal to the activities of the Party of European Socialists (in particular, the Nordic social democrats) and its 'European Employment Initiative' from 1993 onwards: ibid., at 89–92.

[23] Reflection Group, n. 20 above, at para 60.

[24] Ibid., at Part One, I: The Citizen and Europe.

[25] Ahlberg, n. 8 above.

[26] Portuguese Foreign Ministry document of March 1996, summarized in *White Paper on the 1996 Intergovernmental Conference*, n. 13 above.

[27] European Parliament, 'IGC Briefing No 37 (First update: 2nd April 1997): Employment and the IGC', Section VIII; available at *http://www.europarl.eu.int/igc1996/fiches/fiche37_en.htm* [accessed on 10 April 2005].

economic policy must be reconceived to give priority to the achievement or maintenance of a high level of employment. Further, in a memorandum on the IGC from the Benelux governments, 'while not denying the primary responsibility of Member States' for employment, it was suggested that the Community make 'a greater contribution to job-creating investment in the Member States',[28] which would appear to run counter to the view of the majority that, if there were to be a new Title, it should not have any budgetary impact.

It was at this stage in the negotiations that the goal of achieving 'full employment' (as opposed to the eventual objective of 'a high level of employment') was raised,[29] only to be abandoned.[30] Such terminology was always likely to be contentious, especially as some Member States were all too wary of even mentioning employment policy provisions in the Treaty, for fear of raising expectations which the Union could not possibly meet.[31] Moreover, it was extremely unlikely that the Member States would bind themselves, in a treaty, to resurrecting a political commitment to a policy which had long been forsaken, closely linked as it was to now fragmenting conventions of social responsibility and labour markets contained within national boundaries.[32] What was particularly interesting about the suggestion that the new Treaty should bind the Community and Member States to the achievement of full employment, rather than the mere promotion of employment, was the way in which this goal was inevitably linked to calls for greater intervention to bolster the Union's social dimension, and a dilution of the core of EMU. Thus, the submission to the Reflection Group from the representative of the Swedish government called for an employment chapter designed to promote the goal of full employment, and an intensification of social dialogue. This was necessary since '[a] strengthened framework for employment policy in the treaty would serve to reconcile the Union's economic, social and environmental goals with the commitment to

[28] 'Dans le respect des dispositions en vigueur en matière de discipline budgétaire, la Communauté doit davantage affecter les moyens financiers existants à des investissements créateurs d'emploi dans les Etats membres, en particulier là où ceux-ci produiront un avantage transnational': 'Mémorandum de la Belgique, des Pays-Bas et du Luxembourg en vue de la CIG', 7 March 1996 ('Memorandum on the IGC from the Governments of Belgium, Luxembourg and the Netherlands'), available on the 1996 IGC Retrospective Database, at *http://www.europarl.eu.int/igc1996/pos-toc_en.htm* [accessed on 10 April 2005]. Document summarized in *White Paper on the 1996 Intergovernmental Conference*, n. 13 above.

[29] Conference of the Representatives of the Governments of the Member States, Note No 6, CONF/3806/96, Brussels, 2 April 1996. For a discussion of this note outlining the different options for employment policy, see Ahlberg, n. 8 above.

[30] Conference of the Representatives of the Governments of the Member States, 'The European Union Today and Tomorrow: Adapting the European Union for the Benefit of its Peoples and Preparing it for the Future. A General Outline for a Draft Revision of the Treaties', Brussels, 5 December 1996.

[31] Reflection Group, n. 20 above.

[32] Bo Stråth, 'After Full Employment and the Breakdown of Conventions of Social Responsibility' in Bo Stråth (ed.), *After Full Employment: European Discourses on Work and Flexibility* (Brussels: PIE–Peter Lang, 2000) at 14–15.

price stability and sound public finances laid down in the Economic and Monetary Union'.[33] In other words, growth and employment would not be achieved if monetary stability were pursued single-mindedly. Supporters of the Swedish proposal, namely the European Parliament, were more specific, calling for the creation of an Employment Committee of equal status to the Committee on Monetare Affairs, to balance its role, and for social policy to be made a core competence of the Union to offset Economic and Monetary Union.[34]

The term 'full employment' would eventually be reintroduced into policy debate again (as a policy goal, but not as a Treaty objective) by the Portuguese and Swedish Presidencies.[35] However, as will be argued in Section 4 below, the eagerness to move beyond the post-war concept of full employment may have resulted in a rather modest version of full employment,[36] lacking the social solidarity of the post-war version, and which would essentially embody a neo-liberal route to full employment.[37]

A key draft of the Employment Title was the text proposed in December 1996 by the Irish Presidency of the European Council,[38] based on the options proposed earlier by the Member States' representatives.[39] The approach to employment in this draft revision of the Treaties was largely inspired by, and built on, the coordination mechanisms which had been put in place on a less formal footing as part of the 'Essen process'.[40] In essence, the suggested text on employment would (a) specify the promotion of a high level of employment as an objective of the Union and the Community, amending Article B of the TEU and Article 2 of the EC Treaty; and (b) introduce a new Title on employment into the EC Treaty. The provisions of this new Title would establish a coordination

[33] Gunner Lund, 'Strengthening the fight against unemployment: An issue for the Intergovernmental Conference', paper presented to the Reflection Group, 1 September 1995; available at *http://europa.eu.int/en/agenda/igc-home/msspeech/state-sv/lund.html* [accessed on 10 April 2005].

[34] See summary by David Martin, MEP, '1996 And All That', unpublished paper on file with the author (Strasbourg, 1996). David Martin was the European Parliament's *Rapporteur* on the 'Functioning of the Treaty on European Union in view of the Intergovernmental Conference in 1996'.

[35] Presidency Conclusions, Lisbon European Council, n. 1 above, at para 6 and throughout; and Presidency Conclusions, Stockholm European Council, 23 and 24 March 2001, Bull EU-3/2001, 1–40, Part I.

[36] This more 'modest' version of full employment being promoted at EU level can be contrasted with the efforts of individual Member States: see Chapter 6; see also Rodney Smith, 'Full employment for Europe', *BBC News Online: Business*, 11 February 2000, available at *http://news.bbc.co.uk/1/hi/business/639888.stm* [accessed on 10 April 2005]: 'Now [France] appears to be aiming for a more modern version of the post war full-employment consensus, based on social tools like the minimum wage and the 35-hour working week'.

[37] European Economists for an Alternative Economic Policy in Europe, *Alternative Economic Policy Guidelines for Full Employment and Social Cohesion in Europe* (Bremen: University of Bremen, 2000) at 5; available at *http://www.memo-europe.uni-bremen.de* [accessed on 10 April 2005].

[38] Dublin European Council, 13 and 14 December 1996, Bull EU-12/1996, 1–38.

[39] Above, n. 29; and Conference of the Representatives of the Governments of the Member States, 'Report from the Presidency to the European Council', Brussels, 17 June 1996, CONF 3860/1/96.

[40] European Parliament, 'IGC Briefing No 37' n. 27 above.

process on employment policy at Community level, involving:

- a significant role for the European Council in giving political impetus;
- adoption by the Council of Ministers of common guidelines on employment;
- annual assessments of national measures with a view to ensuring consistency and in the light of which the Council would be entitled to address recommendations to Member States;
- provision for the adoption of incentive measures designed to encourage cooperation on a transnational basis in relation to employment; and
- ensuring a coherent approach to employment through the establishment of an Employment Committee with an advisory role which would include two members from each Member State and from the Commission.[41]

The likely *content* of such guidelines was indicated by a separate, but related, development in which the European Council adopted the Dublin Declaration on Employment. This Declaration built on the priority areas for action identified at Essen,[42] and emphasized the importance of continuing the macro-economic strategy 'oriented towards stability, growth and employment' in line with agreed economic policy guidelines, with an emphasis on 'budgetary consolidation' and the 'selective restructuring of public expenditure'. Other indications of the likely substance of the new Employment Strategy could be found in the recommendation to Member States to make increasing efforts to 'modernize the markets for goods and services and to exploit new sources of employment', and to focus on labour market efficiency and investment in human resources. Finally, taxation and social protection systems were to be made 'more employment-friendly'.[43] However, a possibly even more significant decision of the Dublin Council was the agreement reached on the principles and main elements of the Stability and Growth Pact for ensuring budgetary discipline in EMU.[44] The impact of this economic policy framework for the realization of the Employment Strategy will be discussed in greater detail below.

At this stage in the IGC, there was a 'broad measure of support for provisions along the lines suggested' from the Member States, although some delegations were still unconvinced that a new Title or Chapter on employment could be justified, or favoured the status quo and argued against any new Treaty provisions in this area.[45] Some of those in favour of an Employment Title further

[41] 'General Outline for a Draft Revision of the Treaties' prepared by the Conference of the Representatives of the Governments of the Member States, n. 30 above; Section II, Chapter 4: Employment.

[42] See Chapter 3, Section 3.2.

[43] Dublin European Council, n. 38 above, Annex II.

[44] It was left to the later, Amsterdam, European Council to establish the *legal framework* of the Stability and Growth pact, in two regulations, one on the strengthening of surveillance and coordination of budgetary positions, and the other on clarification of the implementation of the excessive deficit procedure; see Section 2.2 below.

[45] 'General Outline for a Draft Revision of the Treaties' prepared by the Conference of the Representatives of the Governments of the Member States, n. 30 above, 'Comments'.

advocated a more binding procedure based, for example, on quantified criteria and possible sanctions; and the objective of 'full employment' rather than a 'high level of employment'. Neither of these proposals won the day in the final version. Further, the proposed amendment to Article 3 of the EC Treaty (the activities of the Community) to include employment policy, and the first article of the new Employment Title, both referred to the development of 'a *common* strategy for employment'.[46] However, this was carefully modified to 'a *coordinated* strategy' in the final versions, betraying an unwillingness by those Member States still opposed to a new Title to tolerate a centralized policy imposed on Member States, rather than the simple European-level coordination of national policies.[47] Finally, it was suggested that the principles guiding employment policy should be set out in detail in the proposed Title. This was only partially the case, in what became Article 125 of the EC Treaty. As the European Parliament points out:

> '[c]ompared with the text proposed in December by the Irish Presidency, the text finally adopted has scarcely been modified except to emphasize the objective of promoting a skilled, trained and adaptable workforce, to stress national responsibilities for employment, to make clear that the employment guidelines must be "consistent with" (and no longer "conform to") the broad guidelines adopted pursuant to Article 103 (2), and to formulate the aims of incentive measures.'[48]

Whilst welcoming the explicit inclusion of the promotion of a high level of employment and social protection amongst the general objectives and tasks of the Union as a milestone in the process of European integration,[49] the European Parliament was nevertheless highly critical of the formulation of this policy, and of the final version of the Employment Title. The Parliament bemoaned the lack of sufficiently robust guiding principles for employment policy, arguing that the Community and Member States should have been required to meet far stricter, more prescriptive, guidelines—including strengthening productivity to enable real incomes to increase, eliminating the qualitative disparity between supply and demand on the labour market, and preventing long-term unemployment and

[46] 'General Outline for a Draft Revision of the Treaties' prepared by the Conference of the Representatives of the Governments of the Member States, n. 30 above, 'Comments', Section II, Chapter 4.

[47] Cf. the view of the integrationist-minded European Parliament, commenting on the Dublin European Council: '... therefore invites the Council and the Commission to translate the [Dublin Declaration on Employment] into action without delay, through reinforced integration of employment policies'. European Parliament, Resolution on the Dublin European Council of 13 and 14 December 1996, OJ C 33/63, 03.02.1997.

[48] European Parliament Directorate-General for Committees and Delegations, Committee on Institutional Affairs, *Initial Analysis of the Treaty of Amsterdam, Based on a Provisional Version of the Treaty*, Conf 4001/97 of 19 June 1997.

[49] European Parliament General Secretariat Working Party, Task Force on the Intergovernmental Conference, *Note on the European Parliament's Priorities for the IGC and the new Amsterdam Treaty: Report and Initial Evaluation of the Results*, 15 July 1997, paragraph 1.3.1; available at *http://www.europarl.eu.int/topics/treaty/report/part1_en.htm* [accessed on 10 April 2005].

social exclusion.[50] Thus, the adoption of the 'limited instrument' of promoting coordination between employment policies of the Member States, and the 'limited amount of budgetary resources' allocated to employment policy threatened, in the Parliament's view, to make all the new provisions 'a dead letter'.[51] The Parliament wanted a more mandatory provision, in particular, placing employment amongst the guiding principles for EMU, as laid down in what is now Article 4 (3) of the EC Treaty. This would have meant that the objective of a high level of employment would be on an equal footing with the maintenance of price stability, sound public finances and a sustainable balance of payments.

Ultimately, what the Parliament had in mind, in stark contrast to the wishes of the majority of Member States, was an employment policy which, far from being subservient to the dictates of economic policy, should be put 'at the centre' of all Community policies, including EMU. The argument is that the broad guidelines for economic policy, produced under what is now Article 99 of the EC Treaty, should in fact take account of the impact of economic policies on employment, and ensure the achievement or preservation of a high level of employment and the combating of economic and social exclusion.[52]

To return to the tensions highlighted at the beginning of this section, between competing approaches to European integration, Towers and Terry describe this disagreement in the following terms:

'The need to find an effective employment strategy to reduce unemployment and to offset the potentially adverse effects of EMU on jobs has been handicapped by the continuing differences between those pressing for greater labour market deregulation and those advocating an increase in expansionist macro-level intervention. . . . [T]he differences between "interventionists" and "deregulators" have manifested themselves primarily in differences between the Parliament and Commission promoting macro-level intervention as against the Council's stronger preference for labour market flexibility, led by the British'.[53]

In the end, however, the European Council meeting in Amsterdam on 16 and 17 June 1997 successfully concluded the IGC with full agreement on a draft Treaty, including a new Title on employment. Whilst it is true, as Janine Goetschy points out, that 'elections in France and in the UK isolated Germany in its rejection of an employment title in the Treaty reform',[54] nevertheless, the final Treaty provisions can be seen as a compromise which conceded much to the

[50] European Parliament, n. 48 above, referring to the proposals of Elisabeth Gigou and Elmar Brok, representatives of the European Parliament to the 1996 IGC; see Letter from Elisabeth Gigou and Elmar Brok, to Noel Dorr, President of the Conference of the Representatives of the Governments of the Member States, 24 July 1996, CONF 3891/96.

[51] European Parliament, n. 49 above. [52] European Parliament, n. 48 above.

[53] Brian Towers and Michael Terry, 'Editorial: Unemployment and Social Dialogue' (1999) 30:4 *Industrial Relations Journal: European Annual Review 1998*, 272–6, at 274.

[54] Janine Goetschy, 'The European Employment Strategy from Amsterdam to Stockholm: Has it Reached its Cruising Speed?' (2001) 32:5 *Industrial Relations Journal: Annual Review 2000/2001*, 401–18, at 401.

long-standing reservations of these three Member States. The last ditch attempt by the French government (after the *Parti Socialiste* came into power following elections in June 1997) to resuscitate an expansionary macro-economic policy, by using Community resources to stimulate job creation, were again blocked by other Member States,[55] although the Parliament gave its support to such measures.[56] Not only had the goal of achieving 'a high level of employment' replaced the proposed aim of 'full employment', but further, employment was now also linked with the pursuit of 'competitiveness',[57] such that any job creation was to be achieved through flexibility in wage-setting and employment conditions—essentially through a form of deregulation. Also, as Deakin and Reed point out, although a change of government in the UK enabled the Fifteen to agree to the incorporation of the Maastricht Agreement on Social Policy into the body of the EC Treaty, in the form of a Title on Social Policy,[58] this was 'largely symbolic'.[59]

The Amsterdam summit as a whole placed particular emphasis on the employment situation, adopting, in addition to the new Title, a Resolution on Growth and Employment 'which together with the Stability and Growth Pact will create favourable conditions for economic growth and new job opportunities'.[60] Thus, the context in which the Employment Title was finally agreed must be seen as one which privileged 'stability' above all else:[61] employment had to be secondary to the attainment of a stable macro-economic policy based on meeting the convergence criteria for EMU.

[55] As George Ross argues, 'French social democracy as a party gave very little thought to EMU until it had already been decided', and then attempted to ameliorate its negative impact on employment, hence Lionel Jospin's proposal at the Amsterdam IGC to revise the Dublin Stability and Growth Pact to allow explicit EMU commitments to growth and employment and the creation of a 'European growth fund', following the recommendations of the 1993 *Growth* White Paper. George Ross, 'French Social Democracy and the EMU', ARENA (Advanced Research on the Europeanisation of the Nation-State), University of Oslo, Working Papers, WP 98/19.

[56] 'Though Parliament has supported the limitations on national public deficits and borrowing, it has also supported Commission's 1993 proposals for increased public investment at Community level': European Parliament, 'Parliament and EMU', 27 April 1998, available at *http://www.europarl.eu.int/euro* [accessed on 10 April 2005].

[57] Simon Deakin and Hannah Reed, 'The Contested Meaning of Labour Market Flexibility: Economic Theory and the Discourse of European Integration' in Jo Shaw (ed.), *Social Law and Policy in an Evolving European Union* (Oxford: Hart Publishing, 2000) at 88.

[58] Title XI (formerly Title VIII) Social Policy, Education, Vocational Training and Youth; the Social Policy Agreement is now contained in Articles 136–145 of this Title.

[59] Deakin and Reed, n. 57 above, at 88.

[60] Presidency Conclusions, Amsterdam European Council, 16 and 17 June 1997, Bull EU 6-1997, 1–31. The European Council adopted two separate Resolutions: the first laid down 'the firm commitments of the Member States, the Commission and the Council regarding the implementation of the Stability and Growth Pact' (Resolution of the European Council on the Stability and Growth Pact, 17 June 1997, OJ C 236/1, 2.8.97); the second was on Growth and Employment, reinforcing the 'firm commitment of the Member States, the Commission and the Council to give a new impulse for keeping employment firmly at the top of the political agenda of the Union' (Resolution of the European Council on Growth and Employment, Amsterdam, 16 June 1997, OJ C 236, 2.8.1997).

[61] Even above 'growth'? 'Stability rather than growth is the priority of the mis-named Stability and Growth Pact', Deakin and Reed, n. 57 above, at 98.

## 2.2 The economic context of the Employment Title

The Amsterdam Treaty introduced a new Title on Employment into the EC Treaty (Title VIII), together with the Title on Economic and Monetary Policy (Title VII), which not only follow each other numerically, but are also to be read together: the combined effect of these two titles is a strategy to promote employment based on the coordination of Member States' macro-economic policies and structural reforms. Put formally, the Employment Title obliges Member States to pursue their employment policies 'in a way consistent with the broad guidelines of the economic policies of the Member States and of the Community'.[62] The importance of this interaction between economic and employment policy cannot be overstated: it is essential to understand the economic context of the employment strategy in order to appreciate the agenda to which the Community and Member States were committing themselves, and in particular, the significance of the Stability and Growth Pact, which had been agreed at the Dublin European Council, and was given a legal basis at the Amsterdam European Council. The Stability and Growth Pact consisted of a Resolution[63] and two Council Regulations, one on the strengthening of the surveillance of budgetary positions and the surveillance and coordination of economic policies,[64] and the other on speeding up and clarifying the implementation of the excessive deficit procedure.[65]

The emphasis is very much on the avoidance of excessive general government deficits.[66] The provisions governing excessive levels of national debt and excessive budget deficits (Article 104 EC, applying only to those Member States participating in the third stage of EMU) establish a monitoring and reporting procedure under which, in contrast to the employment policy procedure, Member States are subject to sanctions for non-compliance. The monitoring procedure, under Regulation 1466/97, requires participating Member States to submit annual 'stability' or 'convergence' programmes, and establishes an 'early warning system' designed to 'alert the Council to the possibility that a Member State . . . may be running up an excessive deficit'.[67]

[62] Article 126 (1) EC.

[63] Resolution of the European Council on the Stability and Growth Pact, n. 60 above.

[64] Council Regulation (EC) No 1466/97 of 7 July 1997 on the strengthening of the surveillance of budgetary positions and the surveillance and coordination of economic policies, OJ L 209, 2.08.1997.

[65] Council Regulation (EC) No 1467/97 of 7 July 1997 on speeding up and clarifying the implementation of the Excessive Deficit Procedure, OJ L 209, 2.08.1997.

[66] This is a Treaty obligation: under Article 104(1) of the EC Treaty (ex Article 104(c)(1)) 'Member States shall avoid excessive government deficits'. This applies *only* to those Member States participating in the third stage of EMU (full monetary union leading to a single currency, the euro). However, under Article 116(4) EC (ex Article 109e (4)), dealing with the second stage of EMU, *all* Member States, including the UK, shall endeavour to avoid excessive deficits.

[67] Deakin and Reed, n. 57 above, at 89.

However, what has been described as the 'least defensible and most mischievous'[68] provision of the Stability and Growth Pact is the Excessive Deficit Procedure (EDP) within Regulation 1467/97, which details the measures to be taken when a Member State breaches the '3 per cent budget deficit rule'. If a Member State runs a budget deficit of more than 3 per cent of GDP, or if total government debt exceeds 60 per cent of GDP, it will be required to make an annual interest-free deposit with the European Commission up to a maximum of 0.5 per cent of GDP; if the excessive deficit is not rectified within two years, the deposit will be converted into a fine.[69] Despite the seeming consensus over the need for macro-economic stability and fiscal prudence,[70] the Stability and Growth Pact—above all, the EDP—has had a troubled history, criticized in particular for imposing rules which lack a clear economic rationale, for setting mechanistic targets, and for a lack of transparency and consistency.[71] A principal concern has been the inability of the Stability and Growth Pact and EDP to police the activities of the Member States, indeed '[a] pessimistic appraisal would say that large countries in particular would never allow themselves to be subject to the full rigors of the EDP'[72] and so it has proved.[73]

For example, in November 2003, the Economic and Financial Affairs Council (ECOFIN) again revealed its lenient attitude towards infringements,[74] when it voted to suspend the EDP against France and Germany, even though their annual net borrowing exceeded 4 per cent of GDP.[75] The Council rejected the

[68] David Purdy, 'Welfare Reform, Social Citizenship and European Integration' in Lars Magnusson and Bo Stråth (eds.), *From the Werner Plan to the EMU: In Search of a Political Economy for Europe* (Brussels: PIE–Peter Lang, 2001) at 404.

[69] Council Regulation (EC) No 1467/97 of 7 July 1997, n. 65 above, Articles 12 and 13. See also Ton Notermans, 'The Werner Plan as a Blueprint for EMU?' in Lars Magnusson and Bo Stråth (eds.), n. 68 above, at 336–7.

[70] For example, 'The UK supports the principle of a strong SGP founded on sensible fiscal policy co-ordination, recognising that fiscal sustainability is a prerequisite for macroeconomic stability, and that collective fiscal discipline and co-ordination are essential for a successful monetary union': HM Treasury, *The Stability and Growth Pact: A Discussion Paper* (London: HMSO, 2004) at para 1.3.

[71] HM Treasury, n. 70 above, at para 3.37.

[72] Anthony Annett, Jörg Decressin, and Michael Deppler, 'Reforming the Stability and Growth Pact', IMF Policy Discussion Paper, February 2005 (Washington: IMF, 2005) at 13. See also Marco Buti and Lucio R. Pench, 'Why Do Large Countries Flout the Stability Pact? And What Can Be Done About It?' (2004) 42:5 *Journal of Common Market Studies*, 1025–32.

[73] Leading some to refer to the EDP as 'the dog that did not bite': Martin Heipertz and Amy Verdun, 'The dog that would never bite? What we can learn from the origins of the Stability and Growth Pact' (2004) 11:5 *Journal of European Public Policy*, 765–80.

[74] Dermot Hodson and Imelda Maher, 'Soft Law and Sanctions: Economic Policy Co-ordination and Reform of the Stability and Growth Pact' (2004) 11:5 *Journal of European Public Policy*, 798–813, at 799.

[75] The EDP had been used for the first time in January 2002 when the Commission made a recommendation to the ECOFIN Council meeting that it should activate the preventative mechanisms envisaged by the Stability and Growth Pact, designed to help Member States prevent deficits from approaching the 3 per cent of GDP reference value. The 'early warning' which, if the Council agreed, would be issued to Germany and Portugal, would aim to ensure that the 3 per cent of GDP reference value was not breached, and that the Member States concerned would resume the process of budgetary consolidation when the economic situation improved: see European

Commission's recommendations that France and Germany be subject to legally binding obligations to reduce their deficits within time limits.[76] Following a judgment of the European Court of Justice, in answer to the Commission's challenge to this decision of ECOFIN, the respective powers of the institutions in the EDP were clarified,[77] and ultimately the entire Stability and Growth Pact was reformed by the European Council in 2005. Whilst the two thresholds—60 per cent for the debt and 3 per cent for the deficit—remain unchanged, the pact was reformed to provide greater flexibility in its implementation.[78] In particular, Member States can avoid an EDP if they experience any negative growth at all (previously −2 per cent), can draw on more 'relevant factors' to avoid one, and will have longer deadlines if they do move into an EDP.[79]

What did not change, however, following this review of the first five years of the operation of the Stability and Growth Pact, was its approach to employment and employment creation, and their role within economic policy. The formalization of economic policy coordination begun with the original version of the Stability and Growth Pact is maintained, with slight shifts in the balance of power as amongst the Council of Ministers, the Member States and the Commission. As Hodson and Maher point out, '[t]he extent to which ECOFIN remains the driver in economic co-ordination is seen in how the Commission's traditional role as agenda-setter is curtailed. Its recommendations under the EDP can, unlike under the Monnet method, be adopted or amended by qualified majority voting . . . and if there are not the requisite votes, the EDP is left in *de facto* abeyance'.[80] Although the *implementation* of the EDP was clarified by the Court of Justice in July 2004 and amended by the European Council in

Commission, Press Release, SPEECH/02/33, 'Pedro Solbes, Member of the European Commission responsible for Economic and Monetary Affairs, Press conference on stability and convergence programmes, Brussels, 30 January 2002'; see also 'EU issues warning as German economy flounders', *The Guardian*, 30 January 2002. However, the ECOFIN Council decided *not* to endorse the Recommendation of the Commission for an early warning, because the German and Portuguese governments had given firm political commitments that the 3 per cent of GDP reference value for deficits would not be breached: 2407th Council Meeting, Economic and Finance Ministers, Brussels, 12 February 2002, Press Release DN: PRES/02/28.

[76] 2546th Council Meeting, Economic and Finance Ministers, Brussels, 25 November 2003, Press Release No 14492/03.

[77] The Court of Justice annulled the conclusions, holding that ECOFIN could not 'break free' of the EDP procedures. The Council was held to have a discretion in this field, in that it could modify the measure recommended by the Commission on the basis of a different assessment of the economic data, of the measures to be taken and of the timetable to be met by the Member State concerned. However, the Council could not depart from the rules laid down by the EC Treaty or those which it set for itself in Regulation No 1467/97: Case C-27/04 *Commission v. Council*, judgment of 13 July 2004, not yet reported. According to Hodson and Maher, the Court's judgment shows that 'even within the realm of soft law, procedures must be respected and followed': see Hodson and Maher, n. 74 above, at 801.

[78] Presidency Conclusions, Brussels European Council, 22 and 23 March 2005, Bull EU 3/2005, Annex II, 'Improving the implementation of the Stability and Growth Pact'.

[79] 'Stability and Growth Pact reform' *EurActiv: EU Policy Portal* available at: *http://www.euractiv.com/* [accessed 10 April 2005].

[80] Hodson and Maher, n. 74 above, at 801.

March 2005, the *underlying economic objectives* remain mostly unchanged from the time of the Treaty of Amsterdam. The Amsterdam European Council had underlined the importance of safeguarding sound government finances as a means to strengthen the conditions for price stability and for strong sustainable growth conducive to employment creation.[81] Two observations may be made here about what the tenets of the Stability and Growth Pact mean for employment. *First*, the rules establishing the Stability and Growth Pact would seem to privilege 'stability' over 'growth', certainly to the extent that Member States can no longer hope to spend their way into employment creation. The European Trade Union Confederation, for one, has been consistently critical of the Stability and Growth Pact for unnecessarily constraining the economic growth of the European economy. The argument here is that the goals of the Employment Title, fleshed out over the years in the Employment Strategy, require investment in human capital, and that such investment—made all the more necessary by the post-Lisbon version of the Employment Strategy with its stress on a 'dynamic knowledge-based economy'—requires public investment, thus potentially pitting the Lisbon Strategy against the Stability and Growth Pact.[82] *Second*, the logic of European economic policy coordination from Amsterdam onwards suggested that job creation would require labour markets to be made more competitive:

'we will need to strengthen the links between a successful and sustainable Economic and Monetary Union, a well-functioning Internal Market and employment. To that end, it should be a priority aim to develop a skilled, trained and adaptable workforce and to make labour markets responsive to economic change.[83] Structural reforms need to be comprehensive in scope, as opposed to limited or occasional measures, so as to address in a coherent manner the complex issue of incentives in creating and taking up a job.'[84]

The place reserved for social policy and social protection highlights its subservient role, in that it should be made more 'employment friendly'[85] and not undermine the goals of controlling inflation and reducing public expenditure:

'[e]conomic and social polices are mutually reinforcing. Social protection systems should be modernized so as to strengthen their functioning in order to contribute to competitiveness, employment and growth.'[86]

Employment policy (and social policy for that matter) would seem to be subordinated to macro-economic policy; where there are tensions between the

[81] Resolution of the European Council on the Stability and Growth Pact, n. 60 above, para I.
[82] Jean-Louis Arnaud, 'Budgetary Discipline and Macroeconomic Policy in the European Union: Are the Stability pact and the Lisbon Strategy compatible?' Report on seminar organized by Notre Europe, Paris, 8 March 2003, available at *http://www.notre-europe.asso.fr/IMG/pdf/Semi18-en.pdf* [accessed on 10 April 2005].
[83] Cf. the wording of the first Article of the Employment Title.
[84] Resolution of the European Council on Growth and Employment, n. 60 above, para 1.
[85] Ibid., para 4. [86] Ibid., para 1.

two, it is likely that economic policy concerns will predominate.[87] As the 1997 Council Recommendation on the broad economic policy guidelines makes clear,[88] the main objectives of EU employment policy are 'growth, employment and convergence' and 'since structural deficiencies continue to restrain both growth and the degree to which growth can be translated into additional employment, most Member States need to implement structural reforms'. In the context of the labour market, these 'structural reforms' mean measures to make the labour market more efficient. For example, priority should be given to: wage flexibility in the form of greater labour cost dispersion, so that wage levels take greater account of differences in productivity;[89] reductions in non-wage labour costs and lower income taxation; reform of the taxation and social protection systems; new patterns of work organization, including more flexible working-time arrangements; and adaptation of educational and vocational training to the needs of markets and to improve human capital, in particular, to 'improving the employability of the unemployed'.[90]

The extent to which the economic context the Employment Title and the prevailing economic discourse at the time have in fact changed, if at all, will be considered below. But, in essence, without once using the word 'flexible', the economic policy guidelines at the foundation of the Employment Title (guidelines with which employment policies must be consistent) dictate greater flexibility of the labour market, in particular, in wage-setting systems and downward wage flexibility. In other words EMU, and EU economic policy in general, appeared to necessitate an employment policy based on very strict fiscal policy, restrictions on public expenditure, 'modernization' of social protection systems, and 'structural reforms' to make labour markets economically responsive and enhance their competitiveness. All this bears a close similarity to the orthodox neoclassical perspective on the labour market flexibility debate, as elaborated in Chapter 2; and to the neoliberal policy prescriptions of the OECD, as discussed in Chapter 3. As mentioned in Chapter 3, there are strong similarities between

[87] Sally Ball provides a telling example, in the conflict between the constraints on public expenditure envisaged by the economic policy guidelines, and the promotion of active labour market policies envisaged by the employment strategy: 'The European Employment Strategy: The Will but not the Way?' (2001) 30:4 ILJ 353–74, at 361.

[88] Council Recommendation of 7 July 1997 on the broad guidelines of the economic policies of the Member States and of the Community (97/479/EC) OJ L 209, 2.08.97. Under Article 99 (ex Article 103) of the EC Treaty, the Council, acting by qualified majority on a recommendation from the Commission, has a duty to formulate a draft of the broad guidelines of the economic policies of the Member States and the Community. After reporting to the European Council, which reaches a conclusion on the broad guidelines, the Council must then adopt a recommendation, setting out these broad guidelines.

[89] Para 6(i) of Council Recommendation 97/479 n. 88 above, states that priority should be given to 'higher employment growth fostered by the maintenance of appropriate wage trends and by wages that better take into account differences [in] qualifications and regions'.

[90] Council Recommendation 97/479, n. 88 above, para 6. For a discussion on the Council Recommendation and the impact of economic policy on employment policy more generally, see Deakin and Reed, n. 57 above, at 88–92.

the EU's (economic and) employment policy, and the OECD's Jobs Strategy, which had urged its member countries to pursue employment policies based on: (a) the use of stability-orientated macro-economic policy frameworks which focused on reducing public sector deficits and debt and controlling inflation; (b) the implementation of a broad range of structural reforms in labour and product markets; and (c) a preparedness to undertake reforms that moderated the bargaining power of labour market insiders.[91] Indeed, the influence of the OECD Jobs Strategy on that of the EU has been recognized by the OECD itself:

> 'The Jobs Strategy shares many common features with the European Employment Strategy which was first launched in 1997. Since its inception, the OECD Jobs Strategy has played an influential role in the policy debate in member countries. And a Secretariat evaluation in 1999 suggested that those countries that had applied the Jobs Strategy the most had tended to perform relatively well in terms of improved labour market performance.'[92]

Thus, it is arguable that, whatever the social democratic or 'Third Way'[93] inclinations of the respective Member States' governments at the time of the drafting of the Employment Title,[94] the common EU approach effectively amounts to a neoliberal economic agenda favouring unduly narrow objectives.[95] Is there no alternative? The success or otherwise of the attempts made since the Lisbon European Council in March 2000 to forge a more equal balance between economic, employment and social policies, by 'modernising the European Social Model'[96] will be discussed in Section 4 below. But to begin with, the question is

[91] OECD, *Implementing the OECD Jobs Strategy: Lessons from Member Countries' Experience* (Paris: OECD, 1997) 1; and also, Labour Market and Social Policy Occasional Papers No 31, 'Key Employment Policy Challenges Faced By OECD Countries'; OECD Submission to the G8 Growth, Employability and Inclusion Conference, London, 21–22 February 1998 (Paris: OECD, 1998).

[92] OECD, *OECD Employment Outlook 2004* (Paris: OECD, 2004) at 11.

[93] For definitions of 'Third Way' thinking, and the relevance of such analysis to the EU Employment Strategy, see Section 4.3 below.

[94] Jos de Beus, 'Are Third Way Social Democrats Friends or Enemies of European Integration? A Tocquevillean Tale on the Politics of Administration' in Lars Magnusson and Bo Stråth (eds.), n. 68 above, 361–88

[95] Memorandum of European Economists, *Full Employment, Social Cohesion and Equity for Europe: Alternatives to Competitive Austerity*, (Bremen: University of Bremen, May 1997), 6; available at *http://www.memo-europe.uni-bremen.de/* [accessed on 10 April 2005]. Established in September 1995, the Working Group on Alternative Economic Policy in Europe is a group of economists from different EU and eastern European countries who are critical of the current economic policy stance in the EU, which they consider to be largely neoliberal, and who believe that there are viable alternatives to this course. They offered a critique of the 'monetarist draft of a European Monetary Union with its consequences: welfare cuts, labour-market deregulation, the destruction of natural environment and further increase of unemployment'. On the basis of its discussions, the Working Group formulated a declaration and a memorandum, supported by more than 250 European economists from all 15 EU Member States. The declaration and the memorandum were published in May 1997, shortly before the European summit in Amsterdam.

[96] The phrase 'European Social Model' is used so often in discussions of European social/employment policy, as if it does not require definition. A typical example is the Commission's Communication on the Social Policy Agenda which fails to provide a definition of the 'European

whether the Employment Title, as originally conceived, in any way softened what has been called a 'deregulatory, neo-liberal approach' to economic policy.[97]

## 3. The Employment Title

The core of the Employment Strategy, set out in Articles 125 to 130 EC, is a power vested in the Union, *supplementary* to that of the Member States (another concession to Member States' anxiety over supranational encroachment into their sovereignty over domestic policy) to promulgate common guidelines similar to those adopted at the Essen Council. Whilst the Treaty articles establishing this broad framework for the creation and implementation of employment policy remain unchanged, the details of the procedure envisaged under the Employment Title have been modified in response to successive reviews of the Employment Strategy. In particular, a concern that years of faithful implementation of the Employment Strategy had nonetheless resulted in relatively weak growth performance and insufficient job creation led the European Council to relaunch the Lisbon Strategy in March 2005, promulgating 'integrated guidelines' for growth and employment, so as to refocus on these two goals.[98] The annual, iterative process of policy-formation, policy-implementation and policy-monitoring which had been the hallmark of the Employment Strategy as originally conceived, was streamlined, simplified and transformed into a three-year policy cycle in 2003, in response to the evaluation of the first five years of the Employment Strategy, only to be overtaken by further procedural changes two years later in a radical relaunch of the Employment Strategy and the Lisbon Strategy to focus on achieving results.[99]

social model' despite spending over 30 pages examining how it will be 'modernized'. CEC, Communication from the Commission to the Council, the European Parliament, the Economic and Social Committee and the Committee of the Regions: Social Policy Agenda, COM (2000) 379 final, Brussels, 28.6.2000. However, the Commission's Communication on 'quality' in employment and social protection does state that 'Quality is at the heart of the European social model'; which 'in its diverse forms within the Union, has played a crucial role in helping maintain continually rising productivity and living standards across the Union, while helping ensure that the benefits are widely shared'; and that the European social model is 'distinguished from others by its framework and design, and by the nature, focus and distribution of the policies.... [F]unding is mainly public in Europe, and much more private in the US ... the benefits appear to be much more evenly spread in Europe than they are in the US'. CEC, Communication from the Commission to the Council, the European Parliament, the Economic and Social Committee and the Committee of the Regions: *Employment and Social Policies: A Framework for Investing in Quality*, COM (2001) 313 final, Brussels, 20.6.2001, at 3 and 5.

[97] Deakin and Reed, n. 57 above, at 91.

[98] Presidency Conclusions, Brussels European Council, n. 78 above, at 2 ('Relaunching the Lisbon Strategy: A Partnership for Growth and Employment'); and CEC, Recommendation/Proposal for Integrated Guidelines for Growth and Jobs (2005–2008), Brussels, 12.4.2005 COM (2005) 141 final.

[99] 'The overall Lisbon goals were right, but the implementation was poor. The lesson from the last five years is that we must re-focus this agenda to deliver results': Commission President José

The relaunched Lisbon Strategy has nevertheless retained key elements of the original annual procedure for the creation of Employment Guidelines, although this process follows a three-year rather than annual cycle. The creation of guidelines for employment policy begins with the adoption by the European Council of conclusions on the employment situation in the Union, on the basis of a joint annual report prepared by the Council and the Commission (Article 128: the 'Joint Employment Report'); these conclusions enable the Commission to propose employment policy guidelines, which must be consistent with the economic guidelines established under Article 99(2) (the 'Broad Economic Policy Guidelines'). Now, as if to strengthen the symbolic interdependence between the Union's employment policy and its economic policy, from 2005 both sets of guidelines are to be promulgated jointly.[100] The Council then adopts the Employment Guidelines by qualified majority after consulting the European Parliament, the Economic and Social Committee, the Committee of the Regions and the Employment Committee, newly established in 1997 (Article 128(2)). The second strand of the Employment Strategy involves action by Member States, which are obliged to report *annually*, in National Action Plans for Employment (NAPs), on the principal measures taken to implement employment policy in light of the Broad Economic Policy Guidelines and the Employment Guidelines (Article 128(3)).

Subject to the strategic review by the European Council, the guiding principles of employment policy (to the extent that they have not already been prescribed by economic policy, as described above) are stated in Article 125, which provides:

'Member States and the Community shall, in accordance with this Title, work towards developing a coordinated strategy for employment and particularly for promoting a skilled, trained and adaptable workforce and labour markets responsive to economic change with a view to achieving the objectives defined in Article 2 of the Treaty on European Union and in Article 2 of this Treaty.'[101]

Member States' responsibilities are spelled out again in Article 126, which obliges them to make their employment policies consistent with the Broad Economic Policy Guidelines, whilst considering the promotion of employment as a matter of 'common concern'. With regard to the Community, its *supplementary* role is again emphasized, with the language of Article 127 limiting its

Manuel Barroso, quoted in CEC, 'Commission launches ambitious Growth and Jobs Strategy for the EU', Press Release IP/05/130, Brussels, 2 February 2005.

[100] 'Overall consistency is reinforced even further by incorporating both texts into one and the same document, thus making it possible to present to the Union and the Member States a clear strategic vision of the challenges facing Europe in the macroeconomic, microeconomic and employment fields': CEC, Integrated Guidelines for Growth and Jobs (2005–2008), n. 98 above, at 7.

[101] Article 2 TEU enumerates the objectives of the Union, which now include the promotion of 'economic and social progress and a high level of employment'; Article 2 EC lists the tasks of the Community, which include 'a high level of employment and of social protection'.

scope of action to 'encouraging' cooperation between Member States, and 'supporting', or (if necessary) 'complementing' Member State action. In addition, 'the competences of the Member States shall be respected'.

Under Article 129, the Council may adopt 'incentive measures' to promote employment, acting by qualified majority. Such measures are designed to encourage cooperation between Member States; to help develop exchanges of information and best practices; and to promote innovative approaches, in particular by recourse to pilot projects. However, none of these measures shall include harmonization of the laws and regulations of the Member States. Furthermore, two Declarations annexed to the Amsterdam Treaty[102] sought to define the scope of incentive measures in a 'somewhat restrictive manner':[103] the incentive measures must specify the grounds for their adoption, their duration (a maximum of five years) and the maximum amount of funding. In addition, the funding for incentive measures as a whole is limited, since it cannot be obtained from the Structural Funds' expenditure,[104] but must be provided under the so-called 'Heading 3 of the Financial Perspectives', which amounts to an insignificant proportion (approximately 6 per cent) of the Community budget, and covers other areas such as social action and the environment.[105]

Together, Articles 127 to 129 reveal a sustained emphasis on subsidiarity and a clear exclusion of harmonizing legislation to the extent that, as Barnard and Deakin suggest, 'the coordinating role accorded to the central organs of the Community is a very weak one and in some respects provides little more than a basis for the exchange of information'.[106] This was certainly the view of at least one UK government representative, who believed the consensus was for employment policy to remain a national matter, and for the process instigated by the Employment Title to remain one of 'peer review' and 'exchange of best practice'.[107] The reluctance (most strongly voiced by the UK and Germany) to sanction significant centralized expenditure aimed at boosting job creation, or to confer competence on central institutions, yet again resulted in restrictive policy provisions.[108] In another example of how jealously Member States guarded their control over national employment policies, although the employment policy procedure was modelled on the convergence arrangements for national economic

[102] Declaration (No 23) on incentive measures referred to in Article 129 (ex Article 109r) of the Treaty establishing the European Community; Declaration (No 24) on Article 129 (ex Article 109r) of the Treaty establishing the European Community.

[103] European Parliament, n. 48 above, Chapter 3.

[104] See Chapter 5, Section 2.

[105] CEC, *The Amsterdam Treaty: A Comprehensive Guide*, (1998) available on the SCAD Database, at: *http://europa.eu.int/scadplus/leg/en/s50000.htm* [accessed 10 April 2005]. See also Janine Goetschy and Philippe Pochet, 'The Treaty of Amsterdam: A New Approach to Social Affairs?' (1997) 3 *Transfer: European Review of Labour and Research*, 607–20.

[106] Barnard and Deakin, n. 19 above, at 356.

[107] Douglas Henderson, 'The UK Presidency: An Insider's View' (1998) 36 *Journal of Common Market Studies*, 563–72, at 567. Douglas Henderson served as Minister of State at the Foreign and Commonwealth Office, with responsibility for Europe, from May 1997 to July 1998.

[108] Barnard and Deakin, n. 19 above, at 358–9.

policies, in comparison with the EDP described above, there are no real sanctions which can be applied against a Member State which fails to comply with the Employment Guidelines. It is true that the Council audits Member States' NAPs, in light of the Employment Guidelines, but the only 'penalty' for a Member State's failure to comply is the issuing of a (non-binding) recommendation by the Council. Whether the processes of employment policy coordination at EU level can be described as solely intergovernmental is, however, by no means straightforward. Certainly, it is true that the intergovernmental European Council has taken a greater lead in determining strategy (witness the Lisbon Strategy, and its relaunch in 2005); nevertheless, such a system of peer review, benchmarking and 'mutual learning' can wield a great deal of 'moral persuasion', particularly in the context of the increasing intensity and prescription of the benchmarks and indicators deployed since 1997.[109]

Article 130 EC establishes the 32-member Employment Committee, consisting of two members appointed by each Member State and by the Commission, whose role is 'to promote coordination between Member States on employment and labour market policies'. The Treaty grants the Employment Committee a broad role, but its status is, nevertheless, only 'advisory',[110] contrary to a proposal by the European Parliament that it have equal status to the Committee on Monetary Affairs, presumably in order to enable employment issues to provide a counterbalance to macro-economic concerns—especially with regard to labour market reforms—and to place employment 'at the heart' of all economic policies, including EMU.[111] Certainly, there is no centralized Community institution to play a role analogous to that of the European Central Bank.[112]

## 3.1 Luxembourg, Cardiff, Cologne: three forms of economic governance?

In order to pre-empt the process for the production of employment policy envisaged by the Employment Title, an Extraordinary European Council

[109] See Chapter 5.

[110] The Employment Committee replaced the Employment and Labour Market Policy Committee, which had been established following the Florence European Council of June 1996 (Bull EU-6/1996, 1–23), on a proposal from the Commission. The role of the Employment and Labour Market Policy Committee had been restricted to developing instruments for the effective monitoring and evaluation of employment and labour market policies and the identification of good practice; whereas the new Employment Committee would have a wider remit: to promote coordination between Member States on employment and labour market issues; to monitor the employment situation and employment policies of the Member States; to formulate opinions—at the request of the Council or the Commission, or on its own initiative.

[111] Martin, n. 34 above; and European Parliament, n. 27 above.

[112] Silvana Sciarra, 'The Employment Title in the Amsterdam Treaty: A Multi-language Legal Discourse' in David O'Keefe and Patrick Twomey (eds.), *Legal Issues of the Amsterdam Treaty* (Oxford: Hart Publishing, 1999), 157–70, at 165.

Meeting was held in Luxembourg in November 1997 ('the Jobs Summit'). The role of the Jobs Summit was to consider the employment situation in the Community, as presented in the *Joint Employment Report* produced by the Commission and the Council, and to discuss the draft of the first set of Employment Guidelines, prepared by the Commission. With some reservations, the European Council gave its blessing to the Commission's draft Employment Guidelines—which would be formally adopted by the Council in December, anticipating what would be the new Article 128(2) of the EC Treaty, following ratification of the Amsterdam Treaty. Once again, the Member States, as embodied by the heads of state and governments, were reluctant to commit the Community to strict employment targets. As a result, the Commission's proposed target of increasing the employment rate (from an average of 60.4 per cent to a rate of 65 per cent within five years, which would require the creation of at least 12 million new jobs[113]) was rejected in favour of committing the Member States and the Community to 'a significant increase in the employment rate in Europe on a lasting basis'.[114] Further, the Commission's target of reducing the *unemployment* rate to 7 per cent of the working population was also rejected.[115] The view of the Luxembourg European Council was that the Employment Guidelines would:

> '[draw] directly on the experience built up in the multilateral surveillance of economic policies, with the success observed in the case of convergence. The idea is, while respecting the differences between the two areas and between the situations of individual Member States, to create for employment, as for economic policy, the same resolve to converge towards jointly set, verifiable, regularly updated targets.'[116]

A form of convergence is envisaged, but it is perhaps better described as coordination, since what is foreseen is not convergence of Member States' employment policies as such,[117] but of their procedures for measurement, assessment and monitoring of the progress on employment.[118] The coordinated strategy for employment launched at the Luxembourg European Council, based on this iterative, 'soft law' procedure, became known as the 'Luxembourg process', and, in spite of its somewhat circumscribed beginnings, the Luxembourg

[113] Commission Communication, *Proposal for Guidelines for Member States' Employment Policies 1998*, COM (97) 497, Section I.

[114] Presidency Conclusions, Extraordinary European Council Meeting on Employment, Luxembourg, n. 5 above, para 22.

[115] CEC, n. 113 above. See also Erika Szyszczak, 'The Evolving European Employment Strategy' in Jo Shaw (ed.), n. 57 above, at 209; and Janine Goetschy, 'The European Employment Strategy: Genesis and Development' (1999) 5: *European Journal of Industrial Relations*, 117–37, at 128.

[116] n. 114 above, para 3.

[117] 'The differing situations of the Member States in relation to the problems addressed by the "guidelines" will result in differing solutions and emphases, in line with individual situations', n. 114 above, para 15.

[118] Marco Biagi, 'The Implementation of the Amsterdam Treaty with Regard to Employment: Co-ordination or Convergence?' (1998) 14:4 *International Journal of Comparative Labour Law and Industrial Relations*, 325–36.

process took on a life of its own, such that the 'rather vague criteria' contained within the Employment Title and guidelines have been 'accompanied by a close monitoring of national initiatives',[119] and have acquired a normative status.[120] The Council adopted the first set of Employment Guidelines on 15 December 1997,[121] structured around four main strategic priorities, or 'pillars'—improving employability, developing entrepreneurship, encouraging adaptability in businesses and their employees, and strengthening the policies for equal opportunities—which were further elaborated through 19 Guidelines.[122]

The first five sets of Employment Guidelines, for the years 1998–2002, were structured around the four pillars, which were further elaborated through an ever-changing number of guidelines. The Commission belatedly recognized that the Employment Guidelines had become complex and should be simplified, so as to provide more general guidance and identification of priority areas.[123] This was accordingly put into practice by means of 'fewer and simpler guidelines reflecting key common challenges'.[124] Whilst retaining annual proposals for Guidelines, as required by the EC Treaty,[125] the yearly policy cycle was simplified as from 2003, so that the Employment Guidelines, the BEPGs and the Employment Recommendations covered a three-year period and would only be fully reviewed every three years. Furthermore, instead of 'pillars' and 'guidelines', the emphasis was on *good governance*, and on three overarching objectives identified by the Lisbon European Council: full employment, quality and productivity at work, and cohesion and an inclusive labour market.

[119] Silvana Sciarra, 'Integration Through Coordination: The Employment Title in the Amsterdam Treaty' (2000) 6:2 *Columbia Journal of European Law*, 209–29, at 220.

[120] Szyszczak, n. 115 above, at 211. This point will be discussed in greater detail below.

[121] Council Resolution of 15 December 1997 on the 1998 Employment Guidelines, OJ C 30/98, 28.01.1998.

[122] The five sets of Employment Guidelines for the years 1998–2002 are available as follows:

Council Resolution of 15 December 1997 on the 1998 Employment Guidelines, OJ C 30/98, 28.01.1998;

Council Resolution of 22 February 1999 on the 1999 Employment Guidelines, OJ C 69, 12.03.1999;

Council Decision of 13 March 2000 on guidelines for Member States' employment policies for the year 2000 (2000/228/EC), OJ L 72/15, 21.03.2000;

Council Decision of 19 January 2001 on guidelines for Member States' employment policies for the year 2001 (2001/63/EC), OJ L 22/18, 24.1.2001;

Council Decision of 18 February 2002 on guidelines for Member States' employment policies for the year 2002 (2002/177/EC), OJ L 60/60, 1.3.2002.

[123] CEC, Communication from the Commission, *The Future of the European Employment Strategy (EES): A Strategy for Full Employment and Better Jobs for All*, COM (2003) 6 final, 14.1.2003, at 6.

[124] CEC, 'Proposal for a Council Decision on Guidelines for the Employment Policies of the Member States' COM (2003) 176 final, Brussels, 08.4.2003, Explanatory Memorandum.

[125] Article 128(2) EC provides that the Council shall 'each year draw up guidelines which the Member States shall take into account in their employment policies'; however Article 99(2) EC on the drafting of the BEPGs does not specify the frequency.

**Table 4.1** Employment pillars and guidelines for 1998

| Pillars | Guidelines |
|---|---|
| Employability | Tackling youth and long-term unemployment (Guidelines 1 and 2)<br>Adapting benefit and training systems to move people from welfare to work and training (3)<br>Encouraging (social) partnership in the provision of training and lifelong learning (4 and 5)<br>Improving the quality of education and easing the transition from school to work (6 and 7) |
| Entrepreneurship | Reducing overhead and administrative costs for businesses, especially small and medium-sized enterprises (8)<br>Promoting self-employment (9)<br>Promoting job creation at local level and in the social economy (10)<br>Reducing the tax burden on labour and non-wage labour costs (11)<br>Examining ways of reducing VAT on labour-intensive services (12) |
| Adaptability | Promoting agreements by the social partners to modernize the organisation of work, while achieving a balance between flexibility and security (13)<br>Introducing more adaptable types of contract, while ensuring adequate levels of security (14)<br>Encouraging investment in human resources and in-house training (15) |
| Equal Opportunities | Tackling gender gaps in employment rates and in unemployment (16)<br>Reconciling work and family life (17)<br>Facilitating return to the paid workforce (18)<br>Promoting the integration of people with disabilities into working life (19) |

The rationale for this change in emphasis was to provide for greater stability, in order to facilitate better implementation of policy—especially pertinent in light of the 2010 target for the strategic goals set at Lisbon—and to avoid the impression that policy strategy was incomplete or in a perpetual state of redefinition.[126]

In other words, there has been a remarkable consistency in the policy objectives behind these 'soft law' pronouncements, and the intensity (or otherwise) of attempts to reconcile the objectives of economic policy, employment creation and social protection. So, the questions to be asked are: what do the various pillars, guidelines and overarching objectives mean in practice, or rather, how have they been interpreted by the Community institutions; and how does the Luxembourg process fit in to the tensions identified above, between regulatory and deregulatory agendas, and intergovernmentalism versus supranationalism? However, before exploring the impact of the Employment Strategy and how it has evolved, it is first necessary to appreciate how the Luxembourg process of

[126] CEC, Communication from the Commission: *Streamlining the Annual Economic and Employment Policy Co-ordination Cycles*, COM (2002) 487 final, 3.9.2002, at 5.

Joint Employment Reports, guidelines and NAPs has been formally (re)positioned within economic policy discourse, in a much more detailed way than that envisaged by the Treaty strictures that employment policies must be consistent with economic policy—so that the Luxembourg process has arguably 'come under pressure from other processes rapidly emerging in the field of economic governance of the EU'.[127]

As requested by the Council Resolution of 15 December,[128] Member States submitted their first NAPs based on the Employment Guidelines in the first quarter of 1998, sufficiently early for the NAPs to be examined by the Council and the Commission prior to the Cardiff European Council.[129] The European Council meeting which took place under the UK Presidency in Cardiff on 15 and 16 June 1998 predictably focused on the issues of Economic and Monetary Union and employment, in light of the transition to the third stage of EMU and the planned introduction of the euro on 1 January 1999. As a result, the 'Cardiff process' was initiated, in recognition of the need for far-reaching structural reform and modernization, with a view to promoting innovation and increasing the efficiency of the labour market and the markets in goods, services and capital.[130] As if to reinforce the extent to which employment policy is subsumed within economic policy, the Cardiff Presidency Conclusions discuss action for employment under the heading 'Economic Reform and Sound Public Finances: The Basis for Growth, Prosperity and Jobs'.

The subsequent Vienna European Council called for greater 'synergy' between the Employment Guidelines and the BEPGs;[131] however, it was not until the Cologne European Council in 1999[132] that the attempt was made more clearly to delineate the relationship between economic and employment policies. The Cologne Council reaffirmed that higher employment continued to be Europe's 'top objective' and therefore launched a European Employment Pact,[133] which embodied a comprehensive approach, bringing together all the Union's employment policy measures. The Employment Pact consisted of three 'pillars' or processes, intended to dovetail together to attain a sustainable reduction in unemployment. Thus, in addition to the coordinated employment strategy to improve the efficiency of labour markets (the Luxembourg process), and the policy of comprehensive economic reform (the Cardiff process) there was now to

[127] Szyszczak, n. 115 above, at 212.

[128] Council Resolution of 15 December 1997, n. 121 above, at para 5.

[129] Presidency Conclusions, Cardiff European Council, 15 and 16 June 1998, Bull EU-6/1998, 1–35.

[130] Presidency Conclusions, Cologne European Council, 3 and 4 June 1999, Bull EU-6/1999, 7–37, at para 7.

[131] Presidency Conclusions, Vienna European Council, 11 and 12 December 1998, Bull EU-12/1998, at para 34.

[132] Presidency Conclusions, Cologne European Council, n. 130 above.

[133] Ibid., Annex I, Resolution of the European Council on the European Employment Pact, and Report to the European Council on the European Employment Pact: Closer Cooperation to Boost Employment and Economic Reforms in Europe.

be the 'Cologne process', aimed at 'macroeconomic dialogue'. More specifically, Cologne was intended to focus attention on the coordination of economic policy and to improve the interaction between fiscal policy, monetary policy and wage developments, through macro-economic dialogue aimed at preserving non-inflationary growth. Such macro-economic dialogue would involve 'all those who decide on or influence economic and employment policy',[134] including the Council, the Commission, the European Central Bank and the social partners. The innovative multi-annual employment monitoring procedure which was the hallmark of the Luxembourg process was accordingly extended to the other two 'pillars' of the Employment Pact:[135] not only would Member States and the Community agree annually on the main elements of the coordinated employment strategy, they would also produce 'Cardiff reports' on economic reform, and engage in a macro-economic dialogue within the framework of the ECOFIN Council, in cooperation with the Labour and Social Affairs Council.[136]

As the Cologne European Council asserts: '[t]he task of creating the conditions for more employment and growth, which is primarily a matter for Member States, must be based on a European strategy of structural reforms and a balanced macroeconomic policy mix'.[137] If this is the case, it would seem that the Luxembourg process is very much circumscribed by the other two pillars of the Employment Pact. How, then, do the traditional concerns with social protection and the European social model, and the objectives of the new Title on Social Policy fit into the development of employment policy? The Employment Pact does make mention of social justice and cohesion in the fight against unemployment, and of course importance is attributed to the role of the social partners in the macro-economic dialogue. This is how the Employment Pact seeks to reconcile the concerns of social policy/employment policy with the other two processes:

> 'In order to improve employment trends in Europe, it is important to ensure that competitiveness, flexibility of employment and social protection of employees are in a balanced relationship with one another. To this end, it is desirable to develop further a core of minimum social standards, in accordance with the provisions of the EC Treaty relating to the improvement of living and working conditions.'[138]

[134] Ibid., Annex1, Resolution of the European Council on the European Employment Pact, para 5.

[135] Of course, this monitoring procedure was not entirely new, as it had first been adopted at the Essen European Council. However, the process developed at Essen had had minimal impact since it was mainly disseminated by means of national seminars. What was different now was the greater influence exerted by the Community level: the annual scrutiny by the Council of Member States' efforts, and the possibility to 'make recommendations' to Member States. The annual production of Employment Guidelines would 'constitute the driving force and the key component of the co-ordination process': Goetschy and Pochet, n. 105 above, at 609–10.

[136] Annex 1 to the Presidency Conclusions, n. 133 above, Resolution of the European Council on the European Employment Pact, paras 4–6.

[137] Annex I to the Presidency Conclusions, n. 133 above, at 7.

[138] Ibid., at 11.

Thus, social standards (at a minimum level) are to be developed under the social policy title,[139] *to the extent that they play a role in maintaining the conditions of economic growth and competitiveness.* Referring to the social policy agreements so far concluded, on parental leave, part-time work and fixed-term work,[140] the European Council urges the social partners to continue along this road, taking, in doing so, 'full account of the impact of [any] new regulations on job creation and employment'.[141] From the foregoing, it can be seen that the interaction between the three processes of economic governance—Luxembourg, Cardiff and Cologne—resulted in an Employment Strategy which gave priority to structural adjustment, with any 'balancing' of competitiveness and social protection very much biased in favour of the former.

## 3.2 The Integrated Guidelines for Growth and Jobs

As mentioned above, the concern to ensure a policy mix, namely to recognize the interdependence between employment and economic policy, has reached its apogee in the development of Integrated Guidelines. The logic of merging the Broad Economic Policy Guidelines and Employment Guidelines is that the delivery mechanisms of the Lisbon Strategy need to be improved, and that this integrated approach will, in the rhetoric of the Commission, 'leverage the guidelines', which are the cornerstones of EU economic policy, and make them a driving force of the Lisbon strategy.[142] These Integrated Guidelines are not yet definitive; they consist of a *recommendation* from the Commission on the Broad Economic Policy Guidelines, and a *proposal* for a Council decision on the Employment Guidelines; nonetheless, there appears to be remarkable unity from all the EU institutions on the need for a relaunched Lisbon Strategy with a sharper focus, thus making the endorsement of these guidelines by the European Council, and their subsequent formal adoption by the Council of Ministers a foregone conclusion. As had become apparent from the mid-term review of the Lisbon Strategy in 2005, the attainment of the 'full employment' targets by 2010 was looking extremely unlikely, as was attainment of the other Lisbon targets. For example, between 1999 and 2003, the number of employed persons in the EU15 increased by 6.5 million people. However, in order to meet the

[139] Articles 136 to 145 of the EC Treaty, previously the Social Policy Agreement.

[140] Council Directive 96/34/EC of 3 June 1996 on the framework agreement on parental leave concluded by UNICE, CEEP and the ETUC, amended by Council Directive 97/75/EC of 15 December 1997, OJ L 145, 19.06.96 and OJ L 10, 16.01.1998. Council Directive 97/81/EC of 15 December 1997 concerning the framework agreement on part-time working concluded by UNICE, CEEP and the ETUC, amended by Council Directive 98/23/EC of 7 April 1998, OJ L 14, 20.01.98 and OJ L 131, 05.05.98. Council Directive 99/70/EC of 28 June 1999 concerning the framework agreement on fixed-term work concluded by UNICE, CEEP and the ETUC, OJ L 175, 10.07.1999.

[141] Annex I to the Presidency Conclusions, n. 133 above, at 11.

[142] CEC, 'The new Integrated economic and employment guidelines', MEMO/05/123, Brussels, 12 April 2005.

**Table 4.2** Integrated Guidelines for Growth and Jobs 2005–2008

| | |
|---|---|
| Macro-economic guidelines | |
| 1 | To secure economic stability. |
| 2 | To safeguard economic sustainability. |
| 3 | To promote an efficient allocation of resources. |
| 4 | To promote greater coherence between macro-economic and structural policies. |
| 5 | To ensure that wage developments contribute to macro-economic stability and growth. |
| 6 | To contribute to a dynamic and well-functioning EMU. |
| Micro-economic guidelines | |
| 7 | To extend and deepen the internal market. |
| 8 | To ensure open and competitive markets. |
| 9 | To create a more attractive business environment. |
| 10 | To promote a more entrepreneurial culture and create a supportive environment for small is and medium-sized enterprises (SMEs). |
| 11 | To expand and improve European infrastructure and complete agreed priority cross-border projects. |
| 12 | To increase and improve investment in R&D. |
| 13 | To facilitate innovation and the take-up of information and communication technology (ICT). |
| 14 | To encourage the sustainable use of resources and strengthen the synergies between environmental protection and growth. |
| 15 | To contribute to a strong industrial base. |
| Employment guidelines | |
| 16 | To implement employment policies aimed at achieving full employment, improving quality and productivity at work, and strengthening social and territorial cohesion. |
| 17 | To promote a lifecycle approach to work. |
| 18 | To ensure inclusive labour markets for jobseekers and disadvantaged people. |
| 19 | To improve matching of labour market needs. |
| 20 | To promote flexibility combined with employment security and reduce labour market segmentation. |
| 21 | To ensure employment-friendly wage and other labour cost developments. |
| 22 | To expand and improve investment in human capital. |
| 23 | To adapt education and training systems in response to new competence requirements. |

Lisbon employment targets for 2010, the required annual growth in the overall employment rate should have been of the same order of magnitude as the employment increase during the best years in the late 1990s.[143] With regard to productivity, having peaked in the mid-1990s at around 97 per cent of levels in the United States, 'European Union labour productivity per hour [was] projected to deteriorate to around 88% in 2005 which is close to its relative level in the early 1980s'.[144] Similarly, in respect of investment, this had on average been growing by only 1.7 per cent per year compared with 5.4 per cent per year in the US. Finally, the average growth of the Euro area was a 'meagre'

[143] CEC, *Commission Staff Working Document in support of the report from the Commission to the Spring European Council, 22–23 March 2005, on the Lisbon Strategy of economic, social and environmental renewal*, Brussels, 28.1.2005 SEC(2005)160, at 7.

[144] Ibid., at 8.

2.2 per cent, whilst the US economy had grown by 4.3 per cent and Japan by 4.4 per cent.[145]

That the Lisbon Strategy was proving woefully inadequate to increase growth and employment within the EU had been forcefully highlighted in the findings of the Kok Report in 2004.[146] The recommendations of the Kok Report, as far as the labour market is concerned, concentrated on the familiar goals of increasing adaptability of workers and enterprises; attracting more people to the labour market by making work a real option for all; investing more effectively in human capital; and ensuring effective implementation of reforms through better governance.[147] But the central message of the Kok Report was the urgent need to improve governance, and to engender a sense of 'ownership' of the Lisbon Strategy, not only within national governments, but in wider civil society; the Report concluded that the disappointing delivery of the Strategy had been due primarily to a lack of 'determined political action', and that the agenda had been overloaded, with poor coordination and conflicting priorities.[148] As can be seen from Table 4.2, the Integrated Guidelines took note of the recommendations of the Kok Report and of the Commission's own mid-term review of the Lisbon Strategy, to include policy prescriptions on macro-economic policy (fiscal discipline and growth-orientated spending), micro-economic reforms (internal market, entrepreneurship, R&D spending) as well as employment (labour market reform, education, and modernizing social protection systems). The Integrated Guidelines usher in a new governance cycle, a complete overhaul of how the renewed Lisbon Strategy is implemented, as follows. On the basis of the Integrated Guidelines, Member States will draw up three-year national reform programmes (in place of the existing National Action Plans for Employment). This single National Action Programme for growth and jobs, adopted by national governments after discussion with their parliaments, is intended to become the major reporting tool on economic and employment measures, so as to simplify greatly the myriad of existing reports under the 'open method of coordination', which itself will be subject to review by Commission.[149]

Whilst the language framing the Integrated Guidelines suggests that '[m]aking growth and jobs the immediate target goes hand in hand with promoting social

[145] An even greater set of contrasts is with the growth of India (6.4 per cent) and China (9 per cent): CEC, 'Question & Answer: A new start for the Lisbon Strategy' MEMO/05/34, Brussels, 2 February 2005.

[146] *Facing the Challenge: The Lisbon Strategy for Growth and Employment.* Report from the High Level Group chaired by Wim Kok (Luxembourg: OOPEC, 2004).

[147] Ibid., at 6. The 2004 Kok Report drew heavily on the recommendations of the Employment Taskforce of 2003, also chaired by Wim Kok: *Jobs, Jobs, Jobs: Creating more employment in Europe.* Report of the Employment Taskforce chaired by Wim Kok (Luxembourg, OOPEC, 2003).

[148] CEC, 'Kok report calls for more determined political action to revitalise Lisbon strategy', Press Release, Brussels, November 3 2004.

[149] CEC, 'Question & Answer', n. 145 above; CEC, *Commission Staff Working Document*, n. 143 above.

or environmental objectives',[150] nevertheless, it is unarguable that only economic and employment objectives are formally foregrounded in the search for 'growth and jobs'. Doubtless, other values are acknowledged; the Commission responds directly to the concern that this new focus on growth and jobs will sideline the environment and social aspects of the Lisbon Strategy, with the assertion that the focus on growth and jobs 'clearly incorporates a social dimension'.[151] But does the formalized integration of economic and employment policy at the relaunch of the Lisbon Strategy serve to dilute the original impetus behind this Strategy, which was precisely to ensure that a (modernized) version of the European social model, and a concern for economic and environmental sustainability were understood to be indispensable to economic progress?

## 4. The Lisbon Strategy

'The Lisbon European Council on 23 and 24 March 2000 set a new strategic goal for the European Union to become the most competitive and dynamic knowledge-based economy in the world capable of sustainable economic growth with more and better jobs and greater social cohesion. The attainment of this goal will enable the Union to regain the conditions for full employment.

The Nice European Council on 7, 8 and 9 December 2000 approved the European Social Agenda, which states that the return to full employment involves ambitious policies in terms of increasing employment rates, reducing regional gaps, reducing inequality and improving job quality.' (European Commission, 2002)[152]

The Lisbon European Council in March 2000 did not create any new 'process' to add to the Luxembourg, Cardiff and Cologne processes, but instead set an overarching strategic goal for the Union for the coming decade, to become 'the most competitive and dynamic knowledge-based economy in the world capable of sustainable economic growth with more and better jobs and greater social cohesion'.[153] In other words, the Employment Strategy (ie the Luxembourg, Cardiff and Cologne processes) becomes *subsumed within* the Lisbon Strategy. Crucially, and in striking contrast to the debates within the IGC leading to the Employment Title, the new strategy was 'designed to enable the Union to regain the conditions for full employment'.[154] Whilst there was no explicit definition of full employment, an indication was given in the targets set for Member States: raising the overall employment rate to as close as

[150] CEC, Communication to the Spring European Council, *Working together for growth and jobs: A new start for the Lisbon Strategy*, Brussels, 02.02.2005 COM (2005) 24, at 4.

[151] CEC, 'Question & Answer', n. 145 above.

[152] CEC, Proposal for a Council Decision on Guidelines for Member States' employment policies for the year 2002, Brussels, 12.9.2001, COM(2001) 511 final, at paras 2 and 3.

[153] Presidency Conclusions, Lisbon European Council, n. 1 above, at para 5.

[154] Ibid., at para 6.

possible to 70 per cent by 2010, and the female employment rate to more than 60 per cent.[155]

For the first time since the introduction of the Employment Title, an explicit attempt was made to fully integrate policies on employment, economic reform and social cohesion. What was significant about the Lisbon Summit was the assertion of the European Council's strategic responsibility for agenda setting, now 'taking on a pre-eminent guiding and coordinating role to ensure overall coherence and the effective monitoring of progress towards the new strategic goal',[156] and the decision to devote an additional European Council meeting every spring to economic *and* social questions. Such ring-fencing, allocating a summit especially to the issue of reconciling the Union's economic and social goals, is particularly important in redressing the imbalance which had long existed between the different Council formations: economic and finance ministers represented within ECOFIN had dominated policy by comparison with the Labour and Social Affairs Council. Lisbon led to institutional changes, designed to ensure wider input into the development of economic policy, so as to give voice to social policy concerns. As stated in the first set of BEPGs after the Lisbon European Council:

'In order to allow the European Council to give effective political guidance in a timely manner at its annual spring meeting *and to ensure that the Ecofin Council is able to draw on the work of other Council formations*, the organisation of the preparation of the BEPGs will be modified.

From this year on, the BEPGs will be forwarded to other relevant Council formations for them to assume responsibility for implementation in their respective areas. At the same time, these Council formations will be invited to pursue work with a view to the formulation of the BEPGs for the coming year, and to make their contributions available by the end of January of the following year.'[157]

Whether this will lead to 'a primacy of politics over the economy', as suggested by the Portuguese Prime Minister at Lisbon, is another matter.[158] Development of employment policy is placed under the broad umbrella of the BEPGs, but an attempt has been made to dilute somewhat the dominance of the 'economic', by developing an integrated strategy across various policy fields: macro-economic policy (the Cologne process), economic reform (the Cardiff process), labour market reform (the Luxembourg process), social exclusion and modernization of

[155] Presidency Conclusions, Lisbon European Council, n. 1 above, at para 30. The Stockholm European Council set intermediate targets, aiming for employment rates of 67 per cent overall and 57 per cent for women by January 2005, as well as a new target of 50 per cent employment for older workers (aged 55 to 64) by 2010: Presidency Conclusions, Stockholm European Council, n. 35 above, at para 9.

[156] Ibid., at para 36.

[157] Council Recommendation of 19 June 2000 on the broad guidelines of the economic policies of the Member States and the Community, 2000/517/EC, OJ L 210, 21.08.2000, 1–40; emphasis added.

[158] The then Portuguese Prime Minister, Antonio Guterres, quoted in *Agence Europe*, 25 March 2000; cf. the discussion in Chapter 2, Section 3, on the embeddedness of the market in the social.

social protection. This goes some way towards redressing the lacuna in the post-Amsterdam EC Treaty, wherein provisions under Title XI on Social Policy—for example, on social security and social protection of workers, or social dialogue between management and labour—were presented almost in a vacuum, unrelated to questions of employment creation (the Employment Title) or macro-economic policy (Title VII on Economic and Monetary Policy).

The *procedural* innovations introduced at Lisbon will be discussed in Chapter 5; what of the *substantive* changes in policy? The new overall strategy launched at Lisbon had as its goal enabling the Union to 'regain the conditions for full employment'.[159] Crucially, the emphasis was not just on *more*, but also *better* jobs.[160] It is clear that a new consensus had been reached, along the lines that greater growth necessitates a balance between economy, employment and social welfare.[161] But what does this mean in practice? Does it amount to a strategic turning point in EU social and economic policy?[162] What did Lisbon mean for the tension between social protection and deregulation of Europe's labour markets? Martin Rhodes confidently suggests that Lisbon should be seen as Europe's 'Maastricht for welfare', viewing it as a genuinely progressive attempt to forge a new social policy agenda, which combines 'a shift towards a more liberal social policy and employment system . . . with a more traditional European emphasis on social dialogue and solidarity'.[163]

Perhaps it is more than one can legitimately expect of an integrating Europe that it replicate the national-level welfare coverage. Even if Streeck's rather harsh predictions of neo-voluntarism have not come to pass,[164] it is arguable that a more realistic scenario (given the 'competency gap' and the regulatory dilemmas identified by systems theory)[165] is for the EU to provide a framework within which national welfare states can continue to operate, rather than creating a uniform system of social rights. On a fairly sanguine note, Jos de Beus observes that 'the ongoing modification of neo-liberalism does not serve the goal of a European welfare state but boils down to soft coordination of a partly open-ended restoration of welfare states at the national level'.[166] Indeed, the

[159] Presidency Conclusions, Lisbon European Council, n. 1 above, at para 6.

[160] Ibid., at para 5. A similar language has also been adopted by the OECD in its policy recommendations on boosting labour market participation: OECD, *OECD Employment Outlook 2003: Towards More and Better Jobs* (Paris: OECD, 2003).

[161] Ministry of Industry, Employment and Communications/Ministry of Health and Social Affairs, Sweden, *A Europe for Full Employment and Social Cohesion: Swedish Presidency Priorities*, (Stockholm, Ministry of Industry, 2001) at 4.

[162] Goetschy, n. 54 above, at 405.

[163] Martin Rhodes, 'Lisbon: Europe's "Maastricht for Welfare"?' (2000) 13:3 *European Community Studies Association (ECSA) Review*, 2–7.

[164] Wolfgang Streeck, 'Neo-Voluntarism: A New European Social Policy Regime?' (1995) 1:1 *European Law Journal*, 31–59.

[165] Explored in Chapter 5: see Fritz W. Scharpf, *Governing in Europe: Effective and Democratic?*, (Oxford: OUP, 1999), at 76–7; and Gunther Teubner, 'Juridification: Concepts, Aspects, Limits, Solutions' in Gunther Teubner (ed.), *Juridification of Social Spheres: A Comparative Analysis in the Areas of Labor, Corporate, Antitrust and Social Welfare Law* (Berlin/New York: Walter de Gruyter, 1987) at 22 ff.

[166] Jos de Beus, n. 94 above, at 380.

Commission admitted something of the sort in its Communication on the Social Policy Agenda, which it was requested to draft by the Lisbon European Council:

'This new Social Policy Agenda does not seek to harmonise social policies. It seeks to work towards common European objectives and increase co-ordination of social policies in the context of the internal market and the single currency.'[167]

Thus, in the course of integrating economic, employment and social policy, the real significance of Lisbon may well be to signal a *continuation* of hard-headed economic policies (restrictive fiscal policy and liberalization of markets), alongside an acceptance of the importance of social cohesion, but a version of social cohesion which is predicated on equalizing the marketability and employability of individuals, rather than protecting them from the market.[168] Such 'modified neoliberalism' does sound suspiciously like a 'Third Way' solution, an approach whose shortcomings will be explored in due course.

## 4.1 The European Employment Strategy: experimentation with governance by guideline

In light of the way in which the Employment Strategy (and in particular, the Luxembourg process) has been being repositioned as a key tool to underpin the Lisbon Strategy, it is useful to consider what the Employment Strategy contributes to the attempt at Lisbon to reconcile the Union's economic, employment and social values, and to resolve the tensions between regulation and deregulation, intergovernmentalism and supranationalism highlighted earlier. Further, what difference is made by the process of streamlining and consolidation post-Lisbon?

A Commission Communication of May 1998 analysed the Member States' first set of National Action Plans and assessed whether the commitments contained therein were in keeping with the tenor and aims of the 1998 Employment Guidelines.[169] Member States also submitted their own 'Implementation Reports' in July 1998, detailing the manner in which policy commitments were being implemented. These reports, together with other relevant work on indicators of performance and policy inputs served as the basis of yet another report—the 1998 *Joint Employment Report* of the Commission and Council—which underpinned the revision of the Employment Guidelines for 1999, in accordance with Article 128(5) EC. The *Joint Employment Report* concluded that the four-pillar structure of the 1998 guidelines should be maintained,

[167] CEC, *Communication on the Social Policy Agenda*, n. 96 above, at 7.

[168] Wolfgang Streeck, 'Competitive Solidarity: Rethinking the "European Social Model"' Max Planck Institute for the Study of Societies (MPIfG) Working Paper 99/8.

[169] CEC, *From Guidelines to Action: The National Action Plans for Employment*, including a Commission Communication, and a Background Report, COM(98) 316 final (Luxembourg: OOPEC, 1998).

since it 'commanded wide political support' and keeping the structure of the guidelines would 'enhance their transparency and facilitate implementation and monitoring'.[170] However, the number of guidelines was increased to 22, in order to 'reflect the most important new challenges . . . as well as any gaps and need for clarification identified in the implementation of the NAPs'.[171] Under the Employability pillar, a new Guideline 4 urged Member States to review tax and benefit systems to provide incentives for unemployed and inactive people to enhance their employability; and to develop a policy for 'active ageing'; Guideline 9 proposed preventative and active policies to promote the integration into the labour market of people with disabilities, ethnic minorities and other disadvantaged groups. Under the Entrepreneurship pillar, a new Guideline 13 exhorted Member States to exploit the employment potential of the service sector. Finally, the Equal Opportunities pillar was reconceived to focus on *gender* equality, so that the guideline on promoting the integration of people with disabilities was replaced by the adoption of a gender mainstreaming approach, integrating gender throughout all four pillars.[172]

Having learnt from the experience of the first round of Employment Guidelines, the 1998 *Joint Employment Report* also initiated a new annual timetable for the Luxembourg process, in order to allow more time for the preparation and evaluation of the NAPs. Further consolidation was deemed necessary, to streamline the bureaucracy and improve the basic employment performance indicators. The Commission Communication had highlighted the lack of quantified or precise indicators or policy targets as 'one of the least satisfactory aspects of the NAPs';[173] common indicators were essential to allow 'an easy-to-read overview of key trends in the labour markets and constitute a mechanism to monitor whether Member States are converging towards reference standards of best overall performance'.[174]

Whilst such terminology—aiming at convergence of indicators rather than convergence of actual policies—should keep Douglas Henderson's mind at ease that the process instigated by the Employment Title remained one of 'peer review' and 'exchange of best practice',[175] nevertheless, it soon became apparent that, for the Commission at least, the Luxembourg process was moving further along the spectrum from cooperation/peer review towards coordination and ultimately towards aspirations of convergence. In its assessment of the first set of NAPs, the Commission had praised some aspects of the action plans—the

[170] CEC and Council, *Employment Policies in the EU and in the Member States: Joint Report 1998* (Luxembourg: OOPEC, 1998) at 15. This report was jointly adopted by the Social Affairs Council and the ECOFIN Council on 1 December 1998, representing a common assessment of the Council and Commission on the NAPs submitted by the Member States in April 1998.

[171] Ibid.

[172] Council Resolution of 22 February 1999 on the 1999 Employment Guidelines, n. 122 above.

[173] CEC, *From Guidelines to Action*, n. 169 above, at 5.

[174] *Joint Employment Report 1998*, n. 170 above, at 15.

[175] Henderson, n. 107 above, and accompanying text.

Member States' commitment to a comprehensive and multi-annual programme, their involvement of national (and even regional) social partners, their transparency, and in two cases, their willingness to engage in critical self-assessment of current problems. However, a number of shortcomings were also identified, namely the vagueness and lack of detail, which made it difficult to discern if measures were underpinned by an integrated strategy; lack of clarity over budget and resource implications; and the lack of an integrated approach to the four pillars.[176]

The second set of NAPs were submitted by Member States in June 1999, and included details on implementation of the 1998 NAPs and details of adjustments made to the NAPs to take account of the changes introduced by the 1999 Employment Guidelines, adopted by the Council in February 1999. However, whilst there were some strong points in these NAPs, the Commission was again very critical of Member States in certain areas:[177] for example, only two Member States—Sweden and the UK—were considered to have implemented policies compliant with the objective of Guideline 2, on preventing adult long-term unemployment. None of the Member States was held to have adequately addressed the new guideline calling on Member States to develop the potential of the services sector. With regard to the aim of modernizing the organization of work and adjusting to structural change, the Commission argued that evidence provided by the majority of Member States suggests 'we are still quite distant from this objective'. Furthermore, the implementation reports presented a piecemeal and disjointed approach which focused almost exclusively on working time. With regard to the objective of mainstreaming gender, the Commission found that Member States had insufficiently integrated the equality objective into measures under the Employability pillar, and had given insufficient attention to increasing the employment rate amongst women. Finally, many Member States still had to upgrade their statistical monitoring systems to provide the appropriate data and to make possible an adequate evaluation of the NAPs.

Therefore, it should come as no surprise that, in preparing for the 1999 *Joint Employment Report* and the 2000 Employment Guidelines, the Commission used the procedure envisaged under Article 128(4) EC, and called upon the Council to make recommendations to individual Member States, to address the major shortcomings in implementing the 1998 Employment Guidelines or in translating into action the 1999 Employment Guidelines.[178] The Commission identified nine priority areas where particular efforts were considered necessary, including preventing long-term unemployment; reforming the tax and benefit systems, with a particular focus on older workers and women; promoting lifelong

[176] CEC, *From Guidelines to Action*, n. 169 above.

[177] The following examples are taken from CEC, Commission Recommendation for Council Recommendations on the implementation of Member States' Employment Policies, COM (99) 445 of 8 September 1999.

[178] Ibid.

learning; modernizing work organization; tackling gender issues in the labour market; improving indicators and statistics.

A revised version of the Commission's proposal was speedily adopted by the Council,[179] a move which Jeff Kenner connects to increased Community intervention in national employment policies.[180] Although the Council asserts, in the third and fourth paragraphs of the preamble to the Recommendation, that 'the competences of the Member States should be respected' and that 'such recommendations should be used sparingly', nevertheless the recommendations to Member States unavoidably give the impression of dictating what the content of Member States' employment policies should be; and their use is far from 'sparing' given that this procedure has led to Council Recommendations on five occasions since the launch of the Employment Strategy. For example, a recommendation is addressed to Spain in 2000, that it '*should* [emphasis added] adopt and implement coherent strategies, encompassing regulatory, fiscal and other measures, designed to reduce the administrative burden on companies, in order to stimulate entrepreneurship and exploit the potential for more stable employment in the service sector'. Similarly-worded entreaties are also directed to Belgium, Germany, Greece, France, Italy and Portugal, giving a strong indication that Member States must take their lead, and the priorities for action to improve the employment situation, from the Community guidelines. By 2003 and 2004, country-specific recommendations are no longer so conscientious about asserting their respect for Member States' competences.[181]

The maturation of the Luxembourg process has led to what Szyszczak describes as a 'decisive shift' in the thinking of the Commission and Member States, and an acceptance of the Community's competence to determine the employment policy of the EU.[182] Clearly, it is important not to overstate the distinction between 'the Community' and the 'Member States', since the latter, after all, directly control two of the 'Community' institutions most involved in the creation of employment policy—the European Council and the Council of Ministers.[183] Nonetheless, whilst the *framework* and *priorities* of employment policy are being set by the (intergovernmentalist) European Council, employment policy is *elaborated* and *policed* by supranationalist institutions. The praise and criticism of Member States' NAPs meted out by the Commission highlights its new role as the ultimate interpreter of the Employment Guidelines, and final arbiter of 'best practice'. This goes beyond what is stipulated in the Treaty.

179 Council Recommendation of 14 February 2000 on the implementation of Member States' employment policies, 2000/164/EC, OJ L 52/32, 25.2.2000.

180 Jeff Kenner, 'Employment and Macroeconomics in the EC Treaty: A Legal and Political Symbiosis?' (2000) 7:4 *Maastricht Journal of European and Comparative Law*, 375–97, at 390–1.

181 Council Recommendation of 14 October 2004 on the implementation of Member States' employment policies (2004/741/EC) OJ L 326/47, 29.10.2004; Council Recommendation of 22 July 2003 on the implementation of Member States' employment policies (2003/579/EC) OJ L 197/22, 5.8.2003.

182 Szyszczak, n. 115 above, at 210–11.

183 I owe this observation to Paul Davies.

Further, guidelines drafted by the integrationist-minded Commission are adopted by the Council of Ministers (a hybrid intergovernmental–supranational body), within which it is quite possible for there to be a mismatch between the rhetoric adopted by Member States acting collectively, and the actual implementation of the Employment Strategy at national level. Another way to explain this disparity between what Member States say within the Council of Ministers, and what they do domestically is the sociological institutionalist perspective, which argues that the crucial coordinating role of the Commission enables it to structure the behaviour of the various actors in a given policy arena, and 'socialize' them into its view of the relevant issues and objectives.[184] Such socialization and collective learning will eventually filter down to the national level, so that the behaviour of national constituents arguably changes in the context of the reform programme suggested at European level.[185]

As borne out by the analysis of the NAPs and, in particular, of the reports of actions to implement the policies originally contained in the Adaptability pillar, it would appear that some of the (deregulatory) assumptions of the Employment Strategy are not yet wholly shared by Member States when it comes to their policies towards their domestic labour markets and labour law regimes.[186] Finally, the absence of a harmonizing agenda, and the related shift from the 'traditional Community method' to a more 'open' method of coordination, does not detract from the fact that the Employment Strategy is having a significant impact, in limiting the policy options of Member States to what is deemed 'acceptable' at EU level. This will be discussed in greater detail in Chapter 6, but for now it is worth noting that the process of experimentation with governance by means of guidelines has led to some *ennui* with the seemingly endless cycle of policy- and guideline-formation. The Barcelona European Council urged the Council and the Commission to streamline the relevant policy processes, with the focus on action for implementation, rather than on the annual elaboration of guidelines.[187] The Commission belatedly recognized that the Employment Guidelines had become complex and should be simplified so as to provide more general guidance and identification of priority areas.[188] This was put into practice by means of 'fewer and simpler guidelines reflecting key common challenges'.[189] Whilst retaining annual proposals for guidelines, as required by

[184] Goetschy, n. 115 above, at 135.

[185] Tania Börzel and Thomas Risse, 'When Europe Hits Home: Europeanisation and Domestic Change', (2000) 4 *European Integration Online Papers* 15, at *http://eiop.or.at/eiop/texte/2000-015a.htm* [accessed 10 April 2005].

[186] See Section 4.2.2 below; and also Chapter 6 on the influence of the Employment Strategy on Member States' employment policies, regulatory strategies and labour law.

[187] Presidency Conclusions, Barcelona European Council, 15 and 16 March 2002, Bull EU 3/2002, 1–56, at para 49.

[188] Commission Communication on 'The Future of the European Employment Strategy', n. 123 above, at 6.

[189] CEC, 'Proposal for a Council Decision on Guidelines for the Employment Policies of the Member States' COM (2003) 176 final, Brussels, 8.4.2003; Explanatory Memorandum.

the EC Treaty,[190] the yearly policy cycle was simplified as from 2003, so that the Employment Guidelines, the BEPGs and the Employment Recommendations now cover a three-year period and will only be reviewed fully every three years. Furthermore, instead of 'pillars', the emphasis will be on *good governance*, and on the three *overarching objectives* identified by Lisbon—full employment, quality and productivity at work, and cohesion and an inclusive labour market. For good measure, the revamped cycle of Employment Guidelines, now integrated with the BEPGs, are centred on the following *priorities for action*: increasing adaptability of workers and enterprises; attracting more people to the labour market and making work a real option for all; investing more, and more effectively, in human capital; and ensuring effective implementation of reforms through better governance.[191]

## 4.2 Regulation and deregulation within the Employment Strategy

In the view of Deakin and Reed,

> 'the employment guidelines are a curious mix of neo-liberal policy objectives, which stress deregulation and individual responsibility for training and labour market mobility, and neo-corporatist strategies, which envisage collective solutions to the reconciliation of flexibility and security.'[192]

I would contend that this curious mix is still an accurate description of European employment policy, even in the wake of the Lisbon Strategy and the 2005 relaunch of this Strategy. The influence of the BEPGs and the Stability and Growth Pact; the three-pillar approach of the European Employment Pact, placing economic reform (the Cardiff process) and macro-economic dialogue (the Cologne process) alongside the coordinated Employment Strategy; the link between employment and competitiveness highlighted at Lisbon and in the Integrated Guidelines—these are all factors which strongly suggest a deregulatory agenda for the Employment Guidelines. In the context of labour market regulation, the 'structural reforms' envisaged by the Employment Pact indicate measures to make the labour market more efficient: thus the 1997 Council Recommendation on the BEPGs advises wage flexibility; reductions in non-wage labour costs; reform of the taxation and social protection systems; new patterns of work organization, including more flexible working-time arrangements; and adaptation of educational and vocational training to the needs of markets.[193]

[190] Art 128(2) EC provides that the Council shall 'each year draw up guidelines which the Member States shall take into account in their employment policies'; however Art 99(2) EC on the drafting of the BEPGs does not specify the frequency.

[191] These priorities were identified by the Employment Taskforce, established by the Heads of State and Government to identify practical reform measures for Member States to implement the revised European Employment Strategy: *Report of the Employment Taskforce*, n. 147 above.

[192] Deakin and Reed, n. 57 above, at 95.

[193] Council Recommendation of 7 July 1997, n. 88 above.

This theme is continued in subsequent BEPGs, culminating in the near-identical exhortation on reform of the labour market in the 2004 guidelines.[194]

However, important as the economic context of the Employment Title is, it does not represent the whole picture. It is worth remembering that Article 2 EC lists amongst the tasks of the Community 'a high level of employment *and of social protection*', whilst Article 2 TEU includes 'economic *and social* progress and a high level of employment' amongst the objectives of the Union [emphasis added]. These texts suggest a balancing of the two sets of values, but the question remains whether they can truly be reconciled.[195] I would argue that, prior to the change of emphasis brought about by the Lisbon European Council in 2000, there had been scant evidence of a genuine middle way within the Employment Strategy, so as to combine economic and social goals on an equal footing.[196] With the relaunch of the Lisbon Strategy, and the introduction of the Integrated Guidelines, it is arguable that there has been yet another change of emphasis. The Lisbon goal, to overtake the US in becoming the most competitive and dynamic economy in the world, has now effectively been abandoned.[197] However, whilst the strategic ambition of becoming the world's dominant economy by 2010 has been quietly dropped, the employment aspects of this goal have been retained, in particular the objectives of full employment, quality and productivity at work, and social cohesion and inclusion.[198] In these three objectives we see a distillation of the values initially expressed in the 'pillar' structure of the Employment Guidelines, and it is useful to trace the evolution of key concepts and to explore the nature of the discourse around regulation and deregulation in the formative

[194] 'It will therefore be essential that policy efforts concentrate on a small number of priority areas that are likely to have the largest impact on labour market performances: ensuring that real wage developments reflect productivity growth; improving the financial incentives to work by reforming tax and benefit systems; improving access to lifelong learning facilities; and, undertaking appropriate reforms of labour market regulations, including a modernisation of the concept of job security to focus on improving employability': Council Recommendation of 5 July 2004 on the 2004 update of the broad guidelines of the economic policies of the Member States and the Community (for the 2003–05 period), in CEC, *European Economy No 4/2004* (Luxembourg: OOPEC, 2004), at 63.

[195] Silvana Sciarra, 'Market Freedom and Fundamental Social Rights' in Bob Hepple (ed.), *Social and Labour Rights in a Global Context: International and Comparative Perspectives* (Cambridge: CUP, 2002).

[196] The attempt to reconcile social justice and economic efficiency has been labelled as a 'Third Way' approach: see Giddens, n. 308 below. See also, Jeff Kenner, 'The EC Employment Title and the "Third Way": Making Soft Law Work?' (1999) 15:1 *The International Journal of Comparative Labour Law and Industrial Relations*, 33–60, who argues that the Employment Title implicitly, and to some extent explicitly, represents an affirmation of the 'Third Way' approach. Without disputing that the 'Third Way' may be the appropriate label for the attempted reconciliation between economic, employment and social policy *post-Lisbon*, what I do question is the benign characterization of this approach as a wholehearted rejection of neoliberalism. See below, Section 4.3.

[197] See discussion below on the Lisbon version of 'full employment' and the attainment of the Lisbon targets. See also Mark Tran, 'EU scales down economic ambitions', *The Guardian*, 2 February 2005.

[198] Commission Communication 'The Future of the European Employment Strategy', n. 123 above, at 9–10.

years of the Employment Strategy leading up to the reassessment of the Lisbon Strategy in 2005.

However, as the following analysis of the discourse of regulation and flexibility within the Employment Strategy and the Lisbon Strategy illustrates, perhaps the most that can be said is that there is an ongoing, unresolved debate over the conflicting goals of social protection on the one hand, and growth, competitiveness and flexibility on the other.[199] Whilst brief mention will be made of two of the original 'pillars'—entrepreneurship and equal opportunities—the focus will be on employability and adaptability as the two concepts which have had such continuity in defining the nature of the Employment Strategy and the wider Lisbon Strategy.

### *4.2.1 Employability, entrepreneurship and equal opportunities*

**Employability**

An example of such unresolved tensions over conflicting goals can be found in the Commission's interpretation of the Employability pillar. According to the *Joint Employment Report 2001*, the main aim of this pillar is improving the employability of workers *and* the unemployed.[200] The focus here is on tackling the skills gap; accordingly, the emphasis is on ensuring that young people and the unemployed (particularly the long-term unemployed) are equipped to take advantage of new employment opportunities in the 'fast-changing labour market'. On the one hand, this would seem to suggest the *absence* of job security in that workers are increasingly expected to be secure by virtue of being employable *across jobs*, rather than in one job. This view is well expressed in Commission's 1997 *Employment in Europe* report:

'[t]here is a need for a radical rethink of all relevant labour market systems—employment protection, working time, social protection and health and safety—to adapt them to a world of work which will be organised differently, in which the concept of security for workers has to be reformulated, *focusing more on security based on employability in the labour market rather than security in a specific job.*'[201]

Hence, a clear link is drawn between employability and flexibility: by emphasizing the fact that workers should improve their skills, education and training so as to be mobile and adaptable, the concept of 'employability' appears to downplay the responsibilities of employers to provide secure employment.[202] On the other hand, at the same time as urging greater flexibility, the Employability

[199] Barnard and Deakin, n. 19 above, at 359: 'it would be a mistake to see the Employment Title as simply a mechanism for deregulation along neo-liberal lines . . . there continues to be an unresolved tension between social policy and the growing clamour for flexibility through deregulation'.

[200] CEC, *Joint Employment Report 2001*, COM (2001) 438 final, Brussels, 12.9.2001, at section 2.2.1.

[201] CEC, *Employment in Europe 1997*, n. 3 above, at 20; emphasis added.

[202] Deakin and Reed, n. 57 above, at 95.

pillar also envisages 'early intervention' and 'the provision of help which is customized and targeted to individual needs', namely a role for state action. However, as Sciarra points out, it is not clear how such goals could be translated into a legal duty: ' "Employability" has no precise legal standing as a word, but is the policy side of a new and peculiar legal command addressed to the Member States'.[203] One path taken by the Employment Guidelines, and subsequent Commission interpretations of the Employability pillar, is to accentuate the role of the state in initiating 'active' labour market policies, as opposed to providing 'passive' systems of benefits and income support for the unemployed:

'Shifting from passive to active policies involves also a thorough review of the tax/benefit systems. The NAPs reflect Member States' recognition that providing income support alone is not sufficient to tackle problems of unemployment and social exclusion. The need to give unemployed persons incentives and opportunities in order to enhance their employability is reiterated.'[204]

One of the few targets in the guidelines from the very beginning was that Member States increase their 'activation' rate—the numbers of unemployed who are offered training or any similar active measure—to the average of the three most successful Member States, and to at least 20 per cent, by 2002. By 2000, fourteen Member States had achieved an activation rate above the 20 per cent target,[205] a requirement which was accordingly removed from the Guidelines for 2002.[206] This target was the nearest to a legal duty on the *state* to provide training, at least for the unemployed; it remains the case that there is even less of an obligation imposed on *employers*. As can be seen from the Integrated Guidelines issued in 2005, this debate on employability within the European Employment Strategy has now largely been subsumed within the larger debate over the attainment of full employment, how individuals can be equipped, encouraged, incentivized and trained to participate in the labour market, whilst ensuring that the focus is not merely on 'more' jobs but also on 'better' jobs.

**Developing entrepreneurship**

The Entrepreneurship pillar of the Employment Strategy as originally designed, emphasized the link between job creation and 'a dynamic and enterprising climate for businesses to expand and hire workers',[207] thus calling on Member States to improve the framework conditions for business to start up and operate, by simplifying and removing administrative burdens, reducing labour taxes and

[203] Sciarra, n. 112 above, at 165.

[204] CEC, *From Guidelines to Action*, n. 169 above, at 7.

[205] CEC, n. 200 above, at section 2.2.1 and Annex 2.

[206] Proposal for Guidelines for the year 2002, n. 122 above.

[207] The Commission's summaries of the four pillars are taken from the website of DG-V on the European Employment Strategy, originally available at: *http://europa.eu.int/comm/employment_social/empl&esf/pillar_en.htm*; now archived at *http://socialpolicy.ucc.ie/Four_pillars_ of_Employment_ Strategy.htm#Pillar1* [accessed 10 April 2005].

tapping the employment potential of services and of the social economy. Measures under this pillar aimed at improving the business environment through removing 'burdens', as distinct from those intended to encourage an enterprise culture throughout the EU, are more straightforwardly deregulatory in character, and clearly resonate with the OECD's Jobs Strategy, which urged member countries to 'nurture an entrepreneurial climate by eliminating impediments to, and restrictions on, the creation and expansion of enterprises'.[208] The Entrepreneurship pillar also connected to deregulation in other areas, since a 'favourable' environment for business would also require competitive markets, access to venture capital, and the 'liberalization' of markets for goods and services.[209] The creation of a more 'entrepreneurial culture' and of a supportive environment for small- and medium-sized enterprises is now contained under the 'micro-economic' section of the Integrated Guidelines. As one would expect, the focus is on alleviating the burden on business by redesigning regulation, since 'the cumulative impact of regulations may impose substantial economic costs'.[210]

**Strengthening the policies for equal opportunities**

The Employment Guidelines for 2003 and 2004 retained the emphasis on gender equality initiated in the four-pillar structure to the Employment Guidelines; indeed, gender is to be 'mainstreamed' or integrated into specific policy areas, with a view to encouraging female labour market participation and achieving a substantial reduction in gender gaps in employment rates, unemployment rates, and pay by 2010.[211] However, by the time of the Integrated Guidelines in 2005, scant mention is made of equal opportunity, beyond the bland assertion that '[e]qual opportunities, combating discrimination and gender mainstreaming are essential for progress'.[212] Rather, the new rhetoric deployed is that of promoting a 'lifecycle approach' to work, as the umbrella concept under which to achieve objectives previously labelled as 'gender' concerns, namely, the elimination of gender gaps in employment, unemployment and pay; better reconciliation of work and private life, and the provision of accessible and affordable childcare facilities.[213] The aims of the 'lifecycle' approach, and before that, of the Equal Opportunities pillar, in particular, the objective of reconciling work and family life, illustrate how 'flexibility' need not necessarily imply deregulation, since in this context it is very much equated with

[208] OECD, *The OECD Jobs Study: Facts, Analysis, Strategies* (Paris: OECD, 1994) at 44.

[209] CEC, *From Guidelines to Action*, n. 169 above, at 8–9.

[210] CEC, Integrated Guidelines for Growth and Jobs (2005–2008), n. 98 above, at 20.

[211] Council Decision of 22 July 2003 on guidelines for the employment policies of the Member States (2003/578/EC) OJ L 197/13, 5.8.2003; and Council Decision of 4 October 2004 on guidelines for the employment policies of the Member States (2004/740/EC) OJ L 326/45, 29.10.2004—the 2004 Guidelines contained a sole article, which simply maintained in force the 2003 Guidelines.

[212] CEC, Integrated Guidelines for Growth and Jobs (2005–2008), n. 98 above, at 27.

[213] Ibid.

employee-friendly, supply-side flexibility. The meaning of flexibility in the EU discourse is by no means clear or precise, but a significant component of this discourse is a tension between the emphasis on demand-side flexibility, focusing on the improvement of employment and competitiveness through a better (ie more flexible) organization of work at the workplace,[214] and a perspective which sees flexibility as an issue of labour supply.[215] In the latter case, 'flexibility' would involve promoting 'atypical' forms of work (eg part-time work, temporary work, teleworking) to suit the priorities and lifestyle choices of workers, especially those with family commitments, in stark contrast to 'demand-side flexibility' which would 'grant employers greater autonomy to shape personnel practices to changing market conditions'.[216]

The two notions of flexibility often exist in parallel. The Commission described the Equal Opportunities pillar as recognizing 'both the social need to counter discrimination and inequalities between women and men, and the economic loss resulting from not making full and effective use of the productive capacities of all sections of the population',[217] suggesting the use of non-standard work as a means of boosting the human capital of those formerly excluded from the labour market. This is particularly important in view of women's low participation rates: in 1998, the proportion of women employed in the EU (ie for the EU15) was still only around 51 per cent of women of working age, some 20 percentage points below the rate for men,[218] a gap which only narrowed to 16.2 percentage points by 2003 for the EU15.[219] However, the Commission has *also* advocated the use of non-standard patterns of work and employment contracts primarily because such flexibility of labour is seen as a logical response to flexibility in goods and services markets.[220] This rather pragmatic, economic justification for liberalizing labour market regulation to permit more forms of 'atypical' work, is at odds with the rationales given in the debates leading up to the adoption of the Part-Time Workers Directive, and in the Directive itself, which traditionally stressed the question of equality of treatment of 'atypical' workers. The stated aims of the Directive are, *first* and foremost, to provide for the removal

[214] CEC, Green Paper: *Partnership for a New Organisation of Work*, (Luxembourg: OOPEC), COM (97) 128 final.

[215] Deakin and Reed, n. 57 above, at 74.

[216] Ibid., at 74–5.

[217] CEC, n 207 above.

[218] CEC, Green Paper: *Partnership*, n. 214 above, at 74.

[219] CEC, *Employment in Europe 2004: Recent Trends and Prospects* (Luxembourg: OOPEC, 2004) at 237 (Statistical Annex). As the *Joint Employment Report 2001* argued: 'A re-balancing of policies is essential to actively encourage women's participation in the labour market, not only at the point of entry, also especially at mid-career, to help women stay in the labour market for longer. Fundamental in this respect are the issues of equal pay, adequate care facilities combined with reconciliation of work and family life, and lifelong learning', *Joint Employment Report 2001*, n. 200 above, at 36.

[220] CEC, Green Paper: *Partnership*, n. 214 above; see also CEC, *Employment in Europe 1997*, n. 3 above, at 17: 'Flexibility in product markets means flexibility at the level of the firm. Such flexibility will require an increasing focus on new types of work organization, which may lead to more flexible patterns of working time. The "flexible firm" should become the norm, not the exception'.

of discrimination against part-time workers and to improve the quality of part-time work; *second*, to facilitate the development of part-time work on a voluntary basis; and only *thirdly* to contribute to the flexible organization of working time in a manner which takes into account the needs of employers and workers.[221]

A key decision early on in the Employment Strategy was that, following the 1999 Guidelines, gender equality was to be 'mainstreamed' throughout the entire Strategy. However, this served to highlight the difficulty of pursuing a job creation agenda whilst also attempting to realize fundamental rights—in this case, the right to gender equality. Under the Adaptability pillar, Member States were urged to revise their systems of employment legislation in order to permit more adaptable forms of labour, whilst at the same time those working under such contracts should enjoy adequate security and higher occupational status, *compatible with the needs of business*.[222] The current discourse on reconciliation is similar: Guideline 20 of the Integrated Guidelines urges Member States to 'promote flexibility combined with employment security' and to allow 'more flexibility combined with employment security to meet the needs of companies and workers'. However, if the tortuous history behind the adoption of the Part-Time Workers Directive[223] and the case law of the European Court of Justice (ECJ) on part-time workers' rights[224] shows us anything, it is the fact that 'atypical' work, in its many forms, is precisely the sort of area where many Member States are most resistant to extending the full protection and benefits afforded to 'typical' workers. The Guidelines promote the use of atypical forms of work because these are considered to have advantages over traditional forms of work: encouraging the use of part-time work is seen as a means of increasing the level of employment[225] as well as improving competitiveness and productivity.[226] However, these advantages exist principally because atypical workers have

221 The Directive merely enacts a Framework Agreement concluded by the social partners, the full text of which is attached to the Council Directive as an annex. Directive 97/81/EC, OJ L 14/9, 20 January 1999 and Annex, UNICE, ETUC and CEEP 'Framework Agreement on Part-Time Work', OJ L 14/12; see also Mark Jeffery, 'Not Really Going to Work? Of the Directive on Part-Time Work, "Atypical Work" and Attempts to Regulate It' (1998) 27:3 ILJ, 193–213, at 195.

222 Originally Guideline 13, then Guideline 14; emphasis added. The 2001 Employment Guidelines, the first revision following the Lisbon European Council, however, added that such security and higher occupational status also had to be compatible with 'the aspirations of workers': Council Decision on Guidelines for the year 2001, n. 122 above.

223 Mark Jeffery, 'The Commission Proposals on "Atypical Work": Back to the Drawing-Board . . . Again' (1995) 24:3 ILJ, 296–9, and Jeffery, n. 221 above.

224 Since 1986 (Case 170/84 *Bilka-Kaufhaus* [1986] ECR 1607) atypical workers have benefited from European Community sex discrimination law, on the grounds that in some circumstances it may be indirectly discriminatory to exclude part-time workers from employment protection provisions, since this group is predominantly female. However, the ECJ's jurisprudence on the circumstances under which such less favourable treatment of part-time workers can be objectively justified is far from predictable. For example, in *Nolte*, Case C-317/93 [1995] ECR I-4625 and *Megner and Scheffel*, Case C-444/93 [1995] ECR I-4741, the ECJ took an approach which was much more tolerant of state-level exemptions of part-time work from protective legislation.

225 CEC, *From Guidelines to Action*, n. 169 above, at 18.

226 CEC, Green Paper: *Partnership*, n. 214 above, Introduction.

traditionally been excluded from high levels of employment protection; often, the very *purpose* of atypical work was to provide a way of circumventing legislative and collective regulations, and their associated costs.[227] As Sandra Fredman shows, in recent years there has been a 'remarkable convergence' between arguments based on market efficiency and fundamental rights rationales; however, particularly in the case of the Part-Time Workers Directive and the Fixed-Term Work Directive,[228] the result has been a 'significant dilution of standards'.[229]

### *4.2.2 'Flexibility' and 'adaptability' in the European Employment Strategy and the Lisbon Strategy*

Of the original four pillars, the Adaptability pillar demands closer scrutiny, as the one which, in incorporating the long-standing discourse on 'flexibility' within labour markets, seems to have most implications for the attempt to reconcile economic and social goals, and offers greatest continuity with the relaunched Lisbon Strategy. As the above discussion of the Employability, Entrepreneurship and Equal Opportunities pillars has shown, despite the rhetoric, it is difficult to find evidence, beyond mere assertion, that the EU institutions have indeed demonstrated the possibility of reconciling these two seemingly contradictory goals. In the context of the discourse on flexibility, just how is the existing commitment to social protection to be reconciled with the simultaneous, and equally strong, commitment to competitiveness and efficiency? First, it will be necessary to explore the competing understandings of 'flexibility'.

#### **Competing conceptions of flexibility**

'Flexibility is a politically attractive concept in general terms because its precise meaning can be disputed.' (Stråth, 2000)[230]

The definition of flexibility used within EU discourse can be difficult to isolate, and the use of the term may even be internally contradictory. In addition to the dichotomy between supply-side and demand-side flexibility,[231] there is also the distinction between internal and external flexibility—the external flexibility of the labour market and the internal flexibility of the firm. Both forms have resonance within the 'labour market flexibility' or 'labour market rigidities' debate, since both can be subsumed within a discourse which sees flexibility as a function of the system of labour market regulation: 'flexibility, then is the

[227] Mark Jeffery, n. 221 above, at 210; see also Simon Deakin and Gillian Morris, *Labour Law*, 3rd edn. (London: Butterworths), Chapter 3.

[228] Council Directive 99/70/EC of 28 June 1999 concerning the framework agreement on fixed-term work concluded by UNICE, CEEP and the ETUC, OJ L 175, 10.07.1999.

[229] Sandra Fredman, 'Discrimination Law in the EU: Labour Market Regulation or Fundamental Rights?' in Hugh Collins, Paul Davies and Roger Rideout (eds.), *Legal Regulation of the Employment Relation*, WG Hart Legal Workshop Series (London/The Hague: Kluwer, 2000) at 191.

[230] Bo Stråth, n. 32 above, at 22.

[231] See above, nn. 215 and 216, and related text.

consequence of the *absence of regulation*. More precisely, flexibility is a condition of "unregulated" markets in which the price mechanism is able to operate unimpeded'.[232] For example, in its draft for the 1997 *Joint Employment Report*,[233] the Commission highlighted internal flexibility, in the organization of work and of working time, as one of the means by which the necessary structural change in the labour market would be brought about. By the time of the 1998 *Joint Employment Report*, the Commission was able to report, with regard to the Adaptability pillar, that 'Member States and social partners are now in the process of implementing reforms or policy initiatives that have been sign-posted in the NAPs in order to bring about a higher degree of flexibility in their productive systems and in their working relations'.[234] The need to promote flexibility combined with security was also emphasized by the report of the Employment Taskforce chaired by Wim Kok, which stated that better responsiveness of EU economies to change requires a high degree of flexibility in labour markets, in particular through modern work organization and a diversity of contractual and working arrangements. However, the Employment Taskforce also pointed out that greater flexibility could only succeed if combined with adequate security for workers. Nevertheless, in the dynamic framework that was needed to capture the increasingly transitional nature of modern labour markets, security is increasingly associated not with the fact of preserving a job for life, but rather with building and preserving people's ability to remain and progress in the labour market, whilst using the welfare system as an instrument of last resort.[235]

The established orthodoxy within EU discourse on unemployment is that a more flexible organization of work is a key component in increasing the employment-intensiveness of growth. This belief was first stated as long ago as the Essen Council,[236] and has been often repeated since. In the context of the emergent Employment Strategy, the Commission identified at least five areas of the labour market where more flexibility was required.[237] Not all of these forms of labour market flexibility necessarily require the removal of the sort of 'labour market rigidities' examined in Chapter 2, but are discussed briefly in order to illustrate the long-standing preoccupation with flexibility in its varied forms as a remedy for the Union's unemployment ills. *First*, the Commission identifies a link between flexibility and employability, as discussed above. This notion of flexibility consequently has implications for forms of labour market regulation which are perceived to impose burdens on business since, in the Commission's view, a policy of skills-upgrading requires the overall cost of employment,

[232] Deakin and Reed, n. 57 above, at 76; and the discussion in Chapter 2, Section 4. Emphasis in the original.

[233] CEC, Commission Draft for the *Joint Employment Report 1997* (Luxembourg: OOPEC, 1997) para 3.3.2.

[234] *Joint Employment Report 1998*, n 170 above, at 33.

[235] *Report of the Employment Taskforce*, n. 147 above, at 27–8; see also CEC, *Employment in Europe 2004*, n. 219 above, at 159–60.

[236] Presidency Conclusions, Essen European Council, 9–10 December 1994, Bulletin of the EU-12/1994.

[237] CEC, *Employment in Europe* 1997, n. 3 above.

including the non-wage element, to be kept low, and for 'artificial barriers inhibiting job creation' to be removed.

The *second* area of labour market flexibility referred to by the Commission is the, by now, familiar discussion on flexibility in working patterns and in work organization. The Commission anticipates that the growing flexibility in product and services markets will lead to an (inevitable) flexibilization of working practices. This theme was taken up with enthusiasm in the Green Paper *Partnership for a New Organisation of Work*, which echoed the discourse on the future 'flexible firm',[238] resulting from the shift away from industrial mass production and the traditional structures of work which came with it. Other, non-Commission, observers have also detected a change in the traditional 'Fordist model' of industrial relations, although their conclusions as to how labour law systems should respond to these changes are not necessarily identical to those of the Commission.[239] The Green Paper concentrated most of its policy prescriptions on 'developments in work organization in firms and public bodies', namely on the internal flexibility of the firm as opposed to the external flexibility of the labour market, whilst the Employment Taskforce adopted a wider focus to consider the business climate more generally.

The *third* type of labour market flexibility identified by the Commission relates to flexibility in labour cost dispersion, namely wages and salaries. That wage developments should thus take greater account of productivity and skills differentials has proven to be a continuing theme of BEPGs and European Council Presidency Conclusions up to and including the Integrated Guidelines and the Spring European Council meeting in 2004.[240] The considerable variation in labour costs across the Union can largely be accounted for by differences in productivity, so this in itself is not seen as a major cause for concern. What does occupy the Commission, however, is the extent to which this variation may be due to regional problems of inadequate infrastructure, to the structure of the tax system in Member States and to the scale of the 'tax wedge'.[241] Thus, the Commission talks of the need to make tax and social security systems more employment-friendly, and to create a tax environment that stimulates enterprise and the creation of jobs, in particular by giving Member States flexibility to reduce taxes on labour. Such flexibility in labour costs can, of course, mean

[238] CEC, Green Paper: *Partnership*, n. 214 above, Executive Summary.

[239] Alain Supiot (with Pamela Meadows), *Beyond Employment: Changes in Work and the Future of Labour Law in Europe* (Oxford: OUP, 2001). The book defines the 'Fordist model' as being centred on 'a large industrial business engaging in mass production based on a narrow specialisation of jobs and competencies and pyramidal management', at 1. This book originally appeared as *Transformation of Labour and the Future of Labour Law in Europe*, Final Report of the Expert Group established by the European Commission V/98/776 (Luxembourg: OOPEC, 1998).

[240] See, for example, Presidency Conclusions, Barcelona European Council, n. 187 above, at para 32; Presidency Conclusions, Brussels European Council, 25 and 26 March 2004, Bull EU 3/2004, 1–50, at para 37.

[241] The difference between the cost of labour to employers and employees' take-home pay.

upward flexibility of wages, but—in line with the thinking of the OECD, and in order to meet the aim of encouraging job creation—is much more likely to mean freedom for employers to engage in *downward* wage flexibility.

In the view of the Commission, a *fourth* example of labour market flexibility, namely geographical mobility of labour, is impeded by obstacles which have as much to do with 'cultural and linguistic difficulties', as with 'rigidities in regulations'.[242] These regulations are, in the main, the sort of remaining restrictions to free movement of labour which have stubbornly survived even the completion of the internal market,[243] and which are not actually linked to the labour market, such as pensions and housing.[244]

The *fifth* example of flexibility identified by the Commission, that of sectoral and occupational mobility, does, however, have implications for the future shape of labour market regulation. This understanding of flexibility raises an extremely important theme, developed in the debate under the Employability pillar and in the discussion on the promotion of training and 'lifelong learning'. In other words, the old certainty that workers, or at least 'typical' workers, can expect a 'job for life' is fast disappearing: security in a job is increasingly being replaced by security throughout one's working life, as workers become more mobile over occupations and sectors. This thinking is very much echoed in the classification of changes to the labour market adopted by Guy Standing. Job security, now much weakened, is one of the seven forms of security Standing has identified, which globalization is transforming into flexibility: labour market security, employment security, job security, work security, skill reproduction security, income security and representation security.[245] However, it seems that potentially, the notion of security based on employability in the labour market could, be limited to only a privileged minority of workers (eg those able to acquire transferable skills) in the way that the traditional 'job for life' protected only 'typical' workers. Together with the notion of 'flexibility through employability', such sectoral or occupational mobility takes on a particular importance in the EU discourse on full employment post-Lisbon, as will be seen below.

These five examples of the sort of flexibility the Commission envisages as necessary for achieving an 'adaptable workforce' and 'labour markets responsive to economic change' amount to just one way of categorizing the wide-ranging discourse on flexibility within EU law- and policy-making. My focus is on *explaining* and *clarifying* the way in which the EU institutions have identified the concept of flexibility, rather than *creating* a new and unnecessarily complex taxonomy of 'flexibility', to compete with the manifold ways in which this term

242 CEC, *Employment in Europe 1997*, n. 3 above, at 19.

243 One of the founding principles of the original Treaty of Rome was of course free movement of persons (labour), seen as a necessary corollary to the other three freedoms—capital, goods and services: Articles 3(c) and 39–48 (ex Articles 48–58) EC.

244 CEC, *Employment in Europe 1997*, n. 3 above, at 19.

245 Guy Standing, 'Globalization, Labour Flexibility and Insecurity: The Era of Market Regulation' (1997) 3:1 *European Journal of Industrial Relations*, 7–37, at 8–9.

has been described.[246] The main reason for attempting a more precise definition of 'flexibility' is so as to ascertain the extent to which this term correlates with 'deregulation', both generally, and specifically in the EU discourse. This is particularly important since, as Brian Towers cautions, 'the terms "deregulated," and "competitive," and "flexible" are frequently used interchangeably and without clear meaning' in policy discussion about labour markets.[247] It is, however, important to bear in mind, *first*, that the policy implications of any particular meaning of flexibility are likely to be indeterminate, and *second*, that it is by no means clear that all forms of flexibility necessarily imply a downward pressure on actual or social wages.[248]

In its preparations for the Extraordinary European Council meeting in Luxembourg, the Commission had argued that

> '[the] employment challenge must be met if the Union is to attain its ambitious objectives to provide for material well-being and social justice for all its citizens. Indeed, the challenge is to demonstrate that higher levels of employment and more flexibility in the labour markets can be achieved without abandoning the basic foundations of solidarity and social rights upon which the European societies are built.'[249]

The long-standing debate on the need to modernize systems of social protection has given prominence to finding a middle, or 'third', way between the deregulatory path to employment creation favoured by the US (and, to a lesser extent, the UK), and the high protection systems of some Member States. This debate crystallized, prior to the Amsterdam Treaty, in the concept mooted by the Dutch Presidency[250] of 'social policy as a productive factor', namely that social protection systems had to be sustainable and more employment-friendly, but that they could also be an *input* into the productive process and an aid to competitiveness.[251] In other words,

> '[t]he process of economic restructuring can be facilitated by a combination of employment and social policies which ensures the appropriate balance between flexibility and security. Social protection systems can help workers to embrace new forms of work

[246] However, a useful attempt to provide an overview of the discourse on flexibility is: Supiot *et al.*, n. 239 above, at 191: 'Flexibility is defined in this chapter to be the pursuit of a collectively efficient response to economic contingencies'.

[247] Brian Towers, 'Employee Protection Policy, the Labor Market, and Employment: The UK Experience' in Christoph F. Büchtemann (ed.), *Employment Security and Labor Market Behavior: Interdisciplinary Approaches and International Evidence* (Ithaca, New York: ILR Press, 1993) at 337.

[248] I am grateful to Karl Klare for these observations.

[249] CEC, *The European Jobs Summit*, available at *http://europa.eu.int/comm/employment_social/elm/summit/en/what/what.htm*, [accessed 10 April 2005].

[250] Dutch Presidency Conference, *Social Policy and Economic Performance: Employment, Activating the Welfare State and Economic Competitiveness*, Amsterdam 23–25 January 1997; discussed in the Commission Communication, *Modernising and Improving Social Protection in the European Union*, COM (97) 102, adopted on 12 March 1997.

[251] CEC, *Modernising and Improving Social Protection in the European Union*, n. 250 above, at sections 2.1 and 2.2.

organisation and working time arrangements as well as to acquire new skills, thereby enhancing adaptability within the labour market.'[252]

This discourse has subsequently been sharpened by increased economic integration brought about by the transition to the third stage of EMU, the introduction of the euro and the development of the Employment Strategy and the Lisbon Strategy. More specifically, systems of social protection and employment protection legislation now have to 'contribute to competitiveness, employment and growth',[253] and 'Member States, especially those combining relatively generous benefit systems and high employment protection, should review their relevant legislation with a view to reconciling security with flexibility while making their benefit systems more efficient'.[254] To this, a 'disincentive' discourse has been added in recent years:

'Member States will reform financial incentives with a view to making work attractive and encouraging men and women to seek, take up and remain in work. . . . Whilst preserving an adequate level of social protection, Member States will in particular review replacement rates and benefit duration; ensure effective benefit management, notably with respect to the link with effective job search, including access to activation measures to support employability, taking into account individual situations; consider the provision of in-work benefits, where appropriate; and work with a view to eliminating inactivity traps.'[255]

It is arguable that the traditional 'European social model' (if it ever existed) is being undermined. A shift in emphasis is discernible, as the EU institutions become more preoccupied with the institutional organization of the labour market as a solution to high unemployment; there is a concern within the economic and employment policy discourse that high levels of employment and social protection impede jobs growth. As Barnard and Deakin argue, it has proven easier to build a political consensus around measures to tackle unemployment than the enactment of more employment law at EU level.[256] The Commission, for one, has become more doubtful of the merits of strong labour market intervention, and has been 'shying away from making any new full-blooded commitments on labour market regulation'.[257] One can see evidence of this as far back as the 1997 Green Paper *Partnership for a New Organisation of Work*,[258]

[252] CEC, *A Concerted Strategy for Modernising Social Protection*, document drawn up on the basis of COM (99) 347 final, adopted on 14 July 1999, at 8.

[253] Resolution of the European Council on Growth and Employment, n. 60 above, at para 1.

[254] Council Recommendation of 6 July 1998 on the Broad Guidelines of the Economic Policies of the Member States and of the Community (98/454/EC), OJ L 200/34, 16.7.98, para 7.2.

[255] Council Recommendation of 22 July 2003 on the implementation of Member States' employment policies, n. 181 above, at 20.

[256] Catherine Barnard and Simon Deakin, 'European Community Social Law and Policy: Evolution or Regression?' (1998) *Industrial Relations Journal: European Annual Review 1997*, 131–53, at 134.

[257] Paul Teague, *Economic Citizenship in the European Union: Employment Relations in the New Europe* (London: Routledge, 1999) at 151–2.

[258] CEC, Green Paper: *Partnership*, n. 214 above.

which focused on improving employment and competitiveness through more flexible organization of work at the workplace. Admittedly, although an improved organization of work 'will not of itself solve the unemployment problem', according to the Green Paper, it would make a valuable contribution 'firstly, to the competitiveness of European firms, and secondly to the improvement of the quality of working life and the employability of the workforce'.[259] The Green Paper envisages a regulatory framework which is a minimalist one, necessarily so, to keep up with the pace of change in the labour market: the changes in the concepts of workplace, firm, factory, employer, and related organizational developments such as downsizing, outsourcing, subcontracting, teleworking, networking and joint ventures are, it is argued, bringing 'new dimensions to the world of work for which traditional labour law provisions do not appear to have adequate answers'.[260] Thus, the Commission foresees 'the likely development of labour law and industrial relations from rigid and compulsory systems of statutory regulations to more open and flexible legal frameworks'.[261] In addition, the possibility of derogating from legislation through both collective agreements and individual contracts is mooted.[262]

It is worthwhile comparing the Commission's diagnoses with that of the Supiot Report,[263] in particular with regard to the Report's conclusions as to what these fundamental changes in the nature of work will mean for labour law regulation. The Supiot Report analysed changes to the labour market in the late twentieth century in terms of a disintegration of the Fordist model of employment in four areas: a breakdown in the continuity of employment status throughout an entire lifetime; and disintegration of occupation (or job content); in the standardized types of employment status; and in the nature and identity of the employer.[264] Rather radically, what the Report then proposes is a redesigned notion of security, to accommodate these changes whilst providing a certain level of protection for workers: briefly, that employment status should be redefined to guarantee the continuity of a career rather than the stability of specific conditions; that employment status should no longer be determined on the basis of the restrictive criterion of 'employment', but on the broader notion of 'work';[265] and that this broadened employment status should go hand in hand with various types of what are termed 'social drawing rights'.[266]

### 'Flexibility' and 'adaptability' in practice

This is the backdrop against which to examine the impact on labour market regulation of the discourse on flexibility in the most recent Employment

[259] CEC, Green Paper: *Partnership*, n. 214 above, para 4. [260] Ibid., para 42.
[261] Ibid., para 44. [262] Ibid., para 43. [263] Supiot *et al.*, n. 239 above.
[264] Ibid., at 220–1.
[265] For an analysis of the differing conceptions of 'work', 'labour' and 'travail', see Bo Stråth 'The Concept of Work in the Construction of Community' in Bo Stråth (ed.), *After Full Employment: European Discourses on Work and Flexibility* (Brussels: PIE–Peter Lang, 2000).
[266] Supiot *et al.*, n. 239 above, at 56 and 222.

Guidelines, and in the Lisbon Strategy. The desirability, within this discourse, of moving from 'rigid and compulsory' systems of labour market regulation to 'more open and flexible' ones resonates with the long-standing theoretical debate, explored in Chapter 2, that labour market rigidities are at the root of European unemployment, and with the strategy proposed by the OECD for combating such 'Eurosclerosis', discussed in Chapter 3. Adaptability' is especially central to the European Union's project, if one remembers that Article 125 EC commits the Member States and the Community to promoting 'a skilled, trained and adaptable workforce and labour markets responsive to economic change'. The desire to reconcile flexibility with security, and the belief that the Union's economic and social goals can go hand in hand lead to a reluctance, especially on the part of the Commission, to equate flexibility with deregulation, at least in the way this term has come to be understood in the Anglo-American debate.[267] For example, the Commission takes pains to point out that

> '[t]he type of flexibility which will be required of the European economy in a context of a fully-functioning Single Market and Economic and Monetary Union will be much more complex than simply deregulating markets.'[268]

However, merely eschewing the language of regulation and deregulation does not get away from the fact that, of the differing forms of labour market flexibility promoted by the Commission, at least some versions of the term will have deregulatory consequences in some contexts. For example, much of the 1997 Green Paper appears to be pursuing a vision of labour market organization which promotes such notions as the 'flexible firm' alongside the development of 'high trust' employment practices and 'high skill' workplaces,[269] implying a version of flexibility which borrows from earlier thinking on social protection as a 'productive factor'.[270] On the other hand, flexibility is equally used to signify a *reduction* in labour standards: at least this seems a valid reading of the Commission's advocacy of a 'radical rethink of all relevant labour market systems', and the emphasis on 'employability' over traditional forms of employment protection.[271] Modernizing work organization has also been a key theme of the Employment Taskforce, whose recommendations were endorsed by the subsequent Kok Report, which itself formed a central plank of the Lisbon relaunch. Thus, the approach to flexibility in work organization which currently underpins the Lisbon and Employment Strategies urges Member States and social partners to take some of the following measures:

- to examine and, where necessary, adjust the level of flexibility provided under standard contracts, to ensure their attractiveness for employers and workers;

[267] Barnard and Deakin, n. 256 above.
[268] CEC, *Employment in Europe 1997*, n. 3 above, at 16.
[269] See CEC, Green Paper: *Partnership*, n. 214 above, para 19.
[270] CEC, *Modernising and Improving Social Protection*, n. 250 above, at para 2.1.
[271] CEC, *Employment in Europe 1997*, n. 3 above, at 20.

- to review the role of other forms of contract with a view to providing more options for employers and employees depending on their needs;
- to ensure there is adequate security for workers under all forms of contract and prevent the emergence of two-tier labour markets;
- to remove obstacles to the setting up and development of temporary work agencies as effective and attractive intermediaries in the labour market, offering improved job opportunities and high employment standards;
- to promote the use of ICT and working time flexibility as tools to modernize work organization; and
- to remove obstacles to, and raise the attractiveness of, part-time work for employers and workers.[272]

Thus, I would argue that *in practice* the Employment Strategy and the Lisbon Strategy can nevertheless be understood as signalling a deregulatory agenda or having deregulatory implications for labour law. The focus on flexibility of the labour market (of which flexibility in the organization of work is just one aspect) as the key to employment generation, correlates too closely with the orthodox neoclassical economic solution not to imply deregulation. That some form of labour market deregulation is the inevitable consequence of the EU's discourse on flexibility follows, it is argued, if one is to attribute internal coherence to the EU's position on the labour market flexibility debate. The inherent logic of the EU's stance on flexibility surely leads to the conclusion that the requisite adjustment to economic change in EU labour markets is 'likely to entail a wide range of changes, and this argues for a deregulatory approach to wage and employment legislation'.[273] In particular, the EU's reluctance to apply the label of 'deregulation' to its 'flexibilization' policies seems disingenuous if one considers the similarity between the overall direction of these policies, on the one hand (away from 'labour market rigidities' and towards a 'radical rethink of all relevant labour market systems') and the deregulatory strategies of the OECD and of individual Member States, on the other hand.

This view of the deregulatory implications of the EU's flexibility discourse is strengthened when one looks at the Commission's critique of Member States' attempts (and failures) to comply with its recommendations; and also when one sees the sharp change of emphasis wrought by the Lisbon European Council meeting. First, the Commission's assessment of Member States' NAPs. The initial appraisal, put simply, was that the response to the Adaptability pillar 'remains disappointing'.[274] In their *Joint Employment Report 1999*, the Commission and Council found 'little evidence that a comprehensive strategy embracing a partnership approach with the social partners and developing

[272] *Report of the Employment Taskforce*, n. 147 above, at 27.

[273] Richard Jackman, 'The Impact of the European Union on Unemployment and Unemployment Policy' in David Hine and Hussein Kassim (eds.), *Beyond the Market: The EU and National Social Policy* (London: Routledge, 1998).

[274] CEC, *Joint Employment Report 1999* (Luxembourg: OOPEC, 1999) at 69.

efforts to modernize the regulatory framework has been undertaken by any Member State'.[275] What action there was on the use of more adaptable forms of contracts and modernization of the regulatory framework, focused on the issue of working time. In many cases, the early NAPs did not appear to go beyond a report on the relevant measures taken to implement obligations which Member States had anyway, to transpose the Working Time Directive into national law.[276] In 1999, only the Portuguese NAP, and that of the UK, appeared to be addressing the wider questions raised by the second part of the then Guideline 18, about the shape of the entire system of labour law, and how it interacts with employment policy more generally.[277] The Commission's assessment of Member States' NAPs for 1999 was barely changed in subsequent years: Member States continued to adopt 'only piecemeal or incremental reforms'[278] and to focus on working-time issues, to the detriment of progress on modernization of work organization, or a more comprehensive reform of working life.[279] There was some evidence, however, in the *Joint Employment Report 2001*, that there was now 'a general trend towards new and flexible forms of work, facilitating the introduction and use of fixed-term contracts, temporary work and part-time work ... through collective agreements.[280]

One reading of this (non-) implementation of the Adaptability pillar is that the majority of Member States did not share whatever deregulatory assumptions lay behind the pillar, and were unwilling to deregulate their domestic labour markets and labour law regimes. To some extent, the Member States did pay lip service to the need to 'flexibilize' their labour markets, but I would argue that there is by no means the sort of shift towards a process of deregulatory or neo-voluntarist regulation recommended by the various international organizations or envisaged

[275] Ibid.

[276] Council Directive 93/104/EC of 23 November 1993 concerning certain aspects of the organization of working time, OJ L 307, 13.12.1993, 18–24.

[277] In Portugal, labour legislation has been revised in order to modernize the organization of work; in particular, proposals were introduced in 1998 on part-time and temporary work, and in order to revise rules on dismissal. The Portuguese NAP for 1999 particularly highlighted the need to update the legislative framework, which was described as being disorganized and inefficient, so that it could deal with new forms of employment and ensure appropriate legal protection for atypical workers. By 2004, the Portuguese NAP was able to report the approval of a new Labour Code, in particular of Law No 35/2004, of 29 July 2004, which introduced a set of legislative changes to make the labour market more adaptable: see *NAP for Employment 2004: Portugal* (Luxembourg: OOPEC, 2004) at 16. The UK NAP for 1999 simply argued that the UK labour market was 'already relatively lightly regulated', and undertook a commitment to review labour market regulation to ensure that the burdens on business are minimized; for example, a 'Better Regulation Task Force', which was established in 1997, and has subsequently published principles of good regulation, stressing the need for regulation and its enforcement to be transparent, accountable, consistent and proportionate. In ensuing NAPs the UK has been able to point to 'more of the same', for example, that 'flexibility has been at the heart of the UK approach to the labour market': *NAP for Employment: UK* (Luxembourg: OOPEC, 2004) at 11.

[278] CEC, *Joint Employment Report 2000* (Luxembourg: OOPEC, 2000) at 56.

[279] CEC, *Joint Employment Report 2000*, n. 278 above, at 4 and 55–6; and *Joint Employment Report 2001*, n. 200 above, at 33–5.

[280] CEC, *Joint Employment Report 2001*, n. 200 above, at 34.

by the EU institutions. Instead it is arguable that 'flexibility is unlikely to become a viable alternative labour market programme as many governments in Europe remain committed, although to varying degrees, to the idea of a European social model'.[281] In later years, the Commission was able to report a more satisfactory level of compliance with the requirements of the flexibility imperative. In the *Joint Employment Report* for 2003–4, the Commission noted that the need to 'strike a more effective balance' as regards flexibility combined with security in the labour market 'is increasingly recognised' by Member States; furthermore,

> '[t]here is evidence of a trend towards greater flexibility through changes to working time patterns and the working environment. In a number of Member States attention has shifted towards introducing flexibility into standard contracts, improving working conditions, and reducing the number of accidents at work and occupational diseases. Actions to promote geographical mobility remain underdeveloped, and tend to focus on reducing regional disparities.'[282]

Slowly, legislation has been put in place in almost all Member States to 'deregulate' employment practices and work organization, often by creating exceptions to existing labour codes to permit certain types of 'atypical' employment contracts. So, for example, reforms in Austria, Greece and Sweden all facilitated the use and legal recognition of flexible or atypical forms of work, such as part-time work, fixed-term employment and teleworking.[283] More recently, some Member States have begun to introduce more flexibility into 'standard' contracts, for instance, as regards the definition of the thresholds beyond which stricter employment protection is applicable (Denmark), or legislation on dismissals which set out a more transparent framework for both employers and employees; (Spain and Portugal) whilst other Member States have launched comprehensive reviews of employment-related legislation (the Netherlands, Portugal and France).[284] However, there has also been a trend towards *extending* employment protection rights, such as the rights against dismissal and rights of trade union membership, to those groups of workers traditionally excluded from the scope of labour law. 'Atypical' or 'informal' workers (that is, those who have traditionally been described as self-employed) are to be brought within employment protection. So, more flexible forms of employment *have* been introduced, but they have often been balanced by extensions to the coverage of employment protection legislation. In the early years of the Employment Strategy there was certainly no large-scale shift towards labour market flexibility,[285] and in fact 'the response [was] to introduce greater flexibility without dismantling the overall regulatory framework'.[286]

[281] Paul Teague and John Grahl, 'Institutions and Labour Market Performance in Western Europe' (1998) 46:1 *Political Studies*, 1–18, at 2.

[282] CEC, *Joint Employment Report 2003–4* (Luxembourg: OOPEC, 2004) at 7.

[283] See CEC, *Joint Employment Report 1999*, n. 274 above.

[284] CEC, *Joint Employment Report 2003–4*, n. 282 above, at 34.

[285] Teague and Grahl, n. 281 above, at 14. [286] Ibid., at 13.

What impact did Lisbon, with its emphasis on the *quality* of jobs and social cohesion, have on the development of flexibilization policies? Were the 'reluctant modernizers' amongst the Member States now more willing to open up labour markets on the understanding that this need not entail unqualified deregulation? The European Council at Lisbon set a new strategic goal for the Union, 'to become the most competitive and dynamic knowledge-based economy in the world capable of sustainable economic growth with more and *better* jobs and *greater social cohesion*'.[287] The Employment Guidelines for 2001 contained the same commitment to reviewing the existing regulatory framework, reducing barriers to employment, and helping the labour market adapt to structural change in the economy; but there was now more emphasis on adaptability as a component of the improved *quality* of jobs, on meeting the needs of workers as well as the needs of business, and on greater partnership with the social partners. Further, the sixth paragraph of the preamble to the Council decision adopting the guidelines for 2001 essentially 'mainstreamed' the promotion of social inclusion throughout all the guidelines.

In other words, the renewed emphasis on social policy and (modernized) systems of social protection post-Lisbon has thrown into sharp relief the previous neglect of social protection and issues of 'security', for the sake of 'structural adjustment' and competitiveness. The Employment Taskforce casts light on the reasons why some Member States were such reluctant modernizers: '[r]esistance to increased flexibility is fuelled by the view that it automatically leads to increased insecurity and precariousness for workers. Member States must overcome this perception'.[288] The response of the Employment Taskforce, which is worth quoting at length, is adamant that

> '*Flexibility is not just in the interest of employers.* Modern workers also have a need for flexible working arrangements and modern work organisation to help them combine work and care, to make time for education and to respond to their personal preferences and lifestyles. This opens scope for negotiations at plant or branch level and creates perspectives for mutually beneficial solutions, provided all are prepared to put aside old pre-conceptions. While promoting flexibility on the labour market, *it is also important to foster new forms of security.* Security in today's labour markets is not a matter of preserving a job for life. In a more dynamic perspective, security is about building and preserving people's ability to remain and progress in the labour market. It is related to decent pay, access to lifelong learning, working conditions, protection against discrimination or unfair dismissal, support in the case of job loss and the right to transfer acquired social rights when moving jobs.'[289]

As mentioned, the relaunched Lisbon Strategy has, in a somewhat circuitous manner, endorsed the conclusions of the Employment Taskforce. But whilst the Employment Taskforce is premised on supply-side *and* demand-side flexibility,

[287] Presidency Conclusions, Lisbon European Council, n. 1 above, at para 5; emphasis added.
[288] *Report of the Employment Taskforce*, n. 147 above, at 27.
[289] Ibid., at 27–8; emphasis added.

on a notion of flexibility which is both employer- and employee-friendly, the relaunched Lisbon Strategy retains a supply-side orientation, seeing flexibility or a high degree of adaptability as important principally 'to promote productivity growth and to facilitate job creation in rapidly growing sectors'.[290] Has the momentum of the Lisbon European Council, to reinvent social protection, been lost? As will be seen below, it is questionable whether the Lisbon Strategy, with its focus on growth and jobs fully captures the requirements of employee-friendly flexibility.

## 4.3 What did Lisbon mean by 'full employment'?

The Portuguese Presidency, and the subsequent Swedish Presidency, reintroduced the term 'full employment' into policy debate, as a policy goal but not as a Treaty objective. In order to answer the question of the extent to which Lisbon amounts to a strategic turning point in European social and employment policy, it is important to understand what this commitment to full employment might mean: is full employment to be backed by a meaningful sense of social solidarity? What sort of 'incentives' are to be used to encourage labour market participation?

No precise definition of full employment is given, beyond the employment targets set for Member States. Even following the abandonment of the numerical targets for employment set at Lisbon and Stockholm, nevertheless this full employment goal has been retained.[291] The expression 'full employment' is equally ambiguous in the academic literature.[292] Historically, the concept has been used to mean 'having always more vacant jobs than unemployed men',[293] ie seeing employment at a living wage as a basic human right. But another approach, dominant amongst economists, views full employment as the minimum unemployment rate which puts no upward pressure on inflation—the 'natural rate of unemployment' or 'non-accelerating inflation rate of unemployment' (NAIRU).[294] In other words, an economy with full employment is an economy where employment is as high as it can be without labour shortages that

[290] CEC, *A new start for the Lisbon Strategy*, n. 150 above, at 27.

[291] Presidency Conclusions, Lisbon European Council, n. 1 above, and Presidency Conclusions, Stockholm European Council, n. 35 above. As the Commission noted prior to the 2005 Spring European Council, '[t]he overall employment rate has increased, but not sufficiently to have the Lisbon target in view. While the employment target for women is within reach, the target for older worker participation is still a way off, in spite of significant progress, and the average age of exit from the labour force moves up at an insufficient pace': CEC, *Commission Staff Working Document*, n. 143 above, at 2.

[292] Andrew Britton, 'Full Employment in the Industrialized Countries' (1997) 136:3 *International Labour Review*, 293–314.

[293] William Beveridge, *Full Employment in a Free Society* (London: Allen & Unwin, 1944) quoted in Britton, n. 292 above.

[294] Helen Lachs Ginsburg, June Zaccone, Gertrude Schaffner Goldberg, Shelia D. Collins, and Sumner M. Rosen, 'Editorial Introduction: The Challenge of Full Employment in the Global Economy' (1997) 18:1 *Economic and Industrial Democracy*, 5–34, at 7–8.

lead to rising wages and hence prices. But it is clear that the level of unemployment under this version of full employment could be very different from the level at which everyone who wants a job has got one.[295]

It is submitted that a better way to define full employment—a definition compatible with the goal of social cohesion to which the EU has also committed itself—is nearer to the Beveridge perspective. The ILO has long argued that 'the concept of full employment, suitably updated, should remain as a principal objective of economic and social policy',[296] and dismissing the concept of a 'natural rate' of unemployment, defines full employment as 'the absence of involuntary unemployment or the availability of jobs for all active job seekers'.[297]

Ultimately, as Eddy Lee points out, any definition of full employment also has to include notions of what constitutes an acceptable 'job'.[298] This seems to be what the Lisbon Strategy is, in part, trying to contribute to the Employment Strategy, with the focus on the 'quality' of jobs, and on *better*, not just *more*, jobs. This was very clearly elaborated in the Employment Guidelines for 2001. The four pillars were amended to incorporate five 'horizontal objectives', the first of which was as follows:

> 'Enhancing job opportunities and providing adequate incentives for all those willing to take up gainful employment with the aim of moving towards full employment recognising Member States' different starting positions, and recognising the fact that full employment is a goal of overall national economic policy. To this end, Member States should consider setting national targets for raising the rate of employment, in order to contribute to the overall European objectives of reaching by 2010 an overall employment rate of 70 per cent and an employment rate of more than 60 per cent for women. In pursuing these targets, the aim of increasing the quality of jobs should also be taken into consideration.'[299]

Whilst the post-war version of full employment is no longer possible or desirable, due to changes in work organization, increased female labour force participation and related changes in social attitudes,[300] it may be that the eagerness to move beyond this historical understanding is resulting in a rather modest version of full employment, lacking the social solidarity of the post-war ideal. To elaborate: the Commission's Communication in 2000 on the Social Policy Agenda reiterates the commitment to develop quality jobs, in particular

[295] Ed Crooks, 'How Full is Full Employment?' *BBC News Online: Business*, 27 September 1999.

[296] International Labour Organization, *World Employment 1996/97: National Policies in a Global Context* (Geneva: International Labour Office, 1996).

[297] ILO, 'Full Employment: Still Feasible and Highly Desirable', Press Release, Geneva, 26 November 1996, available at: *http://www.ilo.org/public/english/bureau/inf/pkits/emp1.htm* [accessed 10 April 2005].

[298] Eddy Lee, 'Is Full Employment Still Desirable and Feasible?' (1997) 18:1 *Economic and Industrial Democracy*, 35–53, at 47.

[299] Council Decision on Guidelines for the year 2001, n. 122 above.

[300] Britton, n. 292 above, at 297–300.

those linked to the knowledge-based economy.[301] However, the examples given of how such 'quality' will be developed in the context of the Employment Strategy focus almost entirely on what might be termed 'supply-side citizenship'[302] or 'supply-side egalitarianism'.[303] With the exception of 'giving more priority to equal opportunities', examples of 'quality' in employment concentrate on:

- improving people's employability and reducing skill gaps;
- developing and improving education and training systems so as to implement a strategy for the 'lifelong education of all';
- promoting entrepreneurship and job creation;
- removing all remaining barriers to the development of the services sector to enable job creation in services; and
- developing a comprehensive approach on adaptability of the workforce and companies to new forms of work organization.[304]

The 2000 Social Policy Agenda expired in 2005, to be replaced by a new Social Agenda which persevered with the aim of moving towards full employment, whilst acknowledging that the deadline of 2010 for achieving full employment was unrealistic.[305]

As Bo Stråth points out, one of the reasons the political commitment to full employment had originally been abandoned was that it was tied to the existence of labour markets contained within national boundaries, to a belief in Keynesian macro-economics, and to conventions of social responsibility—in particular, that the state would underwrite job security or provide income security—which were now fragmenting.[306]

Essentially, the discourse on 'modernizing' welfare states in the context of full employment means a shift from extensive employment protection and social benefits, towards an emphasis on investment in human capital, thus improving 'employability' and equipping individuals to be self-sufficient. The Employment Strategy has been equated with a 'Third Way' agenda due to its perspective on labour markets.[307] However, prior to the change of emphasis brought about by the Lisbon European Council in 2000, there was scant evidence of a genuine 'Third Way' solution within the Employment Strategy, if the 'Third Way' is correctly understood as an attempt to combine economic and social goals on an equal footing. The theoretical concept of the 'Third Way', which was for a time adopted by Tony Blair's Labour government, has been definitively

301 CEC, *Communication on the Social Policy Agenda*, n. 96 above, at para 4.1.1.1.

302 Raymond Plant, 'The Third Way', Friedrich-Robert-Stiftung, working paper 5/98 (1998).

303 Streeck, n. 168 above: 'Social cohesion is sought, not through equal outcomes, but through equal opportunity; and traditional concepts of solidarity are infused with a bourgeois spirit of efficiency and self-sufficiency, emphasizing individual effort and collective investment in competitiveness at least as much as social entitlements to minimal levels of reward or consumption'.

304 CEC, *Communication on the Social Policy Agenda*, n. 96 above, at para 4.1.1.1.

305 CEC, *Communication from the Commission on the Social Agenda*, Brussels, 9.2.2005, COM(2005) 33 final.

306 Stråth, n. 32 above.

307 Kenner, n. 196 above.

elaborated by Anthony Giddens as a critique of both neoliberalism and traditional social democracy.[308] 'Third Way' politics does, however, involve some commitment to the neoliberal agenda in relation to markets, rejecting planning, wary of state intervention, and believing in a stable fiscal and monetary environment. It does, nevertheless, share social democracy's commitment to social justice and social inclusion.[309]

What does bear comparison with 'Third Way' thinking in the context of *European*-level policy-making, is the post-Lisbon perspective on (national) welfare states. The 'Third Way' view of the welfare state is well captured in Raymond Plant's analysis, which deserves to be quoted at length:

> '[some] social democrats . . . have seen social rights as a form of social integration and cohesion following naturally the sense of belonging to a society and a political community that comes from civil and political rights. On this view, civil, political and social rights define the terms of membership and inclusion in a modern state. For the third way thinker, however, this is a mistake. Instead of social rights creating a robust sense of common citizenship, access as of right to state benefits on an unconditional basis has created privatism, lack of discipline, dependency, and a lack of involvement with the educational and social aspects of the labour market. Receiving a Giro through the post as part of welfare rights does not, in third way views, enhance a sense of citizenship. Like freedom, rights have to be linked to responsibilities and common obligations. Dutiless rights breed alienation, not inclusion.'[310]

The 'Third Way' approach is committed to social justice, but what might be described as a communitarian version of it. In the context of international economic integration and the (contestable) claim that the costs of the social democratic welfare state are no longer supportable, the social democratic version of full employment and social policy based on high public expenditure and national controls on capital are considered to be no longer feasible, *or desirable*. Instead, social justice is to be attained through reforming the welfare state around the work ethic, even around the *obligation* to work. In contrast to the social democratic view of citizenship (a form of citizenship which conferred a bundle of rights, independent of the market),

> 'supply side citizenship stresses that citizenship is an achievement, not a status, it is available through participating in the labour market and reaping the rewards that accrue from that, and investment in skills is part of equal opportunity as a right of citizenship in this new economic context'.[311]

Regardless of whether it is appropriate to equate the post-Lisbon consensus with the 'Third Way' approach,[312] policies to recalibrate ('activate') welfare states promote employability and increase labour market participation rates have a

[308] Anthony Giddens, *The Third Way: The Renewal of Social Democracy* (Cambridge: Polity Press, 1998) and *The Third Way and its Critics* (Cambridge: Polity Press, 2000).

[309] Plant, n. 302 above. [310] Ibid. [311] Ibid.

[312] Individual heads of state have, in the past, clearly identified their policies on recalibration of welfare states with the 'Third Way'. See, for example, the document by UK Prime Minister Tony

strong echo in the 'Third Way' view described above. The 'Third Way' under Tony Blair and 'Die Neue Mitte' under Gerhard Schröder are strongly supply-side orientated, much like the post-Lisbon Employment Strategy.[313] For example, renewed emphasis is placed on an 'active and dynamic welfare state', active rather than passive labour market policies and modernized systems of social protection. The BEPGs for 2000 put what is required more explicitly, and in so doing, mirror the economic orthodoxy of the labour market flexibility debate, explored in Chapter 2:

> 'progress with the reform of labour markets is mixed: while policies towards activation and prevention were implemented in many Member States, employment disincentives in tax and benefit systems have been tackled in only a few. Moreover, excessively rigid employment protection legislation should be reassessed more actively in order to identify means to foster job creation.'[314]

This is the sort of policy statement which prompted my comment, above, that the EU's version of full employment may well fall far short of social democratic ideals of solidarity and social rights. Raymond Plant goes to lengths to show that such a perspective on Welfare States is not purely neoliberal, since it retains as strong a belief in social justice, but it is nevertheless wary of state intervention, and seems perilously close to neoliberalism in its critique of public expenditure and endorsement of 'workfare'. Further evidence of the possible influence of 'Third Way' thinking on the EU strategy, in the context of the attainment of full employment, can be found in the report by Boeri, Layard and Nickell to Prime Ministers Blair and D'Alema:

> 'The Welfare-to-Work approach will not prevent long-term unemployment if individuals who receive offers from employers can instead choose to continue living on benefit. A system of complementary rights and responsibilities is needed, where the citizen can expect high-quality help in finding work, *but in return must take advantage of it or cease to draw benefits*. Once the state is channelling offers of work to everyone within the first year of unemployment, that would become in effect the maximum period for which benefits are available.'[315]

One rather blunt and critical assessment of the Lisbon approach to full employment and the BEPGs for 2000, which *does* equate it with a workfare-inspired Third Way (or even neoliberal) agenda, is provided by the European

Blair and German Chancellor Gerhard Schröder, *Europe: The Third Way/Die Neue Mitte* (London: The Labour Party, 1999).

[313] Kerstin Jacobsson, 'Employment and Social Policy Coordination. A New System of EU Governance' unpublished paper for the Scancor workshop *Transnational Regulation and the Transformation of States*, Stanford, 22–23 June 2001; manuscript on file with the author, at 7.

[314] Council Recommendation of 19 June 2000, n. 157 above, at para 2.1.

[315] Tito Boeri, Richard Layard and Stephen Nickell, *Welfare-to-Work and the Fight Against Long-Term Unemployment: Report to Prime Ministers Blair and D'Alema* (London: Centre for Economic Performance, LSE, 2000) summary available as Department for Education and Employment, Research Brief No 206, June 2000; emphasis added.

Economists for an Alternative Economic Policy in Europe:

'Whereas the concept [of full employment] was for decades embedded in a context of safe jobs, decent wages, social security and a certain standard of workers' rights and protection in a free society it becomes in the new context subordinated to the claims of employers and politicians who want to get everybody at work under whatsoever conditions in order to foster growth and international competitiveness.'[316]

The Alternative Economic Policy group is also extremely critical of what it identifies as an attempt to generalize the British approach to labour market reform, an approach influenced by US models of 'workfare' which are inconsistent with the values of the European social model.[317] Will the pursuit of higher labour market participation rates, so central to the new strategic goal post-Lisbon, inevitably mean a restriction of eligibility criteria for unemployment benefit and a reduction in benefit levels across Member States? Surely the emphasis on the *quality* of jobs since the Stockholm European Council will have an impact on the perceived 'workfare' orientation of the goal of full employment? As far as the first question is concerned, I would argue that the conclusions of subsequent European Council meetings have served to reinforce the assessment made above that the Lisbon version of full employment is a heavily supply-side orientated policy which strongly echoes the workfare-inspired 'Third Way' approach.

Three examples come to mind to support this argument: *first*, in order to 'make work pay' and encourage the search for jobs, Member States are urged to review aspects of tax and benefit systems such as conditionality of benefits, eligibility, duration, the replacement rate, the availability of in-work benefits, the use of tax credits, administrative systems and management rigour.[318] The work ethic is accordingly to be fortified by making prolonged reliance on benefits either impossible or less desirable. *Second* greater wage flexibility in the form of increased labour cost dispersion is deemed necessary to guarantee the EU's competitiveness and increase jobs growth:[319] wage developments should thus take greater account of productivity and skills differentials.[320] Thus, in contrast to traditional concepts of equality based on limiting the extent of wage dispersal throughout European

[316] European Economists for an Alternative Economic Policy in Europe, n. 37 above, at 5.

[317] Ibid., at 12–13.

[318] Presidency Conclusions, Barcelona European Council, n. 187 above, at para 32; Council Recommendation of 26 June 2003 on the Broad Guidelines of the Economic Policies of the Member States and the Community for the period 2003–2005, (2003/555/EC) OJ L 195, 01.08.2003, at 6.

[319] Increased wage flexibility has been a mantra of successive BEPGs since at least 1997, but this recommendation serves as an example of the extent to which employment and social policy must comply with the demands of EMU and EU economic policy more generally. For a fuller discussion of the impact of the Employment Strategy and EMU on Member States' wage bargaining systems, see Chapter 6.

[320] 'Some, particularly the low-skilled or those living in poorer regions, find themselves priced out of jobs, which points to the need both to improve the quality of education and training . . . and to allow wages to better reflect productivity': Council Recommendation of 26 June 2003, n. 318 above, at 6. See also Presidency Conclusions, Barcelona European Council, n. 187 above, at para 32.

economies, equality is now to be achieved by means of equalizing the employability of individuals. *Finally* (very much connected with the intermediate targets established at Stockholm for increasing labour market participation of older workers) there is the blunt rejection of the practice of early retirement as a solution to high unemployment, with Member States advised to pursue policies which both discourage the take-up of early retirement schemes and, more positively, increase opportunities for older workers to remain in the labour market.[321] This all bears striking similarity to the policy prescriptions of the OECD, whose employment and labour ministers were advising, in a contemporaneous reform agenda, that member countries should increase labour market participation by means of a comprehensive strategy for 'more and better jobs', including effective activation measures and employment services, combined with enhanced monitoring of social benefits; as well as changes in taxes and benefits so that work pays.[322]

As far as the second issue is concerned, questions as to the quality of jobs need to be examined in the context of the important developments in social policy and social rights which occurred since 2000, in particular the adoption of the Social Policy Agenda (renewed in 2005) and 'proclamation' of the Charter of Fundamental Rights by the Nice European Council.

## 4.4 The interaction between economic, employment and social policy

In spite of the fact that, since Lisbon, other Council formations are supposed to have an input into the content of the BEPGs, the Guidelines for 2000 were nevertheless devoid of any mention of social cohesion, or 'better' jobs, focusing more on 'employment disincentives in tax and benefit systems', and the removal of 'excessively rigid employment protection legislation' in order to promote job creation.[323] However, in accordance with the conclusions of the Lisbon European Council, and on the basis of the Commission Communication,[324] the Nice European Council approved the European Social Agenda at the end of the IGC in December 2000, the aim of which was to:

'ensure the modernisation and deepening of the European social model and place the emphasis on the promotion of quality in all areas of social policy. Quality of training,

[321] Council Recommendation of 26 June 2003, n. 318 above, at 9; Presidency Conclusions, Barcelona European Council, n. 187 above, at para 32. See Chapter 6 for a discussion of the mutual influence between EU and national policies, in particular, those of the UK which is moving more clearly towards a conditional, selective and work-orientated benefits system.

[322] Other steps in the OECD's recommended strategy included more equal access to lifelong learning; job-related training that enhances career prospects and addresses skill mismatches; and lower barriers to labour demand and improved functioning of labour markets so as to strike a balance between flexibility and security: OECD, Meeting of Employment and Labour Ministers, Paris, 29–30 September 2003, *Communiqué: Towards More and Better Jobs* (Paris: OECD, 2003).

[323] Council Recommendation of 19 June 2000, n. 157 above, at para 2.1.

[324] CEC, *Communication on the Social Policy Agenda*, n. 96 above.

quality in work, quality of industrial relations and quality of social policy as a whole are essential factors if the European Union is to achieve the goals it has set itself regarding competitiveness and full employment.'[325]

The Social Policy Agenda was an ambitious five-year programme of action, at the heart of which was the need to 'ensure a positive and dynamic interaction of economic, employment and social policies'.[326] Such an ambitious agenda was to be implemented through 'all existing Community instruments bar none':[327] the open method of coordination (OMC), legislation, social dialogue, the Structural Funds and the support programmes. Not surprisingly, therefore, there were few proposals for binding legislation.[328]

The European Parliament, however, whilst generally endorsing the goals of the Social Policy Agenda, went slightly further: *first*, in spelling out in no uncertain terms that there must not merely be 'interaction' between economic, employment and social policy, but that 'social policy must be a policy in its own right, with its own objectives and cannot be seen solely as an adjunct of economic and employment policy nor as a by-product of creating the single market'.[329] *Second*, although the Parliament welcomed the development of the open method of coordination, it adopted a rather pessimistic perspective towards the impact of OMC that, since such new forms of governance do not produce binding norms and decentralize decision-making, they *could* result in a rejection of social legislation at the European level, and an eventual erosion of the European social model. The Parliament therefore stressed that

'the Community legislative instrument (in the form of directives, regulations or collective agreements) will often be the most effective tool in the Union's areas of competence because it guarantees enjoyment of social rights, aims to establish minimum social standards at Community level and at the same time maintains democratic parliamentary influence and judicial controls over the Union's decisions.'[330]

Whilst it comes as no surprise that the Parliament is wary of a new form of governance which threatens its hard-won role in law-making (OMC completely side-steps the co-decision procedure of Article 251 EC) nevertheless, it is difficult to envisage how the Social Policy Agenda could be implemented so as to 'create a new balance between flexibility and security'[331] or to 'strengthen the role of social policy as a productive factor',[332] without resort to legislative instruments. There have been some important exceptions, particularly in the equality area: in the course of 2000, using the competence granted by Article 13(1) EC to enact

325 Presidency Conclusions, Nice European Council, 7–9 December 2000, Bull EU 12/2000, 1–37, Annex I: European Social Agenda, at para 26.

326 Ibid., para 8.

327 Ibid., para 28.

328 Phil Syrpis, 'Smoke Without Fire: The Social Policy Agenda and the Internal Market' (2001) 30:3 ILJ, 271–88.

329 European Parliament, Report on the Commission's Social Policy Agenda, A5-0291/2000 final, 16 October 2000, at 6.

330 European Parliament, n. 329 above, at 6.

331 European Social Agenda, n. 325 above, para 32.

332 Ibid., para 9.

equality legislation on a range of grounds, two directives were adopted. The first implemented the principle of equal treatment between persons irrespective of racial or ethnic origin;[333] the second established a general framework for equal treatment in employment, extending the principle of equal treatment to prevent discrimination on grounds of age, disability, religion and sexual orientation.[334] Further, with regard to legislation to impose an obligation on undertakings to inform and consult employees, agreement was finally reached in December 2001, and a directive enacted the following spring.[335]

To these developments, one must also add the Charter of Fundamental Rights of the European Union.[336] The lack of a clear set of *human* rights to balance the *economic* rights guaranteed in the Treaty of Rome has long been regarded as a key failing of a Community/Union which is so much more than a mere customs union. [337] Despite the long gestation of the Charter,[338] nevertheless it was not granted a legally binding status,[339] and was apparently intended to confer no new rights, but merely to make the existing rights protected at European level

[333] Council Directive 2000/43/EC of 29 June 2000 implementing the principle of equal treatment between persons irrespective of racial or ethnic origin, OJ L 180/22, 19.7.2000. See generally, Sandra Fredman, 'Equality: A New Generation?' (2001) 30:2 ILJ, 145–68; Catherine Barnard, Simon Deakin and Richard Hobbs, 'Capabilities and Rights: An Emerging Agenda for Social Policy?' (2001) 32:5 *Industrial Relations Journal*, 464–79.

[334] Council Directive 2000/78/EC of 27 November 2000, establishing a general framework for equal treatment in employment and occupation, OJ L 303/16, 2.12.2000.

[335] Directive 2002/14/EC of 11 March 2002 establishing a general framework for informing and consulting employees in the European Community, OJ L 80/29, 23.3.2002. The proposal for a directive had been around for some time, with the Commission forwarding the proposal based on Article 137(2) EC to the Parliament and the Council on 17 November 1998: Proposal for a Council Directive establishing a general framework for informing and consulting employees in the European Community, COM (1998) 612 final.

[336] Charter of Fundamental Rights of the European Union, adopted by a 'Solemn Proclamation' of the European Parliament, Council and Commission at the Nice European Council in December 2000, OJ C 364/01, 18.12.2000.

[337] Any rights discourse which did emerge all too often seemed derived from a market integrationist rationale. The role of the ECJ in developing what might be called a derivative or parasitical human rights competence is critiqued by Jason Coppel and Aidan O'Neill, 'The European Court of Justice: Taking Rights Seriously?' 29 CML Rev, 669–92. However, in the context of social rights, Gillian More argues how, 'despite the market-oriented origins of the principle of equal treatment, the principle has gradually started to shake off its market shackles': 'The Principle of Equal Treatment: From Market Unifier to Fundamental Right?' in Paul Craig and Gráinne de Búrca (eds.), *The Evolution of EU Law* (Oxford: OUP, 1999) at 517.

[338] Prior to the decision of the Cologne European Council that 'at the present stage of development of the European Union, the fundamental rights applicable at Union level should be consolidated in a Charter and thereby made more evident' (Presidency Conclusions, n. 130 above, at para 44), there had been at least three high-level reports calling for a charter of rights: Comité des Sages, *Report on Civic and Social Rights* (Brussels: CEC, 1996); Comité des Sages Report, *Leading by Example: A Human Rights Agenda for the EU for the year 2000* (Florence: European University Institute, 1998); Report of the Expert Group on Fundamental Rights, *Affirming Fundamental Rights in the European Union: Time to Act* (the Simitis Report) (Luxembourg: European Commission Unit V/D.2, 1999).

[339] Bruno de Witte, 'The Legal Status of the Charter: Vital Question or Non-Issue?' (2001) 8:1 *Maastricht Journal of European and Comparative Law*, 81–9.

'more visible'.[340] In reality, however, new rights have been created. The Charter is intended to contain rights drawn from the sources listed in its Preamble, such as the fundamental freedoms of the Treaty of Rome, the rights guaranteed by the European Convention on Human Rights and Fundamental Freedoms, rights derived from the 'constitutional traditions common to the Member States', from the European Social Charter and from the Community Charter of the Fundamental Social Rights of Workers. However, the Charter *is* innovative rather than merely declaratory, generating new rights, and even including clauses which are not rights as such, but statements of policy. In particular, the unconventional grouping of rights in the Charter, eschewing the traditional dichotomy between civil and political rights on the one hand, and social and economic rights on the other, means there is *potential* for an imaginative reading of these rights. With the rights grouped under six 'Chapters'—Dignity, Freedoms, Equality, Solidarity, Citizens' Rights and Justice—social and economic rights are thus scattered throughout the Charter, a move which places them on the same footing as civil and political rights.[341]

Although not legally binding, the Charter has nevertheless been taken into account by the Commission in its proposals for legislation.[342] Moreover, the Charter may well gain *de facto* legal force by virtue of being included in the general principles of EC law, and through the ECJ's jurisprudence more generally. An important example of the latter, in the case of social rights, is the *BECTU* case, in particular the opinion of the Advocate-General.[343] *BECTU* is significant not only for the affirmation that the Charter provides a 'substantive point of reference' in the Community context,[344] but also for the statement that

[340] Preamble to the Charter, n. 336 above.

[341] Barnard, Deakin and Hobbs, n. 333 above, at 468.

[342] '[I]t is clear that it would be difficult for the Council and the Commission, who are to proclaim it solemnly, to ignore in the future, in their legislative function, an instrument prepared at the request of the European Council by the full range of sources of national and European legitimacy acting in concert': CEC, Communication from the Commission on the Legal Nature of the Charter of Fundamental Rights of the European Union, Brussels, 11.10.2000, COM (2000) 644 final, at para 10. More recently, the Commission adopted a new mechanism to ensure that all future Commission legislative proposals are systematically and rigorously checked for compatibility with the Charter. The new mechanism is based on a process of systematic screening of legislation from the earliest preparatory work through to inter-service consultation: 'President Barroso proposes a new framework to "lock-in" a culture of fundamental rights in EU legislation', Press Release, IP/05/494, Brussels, 27 April 2005. In an internal communication of December 2004, the Commission announced that all important initiatives, particularly legislative initiatives, would be accompanied by an integrated assessment of their likely impact, including an analysis of their compliance with subsidiarity and their respect for fundamental rights as set out in the Charter of Fundamental Rights: see speech of Vice-President Franco Frattini, Commissioner for Justice, Freedom and Security, 25 January 2005, SPEECH/05/34.

[343] Case C-173/99, *R v Secretary of State for Trade and Industry, ex Broadcasting, Entertainment, Cinematographic and Theatre Union (BECTU)* [2001] ECR I-4881. See Giancarlo Ricci, '*BECTU*—An Unlimited Right to Annual Paid Leave', (2001) 30:4 ILJ, 401–8.

[344] Opinion of Advocate-General Tizzano, *BECTU*, n. 343 above, at para 28 of the Opinion; the ECJ, however, avoided making any reference to the Charter in its decision.

social rights, such as improvement of workers' health and safety at work, are not to be 'subordinated to purely economic considerations'.[345] However, whilst the Charter has been relied on in numerous decisions of the Court of First Instance and opinions of various Advocates-General, to date the Court of Justice has continued to draw directly on the European Convention on Human Rights whilst refusing to make any direct reference to the Charter, at least until it becomes legally binding.

Barnard, Deakin and Hobbs see developments such as the Social Policy Agenda, the new equality directives and the Charter as evidence of a 'lock-step progression of social rights and economic integration',[346] which could lend political support to the idea of rights as 'capabilities', as endorsed by the Supiot Report.[347] The concept of 'capabilities' argues that a range of social rights is necessary if meaningful participation in the market is to be possible: 'social rights . . . should be understood as institutionalised forms of capabilities which provide individuals with the means to realise the potential of their resource endowments and thereby achieve a higher level of economic functioning'.[348] The Supiot Report uses the term 'active security'[349] to describe this process, proposing a redesigned notion of security to accommodate the changes in the labour market and work organization. The central argument is that the paradigm of 'employment' should be replaced by the paradigm of 'labour force membership', based on the broader notion of 'work', rather than the restrictive criterion of 'employment', and that this broadened employment status should go hand in hand with various types of what are termed 'social drawing rights'.[350] In addition to recognizing the importance of non-marketable forms of work, such 'social drawing rights' would seem to contradict completely the trend identified in many Member States, towards the imposition of a duty to work (or some other form of benefits conditionality) in assessing eligibility for unemployment benefits, disability benefits and pensions.[351]

That said, it is difficult to accept this optimistic reading of the Charter wholeheartedly, since much of the Charter's innovative potential to entrench social rights and thereby counterbalance the economic agenda has now been put into doubt by the impact of the Treaty establishing a Constitution for Europe. The Charter was drafted 'as if' it would eventually to be incorporated into the Treaties, the understanding being that it would become legally binding if and when the Treaty establishing a Constitution for Europe was ratified.[352] The

[345] *BECTU*, n. 343 above, at para 51 of the Judgment. See the discussion in Sciarra, n. 195 above.

[346] Barnard, Deakin and Hobbs, n. 333 above, at 465.

[347] Supiot *et al.*, n. 239 above. See also Simon Deakin and Frank Wilkinson, 'Capabilities, Spontaneous Order and Social Rights' (2000) ESRC Centre for Business Research, University of Cambridge, Working Paper No 174.

[348] Deakin and Wilkinson, n. 347 above.

[349] Supiot *et al.*, n. 239 above, at 222.

[350] Ibid., at 55–56 and 221–2.

[351] Ibid., at 32–4.

[352] On 29 October 2004, the Heads of State or Government of the 25 Member States and the three candidate countries signed the Treaty establishing a Constitution for Europe which was

Constitutional Treaty, a product of the Convention on the Future of Europe convened by the European Council, was finally published in July 2003 and incorporates the text of the Charter as a sort of Bill of Rights. However, this has not been without some subtle changes to the text of the Charter: in particular, the Constitutional Treaty has arguably introduced a hierarchy between civil and political rights on the one hand, and social and economic rights on the other, by means of the distinction between 'rights' and 'principles'. Such a distinction suggests an unwillingness to give constitutional status to social and economic rights, in particular those which are deemed to require further state implementation or state expenditure.[353] Before the Convention on the Future of Europe some Member States' representatives felt unease that the Charter would commit them to costly social and economic rights. This led to a recommendation from the Convention Working Group on the Charter that the distinction between rights and principles be further clarified.[354] This 'clarification' has resulted in an addition to the Charter's 'General Provisions', Article II-52 of the Constitutional Treaty, which states that

> '[t]he provisions of this Charter which contain principles may be implemented by legislative and executive acts taken by Institutions and bodies of the Union, and by acts of Member States when they are implementing Union law, in the exercise of their respective powers. They shall be judicially cognisable only in the interpretation of such acts and in the ruling on their legality.'

The argument that key elements of the Charter have been diluted on incorporation into the Constitutional Treaty may well become moot if, as increasingly appears likely, the Constitutional Treaty in its present form is abandoned in response to negative plebiscites in a number of Member States.[355]

Whilst it is true that the Charter has the *potential* to add an enormously important supporting beam to the edifice of European social rights, nevertheless it is still the case that the much-emphasized 'interaction' (between economic, social and employment policies or between economic growth, employment and social cohesion),[356] runs the risk of privileging an economic rationale. The post-Lisbon vision of 'full employment' is far removed from the idea of economic security beyond the traditional employment relationship, as elaborated in the Supiot Report. As argued above, and as the examples given by Plant and

unanimously adopted by them on 18 June of that year: Treaty establishing a Constitution For Europe, OJ C 310/1, 16.12.2004. This Treaty can only enter into force when it has been adopted or ratified by each of the signatory countries in accordance with its own constitutional procedures.

[353] Diamond Ashiagbor, 'Economic and Social Rights in the European Charter of Fundamental Rights' (2004) 1 *European Human Rights Law Review*, 62–72.

[354] The work of the Convention was assisted by ten specialist Working Groups, such as the Working Group on the EU Charter of Fundamental Rights.

[355] Wolfgang Munchau, 'EU's misjudged No votes' *Financial Times*, 5 June 2005.

[356] CEC, *Communication on the Social Policy Agenda*, n. 96 above, at paras. 5, 8, 31 and throughout. See also, the CEC, *Communication on the Social Agenda* (2005), n. 305 above, at 2, 4 and 5.

Boeri *et al.* show, a logical end-point of the Employment Strategy's emphasis on 'more jobs' and 'active labour market policies' is a move towards 'workfare': that those who won't accept jobs will have their benefits denied or restricted. The recipe offered by the BEPGs, to meet the challenge of creating better as well as more jobs, is that 'Member States should take advantage of the favourable macroeconomic conditions to make the necessary structural improvements in labour markets'.[357] Particular measures suggested include pursuing equal opportunities, ensuring adequate provision of care facilities for children and other dependants, reforming early retirement schemes and encouraging lifelong learning *in order to* increase participation in the labour market, especially amongst women and older workers.[358] This is a rather instrumental view of social policy, and one is left with the impression that from the perspective of the main instrument for coordinating the economic policies of the European Union (the BEPGs) social policy still has the role that the European Parliament cautioned against—of being merely an adjunct of economic and employment policy.[359] Further, the BEPGs continue the 'disincentive' discourse: better use of the EU's human resource potential 'requires reviewing labour market regulation and institutions to diminish obstacles to labour demand and supply which they may pose'; and 'tax and benefit schemes should be further reformed to strengthen financial incentives for people to take up or stay in a job'.[360]

## 4.5 Jobs growth and the quality of jobs

In this context, one can question whether the Employment Strategy is 'good for employees'.[361] In addition to the emphasis on flexibility leading to possible deregulation of employment protection,[362] there is the concern whether the Employment Strategy can successfully reconcile quality with quantity in job creation. This is not a new dilemma, as the debate over the promotion of atypical work shows. The Employment Strategy promotes the use of atypical forms of work because these are considered to have advantages over traditional forms of work: encouraging the use of part-time work is seen as a means of increasing the level of employment[363] as well as improving competitiveness and productivity.[364] On the other hand, the use of certain forms of atypical work, especially where it is not entirely voluntary on the part of the worker, can lead to precisely the sort of labour market instability and social exclusion which the Employment Strategy is aiming to combat. Atypical workers have traditionally been excluded

[357] CEC, *Communication on the Social Policy Agenda*, n. 96 above, at 12. [358] Ibid., at 13.

[359] European Parliament, Report on the Commission's Social Policy Agenda, n. 329 above, at 6.

[360] Council Recommendation of 15 June 2001 on the broad guidelines of the economic policies of the Member States and the Community (2001/483/EC), OJ L 179/1, 2.7.2001, at 6.

[361] Ball, n. 87 above, at 366 ff.

[362] Ball, n. 87 above, at 368–70; see also the discussion in Section 4.2.2 above.

[363] CEC, *From Guidelines to Action*, n. 169 above, at 18.

[364] CEC, Green Paper: *Partnership*, n. 214 above, Introduction.

from employment protection; often, the very *purpose* of atypical work was to provide a way of circumventing legislative and collective regulations, and their associated costs.[365] This dilemma, highlighting a distinction between 'good' and 'bad' types of atypical work, was evident in the *Joint Employment Report 1999*, which praised the attempts made to reconcile flexibility with security referred to in Member States' implementation reports. However, the Report also noted that: 'this trend towards increased flexibility has reached an *excessive* proportion in Spain, where more than 90% of new contracts are temporary with a high rate of turnover'.[366] Also, as Antonio Lo Faro warns, pointing to the low percentage of 'voluntary' part-time work in Italy,[367]

> 'The fact that part-time work is highly involuntary clearly reveals that such contracts in Italy mainly involve unemployed persons forced to accept part-time employment as second-best, rather than potential participators who would be ready to join the labour force so long as they could work on a part-time basis. . . . The option to work part-time in Italy has more to do with a "negative" choice made by workers reluctantly renouncing a full-time job, than with a "positive" choice on the part of people willingly abandoning inactivity in search of a job compatible with family, study or training commitments.'[368]

Part-time work is one of the most prominent forms of atypical work which Member States are promoting, in the effort to encourage employment creation and modernize work organization, in line with successive Employment Guidelines. But it is by no means clear that Member States are matching the liberalization of labour market regulation (so as to encourage atypical work) with the requisite assurances that those working under such flexible contracts 'enjoy adequate security and higher occupational status, compatible with the needs of business *and the aspirations of workers*'.[369] In the Italian case, in order to meet the Lisbon targets, it is arguable that previous legislation—which was considered as reaching an acceptable trade-off 'between a quantitative spread and a qualitative increase in part-time work'—is to be replaced by legislation which risks privileging quantity over quality.[370]

The increasing importance given to performance indicators as the Employment Strategy has matured is due to their pivotal role in the benchmarking

[365] Jeffery, n. 221 above, at 210.

[366] CEC, *Joint Employment Report 1999*, n. 274 above, at para 4.3; emphasis added.

[367] The share of voluntary part-time workers across Europe—those who declare that they do not want to work more hours—is approximately 60 per cent of all part-time workers. However, this proportion is significantly lower in Spain (about 7 per cent), Belgium (about 8 per cent) and Italy (about 25 per cent): CEC, *Employment in Europe 2001: Recent Trends and Prospects* (Luxembourg: OOPEC, 2001) at 70. See also *Employment in Europe 2003: Recent Trends and Prospects* (Luxembourg: OOPEC, 2003) chapter 4: Flexibility, security and quality in work.

[368] Antonio Lo Faro, 'Adaptable Employment and Private Autonomy in the Italian Part-time Reform', in Silvana Sciarra, Paul Davies and Mark Freedland (eds.), *Employment Policy and the Regulation of Part-Time Work in the European Union: A Comparative Analysis* (Cambridge: CUP, 2004) at 166.

[369] Guideline 14, Council Decision of 19 January 2001, n. 122 above; emphasis added.

[370] Lo Faro, n. 368 above, at 167–8.

process, and in the open method of coordination more generally: indicators are essential to enable 'progress evaluation and international comparability' and to facilitate peer review of Member States' performance.[371] Inevitably, such indicators measure *quantity* rather than *quality* of new jobs. The focus on quantitative indicators is not surprising, given the desire for international comparability—the comparison of EU and Eurozone (un)employment rates with those of the US (and to a lesser extent, Japan) being a perennial feature of Eurostat reports on unemployment. The preoccupation with quantity is, however, ironic given the extensive debate among policy-makers and academics over the *quality* of the jobs created by the US economy, with some arguing that the growth in jobs in the US during the 1980s and 1990s is linked to an increase in inequality, in particular, wage inequality.[372]

The question for the EU, therefore, is whether the push towards 'full employment' can avoid this apparent trap.[373] The *Joint Employment Report 1997* relied on eight underlying labour market indicators, which were then transformed into 'radar charts'.[374] By 2000, the number of key indicators had grown, but they remained heavily biased towards measurements of the numbers of jobs created.[375]

[371] CEC, *Joint Employment Report 2000*, n. 278 above, at 82. See also the discussion in Chapter 5.

[372] See Chapter 2, Section 3. A critical examination of the evidence on jobs growth and quality is provided by Susan Houseman, who argues that 'evidence on the quality of net new jobs being generated in the U.S. economy in recent years is mixed.... Arguably the real story about deteriorating quality in the United States is one of deteriorating real wages across a broad spectrum of middle and low wage jobs—new and existing—and the accompanying increase in wage inequality': 'Job Growth and the Quality of Jobs in the US Economy' (1995) *Labour: Review of Labour Economics and Industrial Relations*, (IIRA) S93–S124, at S107.

[373] Gosling and Lemieux argue that the extent and pattern of wage inequality in the UK and the US became increasingly similar between 1979 and 1998, attributing this convergence to 'US style' reforms in the UK labour market: Amanda Gosling and Thomas Lemieux, 'Labour Market Reforms and Changes in Wage Inequality in the United Kingdom and the United States' in David Card, Richard Blundell, Richard Freeman (eds.), *Seeking a Premier Economy: The Economic Effects of British Economic Reforms, 1980–2000* (Chicago: University of Chicago Press, National Bureau of Economic Research Comparative Labour Market Series, 2004). See also John Schmitt, Lawrence Mishel and Jared Bernstein, 'Dangers for European Workers in the U.S. Economic Model', (1998) *WorkingUSA*, May/June 1998, 73–85.

[374] '[G]eneric radar charts are merely another mode of presentation of data found in many standard statistical and graphics software programs.... Radar charts have four (or more) axes integrated into a single radial figure on which data for one or more countries (cases) can be presented simultaneously. Radar charts are useful in particular for comparing performance on multiple dimensions simultaneously or for comparing cases with multiple performance dimensions. The name "radar" chart comes from their resemblance to a radar screen', Hugh Mosley and Antje Mayer, 'Benchmarking National Labour Market Performance: A Radar Chart Approach' Discussion Paper FS I 99–202, Wißenschaftszentrum Berlin für Sozialforschung, 1999. This working paper was also published as a report prepared for European Commission, Directorate-General V, Employment, Industrial Relations and Social Affairs (DGV/A2).

[375] By 2001, there were 9 employment indicators: total employment rate, rate for males, females, ages 15–24, 25–54, 55–64, full-time equivalent (FTE) employment rate, FTE rate for males, FTE for females; 9 unemployment indicators: total unemployment rate, rate for males, females, youth unemployment, youth unemployment male, youth unemployment female, long-term unemployment (LTU) rate, LTU male, LTU female. Other key indicators include: participation in training,

This bias is briefly noted in the *Joint Employment Report 2001*: '[f]ollowing the Stockholm Summit, priority areas for the further development of indicators are quality of work and equal opportunities (gender pay gap and care services for children/other dependants)'.[376] Thus, by the time of the Laeken Summit, the European Council was able to report on the adoption of 'a series of economic and social structural indicators', including indicators on quality in work and social exclusion, as well as key indicators for sustainable development, which would make it possible to see more clearly how each Member State is performing.[377] Nevertheless, Laeken simultaneously argued that '[w]e must accelerate our efforts to achieve by 2010 the 70 per cent employment rate agreed in Lisbon. That must be the first objective of the European Employment Strategy'.[378]

The Lisbon, Stockholm and Nice European Councils all affirmed the importance of 'better' jobs or 'quality' in employment. The finishing touches to the Lisbon Strategy were made by the Göteborg European Council, which added a third, environmental, dimension to the Union's political commitment to economic and social renewal, and confirmed, with the European Union's Sustainable Development Strategy, the need to ensure the consistency of the different policy strands with long-term objectives.[379]

Does this mean that the discourse on full employment is less guided by market rationality? The 'disincentive discourse' is, however, still prevalent in the BEPGs: extensive work protection and social benefits are regarded as a disincentive to take up work and therefore as an obstacle to more jobs,[380] a perspective which accords with the neoclassical theories on unemployment surveyed in Chapter 2, but reflects something of a discrepancy in the views of the Employment and Social Affairs Directorate-General of the Commission and the DG for Economic and Financial Affairs, and correspondingly between labour market and social affairs ministers and finance ministers.[381]

The Stockholm European Council, the first of the new 'Spring European Councils' especially devoted to economic and social issues, is particularly important in reinforcing the Lisbon commitment to 'better' jobs. Whilst setting intermediate targets for achieving full employment, aiming for employment rates of 67 per cent overall and 57 per cent for women by January 2005, as well as a

early school leavers, rate of self-employment, share of employees in non-standard employment; and economic indicators such as real GDP growth and labour productivity growth. CEC, *Joint Employment Report 2001*, n. 200 above, at 92–3. See n. 386 below and accompanying text for a discussion of the growing importance of qualitative indicators.

[376] CEC, *Joint Employment Report 2001*, n. 200 above, at 19.

[377] Presidency Conclusions, Laeken European Council, 14 and 15 December 2001, Bull EU-12/2001, 1–26, at para 22.

[378] Presidency Conclusions, Laeken European Council, n. 377 above, at para 23.

[379] Presidency Conclusions, Göteborg European Council, 15 and 16 June 2001, Bull EU-6/2001, 1–43, at paras 19–21.

[380] Council Recommendation of 19 June 2000, n. 157 above, at para 2.1.

[381] Jacobsson, n. 313 above, at 7.

new target of 50 per cent employment for older workers (aged 55 to 64) by 2010,[382] the Stockholm Council also gave a much fuller definition of what 'quality' would involve:

'Regaining full employment not only involves focusing on more jobs, but also on better jobs. Increased efforts should be made to promote a good working environment for all including equal opportunities for the disabled, gender equality, good and flexible work organisation permitting better reconciliation of working and personal life, lifelong learning, health and safety at work, employee involvement and diversity in working life'.[383]

It was also here that the decision was taken to include quality of work as a general objective in the Employment Guidelines for 2002. What is arguably implicit in the above definition of quality is that improving the quality of work would also involve recourse to traditional regulatory methods: the Swedish Presidency very much considered itself responsible for providing the impetus for the Employment and Social Affairs Council to be able reach political agreement in June 2001 on a common position on three directives—equal treatment between men and women in the workplace, information and consultation of employees, and protection of employees exposed to risks from noise.[384] As the Swedish Secretary of State for Employment has argued, social matters also require old, hard law methods.[385]

Drawing on the conclusions of the Stockholm European Council, the Commission's Communication on Quality recognized the relative and multi-dimensional nature of employment quality, and thus proposed a set of indicators covering ten main elements of quality, along two broad dimensions. The first dimension, the objective and intrinsic characteristics of the job, would include job satisfaction, remuneration, non-pay rewards, working time, skills and training and prospects for career advancement, job content, match between job characteristics and worker characteristics. The second, the work and wider labour market context, would include gender equality, health and safety, flexibility and security, access to jobs, work–life balance, social dialogue and worker

[382] Presidency Conclusions, Stockholm European Council, n. 35 above, at para 9.

[383] Ibid., at para 26.

[384] Council, Employment and Social Policy, Press Release No 9397/01, 11 June 2001, Luxembourg. All three proposed directives were enacted not long after: Directive 2002/73/EC of 23 September 2002 amending Council Directive 76/207/EEC on the implementation of the principle of equal treatment for men and women as regards access to employment, vocational training and promotion, and working conditions OJ L 269/15, 5.10.2002; Directive 2002/14/EC of 11 March 2002 establishing a general framework for informing and consulting employees in the European Community, OJ L 80/29, 23.3.2002; Directive 2003/10/EC of the European Parliament and of the Council of 6 February 2003 on the minimum health and safety requirements regarding the exposure of workers to the risks arising from physical agents (noise) (Seventeenth individual Directive within the meaning of Article 16(1) of Directive 89/391/EEC) OJ L 42/38, 15.2.2003.

[385] Anna Ekström (Secretary of State for Employment Policy during the 2001 Swedish Presidency), 'Employment Policy During the Swedish Presidency: Results and Conclusions for the Future', speech given at the European University Institute, Florence, 29 October 2001.

involvement, diversity and non-discrimination.[386] Such a categorization is intended to provide a framework of analysis of quality in work, so that clear policy objectives and standards can be identified, and appropriate indicators developed to measure performance against those objectives. The imprimatur of the Swedish Presidency is very evident in the Commission's discourse on quality: the emphasis on quality envisages a virtuous circle wherein 'social policies are not simply an outcome of good economic performance and policies but are at the same time an input and a framework':[387]

> 'increasing quality in work by increasing skills and/or by increasing job satisfaction may increase productivity. Increasing quality by providing a better work–life balance, and by increasing the attractiveness of work, may contribute to increasing the overall employment rate and the employment rate of women and older workers. Increasing quality may contribute to increasing employability and adaptability, it may facilitate organisational change and increase access. In this way, increasing quality in work can form part of a virtuous circle of increasing productivity, rising living standards and sustainable economic growth'.[388]

Accordingly, a broad approach to quality in work implies not only pay and minimum standards but attention to the character of individual jobs and the character of the wider work environment including how the labour market works as a whole, particularly with respect to movement between jobs, and in and out of the labour market.[389]

Performance indicators are again important, and as the Employment Strategy has evolved post-Lisbon, so too have the indicators. Post-Lisbon, in an effort to promote 'better' not just 'more' jobs, there has been a shift to measuring 'qualitative' aspects of employment, where hitherto the emphasis had been on observing quantitative indicators. Numerous indicators of quality in work are now embedded in the Employment Strategy, building on those adopted at the Laeken summit. Accordingly, Member States are judged by how successfully they meet targets in relation to factors such as the percentage of undeclared work, the numbers of working poor, job satisfaction rates, the gender pay gap, and rates of gender segregation.[390] Even with the development of indicators to evaluate quality in work and social inclusion, there remain difficulties in reconciling the promotion of flexibility and wage dispersion, on the one hand, with the labour standards necessary to achieve work of 'high skill, high trust and high quality', on the other. This is likely to continue to be the case as long as labour standards, such as gender equality, are seen as means to a particular goal (full employment and competitiveness) rather than as objectives in themselves.

[386] CEC, *Framework for Investing in Quality*, n. 96 above, at 8 and 10.
[387] Ibid., at 5; reference omitted. [388] Ibid., at 8. [389] Ibid., at 7.
[390] Employment indicators have grown in number, type and complexity from the relatively straightforward first generation of indicators in 1997, numbering eight in total, to over sixty indicators in 2004: CEC, *Joint Employment Report 2003–4*, COM (2004) 24 final (Luxembourg: OOPEC, 2003) at 97–116.

Repeated annual *Employment in Europe* reports have analysed quality in work in European labour markets, finding wages—as well as job security, access to training, and career development—to be 'crucial determinants of both subjective job satisfaction and objective job quality'. Whilst generally dismissing fears that increasing employment in the service sector would lead to a proliferation of dead-end jobs of low quality,[391] this upbeat assessment of the harmonious interaction between social and economic policy does acknowledge that new and flexible employment patterns may conflict with some of the main dimensions of job quality, especially in jobs which combine low or no skills with temporary or precarious status and lack of career development opportunities.

Indeed, the Commission's own report on trends in employment[392] found some evidence that changing forms of employment and ever-tighter rhythms of work have prevented working conditions from improving.[393] Although part-time workers report rates of job satisfaction similar to full-time workers, the quality of their jobs—in terms of earnings, job protection and career prospects—is mixed. More worryingly, over a third of temporary contractual relationships can generally be described as involuntary: 'Involuntary temporary contracts seem particularly pronounced in Spain, Greece, Belgium, Portugal, Sweden and Finland, with more than half of all employed in temporary contracts declaring themselves to be so [involuntarily]'.[394] Therefore, an increase in the employment rate brought about by an increase in the use of temporary contracts or involuntary part-time work is problematic to the aim of ensuring quality in employment, since both these forms of atypical work are generally related to strong degrees of workers' dissatisfaction with their jobs.[395] The conclusion of the report for 2003 is that '[w]hile according to these criteria, the majority of jobs in the EU are of relatively high quality, *up to a quarter of Europeans remain in jobs of relatively low quality*, having either low pay, and/or a lack of job security, access to training or career development'.[396] A separate review of progress in 2003 concluded that, whilst there had been some improvements, for example, in rising levels of educational attainment and skills, nevertheless, there was 'scope for considerable improvement under each of the ten dimensions of quality'.[397]

The policy documents speak of the synergies between quality in work, productivity, and employment, with a recent annual employment report asserting that quality in work and subjective job satisfaction are positively correlated with employment performance and labour market participation. In

[391] CEC, *A Framework for Investing in Quality*, n. 96 above, at 9.
[392] CEC, *Employment in Europe 2001: Recent Trends and Prospects*, above n. 367.
[393] Ibid., at 66.
[394] Ibid., at 69. In 2000, 14.5 per cent of women and 12.5 per cent of men in employment were in temporary contracts: ibid., at 17.
[395] Ibid., at 71.
[396] CEC, *Employment in Europe 2003*, n. 367 above, at 126, emphasis added.
[397] CEC, Communication *Improving Quality in Work: A Review of Recent Progress*, COM (2003) 728 final (Luxembourg: OOPEC, 2003) at 3.

particular, for women, 'greater shares of jobs of higher quality are associated with higher female labour force participation and employment'.[398] There is a 'virtuous circle': improvements in the quality of work are viewed instrumentally in the European employment policy discourse as having a key role to play in increasing labour force participation. The post-Lisbon aim of reconciling economic, employment and social policy is thereby reinforced by the assertion that there is a 'positive link' between overall employment performance and job quality: for example, that those who move from unemployment to jobs of low quality, in particular jobs without training opportunities, often remain at high risk of becoming unemployed again, with almost a third of these workers unemployed again a year later, in comparison to around 10 per cent for those in jobs of high quality.[399]

It is not clear how quality in employment, among the dimensions mentioned above, is to be reconciled with the requirements of full employment, since this is understood in the EU discourse to require a repositioning of welfare state provision and employment protection away from 'protecting' those in jobs towards 'facilitating' workers' employability and mobility between jobs. The Lisbon version of full employment would appear to necessitate greater wage flexibility in the form of increased labour cost dispersion, and relaxation of the 'overly restrictive elements of employment protection legislation';[400] in all, a risk of privileging quantity over quality. It therefore remains to be seen whether the efforts of the EU institutions to incorporate a discourse on 'quality' into the discourse on 'quantity' can prevent the pursuit of higher labour market participation rates leading to low quality jobs or a workfare agenda.

## 5. Conclusions: the legacy of Lisbon

'Just think what Europe could be. Think of the innate strengths of our enlarged Union. Think of its untapped potential to create prosperity and offer opportunity and justice for all its citizens. Europe can be a beacon of economic, social and environmental progress to the rest of the world.' (European Commission 2005)[401]

The above quotation would seem to suggest that, far from scaling down the ambitions of the Lisbon European Council meeting, the relaunch of the Lisbon Strategy is seen within the EU institutions as an opportunity to promote, and possibly even to export, the European model. However, the reality is that, in

[398] CEC, *Employment in Europe 2002: Recent Trends and Prospects* (Luxembourg: OOPEC, 2002) at 10.
[399] Ibid., at 6
[400] Council Recommendation of the 25 June 2003 on the Broad Guidelines of the Economic Policies of the Member States and the Community for the period 2003–2005, OJ L 195, 01.08.2003, at para 2.2.
[401] CEC, 'A new start for the Lisbon Strategy', n. 150 above, at 3.

the wake of the economic downturn which EU Member States experienced in the years immediately following the Lisbon meeting, it was clear that the ambitious targets of Lisbon had to be modified. It was hoped that the Barcelona European Council, coming two years after the 'bold and ambitious' Lisbon Council, would give new impetus to the Lisbon strategy and to economic policy coordination.[402] However, the economic context was to be much less favourable than at Lisbon: the economic slowdown in the United States, exacerbated by the uncertainty following the terrorist attacks on the United States and the subsequent political and military situation, has had major repercussions in the European Union. As the Commission's Synthesis Report to the 2002 Spring European Council highlighted, business and consumer confidence, already fragile, weakened further; growth forecasts for the EU for 2001 and 2002 were sharply cut back; business investment slowed considerably as firms of all sizes in the EU waited to see the direction in which the economy was heading; the four-year fall in unemployment was interrupted and job creation slowed considerably.[403]

Nevertheless, the preparations for the Spring European Council suggested a consensus *first*, that European financial markets would be able to absorb the shock well, greatly aided by the arrival of the euro, and that the downturn reflected a largely cyclical change in the global economy, which had been compounded by an unprecedented set of political and economic events. *Second*, that there was no need to question 'basically sound economic fundamentals' or the need to pursue the Lisbon strategy.[404] In this context, the Barcelona European Council focused its priorities on closing the 'delivery gap' on economic and structural reforms, by speeding up progress towards the Lisbon goals. The main priority of the then Spanish prime minister José María Aznar, when outlining his hopes for the Barcelona summit, was the need to inject 'more momentum' into the Lisbon strategy.[405] Similarly, the UK prime minister Tony Blair branded the summit a 'make or break' one for the EU,[406] and argued in his foreword to the Treasury White Paper *Economic Reform in Europe*, that Barcelona must speed up the pace of progress and give a clear signal with regard to reforming Europe's labour markets.[407] Barcelona's main outcome, on liberalization of energy (as opposed to labour) markets, nevertheless fell short of the original hopes of the Commission and the Spanish Presidency: the European

[402] CEC, Communication from the Commission to the Spring European Council in Barcelona (Synthesis Report) *The Lisbon Strategy: Making Change Happen*, Brussels, 15.1.2002, COM (2002) 14 final, at 1 and 3.

[403] Ibid., at 5–6.

[404] Ibid., at 6.

[405] Peter Norman, 'EU leaders take positive view of talks outcome', *Financial Times*, 18 March 2002.

[406] Ian Black, 'Blair allied with European right in summit labour talks', *The Guardian*, 16 March 2002.

[407] HM Treasury White Paper, *Realising Europe's Potential: Economic Reform in Europe*, Cm 5318 (London: HMSO, 2002) at ii.

Council only managed to reach agreement on the liberalization of the *commercial* energy market 'as of 2004'.[408]

Taking the summit as a whole,[409] the key philosophy behind Barcelona can be summed up in three oft-repeated words: simplification, implementation, liberalization. With regard to liberalization of markets, under the heading of 'connecting European economies', the summit reached conclusions on integrating financial markets, and opening up European energy, transport and communications markets.[410] Further, in order to create a favourable environment for entrepreneurship and competitiveness, and hence job creation, it was held essential to have a well functioning internal market, which would necessitate full implementation of all internal market legislation.[411] The Barcelona summit also echoed the conclusions of the Laeken European Council, in endorsing the recommendations of the Mandelkern Group on Better Regulation[412] for improving and simplifying the regulatory environment, with particular emphasis on the need to reduce the administrative burden on small-and medium-sized enterprises.[413] Moreover, having reviewed progress made in the first two years of the Lisbon strategy, the European Council concluded that although there had been important successes, progress had been too slow, so that the objective was now to 'simplify and consolidate' the Lisbon strategy, so as to ensure more effective implementation of the decisions already taken.[414] This focus on 'delivery' and 'effective implementation' became a mantra repeated at the following Spring European Council meetings in 2003 and 2004.[415]

[408] Presidency Conclusions, Barcelona European Council, n. 187 above, at para 37. The original goal, the full liberalization—including household users—of the electricity market in 2003 and of gas in 2004 was blocked by the two French presidential contenders, President Jacques Chirac and Prime Minister Lionel Jospin, who feared a trade union backlash during the 2002 election campaign: Norman, n. 405 above.

[409] I refer to Part I of the Presidency Conclusions (n. 187 above), which deals with the traditional subject matter of the Spring European Council; Part II deals with the future of Europe and external relations.

[410] Presidency Conclusions, Barcelona European Council, n. 187 above, at paras 35–42.

[411] Ibid., at paras 15 and 16.

[412] High-Level Advisory Group (the 'Mandelkern Group') on Better Regulation, Final Report, 13 November 2001 (Luxembourg: OOPEC, 2001). This group was established by EU Ministers for Public Administration in November 2000, following the long-expressed desire to simplify regulation as a prerequisite for the achievement of the EU-wide single market. The conclusion of the group was that, although regulation is essential to achieve the aims of public policy in many areas, it is also essential to ensure that regulation is only used when appropriate, and that it is of high quality, so as to avoid imposition of unnecessary burdens on businesses, citizens and public administrations, or the damage to firms' competitiveness that comes from increased costs and market distortions (particularly for small firms).

[413] Presidency Conclusions, Barcelona European Council, n. 187 above, at para 19.

[414] Ibid., at para 4.

[415] Presidency Conclusions, Brussels European Council, 20 and 21 March 2003, Bull EU 3/2003, 1–49; Presidency Conclusions, Brussels European Council, 25 and 26 March 2004, n. 240 above.

The overall tone of the recommendations on the Employment Strategy is to further reinforce the Lisbon emphasis on increasing labour market participation: 'the revised Employment Strategy should focus on raising the employment rate by promoting employability and by removing obstacles and disincentives to take up or remain in a job, while preserving high protection standards of the European social model'.[416] One of the consequences of the Lisbon strategy is that some of the objectives which advocates of the original Employment Title had failed to get included in the Amsterdam Treaty, have now been introduced into the Employment Strategy by means of 'soft law'. One example is the objective of 'full employment', which was rejected during the Amsterdam IGC in favour of a commitment to a 'high level of employment'; another is the Parliament's proposal that the BEPGs should take account of the impact of economic policies on employment, and ensure the combating of economic and social exclusion.[417] After Lisbon, the BEPGs are now supposed to 'focus increasingly on the medium- and long-term implications of structural policies and on reforms aimed at promoting economic growth potential, employment and social cohesion'.[418] Furthermore, after Göteborg, the Lisbon Strategy is also concerned with the interaction of economic, employment, social *and* environmental policies—economic, social and environmental policies must be dealt with in a 'mutually reinforcing way'.[419]

However, as far as the employment/economic policy axis is concerned, it is arguable that in spite of the new emphasis on 'better' jobs and the requirements of the Social Policy Agenda, the Luxembourg process is still very much circumscribed by other processes in the field of economic governance. To elaborate: the Lisbon strategy is based on the understanding that 'no new process' is needed, that the existing Broad Economy Policy Guidelines and the Luxembourg, Cardiff and Cologne processes offer the necessary instruments, provided they are simplified and better coordinated.[420] Naturally, this leaves unchanged the Treaty requirements that national employment policies must be consistent with the BEPGs (Article 126(1) EC), as must the annual Employment Guidelines (Article 128(2) EC). Thus, the BEPGs are the cornerstone of the whole strategy, and the site where any 'balancing' of competing values must occur. Furthermore, by continuing with the three 'processes', albeit better coordinated, Lisbon is also essentially ensuring that the Employment Pact which was launched at the Cologne European Council is very much intact. The statement of the Cologne European Council therefore still holds true, that '[t]he task of creating the conditions for more employment and growth, which is primarily a matter for

[416] Presidency Conclusions, Barcelona European Council, n. 187 above, at para 31.
[417] European Parliament, DG for Committees and Delegations, *Initial Analysis of the Treaty of Amsterdam*, n. 48 above.
[418] Presidency Conclusions, Lisbon European Council, n. 1 above, at para 35.
[419] Presidency Conclusions, Göteborg European Council, n. 379 above, at para 19.
[420] Presidency Conclusions, Lisbon European Council, n. 1 above, at para 35.

Member States, must be based on a European strategy of structural reforms and a balanced macroeconomic policy mix'.[421] This process was ultimately consolidated and formalized in 2005, with the incorporation of the Employment Guidelines into the Integrated Guidelines.

In addition, even allowing for the BEPGs' proposed focus on employment and social cohesion, the interaction between the BEPGs and the three processes of economic governance results in an Employment Strategy which gives priority to structural adjustment, with any 'balancing' of competitiveness and social protection very much biased in favour of the former. This is further illustrated by the direction taken within the Barcelona European Council, and the earlier Commission Report on the Implementation of the 2001 Broad Economic Policy Guidelines, written by the Directorate-General for Economic and Financial Affairs.[422] Whilst commending Member States' progress in invigorating labour markets—due in part to wage moderation, more flexible contracts and tax reductions targeted to the low end of the wage distribution—the Commission reports that efforts need to be stepped up:

> 'Advancement in reforming tax and benefit systems to make them more employment friendly has been limited in 2001. The recent tax cuts need to be followed up by broader reforms of employment protection legislation and benefit systems in order to increase the incentive to employ and supply labour.'[423]

Such emphasis on reform of protective legislation, benefit systems and other 'disincentives' to job creation can be seen as one of the true legacies of Lisbon, a thread running consistently through post-Lisbon policy pronouncements from Presidency Conclusions and BEPGs to the report of the Economic and Financial Affairs Directorate-General. Such a discourse resonates strongly with the 'supply-side citizenship' approach of the Third Way, and is committed to integrating economic policy objectives with social policy concerns *on its own terms*. The Lisbon strategy talks of 'modernizing the European social model by investing in people and building an active welfare state'. To this, Barcelona adds that '[a]n active welfare state should encourage people to work, as employment is the best guarantee against social exclusion'. Ultimately, this discourse on 'modernizing' welfare states in order to achieve full employment necessitates a shift from extensive employment protection and social benefits, towards investment in human capital, with the aim of improving 'employability' and self-sufficiency of individuals. Thus, social inclusion is to be achieved by equalizing the marketability and employability of individuals, rather than protecting them from the

[421] Presidency Conclusions, Cologne European Council, n. 130 above; Annex I to the Presidency Conclusions, at 7.

[422] CEC, Report on the Implementation of the 2001 Broad Economic Policy Guidelines, Brussels, 21.02.2002, ECFIN/16/02-EN.

[423] CEC, Press Release 'Commission assesses the implementation of the 2001 Broad Economic Policy Guidelines', Brussels, 21 February 2002, DN: IP/02/282.

market. In response to the question whether Lisbon amounts to a strategic turning point in EU social and economic policy, the answer is a qualified affirmative, with the caveat that this transition is occurring concurrently with a *continuation* of growth- and stability-orientated macro-economic policies, sound public finances and comprehensive structural reforms of labour, product and capital markets.

The achievement of Lisbon was to synthesize competing ideological perspectives, by urging that EU economic reform and liberalization of markets could co-exist with the European social model: that social policies were a necessary component of successful economic performance; and that reforms such as reductions in employment protection legislation, reductions in non-wage labour costs, and 'activation' of benefit and pensions systems would not lead to a deterioration of the welfare state. Barcelona developed this strategy further, with an even greater emphasis on the need to 'liberalize' markets and reform benefits and pensions systems. Most recently, the Spring European Council in 2005 has further underlined the philosophy of 'harmonious synergies'—that the quest for full employment through raising employment rates and extending working life is the best hope for retaining the European social model. However, as we have seen, the measures chosen to attain the goal of full employment, against the backdrop of the BEPGs, do not yet provide firm evidence that such contradictory objectives can be adequately reconciled.

# 5

# 'Soft law', new governance and the Employment Strategy

## 1. Introduction

The regulatory *objectives* behind the change in policy post-Lisbon, which were explored in Chapter 4, are closely connected to the regulatory *techniques* required to bring such policies to fruition. This chapter will accordingly discuss in more detail the wider constitutional and institutional implications of the innovative forms of governance to which the Employment Strategy has given rise, in particular, the 'open method of coordination'.

The emergence of the new regulatory techniques has been evolutionary, rather than revolutionary: indeed, the core of the Employment Strategy, the Luxembourg Process, owes much to the multilateral employment monitoring procedure introduced by the Essen European Council in 1994. Instead of a dramatic transition from one form of governance to another, what we are witnessing with the evolution of the Employment Strategy is coexistence of several forms of governance. Long-standing departures from the 'classic' Community method of law- and policy-making, such as 'comitology' and social dialogue, will therefore be explored, for the light they cast on the new 'soft law' mechanisms of the Employment Strategy.

Adopting a critical perspective on the new 'open method of coordination', this chapter argues that, through its creative use of 'soft law' mechanisms, the evolving Employment Strategy has the *potential* to forge a middle course through the regulatory choices facing the EU, between full harmonization, on the one hand, and mutual recognition or regulatory competition, on the other. But difficulties and tensions remain within this approach: I argue that the 'soft' coordination of the open method does in fact have quite a 'hard' impact, placing powerful political pressure on Member States to comply with centrally designed policies, and constraining their policy choices. Further, I question whether—in the context of an explicitly 'hard' economic policy coordination backed by sanctions—a form of governance which eschews centralized social policy norms can adequately ensure a core of social rights, below which no Member State can fall. In other words: how can 'soft law' steer this middle course without resort to 'hard law' mechanisms establishing the normative framework?

## 2. The institutional and constitutional impact of the Employment Strategy

The roles of the Member States, the European Council, the Council of Ministers and the Commission in the Employment Strategy have been considered in Chapter 4, but what of the institutional framework as a whole?

The Employment Title became *formally* applicable only when the Treaty of Amsterdam entered into force on 1 May 1999, although the 'wide consultation of European institutions and bodies' envisaged by the Title had already been taking place.[1] According to Article 128(2) EC, the Council can adopt the Employment Guidelines, drawn up on a proposal by the Commission, only after consulting with the European Parliament, the Economic and Social Committee, the Committee of the Regions and the Employment Committee.

The European Parliament's request that decisions on employment policy in the Council be taken by qualified majority voting was accepted,[2] but not its proposals concerning its own competences:[3] it had requested qualified majority voting and generalized codecision,[4] but only managed to secure consultation and, by way of exception, the codecision procedure *may* be used in formulating incentive measures (Article 129 EC). Thus the position of the Parliament within the Employment Strategy is rather marginal, limited to a consultative role. This must be a cause for frustration, given the Parliament's long-standing enthusiasm for a European-level employment strategy,[5] and its active efforts during the Amsterdam IGC to ensure a higher priority for employment in the Amsterdam Treaty.

The newest institutional actor is the Employment Committee, which was foreseen in Article 130, but only formally brought into being in 2000.[6] With a

[1] CEC, *Joint Employment Report 1999* (Luxembourg: OOPEC, 1999) at 13.

[2] The Council is to use qualified majority voting in adopting the Employment Guidelines (Article 128(2) EC) and in making recommendations to Member States on their employment policies (Article 128(4) EC).

[3] European Parliament General Secretariat Working Party, Task Force on the Intergovernmental Conference, *Note on the European Parliament's Priorities for the IGC and the new Amsterdam Treaty: Report and Initial Evaluation of the Results*, 15 July 1997, at para 1.3.2; available at *http://www.europarl.eu.int/topics/treaty/report/part1_en.htm* [accessed 10 April 2005].

[4] The codecision procedure, set out in Article 251 (ex Article 189b) EC, gives the Parliament the right to propose amendments to Commission-initiated legislation being considered by the Council, and essentially confers a formal right to veto proposals.

[5] 'The EP considers **employment as the most important priority for the EU** and has always been of the opinion that the Community and the Member States have to co-ordinate their efforts and that working towards full employment should be made an explicit goal of the Member States and the Community. Since April 1983, when the EP held a special part-session on combating unemployment, it has adopted many resolutions on the issue': European Parliament Fact Sheets, No 4.8.3. *Employment Policy*, 23.10.2000; emphasis in the original.

[6] Council Decision of 24 January 2000 establishing the Employment Committee (2000/98/EC), OJ L 29/21, 4.02.2000.

membership dominated by Member State nominees, the role of the Employment Committee is to promote coordination between Member States' employment policies, and to advise and contribute to the work of the Council and the Commission, in particular, ensuring that the Luxembourg, Cardiff and Cologne processes are 'formulated and implemented in a consistent and mutually supportive way'.[7] One example of the functioning of the Committee is the 'mid-term review' of the Employment Strategy, undertaken by the Commission and the Member States under the auspices of the Employment Committee, the purpose of which was to translate the conclusions of the Lisbon Summit into new proposals for enriching subsequent Employment Guidelines, notably by giving them more concrete targets. In particular, the 'Indicators Group' of the Employment Committee has worked with the Commission to produce some twenty new indicators to assist the monitoring of the Guidelines, specifically in relation to lifelong learning, adaptability and work organization, taxation and tax/benefits systems, regional disparities, exclusion and discrimination.[8] The Employment Committee also frequently submits opinions to the Council of Ministers and the European Council, lending support to the emerging consensus within and between the EU institutions and the Member States as to the appropriate policy responses to unemployment. This much can be seen in Employment Committee papers such as the report *Making Work Pay*, which resonates so strongly with the discourse of the Broad Economic Policy Guidelines (BEPGs) (as well as that of the OECD, which is quoted extensively in the report) on questions such as the need to make benefits systems more work-orientated and selective.[9]

The role of the social partners (namely, trade unions and works councils, industry and professional associations, and individual companies) is not mentioned in a formal institutional sense in the Employment Title.[10] However, whilst the social partners do not have the sort of powers granted to them under the social dialogue procedure (now contained in Articles 136–139 EC), nevertheless, the consultation of management and labour is envisaged at several stages in the articulation and implementation of employment policy. For example, the Employment Committee is obliged to consult management and labour at the European level, in fulfilling its mandate.[11] More crucially, however, the contribution of the national level social partners to the NAPs is constantly reiterated by the EU institutions. Throughout the Employment Guidelines, there is a

[7] Ibid., 3rd para of the Preamble and Article 1.

[8] CEC, *Joint Employment Report 2001*, COM(2001) 438 final, Brussels, 12.9.2001, at 19.

[9] Employment Committee, *Making work pay: Facts, figures and policy options*, 1 October 2003, EMCO/21/091003/EN. The Employment Committee report makes frequent reference to the analysis contained in *OECD Employment Outlook 2003: Towards More and Better Jobs* (Paris: OECD, 2003).

[10] Erika Szyszczak, 'The New Paradigm for Social Policy: A Virtuous Circle?' (2001) 38 *CML Rev*, 1125–70, at 1148.

[11] Article 130 EC and Article 5 Council decision establishing the Employment Committee.

recognition that the social partners can play a vital part in employment creation: thus, the first set of Guidelines conferred a particular responsibility on the social partners for the promotion of adaptability through modernizing the organization of work, and for promoting employability through 'partnership' and developing lifelong learning. Subsequently, the Lisbon European Council further legitimized the role of the social partners, who were to be 'more closely involved in drawing up, implementing and following up the appropriate guidelines'.[12] The post-Lisbon Employment Guidelines introduced five 'horizontal objectives', to be incorporated into all four pillars, in order to meet the new strategic goal of making the Union the most competitive and dynamic knowledge-based economy in the world. The third horizontal objective is as follows:

> 'The social partners at all levels are invited to step up their action in support of the Luxembourg process. Within the overall framework and objectives set by these guidelines, the social partners are invited to develop, in accordance with their national traditions and practices, their own process of implementing the guidelines for which they have the key responsibility, identify the issues upon which they will negotiate and report regularly on progress, in the context of the National Action Plans if desired, as well as the impact of their actions on employment and labour market functioning. The social partners at European level are invited to define their own contribution and to monitor, encourage and support efforts undertaken at national level'.[13]

Similarly, the Integrated Guidelines for Growth and Jobs in 2005 also envisage that Member States should 'take every opportunity' to involve social partners (as well as regional and local governments, and civil society) in the implementation of the integrated guidelines.[14] *Joint Employment Reports* had in the past criticized Member States for the uneven involvement of the social partners in the NAP process, especially important with regard to the promotion of adaptability and flexibility since 'it is evident that the social partners are the prime movers in this context'.[15] The Guidelines for 2001 therefore moved to involve the social partners more clearly in their own 'mini-process'. The new obligations to monitor and report back annually on progress impose on management and labour duties similar to those imposed on the Member States under the Essen process, and mirror the 'benchmarking' methodology (see Section 3.2 below) to which Member States are currently subject under the Luxembourg process. Moreover, the decision to hold a 'Tripartite Social Summit for Growth and Employment' before each spring European Council has provided yet another forum for social partner involvement in the Employment

[12] Presidency Conclusions, Lisbon European Council, 23 and 24 March 2000, Bull EU-3/2000, 7–17, at para 28.

[13] Council Decision of 19 January 2001 on guidelines for Member States' employment policies for the year 2001 (2001/63/EC), OJ L 22/18, 24.1.2001.

[14] CEC, Recommendation/Proposal for Integrated Guidelines for Growth and Jobs (2005–2008), Brussels, 12.4.2005 COM (2005) 141 final.

[15] CEC, *Joint Employment Report 2000* (Luxembourg: OOPEC, 2000) at 55.

Strategy.[16] What this means is that the institutional framework for the promulgation and enforcement of employment policy envisaged by the Treaty is being creatively expanded, an expansion brought about through 'soft law' mechanisms.

A key part in the implementation of the Employment Strategy is played by the Structural Funds of the European Union, the collective title for the Regional Development Fund (ERDF), the Social Fund (ESF), the fisheries fund (Financial Instrument of Fisheries Guidance, or FIFG) and the Guidance and Guarantee Fund (European Agricultural Guidance and Guarantee Fund, EAGGF). The Structural Funds are a long-standing example of governance, or policy-delivery, by means of direct EU expenditure. Established by the Treaty of Rome, and operational since 1960, the European Social Fund is the main financial tool through which the European Union translates its strategic employment policy aims into action.[17] It has had a dual role: to improve employment opportunities for workers in the internal market by increasing their mobility and facilitating their adaptation to industrial changes, in particular through vocational training and retraining, and contributing thereby to raising the standard of living (Article 146 EC); and to contribute to strengthening economic and social cohesion in the Community (Article 159 EC).

These provisions have existed in similar form since the Treaty of Rome, so that the ESF can be viewed as an early instrument of Community employment policy,[18] alongside provisions for freedom of movement for workers and social security for migrant workers. What distinguishes the ESF from the other two sets of provisions, however, is that it has been able to give financial support to active labour market measures in Member States, by means of vocational training, retraining and job creation schemes. The vital role which the Structural Funds, and the ESF in particular, have played over the years in supporting national labour market policies is strengthened now that the central aims of the ESF (encouraging the growth of job opportunities and the geographical and

[16] ETUC, UNICE, CEEP and UEAPME, 'Tripartite Social Summit: Social Partners Take Actions to Promote Growth and Employment', Press Release, Brussels, 21 March 2005; available at *http://www.unice.org/* [accessed 10 April 2005]. The social summit involved representatives of the social partners—the European Trade Union Confederation, UNICE (the private employers' confederation), UEAPME (small business confederation), CEEP (public employers)—and representatives of the heads of government of the current and two subsequent EU Presidencies, as well as Commission representatives. The first official Tripartite Social Summit was held in March 2003 under the Greek EU Presidency, but three 'unofficial' social summits had already taken place on the eve of the annual spring European Council meeting in March 2001 (Stockholm), December 2001 (Laeken) and March 2002 (Barcelona).

[17] 'The ESF is likely to account for about 35% of the entire Structural Funds budget in the new programming period, i.e. approximately ECU 70 billion': European Parliament Fact Sheets, No 4.8.2. *The European Social Fund*, 1.12.2000.

[18] Fernando Valdés Dal-Ré, 'Economic and Social Cohesion and the European Social Fund' in Paul Davies, Antoine Lyon-Caen, Silvana Sciarra and Simitis Spiros (eds.), *European Community Labour Law: Principles and Perspectives, Liber Amicorum Lord Wedderburn* (Oxford: Clarendon Press, 1996) at 261–2, 267–8; see also Mark Freedland, 'Employment Policy' in ibid. at 294–5.

occupational mobility of workers) have been incorporated into the Employment Strategy. Despite Member States' rejection of an expansionary fiscal policy and centralized expenditure to stimulate employment at Essen, and again at the Amsterdam IGC, the amount of Structural Funds devoted to employment creation is not insignificant: the ESF accounts for about 35 per cent of the entire Structural Funds budget in the period 2000–2006, ie approximately €70 billion. The ESF alone represents up to half of the total spending on employment policy in some Member States[19] (in particular those where regions have specific competence over employment policy, and in the 'cohesion countries' such as Spain, Greece and Portugal), and an estimated 8 per cent of expenditure on active labour market policies.[20] More specifically, in the period 2000–2006, about €60 billion will be available through the ESF to support the Member States in the development and implementation of the Employment Strategy, such as promoting job creation and competitiveness by investing in skills development; supporting the specific labour market development needs of those regions lagging behind the rest of the EU; and underpinning the commitments made at the Lisbon European Council to promote a dynamic knowledge-based economy.[21]

Not surprisingly, the Member States have been criticized for according insufficient recognition in their NAPs to the contribution of the ESF in underpinning their labour market policies.[22] The Structural Funds Regulations for the period 2000–2006, and the Guidelines for their operation, therefore required Member States to integrate the programming of the Structural Funds interventions, in particular ESF-supported programmes, into the implementation of the Employment Guidelines and into the Employment Strategy more generally.[23] The Commission's proposal for an ESF Regulation for 2007–2013 continues this use of the ESF to provide the sort of investment in human capital envisaged by the post-Lisbon Employment Strategy.[24] Over the years, the role of the ESF has thus been sharpened to assist measures taken in line with the guidelines on employment, so that the key policy fields for ESF intervention now mirror the Employment Guidelines, and focus on a preventative strategy, on increasing labour market participation and on other measures under what used to be the Employability pillar. Substantively, the ESF has now become the source of

[19] CEC, *From Guidelines to Action: The National Action Plans for Employment*, including a Commission Communication, and a Background Report COM (98) 316 final (Luxembourg: OOPEC, 1998) at 13 of the Communication.

[20] CEC, Communication on European Social Fund Support for the European Employment Strategy, COM (2001) 16 final/2, Brussels, 23.01.2001, at 5.

[21] Ibid., at 4.

[22] See CEC, *From Guidelines to Action*, n. 19 above, at 14; CEC, *Joint Employment Report 1999*, n. 1 above, at 40; for evidence of increased recognition by Member States of the contribution of the ESF, see CEC, *Joint Employment Report 2003–4* (Luxembourg: OOPEC, 2004) at 39.

[23] Regulation (EC) No 1784/1999 of the European Parliament and of the Council of 12 July 1999 on the European Social Fund, OJ L 213, 13.08.1999.

[24] Proposal for a Regulation of the European Parliament and of the Council on the European Social Fund, COM (2004) 493 final, Brussels, 14.7.2004.

much of the financial assistance required to enable Member States to pursue policies on vocational training, retraining and job creation schemes, aimed particularly at unemployed youth, the long-term unemployed, socially disadvantaged groups, and women.

At the same time as contributing to the substantive development of the Employment Strategy, the decision-making structures at the heart of the Structural Funds have lent weight to the view of the Employment Strategy as a source of innovative forms of governance. Central to the implementation of the Structural Funds is the idea of 'partnership' which is 'predicated upon a sharing of responsibility across different levels of government, and between a variety of actors, both public and private'.[25] ESF programmes are planned by Member States together with the European Commission and then implemented through a wide range of 'provider organizations' in the public and private sectors, such as national, regional and local authorities, educational and training institutions, voluntary organizations and the social partners.[26] The Structural Funds have always been a means of using the Community as 'the instrument of member state restructuring'.[27] The *Joint Employment Reports* now place increasing emphasis on reforming the management of Structural Fund interventions so that they more fully implement the priorities of the Employment Strategy. For example, the *Joint Employment Report 2000*[28] reports how the ESF would be used in the new programmes initiated to comply with the Council's Recommendations on the implementation of Member States' employment policies,[29] and the *Joint Employment Report 2001* recommends that 'regional disparities need to be addressed and fuller use should be made of the Structural Funds, especially the European Social Fund, to support the Employment Strategy'.[30] The proposed ESF Regulation for 2007–2013 continues this theme, placing particular importance on the promotion of good governance, with less red tape, simpler rules and more decentralization to the Member States.[31]

The interesting question now is the extent to which the interaction between the methodology of the Employment Strategy and the decision-making procedures of the Structural Funds has altered the balance between intergovernmentalism and supranationalism within the operation of the Structural Funds. Perhaps such terminology is now partially defunct in the context of the

[25] Joanne Scott, 'Regional Policy: An Evolutionary Perspective' in Paul Craig and Gráinne de Búrca (eds.), *The Evolution of EU Law* (Oxford: OUP, 1999) at 625–6.

[26] CEC, 'ESF 2000–2006' available at *http://europa.eu.int/comm/employment_social/esf2000/introduction-en.htm* [accessed 10 April 2005].

[27] Susan Milner, 'Training Policy: Steering Between Divergent National Logics', in David Hine and Hussein Kassim (eds.), *Beyond the Market: The EU and National Social Policy* (London: Routledge, 1998) at 157.

[28] CEC, *Joint Employment Report 2000*, n. 15 above, at 72.

[29] Council Recommendation of 14 February 2000 on the implementation of Member States' employment policies, 2000/164/EC, OJ L 52/32, 25.2.2000.

[30] CEC, *Joint Employment Report 2001*, n. 8 above, at 8.

[31] CEC, 'New streamlined funding for European Social Fund and social policy', Press Release IP/04/928, Brussels, 15 July 2004.

Structural Funds. In recent years, there has been a trend towards 'supervised self-management',[32] wherein the *implementation* of the Structural Funds is increasingly decentralized, but with greater emphasis on partnership and 'procedural prescription'[33] in relation to the institutional framework for decision-making—a development which echoes the 'soft law' approaches of the Employment Strategy as a whole, in particular the transition to the 'open method of coordination', which will be explored below.

## 3. The evolution of new forms of governance

Although the Employment Guidelines have a clear Treaty basis, in Title VIII and Article 128 in particular, they can be seen as examples of 'soft law' in that they are not produced in the form of legally binding instruments, such as directives or regulations, which the EU institutions have at their disposal. Nevertheless, as was seen in Chapter 4, these guidelines have important implications for the legal rights and duties of Member States and within Member States. In spite of the oft-repeated assertion that employment policy is primarily a matter for the Member States, and the stress on subsidiarity in Articles 127–129 EC, nevertheless it is true to say that the initiative has increasingly come from the Community institutions.[34] Whilst certain provisions of the Employment Title do envisage a central role for the Community institutions, in monitoring national policies and drawing up guidelines, it is arguable that this role has been greatly expanded in practice, especially by the Commission. This and the ensuing chapter will show how, although framed in the language of 'soft law', the Luxembourg process has nevertheless acquired a normative status. As Szyszczak argues,

> 'Through the soft law tools the Commission has created a frame of reference as well as a monitoring process for a European Employment Strategy. Soft law, which was used in the early 1990s to manage social policy pluralism, has ended the decade as the principal legal tool for coercing Member States to address labour market regulation in line with European policies.'[35]

The issue to be examined is the extent to which the various soft law mechanisms to which the Employment Strategy has given rise can and do in fact 'coerce' Member States into some form of convergence or uniformity in the *content* of their employment policies, as opposed to convergence of their procedures for measurement, assessment and monitoring of such policies.

[32] Scott, n. 25 above, at 641. [33] Ibid., at 640.

[34] Silvana Sciarra, 'The Employment Title in the Amsterdam Treaty: A Multi-language Legal Discourse' in David O'Keefe and Patrick Twomey (eds.), *Legal Issues of the Amsterdam Treaty* (Oxford: Hart Publishing, 1999) 157–70, at 164.

[35] Erika Szyszczak, 'The Evolving European Employment Strategy' in Jo Shaw (ed.), *Social Law and Policy in an Evolving European Union* (Oxford: Hart Publishing, 2000) at 213.

Traditionally, 'soft law' has been used either because there is no Community competence in a particular area, or in order to initiate new kinds of policy for which there is no adequate legal basis.[36] In the case of the European Employment Strategy, there *is* a Treaty basis, but it is a rather narrow one, so we can also include the resort to 'soft law' as a means of finding a middle ground between legal and political intervention,[37] particularly important whilst Member States continue to be so reluctant to sanction further inroads into their sovereignty. In the context of the subsidiarity debate,[38] 'soft law' also appears as a possible means to ensure that any action which is deemed suitable to be taken at EU level, will be of a non-binding nature:

'The form of action should be as simple as possible, consistent with satisfactory achievement of the objective of the measure and the need for effective enforcement. The Community should legislate only to the extent necessary ... Non-binding measures such as recommendations should be preferred where appropriate. Consideration should be given where appropriate to the use of voluntary codes of conduct.'[39]

'Soft law' therefore seems to be an ideal *medium* through which to further the Employment Strategy: strictly speaking, the Council's Recommendations on Member States' employment policies are non-binding, and are used 'sparingly'[40] and Article 128(2) EC states only that Member States 'shall take into account' the annual Employment Guidelines. Nevertheless, the *tools* adopted—of peer review, benchmarking, culminating in the open method of coordination—have resulted in very powerful political pressure on Member States to comply with the centrally designed policies.[41]

## 3.1 Peer review and benchmarking

Since the Essen European Council, Member States had been obliged to submit 'Multi-Annual Action Plans' on their progress under the five 'priority areas', to improve efficiency by exposing national policies to scrutiny, and to learn from examples of 'best practice'. However, as discussed in Chapter 4, this early

[36] K. C. Wellens and G. M. Borchardt, 'Soft Law in European Community Law' (1989) 14 ELR, 267–321, at 302. [37] Ibid., at 270.

[38] Article 5 (ex Article 3b) EC: 'In areas which do not fall within its exclusive competence, the Community shall take action, in accordance with the principle of subsidiarity, only if and insofar as the objectives of the proposed action cannot be sufficiently achieved by the Member States and can therefore, by reason of scale or effects of the proposed action, be better achieved by the Community'.

[39] Presidency Conclusions, Edinburgh European Council, 11 and 12 December 1992, Bulletin of the EC-12/1992, Annex I to Part A, 'Overall Approach to the Application by the Council of the Subsidiarity Principle and Article 3b of the Treaty on European Union', at 9; see also Francis Snyder, 'Soft Law and Institutional Practice in the European Community', European University Institute, Working Papers in Law No 93/5, at 7.

[40] See, for example, Council Recommendation of 19 January 2001, n. 13 above.

[41] Sally Ball, 'The European Employment Strategy: The Will but not the Way?' (2001) 30:4 ILJ 353–74, at 357–8.

example of 'peer review' was relatively weak. The surveillance system of the Luxembourg process, though stronger than that of Essen, still needed to be further elaborated. As late as 2000, the Commission and Council, under the heading of 'Improving the monitoring and review of good practices', were urging that

'[t]he development of indicators should be continued with the aim to dispose of the widest possible set of indicators allowing progress evaluation and international comparability; Member States' good practices should be further subject to peer review and better disseminated.'[42]

Such comparative indicators are important in order to be able to identify target groups for each measure, to measure policy effort (in terms of financial resources, staff and technical support), and to compare policy outcomes.[43] But what does such formalized comparison, or 'benchmarking', actually mean in practice? The practice of benchmarking originated in management theory, well exemplified in the title of one book from 1989, *The Search for Industry Best Practices That Lead to Superior Performance*.[44] Essentially, benchmarking involves the process of gathering information about other companies in the same industry, in order to compare performance and to set goals. Competition is a crucial element; in particular, benchmarking can mean recognizing 'the importance of understanding how the best of the competition is performing and of a commitment to implement changes to match or exceed them'.[45] Accordingly, benchmarking in the management or business environment can cover three main areas of activity, which would all apply happily in the context of the Employment Strategy:

- *first*, simple information provision, enabling comparisons to be made, experiences shared and mutual learning to take place;
- *second*, the identification of best practice/preferred practice, which people are encouraged to follow; or
- *third*, agreement on a set of targets, which the parties commit themselves to following, with some form of peer group review to back up moral persuasion.[46]

This might suggest that one should see benchmarking as a way of improving labour market convergence, not just as a methodological means of comparing

[42] CEC, *Joint Employment Report 2000*, n. 15 above, at 82.

[43] CEC, *From Guidelines to Action*, n. 19 above, at 5.

[44] Robert C. Camp, *Benchmarking: The Search for Industry Best Practices That Lead to Superior Performance* (Milwaukee, WI: ASQC Quality Press, 1989).

[45] Keith Sisson and Paul Marginson, 'Benchmarking and the "Europeanisation" of Social and Employment Policy', ESRC 'One Europe or Several?' Programme, Briefing Note 3/01, April 2001. See also James Arrowsmith, Keith Sisson and Paul Marginson, 'What can "benchmarking" offer the open method of co-ordination?' (2004) 11:2 *Journal of European Public Policy*, 311–328.

[46] Sisson and Marginson, n. 45 above, at 1.

performance.[47] However, such convergence would be at odds with the original rationale for borrowing the concept of benchmarking from the world of business, where it is primarily seen as a tool for increasing competitive performance. In light of the origins of benchmarking in management theory, it is instructive to consider what the business perception is of the use of indicators and benchmarking within the Employment Strategy. As Keith Richardson, one-time Secretary General of the European Round Table of Industrialists (ERT)[48] shows, benchmarking was attractive *because* it was equated with maintaining national control over the content of policy:

'The idea was to establish criteria relevant to competitiveness and then publish figures in a regular and systematic way that would encourage each country to try to catch up with the best practice elsewhere, but without dictating the specific policy measures needed. It was the Irish presidency that first grasped the political attraction to member states, that here was a tool that would help them to work together towards common goals *without jeopardising their freedom to take their own decisions in the light of their own circumstances*, and benchmarking rapidly found its way on to the Council of Ministers agenda.'[49]

Particularly interesting is the ERT view of benchmarking as an *alternative* to more labour market regulation:

'Benchmarking passed into the main stream of EU thinking, and ERT pressure may have helped to ensure that the jobs summit of 1997 adopted a benchmarking approach, geared to such topics as entrepreneurship, skills and innovation, rather than a renewed round of social regulations as had at one stage seemed likely.'[50]

In other words, benchmarking was championed by business leaders precisely because it appeared to offer a means to solve two sets of conflict which intersect: the conflict between state action/intergovernmentalism (ie giving states 'the freedom to take their own decisions') and Community competence/supranationalism; and the conflict between regulation and deregulation. Benchmarking, by avoiding more social regulations, would seem to neutralize the fears of those concerned about centralization and over-regulation. The ability of the benchmarking methodology to neutralize the first conflict is in part what endeared this form of governance to policy-makers at the European level—a procedure which could help strike a balance between what one might label 'heteronomy' and 'autonomy' in the enterprise, may well assist in resolving similar issues of autonomy and heteronomy in relation to policy coordination between the Member States.[51]

[47] Leonello Tronti, 'Benchmarking Employment Performance and Labour Market Polices: The Results of the Research Project' (1999) 4 *Transfer: European Review of Labour and Research*, 542–62.

[48] The ERT's memberships consists of 40–50 chairmen or chief executives of leading European companies, mostly in the manufacturing sector.

[49] Keith Richardson, 'Big Business and the European Agenda', Sussex European Institute, SEI Working Paper, No 35, September 2000, at 8; emphasis added.

[50] Ibid.

[51] Arrowsmith, Sisson and Marginson, n. 45 above at 311 and 314–15.

In the European context, this conflict can be seen in the debates around the shape which an EU-level policy on employment should take. The decision to use objectives, targets and indicators as the mechanisms by which to promote a high level of employment was, in part, a result of the political compromises reached in the Intergovernmental Conference (IGC) leading up to the Treaty of Amsterdam. The debate at the Amsterdam IGC, and within the Reflection Group,[52] mirrored that which had occurred at Essen in 1994 in response to the Commission's advocacy of an expansionary fiscal policy and large-scale infrastructure and public works programmes as the route to job creation.[53] Ultimately, the proposals of the Delors Commission, contained in its 1993 White Paper *Growth, Competitiveness and Employment*, were blocked by Member States, who refused to sanction the centralization of expenditure and competence over employment policy which this would have necessitated. The Amsterdam IGC was similarly reluctant to endorse expansion of public investment as the means to increase jobs, leading to an Employment *Strategy* and an Employment *Title* based on the central coordination of national employment policies, rather than a more distinctly European programme of job creation. The shape of the Employment Title changed in the course of the IGC negotiations: from a *common* to a *coordinated* policy; away from *harmonization*, toward coordination of national policies. Consequently, tools for comparison of national practices—such as targets, indicators, statistics, benchmarking and peer review—become central.

So, from the earliest days of the Employment Strategy, it was necessary for Member States to find ways to facilitate mutual learning and to share knowledge of best practices, in order to improve their records on employment. Thus the early comparative method dating from Essen was called in aid. Even before the introduction of the Employment Title, the Commission and Council had received a mandate from the Dublin European Council to assess the possibilities of benchmarking as an instrument for the effective monitoring and evaluation of employment and labour market policies and the identification of good practice. Their *Joint Employment Report 1997*[54] subsequently took up this mandate, and published preliminary results, based on eight underlying labour market indicators,[55] showing employment indicators for the years 1992 and 1997 transformed into 'radar charts'.[56] In view of the multiple goals pursued by

[52] *Reflection Group's Report*, Messina, 2nd June 1995 (Brussels: OOPEC, 1995).

[53] CEC, White Paper *Growth, Competitiveness' Employment: The Challenges and Ways Forward into the 21st Century*, COM (93) 700 final, Luxembourg: OOPEC.

[54] CEC, *Commission Draft for the Joint Employment Report 1997* (Luxembourg: OOPEC, 1997) at section 3.

[55] For *employment*, these are: the employment rate, employment growth, employment of those aged 55–64, the employment gender gap; for *unemployment*: the unemployment rate, long-term unemployment, youth unemployment and the unemployment gender gap. See CEC, *Commission Draft for the Joint Employment Report 1997*, n. 54 above, at Annex 1.

[56] Hugh Mosley and Antje Mayer, 'Benchmarking National Labour Market Performance: A Radar Chart Approach' Discussion Paper FS I 99-202, Wißenschaftszentrum Berlin für Sozialforschung, 1999.

the Employment Strategy, this methodological approach enables multiple performance indicators to be compared or 'benchmarked' and presented in an accessible visual form.[57]

Benchmarking consists of evaluating performance against a common yardstick—in the case of the European Employment Strategy, the average of the three best-performing Member States for that given indicator. As such, it forms the heart of the open method of coordination of employment. One of the earliest tasks of the Employment Committee, once it was formally brought into being in 2000,[58] was to sharpen up the employment indicators. The Employment Committee approves the list of indicators on an annual basis so that, for example, the 'Indicators Group' of the Employment Committee worked with the Commission in 2001 to produce some twenty new indicators to assist the monitoring of the guidelines, specifically in relation to the new post-Lisbon priorities, such as lifelong learning, adaptability and work organization, taxation and tax/benefits systems, regional disparities, exclusion and discrimination.[59]

In 2003, a complete review of all indicators was conducted, as part of the wider review and streamlining of the Employment Strategy more generally, and the introduction of a 'new generation' of Employment Guidelines. A central recognition of the review of the first five years of the Employment Strategy was that in order to monitor effectively Member States' progress towards the Lisbon goals, and the specific objectives of the Luxembourg process, policy attention would need to be directed towards the development of 'adequate and comparable' statistics and indicators.[60] This renewed focus on indicators arose from the sense that the iterative nature of the Employment Strategy, the annual cycle of revisions to the Employment Guidelines undermined the actual implementation of such policy. Effectiveness called for more *result-orientated guidelines*, based, where possible, on appropriate quantitative targets.[61] As the *Joint Employment Report 2003–4* shows, progress towards the Lisbon target of a 70 per cent overall employment rate for the EU has come to a standstill, and it is clear that the EU will miss the intermediate employment rate target for 2005 agreed in Stockholm, of 67 per cent.[62] A consensus has therefore emerged within the European institutions that rather than engaging in a process of further changes in guidelines, the emphasis at EU level should now be on *stronger monitoring* of reforms undertaken by the Member States.[63]

[57] Mosley and Mayer, n. 56 above, at 6–7; see also Tronti, n. 47 above, at 554–5.

[58] Council Decision of 24 January 2000 establishing the Employment Committee (2000/98/EC), OJ L 29/21, 4.02.2000.

[59] CEC, *Joint Employment Report 2001*, n. 8 above at 19.

[60] CEC, *Taking Stock of Five Years of the European Employment Strategy*, COM (2002) 416 final, 17.07.2002, at 19.

[61] CEC, Communication from the Commission: *The Future of the European Employment Strategy (EES): A Strategy for Full Employment and Better Jobs for All*, COM (2003) 6 final, 14.1.2003, at 6.

[62] CEC, *Joint Employment Report 2003–4* (Luxembourg: OOPEC, 2004) at 18.

[63] Ibid., at 16.

In response, employment indicators have grown in number, type and complexity from the relatively straightforward first generation of indicators in 1997, numbering just eight in total.[64] There are now in total 40 *key indicators* and 26 *context indicators*, the former designed to measure progress in relation to the objectives defined in the Employment Guidelines, the latter intended to support the analysis of the National Action Programmes by putting national policies and performance into perspective. In keeping with the principle underpinning benchmarking, that all targets and essential objectives in the Employment Guidelines should be monitored by corresponding key indicators, as the Employment Strategy has evolved post-Lisbon, so too have the indicators. So, for example, numerous indicators of quality in work are now embedded within the key indicators and the context indicators. These quality indicators build on those adopted at the Laeken summit in December 2001,[65] and include such issues as intrinsic job quality, participation in education and training, gender segregation, health and safety at work, work organization and work–life balance.[66]

As the above has shown, this new method for comparison of national practices, centred around targets, indicators, statistics, benchmarking and peer review, now seems a far cry from the original use of benchmarking and competitive comparison in industry, However, how successfully can this methodology make the transition from being a management tool to being an instrument of high-level policy formation? Can it address the tensions as to the level and the content of regulation which have for so long dominated European social and employment policy? These questions will be addressed in the discussion of the open method of coordination more broadly, but a subsidiary question for now is whether the benchmarking methodology can have a sufficiently powerful impact such as to lead to policy change or policy learning. Two potential ways that this can occur are suggested in the literature: a 'spill-over effect'[67] and the process of 'naming and shaming'. In respect of the former, Terry and Towers observe how the social partners can make strategic use of benchmarked standards to advance national bargaining agendas, being familiar with the usefulness of comparison as a basis for bargaining: 'many have sought, both nationally and internationally, to use the achievements of those with greater bargaining power to establish new norms'.[68]

With regard to the latter, peer *review*, which is the logical corollary to benchmarking, can involve a rather detailed assessment of the performance of each Member State by the others, amounting to an intense form of peer *pressure* to

[64] CEC, *Commission Draft for the Joint Employment Report 1997*, n. 54 above, at Annex 1.

[65] Presidency Conclusions, Laeken European Council, 14 and 15 December 2001, Bull EU-12/2001, 1–26.

[66] CEC, Communication *Improving Quality in Work: A Review of Recent Progress*, COM (2003) 728 final (Luxembourg: OOPEC, 2003) Annex 1.

[67] Catherine Barnard, 'The Social Partners and the Governance Agenda' (2002) 8:1 *European Law Journal*, 80–101, at 100.

[68] Michael Terry and Brian Towers, 'Editorial: Developing Social Policy in the EU: Prospects and Obstacles' (2000) 31:4 *Industrial Relations Journal*, 242–6, at 245.

change policy. The peer review programme established by the European Commission involves representatives of Member State governments, independent labour market experts and representatives from the European Commission. Good practices to be reviewed are selected by Member States from amongst those published in the *Joint Employment Reports* or the NAPs. They are based on existing evaluation or early monitoring data and thematically linked with the pillars and guidelines of the Employment Strategy. Each peer review is hosted by a Member State which presents the selected good practice. It is attended by a group of peer countries with a special interest in the experience and in the transfer of the policy.[69] An interesting insight into the effectiveness of 'naming and shaming' resulting from peer review is offered by Sisson and Marginson:

> 'One of us attended a recent seminar attended by a senior official of the UK Treasury, who spoke from personal experience about what it felt like to be involved in international bench marking with peer group review. He said that, like many people, he had been somewhat scornful about the "naming and shaming" as a method of enforcement. Having been personally exposed to the process, however, he could vouch for its impact. It was not at all a comfortable position, he pointed out, for senior officials and ministers of governments to be put in the dock in such a public way.'[70]

The above form of peer review is built around the benchmarking of labour market indicators, as is the 'peer' review by the Council and the Commission of Member States' NAPs. This latter form of review has led, on at least two occasions, to Recommendations based on comparisons with the best performers, which can bring about real pressure on Member States to change their policies:

> 'although the European Employment Guidelines or recommendations issued to specific member states do not have a binding character, the yearly categorization of the performance of each country individually has proved to be an uncomfortable finger-pointing session, putting pressure on the member states to converge towards the benchmark that has been selected as the ideal goal to achieve. In order to improve their respective situations in the overall competition, some countries need to implement structural reforms, which are not necessarily in tune with their dominant national policy objectives or traditions.'[71]

There is a danger of the strategies of the 'best performers' being used as blueprints, perhaps inappropriately, in different institutional contexts.[72] This

[69] See the website of the Peer Review Programme on Active Labour Market Policy, set up by ÖSB/INBAS, the partnership managing the peer review programme on behalf of the European Commission: *http://peerreview.almp.org/en/* [accessed 10 April 2005].

[70] Keith Sisson and Paul Marginson, ' "Soft Regulation"—Travesty of the Real Thing or New Dimension?', ESRC 'One Europe or Several?' Programme Working Paper 32/01, at 24.

[71] Caroline de la Porte, Philippe Pochet and Graham Room, 'Social Benchmarking, Policy Making and New Governance in the EU' (2001) 11:4 *Journal of European Social Policy*, 291–307, at 295.

[72] Holger Schütz, Stefan Speckesser and Günther Schmid, 'Benchmarking Labour Market Performance and Labour Market Policies: Theoretical Foundations and Applications', Discussion Paper FS I 98–205, Wißenschaftszentrum Berlin für Sozialforschung, 1998.

concern is echoed by Tronti, who points out that 'evaluation studies are needed to provide convincing evidence that a specific labour market policy or programme is successful in increasing employment and workers' earnings in a cost-effective way'.[73] One should not just assume that a particular country's labour market policies should be emulated simply because its labour market performance is superior to the others, since many factors (industrial policies, demographic factors, monetary and fiscal policies) affect labour market performance. For example, the current indicators on activation and prevention do not reveal differences in the *quality* of the approach used. The impact evaluation of the Employment Strategy has shown that the concept of a 'new start' has been interpreted in very different ways by Member States, ranging from an interview to a specific active labour market policy, through to individual action plans of varying depth and quality.[74] For instance, although the UK is now one of eight Member States which has attained or exceeded the new 25 per cent target on activation according to the *Joint Employment Report 2003–4*, nevertheless it still has one of the lowest levels of expenditure on active labour market policies.[75]

However, benchmarking and peer review appear to have acquired an unstoppable momentum, adopted by international organizations such as the International Monetary Fund and the World Trade Organization, although the practice has been most extensively developed at the OECD.[76] The synergies between the European Employment Strategy and the OECD Jobs Strategy are thus not limited to their respective policy prescriptions, but can be seen to extend to the regulatory techniques adopted for implementation. The combined methodology of benchmarking and peer review, involving the dissemination of best practice and mutual learning, is similarly a hallmark of the follow-up to the OECD's Jobs Strategy. Indeed, it has been argued that

> '[o]ne reason behind the success of the OECD's 1994 Jobs Strategy was commitment among members to adhere to principles and benchmarks for creating and maintaining stable employment and to collectively review the measures which have been implemented. Those that performed best tended to be those that adopted most of the strategy. The method produced positive results largely because the "rules of the game" were clear from the start and all the countries involved accepted them.'[77]

In the years immediately following the launch of the Jobs Strategy, the OECD's Economic and Development Review Committee (EDRC), mandated by OECD Ministers to examine implementation of the *Jobs Study* recommendations in individual member countries, made use of peer review, namely

[73] Tronti, n. 47 above, at 556.

[74] CEC, *Joint Employment Report 2002* (Luxembourg: OOPEC) at 32.

[75] CEC, *Joint Employment Report 2003–4*, n. 62 above, at 27.

[76] OECD, Policy Brief, *Peer review: a tool for co-operation and change*, December 2003 (Paris: OECD, 2003).

[77] Fabrizio Pagani, 'Peer review: A tool for global co-operation and change' *OECD Observer* No 235, December 2002 (Paris: OECD, 2002).

multilateral surveillance of countries by one another, to assess compliance with its objectives. An ongoing part of the work of the EDRC has been to conduct an Economic Survey of each OECD member country every 18 months to 2 years, the focus of which is primarily on policies with potential to improve the economy's long-run performance, such as labour market reform and investment in human capital. Part of the OECD Economic Survey procedure involves the country subject to survey being reviewed by two other member countries, which comment upon a draft produced by the Secretariat.[78] What is striking about this procedure is that a near-identical methodology is deployed in such different institutional contexts as the OECD and the EU. Whilst the nature and structure of the OECD precludes the sort of tension between autonomy and heteronomy present within the EU (there is not the same anxiety between central regulation and local competence) nonetheless, there is a similar concern to ensure policy implementation is 'effective'. In considering why peer review is such a successful tool, OECD observers cite the 'peer pressure' exerted during the process by the states carrying out the review, and the willingness of the state concerned to accept it.[79] Nevertheless, this amounts to a weaker form of peer review and benchmarking than that operated within the EU, making less use of the types of increasingly prescriptive indicators which have become the hallmark of the post-Lisbon Employment Strategy, and certainly not backed up by the 'hard' mechanisms of the EU's BEPGs and the Stability and Growth Pact. What we do have, nonetheless, is an example of how powerful peer pressure can be, even without recourse to the stricter regime which the European Employment Strategy has at its disposal. Whilst in the European Employment Strategy version of the benchmarking/peer review process, peer review follows on from an ever tighter system of benchmarking, in the OECD version, peer review is relatively free-standing; the standards to be benchmarked within the OECD context are not as prescriptive, they are certainly not subject to iterative, annual revision nor do they feature numerical targets in the way that the European Employment Strategy does.

In conclusion, and drawing on the comparison with the OECD, peer review and benchmarking within the European Employment Strategy can be said to have normative effects—despite the fact that these are tools of 'soft law'—and are in fact resulting in a form of convergence. I would argue that the intensification of the processes at the heart of the open method of coordination (benchmarking and peer review), albeit processes of 'soft law', has led to the narrowing of the range of legitimate responses to unemployment. The growing sophistication in the use of indicators evidences a strengthening of the system of *management by objectives* and a tightening of the permissible range of policy options open to

[78] Bernard Casey, 'The OECD Jobs Strategy and the European Employment Strategy: Two Views of the Labour Market and of the Welfare State' (2004) 10 *European Journal of Industrial Relations*, 329–52.

[79] OECD, Policy Brief, *Peer review*, n. 76 above, at 2.

Member States. But in the absence of what one might label 'social benchmarking'[80] there is the danger that such convergence will inevitably follow the dominant criterion by which progress in employment policy and labour market reform is currently evaluated, namely, an economic criterion. Further, there is the fear, identified by Trubek and Mosher, that 'by moving away from efforts to mandate uniform social and employment standards, the Union might contribute to the gradual erosion of social programmes and policies' that make up the European Social Model.[81]

## 3.2 The 'open method of coordination'

'The open method of co-ordination (OMC) was presented at the 2000 Lisbon European Council as a new method intended to facilitate the implementation of the ambitious strategic goal set at that occasion. Its main "raison d'être" is the fact that many of the Lisbon Strategy objectives fall into areas where the competence largely lies with Member States and hence the Community method cannot be applied.' (European Commission, 2005)[82]

It was clear that the Employment Strategy represented something new, but the constitutional implications of this new form of governance only fully crystallized at the Lisbon European Council meeting in March 2000. The use of guidelines, benchmarking and peer review had evolved considerably after the Luxembourg European Council, and since Lisbon, these tools have become subsumed within the wider 'open method of coordination' (OMC). In fact, the European Council described the OMC in a way which draws almost completely on the methodology of the Employment Strategy:

'This method, which is designed to help Member States to progressively develop their own policies, involves:

- fixing guidelines for the Union combined with specific timetables for achieving the goals which they set in the short, medium and long terms;
- establishing, where appropriate, quantitative and qualitative indicators and benchmarks against the best in the world and tailored to the needs of different Member States and sectors as a means of comparing best practice;

[80] The Lisbon European Council raised the possibility of extending the benchmarking procedure to social protection, and the combating of poverty and social exclusion. However, this is unlikely to amount to the sort of 'institutional means by which the harmonization of social rights can be built into the employment strategy' as envisaged by Deakin and Reed: see Simon Deakin and Hannah Reed, 'The Contested Meaning of Labour Market Flexibility: Economic Theory and the Discourse of European Integration' in Jo Shaw (ed.), n. 35 above, at 97.

[81] David M. Trubek and James S. Mosher, 'Alternative Approaches to Governance in the EU: EU Social Policy and the European Employment Strategy' (2003) 41:1 *Journal of Common Market Studies*, 63–88, at 64.

[82] CEC, *Commission Staff Working Document in support of the report from the Commission to the Spring European Council, 22–23 March 2005, on the Lisbon Strategy of economic, social and environmental renewal*, SEC (2005) 160, Brussels 28.1.2005, at 46.

- translating these European guidelines into national and regional policies by setting specific targets and adopting measures, taking into account national and regional differences;
- periodic monitoring, evaluation and peer review organised as mutual learning processes'[83]

With its creative use of 'soft law' mechanisms, which nevertheless have an impact on Member States' policies, the evolving Employment Strategy has come to represent a middle course between full harmonization, on the one hand, and mutual recognition or regulatory competition, on the other. At Lisbon there was a *substantive* change in policy, involving a recognition of the need to renew the European social model, and to tackle poverty and the lack of social cohesion in the drive to become the 'most competitive and dynamic knowledge-based economy in the world'. Whilst some of the specific targets of the Lisbon Strategy have now been abandoned, nevertheless grand aspirations remain, such as the key strategic goal of 'full employment'. How these objectives were to be achieved was the subject of an important *procedural* innovation. The European Council recognized that the methodology of the Employment Strategy was a new form of governance which could be usefully applied in other policy areas such as: the use of information technology to aid job creation;[84] in promoting Research and Development;[85] and in promoting social inclusion and reducing poverty.[86] Following the Stockholm European Council in 2001, the 'open method of coordination' was also extended to education and training policy, and reform of pension systems.[87] Indeed, the Employment Strategy is now a paradigm case of the application of the open method of coordination, forming a point of departure for other 'OMCs' which sometimes differ significantly from the model articulated by the Lisbon European Council and applied in the Employment Strategy. To date, the open method of coordination has been established in the areas of 'eEurope', research and development policies (covering five areas), innovation, enterprise policy, the European Charter for Small-and Medium-sized Enterprises, social inclusion, pensions, and education and vocational training.[88] The various open *methods* of coordination exhibit varying degrees of intensity of policy coordination and utilize subtly divergent *modus operandi.*

[83] Presidency Conclusions, Lisbon European Council, n. 12 above, at para 37.

[84] Ibid., at para 8. [85] Ibid., at para 13. [86] Ibid., at para 32.

[87] Presidency Conclusions, Stockholm European Council, 23 and 24 March 2001, Bull EU-3/2001, 1–40. It is noteworthy that the areas to be subjected to European level coordination (education, pensions) have traditionally been exclusively *national* concerns. The EU has not acquired *competence* over these areas, in the traditional sense, but policy is to be 'Europeanized' in the sense that these areas will become subject to comparison and benchmarking. One reason for this is, as Jacobsson points out: 'The failure to reform, say, the German pension system, is expected to have effects on the other member states, and thus to be a legitimate concern for all of them'. Kerstin Jacobsson, 'Employment and Social Policy Coordination. A New System of EU Governance' unpublished paper for the Scancor workshop on Transnational Regulation and the Transformation of States, Stanford, 22–23 June 2001; manuscript on file with the author.

[88] CEC, *Commission Staff Working Document*, n. 82 above, at 47.

Following close on the heels of the use of the open method to coordinate employment policy, the application of the open method to the fight against poverty and social exclusion is perhaps the nearest to that in the Employment Strategy, in terms of detail and prescriptiveness.[89] A key feature of the open method shared by the employment OMC and the social inclusion OMC is the joint analysis and assessment by the Commission and the Council of National Action Plans submitted by the Member States. As with the Joint Employment Reports, the Joint Reports on Social Inclusion assess progress made in the implementation of the OMC, set key priorities and identify good practice and innovative approaches of common interest to the Member States.[90] OMC in the context of social inclusion policy is prescriptive in the sense that it emulates the Employment Strategy in seeking to coordinate (rather than harmonize) national policy, but undertakes this coordination within strict parameters which place limits on Member States' choices. That the open method in employment policy coordination can nevertheless have a relatively 'hard' edge which constrains Member States' actions will be explored in greater detail below, but as far as the 'openness' of the open method for social inclusion is concerned, it is arguable that 'the space which OMC inclusion occupies is constrained by the EES'.[91]

The Commission defines social inclusion as 'a process which ensures that those at risk of poverty and social exclusion gain the opportunities and resources necessary to participate fully in economic, social and cultural life and to enjoy a standard of living and well-being that is considered normal in the society in which they live';[92] and in keeping with this definition, social inclusion policy places a great deal of emphasis on improving participation in economic activity and on strengthening fragile attachments to the labour market. At the risk of oversimplification, a central part of the policy to combat social exclusion replicates the initiatives to ensure full employment, starting from the premise that work is the best route out of poverty. So, whilst the key priorities of social inclusion policy include decent housing, quality health, preventing early school leaving and so on, nevertheless, many of the social cohesion and social inclusion objectives touch on social and labour market integration. Accordingly, the National Action Plans for social inclusion must be closely coordinated with the NAPs for employment (and, by extension, closely coordinated with the BEPGs), and both plans should be read together to get a fuller picture of the measures

[89] For a critical exploration of the use of OMC in combating social exclusion, see Kenneth Armstrong, 'Tackling Social Exclusion Through OMC: Reshaping the Boundaries of EU Governance' in Tania Börzel and Rachel Cichowski (eds.), *State of the Union: Law, Politics and Society* (Oxford: OUP, 2003).

[90] Communication from the Commission, *Joint Report on Social Protection and Social Inclusion*, COM (2005) 14 final, Brussels, 27.01.2005. Prior to this, there had been two Joint Reports on Social Inclusion, adopted in 2002 and 2004, drawing respectively upon the National Action Plans on Social Inclusion of 2001–2003 and 2003–2005.

[91] Armstrong, n. 89 above, at 179.

[92] CEC, *Joint Report on Social Inclusion 2004* (Luxembourg, OOPEC, 2004) at 8.

being taken to combat social exclusion through participation in the labour market,[93] narrowing the range of options open to Member States.

OMC is far less prescriptive in policy areas other than employment and social inclusion. For example, common statistical indicators or benchmarks have been established for economic policy, structural reforms, employment policy, and social inclusion (as we have seen) as well as for education, but not yet for pensions or health care.[94] Following the endorsement at the Göteborg European Council of three broad principles for modernizing pension systems, namely safeguarding the capacity of systems to meet their social objectives, maintaining their financial sustainability and meeting changing societal needs, the open method of coordination in pensions was formally launched on the basis of eleven common objectives under these three headings.[95] In contrast to the National Action Plans for employment and social inclusion, Member States are required to produce 'National Strategy Reports' in the coordination of pensions policy, for which they are merely obliged to describe their strategies for securing the sustainability of pension provisions and, where necessary, for modernizing pension systems.[96] As the then Belgian Minister for Social Affairs and Pensions observed, '[o]pen co-ordination is not some kind of fixed recipe that can be applied to any issue', but rather 'a cookbook that contains various recipes, lighter and heavier ones'.[97] OMC-like processes in policy areas such as pensions are 'light' in comparison with the open method of coordination of employment policies, and depart so far from the model outlined by the European Council at Lisbon as to challenge any meaningful attempt to theorize or classify OMC within the array of regulatory techniques open to non-state actors such as the EU.

As a precursor to the attempt to theorize the nature of the open method of coordination, it is useful to think of OMC—at least, the type of OMC adopted to coordinate employment policy—as being at one end of a continuum,[98] at the other end of which is the 'classic Community method'. This method can be summed up as the style of decision-making established in the Treaty of Rome, within which the Commission has the sole right of initiative with regard to

[93] Ibid., at 46.

[94] Jonathan Zeitlin, 'Introduction: The Open Method of Coordination in Question' in Jonathan Zeitlin and Philippe Pochet with Lars Magnusson (eds.), *The Open Method of Coordination in Action: The European Employment and Social Inclusion Strategies*, (Brussels: PIE–Peter Lang, forthcoming 2005) at 3; page numbers refer to manuscript.

[95] Presidency Conclusions, Göteborg European Council, 15 and 16 June 2001, Bull EU-6/2001, 1–43, at para. 43.

[96] Social Protection Committee and the Economic Policy Committee, *Joint report on objectives and working methods in the area of pensions: Applying the open method of coordination*, Report submitted to the Council of the European Union, SOC 469/ECOFIN 334, Brussels, 23 November 2001, at 4.

[97] Frank Vandenbroucke, 'The EU and Social Protection: What Should the European Convention Propose?' Max Planck Institute for the Study of Societies (MPIfG) Working Paper 02/6, June 2002.

[98] Joanne Scott and David M. Trubek, 'Mind the Gap: Law and New Approaches to Governance in the European Union' (2002) 8:1 *European Law Journal*, 1–18.

legislative and policy proposals, the European Parliament has an increasingly important voice, the Council of Ministers takes the final decision—often now by qualified majority voting—and the resulting Community law is enforced by the European Court of Justice.[99]

But, rather than a sharp shift from one method of governance to the other, we can instead perceive an evolving process, in which (a) different forms of governance are used at the same time, and (b) that most innovative regulatory tool, OMC, is revealed to have long-standing antecedents. As to the latter point, it is arguable that the 'classic' Community method always contained elements of more 'open' or flexible methods of governance, both with regard to the 'input' and the 'output' stages.[100] The success of the Community project and the 'classic' Community method has been that, whilst constructing a constitutional order with state-like properties—as a result of doctrines such as direct effect and supremacy, and the uniform application of Community law—there has been flexibility and differentiation, even within the common market 'core'.[101] Experiments with alternatives to the classic Community method have emerged over decades; whilst being innovative, the open method did not spring fully formed from the heads of state and government at the European Council meeting in Lisbon, but rather drew upon a history of experimentation with 'softer' forms of governance.[102] One early case in point was the adoption of the 'new approach' to harmonization, such that 'positive integration' directives no longer aimed to harmonize a subject exhaustively, avoiding the excessive 'Euro-uniformity' of the old approach.[103] As the 1985 White Paper on completion of the internal market had recommended, there was now a move away from exhaustive harmonization, and greater reliance on mutual recognition and equivalence—formalizing the acknowledgement of practices in other Member States in a way which prefigures the mutual learning of the open method.[104] A further example of departure from the standard Community method is comitology, namely, the increasing use of committees in the process of EC

[99] CEC, *European Governance: A White Paper*, Brussels, 27.7.2001, COM(2001) 428, at 8.

[100] Scott and Trubek, n. 98 above, at 2.

[101] Gráinne de Búrca, 'Differentiation within the Core: The Case of the Common Market', in Gráinne de Búrca and Joanne Scott (eds.), *Constitutional Change in the EU: From Uniformity to Flexibility?* (Oxford: Hart Publishing, 2000).

[102] For a discussion of the 'newness' of OMC, see Claire Kilpatrick, who argues that 'it is not the case that EU employment regulation creates governance tools and structures which have never existed before. Recognising the important *but limited and specific* ways in which EU employment regulation is new can help us to make progress in considering both the governance and constitutionalism implications of these changes': 'New EU Employment Governance and Constitutionalism' unpublished paper presented to the workshop on New Governance and Constitutionalism, Faculty of Law, University of Cambridge, 19–20 July 2004. Emphasis in the original.

[103] For example, under the comitology procedure a directive intended to harmonize product safety would only lay down in general terms the health and safety requirements which goods had to meet, with the task of setting detailed technical requirements delegated to specialist committees.

[104] CEC, *White Paper on Completing the Internal Market*, COM (85) 310 final.

policy-making, particularly in regulatory fields.[105] 'Here the nature of the departure is distinct in that it relates not to the character of the emerging norm, but to the institutional setting in which that norm is conceived and adopted'.[106] A good example of a *convergence* between the old and the new forms of governance is social dialogue, wherein agreements by the social partners are transformed into binding directives by virtue of Council decisions. The social dialogue provisions of the EC Treaty not only oblige the Commission to consult with management and labour prior to the submission of legislative proposals; they also empower the social partners, if they so wish, to negotiate 'collective agreements'[107] which can be implemented by Community instruments (directives) or national practice. Also, not only does the *process* by which these directives are drafted differ from the 'classic' Community method in which the Commission initiates legislative proposals; the actual *content* of the framework directives so far produced under the social dialogue procedure has eschewed the prescriptive approach traditionally favoured in directives.[108] Such framework directives do not aim at harmonization, but set out certain of the goals of European social policy, and leave a space for diversity and for self-regulation—either by management and labour, or at the national level.

The new approach to harmonization, comitology and social dialogue can all be understood as reactions to the difficulties inherent in attempting to regulate complex fields, and to regulate for a diverse number of jurisdictions, by means of conventional 'command and control' mechanisms.[109] In the context of comitology, the Single European Act of 1986 accelerated the expansion of the committee system, enabling the Council to delegate to the Commission the task of specifying the detailed technical or scientific requirements and standards of general Council directives. This delegation was not unfettered, due to

[105] Ellen Vos, 'The Rise of Committees' (1997) 3:3 *European Law Journal*, 210–29; and Christian Joerges and Jürgen Neyer, 'From Intergovernmental Bargaining to Deliberative Political Processes: The Constitutionalisation of Comitology' (1997) 3:3 *European Law Journal*, 273–99.

[106] Scott and Trubek, n. 98 above, at 2–3.

[107] Such 'collective agreements' are not recognizable as the product of collective bargaining in the traditional sense, due to the relative weakness of the social partners at European level; thus European collective bargaining is not so much an expression of collective autonomy, as an instrument of European law-making used to circumvent institutional obstacles. See Antonio Lo Faro, *Regulating Social Europe: Reality and Myth of Collective Bargaining in the EC Legal Order* (Oxford: Hart Publishing, 2000).

[108] Social dialogue has led to three directives, on parental leave, part-time work and temporary work: Council Directive 96/34/EC of 3 June 1996 on the framework agreement on parental leave concluded by UNICE, CEEP and the ETUC, amended by Council Directive 97/75/EC of 15 December 1997, OJ L 145, 19.06.96 and OJ L 10, 16.01.1998. Council Directive 97/81/EC of 15 December 1997 concerning the framework agreement on part-time working concluded by UNICE, CEEP and the ETUC, amended by Council Directive 98/23/EC of 7 April 1998, OJ L 14, 20.01.98 and OJ L 131, 05.05.98. Council Directive 99/70/EC of 28 June 1999 concerning the framework agreement on fixed-term work concluded by UNICE, CEEP and the ETUC, OJ L 175, 10.07.1999.

[109] Nick Bernard, 'Legitimising EU Law: Is the Social Dialogue the Way Forward? Some Reflections Around the *UEAPME* Case', in Jo Shaw (ed.), n. 35 above, at 280.

the Member States' insistence on national representatives in comitology procedures but, as Joerges and Neyer argue, the end result is to '[bridge] the gap between intergovernmentalist bargaining and centralised rule-making'.[110] The difficult process of bargaining over divergent national interests in types and levels of regulation has been converted into a 'deliberative' process, leading to 'non-hierarchical governance structures', and mutually acceptable standards.[111] Social dialogue also potentially leads to a comparable shift away from a 'hierarchical to a network style of governance', which is characterized by 'cooperative rather than competitive interaction patterns among a large variety of actors'.[112]

The open method of coordination, which is even further along the continuum from the 'classic' Community method, can similarly be seen as a response to regulatory failure, as well as a response to the 'joint decision trap' or the 'competency gap' in social policy and other policy areas.[113] The 'competency gap' describes the situation in which the national capacity to regulate markets is severely reduced as a result of economic integration (with its associated mobility of financial assets and firms), whilst the problem-solving capacity at European (or international) level is constrained by conflicts of interest amongst governments. In the context of social and employment policy, economic integration can be expected to result in regulatory competition: the reduced capacity to control their economic borders limits the freedom of national governments to raise the regulatory and wage costs of firms, and places pressure on them to deregulate to remain competitive. OMC, as a form of governance which has the potential to achieve policy coordination without threatening jealously guarded national sovereignty, *and* to allow Member States to implement policy in accordance with their socio-economic development, thus offers a potential solution to the tension between autonomy and heteronomy/community, and speaks to both elements of the equation referred to in Chapter 4: the tension between state action (intergovernmentalism) and Community competence (supranationalism), on the one hand, and that between regulation and deregulation, on the other.

As Scharpf notes, the open method of coordination presupposes that Member States should define certain policy areas as a 'common concern', whilst the actual

[110] Joerges and Neyer, n. 105 above.

[111] This is the *ideal*: comitology in practice does not live up to this ideal of deliberative supranationalism due to the lack of transparency and pluralism, amongst other flaws.

[112] Gerda Falkner, 'European Social Policy: Towards Multi-level and Multi-actor Governance' in Beate Kohler-Koch and Rainer Eising (eds.), *The Transformation of Governance in the European Union* (London: Routledge, 1999) at 93.

[113] Fritz W. Scharpf, *Governing in Europe: Effective and Democratic?* (Oxford: OUP, 1999) at 76–7; and Scharpf, 'Negative and Positive Integration in the Political Economy of European Welfare States' in Gary Marks, Fritz W. Scharpf, Philippe C. Schmitter and Wolfgang Streeck (eds.) *Governance in the European Union* (London: Sage, 1996) at 15.

choice of policies remains a national responsibility.[114] There are two possible outcomes here: from the viewpoint of one concerned to preserve (a version of) the European social model, a pessimistic interpretation is that, since such new forms of governance do not produce binding norms, and decentralize decision-making, they signal a rejection of social legislation at the European level, which will eventually lead to an erosion of the European social model. In 1995, Streeck critically referred to this scenario as 'neo-voluntarism', that is, 'a type of social policy that tries to do with a minimum of compulsory modification of both market outcomes and national policy choices, presenting itself as an alternative to hard regulation as well as to no regulation at all'.[115] A more optimistic reading is that the open method of coordination can provide an innovative regulatory strategy which in fact leads to more effective coordination of social policy, by providing a flexible framework in which Member States can achieve the aims of European social policy on their own terms. OMC, like the new regulatory methods applied to the social policy area since the 1990s, has the potential to bridge the gap between community and autonomy. As with the directives on European Works Councils, parental leave and part-time work, the key elements of this new approach are:

> 'minimum harmonisation (the member states may uphold or set up more stringent standards); framework legislation (only some basis principles are set up at the EC level while most details are decided at the lower tiers of the European multi-level system); and double subsidiarity (both the national level and the social partners precede traditional EC legislation by the Council)'.[116]

Thus, on an positive reading, the open method of coordination has the potential to solve the collective action problem which plagues European social and employment policy, and to reach a balance between centralized regulation on the one hand, and deregulation on the other.

## 4. Theorizing regulation

'OMC's principal advantages are that it provides the means to move towards common solutions to common problems without demanding the sort of harmonisation that would be anathema to many governments, and that it can be implemented by governments

[114] Fritz W. Scharpf, 'European Governance: Common Concerns vs the Challenge of Diversity' Jean Monnet Working Paper No 6/01, New York University Law School, Symposium: *Responses to the European Commission's White Paper on Governance*, at 9.

[115] Wolfgang Streeck, 'From Market-Making to State-Building? Some Reflections on the Political Economy of European Social Policy', in Stephan Leibfried and Paul Pierson (eds.), *European Social Policy: Between Fragmentation and Integration* (Washington DC: The Brookings Institute, 1995).

[116] Gerda Falkner, *EU Social Policy in the 1990s: Towards a Corporatist Policy Community* (London: Routledge, 1998) at 152.

without recourse to major and potentially contested legislative change. . . . Such *differentiated policy harmonisation* would represent an artful compromise between policy integration and subsidiarity.' (Ardy and Begg, 2001)[117]

In a pragmatic and sanguine assessment of the reluctance of Member States to cede competence to the EU-level institutions over issues such as labour market regulation, the Commission acknowledges that it is in part this resistance on the part of the Member States which has by necessity led to the invention of these softer methods of coordination: '[t]he experience to date suggests that Member States are willing to consider concertation and some degree of co-ordination between national policies, but that a higher level of involvement will be needed to commit the resources necessary to address sensitive issues requiring co-ordination between several Member States'.[118] Whether we label this, and related, processes 'differentiated policy harmonization', a 'responsive form of regulation',[119] 'regulated autonomy',[120] 'soft regulation',[121] a 'post-regulatory approach to governance'[122] 'reflexive harmonization',[123] or 'deliberative polyarchy',[124] in the context of employment and social policy the very 'openness' of the open method of coordination means that it requires some form of underpinning by a European-level core of fundamental rights and principles, if it is not to signal the promotion of labour market deregulation and convergence around a deregulated model. As Streeck warns, even in an entirely decentralized system, there exists an

'obligation of the "higher level" of governance under the classical concept of subsidiarity to ensure the outcomes of self-regulation are compatible with general political objectives and norms of social justice, instead of being merely market outcomes or results of a contingent distribution of power.'[125]

[117] Brian Ardy and Iain Begg, 'The European Employment Strategy: Policy Integration by the Back Door?' South Bank European Papers, No 4/2001, South Bank University European Institute, at 11; emphasis in the original.

[118] CEC, *Commission Staff Working Document*, n. 82 above, at 18.

[119] Kenneth A. Armstrong, 'Governance and the Single European Market' in Paul Craig and Gráinne de Búrca (eds.), n. 25 above, at 768. See also, Simon Deakin and Jacqueline Cook, 'Boundaries of Law and Regulation' in ESRC Centre for Business Research, *Literature Survey on Factual, Empirical and Legal Issues*, 2000, ch. 9, at 9.2.2. Papers prepared for the DTI Company Law Review (London: HMSO, 2000).

[120] Sisson and Marginson, n. 70 above, at 19.

[121] Ibid.

[122] Jim Mosher, 'Open Method of Coordination: Functional and Political Origins', (2000) 13:3 *European Community Studies Association Review*, 2–7.

[123] Simon Deakin 'Two Types of Regulatory Competition: Competitive Federalism versus Reflexive Harmonisation. A Law and Economics Perspective on *Centros*' (1999) 2 *Cambridge Yearbook of European Legal Studies*, 231–60; Catherine Barnard and Simon Deakin, 'In Search of Coherence: Social Policy, the Single Market and Fundamental Rights' (2000) 31:4 *Industrial Relations Journal*, 331–45, at 332 and throughout.

[124] Charles Sabel and Joshua Cohen, 'Sovereignty and Solidarity in the EU' in Jonathan Zeitlin and David Trubek (eds.), *Governing Work and Welfare in a New Economy: European and American Experiments* (Oxford: OUP, 2003).

[125] Wolfgang Streeck, 'European Social Policy after Maastricht: The "Social Dialogue" and "Subsidiarity"' (1994) 15:1 *Economic and Industrial Democracy*, 151–77, at 171.

How can we understand the development, and possible application, of the open method of coordination in a theoretical light? Can the open method of coordination truly represent a middle route between the tired dichotomies of intergovernmentalism versus supranationalism and regulation versus deregulation?

## 4.1 Reflexive law

One lens through which to view the open method of coordination is that offered by systems theory; but how convincing is this approach in the endeavour to explain or rationalize the new forms of governance within the EU? Social theorists, such as Talcott Parsons and Niklas Luhmann,[126] have argued that primitive societies are characterized by a low degree of differentiation into social subsystems, whereas modern societies are characterized by structural differentiation into functional subsystems—such as the economic system, the political system, the legal system and the cultural system—each of which has its own specialized 'communications medium' or 'system reference' that determines the way it interacts with its environment.[127] What Gunther Teubner refers to as the problem of 'mutual indifference' is that these social systems become so complex internally that they seek their validity only by reference to their internal rules and values; economics, for example, does not seek its legitimacy by reference to legal rules.[128] So as these systems become more autonomous of each other in modern society, it becomes harder for the state to use law to intervene to regulate areas of social life. This, in part, leads to a 'crisis of the regulatory state', since law can no longer be used to 'control' markets.

Another element of the crisis of regulation is the bureaucratization or juridification of law and the state which has occurred as the welfare state has matured and law is used in an attempt to 'tame' markets. As part of this process, 'formal rationality' (the exclusion of non-legal considerations from law-making and adjudication) has given way to 'substantive rationality' in which law is used as an instrument for purposive, goal orientated intervention.[129] Such a transition,

[126] Talcott Parsons, *The Social System* (Glencoe: Free Press, 1951); Niklas Luhmann, *Soziale Systeme: Grundriß einer allgemeinen Theorie* (Frankfurt/am Main: Suhrkamp, 1984); English translation, *Social System* (Stanford: Stanford University Press, 1995).

[127] The argument that social systems have their own 'communications medium' or 'system reference' means, for example, that the legal system is specialized for processing information in terms of the distinction legal/illegal, and the economy is specialized for doing so in terms of the distinction profitable/unprofitable: Alex Viskovatoff, 'Foundations of Niklas Luhmann's Theory of Social Systems' (1999) 29:4 *Philosophy of the Social Sciences*, 481–516, at 500–1.

[128] Gunther Teubner, 'Juridification: Concepts, Aspects, Limits, Solutions' in Gunther Teubner (ed.), *Juridification of Social Spheres: A Comparative Analysis in the Areas of Labor, Corporate, Antitrust and Social Welfare Law* (Berlin/New York: Walter de Gruyter, 1987) at 22 ff.

[129] Gunther Teubner, 'Substantive and Reflexive Elements in Modern Law' (1983) 17:2 *Law and Society Review*, 239–85, at 240.

from the 'rule orientation' of formal law to the 'result orientation' of substantive law, is a feature of juridification as the legislature 'increasingly believes it is both necessary and legitimate to intervene (for example, in markets), with the aim of steering economic and social developments in a direction which conforms with its own broad political and social objectives'.[130] Formal legal rationality can be criticized for its assumption that the freedoms guaranteed by private law (in particular, property rights and contractual freedom) and the 'spontaneous' workings of the market are sufficient to ensure social justice. The problem with substantive legal rationality, however, is that such state regulatory intervention can rigidify the social sphere—commerce, the family, industrial relations, social welfare—in ways which limit the autonomy of individuals or groups to determine their own affairs.[131]

One way out of this crisis[132] is the possibility of a transition towards more indirect means of regulatory intervention, once the direct regulation of human behaviour reaches its limits. This sort of indirect legal regulation, Teubner considers, is more likely to lead to flexible solutions to the continued need for regulation. Thus, Teubner argues, one has to abandon the idea of effective external control by law, and shift towards more indirect means of regulatory intervention.[133] The role of regulatory law must be seen instead as merely triggering the self-regulatory process within the economy—the regulation of schemes of self-regulation and the structuring of negotiating systems. In this theory of 'reflexive law', Teubner tries to find a middle way between formalism and substantive law. Thus, reflexive or regulatory law operates to provide a framework, a set of background rules, leaving actors to operate, deliberate or bargain 'in the shadow of the law':

'The mere existence of substantive law with its threat of sanctions creates negotiation positions for the parties . . . which ultimately affect the result of negotiations. . . . The advantages here are clear to see: *this method is more likely to lead to flexible, cooperative solutions geared to specific situations as opposed to rigid, approximative and authoritative solutions*. The problem of structural coupling is tackled in such a way that the official function of law, which is to decree changes of behaviour recedes into the

[130] Jon Clark, 'The Juridification of Industrial Relations: A Review Article' (1985) 14 ILJ, 69–90, at 70. [131] Ibid., at 86.

[132] Teubner identifies a third facet to the crisis of law as an effective regulatory mechanism, that he refers to as a 'regulatory trilemma', namely the danger of 'legal disintegration through society'. What this means is that increased regulation of social spheres is problematic because the forced inclusion of political criteria within legal rules endangers the integrity of the law; law loses its autonomy from politics if its only role is to pursue social objectives. See Teubner, n. 128 above, at 25–6. Of course, legal realists (and, to some extent, critical legal scholars) would argue for an open articulation of the political values inherent in law: see Felix S. Cohen 'Transcendental Nonsense and the Functional Approach' (1935) 35 *Columbia Law Review*, 809–49. However, see Duncan Kennedy 'Legal Formality' (1973) 2 *Journal of Legal Studies*, 351–98, esp. at 377 ff., where he argues, in the context of adjudication, that there is a 'third way', a judicial method distinct from both formal rule application and substantive rationality, namely reasoned elaboration.

[133] Teubner, n. 128 above, at 21.

background, whereas its latent function, which is to regulate systems of negotiation becomes crucial.'[134]

The strength of reflexive law is that rather than attempting to control markets or impose certain distributive outcomes, law is essentially procedural.[135] However, Teubner also describes reflexive law as structuring bargaining relations so as to *equalize* bargaining power; further, that reflexive law in the context of the contract relation, seeks to 'subject contracting parties to mechanisms of "public responsibility" that are designed to ensure that bargaining processes will take account of various externalities'.[136] So does reflexive law have a normative content? I would agree with de Schutter and Deakin that the reflexive law approach to issues of regulation, by placing such faith in self-regulation within subsystems, raises the question of whether safeguards need to be imposed, whether it might be necessary to impose substantive standards from above to limit the risk of abuse in power relationships.[137] Without returning to the sort of result orientation of substantive rationality which was rejected in favour of reflexive law, this form of regulation nevertheless still bears some of the hallmarks of juridification, since the state is indirectly 'steering' social actors to a desired goal; it would seem essential for the regulatory framework to have such normative underpinnings if it is not merely to replicate formal law. A helpful comparison with Teubner's threefold distinction between formal, substantive and reflexive law is Habermas' categorization of the paradigms of law. Habermas finds a solution to the 'hopeless competition' between the liberal paradigm and the welfare-state paradigm in the 'proceduralist' paradigm of law, and answers the question of how the proceduralist paradigm (or reflexive law) can revitalize the liberal democratic project, and provide scope for solidarity, without succumbing to the two extremes of 'market' or 'state':

'The proceduralist paradigm is not distinguished from the two earlier paradigms by its being "formal" in the sense of "empty" or "poor in content". In pointing to civil society and the political public sphere, it forcefully singles out points of reference from which the democratic process acquires a different weight and a role previously neglected in the realization of the system of rights. In complex societies, the scarcest resources are neither the productivity of a market economy nor the regulatory capacity of the public administration. It is above all the resources of an exhausted economy of nature and of a disintegrating social solidarity that require a nurturing approach. The forces of social

[134] Teubner, n. 128 above, at 34; emphasis added.

[135] Deakin, n. 123 above, at 245: 'regulatory interventions are most likely to be successful when they seek to achieve their ends not by direct prescription, but by inducing "second-order effects" on the part of social actors. In other words, this approach aims to "couple" external regulation with self-regulatory processes. Reflexive law therefore has a *procedural orientation*'; emphasis in the original.

[136] Teubner, n. 129 above, at 256.

[137] Olivier de Schutter and Simon Deakin, 'Reflexive Governance and the Dilemmas of Social Regulation' in Olivier de Schutter and Simon Deakin (eds.), *Social Rights and Market Forces: Is the Open Coordination of Employment and Social Policies the Future of Social Europe?* (Brussels: Bruylant, forthcoming 2005) at 5; page numbers refer to manuscript.

solidarity can be regenerated in complex societies only in the forms of communicative practices of self-determination.'[138]

Whilst the Habermasian perspective on the three paradigms of law does go some way towards answering the question as to the normative content of 'reflexive' or 'procedural' law, nevertheless, it is difficult to see in Teubner's reflexive theories a means by which societies can institutionalize values. Teubner does, though, point out that

'[t]he term "proceduralization" is easily misunderstood from a technical-legal point of view. To interpret it as a recommendation to a "post-interventionist" legislator to do without substantive legal norms and rely exclusively on procedural law instead would be to miss the point.... It is obvious that every act of procedural regulation has substantive premisses and consequences.'[139]

Nevertheless, in common with legal formalism, systems theory asserts the independence of law from other (value) systems, whereas Habermas argues that the responsibility for the failure of democracy in modern western societies lies in part with the ethic of liberal legalism which has hidden behind a methodology that law is somehow a discipline distinct from politics and power. There is, with Teubner and Luhmann a (deliberate) conflation of the use of reflexive law (and systems theory) as a descriptive and as a normative term. Teubner, on the one hand describes the crisis of regulatory/substantive law and the evolution of reflexive law; on the other hand he seems to argue that reflexive law *should* be seen as an answer to the crisis.[140]

Reflexive law remains, however, an ambiguous concept. For me, there remains in the notion of reflexive law an unresolved tension between an equation of the normative with the factual on the one hand and inclinations towards Habermasian regulative ideals on the other. This same tension characterizes many positive evaluations of OMC as an example of reflexive harmonization. As will be seen below, reflexive law approaches do have some explanatory power, and can help shed light on the genesis and ongoing evolution of the open method of coordination although, ultimately, I would contend that there is an imperfect 'fit' between theories of reflexive law and the development of new forms of governance within the EU.

## 4.2 OMC as a form of 'reflexive harmonization'?

In the UK, the policy of the Thatcher governments to remove 'rigidities' in the labour market through 'deregulation' was designed to contribute to the reduction

[138] Jürgen Habermas, *Between Facts and Norms: Contribution to a Discourse Theory of Law and Democracy* (Cambridge, MA: MIT Press, 1996) at 445.

[139] Gunther Teubner, *Law as an Autopoietic System* (Oxford: Blackwell, 1993) at 66.

[140] 'Here my aim is to defend the dual character of the idea of reflexive law as both normative and analytic. Reflexion in law means both empirical analysis and normative evaluation', Teubner, n. 139 above, at 69.

of inflationary pressures and to the promotion of a competitive economy.[141] The use of labour law as tool of economic policy is, accordingly, familiar at national level; but in the context of European integration, how effective can '*soft* law' be as an instrument of economic steering?[142]

Catherine Barnard and Simon Deakin have argued that the emergence of the open method as a technique of regulation in economic and social policy can best be understood in terms of reflexive theory. In other words, the open method is an example of the EU forsaking direct regulatory intervention in Member States, and instead seeking to achieve common goals not by imposing them, but through establishing a framework within which Member States are free to be self-regulating. The open method is thus a form of regulation which aims to 'preserve spaces for experimentation in rule-making, and . . . promote regulatory learning through the exchange of information between different jurisdictional levels'.[143]

It is certainly true that the open method allows for regulation at one step removed. In one of the areas where the open method was first applied, the coordination of employment policies, the overall objectives are set by the European Council, but it is left to the Member States to set national and regional level targets to reach these objectives.[144] Where benchmarks or targets *are* set at European level, Member States are responsible for 'translating' these guidelines into national and regional policies, 'taking into account national and regional differences'.[145] Indeed, OMC is applied precisely in those areas where there is little or no Community competence and where the main field of action is national, since it nevertheless enables Member States and the Community to coordinate their policies. OMC thus eases the tension between inter-governmentalism and supranationalism since it aims to achieve common goals without threatening jealously guarded national sovereignty. In sensitive political areas, the use of the 'classic' Community method, with its 'centralization of policy formation' is a problematic way of achieving policy convergence, whereas the open method would seem to be an ideal means of facilitating further

[141] Simon Deakin and Keith Ewing, 'Inflation, Economic Performance and Employment Rights' ESRC Centre for Business Research, University of Cambridge, Working Paper No 45, 1996, at 2. Governmental policy followed a strategy perhaps most clearly elaborated in the 1985 White Paper *Employment: The Challenge for the Nation*, UK Department of Employment (London: HMSO, 1985).

[142] Michael Wynn, 'European Social Dialogue: Harmonisation or New Diversity?' in Hugh Collins, Paul Davies and Roger Rideout (eds.), *Legal Regulation of the Employment Relation*, WG Hart Legal Workshop Series (London/The Hague: Kluwer, 2000) at 492.

[143] Catherine Barnard and Simon Deakin, 'Market Access and Regulatory Competition' in Catherine Barnard and Joanne Scott (eds.), *The Law of the Single European Market: Unpacking the Premises*, (Oxford: Hart Publishing, 2002) at 218–19. See also Barnard and Deakin, n. 123 above.

[144] Caroline de la Porte, 'Is the Open Method of Co-ordination Appropriate for Organising Activities at European Level in Sensitive Policy Areas?' (2002) 8:1 *European Law Journal*, 38–58.

[145] Presidency Conclusions, Lisbon European Council, n. 12 above, at para 37.

Europeanization 'outside existing institutional forms'.[146] In certain areas of policy-making, the 'Monnet' method is abandoned for a new form of governance, which draws upon and weaves together concepts which have been developed over the years, such as subsidiarity, benchmarking and 'partnership'.[147] As the European Council puts it:

> 'A fully decentralised approach will be applied in line with the principle of subsidiarity in which the Union, the Member States, the regional and local levels, as well as the social partners and civil society, will be actively involved, using variable forms of partnership. A method of benchmarking best practices on managing change will be devised by the European Commission networking with different providers and users, namely the social partners, companies and NGOs.'[148]

Although the Commission's White Paper on *Governance* provided a less than wholehearted endorsement of the open method, elsewhere within the Commission, there was enthusiasm for what this new method could offer.[149] In particular, other voices within the Commission pointed to the ability of OMC to engender a gradualist approach to the development of an EU policy in difficult areas such as immigration, based on the identification and development of common objectives to which it is agreed that a European response is necessary. Only then, after this 'phasing in period' and in the light of the evaluation of the implementation of the coordination method, would the Commission consider introducing legislative instruments to provide for the coordination of the common policy.[150] Developed in the context of the Employment Strategy, but with wider application, the Commission has identified five principles which underpin the open method: subsidiarity, convergence, management by objectives, country surveillance and an integrated approach.[151] These principles resonate with the conceptualization of OMC as a form of reflexive harmonization. In particular, the Commission describes OMC's respect for subsidiarity as establishing an 'equilibrium' between European Union level coordination of common objectives and outcomes, and Member States' responsibilities in deciding the detailed content of action.[152] Here, one can see 'second-order effects' of the sort described

[146] Dermot Hodson and Imelda Maher, 'The Open Method as a New Mode of Governance: The Case of Soft Economic Policy Co-ordination' (2001) 39:4 *Journal of Common Market Studies*, 719–46, at 721–2.

[147] For a discussion of the concept of 'partnership' in the context of the implementation of regional policy, see Joanne Scott, 'Law, Legitimacy and EC Governance: Prospects for "Partnership"' (1998) 36:2 *Journal of Common Market Studies*, 175–94.

[148] Presidency Conclusions, Lisbon European Council, n. 12 above, at para 38.

[149] CEC, *European Governance: A White Paper*, n. 99 above. For a fuller discussion, see Section 5 below.

[150] CEC, Communication from the Commission to the Council and the European Parliament on an *Open Method of Coordination for the Community Immigration Policy*, COM (2001) 387 final Brussels, 11.7.2001, at 5.

[151] CEC, 'Introduction to the EES: The Added Value of an "Open Method of Co-ordination"' available on the Europa website, at *http://europa.eu.int/comm./employment_social/employment_strategy/index_en.htm* [accessed 10 April 2005].

[152] Ibid.

by reflexive theories: common objectives, guidelines, indicators and benchmarks are set at EU level, whilst the definition of the means and conditions under which programmes and policies are implemented is left to a large extent to individual Member States. The European Employment Strategy, the Lisbon Strategy and the instruments of economic governance (the BEPGs and the Stability and Growth Pact) establish the parameters within which Member States are free to be self-regulating. As I will argue below and in Chapter 6, although the space within which Member States have autonomy may in truth be seriously curtailed as far as *employment* policy is concerned, in other policy areas where the open method is deployed, coordination is more 'light' or 'open', thus suggesting that reflexive harmonization may well be an apposite analytical framework by which to understand OMC more generally. In the context of social inclusion policy, as the *Joint Inclusion Report* for 2004 explains, '[o]ne important methodological principle for the selection of the commonly agreed indicators is that they must measure social outcomes rather than the means by which they are achieved'.[153] In other words, the essence of the open method of coordination is that Member States agree on objectives but are left free to choose the policies by which these objectives are to be met, so that, in theory 'one country may achieve low poverty rates by active labour market policy; another may place more reliance on social transfers'.[154]

To gain a better understanding of the extent to which Member States can truly be 'self-regulating' it is instructive to compare this assessment of OMC with a Member State's perspective on what the open method means for the traditional choice between harmonization and regulatory competition. It is therefore worth quoting at length the UK government's position:

'Lisbon marked a recognition not only that all EU economies needed to undertake further structural reforms, but also that the traditional Community method, which had served the EU well in the construction first of a Customs Union and then of a Single Market, would not always be appropriate to this challenge. The construction of a Single Market had inevitably entailed . . . a raft of Community legislation. In the bulk of other areas covered by Lisbon, however, national reforms tailored by, and designed to fit, individual Member States' circumstances will be more appropriate and effective.

Even in those areas in which new Community-level legislation is required to complete, maintain and strengthen the Single Market, the Government believes that, consistent with the Lisbon approach, this legislation should be no more prescriptive for Member

[153] CEC, *Joint Report on Social Inclusion 2004*, n. 92 above, at 23. See also Tony Atkinson, 'Social Europe and Social Science', The 13th ESRC Annual Lecture, 17 October 2002 (Swindon: ESRC, 2002).

[154] Atkinson, n. 153 above, at 6. Having said that, in exercising this choice over policy input, Member States must nevertheless ensure that they also promote active labour market policies, as agreed in the context of the Employment Strategy, and are careful that social transfers do not cause public expenditure to exceed the parameters set by the requirements of macro-economic stability and fiscal prudence.

States than it needs to be. It should also avoid excessive harmonisation in favour of promoting the role of *mutual recognition* in constructing a true Single Market.'[155]

Benchmarking was promoted by business interests in great part as an alternative to more labour market regulation. This view of the merits of 'soft law', and, by extension, of the open method, seems to be shared by the UK government. It is no coincidence that the UK government (in particular the Treasury, which produced the Economic Reform White Paper) is so enthusiastic about the open method: in the Treasury's understanding, OMC is not only a means to favour intergovernmentalism over supranational harmonization, it is also a useful technique to minimize reliance on regulation, instead adopting a 'light touch'.[156]

Although the UK government uses the language of mutual recognition, seemingly equating the open method with 'negative integration', I would argue—in some sympathy with the view of OMC as a form of reflexive harmonization—that OMC is better understood as offering a *compromise* between negative and positive integration, between regulatory competition and full harmonization. The Treasury White Paper starts with the traditional definition of mutual recognition, from the classic European Court decision on free movement of goods,[157] yet broadens it out to cover the same territory that the open method does today. Recognizing that mutual recognition will lead to regulatory competition, the Treasury White Paper disputes that this is necessarily a bad thing. In fact, the Treasury White Paper take pains to point out that so long as there are high levels of trust between national regulators, sustained by full and transparent exchange of information and agreement on the core standards national regimes need to embody, regulatory competition can in fact result in a 'race to the top' rather than a 'race to the bottom':

'In economic terms, the continuing presence of some regulatory competition, *coupled with Lisbon-type processes* to benchmark and peer review Member State regulatory regimes, will lead to better outcomes for the EU as a whole than would a single harmonised regulatory model.'[158]

If the word 'harmonization' were not such anathema to the UK government, then one could describe its assessment of regulation in the era of OMC as a process of reflexive harmonization, not as an example of mutual recognition.[159]

[155] HM Treasury White Paper, *Realising Europe's Potential: Economic Reform in Europe*, Cm 5318 (London: HMSO, 2002) at paras 3.6 and 3.9; emphasis in the original.

[156] 'The new policy framework, overseen by the European Council and supported by the Commission, tilts the balance away from the traditional reliance on intervention and regulation, and towards a lighter approach intended to foster enterprise, innovation and competition': ibid., at 3.3.

[157] Case 120/78, *Rewe-Zentrale AG v Bundesmonopolverwaltung für Branntwein (Cassis de Dijon)* [1979] ECR 649.

[158] HM Treasury, n. 155 above, at 3.12; emphasis added.

[159] Barnard and Deakin n. 143 above, at 220: 'Reflexive harmonisation operates to induce individual states to enter into a "race to the top".... This is done by giving states a number of options for implementation as well as by allowing for the possibility that existing, self-regulatory

The concept of reflexive law thus offers a very valuable intellectual tool, and the most promising analytical framework, with which to understand the open method. But for me there remain a number of caveats. First, reflexive theories do not capture the whole reality of OMC, in terms of being descriptively precise. OMC only partially fits into the paradigm model of governance envisaged by reflexive harmonization, which is not to say that the open method could not over time approximate towards this model. Despite the extensive analysis of OMC by EU scholars and within political circles, it is arguable that the open method has not been fully internalized by key policy-makers; there is a lack of 'ownership' of the Lisbon Strategy, and of the open method within that.[160] The model of regulation favoured by theories of reflexive harmonization does not fully account for this reluctance on the part of the relevant actors to engage with the process in its entirety, or for the insufficient involvement of stakeholders other than national governments. Further, account needs to be taken of the political reality of the operation of OMC, wherein Member States seek to conceal the European origins of certain policy initiatives. In the course of 'translating' European guidelines into national and regional policies, Member States appear reluctant to acknowledge the external sources influencing the domestic policy agenda, or seek to recycle existing domestic policies by adopting the rhetoric of the open method and the Lisbon Strategy to describe pre-existing policies. Such developments are inadequately accounted for in notions of 'mutual learning'.

Second, even if reflexive harmonization is *descriptively* an appropriate name for the open method, there is the question whether, *normatively*, it is right to adopt a reflexive approach to regulation, to the extent that such an approach eschews a normative content for policy coordination in areas such as employment. The earlier enquiry into the apparent lack of a normative content of reflexive law arises equally in the context of the open method: if what we are witnessing is a rejection of the failures of both formal and substantive rationality, a rejection of intervention which seeks to impose particular distributive outcomes, does this mean that reflexive regulation by means of 'soft law' must also reject the values which had previously informed labour market regulation? I will return to these questions in the conclusion to this chapter, and in Chapter 7, by means of the discussion of 'soft harmonization' through 'hard law'. However, it is worth noting that even on their own terms, theories of reflexive law would surely recognize the need for some substantive content—so that in the context of

mechanisms can be used to comply with EU-wide standards. In these ways, far from suppressing regulatory innovation, harmonisation aims to stimulate it'.

[160] 'The governance of the Lisbon Strategy needs radical improvement to make it more effective and more easily understood. Responsibilities have been muddled between the Union and its Member States. There are too many overlapping and bureaucratic reporting procedures and not enough political ownership': CEC, Communication to the Spring European Council, *Working together for growth and jobs: A new start for the Lisbon Strategy*, Brussels, 02.02.2005 COM (2005) 24 at 10.

employment policy coordination, policies are underpinned by the principles contained in the EU's Social Policy Agenda or the EU Charter of Fundamental Rights. As Teubner acknowledges, 'reflexive law does not merely adapt to or support "natural social orders". Quite to the contrary, it searches for "regulated autonomy".'[161]

## 4.3 OMC as an example of 'democratic experimentalism'?

In a development which echoes the application of reflexive theories to the open method of coordination, theories of deliberative democracy have also been deployed to provide an explanatory framework for OMC and related developments in EU governance. For instance, Charles Sabel and Joshua Cohen have adapted earlier work on deliberative democracy and democratic experimentalism to new forms of governance within the EU, arguing that the open method of coordination can be seen as a form of 'directly-deliberative polyarchy', because it encourages a form of problem solving which is more experimental and open, and better suited to the regulation of complex fields than traditional forms of regulation.[162] The relevance of theories of deliberative democracy to the open method can be seen in the ideas developed in two companion pieces by Dorf and Sabel, and Cohen and Sabel.[163] Dorf and Sabel identify a new form of government, based on the premise that deliberation lies at the heart of democratic and effective decision-making. This form of government, democratic experimentalism, centres on the coordination of local-level decision-making:

> 'In democratic experimentalism, subnational units of government are broadly free to set goals and to choose the means to attain them. Regulatory agencies set and ensure compliance with national objectives by means of best-practice performance standards based on information that regulated entities provide in return for the freedom to experiment with solutions they prefer.'[164]

The authors of the theory use 'democratic experimentalism' as a generic term for a political system that follows the logic of decentralized problem-solving.[165] Such governance is 'democratic' in the sense that power is decentralized to enable citizens to participate in decisions affecting them; and it is 'experimental' in that there is the freedom to try out alternatives at local level. In contrast to traditional regulation, based on rigid, authoritative standards, the hallmark of democratic

[161] Teubner, n. 129 above, at 254–5.

[162] Joshua Cohen and Charles Sabel, 'Directly-Deliberative Polyarchy' (1997) 3:4 *European Law Journal*, 313–42; Joshua Cohen and Charles Sabel, 'Sovereignty and Solidarity: EU and US' in Jonathan Zeitlin and David Trubek (eds.), *Governing Work and Welfare in a New Economy: European and American Experiments* (Oxford: OUP, 2003).

[163] Michael Dorf and Charles Sabel, 'A Constitution of Democratic Experimentalism' (1998) 98: 2 *Columbia Law Review*, 267–473.

[164] Dorf and Sabel, n. 163 above, at 267.

[165] Burkard Eberlein and Dieter Kerwer, 'New Governance in the European Union: A Theoretical Perspective' (2004) 42: 1 *Journal of Common Market Studies*, 121–42, at 131.

experimentalism is the use of 'rolling [i.e. continually evolving] best-practice rules' based on benchmarking.[166] The term 'directly-deliberative polyarchy' is used, more specifically, to refer to the polity itself. The term arises from the fact that such a polity relies on direct or participatory forms of governance; it requires collective decisions to be made through public deliberation in arenas open to citizens; and it is polyarchic in the sense that virtually all adults have rights of suffrage, political expression, association, and so on.[167]

'Ideally, then, directly-deliberative polyarchy combines the advantages of local learning and self-government with the advantages (and discipline) of wider social learning and heightened political accountability that result when the outcomes of many concurrent experiments are pooled to permit public scrutiny of the effectiveness of strategies and leaders.'[168]

Taken together, these two perspectives on deliberative democracy provide an uncanny prefiguring of the open method of coordination, or at least a far-sighted prediction of the changing nature of supranational governance, as it seeks to resolve the problems of institutional failure, or what Scharpf has called the 'joint decision trap'. However, as with reflexive theories, a key question to ask is the extent to which the lived reality of OMC matches up to these ideal types; are democratic experimentalism and directly-deliberative polyarchy *descriptively* appropriate names for the open method of coordination? Moreover, despite assertions to the contrary, part of the deliberative democracy project with regard to new governance *is* normative, and may well overstate the extent to which the open method of coordination is truly 'open' and participatory.[169] The 'openness' of the open method of coordination can refer to the possibility that the input is open (that there is deliberative input), as well as to the possibility that the output or outcomes are open (possibly less so in the case of employment policy coordination and economic policy coordination). However, empirical analyses of the operation of the open method in the context of the Employment Strategy do point to signs of it being much more 'top down' (ie that the regional level should simply ensure implementation of the Employment Strategy) than 'bottom up' (ie recognizing national diversity and the need for experimentation).[170] How

[166] Dorf and Sabel, n. 163 above, at 350. They explain this more fully, thus: 'Although benchmarking is formalized in a fully fledged system of democratic experimentalism, it can begin informally as a rough comparison of competing models and alternative performance measures. So long as the comparisons meet the pragmatist criterion of casting doubt on the assumption that current arrangements cannot be improved and suggest directions for improvement (including refinement of the comparisons), they count as polyarchic benchmarking, and encourage the generalization of forms of deliberation on which their own improvement depends, whether institutionalized or not': ibid, at 321.

[167] Cohen and Sabel (1997) n. 162 above, at 313–14 and 317–18.

[168] Cohen and Sabel (1997) n. 162 above, at 314.

[169] Cohen and Sabel indeed contend that their aim is 'neither to articulate a set of normative principles and deduce institutional conclusions from them, nor to predict the course of current institutional evolution': ibid., at 317.

[170] Cécile Barbier, Caroline de la Porte and Philippe Pochet, 'European Briefing' (2002) 12:3 *Journal of European Social Policy*, 241–8, at 242.

much is the open method of coordination of employment policy truly deliberative, democratic or open to experimentation? The understanding by the European institutions of the process points in opposite directions, even at the level of rhetoric. Compare:

'We have done this [making progress towards sustainable development] by acting in partnership—Europe's institutions, government and administrations at a national, regional and local level, our social partners, civil society—all moving together towards a common goal.'[171]

with:

'Making sure that these objectives and reforms are taken on board by all the various players: The Lisbon Strategy failed to commit the key players sufficiently in terms of delivery, particularly at national level. Mobilisation is possible only if the various players feel that the policies proposed concern them, and that they are truly involved in the decision-making and implementation process'.[172]

One of the key themes of the 'new start' for the Lisbon Strategy in 2005 was precisely the concern, identified by the Commission and endorsed by the European Council, that the Lisbon Strategy had been less than successful because of its failure to engage fully the relevant stakeholders at EU, national, regional and local levels—namely, Member States, citizens, parliaments, social partners and civil society, as well as all Community institutions. If the open method of coordination of employment policy is not sufficiently enthusing and engaging these stakeholders, is it more accurately seen as an example of 'bureaucratic management' than as a precursor to a brave new world of 'new democratization'?[173] Democratic participation is, arguably, impeded by the mountain of documentation to which the various open methods give rise in the reiterative process of agreeing and refining indicators, benchmarking and peer review; hence the call by the European Council to simplify and streamline coordination of economic policy and coordination of employment policy in the new Integrated Guidelines for Growth and Jobs.[174] Nevertheless, this streamlining may be insufficient to ensure the sort of transparency which is surely a prerequisite for public participation and deliberation. Furthermore, the extent to which stakeholders such as social partners are able to participate in the formation and implementation of employment policy—for example in contributing to Member

[171] CEC, A *new start for the Lisbon Strategy*, n. 160 above, at 3.

[172] Ibid., at 14. The European Council endorses the need to extend the sense of 'ownership' of the Employment and Lisbon Strategies: 'Alongside the governments, all the other players concerned—parliaments, regional and local bodies, social partners and civil society—should be *stakeholders* in the Strategy and take an active part in attaining its objectives': Presidency Conclusions, Brussels European Council, 22 and 23 March 2005, Bull EU 3/2005, at para 6; emphasis added.

[173] Susana Borrás and Bent Greve, 'Concluding remarks: New method or just cheap talk?' (2004) 11:2 *Journal of European Public Policy*, 329–36, at 333.

[174] Presidency Conclusions, Brussels European Council, n. 172 above, at paras 38–41; CEC, *A new start for the Lisbon Strategy* n. 160 above, at 5, 10 and 12.

States' National Action Plans—may well be determined by the question of path dependency,[175] so that states with a stronger tradition of social partner involvement more readily provide mechanisms and platforms for participation by social partners. For example, reporting on the Member States' progress towards the Lisbon goals as evidenced in their National Action Plans, the first *Joint Employment Report* after the launch of the Employment Strategy noted that, whilst the role of the social partners in the UK was substantially different from that in most other EU countries, they were nevertheless *involved* in the NAP implementation.[176] However, successive *Joint Employment Reports* continued to observe that such involvement has been 'still too much focused on a few aspects of the NAP',[177] or that consultation with the devolved administrations and the English regions could be developed, or that whilst the NAP is made available to the UK Parliament 'visibility remains low' and the devolved administrations and the social partners are only 'consulted' during the preparation of the NAP.[178]

The relatively limited role given to social partners, other civil society actors and sub-national levels of government in the development of NAPs, in the UK at least, would appear to undermine claims that the process of employment policy coordination is in practice either democratic (in the sense of being fully participatory) or indeed an instrument of directly deliberative polyarchy. As for *experimentalism*, with much of the agenda and many of the objectives, targets and indicators agreed centrally, what scope can there be for Member States and sub-national actors to exercise choice over policy outcomes in the context of the Lisbon Strategy, and the Employment Strategy within that? As will be seen below in the analysis of policy transfer, the structure of the open method of coordination of employment policy means that there is a limited space within which Member States are truly free to experiment.

There is much overlap between the theoretical approach to OMC just described, seeing it as an example of deliberative democracy, and the perspective of reflexive harmonization, in particular in that both perceive OMC as allowing for 'bottom-up' governance.[179] What is undoubtedly clear is that OMC does not fit neatly into the classic Community method of governance; it cannot be readily classified as either 'negative' or positive integration.[180] However, neither can it be straightforwardly categorized as promoting experimental learning and

[175] Borrás and Greve, n. 173 above, at 334.

[176] CEC, *Employment Policies in the EU and in the Member States: Joint Report 1998* (Luxembourg: OOPEC, 1998) at 115.

[177] CEC, *Joint Employment Report 1999*, n. 1 above, at 90.

[178] CEC, *Joint Employment Report 2004–5—Addendum 1: Country Fiches* (Luxembourg: OOPEC, 2005) at 95.

[179] Stijn Smismans goes so far as to argue for a synthesis of these two approaches, and proposes a new theoretical model, which he labels 'reflexive deliberative polyarchy': Stijn Smismans, 'Reflexive Law in Support of Directly Deliberative Polyarchy: Reflexive-Deliberative Polyarchy as a Normative Frame for the OMC' in Olivier de Schutter and Simon Deakin (eds.), n. 137 above.

[180] Armstrong, n. 89 above, at 172.

deliberative problem solving. Theories of new governance seeking to explain OMC often lack empirical grounding or authority; but as will be seen below and in Chapter 6 on the influence of the Employment Strategy, the empirical evidence points to a process which, whilst internally contradictory, is at least *capable* of providing an alternative to both intergovernmentalism and supranationalism, at the same time as seeking to redress the imbalance the EU's social and economic objectives.

## 4.4 OMC as (voluntary) policy learning or (coercive) policy transfer?

However, an altogether different lens through which to view the open method of coordination of employment policy is to ask how much freedom of action Member States really have, without risking breach of their obligations to implement national policy in light of the Employment Guidelines? What counts as compliance with such 'soft law'? To what extent are Member States constrained in what they can do with their employment policy? As Caroline de la Porte shows, although the open method is supposed to respect 'national practices, discourses and frames of reference',[181] in practice it requires more fundamental structural alterations for some Member States. Arguably, countries with 'Southern' and 'Continental' welfare state regimes[182] have to make radical adjustments to their welfare provisions in order to be in a position to engage with the European-level objectives for employment policy. It is apparent that the objective of raising the employment rate,[183] in particular, enjoys a closer fit with the welfare state models of the Scandinavian countries, and to some extent the Anglo-Saxon countries, which already have high participation rates, especially amongst women. For example, the Member States with the highest employment rates are Denmark, Sweden and the UK, whilst those with the lowest include Italy, Spain and Greece.[184] The latter group are therefore under particular

[181] de la Porte, n. 144 above, at 56.

[182] Gøsta Esping-Andersen, *The Three Worlds of Welfare Capitalism* (Cambridge: Polity Press, 1990) and Gøsta Esping-Andersen (ed.), *Welfare States in Transition: National Adaptations in Global Economies* (London: Sage, 1996).

[183] From an overall average of 61 per cent to 70 per cent by 2010, with the related target of raising the female employment rate from an average of 51 per cent to more than 60 per cent;.

[184] At the time the Lisbon employment targets were set in 2000, Italy had an employment rate of 53.5 per cent overall and 39.6 per cent for women; Spain 55.0 per cent and 40.3 per cent; Greece 55.6 per cent and 40.9 per cent; Denmark 76.3 per cent and 71.6 per cent; Sweden 73.0 per cent and 71.0 per cent; the UK 71.2 per cent and 64.6 per cent: CEC, *Joint Employment Report 2001*, n. 8, above at 14. The Netherlands was as an exception, then and now, in that although its welfare regime belongs to the 'Continental' family, it has undergone adjustment strategies, and its overall employment rate was 73.2 per cent, and 63.7 per cent for women. The most recent available statistics show some improvement in the employment rates for the southern European countries, although the gap between these and the Scandinavian/Anglo-Saxon countries remains mostly unchanged: see CEC, *Employment in Europe 2004: Recent Trends and Prospects* (Luxembourg: OOPEC. 2004) Statistical Annex.

pressure to converge with the benchmark standards, to reformulate their welfare state systems away from the male breadwinner/female carer model. A typical example of the sort of change required by such Member States was that indicated in the recommendation to Spain, contained in the *Joint Employment Report 2001*, that '[t]he aim of increasing female employment rates needs the urgent implementation of critical efficient measures, especially to promote the reconciliation of family and work and, in particular, childcare and other dependant care'.[185]

The argument raised earlier, that the benchmarking methodology runs the risk of ignoring certain institutional characteristics,[186] could equally be applied to the open method as a whole. The Lisbon target for employment rates is an example of a policy where the 'mutual learning' which is one of the core features of OMC may in fact necessitate a rather '*discontinuous* jump towards new ways of organizing knowledge'[187] for a Member State whose labour market is structured according to a different paradigm. In contrast, Trubek and Mosher would argue that this facet of the Employment Strategy is no bad thing: '[t]he guidelines and the underlying strategy they reflect do, to varying degrees, challenge national policies in many countries and thus *should* destabilize prior understandings'.[188] New understandings in Member States, brought about by 'learning-promoting mechanisms'[189] such as the exchange of best practice and the setting of numerical targets for increasing labour market participation, are considered necessary if the Employment Strategy is to be effective.

The question at the heart of this distinction is whether the Employment Strategy, and the open method more generally, are best understood as forms of (coercive) policy transfer, or merely as forms of policy learning—although both could arguably lead to policy convergence.[190] Whilst attracting growing attention in recent years, political science literature on 'policy transfer' in the context of Europeanization is still in its infancy,[191] but policy transfer is generally understood as follows:

> 'Through informal or more institutionalised exchanges, governments study each other's different methods, gauge the success of various policy alternatives, and mimic 'best practices' employed elsewhere. Successful policies become transferred deliberately and willingly.'[192]

[185] CEC, *Joint Employment Report 2001*, n. 8 above, at 55.

[186] See n. 72 above, and accompanying text.

[187] Claudio Radaelli, 'Discourse and Institutional Change: The Case of Italy in the Euro-Zone', Queen's Papers on Europeanisation, No 5/2000; emphasis added. Paper available at: *http://www.qub.ac.uk/schools/* [accessed 10 April 2005].

[188] Trubek and Mosher, n. 81 above, at 77; emphasis added. [189] Ibid.

[190] For a discussion of policy transfer in the context of EMU, see Hodson and Maher, n. 146 above, at 727.

[191] See, however, Elizabeth Bomberg and John Peterson, 'Policy Transfer and Europeanisation: Passing the Heineken Test?' Queen's Papers on Europeanisation, No 2/2000. Paper available at: *http://www.qub.ac.uk/schools/* [accessed 10 April 2005].

[192] Bomberg and Peterson, n. 191 above, at 10.

This would seem to have some explanatory power in light of the benchmarking and peer review methodology adopted within the EU for implementing the Employment Strategy. However, policy transfer can also be more coercive: Dolowitz and Marsh suggest a continuum that runs from voluntary lesson-drawing (or policy learning) which does not necessarily result in institutional change, to coercive policy transfer—the direct imposition of a programme, policy or institutional arrangement on one political system by another.[193] How does this concept of policy transfer help us to understand the likely impact of the open method of coordination? Ferrera *et al.* are critical of anything that would amount to an 'ill-thought out strategy of policy transfer' which ignores differences in existing policy mixes and institutional settings.[194] What should be resisted, in their view, is the idea that there is 'one best way'. Ferrera *et al.* therefore welcome 'soft co-ordination procedures' since the iterative character of these procedures

> 'helps create trust and co-operative orientations among actors, encourages learning and promotes a general dynamic of institutionalisation, whereby actors internalize norms of conduct, stabilize expectations and start to behave according to a logic of "appropriateness" '[195]

Certainly, one way in which the open method is achieving policy convergence is through the emergence of a common discourse among elite actors (EU institutions, national ministries, the social partners). It is arguable that the process of communication and socialization in transnational political-administrative networks is leading to the development of common perceptions of problems and solutions, a form of 'integration through coordination'.[196] In this way, the open method can be equated with policy learning, or a voluntary form of policy transfer. However, to return to the questions raised earlier (to what extent are Member States constrained in what they can do with their employment policies, and how *discontinuous* is the shift to new policies?), it is also the case that the open method contains elements of coercive, as well as voluntary, policy transfer. States may face internal as well as international pressure to mimic practices from elsewhere. Using the case study of workfare policies, Dolowitz and Marsh show how the decision of the Thatcher government to adopt American-style welfare-to-work programmes in the mid-1980s was due to a mix of voluntary and coercive forces (the twin fears of losing the next general election and of falling behind the international market for jobs and products).[197] Similarly, when other

[193] David P. Dolowitz and David Marsh, 'Learning from Abroad: The Role of Policy Transfer in Contemporary Policy-Making' (2000) 13:1 *Governance: An International Journal of Policy and Administration*, 5–24, at 13 ff.

[194] Maurizio Ferrera, Anton Hemerijck and Martin Rhodes, *The Future of Social Europe: Recasting Work and Welfare in the New Economy* (Oeiras: Celta Editora, 2000) at 53–4.

[195] Ibid., at 84.

[196] Silvana Sciarra, 'Integration Through Coordination: The Employment Title in the Amsterdam Treaty' (2000) 6:2 *Columbia Journal of European Law*, 209–29.

[197] Dolowitz and Marsh, n. 193 above, at 15.

European countries began looking to American and British workfare programmes, some, such as Belgium, were doing so voluntarily; others, such as Norway, were doing so because of a perception amongst key policy-makers that they were falling behind an international trend.[198]

Although any policy transfer which does occur as a result of OMC may well be weak in comparison to the way in which ideas, policies and rules contained in traditional, hierarchical, 'hard law' influence Member States' governance,[199] nevertheless I would identify a transfer effect generated by the Employment Strategy via the open method of coordination. The use of 'soft' mechanisms to persuade Member States to change their policies—such as identification of best practice, peer review and benchmarking of standards to be attained—can nevertheless have the effect of changing not only the direction of Member States' policies (for example, in shifting from passive to active labour market policies), but also the discourse itself, altering the boundaries of what is considered an acceptable range of policy choices for EU states.

Accordingly, I would argue that elements of the open method are indeed quite 'hard' or coercive, especially if one considers that any implementation measures formulated at national level must comply not only with the Employment Guidelines, but also with the BEPGs. Further, although the Council Recommendations on the implementation of Member States' employment policies are not legally binding, they do carry a normative weight, and in this context in particular have the additional authority of being part of a common employment strategy *to which Member States have already committed themselves* in the Treaty and at each European Council meeting. Whilst there may well be a gap between what Member States say in the context of the Council of Ministers and the European Council, and what they do in their domestic policies, any such mismatch will not remain unnoticed, thanks to the multi-annual surveillance and system of peer review and benchmarking.[200]

Three examples should suffice. The BEPGs for 2002 make the following country-specific policy guidelines in the case of Greece: after surveying the country's economic activity and budgetary policy, the Council notes that, despite recent reform measures, the Greek labour market 'still displays a number of

198 Ibid., at 14.

199 See, for example, Bulmer and Padgett, who describe transfer outcomes in employment policy as characterized by 'diffuse influence': Simon Bulmer and Stephen Padgett, 'Policy Transfer in the European Union: An Institutionalist Perspective' (2005) 35:1 *British Journal of Political Science*, 103–26, at 123. They also argue that 'transfer outcomes under governance by facilitated unilateralism [such as OMC] are significantly weaker than under hierarchical modes of governance [such as the classic Community method]. Informal rules and "soft" compliance mechanisms... entail, at best, only the very weakest forms of transfer effect'; ibid., at 124.

200 Contrast this assessment of OMC in the context of employment policy with that of Daguerre and Taylor-Gooby, who consider OMC to be a 'typical example of voluntary policy transfer': Anne Daguerre and Peter Taylor-Gooby, 'Neglecting Europe: Explaining the Predominance of American Ideas in New Labour's Welfare Policies Since 1997' (2004) 14:1 *Journal of European Social Policy*, 25–39, at 26.

problems including: heavy labour market regulation; insufficient wage differentiation; and distortions to incentives to work in the formal sector embedded in pension entitlements and in the tax system'.[201] Accordingly, priorities for Greece are identified, which include ensuring the full implementation of recent labour market reform packages; further loosening of 'restrictive employment protection legislation'; and ensuring that wages take into account productivity and local labour market conditions better.[202] Such Recommendations to reform labour markets which have been characterized as heavily regulated, and to link wages more closely to productivity, really leave very little room for an alternative strategy to that of labour market deregulation and downward wage flexibility.

A second example is that of low participation rates amongst older people in Belgium,[203] which have prompted the Council to recommend that Belgium should examine disincentives to labour market participation within the tax and benefit system, particularly those affecting older workers, and in particular focus on measures to prevent the early withdrawal of workers from work and consider strengthening disincentive measures in this area.[204] This forecloses the option, once common across many EU countries, of encouraging early withdrawal from the labour market (into early retirement, or on to forms of disability or sickness benefit) so as to decrease the numbers officially registered as unemployed.[205]

Thirdly, to take an example from the old 'Employability pillar', one of the few targets in the first set of guidelines (as discussed in Chapter 4), was that Member States increase their 'activation' rate—the numbers of unemployed who are offered training or any similar active measure—to the average of the three most successful Member States, and to at least 20 per cent, by 2002. By 2000, all Member States save the UK had achieved an activation rate above the 20 per cent target.[206] With an activation rate only slightly above 12 per cent, the Council not surprisingly recommended that the UK reinforce active labour market policies for the adult unemployed before the 12 month point, and supplement the support provided by the Jobseekers' Allowance regime. In actual fact, active labour market policies, such as the New Deal, are already an important part of the UK government's agenda to combat unemployment; the Council Recommendations are thus pushing policy along a course already established at national level.

[201] Council Recommendation of 21 June 2002 on the broad guidelines of the economic policies of the Member States and the Community, (2002/549/EC) OJ L 182/1, 11.7.2002, at 28.

[202] Ibid.

[203] For years the lowest in the Union, in 2003 this figure was 28.1 per cent as against the EU15 average of 40.2 per cent: CEC, *Employment in Europe, 2004*, n. 184 above, Statistical Annex; figures for the employment rate as a percentage of the population aged 55–64.

[204] Council Recommendation of 18 February 2002 on the implementation of Member States' employment policies, (2002/178/EC) OJ L 60/70, 1.3.2002.

[205] See Chapter 6, Section 2 for a fuller discussion of what 'compliance' with the Employment Strategy entails for this and other policy areas.

[206] CEC, *Joint Employment Report 2001*, n. 8 above, at 21.

These three examples indicate how far Member States can, or rather cannot, stray from the centrally agreed agenda for employment and economic policy, a point which will be explored again in Chapter 6. For instance, the adoption of *passive* labour market policies, or a reluctance to flexibilize labour market regulation, would be clear examples of non-compliance. Similarly, it would not be an option for a Member State to continue, say, encouragement of early retirement, or other policies which endorsed existing low rates of participation.

## 5. Conclusions: The European Employment Strategy and new forms of governance

The open method of coordination of employment policy is modelled on—and subject to—coordination of monetary policy for the Union as a whole, and particularly for Member States participating in the euro. As examined in Chapter 4, the version of OMC in operation for economic policy involves some rather 'hard' monetary policy coordination, especially in the context of the Stability and Growth Pact, enforced through multilateral surveillance and the excessive deficit procedure (the '3 per cent budget deficit rule'). Is there anything to prevent the open method for employment leading to similar 'hard' coordination? Writing prior to the formalization of the open method by the Lisbon European Council, Laura Cram points out how the Commission, as an accomplished policy entrepreneur, is not unfamiliar with using non-binding policy instruments ('soft law' provisions such as Recommendations or Opinions) in order to gain a 'toe-hold' in contentious policy areas.[207] Further, in the context of economic policy coordination, Hodson and Maher argue that

> 'by its very nature, the open method does not *preclude* a shift to positive co-ordination, no matter how unlikely it looks in the current political and economic climate. Should there be such a shift, the open method could be seen as a transitional mechanism leading to transfer of competence and a precursor to other, more familiar forms of EU governance.'[208]

Support for this view—that the open method of coordination may lead back to traditional forms of governance and the use of 'hard law'—can be found in the Commission's analysis of the appropriate balance between traditional and newer methods of law- and policy-making, which set the agenda for the ensuing debate on 'new governance' within the EU. The Commission's White Paper on *Governance*[209] emphasized the importance of renewing the Community method of policy-making, to make it more inclusive, accountable, and

[207] Laura Cram, *Policy-making in the European Union: Conceptual Lenses and the Integration Process* (London: Routledge, 1997) at 99.
[208] Hodson and Maher, n. 146 above, at 740; emphasis added.
[209] CEC, *Governance* White Paper, n. 99 above.

open to 'non-legislative instruments', thus recognizing the importance of the open method of coordination. However, this was not without some reservations: in particular, that use of the open method should not upset the institutional balance or dilute the achievement of common objectives in the Treaty.[210] *On the one hand*, the Commission valiantly argued that the open method should not be allowed to continue to sideline the voice of the European Parliament, as the process, as it stood, had little room for intervention by the Parliament. The White Paper therefore recommended that regular mechanisms for reporting to the European Parliament should be established within the open method of coordination and, further, that the data and information generated through the open method should provide the basis for determining 'whether legislative or programme-based action is needed'.[211]

*On the other hand*, by urging that the Community method be 'revitalized', and that all institutions should concentrate on their 'core tasks',[212] the Commission was in fact implying an enlarged role for itself, at odds with the increased role for Member States and sub-national actors which is the hallmark of the open method. The White Paper envisaged that the legislative role of the Parliament and the Council should be limited to a definition of 'essential principles' whilst the Commission got on with the specification of 'technical detail'.[213] The main responsibility for executing policy and legislation by adopting implementing regulations or decisions would be conferred on the Commission, as the executive, with the legislature (the Council and European Parliament) monitoring and controlling the actions of the Commission against the principles and political guidelines adopted in the legislation. This, the Commission imagines, would most likely put the continued existence of regulatory and management committees (the comitology procedure) into question, thus undermining the Council's instrument of control over Commission implementation,[214] as well as removing what had been seen as a useful means of democratic legitimation of EU policy-making.[215] As Scharpf and Héritier so clearly demonstrate,[216] the White Paper on *Governance*, whilst recognizing the need for change in the Community method—supporting greater use of framework directives, partnership and the involvement of civil society—nevertheless favoured new forms of governance only in so far as they ensured a significant role for the Commission in initiating and implementing policy. To this, Scott and Trubek add that the accepted need for greater flexibility is also subject to the Commission's desire to maintain at least some degree of Union-wide uniformity.[217]

210 CEC, *Governance* White Paper, n. 99 above, at 22. 211 Ibid. 212 Ibid., at 29.
213 Ibid., at 20 and 34.
214 Adrienne Héritier, 'The White Paper on European Governance: A Response to Shifting Weights in Inter-institutional Decision-Making', Jean Monnet Working Paper No 6/01, New York University Law School, Symposium: *The Commission White Paper on Governance*.
215 Joerges and Neyer, n. 105 above. 216 Scharpf, n. 114 above; Héritier, n. 214 above.
217 Scott and Trubek, n. 98 above, at 16.

In this context, therefore, it is not surprising that the White Paper was rather suspicious of the open method of coordination, asserting that the Commission 'should be closely involved and play a co-ordinating role', whilst listing the circumstances under which the open method should be used—in fact concentrating on when it should *not* be used.[218] Scharpf considers that this was motivated by 'fear that the Commission could lose ground in its turf battle against national governments',[219] particularly important if one accepts that the Commission has already lost ground under the classic Community method, since the revision of the co-decision procedures after the Amsterdam Treaty (now Article 251 EC) has resulted in increased bilateral links between the Council and the Parliament, sidelining the Commission.[220] If, therefore, the consequence of the White Paper's proposals would be to enlarge the role of the Commission at the expense of Member State governments, it would appear to suggest a willingness to resort to 'hard law' for the sake of the Commission retaining a grip over policy-making, and to safeguard uniformity: '[t]he use of the open method of co-ordination must not dilute the achievement of common objectives in the Treaty or the political responsibility of the Institutions. It should not be used when legislative action under the Community method is possible'.[221]

This is not to say that the Commission was proposing to abandon resort to the open method. It is important to bear in mind, *first*, that the Commission does not speak with one voice. Not only is the Commission an internally complex institution, comprising a college (the Commissioners) and administrative units (the Directorates-General, which have considerably internal autonomy) but, more importantly in this context, it is also arguable that the Commission is a 'purposeful opportunist',[222] which seeks to maximize its influence within the EU system—and is thus an organization aware of its objectives but quite flexible about the way it achieves them.[223]

The opportunism of the Commission helps to explain how, in the same month as the *Governance* White Paper was published, damning the open method with faint praise, the Commission issued a Communication recommending its extension to immigration policy.[224] Even more so than in the case of

[218] CEC, *Governance* White Paper, n. 99 above, at 22.

[219] Scharpf, n. 114 above, at 10.

[220] Héritier, n. 214 above, at 1. The elevation of co-decision to the status of the 'default' legislative procedure by the Treaties of Amsterdam and Nice has now been codified by the Treaty establishing a Constitution for Europe, which envisages extending the co-decision procedure, renamed the 'ordinary legislative procedure', to a large number of articles so that the Parliament will become co-legislator in almost all cases: OJ C 310, 16.12.2004.

[221] CEC, *Governance* White Paper, n. 99 above, at 22.

[222] Cram, n. 207 above, at 155–7.

[223] Bryan Wendon, 'The Commission as Image-Venue Entrepreneur in EU Social Policy' (1998) 5:2 *Journal of European Public Policy*, 339–53, at 340.

[224] CEC, Communication from the Commission to the Council and the European Parliament on an *Open Method of Coordination for the Community Immigration Policy*, COM (2001) 387 final, Brussels, 11.7.2001.

employment and social policy, immigration had been dealt with largely as an intergovernmental matter, with Community competence in the areas of immigration and asylum granted only in the Amsterdam Treaty. The Commission Communication therefore considered the open method an ideal regulatory tool, bearing in mind the anxiety to preserve subsidiarity in this policy area, and envisaged that any increased role for the Union would fall far short of a full-scale 'Europeanization' of immigration policy:

'The use of an open method of co-ordination, specifically adapted to the immigration field, and *as a complement to the legislative framework*, will provide the necessary policy mix to achieve *a gradual approach to the development of an EU policy*, based, in a first stage at least, on the identification and development of common objectives to which it is agreed that a European response is necessary.'[225]

A *second* factor to bear in mind is that the right to initiate legislative proposals is not the only form of influence the Commission has over law- and policy-making. The Commission has an important coordination role in the open method. Where legislation is considered appropriate, the Commission will of course retain its right to initiate proposals and thus set the legislative agenda; for matters subject to the open method, the political guidelines and concrete objectives decided by the European Council will naturally be elaborated by the Commission, which will be responsible for drawing up indicators and evaluating Member States' performance. This is equally true in the case of immigration policy,[226] with the Commission further elaborating the political objectives established by the Tampere European Council.[227] Furthermore, one can see that the Directorate-General for Employment and Social Affairs is an OMC enthusiast, which is to be expected in view of the number of policy areas under its remit in which the extension of OMC has in fact enlarged Community competence—employment policy, coordination of social security schemes, social inclusion and reform of pension systems. In the context of employment and social policy, the Commission is the ultimate interpreter of the Employment Guidelines, and final arbiter of 'best practice'. As discussed above, the 'soft' coordination of the open method can in fact lead to some quite 'hard' results, in terms of dictating the direction of Member States' policy. This is a process over which the Commission has a great deal of control: together with the

[225] CEC, Communication from the Commission to the Council and the European Parliament on an *Open Method of Coordination for the Community Immigration Policy*, COM (2001) 387 final, Brussels, 11.7.2001, at 5; emphasis added.

[226] 'At the same time, as a complement to the establishment of the legislative framework, the Commission will support the implementation of the open co-ordination method by presenting proposals for European guidelines, ensuring co-ordination of national policies, the exchange of best practice and evaluation of the impact of the Community policy, as well as through regular consultations with third countries concerned': CEC, Communication on *Immigration Policy*, n. 224 above, at 6.

[227] Presidency Conclusions, Tampere European Council, 15 and 16 October 1999, Bull EU-10/1999, 1–16.

Employment Committee, the Commission's work on developing new indicators and reformulating the Employment Guidelines has gradually led to targets becoming more detailed and prescriptive.

The Commission's evaluation of the first five years of the Employment Strategy identified better governance and strong involvement of all stakeholders (including civil society, the social partners, regional and local actors) as a key for the strategy's future effectiveness.[228] This has been followed by the European Council at its relaunch of the Lisbon Strategy, during which it placed equal emphasis on the need to improve governance and sharpen delivery. Such developments raise the question of how the position of OMC in the Community's array of legislative and non-legislative instruments should be formalized, a point discussed at length in the Constitutional Convention leading to the Treaty establishing a Constitution for Europe.[229] As far as the place of OMC in the Constitutional Treaty is concerned, the four Convention Working Groups which examined the issue—those on Economic Governance, Social Europe, Simplification, and Complementary Competences—all recommended conferring constitutional status on OMC, for example that it should be included within the chapter on Union instruments which constitute non-legislative measures.[230] The European Parliament passed two resolutions calling for the OMC to be incorporated into the Constitutional Treaty and for an inter-institutional agreement with the Council and the Commission, 'laying down rules for governing the selection of policies for open coordination', as well as 'a procedure for developing the open method of coordination into the Community Method', which could be formalized by the Intergovernmental Conference.[231] However, the final text of the Constitutional Treaty contains no generic constitutional provision on OMC,[232] or even any explicit mention of OMC. OMC has instead been *de facto* included in the Constitutional Treaty: in the areas of public health, industry, social policy and employment, the Commission has

[228] CEC, 'Proposal for a Council Decision on Guidelines for the Employment Policies of the Member States' COM (2003) 176 final, Brussels, 08.4.2003; Explanatory Memorandum.

[229] Treaty establishing a Constitution for Europe, OJ C 310, 16.12.2004. See generally *http://european-convention.eu.int/* [accessed on 10 April 2005].

[230] The Convention on the Future of Europe was dominated by representatives from the Member States, one each from the existing states, and also from the candidate countries; as well as two representatives from each national parliament. There were just sixteen representatives from the European Parliament, and two from the Commission. The Convention meet in Plenary sessions which were open to the public as well as eleven specialist Working Groups, on subjects ranging from the 'EU Charter of Fundamental Rights' to 'Social Europe' and 'Economic Governance': Presidency Conclusions, Laeken European Council, n. 65 above, at Annex I, Laeken Declaration on the Future of the European Union.

[231] European Parliament resolution on the application of the open method of coordination, 5 June 2003, OJ C 68 E/604, 18.3.2004; see also Zeitlin, n. 94 above, at 8.

[232] Gráinne de Búrca and Jonathan Zeitlin, 'Constitutionalising the Open Method of Coordination: What Should the Convention Propose?', Centre for European Policy Studies, CEPS Policy Brief No 31, March 2003.

been given the role of promoting, encouraging and facilitating cooperation amongst the Member States.[233]

Despite the failure to 'constitutionalize' or formalize OMC within the Constitutional Treaty, nevertheless OMC has grown to take on some features of hard law, dictating the direction of Member States' policy as far as employment creation and economic governance are concerned; in particular, the processes of peer review and benchmarking have intensified beyond those envisaged in the Employment Title, leading to a narrowing of the range of legitimate responses to unemployment. That said, Member State governments, such as that in the UK which spurns harmonization, appear to welcome the open method. They see it as a new form of mutual recognition, or regulatory competition, since Member States are responsible for 'translating' guidelines into national and regional policies, 'taking into account national and regional differences'.[234]

Even allowing for the growth of a rich and varied literature from legal and political scientists and the actors themselves (the social partners, the European institutions and the Member States in their NAPs), it is still too early in the development of the open method of coordination for a full assessment of its meaning and impact to be made. It is clear, though, that the many different ways of interpreting the open method still leave unanswered the question of how it can successfully ensure minimum (social) standards without being too prescriptive, and thus falling into the trap of traditional forms of harmonization. In the area of employment policy and labour market standards, the question remains how the Community and Member States can move from 'rigid and compulsory' systems of statutory regulations to more 'open and flexible legal frameworks',[235] in such a way as to avoid mere deregulation. The European Parliament, for one, whilst broadly welcoming the development and 'innovatory effect' of OMC, nevertheless remains suspicious that such 'soft' norms and decentralized implementation—which do not guarantee social rights or minimum social standards—may erode the European social model.[236] That some of the actors involved consider OMC to be a 'second best' alternative to 'hard law' seems a disloyal perspective, but one expressed by the Commission itself on occasion: '[c]ompared to the co-ordination mechanisms between Member States, the use of regulations and directives (the so-called "Community method") are more effective, as experience has shown, not least because legislation is enforceable'.[237]

On the contrary, one could argue that coordination mechanisms can be effective to achieve employment policy goals; in particular, that the open method is best understood as an alternative to both centralized harmonization and

[233] Articles III-174.2; III-175.2; III-102 and III-97 respectively. See also The Federal Trust, *EU Constitution Project Newsletter*, Vol 1 Issue 4, July 2003.

[234] Presidency Conclusions, Lisbon European Council, n. 12 above, at para 37.

[235] As suggested in the Commission's Green Paper *Partnership for a New Organisation of Work*, COM (97) 128 final (Luxembourg: OOPEC, 1997) at para 44.

[236] European Parliament, *Report on the Commission's Social Policy Agenda*, A5-0291/2000 final, 16 October 2000, at 6.

[237] CEC, *Commission Staff Working Document*, n. 82 above, at 49.

regulatory competition, but only if it is formalized within the non-legislative instruments of the Community. It is questionable whether 'soft' coordination, on its own, is able to provide a sufficiently robust normative framework to balance the economic policy discourse which continues to dominate the Employment Strategy and the Lisbon Strategy. The policy 'experimentation' which is the hallmark of the open method in fact permits diversity only within a framework firmly wedded to sound public finances, comprehensive economic reform and restructuring of labour markets, thus limiting the extent to which Member States can depart from the Employment Strategy without also breaching the BEPGs and the Stability and Growth Pact.

OMC is a form of governance which has the potential to achieve policy coordination without threatening jealously guarded national sovereignty, and to allow Member States to implement policy in accordance with their socio-economic development, *provided that* it is able to establish a normative framework within which such national autonomy can operate. Given a desire to preserve a version of the European social model, I propose that the most appropriate path is not merely the establishment of a minimal framework within which Member States are free to be self-regulating, but what I call 'soft harmonization' through 'hard law'. In other words, social rights and labour standards need to be built into economic policies such as the Employment Strategy, but so as to preserve a space for national diversity. Perhaps coordination (rather than full harmonization) of employment and social policies is as much as one can rightly expect of an integrating Europe. As one group of European economists proclaim, 'our first argument is not for a European social policy as such, but for a Europe which does more to respect and protect national social systems'.[238] In other words, even the indirect regulation envisaged by reflexive theory must have normative underpinnings. In default of what might be labelled 'social benchmarking' or a strengthened framework of social rights, there is a danger that the open method will coalesce around the dominant criterion by which progress in employment policy has been evaluated, namely, an economic criterion.

[238] European Economists for an Alternative Economic Policy in Europe, *Alternative Economic Policy Guidelines for Full Employment and Social Cohesion in Europe* (Bremen: University of Bremen, 2000) at 5; available at *http://www.memo-europe.uni-bremen.de* [accessed on 10 April 2005].

# 6

# The influence of the European Employment Strategy on Member States' employment policies, regulatory strategies and labour law

## 1. Introduction

The appropriateness or 'explanatory fit' of the various theoretical models canvassed to explain the open method of coordination (reflexive harmonization, democratic experimentalism and policy transfer) will be explored further by means of a closer empirical study of the operation of the open method of coordination of employment policy. This chapter will examine the extent to which the European Employment Strategy is influencing the shape and content of national employment and social policies. Rather than attempting to trace direct causal links between the Employment Strategy and Member States' employment policies, regulatory strategies and labour law, the aim of the chapter is to identify the influence of the Employment Strategy on the *discourse* within Member States over the appropriate path for employment and labour market policy to take. Accordingly, this chapter will reconstruct the ways in which Member States have interpreted EU employment policy, by means of a review of the National Action Plans for Employment (NAPs).

As Chapters 4 and 5 have already highlighted, there is little evidence to show that the flexibilization discourse at the EU level is leading to an across-the-board process of deregulation of national labour law. Instead, the NAPs point to a rather piecemeal review of existing legislation in particular areas, such as the liberalization of legislation governing 'atypical' work. However, an important exception exists for those Member States which adopted deregulatory policies from the 1980s onwards: in this case, there are marked similarities between EU- and national-level discourse on the need to remove labour market 'rigidities'. This similarity goes some way towards explaining the apparent eagerness of some Member States to comply with the 'soft law' obligations imposed by the Employment Guidelines and the open method of coordination, and to adapt their legislative systems so as to achieve some form of uniformity or convergence on the question of flexibility. This argument will be developed further by examining the labour market policies of the Netherlands and the UK, where the influence of 'Third Way' thinking on labour market policies raises the issue of the mutual influence of national and European employment policies.

The opacity, vagueness and rhetorical style of the NAPs presents a challenge to analysis, and requires a different methodological approach to that involved in assessing the impact of, say, directives. This, in part, is due to the fact that Member States' responses to the Employment Guidelines generally take the form of administrative rather than legislative measures, which are likely to be less 'visible'. A related question which will be addressed in this chapter is how one can measure 'compliance' with the 'soft law' requirements of the Employment Strategy. This is of particular importance given the arguments that OMC can be seen as an example of either 'bottom-up' governance, or self-regulation. Assessing the extent to which the Employment Strategy has 'Europeanized' national policy will thus involve four levels of analysis: *first*, an analysis of the legal significance of the NAPs; *second*, an examination of the extent to which the interaction between the Employment Strategy and EMU has given rise to new forms of corporatism in national wage and collective bargaining; *third*, a brief overview of Member States' NAPs since 1998, concentrating on the extent to which national labour law systems can be said to be converging in their response to the 'labour market flexibility' debate; and *fourth*, a review of the impact of EU internal market law on national employment and social policy.

The final sections of the chapter will focus on the debate in two Member States: the Netherlands and the UK. Concentrating attention on the interpretation of EU policy within two countries is necessary in order to gain a more precise understanding of the impact of the Employment Strategy. The Netherlands and the UK have been chosen because they provide particularly significant examples of the interaction and similarities between the objectives of EU policy and domestic political agendas for reform of welfare states and labour markets. The centrality of active labour market policies in both countries, and their attempts to balance flexibility with security (known as 'flexicurity' in the Netherlands) mean that these two countries offer an interesting foretaste of how the 'full employment' policies advocated by the EU since the Lisbon European Council may evolve in other Member States.

## 2. The (legal) status of the National Action Plans

According to Article 128(3) EC, each Member State must provide the Council and the Commission with an annual report on the principal measures taken to implement its employment policy in the light of the Employment Guidelines. Article 128 EC remains unchanged, although following the Commission's review of the first five years of the Employment Strategy, and the decision of the European Council in spring 2005 to relaunch the Lisbon Strategy, the reporting obligation will now follow a three-year cycle. The starting-point of the cycle will be a 'synoptic document' (a strategic report) by the Commission, which will be examined in the relevant Council configurations and discussed at the spring European Council meeting—the latter having responsibility for establishing political guidelines for the economic, social and environmental strands of the Lisbon Strategy. In accordance with the procedures laid down in Articles 99 and 128 EC, and on the basis of the European Council conclusions, the Council will then adopt a set of 'integrated guidelines' consisting of broad economic policy guidelines and employment guidelines. On the basis of the integrated guidelines, Member States will draw up 'national reform programmes' (to replace the current National Action Plans) geared to their own needs and specific situation.[1] The NAPs (in future, National Reform Programmes) are thus the main documentary evidence of whether Member States are or are not complying with their obligations under the Employment Strategy and the wider Lisbon Strategy. But could one envisage the Commission initiating infringement proceedings, as provided for under Article 226 EC, against a Member State which had failed to comply with policy recommendations under the Employment Guidelines or the Integrated Guidelines; would such failure be sufficient to amount to a failure to 'fulfil an obligation under this Treaty', as required by Article 226 EC?[2]

To gain an insight into the possible legal status and influence of the NAPs, it is useful to compare the Employment Strategy and NAPs with traditional modes of EU governance, such as directives, and Member States' responses to them. Even existing 'soft law' mechanisms, such as the social dialogue procedure, have a *core of 'hard law'*, in that the social partners' agreements can lead to framework directives. The first two sets of Employment Guidelines for the years 1998 and 1999 were issued in the form of Council Resolutions;[3] since 2000, the Guidelines have taken the form of Council Decisions.[4] Although Article 249 (formerly

[1] Presidency Conclusions, Brussels European Council, 22 and 23 March 2005, Bull EU 3/2005, at paras 38–41.

[2] Article 226 (formerly Article 169) EC provides that: 'If the Commission considers that a Member State has failed to fulfil an obligation under this Treaty, it shall deliver a reasoned opinion on the matter after giving the State concerned the opportunity to submit its observations. If the State concerned does not comply with the opinion within the period laid down by the Commission, the latter may bring the matter before the Court of Justice'.

[3] Council Resolution of 15 December 1997 on the 1998 Employment Guidelines, OJ C 30/98, 28.01.1998; Council Resolution of 22 February 1999 on the 1999 Employment Guidelines, OJ C 69, 12.03.1999.

[4] Council Decision of 13 March 2000 on guidelines for Member States' employment policies for the year 2000 (2000/228/EC), OJ L 72/15, 21.03.2000; Council Decision of 19 January 2001 on guidelines for Member States' employment policies for the year 2001 (2001/63/EC), OJ L 22/18, 24.1.2001; Council Decision of 18 February 2002 on guidelines for Member States' employment policies for the year 2002 (2002/177/EC), OJ L 60/60, 1.3.2002; Council Decision of 22 July 2003 on guidelines for the employment policies of the Member States (2003/578/EC), OJ L 197/13, 5.8.2003; Council Decision of 4 October 2004 on guidelines for the employment policies of the Member States (2004/740/EC), OJ L 326/45, 29.10.2004.

Article 189) EC provides that 'a decision shall be binding in its entirety upon those to whom it is addressed', I do not, however, think that too much should be read into this change in form since the Guidelines would appear to be 'decisions' *sui generis*, that is, without the legal significance of decisions envisaged by Article 249 EC. Therefore, one can say that the Employment Strategy does not have recourse to the 'hard law' machinery of, say, the social dialogue procedure, thus leaving a potentially wide range of legitimate responses to Member States' obligations under the Employment Strategy.[5]

A key aspect of the use of NAPs to evidence Member States' policies is the absence of sanctions for failure to comply with European guidelines. Coordination rather than harmonization of employment policies means that the Commission's role differs from its role under the 'classic' Community method: it can trigger the adoption of critical recommendations by the Council, rather than pursue infringement proceedings. This absence of real sanctions can be linked to the emphasis, in the open method of coordination, on *processes* and *methods*, rather than *outcomes*—the reverse of what is true in the case of directives.[6] Article 249 EC defines a directive as a measure which 'shall be binding, as to the result to be achieved, upon each Member State to which it is addressed, but shall leave to the national authorities the choice of form and methods'. Hodson and Maher suggest that the open method, with its focus on methods rather than outcomes, marks a maturation of the integration process, a key element in this new maturity being the acceptance of diversity in 'legal frameworks, ideational references and popular perceptions and reactions to either the European project generally or the specific policy being co-ordinated'.[7]

OMC's apparent openness to diversity of policy outcomes on the one hand, alongside the rigour of benchmarking and the increasing prescriptiveness of indicators on the other, means that the legal status of NAPs (wherein Member States detail the outcomes of their policies) cannot be easily categorized. I would contend that—as in the case of the Council Decisions containing the Employment Guidelines—the legal nature of the NAPs is *sui generis*. This has the effect that there is scope for Member States to use the NAPs as a platform for existing national programmes and policies, devised independently of the Employment Strategy, so long as these national measures do not explicitly contradict the tenor of the Employment Guidelines. Such 'opportunism' by Member States will be considered further in Section 2.2. To return to the *sui generis* nature of the NAPs, initially, their production could be seen as a reaffirmation of the 'shared commitment', made in the Employment Title, to make progress on employment. Thus the Commission considered it a 'major political achievement' that the first set of NAPs were prepared, adopted and delivered within such a short time

[5] I am grateful to Paul Davies for this observation.

[6] Dermot Hodson and Imelda Maher, 'The Open Method as a New Mode of Governance: The Case of Soft Economic Policy Co-ordination' (2001) 39:4 *Journal of Common Market Studies*, 719–46, at 730–1.

[7] Ibid., at 731.

frame.[8] Subsequently, it has become clear that the long time horizon of the Employment Strategy as a whole means that NAPs are not a 'once and for all' event, so that Member States do not have to 'get it right' first time. Process is more important than outcome, and the iterative nature of the Employment Strategy means that there is scope for a year-on-year improvement. With the exception of a few key targets, such as that for increasing employment rates, there is no final date by which a given measure *must* be transposed into a Member State's legal system, as there is in the case of directives. To compensate for this, the Commission has engaged in very rigorous monitoring and assessment of the NAPs. In assessing the NAPs for 2000, the *Joint Employment Report 2000* gave a strong indication of the view taken by the Commission and the Council on what Member States should be doing in their NAPs:

'There is a clear learning process in the provision and presentation of the Member States' policy. The implementation reports are becoming more focused, while in some Member States, there is still an over-emphasis on individual initiatives, rather than a comprehensive, mutually supportive policy mix.

The process of setting measurable objectives and targets should be strengthened. Under those guidelines that set common targets, policy progress is more visible, and an objective assessment of impact is made possible, on the basis of common indicators, underpinning further policy development.'[9]

For those guidelines where there are no measurable targets, the role of the NAPs is, arguably, more important: the entire benchmarking and peer review process is dependent on what Member States choose to report in their annual NAPs. Thus the emphasis placed at Lisbon on establishing more quantitative and qualitative indicators[10] is essential to buttress the NAPs, by streamlining the management and presentation of policy, and thus increasing scope for comparisons of best practice. Lisbon also drew links between benchmarking, subsidiarity and 'partnership', all under the umbrella of the open method of coordination.[11] Such a multifaceted approach is also important in defining the role performed by the NAPs in this 'soft law' regime: the 'fully decentralized approach' to the development of employment policy means that the regional and local levels, the social partners and civil society, are all to be actively involved by Member States. Indeed, the social partners were even given their own 'mini process'.[12] This suggests that the NAPs are better understood as tools of *management* than as tools of *regulation*. What is important is the process of

[8] CEC, *From Guidelines to Action: The National Action Plans for Employment*, including a Commission Communication, and a Background Report COM(98) 316 final (Luxembourg: OOPEC, 1998) at 1–2 of the Communication.

[9] CEC, *Joint Employment Report 2000* (Luxembourg: OOPEC, 2000) at 3.

[10] Presidency Conclusions, Lisbon European Council, 23 and 24 March 2000, Bull EU-3/2000, 7–17, at para 37.

[11] Ibid., at para 38.

[12] '[T]he social partners are invited to develop, in accordance with their national traditions and practices, their own process of implementing the guidelines for which they have the key responsibility, identify the issues upon which they will negotiate and report regularly on progress, in the context of the National Action Plans if desired': Council Decision of 19 January 2001, n. 4 above.

putting the NAP together, the wide involvement of different parties and actors below the level of the nation state. For example, the *Joint Employment Report 2001* noted with approval the improving quality of the NAPs, and the involvement of an increasing number of partners in their preparation and follow-up.[13]

'The 2001 National Actions Plans for Employment (NAPs) provide a much clearer and more coherent presentation of Member States' employment policies than in previous years. This seems to reflect not only the continued commitment of Member States to the European co-ordination of national employment policies, but also the strengthening of the preparation process at national level. The elaboration of the NAPs involves an ever increasing number of actors at different levels—national, regional or local—and of different origins—different Ministries but also social partners—in a strong partnership approach. This trend is a positive factor for the better integration of employment policies with other related policies.'[14]

However, *any* increase in the involvement of the social partners and civil society groups was bound to be an improvement on the first round of NAPs; subsequent *Joint Employment Reports* report little further improvement.[15] Changes to the way in which policy developments referred to in the NAPs are presented can have an impact on the content of such policy. As Jacobsson argues, the Commission has a central role in managing knowledge and may function as an 'editor' of knowledge and ideas into standards, thereby exerting an indirect influence on policy content.[16] Thus, the legal significance of the NAPs lies not so much in the formal role attributed to them by the Title on Employment, as in the way Member States' interpretation of concepts such as employability and adaptability is managed by the Commission, and by the Council in its Recommendations. Knowledge is transformed into standards in the course of the benchmarking process, and in the tightening of the guidelines and the narrowing of the range of legitimate responses to unemployment.

## 2.1 The development of National Action Plans

In the view of the Commission, the purpose of the NAPs is to enable external scrutiny of what Member States have committed themselves to doing with regard to employment policies, so that it can be seen whether these commitments are in line with the contents and objectives of the Employment Guidelines.[17] NAPs are thus a key stage in the benchmarking process, and within the open method of

[13] CEC, *Joint Employment Report 2001* (Luxembourg: OOPEC, 2002) at 4.
[14] Ibid., at 11.
[15] See for example the JER for 2003–4: 'NAPs need increased political legitimacy involving national parliaments and consulting social partners and civil society should become the norm throughout the EU': CEC, *Joint Employment Report 2003–4* (Luxembourg: OOPEC, 2004) at 61.
[16] Kerstin Jacobsson, 'Employment and Social Policy Coordination. A New System of EU Governance' unpublished paper for the Scancor workshop on Transnational Regulation and the Transformation of States, Stanford, 22–23 June 2001; manuscript on file with the author, at 13.
[17] CEC, *From Guidelines to Action*, n. 8 above, at 1 of the Communication.

coordination more generally, since they permit the Commission to assess the extent to which Member States have translated European guidelines into national and regional policies, by setting specific targets and adopting measures. In other words, NAPs (alongside the Commission's own system of performance indicators) provide an information resource from which Member States' employment performance can be monitored, evaluated and subjected to peer review.

This perspective on the function of NAPs is reinforced when one considers the proliferation of 'National Action Plans'—for social exclusion, for immigration policy, and for pensions reform, all areas which are now to be subject to the open method of coordination. A similar role is attributed to the NAPs in the coordination of policies to tackle social exclusion, which follows the *modus operandi* of the Employment Strategy: a Joint Report, the establishment of common indicators, and then the submission of NAPs. The Stockholm European Council had urged Member States to prioritize the implementation of NAPs for social inclusion, to achieve progress on the basis of the common objectives agreed in Nice, assessed by commonly agreed indicators.[18] In due course, the Laeken European Council in December 2001 was able to report how the first Joint Report on social inclusion and the establishment of a set of common indicators had furthered the policy defined at Lisbon for eradicating poverty and promoting social inclusion.[19] The first NAPs for social inclusion were submitted by Member States during June 2001, and the second in July 2004, in response to the common objectives on poverty and social exclusion agreed in Nice and revised by the Council of Ministers in December 2002. In these plans, each Member State presented its priorities and efforts for the coming two years in promoting social inclusion and combating poverty and social exclusion. In the case of immigration policy, the Commission also foresaw the use of NAPs as a key element in realizing a Community policy in this area:

> 'In order to implement each set of guidelines on immigration, Member States should prepare national action plans which will be reviewed and adapted on an annual basis. These would be in two parts so as to provide both an overview of results of the actions carried out in the previous year in relation to the European guidelines as well as proposals for the implementation of the migration guidelines in the year to come.'[20]

Similarly, with regard to pensions reform, the Laeken European Council took note of the Joint Report on pensions drawn up by the Social Protection Committee and the Economic Policy Committee.[21] Although there has been no

[18] Presidency Conclusions, Stockholm European Council, 23 and 24 March 2001, Bull EU-3/2001, 1–40, at para 28.

[19] Presidency Conclusions, Laeken European Council, 14 and 15 December 2001, Bull EU-12/2001, 1–26, at para 28.

[20] CEC, Communication from the Commission to the Council and the European Parliament on an *Open Method of Coordination for the Community Immigration Policy*, COM (2001) 387 final, Brussels, 11.7.2001, at 12.

[21] Presidency Conclusions, Laeken European Council, n. 19 above, at para 30.

specific reference to NAPs as such in the area of pensions reform, the Stockholm European Council did state that 'the potential of the open method of coordination should be used to the full' in the field of pensions, taking due account of the principle of subsidiarity,[22] with all that the OMC implies for resort to benchmarking, indicators and NAPs. It is not surprising that, in those areas such as immigration and pensions reform where the competence of the Union to act is relatively new and still very much circumscribed, the perceived strength of the open method of coordination as a means of ensuring subsidiarity is brought to the foreground.

To return to the NAPs for Employment, it is clear that, as the open method of coordination has grown in sophistication, the NAPs too have evolved: in place of the rather perfunctory reports (the first set of NAPs were criticized for being too vague in some areas, or consisting of a mere list of initiatives)[23] we can now observe much more detailed accounts of policy implementation. This can be attributed to a number of factors: the intensification of the peer review process; the extension of benchmarking by reference to a greater number of performance indicators; the growing prescriptiveness of the Employment Guidelines and their greater resort to target-setting; and the annual adoption of Council Recommendations on Member States' employment policies—developments which have obliged Member States to use the NAPs to give a more revealing account of and insight into an otherwise opaque system of policy-making. Since most Member States' responses to the Employment Strategy are administrative rather than legislative in character, there is the danger that the elaboration of employment policy takes place at a purely interministerial level, with little scope for public debate.[24] For instance, as the *Joint Employment Report 2003–4* noted, NAPs need to acquire increased political legitimacy through a greater involvement of national parliaments and consultation with social partners and civil society.[25] Commenting on the first set of NAPs for social inclusion, the Commission and Council reported that

> 'most Member States have focused their efforts on improving co-ordination, refining and combining existing policies and measures and promoting partnership, rather than launching important new or innovative policy approaches. . . . Thus, while most 2001 NAPs/Incl are an important starting point in the process, in order to make a decisive impact on poverty and social exclusion further policy efforts will be needed in the coming years.'[26]

[22] Presidency Conclusions, Stockholm European Council, n. 18 above, at para 32.

[23] CEC, *From Guidelines to Action*, n. 8 above, at 4 of the Communication.

[24] See, for example, the French NAP for 2001: 'The National Action Plan for Employment adopted by France for 2001 benefited from extensive interministerial preparations, involving the Ministry for Employment and Solidarity, the Ministry of the Economy, Finance and Industry, the Ministry for Education and the Ministry for Women's Rights and Vocational Training': *France: National Action Plan for Employment 2001*, at 2; NAPs are published by the European Commission and available from the Commission's website at: *http://europa.eu.int/comm/employment_social/employment_strategy/national_en.htm* [accessed 10 April 2005].

[25] CEC, *Joint Employment Report 2003–4*, n. 15 above, at 61.

[26] CEC, *Draft Joint Report on Social Inclusion*, Brussels, 12 December 2001, 15223/01, at 9. This Joint Inclusion Report (JIR) was adopted by the Employment and Social Affairs Council on

The same could be said in the case of the NAPs for Employment, which gradually moved away from describing measures already in train, formulated independently of the Employment Strategy.[27] As the Luxembourg process over the years has become more expertly managed by the Commission, so the NAPs for Employment have developed in the way the Commission envisages the NAPs for social inclusion will develop: less a showcase for Member States' existing policies, and more a response to European-level guidelines and targets.[28] Nevertheless, it remains a struggle to persuade Member States to use the NAPs other than as 'summing-up reports', but instead to treat them as an opportunity to be more proactive and forward-looking.[29]

## 2.2 What does compliance mean?

This question was addressed in Chapter 5, in the context of whether the Employment Strategy, and in particular the open method of coordination, was leading to policy learning or policy transfer between Member States, or allowing a sufficient space for Member State experimentation and diversity in the development of policy. The issue of compliance will now be considered more specifically by looking at what restrictions, if any, the Employment Strategy places on the range of policy options open to Member States.

Arguably, the issue of compliance with the Employment Strategy is much less troublesome than that of compliance with legislation, in particular, with legislation enacted on the basis of qualified majority voting, which a given Member State may have opposed. Member States are being asked, through their NAPs, to show compliance with Guidelines which (a) they themselves have in large measure specified; and which (b) cover such a wide range of labour market policies as to make it much harder for the Commission to measure 'compliance'. One should not overstate the distinction between the Community and the Member States: this distinction is less valid in the case of the Employment Strategy, which is much more intergovernmental than the supranationalist legislative procedures subject to

3 December 2001 and submitted to the Laeken European Council on 14 December 2001. JIRs are published by the European Commission and available from the Commission's website at ***http://europa.eu.int/comm/employment_social/social_inclusion/jrep_en.htm*** [accessed 10 April 2005].

[27] The first UK NAP, in 1998, is an excellent example of this: it was little more than a showcase for the employment policies of the Labour government, which had been in office for one year, and dealt with Labour policies which, for the most part, had the fortune to coincide with the objectives of the European Employment Strategy: (a) macro-economic stability—stable public finances and low inflation; (b) increasing investment in education, training and human resources; (c) active labour market policies, in particular the 'New Deal', a programme designed to provide intensive support to the unemployed, especially the young and long-term unemployed, lone parents, people with disabilities and ex-offenders; (d) labour market flexibility. *UK: Employment Action Plan 1998*, at 3–6.

[28] For example, '[t]he National Action Plan for Employment (NAP) 2001 outlines the progress made by the Netherlands in implementing the targets in the guidelines for 2001': *Netherlands: National Action Plan for Employment 2001*, at 3.

[29] CEC, *Joint Employment Report 2004–5* (Luxembourg: OOPEC, 2005) at 19.

Article 251 or 252 EC (the co-decision and cooperation procedures). Such intergovernmentalism is increasingly the case after the Lisbon summit reaffirmed the European Council's strategic responsibility for agenda setting, so that the heads of state and government are now responsible for 'taking on a pre-eminent guiding and coordinating role to ensure overall coherence and the effective monitoring of progress towards the new strategic goal'.[30]

One significant example of policy divergence which *does* appear to be permitted within the framework of the Employment Strategy relates to the French policy which endeavoured to increase employment by means of reducing working time. The two 'Aubry' laws, of 13 June 1998 and 19 January 2000,[31] imposed an annual ceiling on working hours, to be implemented through collective agreements, which for most workers has been translated into a maximum 35-hour week.[32] The explicit aim of the legislation was to create employment by distributing work, with the requirement that the 35-hour week not be accompanied by a comparable wage cut. According to the French government, hundreds of thousands of jobs have been created or preserved since the adoption of the first Aubry law:

> 'This higher job content can be explained, first of all, by the implementation of the negotiated reduction in working hours, which was accompanied by deeper cuts in social contributions on low and average salaries. The number of salaried jobs created by measures for the reform and reduction of working hours (ARTT) in the competitive sector in 2001 is estimated at 70,000, or nearly 30% of total jobs created for the year. It is estimated that commitments for job creation and maintenance in the agreements on the reduction of working hours signed up until 2001 amount to 410,000.'[33]

Not surprisingly the Aubry laws occupy a predominant position in successive French NAPs. However, as discussed in Chapter 3,[34] economic orthodoxy is extremely dismissive of the idea that an economy supports a fixed level of employment, and that this lump of labour can be apportioned amongst a greater number of workers, with output remaining constant. In the view of the OECD, for example, 'state funded early-retirement programmes and across-the-board work-sharing initiatives, such as legislated reductions in the work week that are not accompanied by adjustment of remuneration to productivity changes, are not viable long-term solutions to the unemployment problem'.[35] The European

[30] Presidency Conclusions, Lisbon European Council, n. 10, above at para 36.

[31] For an analysis, see Sylvaine Laulom, 'France: Part-Time Work—No Longer An Employment Policy Tool' in Silvana Sciarra, Paul Davies and Mark Freedland (eds.), *Employment Policy and the Regulation of Part-Time Work in the European Union: A Comparative Analysis* (Cambridge: CUP, 2004).

[32] This flagship policy of the former Socialist-led government was amended by the National Assembly in March 2005, to allow workers to work up to 48 hours a week if they chose, in return for extra pay: see *http://www.premier-ministre.gouv.fr/en/* [accessed 10 April 2005].

[33] France, *National Action Plan for Employment 2002*, at 4.

[34] At n. 34 and accompanying text.

[35] OECD, *The OECD Jobs Study: Implementing the Strategy* (Paris: OECD, 1995) at 24.

Employment Strategy clearly endorses the first part of this sentiment: one of the key elements in the objective of increasing the employment rate is the targeted increase by 2010 to 50 per cent in the average employment rate amongst older workers (55 to 64),[36] thus reversing previous national policies which had encouraged early retirement.

What of the OECD's critique of legislated reductions in working time? The EU approach to employment creation rests essentially on supply-side principles—improving individuals' skills and employability, flexibilizing work organization and 'activating' welfare states to increase labour market participation rates. This approach by no means endorses the 'lump of labour fallacy' but neither does it appear to rule out the French approach to employment creation through reductions in working time. Indeed, the French NAPs repeatedly make reference to the Aubry laws as a response to many of the Employment Guidelines: for example, the objectives of the legislation happily coincide with the aims of the Employment Guidelines promoting adaptability, and can also be promoted as a means of furthering the reconciliation of work and family life, as required by the requirement to mainstream equal opportunities.

As far as the European response to the French approach is concerned, it would seem that the jury is out on the question whether the improvements in the employment situation in France are truly attributable to the 35-hour week: the *Joint Employment Report 2000* is lukewarm, going only so far as to say that the first Aubry law 'does not appear to be having an adverse effect on the competitiveness of enterprises';[37] whilst the Council Recommendations for 2001 and 2002 both advise that the French government should 'closely monitor the net effects of the implementation of the 35-hour working week legislation'.[38] Finally, the most recent *Joint Employment Report* even to mention this legislation, notes that '[w]hilst aiming at the common objectives, France has followed its own agenda of statutorily reducing working time to 35 hours'.[39] Thus, the French emphasis on the 35-hour week is within the boundaries of what is deemed acceptable within the context of the European Employment Strategy, *provided that* due emphasis is also placed on preventative measures and on increasing labour market participation, especially amongst older people, where the activity rate is amongst the lowest in the EU.

In essence, the French NAPs are a particularly striking example of what occurs to some extent in all the National Action Plans: national policies are being translated into the language of the EU guidelines, such that the NAPs become a platform for what the Member State would be doing anyway. However, it seems

[36] Presidency Conclusions, Stockholm European Council, n. 18 above, at para 9.

[37] CEC, *Joint Employment Report 2000*, n. 9 above, at 123.

[38] Council Recommendation of 19 January 2001 on the implementation of Member States' employment policies (2001/64/EC), OJ L 22/27, 24.1.2001; Council Recommendation of 18 February 2002 on the implementation of Member States' employment policies (2002/178/EC), OJ L 60/70, 1.3.2002.

[39] CEC, *Joint Employment Report 2001*, n. 13 above, at 73.

to me that the success of the French economy in creating jobs has helped to head off any criticism that might have been forthcoming of the economic thinking underlying the French approach to employment creation: the *Joint Employment Report 2001* observed that the French economy had witnessed a growth in employment of 2 per cent and a reduction in unemployment of 1.7 per cent.[40] What is also important is that the French policy *as a whole*, as evidenced in the NAPs, has adopted a growth-orientated macro-economic philosophy in line with that envisaged by the Employment Strategy,[41] with emphasis on active labour market policies and development of human resources, and in particular has made a concerted effort to address the Council's Recommendations to the French government.[42]

But what of policy which *does not* appear to be permitted within the context of the Employment Strategy? One example is that of state-sanctioned early retirement, encouraging workers to exit from the labour market voluntarily, in the attempt to reduce unemployment by reducing labour supply. Such a policy was certainly widespread across all Member States up to the mid-1990s, although those with 'Continental' welfare state regimes relied most heavily on this labour-shedding strategy.[43] The interaction of a number of factors encouraged employers, trade unions and governments to resort to early retirement strategies as a means to combat mass unemployment: for example, the desire to ease industry restructuring by offering 'soft landings' to workers with seniority; the traditionally high normal retirement age (especially for men), combined with a lower age at which workers could receive disability or incapacity benefits; the introduction of pre-retirement schemes (for example, in Sweden, Germany and France) to bridge the gap between early retirement and the normal pension age; and the relatively high replacement rate of public pensions.[44]

The European Round Table of Industrialists (ERT) adopted, as could be expected, a very critical perspective towards the culture of early retirement and early exit from the labour force:

'the Netherlands and the UK have implemented generous policies, not directly related to pensions, which give significant amounts of money to those who are leaving work because of disability or supposed disability. In countries like France and Italy early retirement schemes have been quite specifically used to ease people out of the labour market. All these disincentives, built into the social security systems throughout Europe, create an

[40] Ibid., at 54.

[41] 'Since the first National Action Plan for Employment was drafted in 1998, France's macro-economic and structural policies, together with its proactive employment policy, have resulted in a high rate of growth; it has continued with its efforts to raise its growth potential. Growth has been maintained at more than 3%': *France: National Action Plan for Employment 2001*, n. 24 above, at 6.

[42] Ibid., at 2: 'This dialogue [between four government ministries] resulted in an organised synthesis of the French employment strategy and, for the second year in a row, ensured compliance with the European Council's recommendations for France'.

[43] Bernhard Ebbinghaus, 'When Labour and Capital Collude: The Varieties of Welfare Capitalism and Early Retirement in Europe, Japan and the USA', Working Paper No 4, Center for European Studies, Harvard University, 2000, at 5.

[44] Ibid.

implicit tax on work: workers tend to leave the labour force through any existing loophole when the implicit tax on work is high.'[45]

However, demographic changes throughout the EU—an aging population, increased longevity, plus significant reductions in labour force participation rates since the 1960s—have increased the dependency ratio, so that there are fewer working age employees to support the aging population. Such changes led many Member States, from the 1990s onwards, to adopt more market-orientated pension and retirement policies. Some Member States, notably Italy, are experimenting with the transition from a 'pay as you go' pension scheme, based on solidarity, with the working population paying for the retired population, to privatized or individually funded schemes, where workers invest in stock markets in order to fund their future pensions.[46]

Member States are also responding to this demographic challenge in the context of the Employment Strategy: the Stockholm European Council drew a clear link between, on the one hand, raising employment rates, and on the other, reducing public debt and reforming systems of social protection and pensions, so that these systems are sustainable.[47] However, what remains a very real question, when considering the issue of compliance with the Employment Strategy, is whether a Member State is free to 'solve' the demographic challenge by means other than those recommended by the Employment Strategy, for example, solutions which do not involve major reductions in welfare expenditure? Public opinion would appear to be resistant to any major departures from solidarity-based systems of pensions provision. For example, whilst arguing for a more radical reform of pensions systems, the ERT urged that governments must educate their publics to accept greater reforms of welfare states:

'The current size of the welfare state is supported by public opinion at large, not just by a powerful minority. In all four countries included in this survey [France, Germany, Italy and Spain] there is a majority against cutting it back.'[48]

In the view of the ERT, early retirement is not yet effectively discouraged in some Member States.[49] The reality of such discouragement would be to reduce pension

[45] European Round Table of Industrialists, *European Pensions: An Appeal for Reform. Pension Schemes that Europe can Really Afford* (Brussels: ERT, 1999) at 22; available at *http://www.ert.be* [accessed 10 April 2005].

[46] See 'Italians flock to pension protest', *BBC News Online*, 6 December 2003, at *http://news.bbc.co.uk/* [accessed 10 April 2005]. For a more detailed analysis, see David Natali and Martin Rhodes, 'Trade-offs and Veto Players: Reforming Pensions in France and Italy' (2004) 2:1 *French Politics*, 1–23.

[47] Presidency Conclusions, Stockholm European Council, n. 18 above, at paras 7 and 32.

[48] European Round Table of Industrialists, *Pensions Reform: Europe must seize the limited opportunity* (Brussels: ERT, 2002). A study by Boeri, Börsch-Supan and Tabellini found that a clear majority of voters support the overall size of the welfare state, opposing cuts to social security and welfare spending, but also opposing further increase in taxes and expenditure: Tito Boeri, Axel Börsch-Supan and Guido Tabellini, 'Would You Like to Shrink the Welfare State? A Survey of European Citizens' (2001) *Economic Policy*, 8–50.

[49] European Round Table of Industrialists, High Level Meeting on Pension Reforms in Europe, Brussels, 31 October 2001, Summary of the Discussion, available at *http://www.ert.be* [accessed 10 April 2005].

payments, limit eligibility or otherwise weaken early retirement and ill-health retirement schemes. Although pensions policy is the prerogative of Member States, there is also a shared recognition that a rising EU pensions burden has major implications for the sustainability of public finances.[50] Thus, the Stability and Growth Pact and the BEPGs, to which the Employment Strategy must conform, may well dictate the increased privatization of pensions provision as a means of reducing public expenditure. Does this imply that Member States will be required to adopt a pattern of provision similar to that of the UK?

> 'In the UK, where private schemes make a relatively large contribution to pensioner incomes, the proportion of GDP needed to fund public pension provision should remain stable. In Spain and Greece, by contrast, unchanged policy suggests increases of 8 per cent and over 12 per cent of GDP respectively.'[51]

Successive European Councils have recommended that reform of pension systems be accelerated, to ensure that they are both financially sustainable and meet their social objectives.[52] In particular, the detrimental effect of early retirement on labour market participation has to be tackled. In the context of reinforcing the Lisbon strategy, the Barcelona European Council stated bluntly that

> 'early retirement incentives for individuals and the introduction of early retirement schemes by companies should be reduced. Efforts should be stepped up to increase opportunities for older workers to remain in the labour market, for instance, through flexible and gradual retirement formulas and guaranteeing a real access to life long learning.'[53]

This much is repeatedly reinforced in numerous *Joint Employment Reports* and Council Recommendations, with underperforming Member States warned of the need to develop comprehensive strategies for 'active ageing' to retain older workers longer in employment and to reduce early retirement schemes.[54] Thus, it is likely that a Member State which was unwilling to contemplate disincentives to early retirement *and* was disinclined to reform its pensions provisions radically (for example, to move from a public pension system to a combination of privatized and occupational schemes) would find itself at odds with the requirements of the Employment Strategy, particularly with regard to the restrictive fiscal policy underlying the Strategy and the emphasis on increased labour market

[50] HM Treasury White Paper, *Realising Europe's Potential: Economic Reform in Europe*, Cm 5318 (London: HMSO, 2002) at 23. [51] Ibid.

[52] Presidency Conclusions, Barcelona European Council, 15 and 16 March 2002, Bull EU 3/2002, 1–56, at para 25; see also Presidency Conclusions, Brussels European Council, 20 and 21 March 2003, Bull EU 3/2003, 1–49, at para 49.

[53] Presidency Conclusions, Barcelona European Council, n. 52 above, at para 32.

[54] Council Recommendation of 14 October 2004 on the implementation of Member States' employment policies (2004/741/EC), OJ L 326/47, 29.10.2004, at 53; 'The increase in early retirement and in unemployment with exemption from job-search . . . is in contradiction with EU recommendations and the government's aim to reinvigorate the labour market for older workers': CEC, *Joint Employment Report 2004–5—Addendum 1: Country Fiches* (Luxembourg: OOPEC, 2005) at 37, discussing France.

participation of older workers. To take one example: Belgium has the lowest participation rate amongst older workers and some of the highest taxes on labour in the EU.[55] In order to comply with the Employment Strategy, Belgium would need to implement a range of labour market reforms which, it could be argued, would undermine the social content of the welfare state.[56] In the context of the BEPGs and the Employment Guidelines, Belgium is advised to: introduce further measures aimed at preventing the early withdrawal of workers; create adequate 'incentives' for older people to continue to work or re-enter the labour market; reduce taxes on labour; reduce social security contributions and reform benefit systems; and revise the special arrangements exempting older unemployed people (aged over 50) from active job search.[57] Fortunately for the sake of compliance with the Employment Strategy, the political consensus in Belgium, as evidenced by the NAPs, appears to be in favour of such radical reforms. The Belgian NAP for 2004 makes it clear that '[t]he active ageing issue comes first on Belgium's employment policy priority list', and proceeds to report on initiatives at federal level and within the various communities to keep older workers in employment.[58] Such measures, a continuation of policies begun in 2001, involve a Fiscal Reform Plan, training programmes for older workers, reductions in working time, reductions in social security contributions for workers over 58, and other measures granting financial support to employers who retain or hire older workers.[59] Such measures are entirely in keeping with the Council Recommendations for Belgium and the BEPGs, and illustrate the convergence of policy responses to the demographic and employment challenges facing EU Member States. The language used ('finding inspiration in the example of the Scandinavian countries') also suggests a convergence of discursive frameworks has arisen from the OMC method and from exchange of best practice.

The fact that there is such a convergence of opinion between the Belgian NAPs and the Employment Strategy over both the *necessity for* and the *nature of* reform of the labour market and welfare state, is enormously instructive. It illustrates

[55] The employment rate for older workers (aged 55–64) in 2003 was 28.1 per cent as against the EU15 average of 40.2 per cent: CEC, *Employment in Europe 2004: Recent Trends and Prospects* (Luxembourg: OOPEC. 2004) Statistical Annex.

[56] 'A reduction in social security contributions by enterprises may appear to make the cost of labour cheaper and to encourage inward foreign direct investment. But this overlooks the question of who bears the cost of such contributions and what the costs of alternative provision would be. There are clear dangers that such competition will lead to an all round deterioration of public services and welfare state provision': European Economists for an Alternative Economic Policy in Europe, *Economic Policy against Recession and Polarisation in Europe: Proposals to Overcome Ideological Sterility and Policy Blockades* (Bremen: University of Bremen, 2001) at 5; available at: *http://www.memo-europe.uni-bremen.de* [accessed on 10 April 2005].

[57] Council Recommendation of 19 January 2001, n. 38 above; Council Recommendation of 15 June 2001 on the broad guidelines of the economic policies of the Member States and the Community (2001/483/EC), OJ L 179/1, 2.7.2001, at 19; Council Recommendation of 22 July 2003 on the implementation of Member States' employment policies (2003/579/EC) OJ L 197/22, 5.8.2003, at 23.

[58] *Belgium: National Action Plan for Employment 2004*, at 43–5.

[59] *Belgium: National Action Plan for Employment 2001*, at 10.

how the policy choices of individual Member States—even those which had, until recently, been following diametrically opposed policies or tolerating low rates of labour market participation—are constrained by the *collective consensus* at EU level with regard to fiscal restraint and high participation rates: in this context, early retirement is seen as imposing an unsustainable burden on increasingly fragile social security systems, as well as reducing the tax base. If this consensus extends to the adoption of the ERT's recommendations, it will result in the imposition of drastic reductions in the provision of public pensions, to make pensions less attractive and thus discourage early retirement. It would seem, therefore, that the wide-ranging process of coordinating their employment policies has led to—or speeded up—a process of convergence in Member States' labour market reforms, to the extent that the differences identified by the OECD in the mid-1990s are no longer as valid. For example, the OECD noted that

'The central issue dividing the more comprehensive reformers from the less comprehensive is differences in judgement about potential conflicts between better labour market performance and concerns for equity and social cohesion.

A key reason for slow and sporadic implementation of the OECD Jobs Strategy is the perception that undertaking reform involves conflict with policy objectives concerning equity and social cohesion. In particular, concern has been expressed in some quarters that the Jobs Strategy recommendations to enhance wage flexibility and to reform social transfer systems would be at odds with the policy objectives of ensuring some degree of equity across members of the labour force or the population at large.'[60]

In contrast to English-speaking countries, Continental European countries were identified as the ones most likely to be resistant to the reform measures recommended by the OECD's Jobs Strategy,[61] seeing equity as a more fundamental goal than low unemployment.[62] However, as illustrated by their NAPs, these same countries are now endorsing an EU Employment Strategy which advocates very similar reforms to social security systems, in particular with regard to social transfer systems, to those recommended by the OECD's *Jobs Study*.[63]

Ultimately, one could argue that compliance with the Employment Strategy, and the Guidelines in particular, is best measured not simply by failure or success in meeting a centrally determined 'target' (though that, too, is important) but by assessing the extent to which Member States' understandings of what is a legitimate policy response to unemployment have been conditioned by the process of coordination. I would contend that the range of permissible policies has been narrowed, as Member States develop collective understandings of concepts such as 'full employment', 'employability' and 'active labour market policies'. The consistency with which the supply-side policies of the Employment

[60] OECD, *Implementing the OECD Jobs Strategy: Lessons from Member Countries' Experience* (Paris: OECD, 1997) at 13.

[61] OECD, *The OECD Jobs Study: Evidence and Explanations* and *Facts, Analysis, Strategies* (Paris: OECD, 1994) at 44.

[62] OECD, n. 60 above, at 14.

[63] As to their willingness to reform labour market regulation, see Section 3.2 below.

Strategy are adopted by Member States makes it almost unthinkable for a Member State to contemplate encouraging early retirement, adopting passive labour market measures, or accepting low labour market participation. What remains to be considered, below, is whether policies which leave 'rigid' labour market regulations unreformed still fall within the range of what is permissible or acceptable within the context of the Employment Strategy.

The 'soft law' nature of the Guidelines, the lack of sanctions for failure to meet targets, and the openness to approaches such as the French 35-hour week, mask the fact that Member States face peer pressure to act in accordance with the main thrust of the Employment Strategy and its 'policy mix'. They further mask the fact that the policy 'experimentation' which is the hallmark of the open method of coordination in fact permits experimentation only within a framework firmly wedded to sound public finances, comprehensive economic reform and restructuring of welfare states and the labour market, thus limiting the extent to which Member States can depart from the Employment Strategy and the Lisbon Strategy without also breaching the BEPGs and the Stability and Growth Pact. By this reckoning, therefore, Member State compliance with the Employment Strategy is extremely high.

## 3. The Employment Strategy, EMU and Europeanization of national policy

Assessing the *direct* impact of the Employment Strategy on Member States' labour market regimes and labour market performance is problematic, first because the reforms envisaged by the Employment Strategy have a long time horizon: as the *Joint Employment Report 2000* points out, '[i]nterest rates can be changed overnight, but the impact of human resources investment and institutional reforms in the labour markets require sustained efforts, and can only be expected to yield visible effects over time'.[64] Secondly, and more broadly, it is always difficult to point to a direct correlation between a particular legislative provision or policy goal articulated at European level, a Member State's response and changes in a Member State's labour market performance or (un)employment rates.

Nevertheless, it is possible to trace some trends and observe initiatives taken at national level—such as social concertation, wage restraint, and reform of social security and employment protection legislation—which are clearly in response to the demands of Economic and Monetary Union, the Lisbon Strategy and the Employment Strategy. In particular, as the UK Treasury cautions, labour market flexibility is an important objective irrespective of whether a country is inside or outside a currency union, but it takes on an added importance inside a currency

[64] CEC, *Joint Employment Report 2000*, n. 9 above, at 3.

union such as EMU, when neither the nominal exchange rate nor national interest rates can be adjustment mechanisms in the face of economic shocks.[65] As Hassel and Hoffman point out:

'European Economic and Monetary Union has already had a clear impact on national wages and social policy during the 1990s. All of the Member States of the EU are under considerable pressure to reduce costs, and labour market and social policy are increasingly at the centre of attempts to adapt to this new environment. The need to drive down costs has meant that all countries, irrespective of the political colour of their government or the position of the social partners, have introduced reforms geared towards cutting costs and making the labour market more flexible.'[66]

It is therefore important to place the discussion of Member States' responses to the Employment Strategy in the wider context of their responses to European economic policy, to appreciate the impact that EMU and the BEPGs are having on national industrial relations and labour law.

## 3.1 Neo-corporatism, 'credibility bargaining' and wage determination

The convergence criteria for monetary union laid down in the Maastricht Treaty require those Member States participating in the single currency to maintain retail price inflation within certain limits, restrict national debt to 60 per cent of GDP, and confine budget deficits to no more than 3 per cent of GDP.[67] Even the non-Eurozone Member States are not only obliged to maintain 'sound budgetary positions' in accordance with the Stability and Growth Pact,[68] but are also under a Treaty obligation (Article 116(4), formerly Article 109e(4) EC) to endeavour to avoid excessive budget deficits. In this context, as argued in Chapter 4, employment and social policy are very much circumscribed by the requirements of EMU and European economic policy more broadly. Since 1997, the main objectives of this economic policy—applicable to all Member States, the EU15 then to the EU25—have been 'growth, employment and convergence',[69] necessitating as regards the labour market, comprehensive structural reforms and measures to improve labour market efficiency. Wage flexibility is a vital facet of

65 HM Treasury, *EMU and Labour Market Flexibility* (London: HMSO, 2003) at 5.1.

66 Anke Hassel and Reiner Hoffmann, 'National Alliances for Jobs and Prospects for a European Employment Pact' European Trade Union Institute Discussion and Working Papers, DWP 2000.01.01 (European Trade Union Institute: Brussels, 2000) at 14.

67 The convergence criteria are set out in Protocol No 21 annexed to the EC Treaty. These two thresholds remain unchanged, although the Stability and Growth Pact was reformed in 2005 to provide greater flexibility in its implementation: see Chapter 4, Section 2.2. See also Catherine Barnard and Simon Deakin, 'A year of living dangerously? EC social rights, employment policy, and EMU' (1999) 30:4 *Industrial Relations Journal: European Annual Review 1998*, 355–72, at 362.

68 Council Recommendation of 15 June 2001, n. 57 above, at 11.

69 Council Recommendation of 7 July 1997 on the broad guidelines of the economic policies of the Member States and of the Community (97/479/EC) OJ L 209, 2.8.97.

these labour market reforms, and can be compared to the emphasis on wage flexibility in the neoclassical theories of unemployment analysed in Chapter 2; for instance, the BEPGs for 1997 considered that higher employment growth could be brought about by the maintenance of 'appropriate wage trends' and by wages that 'better take into account differences in qualifications and regions', which would be an important task for the social partners.[70]

Continuity with this emphasis on wage flexibility can be seen in the BEPGs for 2003–5 which recommend 'responsibility' in order for wage developments to contribute to stable macro-economic conditions and to an employment-friendly policy mix. In particular, (i) that any increase in nominal wages be consistent with price stability; (ii) that the increase in real wages not exceed labour productivity growth; and (iii) that wage formation processes take account of productivity differences.[71] Also, in order for labour markets to function in the way envisaged by the Treasury as necessary for a currency union—providing flexibility which is no longer available by other means—the BEPGs play an important role for the social partners, in wage restraint and helping their governments to keep to the tight fiscal constraints imposed by EMU—a role which can be seen as 'neo-corporatist'.[72] To these developments, one must add the 'Cologne process' which along with the Luxembourg and Cardiff processes, is one of the three 'pillars' of the European Employment Pact launched at the Cologne European Council in 1999.[73] The Cologne process is intended to coordinate fiscal policy, monetary policy and wage developments, through macro-economic dialogue aimed at preserving non-inflationary growth. Such macro-economic dialogue would involve 'all those who decide on or influence economic and employment policy', including the Council, the Commission, the European Central Bank and the social partners.

Thus, one can see that the Employment Strategy and EMU are giving rise to new forms of corporatism. First, the social partners are increasingly involved in the articulation and implementation of employment policy—for example, the Employment Guidelines for 2001 required the national level social partners to be more clearly engaged in their own 'mini-process', with new obligations to

[70] Council Recommendation of 7 July 1997 on the broad guidelines of the economic policies of the Member States and of the Community (97/479/EC) OJ L 209, 2.8.97, at para 6(i).

[71] Council Recommendation of the 26 June 2003 on the Broad Guidelines of the Economic Policies of the Member States and the Community for the period 2003–2005 (2003/555/EC) OJ L 195, 01.08.2003, at 5; see also Council Recommendation of 15 June 2001 on the broad guidelines of the economic policies of the Member States and the Community, n. 57 above, at 11.

[72] Barnard and Deakin, n. 67 above, at 363. The BEPGs would thus seem to be reconciled to 'centralized' or 'coordinated' systems of wage formation, but only to the extent that such coordination in fact has the effect of containing wage developments, as the Calmfors–Driffill model would suggest: Lars Calmfors and John Driffill, 'Bargaining Structure, Corporatism and Macro-economic Performance' (1988) 6 *Economic Policy*, 14–61.

[73] Presidency Conclusions, Cologne European Council, 3 and 4 June 1999, Bull EU-6/1999, 7–37, para 7, Annex I, Resolution of the European Council on the European Employment Pact, and Report to the European Council on the European Employment Pact: Closer Cooperation to Boost Employment and Economic Reforms in Europe.

monitor and report back annually on progress. Having said that, such social partnership is clearly having a greater impact in those countries which already have in place mechanisms for negotiations on economic and social policies resulting in economy-wide agreements.[74]

Second, many Member States are witnessing a concerted regulation of wage developments, albeit within a constrained macro-economic environment, at the heart of which is the desire for national competitiveness and wage moderation.[75] Writing in 1998, Paul Teague noted that recent national pay agreements had had a weaker social agenda, being more concerned with helping the Member State in question meet the Maastricht criteria or improve domestic competitiveness.[76] Whilst wage moderation has been the overriding aim of such bargaining on employment and competitiveness, bargaining has also been aimed at reducing indirect labour costs by, for example, reducing employers' social security contributions, a development which has taken place in Belgium, Denmark, Finland, France, Italy and Spain. Some agreements (eg in Austria, Germany, Italy, the Netherlands and Spain) have also included 'opening' and 'hardship' clauses, or special clauses for small and medium-sized enterprises, allowing exemptions from collectively agreed standards, namely derogations *in pejus*.[77]

Several commentators have observed an apparently contradictory tendency in national-level wage and collective bargaining, towards both decentralization *and* coordination, which has been intensified by EMU.[78] Whilst many Member States have witnessed the devolution of functions from higher to lower levels of the system, with greater scope being granted to company-level and plant-level bargaining to conclude agreements which increase flexibility and adaptability in local working practices,[79] this has taken place within a still functioning regulatory framework of higher-level collective bargaining.[80] For example: Ireland

[74] Evelyne Léonard, 'Industrial Relations and the Regulation of Employment in Europe' (2001) 7:1 *European Journal of Industrial Relations*, 27–47, at 33. Léonard takes this point further, to argue that, in the majority of cases, the NAP is essentially a governmental project.

[75] Ibid., at 36–8; see also Paul Teague, 'Macroeconomic Constraints, Social Learning and Pay Bargaining in Europe' (2000) 38:3 *British Journal of Industrial Relations*, 429–52.

[76] Paul Teague, 'Monetary Union and Social Europe' (1998) 8:2 *Journal of European Social Policy*, 117–38, at 122.

[77] These examples are taken from a report compiled for the European Foundation for the Improvement of Living and Working Conditions, on 'pacts for employment and competitiveness' in operation between January 1997 and February 1999: Stefan Zagelmeyer, *Innovative Agreements on Employment and Competitiveness in the European Union and Norway* (Luxembourg: OOPEC, 2000) at 12.

[78] Léonard, n. 74 above, at 34–8; Franz Traxler, 'Farewell to Labour Market Associations? Organized versus Disorganized Decentralization as a Map for Industrial Relations', in Colin Crouch and Franz Traxler (eds.), *Organized Industrial Relations in Europe: What Future?* (Aldershot: Avebury, 1995); Colin Crouch, 'National Wage Determination and European Monetary Union' in Colin Crouch (ed.), *After the Euro: Shaping Institutions for Governance in the Wake of European Monetary Union* (Oxford: OUP, 2000).

[79] Léonard, n. 74 above, at 27.

[80] Keith Sisson and Paul Marginson, 'Co-ordinated Bargaining: A Process for our Times?', ESRC *One Europe or Several?* Programme Working Paper 14/00, at 5; Léonard, n. 74 above, at 34.

has had a system of national wage agreements since 1987, with local bargaining clauses allowing enterprise-level pay productivity negotiations subject to a centrally determined cap;[81] in Denmark, bargaining is conducted at firm or industry level, with the national peak organizations monitoring the outcomes and issuing guidance;[82] in Germany, the short-lived 'Alliance for Employment, Apprenticeship and Competitiveness' (*Bündnis für Arbeit, Ausbildung und Wettbewerbsfähigkeit*) was a federal-level tripartite body which served as an instrument to assist the government in mobilizing the main industrial relations actors to fight unemployment,[83] for example, enlisting social partners in the reform of the social security system.[84] Such federal-level coordination in Germany sat alongside increased resort to company-level bargaining, as evidenced by concession bargaining to save jobs at Volkswagen, Continental, Bayer, Mercedes Benz and more recently at Siemens.[85] In Belgium, a major bipartite economy-wide agreement was signed in 1998, which established a reference framework for *sectoral* bargaining, with pay rises restricted to 5.9 per cent for 1999–2000.[86] In the Belgian case, the signatories to the economy-wide agreement referred explicitly to EMU in the preamble to the agreement. Anticipation of membership of the common currency has similarly led other Member States towards pay moderation, a tendency which has continued within the new 'Eurozone', under the shadow of the Stability and Growth Pact.

Thus, whilst globalization and the prevailing neoliberal ideological climate place strong pressures on states to loosen institutional structures and give freer rein to market forces, leading to deregulation and decentralization of labour regulation to the level of the individual firm, at the same time some form of coordination of labour markets is essential if Member States are to manage the transition to the single currency.[87] Paul Teague labels this combination of decentralization and coordination 'credibility bargaining'.[88] National economic policy-makers are striving for credible reputations in a situation where most

[81] Teague, n. 75 above, at 447.

[82] Crouch, n. 78 above, at 215. Even though Denmark has not yet joined EMU, the government has nevertheless adopted a 'fairly austere' macro-economic programme: Teague, n. 75 above, at 448–9.

[83] Léonard, n. 74 above, at 46.

[84] Zagelmeyer, n. 77 above, at 67. Established in December 1998 under the aegis of Germany's then 'red-green' coalition government, the Alliance for Employment was promoted as one of the government's most important projects to reduce unemployment and to safeguard vocational training. Eight top-level meetings were held prior to January 2002, which covered considerable ground, including the issuing of a number of joint statements on employment-orientated collective bargaining policy. However, enthusiasm for the Alliance waned following failure to reach agreement over a package of sweeping labour market reforms, and talks broke down permanently in 2003: see European Industrial Relations Observatory On-Line, available at *http: //www.eiro.eurofound.eu.int/index.html* [accessed 10 April 2005].

[85] Zagelmeyer, n. 77 above at 76–83. With regard to the agreement between Siemens and the German Metalworkers' Union (IG Metall) which came into force in July 2004, see European Industrial Relations Observatory On-Line, at *http: //www.eiro.eurofound.eu.int/2004/07/feature/de0407106f.html* [accessed 10 April 2005].

[86] Léonard, n. 74 above, at 45.

[87] Crouch, n. 78 above, at 211–13, 224–5; Teague, n. 75 above, at 446.

[88] Teague, n. 75 above, at 430 ff.

economists would agree that the EU does not represent a particularly good optimum currency area to be governed by one money.[89]

'OCA [optimum currency area] theory focuses on characteristics which make stable exchange rates and monetary unification more or less desirable. The most important of these are asymmetric disturbances to output, trade linkages, the usefulness of money for transactions, the mobility of labor, and the extent of automatic stabilizers.'[90]

According to OCA theory, a single currency is more workable where there is a common labour market and where the composition of output is relatively uniform from one country to the next, so that they do not experience trade shocks differentially or 'asymmetrically'.[91] Further, in neoclassical economic theory, if countries or regions have a problem of competitiveness within a single currency zone, they can solve it by a combination of reductions in labour costs and migrations of population.[92] However, despite the free movement provisions of the Treaty of Rome, it is difficult to talk of a 'common' labour market across the EU; further, labour mobility is extremely low in the EU (compared with the US, for example) both within and between Member States.[93] A single currency therefore places an enormous burden on labour, and the question then becomes whether, as Colin Crouch puts it, 'it is possible for labour markets to find alternative means of adaptation to either sudden and unanticipated cost reductions through massive deflations or devaluations'.[94] So, faced with a choice between labour market deregulation and macro-economic stability, European trade unions have chosen the latter, and have been 'willing signatories' to the new centralized agreements.[95] For governments, some form of centralized coordination of bargaining over wages is an essential part of the strategy to convince financial markets and other Eurozone Member States that they can comply with the restrictive fiscal policy regimes and limits on public expenditure, and they have accordingly 'endeavoured to make wage determination systems consistent with the pursuit of tight monetary and fiscal policies'.[96]

[89] Ibid., at 435. See also R. A. Mundell, 'A Theory of Optimum Currency Areas' (1961) 51 *American Economic Review*, 657–67.

[90] Tamim Bayoumi and Barry Eichengreen, 'Ever Closer to Heaven? An Optimum-Currency-Area Index for European Countries', Center for International and Development Economics Research, University of California Berkeley, Working Paper Series No C96-078, December 1996, at 3.

[91] Ronald McKinnon, 'Mundell, the Euro, and Optimum Currency Areas', Stanford University Working Papers in Economics No 009, May 2000, at 2.

[92] Colin Crouch, 'Introduction: The Political and Institutional Deficits of European Monetary Union', in Colin Crouch (ed.), n. 78 above, at 19.

[93] The Barcelona European Council sought to boost geographical mobility of labour by means of, *inter alia*, endorsing the Commission Action Plan to develop and open up new European labour markets, and to facilitate worker mobility (*Commission's Action Plan for skills and mobility*, COM (2002) 72 final, Brussels, 13.2.2002). The aim was to remove the barriers within European labour markets by 2005, for example by lowering regulatory and administrative barriers to professional recognition and increasing (where appropriate) the transferability of social security rights, including pensions, across the European Union: Presidency Conclusions, Barcelona European Council, n. 52 above, at para 33.

[94] Crouch, n. 92 above, at 20.

[95] Teague, n. 75 above, at 435.

[96] Ibid., at 431.

In conclusion, one can see similarities and connections between these new forms of corporatism—coordinated bargaining or credibility bargaining—and the open method of coordination. EMU, the Lisbon Strategy and the Employment Strategy together establish a rigid (macro-economic) framework, which constrains the discretion of governments and social partners, and thus impacts on national industrial relations.[97] Without suggesting that developments such as the social dialogue procedure are leading to the creation of meaningful 'collective bargaining' at European level, one can see that the EU is nevertheless providing a framework within which national and sub-national collective and wage bargaining now takes place. The extent to which a minimalist form of 'collective bargaining' is emerging at European level is well captured by Dølvik:

'What we can expect is probably a continuation of the tendency to restrict the EU role to providing framework regulations that define broad objectives, minimum standards and procedures, while allowing considerable leeway for flexible implementation by national governments and the social partners.'[98]

Thus, governments and national level social partners continue to pursue collective and wage bargaining as before, but the *objectives* are either established in advance at the EU level, or severely constrained by the requirements of economic policy: to this extent, I would disagree with Dølvik that national-level actors are left with 'considerable leeway'. The similarity between such changes in European and national industrial relations and the open method of coordination is striking. The open method of coordination of employment policy involves the elaboration of guidelines, benchmarks and indicators at EU level, their translation into national policies and the periodic monitoring of such implementation. What is happening with 'credibility bargaining' and wage determination is a similar, though much less structured, process—minus the EU monitoring of wage developments, save for recommendations in the BEPGs that wage restraint must be observed. The process is one of 'organized decentralization',[99] whereby the economic and political *context* in which wage bargaining takes place is becoming increasingly 'Europeanized' even though the level at which decisions are reached and implemented may well be increasingly decentralized.[100]

## 3.2 Labour market flexibility and deregulation

The main argument of this section is that, despite the consensus which appears to have been reached at EU level on the path to be taken to achieve full employment and competitive markets, the majority of Member States continue to be reluctant

[97] Teague, n. 75 above, at 446

[98] Jon Erik Dølvik, 'Building Regional Structures: ETUC and the European Industry Federations', (2000) 6:1 *Transfer: European Review of Labour and Research*, 58–77, at 72.

[99] Traxler, n. 78 above.

[100] For a fuller discussion on the 'Europeanization' of industrial relations, see Sisson and Marginson, n. 80 above.

to engage in the wholesale modernization of their regulatory regimes envisaged by the Employment Strategy.

As shown in the discussion in Chapter 4 on the interaction between economic, employment and social policy and the implementation of full employment, the attempt within the EU to reconcile labour market flexibility with social protection has ultimately been unconvincing. The BEPGs continue to recommend the removal of 'excessively rigid employment protection legislation' in order to promote job creation, whilst the philosophy underpinning the Social Policy Agenda is that 'quality' in work and in social policy is essential to attain competitiveness and full employment.

In 1997, the OECD identified a difference of opinion amongst member countries, with Continental European countries the most likely of the western states to reject comprehensive labour market reforms, due to concerns over equity and social cohesion. Much has changed since then within the EU—not least the introduction of the euro and the development of an employment strategy committed to macro-economic stability and major structural reform of labour markets—but this ambivalent attitude towards labour market reforms has not entirely disappeared. As noted above, in the context of economic coordination within the EU the demographic crisis and 'pensions time bomb' have weakened the resistance of these same European countries to undertaking reforms of social transfer systems.[101] Further, the fiscal straitjacket imposed by EMU has obliged national industrial relations systems to practise wage restraint as well as to contemplate allowing greater wage flexibility. However, moves towards the latter policy have been limited: whilst aggregate wage developments appear to be satisfying the requirements of the economic policy guidelines (that increases in nominal wages be consistent with price stability) there still appears to be a reluctance in many Member States to open wage formation processes up fully, with all that this would mean for wage (in)equality. Thus, the Commission report on the implementation of the 2001 BEPGs noted that:

'**Aggregate wage developments**
Overall, wage trends remained moderate in 2001, even though the rise in compensation per employee in the euro area is estimated to have accelerated by half a percentage point to about 3 per cent. While labour market conditions tightened until early 2001, the response in wage settlements to the temporary rise in headline inflation remained muted....

**Wage differentiation**
[However] Moves to achieve wage structures that better reflect productivity differences were limited in 2001. In some countries (Belgium, Germany, Austria) steps were taken

[101] The OECD had identified a concern amongst some member countries that its recommendations to enhance wage flexibility and reform social transfer systems would contradict social policy goals of ensuring some degree of equity across members of the labour force or the population at large: OECD, *Implementing the OECD Jobs Strategy*, n. 60 above, at 13.

that allow, under certain conditions, for deviations from the wage norms fixed in collective agreements at sectoral level.'[102]

By 2004, the Commission was able to report that wage growth had declined by less than the drop in productivity growth, in other words, that wages had responded only modestly to the worsened economic situation, even though wages were nevertheless broadly compatible with price stability in the medium term.[103]

If Member States appear reluctant to engage in wage differentiation, what of systems of labour market regulation more generally? As evidenced in their NAPs, Member States have been slow to flexibilize labour markets fully to the extent demanded by the Employment Strategy. With regard to the obligation to encourage adaptability in business and their employees, the 1999 *Joint Employment Report* stated that '[t]he response to this pillar remains disappointing'.[104] To recall the arguments made earlier,[105] the 1999 *Joint Employment Report* found 'little evidence that a comprehensive strategy embracing a partnership approach with the social partners and developing efforts to modernize the regulatory framework has been undertaken by any Member State'.[106] The *Joint Employment Reports* for 2000 and 2001 reached similar conclusions: Member States continued to adopt 'only piecemeal or incremental reforms'[107] and to focus on working time issues, to the detriment of progress on modernization of work organization, or a more comprehensive reform of working life.[108] By 2005, the message about labour market reform was reinforced by the conclusions of the 2004 Employment Taskforce, and the Commission was able to report a greater recognition by Member States of the need for 'modernization':

'Increasingly, Member States seek to promote a balance between flexibility and security, often through discussion with social partners.... However, labour market segmentation is not significantly addressed across the EU.... In particular, a lot remains to be done to improve work organisation, facilitate mobility and labour market transitions, especially for young people. Ten Member States received a specific recommendation on the modernisation of labour law.'[109]

As previously argued, one reading of this (non-)implementation of the adaptability guidelines is that the majority of Member States, when acting domestically, did not endorse its deregulatory assumptions. To some extent, the Member States have been paying lip service to the need to 'flexibilize' their

[102] CEC, *Report on the Implementation of the 2001 Broad Economic Policy Guidelines*, Brussels, 21.02.2002, ECFIN/16/02-EN, at 19.

[103] CEC, Communication from Commission: *The Implementation of the 2003–05 Broad Economic Policy Guidelines*, COM (2004) 20 final, Brussels, 21.1.2004, at 21.

[104] CEC, *Joint Employment Report 1999* (Luxembourg: OOPEC, 1999) at 69.

[105] In Chapter 4, Section 4.2.2.

[106] CEC, *Joint Employment Report 1999*, n. 104 above.

[107] CEC, *Joint Employment Report 2000*, n. 9 above, at 56.

[108] Ibid. at 4 and 55–6; see also *Joint Employment Report 2001*, n. 13 above, at 33–5.

[109] CEC, *Joint Employment Report 2004–5*, n. 29 above, at 11–12.

labour markets—the *Joint Employment Report* for 2001 noted that there was now 'a general trend towards new and flexible forms of work, facilitating the introduction and use of fixed-term contracts, temporary work and part-time work . . . through collective agreements'.[110] However, I would argue that there is by no means the sort of shift towards a process of deregulatory or neo-voluntarist regulation as recommended by the various international organizations or envisaged by the EU institutions and Member States when acting supranationally.

Tellingly, the Council of Ministers for Economic and Financial Affairs recommended, in its proposals for the Barcelona European Council, that '[p]olicy action should focus on modernising the labour market in order to support the process of employment creation'.[111] This would necessitate not only continuing efforts towards active labour market policies and reducing the tax burden on labour, but also (i) reform of wage formation systems to allow greater differentiation of wages according to productivity developments and skills differentials; (ii) improvement in labour market efficiency through supply-side measures such as increased mobility, and education and training; and (iii) a review of labour legislation, to assess the costs attached to the formulation and termination of employment contracts, with a view to striking a proper balance between flexibility and social protection.[112] These are precisely the sort of labour market reforms envisaged by the European Central Bank, for example, in its report on the labour market matching process, which was also published in March 2002.[113]

However, the Barcelona summit itself, for reasons of intergovernmental politics, was unable to reach agreement on precise details of further labour market flexibility measures. At first sight, this difference of opinion between the Council of Ministers and the European Council is puzzling. I have already emphasized the importance of not overstating the distinction between 'Member States' and 'the Community' in the context of employment policy and when analysing the extent of Member State compliance with 'Community' policies. However, it can be genuinely difficult to discern precisely where individual Member States stand on the issue of further labour market flexibility, in particular, where Finance Ministers appear to be agreeing to one thing (further labour market deregulation) which Heads of State and Government then shy away from.

To appreciate the positions of the Member States, it is helpful to see how the EU-level debates on labour market flexibility are perceived by the social partners and external commentators. Comparing responses to Barcelona in 2002 and Brussels in 2005, one is struck by a strong sense of *déjà vu*. Some, such as *The*

[110] CEC, *Joint Employment Report 2001*, n. 13 above, at 34.

[111] Economic and Financial Affairs Council, 'Key Issues Paper on the 2002 Broad Economic Policy Guidelines', paper annexed to the Presidency Conclusions, Barcelona European Council, n. 52 above, at para 37.

[112] Ibid., at para 39.

[113] European Central Bank, *Labour Market Mismatches in Euro Area Countries* (Frankfurt am Main: ECB, March 2002).

*Economist*, view both Barcelona and Brussels as having failed to fulfil the promise of Lisbon. *The Economist* began with the premise that the Lisbon process was essentially about liberalization of markets, including labour markets, and that the EU Member States had finally accepted the need for major economic reforms to close the gap with the US economy. In consequence, the journal naturally viewed the inability, since Lisbon, to realize reforms (such as the creation of an EU-wide system of patent law and a pan-European code for corporate takeovers) as failures, which were further confounded by 'a new wave of labour-market regulation which runs counter to Lisbon's professed desire to cut unemployment',[114] here referring to the proposed directive extending employment rights to temporary agency workers.[115] The inference seems to be that Member States are in denial over what the strategic goal established at Lisbon will mean for reform (ie deregulation) of labour markets, captured in the assessment of Brussels that '[o]nce again, the Union's leaders have shown that they lack the courage to do what is necessary to boost its sluggish economy'.[116]

Both sets of social partners had warmly welcomed the conclusions reached at Lisbon. For the ETUC,[117] Lisbon 'marked a change of spirit and priority as far as addressing the problems facing the European economy is concerned. Stability is no longer the dominant feature. Growth and employment are also being taken into account'.[118] Of particular importance for the ETUC was the fact that 'full employment is becoming the target of a more efficient economy based on innovation and knowledge and that, at the same time, social cohesion as a basic requirement is being emphasised'.[119] There had been a similarly enthusiastic reception for the Lisbon strategy within the business community. UNICE[120] was 'happy with this new momentum in the EU to tackle the high unemployment rates through economic and structural reforms',[121] but also urged that reforms must be implemented rapidly. However, by 2002, concerned at the slow progress towards the Lisbon goals, UNICE warned that decisive steps must be taken at

[114] 'Barcelona Blues', *The Economist Global Agenda*, 15 March 2002.

[115] The final text of the proposed directive was published by the Commission soon after Barcelona: Proposal for a Directive of the European Parliament and the Council on working conditions for temporary workers, COM (2002) 149 final, Brussels, 20.3.2002.

[116] 'Dodging the difficult stuff', *The Economist Global Agenda*, 29 March 2005.

[117] The European Trade Union Confederation, established in 1973, comprises 74 member organizations from 34 countries in western, central and eastern Europe, as well as 11 European industry federations, representing 60 million members; see *http://www.etuc.org/*.

[118] Emilio Gabaglio (ETUC General Secretary), 'Lisbon marks the way to full employment: The commitments must be felt in the economic orientations to be taken and in the social agenda'. Brussels, 27 March 2000; see also ETUC Resolution for the Lisbon Summit, 'A new opportunity for a strategy for full employment' Lisbon, 22 March 2000. Both documents available at *http://www.etuc.org/* [accessed 10 April 2005].

[119] Gabaglio, n. 118 above.

[120] The Union of Industrial and Employer's Confederations of Europe, created in 1958, consists of 34 central industrial and employers' federations from 27 countries and represents more than 16 million companies; see *http://www.unice.org/unice/*.

[121] UNICE, Press Release, Brussels, 24 March 2000; available at *http://www.unice.org* [accessed 10 April 2005].

Barcelona, if the Lisbon process was not to fail. And in relation to labour market reform, UNICE argued that

'The modernisation of the labour market depends above all on measures taken within Member States. But the European level must avoid imposing additional constraints in the form of ill-conceived social measures. The proposed directive on temporary work, which is currently being discussed by the Commission, is an example of such a measure.'[122]

Again, as in the view of *The Economist*, it is considered that Member States were not sufficiently reform-orientated; that the full implications of the laudable strategic goal set at Lisbon—which include labour market deregulation—were being ignored for the sake of politically inspired social measures.[123] In particular, the journal took the view which has been reflected elsewhere in much of the English-language press, that Continental Europe's 'dismal unemployment levels and disappointing economic growth' would not be solved by any combination of macro-economic policies unless considerable micro-economic reform took place, particularly in its heavily regulated labour markets.[124] However, the ETUC, as could be expected, took the opposite view, welcoming the fact that '[t]he neo-liberal offensive launched on the eve of the Barcelona summit has not succeeded'.[125] The ETUC had been concerned at what it identified as a growing tendency among several governments and European employers to argue simply for 'market deregulation, structural reform and yet more labour flexibility',[126] a unilateral approach which according to the ETUC contradicted the balanced integrated nature of the Lisbon strategy, and stressed economic reforms to the exclusion of social and environmental needs.

On comparing the texts of UNICE and *The Economist* on the one hand, and the ETUC on the other, it would seem safe to conclude that all three are observing the same phenomenon, albeit from differing perspectives: namely, the reluctance of Member States collectively to agree to 'neoliberal' deregulation. In the view of UNICE, it means a danger that what could have been a turning point for the European economy (Lisbon) is being squandered, as Member States continue to avoid making the necessary 'tough choices'.[127] Some Member States, though, do seem happy to make such 'tough choices' and their stance on the issue

[122] UNICE, *European Business says: Barcelona Must Revitalise the Lisbon Process* (Brussels: UNICE, 2002).

[123] See also 'Lisbon's lost legacy', *The Economist Global Agenda*, 14 December 2001: 'Europe's labour markets, meanwhile, are becoming less flexible rather than more. New and tougher regulations are looming on the consultation of workers by management. These will make it harder for employers to fire staff, and thus make them more reluctant to hire as well'.

[124] *The Economist*, n. 116 above. See also, David Smith, 'Sad to say, Europe's big boys are stuck in the mire', *The Sunday Times: Economic Outlook*, 27 March 2005; Wolfgang Munchau, 'Europe's missed chances', *Financial Times*, 27 March 2005.

[125] Emilio Gabaglio, 'Barcelona: The neo-liberal offensive has not been imposed' (ETUC, Brussels, 19 March 2002); available at *http://www.etuc.org/* [accessed 10 April 2005].

[126] European Council in Barcelona: Resolution adopted by the ETUC Executive Committee, Brussels, 11–12 March 2002; available at *http://www.etuc.org/* [accessed 10 April 2005].

[127] UNICE, n. 122 above.

of labour market deregulation is easier to identify. For example, the joint statement issued by Prime Ministers Tony Blair and Silvio Berlusconi following the Anglo-Italian summit in Rome prior to the Barcelona European Council clearly indicates their determination to proceed with further labour market reform.[128] In addition to calling for more flexible labour markets across the EU, the joint statement also argued that

'it is now more than ever important that the reform of European labour markets is tackled in parallel with the reform of product and capital markets. The overriding objective of labour market reform must be the achievement of the ambitious employment targets set by the Lisbon and Stockholm Councils. In particular we need to review existing labour market regulation at both EU and national level to ensure that it takes account of both the business need for flexibility and the employee's need for job security and employability, as well as to press ahead with an ambitious programme of structural reforms.'[129]

This statement is premised on the idea that economic interdependence of Member States (especially in the wake of EMU) means that labour market policy and labour market regulation can no longer be considered merely national concerns. However, in the absence of institutional capacity at EU level to replicate existing national social systems,[130] it is up to the individual Member States to ensure that their systems of labour market regulation are sufficiently flexible. Yet not only are electorates 'relatively firmly (if begrudgingly) committed to their respective national status quos'[131] and unwilling to countenance major reductions in social protection, but the philosophy behind the Blair–Berlusconi statement is not uniformly shared by other Member States: 'the influence of neo-liberal ideology . . . has spread unevenly across member states and remains a salient issue of dispute within them'.[132]

For example, in relation to the annual Country-Specific Economic Policy Guidelines contained in the BEPGs, the 2002 implementation report noted that better and more consistent progress had been made by Member States in implementing the capital market and product market recommendations, than the labour market recommendations.[133] In particular,

'[s]everal Member States (Germany, Spain, France, Italy, Portugal) need to go further in reforming the existing regulatory framework with a view to combining greater

[128] Joint Statement by the Prime Minister, Tony Blair, and Italian Prime Minister, Silvio Berlusconi, at the Anglo-Italian Summit, 15 February 2002, available at *http://www.number-10.gov.uk/* [accessed 10 April 2005].

[129] Ibid.

[130] Paul Teague, 'Deliberative Governance and EU Social Policy' (2001) 7:1 *European Journal of Industrial Relations*, 7–26, at 21.

[131] Philippe C. Schmitter and Michael W. Bauer, 'A (modest) proposal for expanding social citizenship in the European Union', (2001) 11:1 *Journal of European Social Policy*, 55–65, at 55. See also Boeri, Börsch-Supan and Tabellini, n. 48 above.

[132] Schmitter and Bauer, n. 131 above, at 55.

[133] CEC, *Report on the Implementation of the 2001 Broad Economic Policy Guidelines*, n. 102 above, at 37–48.

flexibility with security in order to reduce structural unemployment and labour market segmentation.'[134]

Member States are at different stages of development, so it is inevitable that, with regard to flexibility of capital, labour and product markets, 'the precise nature of such flexibility is likely to differ from one national factor market to another'.[135] So long as Member States do not fall foul of their obligations under the 'hard coordination' mechanisms of EMU and the Stability and Growth Pact, the open method of coordination means that it is difficult to force a Member State to deregulate its labour markets beyond what is feasible in the given domestic political context.[136] Therefore, what seems to be occurring is the scenario mooted by Bertola and Ichino in 1995: 'it is quite possible that a unified Europe should choose a common institutional framework that, while less rigid than previously, does not reach the American or British degree of flexibility'.[137]

As observed in the discussion on compliance with the Employment Strategy and the growing consensus over policy goals—such as increased labour market participation, and investment in skills and training—socialization and collective learning have an influence on the process of policy formation,[138] such that the very way in which Member States understand the unemployment problem changes over time. Nevertheless, as far as wage differentiation and labour market flexibility are concerned, there remains a residual belief within some Member States in the 'trade-off' between horizontal equity and employment objectives, a belief which is sufficiently entrenched to prevent a consensus being reached over further labour market deregulation.

## 3.3 The impact of EU internal market law on national employment policy

'The need to avoid distortion of competition in the Single Market also place[s] limitations on national employment policy. For example the Commission ruling against Italy's subsidisation of new employment by 'contratti di Formazione e Lavoro' (training employment contracts), which were seen to benefit employers (rather than workers). (Ardy and Begg, 2001)[139]

[134] Ibid., at 24. [135] Hodson and Maher, n. 6 above, at 735.

[136] A comparison can be made here with the unwillingness of the French government to liberalize its energy markets fully.

[137] Giuseppe Bertola and Andrea Ichino, 'Wage Inequality and Unemployment: US vs Europe', Centre for Economic Policy Research (CEPR) Discussion Paper No 1186, May 1995, at 33.

[138] Tania Börzel and Thomas Risse, 'When Europe Hits Home: Europeanisation and Domestic Change' (2000) 4 *European Integration Online Papers* 15, at *http://eiop.or.at/eiop/texte/2000-015a.htm* [accessed 10 April 2005].

[139] Brian Ardy and Iain Begg, 'The European Employment Strategy: Policy Integration by the Back Door?' South Bank European Papers, No 4/2001, South Bank University European Institute, at 7.

Article 87 (ex Article 92) EC provides that any aid granted by a Member State which distorts or threatens to distort competition by favouring certain undertakings or the production of certain goods shall, in so far as it affects trade between Member States, be incompatible with the common market. In addition, Article 81 (ex Article 85) EC prohibits agreements or associations between undertakings 'which may affect trade between Member States and which have as their object or effect the prevention, restriction or distortion of competition within the common market'. Finally, Article 82 (ex Article 86) EC prohibits abuse by undertakings of a dominant market position. Together with the 'four freedoms' guaranteed by the EC Treaty—free circulation of goods, persons, services and capital—these provisions 'provide the framework for the establishment and functioning of the common market'.[140]

Although at the time of the founding Treaties, the prevailing wisdom was that the goal of market integration did not require social policy harmonization,[141] that national systems of labour law and industrial relations would be unaffected by European economic integration, it soon became apparent that the potential existed for a very serious clash between the provisions of national social policy and the law of the common market.[142] The European Court of Justice (ECJ), in its decisions on free movement of goods, prompted negative integration by extending Article 28 EC to include a large range of national regulations which might have an effect on free circulation of economic resources, and hence on inter-state trade.[143] In widening the circumstances under which state intervention in national economies would be held incompatible with the single market, the ECJ was, in effect, second-guessing national regulatory policies.[144] In the context of the influence of the Employment Strategy on Member States' policies, the importance of these market-creating provisions and decisions is to raise the question of how EU employment policy can mediate the interaction between EU competition law and the law of the internal market on the one hand, and national labour law on the other.

This conflict between the values of market integration and competition policy at EU level and national level social policy has been scrutinized in a series of ECJ

[140] Simon Deakin, 'Labour Law as Market Regulation: The Economic Foundations of European Social Policy', in Paul Davies, Antoine Lyon-Caen, Silvana Sciarra and Spiros Simitis (eds.), *European Community Labour Law: Principles and Perspectives, Liber Amicorum Lord Wedderburn* (Oxford: Clarendon Press, 1996) at 71.

[141] International Labour Organization, *Social Aspects of Economic Co-operation: Report of a Group of Experts*, Studies and Reports, New Series, No 46 (Geneva: ILO, 1956) (the Ohlin Report); and Comité Intergouvernemental Créé par la Conférence de Messine, *Rapport des Chefs de Délégation aux Minstres des Affaires Etrangères* (Brussels, 1956) (the Spaak Report) summarized in English in 'Political and Economic Planning,' *Planning* No 405 (1956).

[142] Deakin, n. 140 above, at 76.

[143] Case 120/78, *Rewe-Zentral AG v Bundesmonopolverwaltung für Branntwein (Cassis de Dijon)* [1979] ECR 649; Joined Cases C-267/91 and C-268/91, *Keck and Mithouard (Criminal Proceedings against)* [1993] ECR I-6097.

[144] Miguel Poiares Maduro, 'Never on a Sunday—What Has (EU) Law Got to do With It?', in Silvana Sciarra (ed.), *Labour Law in the Courts: National Judges and the European Court of Justice* (Oxford: Hart Publishing, 2001) at 274.

decisions during the 1990s,[145] decisions which have taken on an even wider resonance in the context of the attempts by Member States to implement those parts of the Employment Strategy which demand active labour market measures and new forms of collective bargaining.[146]

The leading case of *Albany* concerned compulsory pension schemes based on collective agreements in the Netherlands, which were alleged to be incompatible with Articles 81, 82 and 86 (ex Articles 85, 86 and 90) EC.[147] Three employers in three different industrial sectors brought a complaint under these Treaty provisions against legislative schemes which made it compulsory for the employers to affiliate to supplementary pension plans based on collective agreements between a multi-employer organization and the trade unions in each sector. The argument was that the Member State legislation making affiliation to the pension fund compulsory favoured or furthered an agreement between undertakings which was contrary to Article 81(1) (ex Article 85(1)) EC. *First*, the ECJ recognized that collective agreements can restrict competition, but that since the Treaty as a whole also recognizes social policy objectives, and promotes freedom of association and collective bargaining, then such agreements must be regarded as falling outside the scope of Article 81(1) EC. But there is a very important proviso to this exemption of social law from the competition provisions: the Court's judgment states that collective agreements are only immune from anti-trust scrutiny if they are in the context of collective bargaining, and if they relate to the traditional subject matter of collective bargaining, ie wages and working conditions.[148] *Second*, the Court held that the pension fund was an undertaking within the meaning of Article 81 EC, because it engaged in an economic activity. It was immaterial that the pension fund was non-profit making, or that it pursued an essential social function, or that it was based on the principle of solidarity.[149]

The Court seems to be saying that collective agreements are outside the scope of Article 81 EC where they are concluded in the context of collective negotiations between management and labour, and are seeking to improve conditions

[145] For a discussion of the ECJ's case law, see Deakin, n. 140 above, and Silvana Sciarra, 'Market Freedom and Fundamental Social Rights' in Bob Hepple (ed.), *Social and Labour Rights in a Global Context: International and Comparative Perspectives* (Cambridge: CUP, 2002).

[146] These decisions on the interaction between internal market law and national social policy have been followed by a series of judgments on the interaction between internal market law and other areas of national regulatory competence, such as provision of health care services; see eg Case C-120/95 *Decker v Caisse de maladie des employés privés* [1998] ECR I-1831; Case C-158/96 *Kohll v Union des caisses de maladie* [1998] ECR I-1931; Case C-157/99 *Geraets-Smits and Peerbooms* [2001] ECR I-5473; and Case C-385/99, *V.G. Müller-Fauré v Onderlinge Waarborgmaatschappij OZ Zorgverzekeringen UA*, and *E.E.M. van Riet v Onderlinge Waarborgmaatschappij ZAO Zorgverzekeringen* [2003] ECR I-4509.

[147] Case C-67/96, *Albany International BV v Stichting Bedrijfspensioenfonds Textielindustrie* [1999] ECR I-5751. For commentary see Stephen Vousden, 'Albany, Market Law and Social Exclusion', (2000) 29:2 ILJ 181–91; and Luc Gyselen, 'Case note' (2000) 37 *CML Rev*, 425–48.

[148] *Albany*, n. 147 above, at paras 59–60 of the Court's decision.

[149] Ibid., at paras 84–7 of the Court's decision.

of work, but possibly not where they exceed these objectives. This is an important recognition of the legitimacy of collective bargaining (and social policy) within the European legal order,[150] and some recognition of its autonomy. However, this autonomy is circumscribed to the extent that collective bargaining must still be subject to scrutiny to see what its *effects* are: 'the agreement at issue in the main proceedings does not, *by reason of its nature and purpose*, fall within the scope of Article 85(1) [now Article 81(1)] of the Treaty'.[151]

Nonetheless, this does leave collective agreements which are not on these *core* areas—the traditional subject matter of collective bargaining—particularly vulnerable to anti-trust scrutiny. In this regard, it is also instructive to consider the Advocate-General's Opinion. Advocate-General Jacobs went further than the ECJ in arguing that the proposed anti-trust immunity for collective agreements should extend only to agreements (a) made within the framework of collective bargaining between both sides of industry; (b) which were concluded in good faith (ie not 'merely a cover for a serious restriction of competition between employers on their product markets'); and (c) which dealt with the core subjects of collective bargaining such as wages and working conditions, and which did not directly affect third parties or markets.[152] An economic rationale is given for the anti-trust exemption, that 'collective agreements between management and labour prevent costly labour conflicts, reduce transaction costs through a collective and rule-based negotiation process and promote predictability and transparency'.[153] Such a 'static definition of a dynamic process'[154] is a cause of concern for labour lawyers, since it artificially restricts the evolution of collective bargaining and negates the very assumption on which such bargaining is based, namely that 'there is no limit to discovering new fields of action and entering new subject areas, while balancing the countervailing powers of the parties involved'.[155]

*Albany* and related cases[156] have major implications for the ability of the social partners to bargain collectively, and for Member States to elaborate social and

[150] Catherine Barnard and Simon Deakin, 'In Search of Coherence: Social Policy, the Single Market and Fundamental Rights' (2000) 31:4 *Industrial Relations Journal*, 331–45, particularly at 331–7.

[151] *Albany*, at para 64 of the Court's decision; emphasis added.

[152] Ibid., at paras 190–4 of the Advocate-General's Opinion.

[153] Ibid., at para 181 of the Advocate-General's Opinion.

[154] Sciarra, n. 145 above, at 108.

[155] Silvana Sciarra, '*Job Centre*: An Illustrative Example of Strategic Litigation' in Silvana Sciarra (ed.), *Labour Law in the Courts: National Judges and the European Court of Justice* (Oxford: Hart Publishing, 2001) at 247.

[156] The Advocate-General in *Albany* referred to the well-known series of decisions in which the ECJ had accepted the principle that competition rules apply to the social field: eg in *Höfner* and *Job Centre*, in respect of the labour market, and *Poucet* as regards pensions: Case C-41/90 *Klaus Höfner and Fritz Elser v Macroton GmbH* [1991] ECR I-1979; Case C-55/96, *Job Centre Coop. Arl. [Job Centre II]* [1997] ECR I-7119; Joined Cases C-159/91 and C-160/91 *Poucet et Pistre* [1993] ECR I-637. More recently, in *van der Woude* the Court held collective agreements concerning voluntary supplementary health insurance *subject* to the competition rules, but nevertheless *compatible with* Articles 81 and 82: Case C-222/98, *Hendrik van der Woude v Stichting Beatrixoord* [2000] ECR I-7111.

employment policy at national level, even though the Court held back from endorsing the Advocate-General's third condition (that the collective bargaining must not directly affect third parties or markets) which would arguably have 'opened up many multi-employer agreements to the review of competition policy authorities'.[157] The reasoning of the ECJ, which exempts collective agreements from the scope of competition law only where those agreements are on the traditional subject matter of collective bargaining, possibly impedes moves being taken by the national level social partners, often at the behest of Member State governments, to engage in bargaining to combat unemployment, such as social pacts or credibility bargaining 'in the shadow of EMU', as discussed above. The neo-corporatist role for the social partners in the articulation and implementation of employment policy at national level is leading to bargaining on issues of job creation and competitiveness, as well as the involvement of the social partners in the reform of social security systems. Thus, a Member State would risk breaching Article 81 EC where it gave legislative or other support to a collective agreement on job creation, or a pact for employment and competitiveness, which did not have the nature or purpose to contribute directly to the improvement of conditions of work.

Although the ECJ has stated that Articles 81 and 82 EC are 'concerned only with the conduct of undertakings and not with national legislation of Member States', it is also the case that Article 81 EC, read in conjunction with Article 10 EC,[158] requires Member States not to 'introduce or maintain in force measures, even of a legislative nature, which may render ineffective the competition rules applicable to undertakings'.[159] As we now know, national labour law is not immune from the logic of market integration. This 'infiltration'[160] of labour law by competition law raises a fundamental issue which goes to questions of 'social sovereignty', since certain forms of state intervention in national economies to ensure provision of what are often referred to as collective goods, might be held to be incompatible with Community law.[161] This is not to say that the Treaties necessarily impose a particular economic paradigm on Member States;[162] after all, social protection and social cohesion are stated aims of the Community, as well as free competition. Nevertheless, it is difficult to envisage how the complete

[157] Barnard and Deakin, n. 150 above, at 335.

[158] Formerly Article 5 EC: Member States shall 'abstain from any measure which could jeopardise the attainment of the objectives of this Treaty'.

[159] Joined Cases C-401/92 and C-402/92, *Heukske vof and J.B.E. Boermans, Criminal Proceedings Against Tankstation 't* [1994] ECR I-2199, at para 16.

[160] Gerard Lyon-Caen, 'L'infiltration du droit du travail par le droit de la concurrence' (1992) *Droit Ouvrier*, 313–21.

[161] Leigh Hancher, 'Community, State and Market', in Paul Craig and Gráinne de Búrca (eds.), *The Evolution of EU Law* (Oxford: OUP, 1999); see also Tamara Hervey, 'Social Solidarity: A buttress against internal market law' in Jo Shaw (ed.) *Social Law and Policy in an Evolving European Union* (Oxford: Hart Publishing, 2000).

[162] Wolf Sauter, 'The Economic Constitution of the European Union' (1998) 4 *Columbia Journal of European Law*, 27–68.

removal of barriers to trade between countries and mobility of economic resources can be compatible with the preservation of national autonomy in the area of employment policy, so as to give Member States the freedom to promote employment whilst also 'progressively develop[ing] their own policies'.[163]

Turning to the implications of Article 87 EC (on state aid) for Member States' employment policies, the relationship between lawful and unlawful training/ employment aid or subsidies was partially clarified at the launch of the Luxembourg process: the European Council concluded that

> 'it is important to focus on aid arrangements which favour economic efficiency and employment without causing distortions of competition. The Commission will ensure that the control of State aid does not constitute an obstacle to labour market policy measures compatible with the Treaty.'[164]

Clearly, measures taken by a Member State to implement the employability guidelines in particular—to promote the development of human resources and implement an active labour market policy—run the risk of falling foul of Article 87 EC, if financial support, incentive measures or subsidies are seen to favour certain undertakings. Therefore, the Commission issued a further clarification, that a training aid measure intended to reduce the costs which certain firms would normally have to bear, in their own interest, to improve their employees' skills, confers on them an advantage over their competitors and is likely to distort competition, in breach of Article 87 EC.[165] Generally, Article 88 EC provides for a system of notification to and supervision by the Commission of all systems of state aid; with regard to employment and training aid, the Commission has over the years issued a series of guidelines and regulations, identifying the types of training and employment aid which are likely to be acceptable, and listing exemptions from the state aids regime.[166]

[163] Presidency Conclusions, Lisbon European Council, n. 10 above, at para 37.

[164] Presidency Conclusions, Extraordinary European Council Meeting on Employment, Luxembourg, 20 and 21 November 1997, Bull EU-11/1997, 7–13, at para 27.

[165] Communication from the Commission, *Framework on Training Aid* (1998) OJ C 343/7, at para 7. For an analysis of the interaction between competition law and national employment measures, see Sally Ball, 'The European Employment Strategy: The Will but not the Way?' (2001) 30:4 ILJ, 353–74, at 363–6.

[166] Guidelines on State Aid for Employment, OJ C 334 of 12.12.1995. In January 2001, the Commission published three 'block exemption Regulations' covering aid to small and medium-sized enterprises; aid for training; and *de minimis* aid (small amounts of aid). Under the 'block exemptions', as long as the state aid fits all the terms of the exemption, the funding body does not need to go through the full notification procedure and await Commission approval. However, it does still need to provide the Commission with summary information on the scheme and submit annual reports on all the activity under the scheme. Commission Regulation (EC) No 68/2001 of 12 January 2001 on the application of Articles 87 and 88 of the EC Treaty to training aid, OJ L 10/20; Commission Regulation (EC) No 69/2001 of 12 January 2001 on the application of Articles 87 and 88 of the EC Treaty to *de minimis* aid, OJ L 10/30; Commission Regulation (EC) No 70/2001 of 12 January 2001 on the application of Articles 87 and 88 of the EC Treaty to State aid to small and medium-sized enterprises, OJ L 10/33, 13.1.2001. Regulation 70/2001 was amended by Commission Regulation (EC) No 363/2004 of 25 February 2004, on the application of Articles 87 and 88 of the EC Treaty to training aid, OJ L 63 of 28.02.2004.

Examples of cases where the Commission has judged Member States' measures to be sufficiently 'general' as to avoid being classed as unlawful aid include the 'New Deal' in the UK; the French 'mesures financières d'accompagnement de la gestion des fins de carrière'; and Swedish 'tax relief for foreign experts'.[167] Three examples of employment policy measures which were, on the other hand, caught by the prohibition on state aids concern social plans in France,[168] the Belgian *Maribel bis/ter* schemes,[169] and the Italian *contratti di formazione e lavoro* (training employment contracts).[170] In *France v Commission* the ECJ ruled that the financial support of the French *Fonds National de l'Emploi* (FNE), a state body, in paying for measures included in the social plan drawn up by a company faced with large-scale redundancies, constituted a state aid contrary to Article 87 EC (then, Article 92 EC), and should therefore have been notified to the Commission. Nothing could more clearly inhibit the freedom of Member States to determine their own employment and social policy than the statement that Article 87(1) EC does not distinguish state intervention by reference to its aims, but only in respect of its effects; thus the social character of FNE assistance is not sufficient to exclude it outright from being categorized as aid under Article 87 EC.[171] The Court accepted that if state funding had been restricted to financing unemployment benefits for the redundant employees, it would not have been a state aid because the benefits went completely to the employees. However, since the funding in this case included payments to employees who were not dismissed but instead made the transition to new half-time and short-term arrangements, the funding partly benefited the firm and could therefore be characterized as a state aid.

The Belgian *Maribel* schemes[172] involved reduced social security contributions for employers in relation to manual workers, with special additional reductions for specified sectors of industry. The Belgian government argued that measures in favour of certain categories of workers could not amount to state aids as they were non-discriminatory, non-discretionary and objectively justified. In the opinion of the Court, however, the fact that certain industrial activities were excluded was sufficient to distinguish the included sectors—the aid favoured certain undertakings or the production of certain goods and therefore breached Article 87(1) EC. The Court again reiterated the view that Article 87(1) EC catches state intervention regardless of its intentions.

[167] CEC, *Commission Report on the Application of the 1995 Guidelines on Aid to Employment*, adopted by the Commission on 21.12.2000 (Luxembourg: OOPEC, 2000) at 3.

[168] Case C-241/94, *France v Commission* [1996] ECR I-4551.

[169] Case C-75/97, *Belgium v Commission* [1999] ECR I-3671.

[170] The following discussion of the *contratti di formazione e lavoro* draws on Marco Biagi and Michele Tiraboschi, 'The Role of Labour Law in Job Creation Policies: An Italian Perspective' in Marco Biagi (ed.), *Job Creation and Labour Law: From Protection Towards Pro-action* (Dordrecht/London: Kluwer Law International, 2000) at 187–8.

[171] *France v Commission*, n. 168 above, at paras 19–21 of the judgment.

[172] For an analysis of *Belgium v Commission*, see Malcolm Ross, 'State Aids and National Courts: Definitions and Other Problems—A Case of Premature Emancipation?' (2000) 37 *CML Rev*, 401–23, at 404.

It was against a similar backdrop that the Commission found the Italian *contratti di formazione e lavoro* to be unlawful state aids. These special contracts, first introduced by statute in 1984 and amended by the Italian Constitutional Court in 1987 to emphasize the job creation function, subsidized companies to take on workers up to the age of 32 under fixed-term contracts for a maximum of 24 months, by permitting reductions to wage levels established by industry-wide agreements and by reductions in employers' fiscal and social contributions.[173] In its decision of 11 May 1999,[174] the Commission held such contracts to be unlawful state aids, contrary to Article 87(1) EC, due to the fact that there was selection (aid was granted on a discriminatory basis) on the grounds of the geographical area and type of company involved. As Marco Biagi and Michele Tiraboschi argued, such decisions on state aids for employment leave national legislators little room for manoeuvre, and have 'effectively eroded significant powers of the Member States in pursuing policies aimed at supporting the productive and employment systems'.[175]

The reasoning in such judgments of the ECJ and decisions of the Commission has the effect that social plans, and other measures aimed at restructuring or providing incentives to retain or create jobs, must be tested for conformity with Article 87 EC in a way which undercuts the independence of national social legislation and can constitute a constraint on its operation. Such decisions have important implications for the more ambitious employment policies pursued by Member States, which attempt to use industrial policy to make a contribution to alternative investment plans. One of the key stumbling blocks in Article 87 EC—as was seen in the Belgian and Italian cases—is selectivity, namely that a measure which is insufficiently 'general' will be an unlawful state aid. The 2001 round of regulations on training aid exempted aid granted for 'general training' from the notification requirements of Article 88(3) EC,[176] since such training 'is not applicable only or principally to the employee's present or future position in the assisted firm, but . . . provides qualifications that are largely transferable to other firms or fields of work and thereby substantially improve the employability of the employee'.[177] The opposition to aid for firm-specific training is that it would 'provide a direct competitive advantage for the firm receiving the aid'.[178] Furthermore, the notion of employability which informs the Regulations, whilst entirely consistent with that contained within the Employment Guidelines, is likewise one which appears to equate employability with flexibility; workers are increasingly expected to be secure by virtue of being employable *across jobs*, rather than in

[173] Biagi and Tiraboschi, n. 170 above, at 187.

[174] Commission Decision of 11 May 1999 concerning aid granted by Italy to promote employment (2000/128/EC) OJ L 42, 15.02.2000.

[175] Biagi and Tiraboschi, n. 170 above, at 188.

[176] Commission Regulation No 68/2001, n. 166 above, Article 4.

[177] Ibid., Article 2(e).

[178] Ball, n. 165 above, at 365.

one job. As the Commission stated in 1997:

'[t]here is a need for a radical rethink of all relevant labour market systems . . . to adapt them to a world of work which will be organized differently, in which the concept of security of workers has to be reformulated, *focusing more on security based on employability in the labour market rather than security in a specific job*.'[179]

Thus, not only does this understanding of the employability concept rather let employers off the hook as regards responsibility for training, placing more emphasis on individual workers' responsibilities for improving their own human capital, but it also serves to undermine state intervention intended to encourage training by employers.

In conclusion, one interpretation of the above is that, in their national measures to implement what they understand to be European employment policy, Member States run the risk of infringing European internal market law. However, a better view, which can help in assessing the influence of the Employment Strategy and the extent to which Member States are constrained by it, is that the internal market and competition *acquis* provide the economic backdrop which further bolsters the 'soft law' of the Employment Strategy. Again, the 'soft law' framework of the Employment Strategy and the open method of coordination is deceptive. As explored in Section 2 above, and in Chapter 5, such 'soft law' can exert a powerful controlling influence on the direction and content of Member States' employment policies, and to this must also be added the limitations imposed by the dictates of internal market and competition law.

## 4. The interaction between EU and national employment policy

### 4.1 The Netherlands and the UK: different versions of the 'Third Way'?

'The Third Way is an attempt to find new answers to the problems of unemployment, inequality and social exclusion, in the awareness that it has become increasingly difficult for any national state to impose standards of good social behaviour on, and extract resources from, capital, firms and other mobile sources.' (Visser, 2000)[180]

The concluding sections of this chapter will analyse the interaction between the European Employment Strategy and the employment policies of two Member States, the Netherlands and the UK. The issue of influence is double-edged: as discussed above, the Employment Strategy is having an impact on the

[179] CEC, *Employment in Europe 1997, including An Employment Agenda for the Year 2000*, COM (97) 479 final (Luxembourg: OOPEC, 1997) at 20; emphasis added.

[180] Jelle Visser, 'From Keynesianism to the Third Way: Labour Relations and Social Policy in Postwar Western Europe' (2000) 21:4 *Economic and Industrial Democracy*, 421–56, at 424.

**Table 6.1** Competitive and corporatist approaches to unemployment

| Competitive | Corporatist |
|---|---|
| • Reduction in union power | • New social consensus |
| • Incentives to work | • Incentives to work & employability |
| • Social security system is less comprehensive | • Reform of social security |
| | • Redistribution of labour |
| • Wage and labour market flexibility | • Labour cost reduction |

discourse within the Member States over the appropriate path to take to combat unemployment and increase employment, but at the same time, policies in Member States are filtering up to the EU level. There is a growing similarity not only between the policy initiatives at national and EU level, but also in the philosophy behind these labour market and welfare state reforms. In the UK context, this supply-side philosophy has been explicitly identified with the 'Third Way', a label which could arguably also be extended to the post-Lisbon Employment Strategy and to the approach adopted in the Netherlands since the early 1990s.

One can see a turn to 'Third Way' politics in the UK, as the response of the Labour government to 18 years of Conservative rule, providing continuity with the supply-side agenda of the Conservatives combined with a communitarian emphasis on the 'rights and responsibilities' of jobseekers and other beneficiaries of the welfare state. In the Netherlands, on the other hand, the social policies pursued by 'purple' coalition governments since 1999—made up of blues and reds, namely liberal (ie right wing) and socialist parties—paved the way for a synthesis of neoliberal and social democratic approaches to social and employment policy, which may also merit the label 'Third Way'. Filip Abraham suggests a useful distinction between 'competitive' and 'corporatist' versions of the 'Third Way', either of which may successfully keep unemployment under control, *provided that* policies take into account the interdependence of unemployment, labour costs and social security, as outlined in Table 6.1.[181]

To this taxonomy, I would add that 'corporatist' versions of the Third Way—a category into which I argue the Netherlands falls—also place emphasis on the importance of labour market flexibility (for instance, the official Dutch policy of encouraging atypical work and flexible work organization). Nevertheless, this remains a valuable way to understand the different types of 'Third Way' thinking to which the Dutch and British employment policies seem to adhere, whilst also 'complying' with the philosophy of the European Employment Strategy. In examining the mutual influence of the European Employment Strategy on

[181] Filip Abraham, 'A Policy Perspective on European Unemployment' (1999) 46:4 *Scottish Journal of Political Economy*, 350–66, at 362.

employment and labour market policies in the Netherlands and the UK, the focus will be on the promotion of employability and adaptability within the Employment Strategy, and how these objectives interact with national policies, as evidenced in the NAPs for Employment from 1998 to 2004.

## 4.2 The 'Third Way' and labour market policy

Anthony Giddens, who has definitively elaborated the 'Third Way' as a critique of both neoliberalism and traditional social democracy, argues that it is now necessary to move beyond the terminology,[182] to recognize that 'Third Way' is merely a useful shorthand term for the renewal of social democracy in contemporary social conditions. Accordingly, the term could apply equally to New Democrats or Clinton-era Democrats in the US, New Labour in the UK, as well as to the doctrinal changes made by left parties or coalitions in Scandinavian countries, the Netherlands or France since the late 1980s.[183] For the purposes of examining the interaction between the European Employment Strategy and the national policies of the Netherlands and the UK, I shall adopt a pragmatic definition, since my aim is to identify similarities in policy prescriptions in response to the perceived need for welfare state and labour market reform.

The core of 'Third Way' thinking is the project of transformation, or modernization, of the welfare state, based on the following assumptions: that Keynesian management of the national economy is no longer feasible ('The ability of national governments to fine-tune the economy in order to secure growth and jobs has been exaggerated'[184]); that 'old' social democracy was statist and bureaucratic ('The belief that the state should address damaging market failures all too often led to a disproportionate expansion of the government's reach and the bureaucracy that went with it'[185]); and that rights were too often elevated above responsibilities, thus neglecting the importance of individual effort. In response, the 'Third Way' approach emphasizes a pragmatism towards, and greater acceptance of, the market: 'the essential function of markets must be complemented and improved by political action, not hampered by it. . . . The weaknesses of markets have been overstated and their strengths

182 Anthony Giddens, 'Introduction' in Anthony Giddens (ed.), *The Global Third Way Debate* (Cambridge: Polity Press, 2001) at 1.

183 Ibid., at 2. For an analysis of social policy in the Netherlands and Belgium, which confirms the 'Third Way' tendencies of recent reforms, see Renaat Hoop, 'Social Policy in Belgium and the Netherlands: Third Way or Not?' in Giuliano Bonoli and Martin Powell (eds.), *Social Democratic Party Policies in Contemporary Europe* (London: Routledge/ECPR Studies in European Political Science, 2003).

184 Tony Blair and Gerhard Schröder, *Europe: The Third Way/Die Neue Mitte* (London: The Labour Party, 1999) at section I.

185 Ibid.; for a critique, see Paul Hirst, 'Has Globalisation Killed Social Democracy?' in (1999) 70:S1 (Special Issue) *The Political Quarterly*, 84–96, at 86–7.

underestimated'.[186] Thus, there exists a belief that a 'robust and competitive' market framework is essential for economic success and employment growth. However, the 'Third Way' approach carefully distances itself from *laissez faire* liberalism, in asserting that flexible markets must be combined with a redefined role for an active state. Giddens, for example, suggests that government has an 'essential role to play in investing in the human resources and infrastructure needed to develop an entrepreneurial culture'.[187] Further, that 'the guideline is investment in *human capital* wherever possible, rather than the direct provision of economic maintenance. In place of the welfare state, we should put the *social investment* state'.[188]

This is where the 'Third Way' approach really becomes more concrete, and resonates with the European Employment Strategy and the Lisbon Strategy, which are similarly concerned with improving employability, and encouraging high rates of labour market participation. As Philip Arestis and Malcolm Sawyer caution, it is 'unlikely that economic policy pursued by any government is fully consistent either internally or with some theoretical paradigm'.[189] Yet, it is in the area of welfare state and labour market reform that one can most clearly see links between 'Third Way' philosophies and the employment policies adopted by Member States and the EU:

> '"third way" policy pragmatism involves both a positive view of the ability of the market to provide certain outcomes and a strong emphasis on the active "social investment state". At the level of policies, the "third way" involves such elements as a robust macro-economic policy, responsive wage bargaining, combining wage moderation and flexibility, active labor market policies, and employment-friendly and efficient tax and social policy.'[190]

The proposals put forward in the Blair–Schröder paper of 1999 are directed to other European social democratic governments who share their modernizing aims, as well as to the European Union, thus contributing to thinking underpinning the Employment Strategy and the genesis of the Lisbon Strategy. The policy recommendations made in the Blair–Schröder paper with respect to the welfare state include a tax policy that promotes sustainable growth, in particular by reducing the burden on business; a macro-economic policy that emphasizes sound public finances; reforms of welfare and benefits systems away from a focus on cash transfers which encourage inactivity; active labour market policies which stress personal responsibility and promote labour market participation; and greater flexibility of the labour market.

186 Blair and Schröder, n. 184 above.

187 Anthony Giddens, *The Third Way: The Renewal of Social Democracy* (Cambridge: Polity Press, 1998) at 99.

188 Ibid., at 117; emphasis in the original.

189 Philip Arestis and Malcolm Sawyer, 'The Economic Analysis Underlying the "Third Way"' (2001) 6:2 *New Political Economy*, 255–78, at 256.

190 Christoffer Green-Pedersen, Kees van Kersbergen and Anton Hemerijck, 'Neo-liberalism, the "Third Way" or What? Recent Social Democratic Welfare Policies in Denmark and the Netherlands' (2001) 8:2 *Journal of European Public Policy*, 307–25, at 309.

# 5. The Netherlands

## 5.1 The 'Dutch miracle' and welfare reform

In the 1980s, the Netherlands had one of the highest unemployment rates in the European Community; now, it (together with Luxembourg) has the lowest unemployment rate of the EU25.[191] Such a revolution in labour market performance, labelled the Dutch employment miracle,[192] has been attributed to wage restraint within the framework of Dutch corporatism, working-time reduction and job redistribution, and the shift from the traditional breadwinner to a dual-earner economy, based on a one-and-a-half jobs per household model.[193] The government has credited the successful labour market performance to the following:

'During recent years the government—in tandem with social partners—has worked to create a confidence-building, macro-economic framework, to strengthen the economic structure, to promote a restrained wage-cost development and to implement measures aimed at the lower end of the labour market. Together these efforts have made a significant contribution to the growth of employment.'[194]

Some commentators, however, question the prominence given to wage moderation as the major causal factor in the Dutch employment miracle, suggesting that economists have perhaps overestimated the importance of wages in fuelling jobs growth: 'comparative considerations seem to suggest that wage levels and wage moderation are not so important for a country's employment performance as supply-siders assert'.[195] In the Dutch case, although unit wage costs have been rising less rapidly in the Netherlands than in Germany, for example, this does not apply across the board, and in any case the difference has been less marked in the

[191] As at December 2004, the unemployment rate in the Netherlands was 4.7 per cent, in comparison to an average of 8.0 per cent for the EU15 and 8.9 per cent for the EU25. This had risen from a low of 2.3 per cent for the Netherlands in February 2002 (although all EU states saw an increase over these years—in February 2002, unemployment averaged 7.7 per cent for the EU15). In June 2001 the Netherlands had overtaken Luxembourg to have the lowest unemployment rate in the EU. Eurostat: Statistical Office of the European Communities in Luxembourg, Euro-indicators News Release No 44/2005, 1 April 2005; News Release, No 40/2002, 3 April 2002; and News Release No 90/2001, 4 September 2001. Dutch unemployment had reached a peak of 14 per cent in the summer of 1983: Uwe Becker, 'The "Dutch Miracle": Employment Growth in a Retrenched But Still Generous Welfare System', Social Policy Research Centre, University of New South Wales, SPRC Discussion Paper No 99, May 1999, at 1.

[192] Jelle Visser and Anton Hemerijck, *'A Dutch Miracle': Job Growth, Welfare Reform, and Corporatism in the Netherlands* (Amsterdam: Amsterdam University Press, 1997); Günther Schmid, 'The Dutch Employment Miracle? A Comparison of Employment Systems in the Netherlands and Germany', Berlin: Wißenschaftszentrum, Discussion paper FS 1 97–202; for a more critical account, see Uwe Becker, 'A "Dutch Model": Employment Growth by Corporatist Consensus and Wage Restraint? A Critical Account of an Idyllic View' (2001) 6:1 *New Political Economy*, 19–43.

[193] Jelle Visser, 'The First Part-Time Economy in the World: Does it Work?' Amsterdam Institute for Advanced Labour Studies (AIAS) University of Amsterdam, Working Paper 00–01, June 2000, at 9 ff, and 22.

[194] *Netherlands: National Employment Action Plan 1998*, at 5.

[195] Becker, n. 191 above, at 13.

1990s.[196] Arguably, therefore a greater share of the Dutch employment miracle is attributable to the creation of part-time jobs, and the related abandonment of traditional male-breadwinner patterns, which led to an increase in the number of women in (part-time) employment. No other OECD country currently has such a high level of part-time employment as the Netherlands,[197] leading to the epithet of the 'first part-time economy in the world'.[198]

The growth in employment and in labour market participation (admittedly, from a low base: labour market participation grew from barely 60 per cent in 1983 to more than 70 per cent in 1998[199]) has occurred in parallel with welfare state reform, such that many argue the two are linked. The orthodox view would be to contend that the Dutch welfare state had been too generous, and needed to be retrenched in order to promote job creation. A Christian-Liberal coalition in power from 1982 brought the Netherlands into line with the 'broad western move to the right', in rejecting state intervention and Keynesianism, and liberalizing the welfare state by emphasizing individual responsibilities and duties as much as or even more than rights.[200] The coalition government tightened eligibility rules for social assistance, reduced the top marginal income tax from 72 to 60 per cent, and raised social security contributions. Between 1986 and 1992 (with a new Christian-Labour coalition from 1989) the government reduced most gross replacement rates from 80 to 70 per cent, reformed the disability scheme, and froze the general child and student allowances.[201] The first 'purple' coalition government of 1994 further tightened eligibility rules, to compel recipients of social assistance to accept a job, and recipients of unemployment assistance to be 'actively seeking work'.[202] The discursive framework within which such changes occurred were crucial to their success: reforms such as those to social security arrangements and taxation were not presented as forming part of a New Right ideology, so that the Dutch Social Democrats were able to support them.[203]

Clearly, the Dutch welfare system has been subject to a degree of retrenchment, but in view of its starting point, it is still generous. Poverty rates remain low in comparison with other EU countries: the high per capita social expenditure levels are well above the EU average, with the percentage of the population at risk of poverty well below the EU average.[204] This is due, in particular, to the

[196] Schmid, n. 192 above, at 9. [197] Ibid., at 10. [198] Visser, n. 193 above.

[199] Uwe Becker, 'Welfare State Development and Employment in the Netherlands in Comparative Perspective' (2000) 10:3 *Journal of European Social Policy*, 219–39, at 220.

[200] Ibid., at 224. [201] Ibid., at 225. [202] Ibid.

[203] A. H. G. M. Spithoven, 'The Third Way: the Dutch Experience' (2002) 31:3 *Economy and Society*, 333–68, at 338.

[204] CEC, *Draft Joint Report on Social Inclusion 2001*, n. 26 above, at 17. There is a lack of commonly defined and agreed indicators on poverty at EU level, with Member States using different definitions for measuring and characterizing current levels of poverty and social exclusion. Most Member States, however, refer to the key indicator of the 'risk of poverty' rate, central factors of which are unemployment (especially when long-term), low income, low quality employment, homelessness, weak health, immigration, low qualifications and early school leaving, gender inequality, discrimination and racism, disability, old age, family break-ups, drug abuse and

retention of a comprehensive system of social benefits which guarantees citizens a high minimum income (relative to other EU states).[205] Although a differential has been introduced, in order to encourage people to leave the benefits system for paid work, nevertheless the minimum subsistence income still amounts to at least 70 per cent of the minimum wage,[206] and attention is paid to the trend in the purchasing power of those on minimum incomes. As between those in work, there remains relatively little income inequality.[207] Although earnings inequality has increased in the Netherlands over the past decade, the increase has been fairly modest: the OECD *Employment Outlook* for 1996 shows that full-time wage earners' gross income inequality has only changed slightly, much of the increase in income inequality being attributable to the decline of welfare benefits (as discussed above), and the large increase of female part-time work.[208] The Dutch employment miracle thus shows that success can be achieved without a sharp rise in earnings inequality,[209] or a cutback of the welfare state towards the United States' level.[210] Indeed, the restructuring of Dutch social security by the two 'purple' governments under Wim Kok has been characterized as a case of 'managed liberalization', implying a public recognition that the Dutch 'Polder model' represented something of an alternative to both neoliberal deregulation and traditional social democracy.[211]

## 5.2 'Flexicurity' and adaptability

In its assessment of the National Action Plans for 1998, the Commission noted the willingness, on the part of the Netherlands and the UK, to engage in

alcoholism and living in an area of multiple disadvantage: ibid., at 7. For more on the different definitions and measurements of social exclusion within the EU, see Diamond Ashiagbor, 'Promoting Precariousness? The Response of EU Employment Policies to Precarious Work' in Judy Fudge and Rosemary Owens (eds.), *Precarious Work, Women and the New Economy: The Challenge to Legal Norms* (Oxford: Hart Publishing, forthcoming 2005).

[205] *Dutch National Action Plan: Against Poverty And Social Exclusion, 1 June 2001*, at para 1.3.1.

[206] Ibid.: the rate of minimum subsistence income for people living alone is 70 per cent of the minimum wage, with 100 per cent for couples, and 90 per cent for single parents.

[207] Michael F. Förster and Michele Pellizzari, 'Trends and Driving Factors in Income Distribution and Poverty in the OECD Area', OECD Labour Market And Social Policy: Occasional Papers No 42, August 2000, at 46.

[208] OECD, *Employment Outlook 1996* (Paris: OECD, 1996) at Chapter 3: Earnings Inequality, Low-paid Employment and Earnings Mobility.

[209] Visser, n. 193 above, at 31.

[210] Becker, n. 199 above, at 236.

[211] Anton C. Hemerijck and Mark I. Vail, 'The Forgotten Center: The State as Dynamic Actor in Corporatist Political Economies' unpublished paper prepared for workshop, *The State after Statism: New State Activities in the Age of Globalization and Liberalization*, University of California Berkeley, 14–15 November 2003, at 19–20; page numbers refer to manuscript. The Kok administration was re-elected in 1998, and after stepping down as prime minister in 2002, Wim Kok went on to chair two reviews of the Employment and Lisbon Strategies, thus putting the seal on the process of 'mutual learning' over approaches to employment which I argue has been occurring between the EU and certain Member States: see *Jobs, Jobs, Jobs: Creating more employment in Europe*. Report of the Employment Taskforce chaired by Wim Kok (Luxembourg: OOPEC, 2003) and Kok Report, *Facing the Challenge: The Lisbon Strategy for Growth and Employment*. Report from the High Level Group chaired by Wim Kok (Luxembourg: OOPEC, 2004).

critical self-assessment of current problems, needs and policies in their labour markets.[212] The Dutch labour market priorities, elaborated in its 1998 NAP, have remained remarkably unchanged: to reduce benefit dependency; to promote labour force participation amongst older people, women, ethnic minorities and less educated people; to increase the quality of the labour supply; and to support the modernization of the labour system in order to achieve a new balance of flexibility and security in the labour market.[213] Although there had been a rapid increase in the female participation rate in the 1990s, it remains well below that for men[214] and, in view of the central goal of increasing the effective supply of labour, the government is therefore keen to increase labour participation amongst women by making it easier to combine work and family responsibilities.[215]

With regard to modernization of working patterns, the main initiative here was the Flexibility and Security Act, which came into force in January 1999, although to some extent the framework of consensual flexibility—more flexible employment relations achieved by means of industrial consensus—had been established with the 'Wassenaar Agreement' of 1982.[216] The 1999 Act, however, further strengthened a legislative framework for the promotion of flexibility, which included new legislation on working hours in 1996, legislation prohibiting discrimination between employees based on working hours in 1996, and the Career Breaks (Funding) Act of 1998.[217] A key aim of the Flexibility and Security Act was to increase labour flexibility, whilst also improving the security of 'atypical' workers, for example, by simplifying dismissals, at the same time as enabling temporary contracts to be a stepping stone to permanent employment.

Accordingly, the Act shortened and simplified notice periods; shortened procedures for dismissal on economic, technical and organizational grounds; liberalized the regulation of temporary work agencies; and widened the circumstances

[212] CEC, *From Guidelines to Action*, n. 8 above, at 2 of the Communication.

[213] *Netherlands: National Employment Action Plan 1998*, at 6–7; *National Action Plan for Employment 2000*, at 7; *National Action Plan for Employment 2001*, at 7–8; *National Action Plan for Employment 2003*, at 3–5; and *National Action Plan for Employment 2004*, at 4–7.

[214] The overall employment rate had risen from 66.3 per cent in 1996 to 73.5 per cent in 2003; the female rate from 55.8 per cent; to 65.8 per cent, surpassing the Lisbon target of 60 per cent by 2010: CEC, *Employment in Europe 2004: Statistical Annex*, n. 55 above, at 255.

[215] *Netherlands: National Action Plan for Employment 2000*, at 7–8; *National Action Plan for Employment 2003*, at 40–1; *National Action Plan for Employment 2004*, at 48.

[216] The 1982 Wassenaar Agreement, reached between the peak trade unions and the main employers' association, is considered by many to mark the origin of the 'Dutch model' or 'Polder model' by providing a transition to a more consensual model of industrial relations: see Steve Nickell and Jan van Ours, 'The Netherlands and the United Kingdom: A European Employment Miracle?' (2000) 30 *Economic Policy*, 136–80, at 152–3. The agreement introduced the flexible reduction of working time as a measure against unemployment, and liberalized the increased use of temporary, part-time and other forms of 'atypical' employment. The Wassenaar Agreement also prompted other agreements concerning wage restraint, labour market flexibility, early retirement and job creation: see Nickell and van Ours, ibid.; and Gustav Heerma van Voss, 'The Flexibility and Security Act', Peer Review Programme on Active Labour Market Policy, Discussion Paper, 26–27 October 2000; available at *http://peerreview.almp.org/en/* [accessed 10 April 2005].

[217] *Netherlands: National Action Plan for Employment 2000*, at 19.

under which firms could use temporary workers—three temporary contracts may succeed one another in the space of three years without the employer being obliged to give the worker a permanent job.[218] As far as 'security' was concerned, the Act clarified the circumstances under which flexible working arrangements could amount to a permanent contract of employment, namely, if there have been three successive contracts, or if the total duration of successive contracts is over three years, although collective agreements may waive these provisions.[219]

The impact of the Flexibility and Security Act on dismissals was mixed, with some employers arguing that dismissals were now more complicated, due to the existence of differing procedures for different categories of workers. However, a second government investigation into the effects of the legislation in August 2000 found over 50 per cent of employers had a positive view of the new Act.[220] Further, in 2000, the Working Hours (Adjustment) Act came into force, the aim of which was to make it easier for employees to combine paid work with other responsibilities by giving them a statutory right to work longer or shorter hours. The right extends to all employees in businesses which employ 10 or more, who can request their working hours to be increased or decreased once every two years. This Act, viewed as a major restriction on employers' freedom since the request for a variation in hours could only be refused for legitimate business reasons, is a sign of the seriousness with which the legislature views the desire to reconcile work and home life, and of the high level of support for part-time work.[221]

The overarching aim of the above measures, to find the right balance between flexibility and security in laws and regulations ('flexicurity'), clearly resonates with the objectives of the Employment Strategy, and offers a potential model for other Member States to follow. Certainly, from the viewpoint of European employment policy, one cannot find fault with the stated aim of the Flexibility and Security Act and related legislation, to create 'balanced, durable and flexible working relationships in such a way that the process of work flexibilization takes place in a responsible and balanced manner for both parties'.[222] As early as the 1999, the Commission was able to report near-complete satisfaction of the

[218] *Netherlands: National Employment Action Plan 1999*, at 47; see also Heerma van Voss, n. 216 above.

[219] The regulation of successive temporary contracts is also governed, at EU level, by the Fixed Term Work Directive: Council Directive 99/70/EC of 28 June 1999 concerning the framework agreement on fixed-term work concluded by UNICE, CEEP and the ETUC, OJ L 175, 10.07.1999. Dutch law required little in the way of amendment to comply with the Directive; this was done by amendments to the Dutch Civil Code in 2002: Susanne Burri, 'Flexibility and Security, Working Time and Work–Family Policies in the Netherlands' in Judy Fudge and Rosemary Owens (eds.), *Precarious Work, Women and the New Economy: The Challenge to Legal Norms* (Oxford: Hart Publishing, forthcoming 2005) at 17; page numbers refer to manuscript.

[220] *Netherlands: National Action Plan for Employment 2001*, at 24.

[221] Heerma van Voss, n. 216 above, at 7–8.

[222] *Netherlands: National Employment Action Plan 1998*, at 29.

country's obligations under the old Adaptability pillar of the Employment Strategy:

'With the introduction of the Flexibility and Security Act (arranging the rights of flex-workers and flex-work) in January 1999, the announcement of the Working Hours (Adjustment) Bill (making it possible [for] the individual to change one's working hours with the same employer) and arrangements making temporary work easier and dismissal procedures shorter, the Dutch system is in a good position to achieve the goals set under the adaptability pillar.'[223]

However, although the Netherlands now has one of the lowest rates of unemployment in the EU, and has caught up with (and surpassed) the average European rates of labour market participation, nevertheless it suffers from what the Council Recommendations for 2002 called a 'a key structural imbalance' in that the labour force is constrained by the high proportion of the working age population drawing on disability, unemployment or welfare benefits.[224] In accordance with the general shift away from early retirement and other forms of 'passivity', and in an echo of the Dutch government's own policy objective of reducing benefit dependency, the Council thus recommended that the Netherlands decrease the inflow into disability benefits, reintegrate people currently drawing such benefits into jobs and address the accumulation of benefits.

From the timing of the various pieces of 'flexicurity' legislation, and their position in a wider framework of labour market and welfare state reform, one can see that the Dutch responses to the requirements of the Employment Strategy that Member States flexibilize their labour markets almost entirely take the form of pre-existing measures, or measures which were the outcome of long-standing national level social dialogue, stretching back to the corporatism of the 1982 Wassenaar Agreement.[225] Although many of the more interesting Dutch policy initiatives were not direct *responses* to the Employment Strategy, but rather outcomes of the existing domestic reform process, nevertheless the objectives overlap with those of the Employment Strategy, and also meet the Lisbon challenge of stimulating employment and economic growth as well as protecting social cohesion. Of particular importance is the *language* of Dutch policy-making: the need to reduce benefits dependency and increase labour market participation by certain groups is to be achieved by measures which talk of social activation without (until recently) resorting to benefits conditionality.[226] The emphasis is on tackling the poverty gap, which arises when people move from benefits to low paying employment, through reforms of the tax-benefit

[223] CEC, *Joint Employment Report 1999* Part II, n. 104 above, at 59.

[224] Council Recommendation of 18 February 2002, n. 38 above. 'Non-employment' has remained high despite the fall in unemployment and the rise in labour market participation, with nearly 14 per cent of the economically active population resorting to the disability scheme: Becker, n. 192 above, at 23.

[225] For example, the Flexibility and Security Act was adopted by the government on the basis of unanimous recommendations from the social partners: *Netherlands: National Employment Action Plan 1998*, at 29.

[226] *Netherlands: National Action Plan for Employment 2001*, at 8–9.

system,[227] in particular, the introduction of a multi-year policy intended to reduce the marginal pressure of income-dependent schemes, which should make working more attractive, and an 'outflow-premium' of €1,815 for the long-term unemployed who completely leave welfare.[228] More recently, however, these measures to make work 'more attractive' have begun to refer to 'push' factors alongside 'pull' factors to promote labour market participation; whilst still holding back from the full-blown language of conditionality which, as will be seen below, is more clearly the hallmark of UK policy and the UK version of the 'Third Way'. The Dutch NAP for 2004 reported on proposals to improve the activating effect of social security schemes such as those provided for under the Occupational Disability Insurance Act (*Wet op de arbeidsongeschiktheidsverzekering* or WAO) and the Unemployment Act (*Werkloosheidswet* or WW). For instance, a revised system of occupational disability insurance was introduced in 2004, providing incentives for employers and employees in order to prevent long-term absenteeism due to illness. The Dutch government also proposed reforms to make the WW work less attractive as an 'exit route' from employment, by tightening the eligibility requirements, restricting compensation for dismissal from mid-2005 onwards, and abolishing the 'short-term benefit' which used to be paid under this law. With regard to labour participation by older people, the favourable tax treatment of voluntary early retirement and 'pre-pension' schemes is to be discontinued from January 2006.[229]

Despite the recent hardening of approach to the generosity of welfare provision, there are important lessons to be learnt from the Dutch experience, namely that (a) elements of consensus, that is, partnership between the social partners in particular over organization of work; (b) wage moderation without resort to massive wage differentiation; (c) reforms of labour market regulation which increase flexibility for employers whilst also improving security for atypical workers 'in jobs' not merely 'on the market'; and (d) reforms to the benefits system aimed at making work pay, without penalizing those on benefit, provide a far more convincing balancing of labour market flexibility and social protection than that suggested by the EU discourse.

It was argued above that the 'Third Way' is characterized by the pursuit of a robust macro-economic policy, a redefined role for an active state, flexible markets and wage moderation, high rates of labour market participation together with investment in human and social capital. Thus, if the (relatively modest) welfare state retrenchment, labour market 'flexicurity' and active labour market policies, which have been the hallmark of the Dutch coalition governments since the 1980s, amount to a 'Third Way' approach, which I contend they do,[230] then

[227] Ibid., at 13. [228] Ibid., at 30.

[229] *Netherlands: National Action Plan for Employment 2004*, at 6.

[230] As Renaat Hoop argues, recent Dutch policies can clearly be viewed 'not as *the* concrete elaboration of Third Way thinking with regard to the shaping of the welfare state, but at least as a *possible* elaboration': Hoop, n. 183 above, at 14; emphasis in the original.

it would appear that the Dutch version of the 'Third Way' differs from the version on offer in the UK (and also from the supply-side citizenship of the Employment Strategy post-Lisbon) in that the Dutch version still adheres to a more 'old' social democratic view of equality and social solidarity, and a greater willingness to accept the limitations of markets.

## 6. The UK

### 6.1 The influence of 'Third Way' philosophies

'The Government is actively working towards the goal of full employment as it is the best means to realise a fair and inclusive society. In the dynamic, modern labour market, this cannot be delivered through jobs for life, but rather through ensuring job opportunities for all throughout their working lives. It is seeking both to reduce levels of unemployment and to bring further into the labour market, groups whose participation has traditionally not been high.' (UK Employment Action Plan, 2000)[231]

The UK government is committed to the 'modern version of full employment', namely to providing employment opportunity for all.[232] Its strategic aims are identified as (a) macro-economic stability—stable public finances and low inflation in order to attain high and stable levels of growth and employment; (b) increasing investment in education, training and 'lifelong learning'; (c) 'welfare-to-work' and active labour market policies to help people take up employment; (d) tax-benefit reforms to 'make work pay'; and (e) the building of a fair and flexible labour market.[233]

The UK has experienced strong labour market performance and favourable yearly employment growth, in comparison with the EU average, since the launch of the Employment Strategy.[234] Further, it has surpassed all the employment targets established at the Lisbon and Stockholm European Councils.[235] What

[231] *United Kingdom: Employment Action Plan for 2000*, at 3. See also, *United Kingdom: National Action Plan for Employment 2004*, at 5: 'Full employment, economic success and social justice go hand in hand'.

[232] *United Kingdom: Employment Action Plan for 2001*, at 4; and Department for Education and Employment (DfEE) Green Paper, *Towards Full Employment in a Modern Society*, Cm 5084 (London: HMSO, 2001) at para 2.3; HM Treasury and Department of Work and Pensions (DWP) *Full Employment in Every Region* (London: HMSO, 2003) at chapter 3.

[233] *United Kingdom: Employment Action Plan 1998*, at 3–6; *United Kingdom: Employment Action Plan for 2000*, at 3; *United Kingdom: Employment Action Plan for 2001*, at 4; *United Kingdom: National Action Plan for Employment 2004*, at 1; HM Treasury and DWP, n. 232 above, at para 1.9.

[234] CEC and Council, *Employment Policies in the EU and in the Member States: Joint Report 1998* (Luxembourg: OOPEC, 1999) at 113; *Joint Employment Report 1999*, n. 104 above, at 97; *Joint Employment Report 2000*, n. 9 above, at 180; *Joint Employment Report 2001*, n. 13 above, at 80.

[235] In 2003, the overall employment rate was 71.8 per cent, compared with the Lisbon target of 70 per cent by 2010; the female employment rate was 65.3 per cent, as compared with the target of 60 per cent; and the employment rate for those aged 55–64 was 55.5 per cent, as against a target of 50 per cent by 2010: CEC, *Employment in Europe 2004: Statistical Annex*, n. 55 above, at 263.

remains, according to the Council Recommendations, are some 'structural challenges', namely the persistence of long-term unemployment and low rates of employment amongst disadvantaged groups and regions (in particular, single parents, certain ethnic minorities, older male workers, the disabled, and the low-skilled); the persistent gender pay gap; and the lack of a coherent approach to social partners' involvement.[236]

Since 1997, the Labour government has been engaged in a project of modernization of the welfare state and labour market, based on the 'Third Way' critique of both 'old' social democracy and neoliberalism highlighted in the Blair–Schröder paper of 1999, as discussed above. However, there has been some continuity with the previous Conservative governments' supply-side policies, in particular the 'Jobseeker's Allowance' (JSA) which was introduced nationally in 1996 as part of a radical restructuring of the benefits regime.[237] It would be an understatement to say that the UK NAPs place a strong emphasis on active labour market policies and employability: employability is more than just a buzzword for Labour, it is the core of its labour market policy and critique of the welfare state.[238] For example, the Chancellor of the Exchequer, Gordon Brown, listed four conditions for high and stable growth and employment, the third of which was employability, defined as 'a strengthening of programmes to ensure all have the opportunity of work' and as 'an active labour market policy matching rights and responsibilities'.[239] Although 'employability' is also a mainstay of the Employment Strategy, the mantra of employability and investment in human capital (in skills and training) has become such an integral part of the policy pronouncements of the Labour government that it becomes almost impossible to determine which policy is influencing the other, to identify in which direction the policy transfer is occurring, especially as the UK government does not shrink from lecturing other EU states on how to achieve full employment.[240]

The encouragement of labour market participation as the solution to social exclusion involves renewed emphasis on the *responsibilities* of jobseekers. As two of the government's economic advisers put it: 'the citizen can expect high-quality help in finding work, but in return must take advantage of it or cease to draw

[236] Council Recommendation of 18 February 2002, n. 38 above; Council Recommendation of 22 July 2003, n. 57 above, at 30; Council Recommendation of 14 October 2004, n. 54 above, at 58.

[237] Jamie Peck and Nikolas Theodore, 'Beyond "Employability"' (2000) 24 *Cambridge Journal of Economics*, 729-49, at 735.

[238] Peck and Theodore, n. 237 above; John Philpott, 'Behind the Buzzword: "Employability"', *Employment Policy Institute Economic Report*, Vol 12, No 10, 1999.

[239] Gordon Brown, 'The Conditions for High and Stable Growth and Employment' (2001) 111 *The Economic Journal*, C30–C44, at C31 and C38; the other conditions are stability (a proactive monetary policy and prudent fiscal policy); high productivity; and international engagement.

[240] Domestic strategy to achieve full employment is set out in the DfEE Green Paper of 2001, n. 232 above, and in the 2003 paper from the Treasury and the DWP, n. 232 above; advice to the rest of the EU is set out in HM Treasury, *A Full Employment Strategy for Europe* (London: HMSO, 2003).

benefits'.[241] In other words, the 'supply-side egalitarianism' discussed in Chapter 4 is very much to the fore: the role of state intervention is not to secure equality of outcomes, but equality of opportunity, to invest in skills so as to improve and equalize the *marketability* of individuals, rather than protecting them from the market.[242] This, I would argue, can be contrasted with the Dutch version of the 'Third Way', which has yet to adopt the language or imagery of individuals fending for themselves on the market, or that of 'workfare' or benefits conditionality. Indeed, the differences in the philosophies underpinning active labour market policies in the UK and those in other EU states such as the Netherlands and some Nordic countries, have led some to argue that the UK approach post-1997 owes more to 'transplants' or selective policy transfer from the US, than to policy transfer from elsewhere within the EU.[243] Undoubtedly, the Labour government approach more clearly signals a rejection of the idea that workers can expect (indefinite) security from social transfers or within one job,[244] instead pursuing the promotion of security through employability across the labour market: 'Employability remains at the heart of our employment policies and we are continuing to work to enable people, through education, training, mobility and other help, to find fulfilling employment in an age when no-one can expect to have only one job throughout his or her career'.[245]

## 6.2 Employability and adaptability

Employability and flexibility/adaptability are linked, not only in the context of the European Employment Strategy, but also in the UK's domestic labour market policy. The government's 1998 White Paper *Fairness at Work*, which set out its legislative programme for individual and collective labour law, is worth quoting at length in order to appreciate the interaction between employability and flexibility which was to inform policy-making:

'For those in work, the Government has two key objectives for the labour market: efficiency and fairness. . . . The keys to securing efficiency and fairness are employability and flexibility. Employability means ensuring that people are well prepared, trained and

[241] Tito Boeri, Richard Layard and Stephen Nickell, *Welfare-to-Work and the Fight Against Long-Term Unemployment: Report to Prime Ministers Blair and D'Alema* (London: Centre for Economic Performance, LSE, 2000); summary available as Department for Education and Employment, Research Brief No 206, June 2000.

[242] Wolfgang Streeck, 'Competitive Solidarity: Rethinking the "European Social Model" ' Max Planck Institute for the Study of Societies (MPIfG) Working Paper 99/8, 1999.

[243] Anne Daguerre and Peter Taylor-Gooby, 'Neglecting Europe: Explaining the Predominance of American Ideas in New Labour's Welfare Policies Since 1997' (2004) 14:1 *Journal of European Social Policy*, 25–39. They argue that 'American workfare policies . . . continued to represent the main source of inspiration for the New Deal, especially in their strong emphasis on individual responsibility and the need to implement a tougher sanction regime on the workshy'; at 30.

[244] Cf. the quotation from Giddens that the state should be less concerned with the direct provision of economic maintenance: Giddens, n. 187 above, at 117.

[245] *United Kingdom: Employment Action Plan 1999*, at 6.

supported, both initially as they enter the labour market, and throughout their working lives. Flexibility means businesses being able to adapt quickly to changing demand, technology and competition. By enabling business success, flexibility promotes employment and prosperity.... To support both employability and flexibility we need a labour market culture and a legislative framework which together promote economic growth, enhance competitiveness, encourage entrepreneurship and foster job creation.'[246]

At the centre of the Labour government's employability strategy lie the 'Jobseeker's Allowance', and the 'New Deal'. The former, which applies to 76 per cent of unemployed people, is the basic form of unemployment benefit and is grounded in conditionality: participation in active labour market measures is a condition for receiving this benefit.[247] From the first day of unemployment, all jobseekers are required to take part in a progressive programme of interviews and job search help, including a series of individually negotiated, specific job-seeking activities—interviews, a job search plan, regular attendance at a jobcentre, eventually leading to a work trial, a place on a job club, and a guaranteed interview with an employer. Such regular and increasingly intensive contact with the Employment Service is designed to 'encourage jobseekers to find a job or develop their employability as early as possible'.[248]

The 'New Deal', which came into operation from 1998, is the core of the 'welfare-to-work' part of the employability strategy, and follows on from the Jobseeker's Allowance, or as Peck and Theodore put it, 'JSA establishes a framework of compulsion within which the New Deal operates, substantially determining participation patterns and internal rule systems'.[249] The New Deal in fact consists of six programmes designed to provide intensive support to the unemployed, especially the young and long-term unemployed, lone parents, people with disabilities, those lacking basic literacy and numeracy skills, and ex-offenders.[250]

The New Deal for Young People aged 18–24 begins after six months' unemployment (thus addressing the Employment Guideline on tackling youth unemployment) when individuals enter an intensive 'gateway' period which consists of counselling, advice and guidance lasting up to four months, after which those who do not find a job have four options: a subsidized job for six months; work in the voluntary sector; work on the Environment Task Force; or

[246] Department of Trade and Industry/President of the Board of Trade, *Fairness at Work: A White Paper*, Cm 3968 (London: HMSO, 1998) at paras 2.12 and 2.13.

[247] *UK: Employment Action Plan 1998*, at 12. The government department with responsibility for governance and delivery of active labour market policies has changed over the years: the Department for Work and Pensions (with responsibility for 'working age' issues including the New Deal) was formed in June 2001 from the Department of Social Security (DSS) and parts of the former Department for Education and Employment (DfEE), the latter becoming the Department for Education and Skills (DfES), with responsibility for education.

[248] Ibid., at 13.

[249] Peck and Theodore, n. 237 above, at 735.

[250] New Deal for Young People, New Deal 25 Plus, New Deal 50 Plus, New Deal for Lone Parents, New Deal for Disabled People, New Deal for Partners: *United Kingdom: Employment Action Plan 1999*, at 4–5 and *United Kingdom: National Action Plan for Employment 2004—Annexes*.

full-time education or training for up to 12 months for those who need it. Those who refuse any of these four options will lose benefits, leading to the phrase 'there is no fifth option' for young people.[251] The New Deal for the Long-term Unemployed is aimed at those aged 25 or over who have been unemployed for 18 months or more (reduced from two years in April 2001). It consists of a case management 'gateway', wherein personal advisers provide support and advice, and there are two main options—either subsidized employment or education and training.[252] Attendance is compulsory for those under 50, although the approach is mildly less prescriptive than that for young people.[253]

The Labour government policy of imposing a windfall tax on the privatized utilities raised £5.2 billion between 1997 and 1999, and all of these funds have been allocated to financing New Deals of some variety.[254] Thus, although the 'stricter benefits regime' of the Conservatives is continued under the Labour government,[255] there are three crucial differences within the overall impression of continuity: *first*, there is greater state assistance with job search and skills upgrading, as well as better resourcing than previous active labour market policies.[256] In addition to increased funding, a key theme of recent years, as evidenced in the UK's NAP for 2004, has been the question of improving governance of (active) labour market policies, and modernizing the New Deals.

[251] As stated by Andrew Smith MP, the then Employment Minister: 'New Figures Reveal that New Deal is Tough on Shirkers', Press Notice 1998/0513 (previously known as 513/98) 4 November 1998, available at *http://www.dfes.gov.uk* [accessed 10 April 2005]; see also House of Commons, Select Committee on Education and Employment, Fifth Report, *New Deal: An Evaluation*, HC 58 20 March 2001 (London: HMSO, 2001) at para 7.

[252] *UK: Employment Action Plan 1998*, at 10–11; see also House of Commons Select Committee on Education and Employment, n. 251 above, at para 9.

[253] *United Kingdom: Employment Action Plan for 2001*, at 9; see also Richard Dickens, Paul Gregg and Jonathan Wadsworth, 'New Labour and the Labour Market' (2000) 16:1 *Oxford Review of Economic Policy*, 95–113, at 101.

[254] John van Reenen, 'No More Skivvy Schemes? Active Labour Market Policies and the British New Deal for the Young Unemployed in Context', The Institute for Fiscal Studies, Working Paper 01/09, 5 May 2001, at 8; see also *United Kingdom: Employment Action Plan for 2000*, at 5: 'The Government is investing £5.2 billion over 5 years in Welfare to Work'.

[255] For example, under the Conservatives, the 1988 Social Security Act had removed 16 and 17 year olds from eligibility for cash benefits: Peck and Theodore, n. 237 above, at 734.

[256] Overall spending on active labour market policies in the UK has almost certainly increased after 1997 and is weighted more towards the youth component, although comparative data post-New Deal is not yet available: van Reenen, n. 254 above, at 13. Having said that, spending is still low by international standards. Peter Robinson argues that to some extent, the New Deal has been a triumph of marketing in that the *projected* increase in spending on active labour market policies under the New Deal, as a proportion of GDP, will bring the UK up to the level of spending in Canada, Australia and Austria, but will still be very modest by international standards: Peter Robinson, 'Active Labour-Market Policies: A Case of Evidence-Based Policy Making?' (2000) 16:1 *Oxford Review of Economic Policy*, 13–26, at 18–19. However, the relatively low spend on such policies has in fact been trumpeted by the government as a virtue: 'The New Deal model is very cost-effective, providing amongst the most cost-effective programmes of their type in the world. Measured in terms of the amount spent on active labour market policies as a percentage of GDP (for each percentage point of unemployment) it is among the lowest in the OECD': *United Kingdom: National Action Plan for Employment 2004—Annexes*, at 44.

Partly in response to the report of the Employment Taskforce chaired by Wim Kok, that effective implementation of active labour market policies depends upon good governance and effective partnership between all stakeholders, the UK government has begun to increase flexibility in delivery of such policies as the New Deal, with greater devolution to local managers and personal advisers to tailor provision according to their local labour markets. Further, whilst certain core functions, such as imposing benefit sanctions, will be performed by the state, many services are being opened up to competition between private and voluntary sectors, and public services.[257] *Second*, the policy as a whole is couched in the language of rights and responsibilities, and the responsibility of the unemployed to make themselves attractive to employers. As the responsible government minister put it:

> 'I made it quite clear from the start that the New Deal would carry responsibilities as well as opportunities and that anyone who was not prepared to comply would risk losing their Jobseeker's Allowance. . . . New Deal is not a soft touch and it would be grossly unfair to all those youngsters gladly seizing the opportunity to enter the jobs market to tolerate the tiny minority abusing the system. You have to put something back into society as well as taking it out.'[258]

Such benefit conditionality suggests a 'workfare' orientation to British labour market policy.[259] Instilling the work ethic is an important part of the government's employability strategy, as is ensuring that people remain attached to the labour market.[260] Thus the active job search requirements of the New Deal are being extended to groups traditionally exempt from such active labour market policies, such as lone parents and people on disability benefits, albeit on a voluntary basis. However, benefits conditionality is gradually being extended to new areas: from April 2004, receipt of full benefit was made conditional on partners of working age benefit recipients taking part in what is known as a 'Work-Focused Interview'.[261]

A *third* way in which the Labour government sought to differentiate itself from the previous Conservative administrations is linked to its advocacy of fairness/flexibility at work, namely through the promotion of 'family-friendly' policies, which in the course of the year 2000 were redefined as 'work–life balance' policies.[262] The government accordingly introduced a legal right to

[257] *United Kingdom: National Action Plan for Employment 2004*, at 3. The Government announced its plans for a new framework for delivery of active labour market policies, devolving more responsibility for the allocation of resources to local Jobcentre Plus managers, 'within a framework of rights and responsibilities': Department of Work and Pensions, *Building on New Deal: Local Solutions Meeting Individual Needs* (London: HMSO, 2004).

[258] Smith, n. 251 above. [259] Peck and Theodore, n. 237 above, at 733.

[260] *United Kingdom: Employment Action Plan for 2000*, at 11.

[261] *United Kingdom: National Action Plan for Employment 2004*, at 7.

[262] Sonia McKay, 'Annual Review Article 2000—Between Flexibility and Regulation: Rights, Equality and Protection at Work' (2001) 39:2 *British Journal of Industrial Relations*, 285–303, at 292.

parental leave—although one could argue that this went only so far as necessary to satisfy the government's obligations to transpose the EC Parental Leave Directive,[263] and even then, the rights were restricted to parents of children born after 15 December 1999, which resulted in a legal challenge by the Trades Union Congress.[264] Shorter working hours have been recognized as another important factor in meeting the aim of enabling workers to have a more appropriate balance between work and home life. However, in contrast to the Dutch Working Hours (Adjustment) Act 2000, the British policy has been to undercut enforceable limits on working hours by allowing individual workers to opt out of the limits on working hours contained in the Working Time Regulations 1998.[265] Although the Regulations (and the EC Directive on which they are based) give workers a choice over whether to opt out of the hours' limits, their wording would appear to undermine the reality of that choice in workplaces with a long hours' culture.[266]

The government has repeatedly endorsed 'family-friendly' and 'work–life balance' policies—as a good in themselves, and also as a means of achieving 'supply-side flexibility' in the labour market.[267] The *Fairness at Work* White Paper contained the following rationale:

> 'Competitiveness depends on the UK making the best use of the talents of as many people as possible. The larger the number of people—particularly skilled people—to which business can look, the better. We also need to ensure that as many people as possible who want to work should have the chance to do so.'[268]

This echoes the rationale behind the 'Equal Opportunities' pillar of the original Employment Strategy, which recognized that not only was there a

[263] Council Directive 96/34/EC of 3 June 1996 on the framework agreement on parental leave concluded by UNICE, CEEP and the ETUC, amended by Council Directive 97/75/EC of 15 December 1997, OJ L 145, 19.06.96 and OJ L 10, 16.01.1998.

[264] Case C-234/00, *R v Secretary of State for Trade and Industry ex p Trades Union Congress*, removed from the register of the ECJ by order of 7 May 2003, OJ C 184/53 of 2.08.2003. A request for a preliminary reference was lodged at the ECJ but withdrawn before a hearing. In April 2001, the UK government announced that it would drop the restriction of statutory parental leave to parents of children born after the entitlement was first introduced in December 1999. All working parents with children under five would now be entitled to parental leave. This move had followed an earlier decision by the Commission to send a 'reasoned opinion' to the UK government in the context of the Article 226 infringement procedure, arguing that the restriction of parental leave rights to parents of children born on or after 15 December 1999 was in breach of the Directive (96/34/EC).

[265] McKay, n. 262 above, at 292–3.

[266] The Working Time Directive 93/104/EC, OJ L 307/18. For an analysis of how the UK's individualized system of workplace bargaining has led to widespread use of the 'opt out' from limits on working time, see Catherine Barnard, Simon Deakin and Richard Hobbs, 'Opting Out of the 48-Hour Week: Employer Necessity or Individual Choice? An Empirical Study of the Operation of Article 18(1)(b) of the Working Time Directive in the UK' (2003) 32:4 ILJ, 223–52. See also Catherine Barnard, 'The Working Time Regulations 1999' (2000) 29:2 ILJ, 167–171.

[267] Simon Deakin and Hannah Reed, 'The Contested Meaning of Labour Market Flexibility: Economic Theory and the Discourse of European Integration' in Jo Shaw (ed.), *Social Law and Policy in an Evolving European Union* (Oxford: Hart Publishing, 2000) at 74–5.

[268] DTI, *Fairness at Work* White Paper, n. 246 above, at para 5.1.

*social* need to counter inequalities between women and men, but that there was an *economic* loss from not making full and effective use of the productive capacities of all sections of the population.[269] However, as the transposition of the Working Time Directive and the Part-Time Workers Directive[270] has shown, in balancing demand-side with supply-side flexibility, it would appear that the UK government is not sufficiently prepared to safeguard employee-friendly flexibility.[271] In the case of the Regulations transposing the Part-Time Workers Directive,[272] the principle of 'no less favourable treatment' between full-time and part-time workers is heavily qualified, with the right limited to comparators working under the same type of contract and at the same location, a limitation considered to be so overwhelming as to 'render [the Regulations] largely irrelevant to the vast majority of part-time workers'.[273] Furthermore, the Regulations neglect *expressly* to prohibit dismissals in connection with a refusal to transfer between part-time and full-time work.[274] Finally, there is no absolute legal obligation on employers to make part-time work available where the employee requests it.[275] Thus, the 'family-friendly' agenda appears to exist only in so far as such policies do not interfere with the agenda of promoting business. The Part-time Workers Regulations, in particular, illustrate how the commitment to respect the work–life balance lost ground to the desire not to be seen to be imposing too many burdens on business. According to the government's own figures the Regulations will potentially benefit just 450,000 part-time workers, ie less than 10 per cent of the total, having been framed narrowly due to government concern that 'any more generous provision might antagonize employers'.[276] A similar tale could be told of the government's lack of enthusiasm for transposition of the Fixed-Term Workers Directive,[277] which it transposed into national law with 'its by

[269] The Commission's summaries of the four pillars are taken from the website of DG-V on the European Employment Strategy, originally available at: *http://europa.eu.int/comm/employment_social/empl&esf/pilar_en.htm;* now archived at *http://socialpolicy.ucc.ie/Four_pillars_of_Employment_Strategy.htm#Pillar1* [accessed 10 April 2005].

[270] Council Directive 97/81/EC of 15 December 1997 concerning the framework agreement on part-time working concluded by UNICE, CEEP and the ETUC, amended by Council Directive 98/23/EC of 7 April 1998, OJ L 14, 20.01.98 and OJ L 131, 05.05.98.

[271] A similar attempt to reconcile these two notions of flexibility is also occurring within EU-level discourse: see Chapter 4, Section 4.2.1.

[272] The Part-time Workers (Prevention of Less Favourable Treatment) Regulations 2000, SI 2000/1551. For an analysis, see Aileen McColgan, 'Missing the Point? The Part-time Workers (Prevention of Less Favourable Treatment) Regulations 2000 (SI 2000, No 1551)' (2000) 29:3 ILJ, 260–7; see also Mark Freedland and Claire Kilpatrick, 'Part-Time Work in the UK: Can EU Governance be Transformative?' in Silvana Sciarra, Paul Davies and Mark Freedland (eds.) *Employment Policy and the Regulation of Part-Time Work in the European Union: A Comparative Analysis* (Cambridge: CUP, 2004).

[273] McColgan, n. 272 above, at 266.

[274] Ibid.

[275] McKay, n. 262 above, at 294.

[276] Ibid., at 295.

[277] Council Directive 1999/70/EC of 28 June 1999 concerning the framework agreement on fixed-term work concluded by ETUC, UNICE and CEEP, OJ L 175, 10/07/1999, 43–48. The Directive was transposed into UK law by the Fixed-Term Employees (Prevention of Less Favourable Treatment) Regulations 2002, SI 2002/2034.

now standard minimalist approach to transposition'[278] and opposition to the proposal for an EC directive on temporary workers.[279]

Thus, the extent to which work–life balance policies are a means to achieving competitiveness suggests that they are vulnerable to being trumped by the dictates of business. For the rest of its adaptability policies, the UK government is relatively sanguine that the UK labour market is sufficiently flexible. For example, with regard to the long-standing employment guideline that Member States should examine the possibility of incorporating in national law more flexible types of contract—the UK NAPs could report as early as 1998 that '[w]e have considered the possibility of more adaptable contracts but do not consider that there is a need to review contract law in this regard'.[280] The core of the approach in the early NAPs was that businesses will be able to create more jobs if they operate in a labour market that is 'not hampered by unnecessary bureaucracy and regulation', at the same time that the UK's more flexible labour market should be underpinned by an 'appropriate framework of minimum standards'.[281] In this, the approach adopted by the UK NAPs has been remarkably consistent, underpinned by the theoretical perspective that 'well-focused regulation' has important economic benefits and plays a vital role in correcting market failures, although it is also important to strike the right balance so that regulations do not impose 'too heavy a burden' on businesses, particularly small businesses, or stifle entrepreneurship.[282]

As to the mutual influence between EU and national policies, it is possible to identify a parallel development in views on welfare state reform: the reforms to the British welfare state, moving towards a more 'conditional, selective and work-orientated' benefits system,[283] have been matched by EU-level recommendations to other Member States. Whilst the BEPGs for 1999 had urged Member States to 'assess' the duration of benefits and their eligibility criteria, in the context of increasing employability,[284] the 2000 BEPGs noted that only a few Member States

[278] Aileen McColgan, 'The Fixed-Term Employees (Prevention of Less Favourable Treatment) Regulations 2002: Fiddling While Rome Burns?' (2003) 32:3 ILJ, 194–9.

[279] Proposal for a Directive of the European Parliament and the Council on working conditions for temporary workers, Brussels, 20.3.2002, COM(2002) 149 final; see Ian Black, 'Employers attack charter for temps as unworkable', *The Guardian*, 21 March 2002: 'The [UK] government and employers' organizations are gearing up to fight a European commission directive that would give Britain's temporary workers the same pay and rights as permanent staff'.

[280] *UK: Employment Action Plan 1998*, at 32; *United Kingdom: Employment Action Plan 1999*, at 19. The Employment Guidelines for 2004 merely maintain in force the guidelines for 2003; these provide that Member States should promote 'diversity of contractual and working arrangements': Council Decision of 22 July 2003, n.4 above, at 18. The original guideline was that 'each Member State [should] examine the possibility of incorporating in its law more adaptable types of contract': Council Resolution of 15 December 1997 on the 1998 Employment Guidelines, OJ C 30/98, 28.01.1998.

[281] *United Kingdom: Employment Action Plan 1999*, at 38.

[282] *United Kingdom: National Action Plan for Employment 2004*, at 9; *United Kingdom: National Action Plan for Employment 2003*, at 11.

[283] Peck and Theodore, n. 237 above, at 746.

[284] Council Recommendation of 12 July 1999 on the broad guidelines of the economic policies of the Member States and of the Community (1999/570/EC) OJ L 217, 17.08.1999, 34–61, at para 3.3(i).

had tackled employment disincentives in tax and benefit systems.[285] So, the BEPGs for 2001 recommended that Member States should ensure that tax and benefit systems make work pay, by reducing labour taxes and high marginal effective tax rates, especially for low-paid workers, and addressing incentive effects, duration, eligibility and enforcement of benefit schemes to make them more employment-friendly.[286] This would seem to require Member States which have not already done so to reduce replacement rates, impose job search and other requirements on the unemployed, and reduce the length of time for which benefits are available, as has occurred in the UK. For example, in successive country-specific employment policy recommendations, Belgium is urged to review tax and benefit systems to remove subsisting unemployment traps and provide adequate incentives for active job search by reviewing the conditionality of benefits;[287] France is required to pay 'particular attention' to income guarantee schemes;[288] as for the Netherlands, its reforms should focus on the 'relatively lax eligibility rules',[289] and Sweden is congratulated for its tightened eligibility criteria for unemployment insurance (in terms of occupational and geographical mobility).[290]

The supply-side agenda adopted in the UK gives rise to labour market policy which seeks to equip individuals to compete in the market, emphasizing employability over social protection. Such developments in labour market policy shed light on what a 'modernized' or 'active' welfare state (as envisaged by the Lisbon Strategy) might look like, and give an indication of one possible future direction of the supply-side agenda adopted by the Employment Strategy in its post-Lisbon stage. However, if we think in terms of the mutual influence of national and European employment policies, it is important to question whether this version of the 'Third Way' can really be seen as a renewal of social democracy as some argue,[291] or rather, more accurately described as no more than 'neo-liberalism with a human face'.[292]

## 7. Conclusions

In respect of the issue of compliance with the Employment Strategy, it has been argued that Member State compliance is in fact extremely high, in spite of the

[285] Council Recommendation of 19 June 2000 on the broad guidelines of the economic policies of the Member States and the Community, (2000/517/EC) OJ L 210, 21.08.2000, 1–40, at para 2.1.

[286] Council Recommendation of 15 June 2001, n. 57 above, at 13.

[287] Council Recommendation of 14 October 2004, n. 54 above, at 50.

[288] Council Recommendation of 15 June 2001, n. 57 above, at 29.

[289] Ibid., at 36.

[290] Council Recommendation of 22 July 2003, n. 57 above, at 29; Council Recommendation of 15 June 2001, n. 57 above at 42.

[291] See, for example, Jos de Beus, 'Are Third Way Social Democrats Friends or Enemies of European Integration? A Tocquevillean Tale on the Politics of Administration' in Lars Magnusson and Bo Stråth (eds.), *From the Werner Plan to the EMU: In Search of a Political Economy for Europe* (Brussels: PIE-Peter Lang, 2001): 'the Third Way can be seen as a coherent public philosophy which is distinctively progressive and compatible with the tradition of social liberalism and reformism. To see it as the triumph of neo-liberalism or as the exhaustion of ideology does not make much sense': ibid., at 362.

[292] Arestis and Sawyer, n. 189 above, at 275.

absence of 'hard law' sanctions, due in part to the self-policing nature of the Employment Strategy, the Commission's intensive scrutiny of Member States' policies in the context of the open method of coordination, and the growing consensus amongst Member States as to the range of 'acceptable' responses to the problem of unemployment. Although the law of the internal market and competition law have placed some difficulties in the way of full realization of these policies at the national level, intruding on Member States' autonomy to regulate their national markets, such restrictions on Member State autonomy in fact reinforce the findings of this chapter that an Employment Strategy consisting almost entirely of 'soft law' mechanisms has nevertheless been able to 'Europeanize' national policy.

The process of coordination of employment (and economic) policies has led to a process of convergence around a growth-orientated macro-economic philosophy, supply-side agendas, active labour market policies (committed to the reduction of benefit dependency and the strengthening of labour market attachment) the promotion of labour market participation, wage restraint, *some* wage flexibility, and flexible work organization. Exceptions remain: Member States continue to display an unwillingness to agree to the levels of wage differentiation envisaged by the BEPGs, and are similarly disinclined to engage in wholesale 'modernization' of their systems of labour market regulation—in part due to the resistance of the (national level) social partners.

By concentrating on the Netherlands and the UK, and in particular reviewing their employability and adaptability policies, this chapter has focused on two Member States, both with labour market performance above the EU average, which could be seen as possible exemplars of the Employment Strategy, in particular in the way they combine the basic tenets of the Employment Strategy with what could be called a 'Third Way' agenda. In doing so, the chapter has underscored the growing convergence in thinking between Member States and the central EU institutions over the legitimate range of employment policies.

# Conclusions

## 1. Introduction

As the preceding chapters have shown, employment policy has become an arena within which competing visions of European integration are being debated: regulation competes with deregulation, intergovernmentalism with supranationalism. These competing visions have resulted in a European Employment Strategy which is itself an uneven synthesis of rival, yet overlapping, policy discourses. That the attempted synthesis is uneven is evidenced by the dominance of economic policy discourses, which emphasize labour market efficiency and flexibility, over social policy discourses which have been traditionally concerned with employment protection and social protection. Furthermore, the Employment Strategy has exposed tensions between the adoption of minimal regulatory standards at EU level, permitting regulatory competition between Member States (negative integration), and centralized harmonization through common European policies to shape the conditions under which markets operate (positive integration).

By bringing together these two themes—national/intergovernmental vs. supranational, and regulation vs. deregulation—this concluding chapter will cast light on how the regulatory choices facing the EU are being dealt with in the Employment Strategy. As Table 7.1 illustrates, these two themes overlap: Streeck, for example, talks of an 'elective affinity' between nationalism and a neoliberal programme of deregulatory market expansion based in decision-rules of intergovernmental diplomacy,[1] namely, as represented by box 4 in the Table. In the case of the Employment Strategy, the EU's regulatory choices can be seen first, in the attempt to reconcile competing policy discourses; and second in the attempt to circumvent the tired dichotomy between intergovernmentalism and supranationalism by means of innovative regulatory techniques, in particular the open method of coordination, which have the potential to construct a middle course between full harmonization and mutual recognition or regulatory competition. The regulatory options open to the EU are mapped out in Table 7.1

[1] Wolfgang Streeck, 'Public Power Beyond the Nation-State; The Case of the European Community' in Robert Boyer and Daniel Drache (eds.), *States Against Markets: The Limits of Globalization* (London: Routledge, 1996) at 305.

**Table 7.1** The interaction between levels and types of rule-making

| | Forum/Level of governance/rule-making | |
|---|---|---|
| Content/ Type of rule-making | Supranational | Intergovernmental |
| Regulation | 1. Positive integration/centralized harmonization: the 'old' approach to harmonization | 2. Regulatory competition: 'reflexive harmonization' |
| Deregulation | 3. Negative integration: the coordinated deregulation of national economic policy | 4. Regulatory competition: 'competitive federalism' |

which will be analysed in more detail below, as will the relative success of the EU in reconciling these competing choices.

## 2. Regulatory choices and the European Employment Strategy

### 2.1 Regulation and deregulation

As Chapters 3 and 4 have demonstrated, the evolution of European employment policy and the subsequent development of the Employment Strategy and Lisbon Strategy have been heavily influenced by the EU's economic policy agenda—whether in the form of the convergence criteria for monetary union, the Stability and Growth Pact or the annual Broad Economic Policy Guidelines (BEPGs). And, in turn, this economic policy has been influenced by neoclassical theories, analysed in Chapter 2, which are so critical of 'exogenous' interference in the operation of the labour market. European economic policy has been increasingly concerned to eliminate labour market 'inefficiencies' or rigidities, as evidenced in successive BEPGs reinforced by the analysis of the European Central Bank (ECB).[2] Indeed, the ECB is one of the European institutions which most clearly concurs with traditional neoclassical critiques of labour market regulation, in identifying the inefficient operation of a number of labour market institutions, such as (overly generous) benefit systems or insufficient wage flexibility and wage differentiation, as the main causal factors behind high unemployment and labour market mismatches.[3]

This book has identified the European Council meeting in Lisbon as the most important turning point in the development of the European Employment Strategy since that Strategy came of age following the Treaty of Amsterdam. The significance of Lisbon can be summarized in the turn to a policy of 'full

[2] European Central Bank, *Labour Market Mismatches in Euro Area Countries* (Frankfurt am Main: ECB, 2002).

[3] Ibid., at 28.

employment', coupled with the attempt to reconcile apparently contradictory objectives, by urging that EU economic reform and liberalization of markets could co-exist alongside a renewed version of the European social model. As argued in Chapter 4, however, the version of full employment embedded in the Lisbon Strategy, lacking the social solidarity of the post-war ideal, is heavily supply-side orientated, with strong echoes of the workfare-inspired philosophy underpinning the 'Third Way' approach to labour markets and welfare states, with all that this implies for equality and social cohesion. The post-Lisbon discourse on 'modernized' and 'active' welfare states focuses on improving the self-sufficiency of individuals in the market, reform of protective legislation, benefit reform and greater incentives to labour market participation *but*—especially since the Social Policy Agenda and the proclamation of the EU Charter of Fundamental Rights—alongside a revitalized discourse on social policy, social rights and quality in employment. Thus, for the first time since Amsterdam an explicit attempt was made to fully (re)integrate policies (and discourses) on employment, economic reform and social cohesion, on the understanding that social policy was essential to economic progress, and that the EU's social protection systems were necessary to provide the 'stable framework required for managing the structural changes involved in moving towards a knowledge-based society'.[4] In due course the first Spring Summit devoted to economic *and* social questions made the assertion that 'economic reform, employment and social policies are mutually reinforcing'.[5] Thus, whilst contending that the EU, post-Lisbon, has adopted a supply-side agenda which ultimately displaces social protection in favour of 'employability', one can nevertheless point to some counter-examples, where such emphasis on equipping individuals to compete in the market can operate to provide a 'human face' to an otherwise neoliberal labour market policy, through the support for investment in human capital;[6] after all, the EC Treaty also committed the Community and Member States to the promotion of 'a *skilled, trained* and adaptable workforce'.[7]

However, notwithstanding this attempt to reconcile differing discourses, what remains unchanged is the economic context of the Employment Strategy: the instruments of economic governance in place prior to Lisbon remain as before, so that the Union's strategic goal to become 'the most competitive and dynamic knowledge-based economy in the world capable of sustainable economic growth with more and better jobs and greater social cohesion', was to have been implemented by means of existing 'processes', albeit simplified and better coordinated. Thus, the BEPGs (at the core of which lie growth- and stability-orientated

[4] Presidency Conclusions, Lisbon European Council, 23 and 24 March 2000, Bull EU-3/2000, 7–17, at para 3.

[5] Presidency Conclusions, Stockholm European Council, 23 and 24 March 2001, Bull EU-3/2001, 1–40, at para 1.

[6] Philip Arestis and Malcolm Sawyer, 'The Economic Analysis Underlying the "Third Way"' (2001) 6:2 *New Political Economy*, 255–78, at 275.

[7] Article 125 EC; emphasis added.

macro-economic policies and comprehensive economic reforms of labour, product and capital markets) provide the overarching framework, governing macro-economic policy (the Cologne process), economic reform (the Cardiff process), labour market reform (the Luxembourg process), and finally, social inclusion and the modernization of social protection. The relaunch of the Lisbon Strategy served to reinforce this tendency: whilst continuing to underline the philosophy of 'harmonious synergies' between economic, employment and social policies, nevertheless, the introduction of 'integrated guidelines' for growth and employment, has resulted in a renewed focus on these two goals, sidelining social policy concerns and the preservation of the European social model.

As this book has shown, in spite of the weight given to 'better' not just 'more' jobs, the dominance of the processes of economic governance has meant that social policy discourse continues to be marginalized. Such marginalization of social policy is connected to the stance taken on the choice between regulation and deregulation, since there has been a growing acceptance of the argument that traditional forms of social protection did not strike the proper balance between flexibility and security needed to promote employment.[8] Hence the recommendation in the BEPGs for 2001 that labour market regulation and institutions should be reviewed to 'diminish obstacles to labour demand and supply which they may pose'.[9] One can observe, in the BEPGs generally and in the documentation of the Commission's Economic and Financial Affairs Directorate, a focus on structural reform of labour markets, to tackle 'rigidities' in external labour markets, which arguably overstates the causal link between labour market institutions and unemployment, and leads to an unbalanced concentration on 'flexibility' at the expense of 'security'.

In contrast, drawing on the conclusions reached in Chapter 2, this book contends that it is essential to disaggregate the effects of labour market institutions on labour market performance and to consider the efficiency arguments for labour market regulation. As Alogoskoufis *et al.* point out: 'appeals for deregulation are frequently founded on a misconceived notion of how rigid European markets are in practice, fail to recognize the role played by regulations in tackling other market failures and ignore issues of political economy in advocating certain reforms'.[10] Indeed, the response of Member States to this deregulatory agenda, as surveyed in Chapter 6, shows that many Member States continue to be reluctant to engage in the wholesale modernization of their regulatory regimes envisaged by the Employment Strategy. Member States remain ambivalent about the need for extensive labour market reforms, contrary to what they may have agreed to

[8] Presidency Conclusions, Barcelona European Council, 15 and 16 March 2002, Bull EU 3/2002, 1–56 at para 32.

[9] Council Recommendation of 15 June 2001 on the broad guidelines of the economic policies of the Member States and the Community (2001/483/EC) OJ L 179/1, 2.7.2001, at 6.

[10] George Alogoskoufis, Charles Bean, Giuseppe Bertola, Daniel Cohen, Juan Dolado and Gilles Saint-Paul, *Unemployment: Choices for Europe* (London: CEPR, 1995) at 8.

collectively in the context of the Council of Ministers or the European Council. This suggests that the attempted reconciliation between economic, employment and social policy discourses has fallen far short of providing a assurance that the European social model will be protected at EU level sufficiently convincing to persuade these reluctant Member States to further 'flexibilize' their labour markets. Furthermore, those issues of political economy may well militate against deregulation where that would function to undermine the chosen mode of coordination of the market economy which is best suited to that country's institutional infrastructure, culture and history.[11]

## 2.2 Harmonization and regulatory competition

'The new policy framework, overseen by the European Council and supported by the Commission, tilts the balance away from the traditional reliance on intervention and regulation, and towards a lighter approach intended to foster enterprise, innovation and competition. Rather than seeking to standardise or harmonise policies at an EU level, it uses, where possible and appropriate, peer review and national benchmarking to develop and promulgate best practice. The Government, recognising the UK's interdependence with other EU economies, and in close cooperation with its European partners, has been at the forefront of developing this approach'. (HM Treasury, 2002)[12]

This account of the governance regime for employment policy—conceived at Essen, modelled on the convergence arrangements for national economic policies, and assigned a new name at Lisbon—represents the open method of coordination as an alternative to centralized harmonization; however, the UK government's enthusiasm for this new form of governance is premised on a reading of the open method which also depicts it as being a form of mutual recognition, as this later extract shows:

'Even in those areas in which new Community-level legislation is required to complete, maintain and strengthen the Single Market, the Government believes that, consistent with the Lisbon approach, this legislation should be no more prescriptive for Member States than it needs to be. It should also avoid excessive harmonisation in favour of promoting the role of mutual recognition in constructing a true Single Market'.[13]

Thus, the open method is conceived as a form of intergovernmentalism coupled with deregulation, occupying box 4 of Table 7.1. If, as I argue, this is not an entirely accurate portrayal of the innovative regulatory techniques to which the Employment Strategy has given rise, how then are these new forms of governance best characterized?

[11] Peter A. Hall and David Soskice, 'An Introduction to Varieties of Capitalism' in Peter A. Hall and David Soskice (eds.), *Varieties of Capitalism: The Institutional Foundations of Comparative Advantage* (Oxford: OUP, 2001) especially at 12–14.

[12] HM Treasury White Paper, *Realising Europe's Potential: Economic Reform in Europe*, Cm 5318 (London: HMSO, 2002) at para 3.3.

[13] Ibid., at para 3.9.

Chapter 4 highlighted the tensions between competing approaches to European integration which underpinned the Amsterdam Intergovernmental Conference, namely the choice between a continuation of integration on the basis of exclusively free-market and largely intergovernmental criteria, with a wide margin of national autonomy and subsidiarity as the golden rule (intergovernmentalism plus deregulation); or the centralization of authority, thus ensuring the operation of generously financed common policies (supranationalism plus regulation). Such a scenario presents a stark choice, which Member States seem unwilling to make. Globalization places pressure on national economies to deregulate to remain competitive, since national capacity to regulate markets is severely reduced due to mobility of capital and fear of capital flight. Yet the regulatory capacity lost at national level is not regained through social regulation at European level[14] since, as we have seen in Chapters 3 and 4, Member States remain reluctant to confer sovereignty over economic and social policy entirely to the EU. National sovereignty, or 'social nationalism' makes Member States unwilling to consent to the EU to becoming a supranational interventionist state (see box 1 of Table 7.1).[15] The result is a 'joint decision trap' or a 'competence gap' in social policy and other policy areas. Whereas the removal of barriers to cross-border trade and distortions of competition require little supranational decision-making power—as seen in the introduction of the principle of mutual recognition as a regulatory principle, and the judicial recognition of such[16]—positive integration requires the agreement of national governments at EU level.[17]

In this context, and given the four freedoms, the prohibition on distortions of competition and the principle of mutual recognition, countries are forced into competition for 'locational advantage'.[18] Such regulatory competition, or 'competitive federalism', *may* result in a 'race to the top' in which competition between states produces optimal, efficient and innovative legislation.[19] This was

[14] Fritz W. Scharpf, 'Balancing Positive and Negative Integration: The Regulatory Options for Europe' EUI/RSC Policy Papers, RSC No 97/4.

[15] Colin Crouch and Wolfgang Streeck, 'Introduction' in Colin Crouch and Wolfgang Streeck (eds.), *Political Economy of Modern Capitalism: Mapping Convergence and Diversity* (London: Sage, 1997) at 12; and Scharpf, n. 14 above.

[16] The Commission's 1985 White Paper *Completing the Internal Market*, COM (85) 310 final, introduced a legislative programme for market integration, under which the 'old approach', the approximation of national legislation, was limited to essential requirements, beyond which the 'new approach' of mutual recognition of national provisions would apply: see Jeanne-Mey Sun and Jacques Pelkmans, 'Regulatory Competition in the Single Market' (1995) 33:1 *Journal of Common Market Studies*, 67–89.

[17] Fritz W. Scharpf, 'Negative and Positive Integration in the Political Economy of European Welfare States' in Gary Marks, Fritz W. Scharpf, Philippe C. Schmitter and Wolfgang Streeck (eds.), *Governance in the European Union* (London: Sage, 1996).

[18] Scharpf, n. 17 above, at 17.

[19] Catherine Barnard, 'Regulating Competitive Federalism in the European Union? The Case of EU Social Policy' in Jo Shaw (ed.), *Social Law and Policy in an Evolving European Union* (Oxford: Hart Publishing, 2000) especially at 50–1. See also HM Treasury White Paper, n. 12 above, at para 3.12.

the prevailing wisdom at the time of the founding Treaties:[20] the theory of comparative advantage, which so influenced the Treaty of Rome, asserted that competition does not necessarily require a complete harmonization of labour law and social policy, but merely strategic interventions in order to avoid distortions of competition or destructive downwards competition. Furthermore, competition between states *theoretically* permits diversity and experimentation, allowing for a better 'fit' between a country's regulatory regime and its legal culture. However, without some sort of legal framework to govern regulatory competition, there is the risk that such competitive federalism will instead result in a 'race to the bottom', or a race to converge, in which an optimal outcome is not guaranteed.[21] As the analysis in Chapter 2 of game-theoretical and new institutionalist perspectives on regulation has shown,

'in the absence of institutional regulation, private ordering can lead to sub-optimal outcomes in bargaining relationships.... One implication of these models, then, is unfettered competition may not be welfare-maximizing, and that regulatory interventions may increase economic welfare'.[22]

In the context of the sort of decentralized rule-making which characterizes regulatory competition, an important question to be asked is 'what kind of institutions are needed to alter the legal environment in such a way as to induce the cooperation which is needed for regulatory competition to function effectively?'[23] As Filip Abraham shows, such sub-optimal outcomes in the social policy area are not inconceivable:

'In principle, EU minimum requirements render a unilateral reduction in social protection more difficult. In practice, the EU legislative framework is gradually expanding over time but nevertheless very partial at this stage. Few directives apply to social security in spite of their important share in total labour costs. And, understandably, the EU does not interfere with the wage determination process of the member countries. For all those reasons, EU social standards will not stop a country from driving down costs if that is what the country wants to do'.[24]

Thus, Member States are faced with a choice: loss of sovereignty through centralized harmonization, or loss of local autonomy in the case of complete autonomy of movement for the factors of production. Rules are therefore

[20] See the discussion of the Spaak and Ohlin Reports in Chapter 3, Section 3.

[21] Simon Deakin, 'Two Types of Regulatory Competition: Competitive Federalism versus Reflexive Harmonisation. A Law and Economics Perspective on *Centros*' (1999) 2 *Cambridge Yearbook of European Legal Studies*, 231–60, at 246; and Catherine Barnard and Simon Deakin, 'Market Access and Regulatory Competition', in Barnard and Scott (eds.), *The Law of the Single European Market: Unpacking the Premises* (Oxford: Hart Publishing, 2001) at 37.

[22] Simon Deakin and Jonathan Michie, 'The Theory and Practice of Contracting' in Simon Deakin and Jonathan Michie (eds.), *Contracts, Co-operation and Competition: Studies in Economics, Management and Law* (Oxford: OUP, 1997) at 9–10.

[23] Deakin, n. 21 above, at 239.

[24] Filip Abraham, 'A Policy Perspective on European Unemployment' (1999) 46:4 *Scottish Journal of Political Economy*, 350–66, at 360.

needed, which 'protect local systems from being destabilized in this way',[25] since in the absence of social regulation at European level, it would appear that there is an inadequate framework within which diverse national systems of labour and social law can co-exist and 'compete' without this regulatory competition resulting in a 'race to the bottom'.

Is there no middle way which would allow diversity in national employment and social policy without permitting destructive downwards competition? In the context of competition law, Imelda Maher observes that the UK Competition Act 1998 exemplifies how a process of 'voluntary harmonization' is under way, in that like most other Member States, the UK has chosen to enact competition norms based on those contained in the EC Treaty, even though this is not a 'hard law' requirement.[26] The result of such 'soft harmonization' is inevitably national variation in competition law, but is, however, considered an advantage, allowing as it does for a better 'fit' between the competition law regime and national legal and business culture. Similarly, Simon Deakin asserts that 'reflexive harmonization' of the sort arguably taking place within European company law, creates 'spaces within which local experimentation and adaptation can take place', as well as increasing the potential for innovation and evolutionary learning.[27]

In the context of employment policy, this book has explored the procedural innovations of the Employment Strategy as examples of either reflexive harmonization or democratic experimentalism. As we have seen, theories of reflexive law describe (and prescribe) an alternative to both direct regulation and deregulation, in the form of indirect means of regulatory intervention, wherein the role of regulatory law becomes merely to trigger the self-regulatory process within the economy—the regulation of schemes of self-regulation. Thus, rather than imposing particular distributive outcomes, economic and social regulation, ideally, establishes a framework for autonomous solutions to emerge in Member States.[28] In similar fashion, democratic experimentalism embodies participatory, decentralized decision-making which leads to open and experimental outcomes.

In predominantly taking the form of 'soft law', the European Employment Strategy has eschewed the 'classic' Community method of hierarchical law-making, but does the open method of coordination amount to a middle course between centralized harmonization and regulatory competition? The open method of coordination involves the elaboration of employment policy at EU level, revolving around the centralized setting of guidelines, benchmarks and indicators, their translation into national policies and the periodic monitoring of such implementation by means, mostly, of peer review. In setting out a definition of the open method, the European Council took pains to stress that this method was 'designed to help Member States to progressively develop their own policies'

[25] Deakin, n. 21 above, at 244.

[26] Imelda Maher, 'Juridification, Codification and Sanction in UK Competition Law' (2000) 63:4 MLR, 544–69.

[27] Deakin, n. 21 above, at 232.

[28] Deakin, n. 21 above, at 245–246.

and that implementation would take into account 'national and regional differences'.[29] The open method of coordination thus has the capacity to ease the tension between intergovernmentalism and supranationalism since it avoids the need to resort to the 'classic' Community method in politically sensitive areas, and involves a wider range of actors in policy-making, through mechanisms such as subsidiarity, benchmarking and 'partnership'.

It was argued in Chapters 1 and 2 that the institutional regulation of the labour market may have positive economic effects, that there are efficiency arguments for labour market regulation. Such insights apply not only to the regulation of the employment relationship, but also to the regulation of the wider labour market and the regulation of competition between (labour) markets. The discussion in Chapter 2 of the efficiency reasons for labour market institutions, and the varied impact of institutions on economic performance highlights the complexity of regulatory regimes. Thus, not only can regulation have an input into economic efficiency, but further, deregulation may in fact *impede* a nation's competitiveness, by unsettling the collective forms of economic coordination most appropriate to a country's social systems of production.[30] Esping-Andersen and Regini underscore how the regulatory regime of any advanced country is a highly complex system since 'it involves different institutions, levels and mechanisms, and has multiple, often contradictory, economic effects'.[31] It is important not to look at labour market institutions in isolation: employment protection legislation, for example, may well be contained within a wider institutional framework which provides incentives to stabilize employment, and a supporting infrastructure that enables firms to benefit from the efficiency advantages of internal labour markets and relational contacts.[32] Accordingly, it is also vital to consider the ability of 'reflexive harmonization' to preserve national institutional diversity against the threat of competitive deregulation. In this context, therefore, a key advantage of the open method of coordination is the national institutional diversity which is permitted by its use of 'soft law'. However, such local autonomy will be threatened where the competition between regimes is insufficiently unregulated.

It is therefore argued that the open method of coordination at the centre of the Employment Strategy—whether one defines it as an example of 'reflexive harmonization', 'democratic experimentalism', or as an instance of 'soft

[29] Presidency Conclusions, Lisbon European Council, n. 4 above, at para 37.

[30] J. Rogers Hollingsworth and Robert Boyer, 'Coordination of Economic Actors and Social Systems of Production' in J. Rogers Hollingsworth and Robert Boyer (eds.), *Contemporary Capitalism: The Embeddedness of Institutions* (Cambridge: CUP, 1997) especially at 2. See also Hall and Soskice, n. 11 above.

[31] Gøsta Esping-Andersen and Marino Regini, 'Conclusions' in Gøsta Esping-Andersen and Marino Regini (eds.), *Why Deregulate Labour Markets* (Oxford: OUP, 1999) at 338.

[32] Christoph F. Büchtemann, 'Introduction: Employment Security and Labor Markets' in Christoph F. Büchtemann (ed.), *Employment Security and Labor Market Behavior: Interdisciplinary Approaches and International Evidence* (Ithaca, New York: ILR Press, 1993) at 65.

harmonization'—is a form of governance which has the potential to achieve policy coordination without threatening jealously guarded national sovereignty, *and* to allow Member States to implement policy in accordance with their socio-economic development, *provided that* it is able to establish a normative framework within which such national autonomy can operate.

## 3. Concluding thoughts: 'soft harmonization' by means of 'hard law'

In summary, this concluding chapter has highlighted how the choices made in the context of the Employment Strategy, between regulation and deregulation, have tended to favour the latter, and that the attempt to reconcile economic, employment and social policy discourses on an equal footing has not, ultimately, been successful, even following the relaunch of the Lisbon Strategy in 2005. Economic policy discourse continues to dominate the Employment Strategy, to the detriment of discourses around social justice and solidarity. By contrast, however, the procedural innovations of the Employment Strategy, as the paradigm example of the evolving open method of coordination, have come to serve as a valuable model for other policy areas, in the course of further European integration. However, as suggested in Chapter 5, in the absence of 'social benchmarking' at EU level, there is a danger that the open method of coordination of employment policy will coalesce around the dominant criterion by which progress in employment policy and labour market reform has traditionally been evaluated, namely, an economic criterion. Chapter 4 reviewed the more recent emphasis on 'quality' in employment and on promotion of social rights and social inclusion, in order to assess the extent to which the attempt to integrate social policy with economic and employment policy discourse can provide sufficiently strong institutional means by which social rights can be built into the Employment Strategy.

In considering the utility of both reflexive theories and theories of deliberative governance to explain new forms of governance of employment policy, I contend that the crucial factor is the *framing* of such self-regulation or of such democratic experimentation: what are the background rules governing the process of self-regulation or of deliberative decision-making? In light of the above characterization of the regulatory techniques at the heart of the Employment Strategy as a form of 'soft harmonization', and given the normative desire to preserve a version of the European social model and the institutions contained within this, I conclude that the most appropriate path is not merely the setting of minimum standards at EU level, but what can be called 'soft harmonization through hard law'. In other words, social rights and labour standards need to be built into economic policies such as the Employment Strategy, in order to counterbalance economic discourse, but in such a way as to preserve a space for national diversity and experimentation. 'Soft law', without more, is unable to provide a sufficiently strong normative framework to balance the economic policy discourse which pervades the Employment Strategy.

As seen in Chapters 5 and 6, certain parts of the Employment Strategy are producing quite 'hard' results: the open method permits not only policy learning, but also (possibly coercive) policy transfer, around a specific model of labour market regulation, in which the emphasis on high participation rates is leading to changes in welfare state and labour market regimes. The examination of Member States' 'compliance' with the Employment Strategy has shown that the policy experimentation which is the hallmark of the open method of coordination in fact permits experimentation only within a framework firmly wedded to sound public finances, comprehensive economic reform and restructuring of welfare states and the labour market, thus limiting the extent to which Member States can depart from the Employment Strategy without also breaching the Broad Economic Policy Guidelines and the Stability and Growth Pact. However, the framework around which the open method is constructed need not be determined solely by an economic policy discourse. The Social Policy Agenda, renewed in 2005, and the Charter of Fundamental Rights of the European Union are both relatively recent stages in the development of the EU into a more complex polity, yet both already exhibit the potential to provide a meaningful and robust framework of social rights at European level, to ensure that European economic and employment policy sufficiently recognize and protect social rights.

# Bibliography

Abraham, Filip (1999), 'A Policy Perspective on European Unemployment' 46:4 *Scottish Journal of Political Economy*, 350–66

Addison, John T. (1998), 'The US Employment Miracle in Comparative Perspective' 19 *Comparative Labor and Policy Journal*, 283–300

Addison, John T. and W. Stanley Seibert (1992), 'The Social Charter: Whatever Next?' 30 *British Journal of Industrial Relations*, 495–513

Adnett, Nick (1996), *European Labour Markets: Analysis and Policy* (London: Longman)

—— (2001), 'Modernizing the European Social Model: Developing the Guidelines' 39:2 *Journal of Common Market Studies*, 353–64

Adserà, Alicia and Carles Boix (2000), 'Must We Choose? European Unemployment, American Inequality and the Impact of Education and Labor Market Institutions' 16 *European Journal of Political Economy*, 611–38

*Agence Europe*, No 6993 (n.s.), Thursday 12 June 1997

Ahlberg, Kerstin (2002), 'The Making of the Employment Title', unpublished manuscript on file with the author (Stockholm: National Institute for Working Life)

Alogoskoufis, George, Charles Bean, Giuseppe Bertola, Daniel Cohen, Juan Dolado and Gilles Saint-Paul (1995), *Unemployment: Choices for Europe* (London: CEPR)

Anon (1996), 'Les Orientations de la France Pour la Conférence Intergouvernmentale de 1996', *Le figaro*, 20 February 1996

—— (1997), 'One lump or two?', *The Economist*, 25 October 1997, Vol 345 Issue 8040, 17

—— (1998), 'Short measure', *The Economist*, 31 January 1998, Vol 346 Issue 8053, 79

—— (2001), 'Lisbon's lost legacy', *The Economist Global Agenda*, 14 December 2001

—— (2002a), 'EU issues warning as German economy flounders', *The Guardian*, 30 January 2002

—— (2002b), 'Barcelona Blues', *The Economist Global Agenda*, 15 March 2002

—— (2003), 'Italians flock to pension protest', *BBC News Online*, 6 December 2003

—— (2004), 'Economics focus: A gentler touch', *The Economist*, 8 July 2004

—— (2005), 'Dodging the difficult stuff', *The Economist Global Agenda*, 29 March 2005

Annett, Anthony, Jörg Decressin and Michael Deppler (2005), 'Reforming the Stability and Growth Pact' IMF Policy Discussion Paper, February 2005 (Washington: IMF)

Ardy, Brian and Iain Begg (2001), 'The European Employment Strategy: Policy Integration by the Back Door?' South Bank European Papers, No. 4/2001, South Bank University European Institute

Arestis, Philip and Malcolm Sawyer (2001), 'The Economic Analysis Underlying the "Third Way"' 6:2 *New Political Economy*, 255–78

Armstrong, Kenneth A. (1999), 'Governance and the Single European Market' in Craig and de Búrca (eds.), *The Evolution of EU Law* (Oxford: OUP)

—— (2003), 'Tackling Social Exclusion Through OMC: Reshaping the Boundaries of EU Governance' in Börzel and Cichowski (eds.), *State of the Union: Law, Politics and Society* (Oxford: OUP)

Arnaud, Jean-Louis (2003), 'Budgetary Discipline and Macroeconomic Policy in the European Union: Are the Stability pact and the Lisbon Strategy compatible?' Report on seminar organized by Notre Europe, Paris, 8 March 2003, available at *http://www.notre-europe.asso.fr/IMG/pdf/Semi18-en.pdf*

Arrowsmith, James, Keith Sisson and Paul Marginson (2004), 'What can "benchmarking" offer the open method of co-ordination?' 11:2 *Journal of European Public Policy*, 311–28

Ashiagbor, Diamond (2004), 'Economic and Social Rights in the European Charter of Fundamental Rights', *European Human Rights Law Review*, 62–72

—— (2005), 'Promoting Precariousness? The Response of EU Employment Policies to Precarious Work' in Fudge and Owens (eds.), *Precarious Work, Women and the New Economy: The Challenge to Legal Norms* (Oxford: Hart Publishing)

Atkinson, Tony (2002), 'Social Europe and Social Science', The 13th ESRC Annual Lecture, 17 October 2002 (Swindon: ESRC)

Ayres, Ian and Robert Gertner (1992), 'Strategic Contractual Inefficiency and the Optimal Choice of Legal Rules' 101 *Yale Law Journal*, 729–73

Baird, Douglas G. (1997), 'The Future of Law and Economics: Looking Forward, Introduction' 64 *University of Chicago Law Review*, 1129–65

Ball, Sally (2001), 'The European Employment Strategy: The Will but not the Way?' 30:4 *Industrial Law Journal*, 353–74

Barbier, Cécile, Caroline de la Porte and Philippe Pochet (2002), 'European Briefing' 12:3 *Journal of European Social Policy*, 241–8

Barnard, Catherine (1995), *EC Employment Law* (Chichester: Wiley)

—— (2000a), 'Regulating Competitive Federalism in the European Union? The Case of EU Social Policy' in Shaw (ed.), *Social Law and Policy in an Evolving European Union* (Oxford: Hart Publishing)

——(2000b), 'The Working Time Regulations 1999' 29:2 *Industrial Law Journal*, 167–71

—— (2002), 'The Social Partners and the Governance Agenda' 8:1 *European Law Journal*, 80–101

Barnard, Catherine and Simon Deakin (1998), 'European Community Social Law and Policy: Evolution or Regression?' *Industrial Relations Journal: European Annual Review 1997*, 131–53

—— (1999), 'A year of living dangerously? EC social rights, employment policy, and EMU', 30:4 *Industrial Relations Journal: European Annual Review 1998*, 355–72

—— (2000), 'In Search of Coherence: Social Policy, the Single Market and Fundamental Rights', 31:4 *Industrial Relations Journal*, 331–345

——(2002), 'Market Access and Regulatory Competition', in Barnard and Scott (eds.), *The Law of the Single European Market: Unpacking the Premises* (Oxford: Hart Publishing)

Barnard, Catherine, Simon Deakin, and Richard Hobbs (2001), 'Capabilities and Rights: An Emerging Agenda for Social Policy?' 32:5 *Industrial Relations Journal*, 464–79

—— (2003), 'Opting Out of the 48-Hour Week: Employer Necessity or Individual Choice? An Empirical Study of the Operation of Article 18(1)(b) of the Working Time Directive in the UK' 32:4 *Industrial Law Journal*, 223–52

Barrell, Ray and Veronique Genre (1999), 'Employment Strategies for Europe: Lessons from Denmark and the Netherlands' *National Institute Economic Review* No 168, April 1999, 82–98

Barrell, Ray, Guglielmo Maria Caporale and James Sefton (1994), 'Prospects for European Unemployment' in Michie and Grieve Smith (eds.), *Unemployment in Europe* (London: Academic Press)

Barrell, Ray, Julian Morgan and Nigel Pain (1996), 'The Impact of the Maastricht Fiscal Criteria on Employment in Europe' EUI Working Paper RSC No 96/61

Bastian, Jens (1998), 'Putting the Cart Before the Horse? Labour Market Challenges Ahead of Monetary Union in Europe' in Hine and Kassim (eds.), *Beyond the Market: The EU and National Social Policy* (London: Routledge)

Bayoumi, Tamim and Barry Eichengreen (1996), 'Ever Closer to Heaven? An Optimum-Currency-Area Index for European Countries', Center for International and Development Economics Research, University of California Berkeley, Working Paper Series No C96-078, December 1996

Bean, Charles R. (1994), 'European Unemployment: A Survey' 32 *Journal of Economic Literature*, 573–619

Beaumont, Paul, Carole Lyons and Neil Walker (2001), (eds.), *European Public Law* (Oxford: Hart Publishing)

Becker, Uwe (1999), 'The "Dutch Miracle": Employment Growth in a Retrenched But Still Generous Welfare System', Social Policy Research Centre, University of New South Wales, SPRC Discussion Paper No 99, May 1999

—— (2000), 'Welfare State Development and Employment in the Netherlands in Comparative Perspective' 10:3 *Journal of European Social Policy*, 219–39

——(2001), 'A "Dutch Model": Employment Growth by Corporatist Consensus and Wage Restraint? A Critical Account of an Idyllic View' 6:1 *New Political Economy*, 19–43

Belot, Michèle and Jan C. van Ours (2004), 'Does the recent success of some OECD countries in lowering their unemployment rates lie in the clever design of their labor market reforms?' 56:4 *Oxford Economic Papers*, 621–42

Bercusson, Brian (1992), 'Maastricht: A Fundamental Change in European Labour Law' 23 *Industrial Relations Journal* 177–90

—— (1994), 'The Dynamic of European Labour Law After Maastricht' 23:1 *Industrial Law Journal*, 1–31

—— (1995), 'The Conceptualization of European Labour Law' 24 *Industrial Law Journal*, 3–18

Bernard, Nick (2000), 'Legitimising EU Law: Is the Social Dialogue the Way Forward? Some Reflections Around the *UEAPME* Case', in Shaw (ed.), *Social Law and Policy in an Evolving European Union* (Oxford: Hart Publishing)

Bertola, Giuseppe, Francine D. Blau, and Lawrence M. Kahn (2002), 'Comparative Analysis of Labor Market Outcomes: Lessons for the US from International Long-Run Evidence', in Krueger and Solow (eds.), *The Roaring Nineties: Can Full Employment Be Sustained?* (New York: Russell Sage Foundation)

Bertola, Giuseppe, Tito Boeri and Sandrine Cazes (1999), 'Employment Protection and Labour Market Adjustment in OECD Countries: Evolving Institutions and Variable Enforcement', International Labour Organization, Employment and Training Papers No 48

—— (2000), 'Employment protection in industrialized countries: The case for new indicators', 139:1 *International Labour Review*, 57–72

Bertola, Giuseppe, Tito Boeri and Giuseppe Nicoletti (2001), (eds.), *Welfare and Employment in a United Europe: A Study for the Fondazione Rodolfo Debenedetti* (Cambridge, MA: The MIT Press)

Bertola, Giuseppe and Andrea Ichino (1995a), 'Crossing the River: A Comparative Perspective on Italian Employment Dynamics', 21 *Economic Policy*, 359–420

——(1995b) 'Wage Inequality and Unemployment: US vs Europe' Centre for Economic Policy Research Discussion Paper No 1186 (London: CEPR)

Bettio, Francesca and Samuel Rosenberg (1999), 'Labour Markets and Flexibility in the 1990s: The Europe–USA Opposition Revisited', 13:3 *International Review of Applied Economics*, 269–79

Beveridge, William (1944), *Full Employment in a Free Society* (London: Allen & Unwin)

Biagi, Marco (1998), 'The Implementation of the Amsterdam Treaty with Regard to Employment: Co-ordination or Convergence?' 14:4 *International Journal of Comparative Labour Law and Industrial Relations*, 325–36

——(2000), 'The Impact of the European Employment Strategy on the Role of Labour Law and Industrial Relations', 16:2 *International Journal of Comparative Labour Law and Industrial Relations*, 157–161

——(2000), (ed.), *Job Creation and Labour Law: From Protection Towards Pro-action* (Dordrecht/London: Kluwer Law International)

Biagi, Marco and Michele Tiraboschi (2000), 'The Role of Labour Law in Job Creation Policies: An Italian Perspective' in Biagi (ed.), *Job Creation and Labour Law: From Protection Towards Pro-action* (Dordrecht/London: Kluwer Law International)

Black, Ian (2002), 'Blair allied with European right in summit labour talks', *The Guardian*, 16 March 2002

——'Employers attack charter for temps as unworkable', *The Guardian*, 21 March 2002

Blair, Tony and Gerhard Schröder (1999), *Europe: The Third Way/Die Neue Mitte* (London: The Labour Party)

Blair, Tony and Silvio Berlusconi (2002), 'Joint Statement at the Anglo-Italian Summit', Friday 15 February 2002, available at *http://www.number-10.gov.uk/*

Blanchard, Oliver J. and Jan Wolfers (2000), 'The Role of Shocks and Institutions in the Rise of European Unemployment: The Aggregate Evidence', 110 *Economic Journal*, C1–C33.

Blanchard, Oliver and Lawrence H. Summers (1986), 'Hysteresis and the European Unemployment Problem', NBER Macroeconomics Annual, Stanley Fischer (ed.) Vol 1 (Cambridge: MIT Press)

Blank, Rebecca M. (undated), 'Is There a Trade-Off Between Unemployment and Inequality? No Easy Answers: Labor Market Problems in the United States versus Europe', Levy Economics Institute Public Policy Brief No 33

Block, Fred (1990), *Postindustrial Possibilities: A Critique of Economic Discourse* (Berkeley: University of California Press)

Boeri, Tito, Axel Börsch-Supan and Guido Tabellini (2001), 'Would you Like to Shrink the Welfare State? A Survey of European Citizens' *Economic Policy*, 8–50

Boeri, Tito, Richard Layard and Stephen Nickell (2000), *Welfare-to-Work and the Fight Against Long-Term Unemployment: Report to Prime Ministers Blair and D'Alema*, (London: Centre for Economic Performance, LSE); summary available as Department for Education and Employment Research Brief No 206, June 2000

Bomberg, Elizabeth and John Peterson (2000), 'Policy Transfer and Europeanisation: Passing the Heineken Test?' Queen's Papers on Europeanisation, No 2/2000, Queen's University Belfast

Bonczar, Thomas P. (2003), 'Prevalence of Imprisonment in the U.S. Population, 1974–2001' Bureau of Justice Statistics (BJS) Special Report (Washington: BJS)

Borrás, Susana and Bent Greve (2004), 'Concluding remarks: New method or just cheap talk?' 11:2 *Journal of European Public Policy*, 329–36

Börzel, Tania and Thomas Risse (2000), 'When Europe Hits Home: Europeanisation and Domestic Change', 4:15 *European Integration Online Papers*, at *http://eiop.or.at/eiop/texte/2000-015a.htm*

Boyer, Robert (1993), 'Labour Institutions and Economic Growth: A Survey and a "Regulationist" Approach' 7:1 *Labour: Review of Labour Economics and Industrial Relations*, 25–72

—— (1996), 'State and Market: A New Engagement for the Twenty-First Century?' in Boyer and Drache (eds.), *States Against Markets: The Limits of Globalization* (London: Routledge)

—— (1997), 'The Variety and Unequal Performance of Really Existing Markets: Farewell to Doctor Pangloss?' in Hollingsworth and Boyer (eds.), *Contemporary Capitalism: The Embeddedness of Institutions* (Cambridge: CUP)

Boyer, Robert and Daniel Drache (1996a), (eds.), *States Against Markets: The Limits of Globalization* (London: Routledge)

—— (1996b), 'Introduction' in Boyer and Drache (eds.), *States Against Markets: The Limits of Globalization* (London: Routledge)

Britton, Andrew (1997), 'Full Employment in the Industrialized Countries' 136:3 *International Labour Review*, 293–314

Brodsky, Melvin M. (1994), 'Labor Market Flexibility: A Changing International Perspective' 117:11 *Monthly Labor Review*, 53–60

Brothwell, John F. (1994), 'Unemployment' in Hodgson, Samuels and Tool (eds.), *The Elgar Companion to Institutional and Evolutionary Economics: L–Z* (Aldershot: Edward Elgar)

Brown, Gordon (2001), 'The Conditions for High and Stable Growth and Employment' 111 *The Economic Journal* C30–C44

Brown, William, Simon Deakin and Paul Ryan (1997), 'The Effects of British Industrial Relations Legislation 1979–1997' 161:3 *National Institute Economic Review*, 69–83

Brunetta, Renato and Leonello Tronti (1995), 'Italy: The Social Consequences of Economic and Monetary Union', *Labour: Review of Labour Economics and Industrial Relations*, 149–201

Buchele, Robert and Jens Christiansen (1998), 'Do employment and income security cause unemployment? A comparative study of the US and the E-4', 22 *Cambridge Journal of Economics*, 117–36

—— (1999), 'Employment and Productivity Growth in Europe and North America: The Impact of Labour Market Institutions', 13:3 *International Review of Applied Economics*, 313–32

Büchtemann, Christoph F. (1993a), (ed.), *Employment Security and Labor Market Behavior: Interdisciplinary Approaches and International Evidence* (Ithaca, New York: ILR Press)

——(1993b), 'Introduction: Employment Security and Labor Markets' in Büchtemann (ed.), *Employment Security and Labor Market Behavior: Interdisciplinary Approaches and International Evidence* (Ithaca, New York: ILR Press)

Bulmer, Simon and Stephen Padgett (2005), 'Policy Transfer in the European Union: An Institutionalist Perspective' 35:1 *British Journal of Political Science*, 103–26

Burda, Michael C. (1997), 'Corporatism, Labor Unions and the Safety Net', 41 *European Economic Review*, 635–46

Burda, Michael and Barbara Dluhosch (1998), 'Globalization and European Labor Markets' CEPR Discussion Paper No 1992 (London: CEPR)

Burlamaqui, Leonardo, Ana Célia Castro and Ha-Joon Chang (2000), (eds.), *Institutions and the Role of the State* (Cheltenham, Edward Elgar)

Burri, Susanne (2005), 'Flexibility and Security, Working Time and Work-Family Policies in the Netherlands' in Fudge and Owens (eds.), *Precarious Work, Women and the New Economy: The Challenge to Legal Norms* (Oxford: Hart Publishing)

Burrows, Paul and Cento G. Veljanovski (1981), 'Introduction: The Economic Approach to Law' in Burrows and Veljanovski (eds.), *The Economic Approach to Law* (London: Butterworths)

——(1981), *The Economic Approach to Law* (London: Butterworths)

Buti, Marco, and Lucio R. Pench (2004), 'Why Do Large Countries Flout the Stability Pact? And What Can Be Done About It?' 42:5 *Journal of Common Market Studies*, 1025–32

Butler, Henry N. and Keith W. Chauvin (1999), 'Economic Analysis of State Employment Law Issues Symposium. Economic Analysis of Labor Markets: A Framework for Analyzing Employment Law Issues', 8 *Kansas Journal of Law and Public Policy*, 1–89

Calabresi, Guido (1968), 'Transaction Costs, Resource Allocation, and Liability Rules—A Comment' 11 *Journal of Law and Economics*, 67–73

——(1991), 'The Pointlessness of Pareto: Carrying Coase Further' 100 *Yale Law Journal*, 1211–37

Calmfors, Lars and John Driffill (1988), 'Bargaining Structure, Corporatism and Macroeconomic Performance', 6 *Economic Policy*, 14–61

Camp, Robert C. (1989), *Benchmarking: The Search for Industry Best Practices That Lead to Superior Performance* (Milwaukee, WI: ASQC Quality Press)

Campbell, David (1994), 'Ayres v Coase: An Attempt to Recover the Issue of Equality in Law and Economics' 21 *Journal of Law and Society*, 434–63

——(1997) 'The Relational Constitution of Contract and the Limits of "Economics": Kenneth Arrow on the Social Background of Markets' in Deakin and Michie (eds.), *Contracts, Co-operation and Competition: Studies in Economics, Management and Law* (Oxford, OUP)

Campbell, David and Sol Picciotto (1998), 'Exploring the Interaction Between Law and Economics: The Limits of Formalism',18 *Legal Studies* 249–78

Campbell, David and Peter Vincent Jones (1996), (eds.), *Contract and Economic Organisation: Socio-Legal Initiatives* (Aldershot: Dartmouth)

Campbell, Thomas J. (1986), 'Labor Law and Economics' 38 *Stanford Law Review*, 991–1064

Card, David and Richard B. Freeman (1993), (eds.), *Small Differences that Matter: Labor Markets and Income Maintenance in Canada and the United States* (Chicago: University of Chicago Press)

Card, David and Richard B. Freeman (2002), 'What Have Two Decades of British Economic Reform Delivered?', National Bureau of Economic Research, NBER Working Paper No 8801

Card, David and Alan Krueger (1994), 'Minimum Wages and Employment: A Case Study of the Fast Food Industry in New Jersey and Pennsylvania', 84 *American Economic Review*, 772–93

——(1995), *Myth and Measurement: The New Economics of the Minimum Wage* (Princeton, NJ: Princeton University Press)

Card, David and W. Craig Riddell (1993), 'A Comparative Analysis of Unemployment in Canada and the United States' in Card and Freeman (eds.), *Small Differences that Matter: Labor Markets and Income Maintenance in Canada and the United States* (Chicago: University of Chicago Press)

Casey, Bernard (2004), 'The OECD Jobs Strategy and the European Employment Strategy: Two Views of the Labour Market and of the Welfare State' 10 *European Journal of Industrial Relations*, 329–52

Casey, Bernard and Michael Gold (1999), 'Institutions and Performance: "Misery Indexes" and "Magic Squares" for Europe and the USA' Paper presented at the workshop *Relations Between Social Protection and Economic Performance ('Social Protection as a Productive Factor'*) European University Institute, 6–7 May 1999

Casey, Bernard Ewart Keep, and Ken Mayhew (1999), 'Flexibility, Quality and Competitiveness' *National Institute Economic Review* No 168

Castro, Alberto, Philippe Méhaut and Jill Rubery (1992), (eds.), *International Integration and Labour Market Organisation* (London: Academic Press)

Cecchini, Paolo (1998), *The European Challenge 1992: The Benefits of a Single Market* (Aldershot: Gower)

Chang, Ha-Joon (2000), 'An Institutionalist Perspective on the Role of the State: Towards an Institutionalist Political Economy' in Burlamaqui, Castro and Chang (eds.), *Institutions and the Role of the State* (Cheltenham: Edward Elgar)

Charnovitz, Steve (1997), 'Trade, Employment and Labour Standards: The OECD Study and Recent Developments in the Trade and Labor Standards Debate' 11:1 *Temple International and Comparative Law Journal*, 131–63

Chirac, Jacques (1996), 'Pour un modèle social européen' *Libération*, 25 March 1996

Clark, Jon (1985), 'The Juridification of Industrial Relations: A Review Article' 14 *Industrial Law Journal*, 69–90

Coase, Ronald (1937), 'The Nature of the Firm' 4 *Economica* (NS), 386–405

——(1988), *The Firm, the Market and the Law* (Chicago: University of Chicago Press)

——(1993), 'Coase on Posner on Coase' 149:1 *Journal of Institutional and Theoretical Economics*, 96–8

——(1996), 'Law, Economics and A. W. Brian Simpson' 25 *Journal of Legal Studies*, 103–9

Cohen, Felix S. (1935), 'Transcendental Nonsense and the Functional Approach' 35 *Columbia Law Review*, 809–49

Cohen, Joshua, and Charles Sabel (1997), 'Directly-Deliberative Polyarchy' 3:4 *European Law Journal*, 313–42

——(2003), 'Sovereignty and Solidarity: EU and US' in Jonathan Zeitlin and David Trubek (eds.), *Governing Work and Welfare in a New Economy: European and American Experiments* (Oxford: OUP)

Collins, Hugh (1989), 'Labour Law as a Vocation' 105 *Law Quarterly Review*, 468–84

——(1992), *Justice in Dismissal: The Law of Termination of Employment* (Oxford, Clarendon)

——(1997), 'The Productive Disintegration of Labour Law' 26:4 *Industrial Law Journal*, 295–309

——(2000), 'Justifications and Techniques of Legal Regulation of the Employment Relation' in Collins, Davies and Rideout (eds.) *Legal Regulation of the Employment Relation*, WG Hart Legal Workshop Series (London/The Hague: Kluwer)

——(2001), 'Regulating the employment relation for competitiveness' 30:1 *Industrial Law Journal*, 17–48

Collins, Hugh, Paul Davies and Roger Rideout (2000), (eds.), *Legal Regulation of the Employment Relation*, WG Hart Legal Workshop Series (London/The Hague: Kluwer)

Comité des Sages (1996), *Report on Civic and Social Rights* (Brussels: Commission of the European Communities)

——(1998), *Leading by Example: A Human Rights Agenda for the EU for the year 2000* (Florence: European University Institute)

Comité Intergouvernemental Créé par la Conférence de Messine (1956), *Rapport des Chefs de Délégation aux Minstres des Affaires Etrangères* (Brussels, 1956), summarized in English in 'Political and Economic Planning', *Planning* No 405

Committee for the Study of Economic and Monetary Union (The Delors Committee) (1989), *Report on Economic and Monetary Union in the Community* (Luxembourg: OOPEC)

*Comparative Labor Law and Policy Journal* (1998), Special Issue, Vol 19

Compston, Hugh (1997), (ed.), *The New Politics of Unemployment: Radical Policy Initiatives in Western Europe* (London: Routledge)

Conaghan, Joanne, Karl Klare and Richard Michael Fischl (2002), (eds.), *Labour Law in an Era of Globalization: Transformative Practices and Possibilities* (Oxford: OUP)

Conceição, Pedro, Pedro Ferreira and James K. Galbraith (1999), 'Inequality and Unemployment in Europe: The American Cure' The University of Texas at Austin Working Paper Number 11, May 18

Cooter, Robert (1982), 'The Cost of Coase' 11 *Journal of Legal Studies*, 1–33

Cooter, Robert and Thomas Ulen (2000), *Law and Economics* (Reading, MA: Addison-Wesley)

Coppel, Jason and Aidan O'Neill (1992), 'The European Court of Justice: Taking Rights Seriously?' 29 *Common Market Law Review*, 669–92

Craig, Paul and Gráinne de Búrca (1999), (eds.), *The Evolution of EU Law* (Oxford: OUP)

Cram, Laura (1993), 'Calling the Tune Without Paying the Piper? Social Policy Regulation: The Role of the Commission in European Community Social Policy' 21 *Policy and Politics*, 135–46

——(1997), *Policy Making in the European Union: Conceptual Lenses and the Integration Process* (London: Routledge)

Crooks, Ed (1999), 'How Full is Full Employment?' *BBC News Online: Business*, 27 September 1999

Crouch, Colin (2000a), (ed.), *After the Euro: Shaping Institutions for Governance in the Wake of European Monetary Union* (Oxford: OUP)

——(2000b) 'Introduction: The Political and Institutional Deficits of European Monetary Union' in Crouch (ed.), *After the Euro: Shaping Institutions for Governance in the Wake of European Monetary Union* (Oxford: OUP)

Crouch, Colin (2000c), 'National Wage Determination and European Monetary Union' in Crouch (ed.), *After the Euro: Shaping Institutions for Governance in the Wake of European Monetary Union* (Oxford: OUP)

Crouch, Colin and Wolfgang Streeck (1997a), 'Introduction' in Crouch and Streeck (eds.), *Political Economy of Modern Capitalism: Mapping Convergence and Diversity* (London: Sage)

—— (1997b), (eds), *Political Economy of Modern Capitalism: Mapping Convergence and Diversity* (London: Sage)

Crouch, Colin and Franz Traxler (1995), (eds), *Organized Industrial Relations in Europe: What Future?* (Aldershot: Avebury)

Cukierman, Alex and Francesco Lippi (1999), 'Central Bank Independence, Centralization of Wage Bargaining, Inflation and Unemployment: Theory and Some Evidence', 43:7 *European Economic Review*, 1395–434

Daguerre, Anne and Peter Taylor-Gooby (2004), 'Neglecting Europe: Explaining the Predominance of American Ideas in New Labour's Welfare Policies Since 1997' 14:1 *Journal of European Social Policy*, 25–39

Davies, Paul (1992), 'The Emergence of European Labour Law' in McCarthy (ed.), *Legal Intervention Industrial Relation: Gains and Losses* (Oxford: Blackwell)

—— (1995), 'Market Integration and Social Policy in the Court of Justice', 24:1 *Industrial Law Journal*, 49–77

Davies, Paul and Mark Freedland (1993), *Labour Legislation and Public Policy: A Contemporary History* (Oxford: OUP)

Davies Paul, Antoine Lyon-Caen, Silvana Sciarra and Simitis Spiros (1996), (eds.), *European Community Labour Law: Principles and Perspectives, Liber Amicorum Lord Wedderburn* (Oxford: Clarendon Press)

Deakin, Simon (1996a), 'Labour Law as Market Regulation: The Economic Foundations of European Social Policy', in Davies, Lyon-Caen, Sciarra and Simitis (eds.) *European Community Labour Law: Principles and Perspectives, Liber Amicorum Lord Wedderburn* (Oxford: Clarendon Press)

—— (1996b), 'Law and Economics' in Thomas (ed.), *Legal Frontiers* (Aldershot: Dartmouth)

—— (1999), 'Two Types of Regulatory Competition: Competitive Federalism versus Reflexive Harmonisation. A Law and Economics Perspective on *Centros*' 2 *Cambridge Yearbook of European Legal Studies*, 231–60

—— (2002), 'The Many Futures of the Contract of Employment' in Conaghan, Klare and Fischl (eds.), *Labour Law in an Era of Globalization: Transformative Practices and Possibilities* (Oxford: OUP)

Deakin, Simon and Jacqueline Cook (2000), 'Boundaries of Law and Regulation' in ESRC Centre for Business Research, *Literature Survey on Factual, Empirical and Legal Issues*, Papers prepared for the DTI Company Law Review (London: HMSO)

Deakin, Simon and Keith Ewing (1996), 'Inflation, Economic Performance and Employment Rights' ESRC Centre for Business Research, University of Cambridge, Working Paper No 45

Deakin, Simon and Jonathan Michie (1997a), 'The Theory and Practice of Contracting' in Deakin and Michie (eds.), *Contracts, Co-operation and Competition: Studies in Economics, Management and Law* (Oxford: OUP)

—— (1997b), (eds.), *Contracts, Co-operation and Competition: Studies in Economics, Management and Law* (Oxford: OUP)

Deakin, Simon and Gillian Morris (2001), *Labour Law* 3rd edn. (London: Butterworths)
Deakin, Simon and Ulrich Mückenberger (1992), 'Deregulation and European Labour Markets' in Castro, Méhaut and Rubery (eds.), *International Integration and Labour Market Organisation* (London: Academic Press)
Deakin, Simon and Hannah Reed (1999), 'Transcending the Flexibility Debate? Deregulation and Employment in Britain 1979–1997' ESRC Centre for Business Research, University of Cambridge, Working Paper No 132
—— (2000), 'The Contested Meaning of Labour Market Flexibility: Economic Theory and the Discourse of European Integration' in Shaw (ed.), *Social Law and Policy in an Evolving European Union* (Oxford: Hart Publishing)
Deakin, Simon and Frank Wilkinson (1992), 'The Law and Economics of the Minimum Wage' 19:3 *Journal of Law and Society*, 379–92
—— (1994), 'Rights vs Efficiency? The Economic Case for Transnational Labour Standards' 23:4 *Industrial Law Journal*, 289–310
—— (1996), 'Contracts, Co-operation and Trust: The Role of the Institutional Framework' in Campbell and Vincent Jones (eds.) *Contract and Economic Organisation: Socio Legal Initiatives* (Aldershot: Dartmouth)
—— (2000), 'Labour Law and Economic Theory: A Reappraisal' in Collins, Davies and Rideout (eds.) *Legal Regulation of the Employment Relation*, WG Hart Legal Workshop Series, (London/The Hague: Kluwer)
—— (2000), 'Capabilities, Spontaneous Order and Social Rights' ESRC Centre for Business Research, University of Cambridge, Working Paper No 174
de Beus, Jos (2001), 'Are Third Way Social Democrats Friends or Enemies of European Integration? A Tocquevillean Tale on the Politics of Administration' in Magnusson and Stråth (eds.), *From the Werner Plan to the EMU: In Search of a Political Economy for Europe* (Brussels: PIE–Peter Lang)
de Búrca, Gráinne (2000), 'Differentiation within the Core: The Case of the Common Market', in de Búrca and Scott (eds.), *Constitutional Change in the EU: From Uniformity to Flexibility?* (Oxford: Hart Publishing)
—— (2002), 'The Case for a European Human Rights Policy' in Beaumont, Lyons and Walker (eds.), *European Public Law* (Oxford: Hart Publishing)
de Búrca, Gráinne and Scott, Joanne (2000), (eds.), *Constitutional Change in the EU: From Uniformity to Flexibility?* (Oxford: Hart Publishing)
de Búrca, Gráinne and Jonathan Zeitlin (2003), 'Constitutionalising the Open Method of Coordination: What Should the Convention Propose?' Centre for European Policy Studies, CEPS Policy Brief No 31, March 2003
de la Porte Caroline (2002), 'Is the Open Method of Co-ordination Appropriate for Organising Activities at European Level in Sensitive Policy Areas?' 8:1 *European Law Journal*, 38–58
de la Porte, Caroline, Philippe Pochet and Graham Room (2001), 'Social Benchmarking, Policy Making and New Governance in the EU' 11:4 *Journal of European Social Policy*, 291–307
Department for Education and Employment (2001), Green Paper, *Towards Full Employment in a Modern Society* Cm 5084 (London: HMSO)
Department of Employment (1985), White Paper, *Employment: The Challenge for the Nation* (London: HMSO)

Department of Trade and Industry/President of the Board of Trade (1998), *Fairness at Work: A White Paper* Cm 3968 (London: HMSO)

Department of Work and Pensions (2004), *Building on New Deal: Local Solutions Meeting Individual Needs* (London: HMSO)

de Schutter, Olivier and Simon Deakin (2005a), 'Reflexive Governance and the Dilemmas of Social Regulation' in de Schutter and Deakin (eds.), *Social Rights and Market Forces: Is the Open Coordination of Employment and Social Policies the Future of Social Europe?* (Brussels: Bruylant)

——(2005b), (eds.), *Social Rights and Market Forces: Is the Open Coordination of Employment and Social Policies the Future of Social Europe?* (Brussels: Bruylant)

de Witte, Bruno (2001), 'The Legal Status of the Charter: Vital Question or Non-Issue?' 8:1 *Maastricht Journal of European and Comparative Law*, 81–9

Dickens, Richard, Paul Gregg and Jonathan Wadsworth (2000), 'New Labour and the Labour Market' 16:1 *Oxford Review of Economic Policy*, 95–113

Dolowitz, David P. and David Marsh (2000), 'Learning from Abroad: The Role of Policy Transfer in Contemporary Policy-Making' 13:1 *Governance: An International Journal of Policy and Administration*, 5–24

Dølvik, Jon Erik (2000), 'Building Regional Structures: ETUC and the European Industry Federations' 6:1 *Transfer: European Review of Labour and Research*, 58–77

Dore, Ronald (1997), 'Good Jobs, Bad Jobs and No Jobs', 28:4 *Industrial Relations Journal*, 262–8

Dorf, Michael and Charles Sabel (1998), 'A Constitution of Democratic Experimentalism' 98:2 *Columbia Law Review*, 267–473

Dostal, Jörg Michael (2004), 'Campaigning on expertise: how the OECD framed EU welfare and labour market policies—and why success could trigger failure' 11:3 *Journal of European Public Policy*, 440–60

Drèze, Jacques H. and Edmond Malinvaud (1994), 'Growth and Employment: The Scope of a European Initiative', 34 *European Economic Review*, 489–504

Dugger, William M. (1993), 'Transaction Cost Economics and the State' in Pitelis (ed.), *Transaction Costs, Markets and Hierarchies* (Oxford: Blackwell)

——(1994), 'Williamson, Oliver E.' in Hodgson, Samuels and Tool (eds.) *The Elgar Companion to Institutional and Evolutionary Economics: L–Z* (Aldershot: Edward Elgar)

Duxbury, Neil (1991), 'Is There a Dissenting Tradition in Law and Economics?' 54:2 *Modern Law Review*, 300–11

——(1995), *Patterns of American Jurisprudence* (Oxford: OUP)

Dworkin, Ronald (1980), 'Is Wealth a Value?' 9:2 *Journal of Legal Studies*, 191–226

Dyson, Kenneth and Kevin Featherstone (1999), *The Road to Maastricht: Negotiating Economic and Monetary Union* (Oxford, OUP)

Ebbinghaus, Bernhard (2000), 'When Labour and Capital Collude: The Varieties of Welfare Capitalism and Early Retirement in Europe, Japan and the USA', Working Paper No 4, Center for European Studies, Harvard University

Eberlein, Burkard and Dieter Kerwer (2004), 'New Governance in the European Union: A Theoretical Perspective' 42:1 *Journal of Common Market Studies*, 121–42

Economic Policy Institute (2005), *The State of Working America: Fact Sheet on Wages* (Washington, DC: Economic Policy Institute)

Editorial (1998), 'The US "Employment Miracle": Employment Protection and Job Generation' 19 *Comparative Labor Law and Policy Journal*, 279

Eichengreen, Barry (1996), 'Unemployment and the Structure of Labor Markets: The Long View' in Giersch (ed.), *Fighting Europe's Unemployment in the 1990s* (Berlin/ New York: Springer)

Ekström, Anna (2001), 'Employment Policy During the Swedish Presidency: Results and Conclusions for the Future', unpublished speech given at the European University Institute, Florence, 29 October 2001

Ellickson, Robert (1989), 'The Case for Coase and Against "Coaseanism"' 99 *Yale Law Journal*, 611–29

Elliot, Larry (2000), 'Markets must deliver what people want' *Guardian Weekly*, 13–19 April 2000

Elmeskov, Jørgen (1998), 'The Unemployment Problem in Europe: Lessons From Implementing the OECD Jobs Strategy' EUI Working Paper RSC No 98/24

Elmeskov, Jørgen John P. Martin and Stefano Scarpetta (1998), 'Key Lessons for Labour Market Reforms: Evidence from the OECD Countries' Experiences' Centro Interdipartimentale di Studi Internazionali sull'Economia e lo Sviluppo, Working Paper No 62, Università degli Studi di Roma 'Tor Vergata'

Elwert, Felix (2002), 'Incarceration, Unemployment, and "Eurosclerosis"', unpublished paper (Cambridge, MA) available at: *http://www.wjh.harvard.edu/~winship/cfa_papers/ ElwertIncarceration.pdf*

Engels, Chris and Manfred Weiss (1998), (eds.), *Labour Law and Industrial Relations at the Turn of the Century: Liber Amicorum in Honour of Roger Blainpain* (The Hague: Kluwer Law International)

Epstein, Richard A. (1983), 'A Common Law for Labor Relations: A Critique of the New Deal Labor Legislation', 92 *Yale Law Journal* 1357–1408

——(1984), 'In Defense of the Contract at Will' 51 *Chicago Law Review*, 947–82

——(1995), *Simple Rules for a Complex World* (Cambridge, MA: Harvard University Press)

——(2004) 'The Optimal Complexity of Legal Rules' University of Chicago, John M. Olin Law & Economics Working Paper No 210 (2nd Series), April

Esping-Andersen, Gøsta (1990), *The Three Worlds of Welfare Capitalism* (Cambridge: Polity Press)

——(1996), (ed.), *Welfare States in Transition: National Adaptations in Global Economies* (London: Sage)

——(1999a), *Social Foundations of Postindustrial Economies* (Oxford: OUP)

——(1999b), 'Who is Harmed By Labour Market Regulations? Quantitative Evidence' in Esping-Andersen and Regini (eds.), *Why Deregulate Labour Markets* (Oxford: OUP)

Esping-Andersen, Gøsta and Marino Regini (1999a) (eds.), *Why Deregulate Labour Markets* (Oxford: OUP)

——(1999b), 'Conclusions' in Esping-Andersen and Regini (eds.), *Why Deregulate Labour Markets* (Oxford: OUP)

Esty, Daniel C. and Damien Geradin (2001), (eds), *Regulatory Competition* and *Economic Integration* (Oxford: OUP)

ETUC Executive Committee (2002), European Council in Barcelona: Resolution adopted by the Committee, Brussels, 11–12 March 2000, available at: *http://www. etuc.org*

ETUC Resolution for the Lisbon Summit (2000), 'A new opportunity for a strategy for full employment' (Lisbon: ETUC)

ETUC, UNICE, CEEP and UEAPME (2005), 'Tripartite Social Summit: Social Partners Take Actions to Promote Growth and Employment', Press Release, Brussels, 21 March 2005

EurActiv (2005), 'Stability and Growth Pact reform' *EurActiv: EU Policy Portal* available at: *http://www.euractiv.com/*

European Central Bank (2002), *Labour Market Mismatches in Euro Area Countries* (Frankfurt am Main: ECB)

European Economists for an Alternative Economic Policy in Europe (1997), *Full Employment, Social Cohesion and Equity for Europe: Alternatives to Competitive Austerity* (Bremen: University of Bremen)

European Economists for an Alternative Economic Policy in Europe (2000), *Alternative Economic Policy Guidelines for Full Employment and Social Cohesion in Europe* (Bremen: University of Bremen)

—— (2001), *Economic Policy against Recession and Polarisation in Europe: Proposals to Overcome Ideological Sterility and Policy Blockades* (Bremen: University of Bremen)

European Round Table of Industrialists (1999), *European Pensions: An Appeal for Reform. Pension Schemes that Europe can Really Afford* (Brussels: ERT)

—— (2001), High Level Meeting on Pension Reforms in Europe, Brussels, 31 October 2001 (Brussels: ERT)

—— (2002), *Pensions Reform: Europe must seize the limited opportunity* (Brussels: ERT)

Ewing, Keith (1995), 'Democratic Socialism and Labour Law' 24:2 *Industrial Law Journal*, 103–32

Expert Group on Fundamental Rights (1999), *Affirming Fundamental Rights in the European Union: Time to Act* (the Simitis Report) (Luxembourg: European Commission Unit V/D.2)

Falkner, Gerda (1998), *EU Social Policy in the 1990s: Towards a Corporatist Policy Community* (London: Routledge)

—— (1999), 'European Social Policy: Towards Multi-level and Multi-actor Governance' in Kohler-Koch and Eising (eds.), *The Transformation of Governance in the European Union* (London: Routledge)

Federal Trust, The (2003), *EU Constitution Project Newsletter*, Vol 1 Issue 4

Ferrera, Maurizio, Anton Hemerijck, and Martin Rhodes (2000), *The Future of Social Europe: Recasting Work and Welfare in the New Economy* (Oeiras: Celta Editora)

Fischel Daniel R. (1984), 'Labor Markets and Labor Law Compared with Capital Markets and Corporate Law' 51 *University of Chicago Law Review*, 1061–77

Fitzpatrick, Barry (1992), 'Community Social Law After Maastricht' 21:3 *Industrial Law Journal*, 199–213

Foreign and Commonwealth Office (1996), *A Partnership of Nations: The British Approach to the European Union IGC*, Cm 3181 (London: HMSO)

Forster, Anthony (1998), 'Britain and the Negotiation of the Maastricht Treaty: A Critique of Liberal Intergovernmentalism' 36:3 *Journal of Common Market Studies*, 347–68

Förster, Michael F. and Michele Pellizzari (2000), 'Trends and Driving Factors in Income Distribution and Poverty in the OECD Area', OECD Labour Market and Social Policy: Occasional Papers No 42, August 2000

Fredman, Sandra (1992), 'The New Rights: Labour Law and Ideology in the Thatcher Years' 12:1 *Oxford Journal of Legal Studies*, 24–44

——(2000), 'Discrimination Law in the EU: Labour Market Regulation or Fundamental Rights?' in Collins, Davies and Rideout (eds.), *Legal Regulation of the Employment Relation*, WG Hart Legal Workshop Series (London/The Hague: Kluwer)

——(2001), 'Equality: A New Generation?' (2001) 30:2 *Industrial Law Journal*, 145–68

Freedland, Mark (1996a) 'Employment Policy' in Davies, Lyon-Caen, Sciarra and Simitis (eds.), *European Community Labour Law: Principles and Perspectives* (Oxford: Clarendon Press)

——(1996b), 'Vocational Training in EC Law and Policy—Education, Employment or Welfare?', 25 *Industrial Law Journal*, 110–120

Freedland, Mark and Claire Kilpatrick (2004), 'Part-Time Work in the UK: Can EU Governance be Transformative?' in Sciarra, Davies and Freedland (eds.), *Employment Policy and the Regulation of Part-Time work: in the European Union: A Comparative Analysis* (Cambridge: CUP)

Freeman, Richard (1996), 'Doing It Right? The US Labor Market Response to the 1980s–1990s' in Giersch (ed.), *Fighting Europe's Unemployment in the 1990s* (Berlin/New York: Springer)

Friedman, Milton (1974), 'Schools at Chicago', *University of Chicago Magazine*, Autumn 1974, 11–16

——(1962), *Capitalism and Freedom* (Chicago: University of Chicago Press)

Friedman, Sheldon and Christian Weller (1998), 'One More Time: Labor Market Flexibility, Aggregate Demand and Comparative Employment Growth in the US and Europe', 19 *Comparative Labor Law and Policy Journal*, 307–19

Fudge, Judy and Rosemary Owens (2005), (eds.), *Precarious Work, Women and the New Economy: The Challenge to Legal Norms* (Oxford: Hart Publishing)

Gabaglio, Emilio (2000), 'Lisbon marks the way to full employment: The commitments must be felt in the economic orientations to be taken and in the social agenda' (Brussels: ETUC)

——(2002), 'Barcelona: The neo-liberal offensive has not been imposed' (Brussels: ETUC)

Gahan, Peter G. (1998), 'European Unemployment: The Role of Labor Market Regulation? A Review Essay', 19 *Comparative Labor Law and Policy Journal*, 455–72

Galbraith, James K. (1997), 'Time to Ditch the NAIRU' 11:1 *Journal of Economic Perspectives*, 93–108

Ganssmann, Heiner (2000), 'Labor Market Flexibility, Social Protection and Unemployment', 2:3 *European Societies*, 243–69

Garibaldi, Pietro and Paolo Mauro (2002), 'Anatomy of Employment Growth' *Economic Policy*, 67–173

Gersbach, Hans (2000), 'Promoting Product Market Competition to Reduce Unemployment in Europe: An Alternative Approach?' 53:2 *Kyklos*, 117–34

Giddens, Anthony (1998), *The Third Way: The Renewal of Social Democracy* (Cambridge: Polity Press)

——(2000), *The Third Way and its Critics* (Cambridge: Polity Press)

——(2001a), (ed.) *The Global Third Way Debate* (Cambridge: Polity Press)

——(2001b), 'Introduction' in Giddens (ed.), *The Global Third Way Debate*

Giersch, Herbert (1985), 'Eurosclerosis', Kiel Discussion Paper No 112 (Kiel: Institute for World Economics)

Giersch, Herbert (1996), (ed.), *Fighting Europe's Unemployment in the 1990s* (Berlin/New York: Springer)

Gill, Colin, Michael Gold and Peter Cressey (1999), 'Social Europe: National Initiatives and Responses' 30:4 *Industrial Relations Journal: European Annual Review 1998*, 313–29

Godbout, Todd (1993), 'Employment Change and Sectoral Distribution in 10 Countries, 1970–1990' 116:10 *Monthly Labor Review*, 3–20

Goetschy, Janine (1999), 'The European Employment Strategy: Genesis and Development', 5:2 *European Journal of Industrial Relations*, 117–37

—— (2001), 'The European Employment Strategy from Amsterdam to Stockholm: Has it Reached its Cruising Speed?' 32:5 *Industrial Relations Journal: Annual Review 2000/2001*, 401–18

Goetschy, Janine and Philippe Pochet (1997), 'The Treaty of Amsterdam: A New Approach to Social Affairs?' 3 *Transfer: European Review of Labour and Research*, 607–20

Goodhart, Charles A. E. (1997), 'Economics and the Law: Too Much One-Way Traffic?', 60:1 *Modern Law Review*, 1–22

Gosling, Amanda and Thomas Lemieux (2004), 'Labour Market Reforms and Changes in Wage Inequality in the United Kingdom and the United States' in Card, Blundell, and Freeman (eds.), *Seeking a Premier Economy: The Economic Effects of British Economic Reforms, 1980–2000* (Chicago: University of Chicago Press, National Bureau of Economic Research Comparative Labor Market Series)

Granovetter, Mark (1985), 'Economic Action and Social Structure: A Theory of Embeddedness' 91 *American Journal of Sociology*, 481–510

Grahl, John and Paul Teague (1997), 'Is the European Social Model Fragmenting?' 2:3 *New Political Economy*, 405–26

Green-Pedersen, Christoffer (2003), 'Small States, Big Success. Party Politics and Governing the Economy in Denmark and the Netherlands from 1973 to 2000' 1:3 *Socio-Economic Review*, 411–37

Green-Pedersen, Christoffer, Kees van Kersbergen, and Anton Hemerijck (2001), 'Neo-liberalism, the "Third Way" or What? Recent Social Democratic Welfare Policies in Denmark and the Netherlands' 8:2 *Journal of European Public Policy*, 307–25

Gregg, Paul and Alan Manning (1997), 'Labour Market Regulation and Unemployment' in Snower and de la Dehesa (eds.) *Unemployment Policy: Government Options for the Labour Market* (Cambridge: CUP)

Gyselen, Luc (2000), 'Case note' 37 *Common Market Law Review*, 425–48

Habermas, Jürgen (1996), *Between Facts and Norms: Contribution to a Discourse Theory of Law and Democracy* (Cambridge, MA: MIT Press)

Hall, Peter A. and David Soskice (2001), 'An Introduction to Varieties of Capitalism' in Hall and Soskice (eds.), *Varieties of Capitalism: The Institutional Foundations of Comparative Advantage* (Oxford: OUP)

Hancher, Leigh (1999), 'Community, State and Market', in Craig and de Búrca (eds.), *The Evolution of EU Law* (Oxford: OUP)

Handler, Joel F. (2000a), 'American Regulatory Policy: Have We Found the "Third Way"?' Symposium Paper: The "Third Way" or the Old Way? 48 *Kansas Law Review*, 765–800

—— (2000b), 'Questions About Social Europe by an American Observer' 18 *Wisconsin International Law Journal*, 437–76

Harris, Donald (1983), 'The Development of Socio-Legal Studies in the United Kingdom' 2 *Legal Studies*, 315–33

Harrison, Paige M. and Jennifer C. Karberg (2004), 'Prison and Jail Inmates at Midyear 2003' *Bureau of Justice Statistics Bulletin* (Washington: BJS)

Hassel, Anke and Reiner Hoffmann (2000), 'National Alliances for Jobs and Prospects for a European Employment Pact' European Trade Union Institute Discussion and Working Papers, DWP 2000.01.01 (Brussels: ETUI)

Hatch, Julie and Angela Clinton (2000), 'Job Growth in the 1990s: A Retrospect' 123:12 *Monthly Labor Review*, 3–18

Hayek, Friedrich A. (1978), 'Competition as a Discovery Procedure' in Hayek, *New Studies in Philosophy, Politics, Economics and the History of Ideas* (Chicago: The University of Chicago Press)

Heerma van Voss, Gustav (2000), 'The Flexibility and Security Act', Peer Review Programme on Active Labour Market Policy, Discussion Paper, 26–27 October 2000

Heipertz, Martin and Amy Verdun (2004), 'The dog that would never bite? What we can learn from the origins of the Stability and Growth Pact' 11:5 *Journal of European Public Policy*, 765–80

Heise, Arne (1997), 'A Different Transatlantic View: The American Job Machine' *Challenge: The Magazine of Economic Affairs*, May/June 1997, 50–56

Hemerijck, Anton C. and Mark I. Vail (2003), 'The Forgotten Center: The State as Dynamic Actor in Corporatist Political Economies' unpublished paper prepared for workshop, *The State after Statism: New State Activities in the Age of Globalization and Liberalization*, University of California Berkeley, 14–15 November 2003

Henderson, Douglas (1998), 'The UK Presidency: An Insider's View' 36 *Journal of Common Market Studies*, 563–72

Henry, David K. and Richard P. Oliver (1987), 'The Defense Buildup, 1977–85: Effects on Production and Employment' 110:8 *Monthly Labor Review*, 3–11

Hepple, Bob (1995), 'The Future of Labour Law' 24:4 *Industrial Law Journal*, 303–22

Herin, Jan (1998), 'Comments on Alan B. Krueger and Jörn-Steffen Pischke: Observations and Conjectures on the US Employment Miracle' 19 *Comparative Labor Law and Policy Journal*, 295–305

Héritier, Adrienne (2001), 'The White Paper on European Governance: A Response to Shifting Weights in Inter-institutional Decision-Making', Jean Monnet Working Paper No 6/01, New York University Law School, Symposium: *The Commission White Paper on Governance*

Hervey, Tamara (2000), 'Social Solidarity: A Buttress against Internal Market Law' in Shaw (ed.), *Social Law and Policy in an Evolving European Union* (Oxford: Hart Publishing)

High-Level Advisory Group (the 'Mandelkern Group') on Better Regulation (2001), Final Report, 13 November 2001 (Luxembourg: OOPEC)

Hine, David and Hussein Kassim (1998), (eds.), *Beyond the Market: The EU and National Social Policy* (London: Routledge)

Hirsch, Barry T., David A. Macpherson and Wayne G. Vroman (2001),'Estimates of union density by state' 124:7 *Monthly Labor Review*, 51–5

Hirst, Paul (1999), 'Has Globalisation Killed Social Democracy?' in 70:S1 (Special Issue) *The Political Quarterly*, 84–96

HM Treasury (2002), *White Paper: Realising Europe's Potential: Economic Reform in Europe* Cm 5318 (London: HMSO)
—— (2003a), *EMU and Labour Market Flexibility* (London: HMSO)
—— (2003b), *A Full Employment Strategy for Europe* (London: HMSO)
—— (2004), *The Stability and Growth Pact: A Discussion Paper* (London: HMSO)
HM Treasury and Department of Work and Pensions (2003), *Full Employment in Every Region* (London: HMSO)
Hodgson, Geoffrey M. (1993), 'Transaction Cost Economics and the Evolution of the Firm' in Pitelis (ed.) *Transaction Costs, Markets and Hierarchies* (Oxford: Blackwell)
—— (1994), 'Institutionalism, "Old" and "New"' in Hodgson *et al.*, *The Elgar Companion to Institutional and Evolutionary Economics: A–K* (Aldershot: Edward Elgar)
—— (2001), 'Frontiers of Institutional Economics' 6:2 *New Political Economy*, 245–53
Hodgson, Geoffrey M., Warren J. Samuels and Marc R. Tool (1994a), (eds.), *The Elgar Companion to Institutional and Evolutionary Economics: A–K* (Aldershot: Edward Elgar)
—— (1994b), (eds.), *The Elgar Companion to Institutional and Evolutionary Economics: L–Z* (Aldershot: Edward Elgar)
Hodson, Dermot and Imelda Maher (2000), 'EMU: Balancing Credibility and Legitimacy in the Policy Mix' ESRC/'One Europe or Several?' Programme, Working Paper 12/00, Brighton: Sussex European Institute
——(2001), 'The Open Method as a New Mode of Governance: The Case of Soft Economic Policy Co-ordination' (2001) 39:4 *Journal of Common Market Studies*, 719–46
—— (2004), 'Soft Law and Sanctions: Economic Policy Co-Ordination and Reform of the Stability and Growth Pact' 11:5 *Journal of European Public Policy*, 798–813
Hollingsworth, J. Rogers and Robert Boyer (1997a), 'Coordination of Economic Actors and Social Systems of Production' in Hollingsworth and Boyer (eds.) *Contemporary Capitalism: The Embeddedness of Institutions* (Cambridge: CUP)
——(1997b), (eds), *Contemporary Capitalism: The Embeddedness of Institutions* (Cambridge: CUP)
Hoop, Renaat (2003), 'Social Policy in Belgium and the Netherlands: Third Way or Not?' in Bonoli and Powell (eds.), *Social Democratic Party Policies in Contemporary Europe* (London: Routledge/ECPR Studies in European Political Science)
Houseman, Susan N. (1995), 'Job Growth and the Quality of Jobs in the US Economy' *Labour: Review of Labour Economics and Industrial Relations* (IIRA) S93–S124
House of Commons, Select Committee on Education and Employment (2001), Fifth Report, *New Deal: An Evaluation*, HC 58 (London: HMSO)
Hylton, Keith N (1993), 'Efficiency and Labor Law' 87:2 *Northwestern University Law Review*, 471–522
Ichino, Pietro (1998), 'The Labour Market: A Lawyer's View of Economic Arguments' 137:3 *International Labour Review*, 299–311
International Labour Office (1956), 'Social Aspects of European Economic Co-operation' 74 *International Labour Review*, 99
International Labour Organization (1956), *Social Aspects of Economic Co-operation: Report of a Group of Experts*, Studies and Reports, New Series, No 46 (Geneva: International Labour Office)

——(1996a), *World Employment 1996/97: National Policies in a Global Context* (Geneva: International Labour Office)

——(1996b), 'Full Employment: Still Feasible and Highly Desirable', Press Release, Geneva, 26 November 1996 (Geneva: International Labour Office)

International Monetary Fund (1999), *World Economic Outlook* (Washington: IMF)

Jacobsson, Kerstin (2001), 'Employment and Social Policy Coordination. A New System of EU Governance' unpublished paper for the Scancor workshop on Transnational Regulation and the Transformation of States, Stanford, 22–23 June 2001

Jackman, Richard (1998), 'The Impact of the European Union on Unemployment and Unemployment Policy' in Hine and Kassim (eds.), *Beyond the Market. The EU and National Social Policy* (London: Routledge)

Jackman, Richard, Richard Layard and Stephen Nickell (1996) 'Combating Unemployment: Is Flexibility Enough?' in OECD, *Macroeconomic Policies and Structural Reform* (Paris: OECD)

Jackson, Craig L. (1995), 'Social Policy Harmonization and Workers' Rights in the European Union: A Model for North America?' 21 *North Carolina Journal of International Law and Commercial Regulation*, 1–63

Jeffery, Mark (1995), 'The Commission Proposals on "Atypical Work": Back to the Drawing-Board... Again' 24:3 *Industrial Law Journal*, 296–9

——(1998), 'Not Really Going to Work? Of the Directive on Part-Time Work, "Atypical Work" and Attempts to Regulate It' 27:3 *Industrial Law Journal*, 193–213

Jimeno, Juan F. (1998), 'EMU and the Labour Market: The Initial Conditions' Centro Interdipartimentale di Studi Internazionali sull'Economia e lo Sviluppo (CEIS) Working Paper No 6362 (Università degli Studi di Roma 'Tor Vergata'

Joerges, Christian and Jürgen Neyer (1997), 'From Intergovernmental Bargaining to Deliberative Political Processes: The Constitutionalisation of Comitology' 3:3 *European Law Journal*, 273–299

Johansson, Karl Magnus (1999), 'Tracing the Employment Title in the Amsterdam Treaty: Uncovering Transnational Coalitions' 6:2 *Journal of European Public Policy*, 85–101

Kahn-Freund, Otto (1977), *Labour and the Law* (London: Stevens)

Kennedy, Duncan (1973), 'Legal Formality' 2 *Journal of Legal Studies*, 351–98

Kenner, Jeff (1994), 'European Social Policy—New Directions' 10:1 *The International Journal of Comparative Labour Law and Industrial Relations*, 56–63

——(1995), 'EC Labour Law: The Softly, Softly Approach' 11:4 *The International Journal of Comparative Labour Law and Industrial Relations*, 307–26

——(1999), 'The EC Employment Title and the "Third Way": Making Soft Law Work?' 15:1 *The International Journal of Comparative Labour Law and Industrial Relations*, 33–60

——(2000), 'Employment and Macroeconomics in the EC Treaty: A Legal and Political Symbiosis?' 7:4 *Maastricht Journal of European and Comparative Law*, 375–97

Kilpatrick, Claire (2003), 'Has New Labour Reconfigured Employment Legislation?' 32:3 *Industrial Law Journal*, 135–63

——(2004), 'New EU Employment Governance and Constitutionalism' unpublished paper presented to the workshop on New Governance and Constitutionalism, Faculty of Law, University of Cambridge, 19–20 July 2004

Klare, Karl E. (1978), 'Judicial Deradicalization of the Wagner Act and the Origins of Modern Legal Consciousness' 62 *Minnesota Law Review*, 265–339

Klare, Karl E. (1988), Workplace Democracy and Market Reconstruction: An Agenda For Legal Reform, 38:1 *Catholic University Law Review*, 1–49

—— (2000), 'Countervailing Workers' Power as a Regulatory Strategy' in Collins, Davies and Rideout (eds.), *Legal Regulation of the Employment Relation*, W G Hart Legal Workshop Series (London/The Hague, Kluwer)

—— (2002), 'The Horizons of Transformative Labour and Employment Law' in Conaghan, Klare and Fischl (eds.), *Labour Law in an Era of Globalisation: Transformative Practices and Possibilities* (Oxford: OUP)

Kohler, Thomas C. (1999), 'The Employment Relation and its Ordering at Century's End: Reflections on Emerging Trends in the United States' 41 *Boston College Law Review*, 103–23

Kohler-Koch, Beate and Rainer Eising (1999), (eds.), *The Transformation of Governance in the European Union* (London: Routledge)

Kok, Wim (2003), *Jobs, Jobs, Jobs: Creating more employment in Europe*. Report of the Employment Taskforce chaired by Wim Kok (Luxembourg: OOPEC)

Kok Report (2004), *Facing the Challenge: The Lisbon Strategy for Growth* and *Employment*. Report from the High Level Group chaired by Wim Kok (Luxembourg: OOPEC)

Krueger, Alan B. (2000), 'from Bismarck to Maastricht: The March to European Union and the Labor Compact' National Bureau of Economic Research Working Paper W7456

Krueger, Alan B. and Jörn-Steffen Pischke, (1997), *Observations and Conjectures on the US Employment Miracle*, National Bureau of Economic Research Working Paper 6146 (Cambridge, MA: NBER)

—— (1998), 'Authors' Responses to Comments on "Observations and Conjecture on the US Employment Miracle"' 19 *Comparative Labor Law and Policy Journal*, 321–9

Krugman, Paul (1995), 'Europe Jobless, America Penniless?' *Foreign Policy*, 19–24

Kuper, Bernd-Otto (1994), 'The Green and White Papers of the European Union: The Apparent Goal of Reduced Social Benefits' 4:2 *Journal of European Social Policy*, 129–37

Kuttner, Robert (1997a), 'The Limits of Labor Markets' *Challenge: The Magazine of Economic Affairs*, May–June 1997, 75–102

—— (1997b), *Everything for Sale: The Virtues and Limits of Markets* (New York: Alfred A. Knopf)

Lachs Ginsburg, Helen, June Zaccone, Gertrude Schaffner Goldberg, Shelia D. Collins and Sumner M. Rosen (1997), 'Editorial Introduction: The Challenge of Full Employment in the Global Economy' 18:1 *Economic and Industrial Democracy*, 5–34

Laulom, Sylvaine (2004), 'France: Part-Time Work—No Longer An Employment Policy Tool' in Sciarra, Davies and Freedland (eds.), *Employment Policy and the Regulation of Part-Time Work in the European Union: A Comparative Analysis* (Cambridge: CUP)

Laursen, Finn and Sophie Vanhoonacker (1994), (eds.), *The Ratification of the Maastricht Treaty: Issues, Debates and Future Implications* (Maastricht: Martinus Nijhoff)

Layard, Richard, Stephen Nickell and Richard Jackman (1991), *Unemployment: Macroeconomic Performance and the Labour Market* (Oxford: OUP)

Lazear, Edward P. (1990), 'Job Security Provisions and Unemployment' 105:3 *The Quarterly Journal of Economics*, 699–726

Lee, Eddy (1997), 'Is Full Employment Still Desirable and Feasible?' 18:1 *Economic and Industrial Democracy*, 35–53

Leibfried, Stephan and Paul Pierson (1995), (eds.), *European Social Policy: Between Fragmentation and Integration* (Washington, DC: The Brookings Institute)

Léonard, Evelyne (2001), 'Industrial Relations and the Regulation of Employment in Europe', 7:1 *European Journal of Industrial Relations*, 27–47

Lewis, Jane (2001), 'Social Insurance and Future Work' in Marsden and Stephenson (eds.), *Labour Law and Social Insurance in the New Economy: A Debate on The Supiot Report* (London: Centre for Economic Performance, LSE)

Lindbeck, Assar (1996), 'The West European Employment Problem' University of Stockholm, Institute for International Economic Studies, Seminar Papers No 616

Lindbeck, Assar and Dennis J. Snower (1989), *The Insider–Outsider Theory of Employment and Unemployment* (Cambridge, MA: The MIT Press)

Lo Faro, Antonio (2000), *Regulating Social Europe: Reality and Myth of Collective Bargaining in the EC Legal Order* (Oxford: Hart Publishing)

——(2002), 'Adaptable Employment and Private Autonomy in the Italian Part-time Reform', in Sciarra, Davies and Freedland (eds.), *Employment Policy and the Regulation of Part-Time Work in the European Union: A Comparative Analysis* (Cambridge: CUP, 2004)

Luhmann, Niklas (1984), *Soziale Systeme: Grundrißeiner allgemeinen Theorie* (Frankfurt am Main: Suhrkamp); English translation (1995) *Social System* (Stanford: Stanford University Press)

Lund, Gunner, 'Strengthening the fight against unemployment: An issue for the Intergovernmental conference' available at *http://europa.eu.int/en/agenda/igc-home/msspeech/state-sv/lund.html* [accessed on 10 April 2005]

Lyon-Caen, Gerard (1992), 'L'infiltration du droit du travail par le droit de la concurrence', *Droit Ouvrier*, 313–21

MacEwan, Arthur (1999), *Neo-liberalism or Democracy? Economic Strategy, Markets, and Alternatives for the 21st Century* (London/New York: Zed Books)

Machin, Stephen (1997), 'The Decline of Labour Market Institutions and the Rise of Wage Inequality in Britain' 41 *European Economic Review*, 647

Machin, Stephen and Alan Manning (1997), 'Minimum Wages and Economic Outcomes in Europe' 41:3–5 *European Economic Review*, 733–42

Macneil, Ian (1974), 'The Many Futures of Contracts', 47 *Southern California Law Review*, 691–816

McCarthy, William (1992), (ed.), *Legal Intervention in Industrial Relations: Gains and Losses* (Oxford: Blackwell)

McColgan, Aileen (2000), 'Missing the Point? The Part-time Workers (Prevention of Less Favourable Treatment) Regulations 2000 (SI 2000, No 1551)' 29:3 *Industrial Law Journal*, 260–7

——(2003), 'The Fixed-Term Employees (Prevention of Less Favourable Treatment) Regulations 2002: Fiddling While Rome Burns?' (2003) 32:3 *Industrial Law Journal*, 194–9

McKay, Sonia (2001), 'Annual Review Article 2000—Between Flexibility and Regulation: Rights, Equality and Protection at Work' 39:2 *British Journal of Industrial Relations*, 285–303

McKinnon, Ronald (2000), 'Mundell, the Euro, and Optimum Currency Areas', Stanford University Working Papers in Economics No 009

Magnusson, Lars and Stråth, Bo (2001a), 'Introduction' in Magnusson and Stråth (eds.) *From the Werner Plan to the EMU: In Search of a Political Economy for Europe* (Brussels: PIE–Peter Lang)

—— (2001b), (eds), *From the Werner Plan to the EMU: In Search of a Political Economy for Europe* (Brussels: PIE–Peter Lang)

Maher, Imelda (2000), 'Juridification, Codification and Sanction in UK Competition Law' 63:4 *Modern Law Review*, 544–69

Majone, Giandomenico (1996), *Regulating Europe* (London: Routledge)

Marks, Gary, Fritz W. Scharpf, Philippe C. Schmitter and Wolfgang Streeck (1996), (eds.), *Governance in the European Union* (London: Sage)

Marsden, David (1995), 'Deregulation or Cooperation? The Future of Europe's Labour Markets?' *Labour: Review of Labour Economics and Industrial Relations*, 68–91

Marsden, David and Hugh Stephenson (2001), (eds.), *Labour Law and Social Insurance in the New Economy: A Debate on the Supiot Report* (London: Centre for Economic Performance, LSE)

Martin, David (1996), '1996 And All That' unpublished paper on file with the author (Strasbourg)

Michie, Jonathan and John Grieve Smith (1994), (eds.) *Unemployment in Europe* (London: Academic Press)

Miles, Thomas J. (2000), 'Common Law Exceptions to Employment at Will and US Labor Markets' 16:1 *Journal of Law, Economics and Organization*, 74–101

Milner, Susan (1998), 'Training Policy: Steering Between Divergent National Logics', in Hine and Kassim (eds.), *Beyond the Market: The EU and National Social Policy* (London: Routledge)

Ministry of Industry, Employment and Communications/Ministry of Health and Social Affairs, Sweden (2001), *A Europe for Full Employment and Social Cohesion: Swedish Presidency Priorities* (Stockholm: Ministry of Industry)

Mishel, Lawrence, Jared Bernstein and Sylvia Allegretto (2005), *The State of Working America* (Ithaca, NY: Economic Policy Institute/Cornell University Press)

More, Gillian (1999), 'The Principle of Equal Treatment: From Market Unifier to Fundamental Right?' in Craig and de Búrca (eds.), *The Evolution of EU Law* (Oxford: OUP)

Mosher, Jim (2000), 'Open Method of Coordination: Functional and Political Origins', 13:3 *European Community Studies Association Review*, 2–7

Mosley, Hugh and Antje Mayer (1999), 'Benchmarking National Labour Market Performance: A Radar Chart Approach' Wißenschaftszentrum Berlin Working Paper FS I 99–202

Mückenberger, Ulrich and Simon Deakin (1989), 'From Deregulation to a European Floor of Rights: Labour Law, Flexibilisation and the European Single Market' 3 *Zeitschrift für ausländisches und internationales Arbeits- und Sozialrecht*, 153–207

Muhl, Charles J. (2001), 'The Employment-at-Will Doctrine: Three Major Exceptions', 124:1 *Monthly Labor Review*, 3–11

Munchau, Wolfgang (2005), 'Europe's missed chances', *Financial Times*, 27 March 2005

—— (2005), 'EU's misjudged No votes', *Financial Times*, 5 June 2005

Mundell, R. A. (1961), 'A Theory of Optimum Currency Areas', 51 *American Economic Review*, 657–67

Natali, David and Martin Rhodes (2004), 'Trade-offs and Veto Players: Reforming Pensions in France and Italy' 2:1 *French Politics*, 1–23

Neumark, David and William L. Wascher (2004), 'Minimum Wages, Labor Market Institutions, and Youth Employment: A Cross-National Analysis' 57 *Industrial and Labor Relations Review*, 223–48

Ng, Gek-Boo (1999), 'Foreword' in Bertola, Boen and Cazes, *Employment Protection and Labour Market Adjustment in OECD Countries: Evolving Institutions and Variable Enforcement*, ILO, Employment and Training Papers No 48, 1999

Nickell, Stephen (1997), 'Unemployment and Labor Market Rigidities: Europe versus North America' 11:3 *Journal of Economic Perspectives*, 55–74

Nickell, Stephen and Richard Layard (1998), 'Labour Market Institutions and Economic Performance', Centre for Economic Performance, London School of Economics, Discussion Paper No 407

Nickell, Steve and Jan van Ours, (2000), 'The Netherlands and the United Kingdom: A European Employment Miracle?' 30 *Economic Policy*, 136–180

Norman, Peter (2002), 'EU leaders take positive view of talks outcome', *Financial Times*, 18 March 2002

Notermans, Ton (2001), 'The Werner Plan as a Blueprint for EMU?' in Magnusson and Stråth (eds.), *From the Werner Plan to the EMU: In Search of a Political Economy for Europe* (Brussels: PIE–Peter Lang) 336–7.

Nunziata, Luca (2003), 'Labour market institutions and the cyclical dynamics of employment' 10:1 *Labour Economics*, 31–53

Organisation for Economic Cooperation and Development (1986), *Labour Market Flexibility: Report of A High-Level Group of Experts to the Secretary-General* (Paris: OECD)

—— (1994a), *The OECD Jobs Study: Facts, Analysis, Strategies* (Paris: OECD)

—— (1994b), *The OECD Jobs Study: Evidence and Explanations* (Paris: OECD)

—— (1995), *The OECD Jobs Study: Implementing the Strategy* (Paris: OECD)

—— (1996a), *Pushing Ahead with the Strategy* (Paris: OECD)

—— (1996b), *OECD Employment Outlook* 1996 (Paris: OECD)

—— (1997), *Implementing the OECD Jobs Strategy: Lessons from Member Countries' Experience* (Paris: OECD)

—— (1998a), 'Key Employment Policy Challenges Faced By OECD Countries', Labour Market and Social Policy Occasional Papers No 31, OECD Submission to the G8 Growth, Employability and Inclusion Conference, London, 21–22 February 1998 (Paris: OECD)

—— (1998b), *OECD Employment Outlook, June 1998* (Paris: OECD)

—— (1999a), *OECD Employment Outlook, June 1999* (Paris: OECD)

—— (1999b), 'OECD Employment Outlook, News Release', 15 June 1999 (Paris: OECD)

—— (1999c), *Implementing the OECD Jobs Strategy: Assessing Performance and Policy* (Paris: OECD)

Organisation for Economic Cooperation and Development (1999d), 'OECD's View on Employment Protection Legislation' *OECD News Release*, 13 July 1999 (Paris: OECD)
—— (2000), *OECD Employment Outlook, June 2000* (Paris: OECD)
—— (2001a), *OECD Employment Outlook, June 2001* (Paris: OECD)
—— (2001b), *Quarterly Labour Force Statistics, 2001/1* (Paris: OECD)
—— (2002), 'Standardised Unemployment Rates, 5 April 2002' (Paris: OECD)
—— (2003a), *OECD Employment Outlook 2003: Towards More and Better Jobs* (Paris: OECD)
—— (2003b), Meeting of Employment and Labour Ministers, Paris 29–30 September 2003, *Communiqué: Towards More and Better Jobs* (Paris: OECD)
—— (2003c), *Policy Brief, Peer review: a tool for co-operation and change*, December 2003 (Paris: OECD)
—— (2003d), *OECD Economic Outlook No 73, June 2003*, Statistical Annex (Paris: OECD)
—— (2003e), Spotlight on Employment, in *OECD Observer* No 239, September 2003
—— (2003f), *OECD Observe* Nos 240/241, December 2003 (Paris: OECD)
—— (2004a), *OECD Employment Outlook 2004* (Paris: OECD)
—— (2004b), *Policy Brief—Employment Protection: The Costs and Benefits of Greater Job Security*, September 2004 (Paris: OECD)
—— (2004c), *Quarterly Labour Force Statistics, 2004/4* (Paris: OECD)
——(2003d), *OECD Economic Outlook No 75, June 2004,* Statistical Annex (Paris: OECD)
—— (2005), *OECD Main Economic Indicators, April 2004* (Paris: OECD)
Ogus, Anthony I. and Cento G. Veljanovski (1984) (eds.), *Readings in the Economics of Law and Regulation* (Oxford: Clarendon Press)
Ó Móráin, Seamus (2000), 'The European Employment Strategy: A Consideration of Social Partnership and Related Matters in the Irish Context' 16:1 *International Journal of Comparative Labour Law and Industrial Relations*, 85–101
O'Keefe, David (1996), 'The Uneasy Progress of European Social Policy' 2:2 *Columbia Journal of European Law*, 241–64
O'Keefe, David and Patrick Twomey (1999) (eds.), *Legal Issues of the Amsterdam Treaty* (Oxford: Hart Publishing)
Pagani, Fabrizio (2002), 'Peer review: A tool for global co-operation and change' *OECD Observer* No 235, December (Paris: OECD)
Parisi, Francesco (2000a), 'Introduction: The Legacy of Richard A. Posner and the Methodology of Law and Economics' in Parisi (ed.), *The Economic Structure of the Law: The Collected Economic Essays of Richard A. Posner* (Cheltenham: Edward Elgar)
—— (2000b), (ed.), *The Economic Structure of the Law: The Collected Economic Essays of Richard A. Posner* (Cheltenham: Edward Elgar)
Parsons, Talcott (1951), *The Social System* (Glencoe: Free Press)
Paul, Joel R. (1994/1995), 'Free Trade, Regulatory Competition and the Autonomous Market Fallacy' 1:1 *Columbia Journal of European Law* 29–62
Peck, Jamie and Nikolas Theodore (2000), 'Beyond "Employability"', 24 *Cambridge Journal of Economics*, 729–49
Peretto, Pietro F (1998), 'Market Power, Growth and Unemployment' Duke University, Economics Working Paper No 98–16
Peters, Torsten (1995), 'European Monetary Union and Labour Markets: What to Expect?' 134:3 *International Labour Review*, 315–32

Pettit, Pascal (1999), 'Sectoral Patterns of Distribution in Slowly Growing Economies: The Case of Nine OECD Countries in the 1980s and 1990s' 13:3 *International Review of Applied Economics*, 333–51

Philpott, John (1999), 'Behind the Buzzword: "Employability"' *Employment Policy Institute Economic Report*, Vol 12, No 10

Pierson Christopher, Anthony Forster, and Erik Jones (1998), 'The Politics of Europe: (Un)employment Ambivalence' in Towers and Terry (eds.), 30:4 *Industrial Relations Journal, European Annual Review 1998*, 277–90

Pigou, A. C. (1932), *The Economics of Welfare* (London: Macmillan)

Pissarides, Christopher A. (1999), 'Policy Influences on Unemployment: The European Experience' 46:4 *Scottish Journal of Political Economy*, 389–418

Pitelis, Christos (1993), (ed.), *Transaction Costs, Markets and Hierarchies* (Oxford: Blackwell)

Plant, Raymond (1998), 'The Third Way', Friedrich-Ebert-Stiftung, Working Papers 5/98

Pochet Philippe (1999), 'The New Employment Chapter of the Amsterdam Treaty' 9:3 *Journal of European Social Policy*, 271–78

Poiares Maduro, Miguel (2001), 'Never on a Sunday–What Has (EU) Law Got to do With It?' in Sciarra (ed.), *Labour Law in the Courts: National Judges and the European Court Justice* (Oxford: Hart Publishing)

Polanyi, Karl (1944), *The Great Transformation* (Boston: Beacon Press)

Posner, Richard (1973), *Economic Analysis of Law* (Boston: Little, Brown & Co)

—— (1980), 'The Value of Wealth: A Comment on Dworkin and Kronman' 9:2 *Journal of Legal Studies*, 243–52

——(1984), 'Some Economics of Labor Law' 51 *University of Chicago Law Review*, 988–1011

——(1990), 'Law and Economics *is* Moral' 24:2 *Valparaiso University Law Review*. 163–73

—— (1992), *Economic Analysis of Law*, 4th edn. (Boston: Little, Brown & Co)

——(1993), 'Ronald Coase and Methodology' 7:4 *Journal of Economic Perspectives*, 195–210

Purdy, David (2001a), 'Economic Theory and Policy from the Keynesian Revolution to the Third Way' in Magnusson and Stråth (eds.), *From the Werner Plan to the EMU: In Search of a Political Economy for Europe* (Brussels: PIE–Peter Lang).

—— (2001b), 'Welfare Reform, Social Citizenship and European Integration' in Magnusson and Stråth (eds.), *From the Werner Plan to the EMU: In Search of a Political Economy for Europe* (Brussels: PIE–Peter Lang).

Quack, Sigrid and Glenn Morgan (2000), 'National Capitalisms, Global Competition and Economic Performance' in Quack, Morgan and Whitley (eds.), *National Capitalisms, Global Competition and Economic Performance* (Amsterdam: John Benjamins Publishing)

Quack, Sigrid, Glenn Morgan and Richard Whitley (2000), (eds.), *National Capitalisms, Global Competition and Economic Performance* (Amsterdam: John Benjamins Publishing)

Radaelli, Claudio (2000), 'Discourse and Institutional Change: The Case of Italy in the Euro-Zone', Queen's Papers on Europeanisation, No 5/2000, Queen's University Belfast

Raphael, Steven (2004), 'The Socioeconomic Status of Black Males: The Increasing Importance of Incarceration' unpublished paper (Berkeley, CA) available at: *http://ist-socrates.berkeley.edu/~raphael/* [accessed on 10 April 2005].

Regini, Marino (1999a), 'Between Deregulation and Social Pacts: The Responses of European Economies to Globalization' Centro Estudios Avanzados en Ciencias Sociales, Estudio/Working Paper 1999/133, March 1999

——(1999b), 'The Dilemmas of Labour Market Regulation' in Esping-Andersen and Regini (eds.), *Why Deregulate Labour Markets*, (Oxford: OUP).

Rhodes, Martin (2000), 'Lisbon: Europe's "Maastricht for Welfare"?' 13:3 *European Community Studies Association Review*, 2–7

Ricci, Giancarlo (2001), 'BECTU—An Unlimited Right to Annual Paid Leave' 30:4 *Industrial Law Journal*, 401–8

Richardson, Keith (2000), 'Big Business and the European Agenda', Sussex European Institute, SEI Working Paper, No 35

Robinson, Peter (2000), 'Active Labour-Market Policies: A Case of Evidence-Based Policy Making?' 16:1 *Oxford Review of Economic Policy*, 13–26

Rogers, Joel (1990), 'Divide and Conquer: Further Reflections on the Distinctive Character of American Labor Laws' 13 *Wisconsin Law Review*, 1–147

——(1993), 'Reforming US Labor Relations' 69 *Chicago-Kent Law Review*, 97–127

Ross, George (1998), 'French Social Democracy and the EMU' ARENA (Advanced Research on the Europeanisation of the Nation-State) University of Oslo, Working Papers, WP 98/19

——(2000), 'Labor Versus Globalization' 570:1 *Annals (The Annals of the American Academy of Political and Social Science)*, 78–91

Ross, Malcolm (2000), 'State Aids and National Courts: Definitions and Other Problems—A Case of Premature Emancipation?' 37 *Common Market Law Review*, 401–23

Royal Commission on Trade Unions and Employers' Associations (1965–8), Cmnd. 3623 (London: HMSO)

Sabel, Charles, and Joshua Cohen (2003), 'Sovereignty and Solidarity in the EU' in Zeitlin and Trubek (eds.), *Governing Work and Welfare in a New Economy: European and American Experiments* (Oxford: OUP)

Saint-Paul, Gilles (1997a), 'High Unemployment from a Political Economy Perspective' in Snower and de la Dehesa (eds.), *Unemployment Policy: Government Options for the Labour Market* (Cambridge: CUP).

——(1997b), 'Labour Rigidities and the Performance of the French Economy' in Siebert (ed.), *Structural Change and Labor Market Flexibility: Experience in Selected OECD Countries* (Tübingen: Institute für Weltwirtschaft an der Universität Kiel/Mohr/Paul Siebeck)

——(1998), 'Assessing he Political Viability of Labor Market Reform: The Case of Employment Protection' Universitat Pompeu Fabra Economics WP No 346

——(2004), 'Why are European Countries Diverging in their Unemployment Experience?' 18:4 *Journal of Economic Perspectives*, 49–68

Salais, Robert (2001), 'Filling the Gap Between Macroeconomic Policy and Situated Approaches to Employment. A Hidden Agenda for Europe?' in Magnusson and Stråth (eds.), *From the Werner Plan to EMU: In Search of a Political Economy for Europe* (Brussels: PIE–Peter Lang)

Salinas de Gortari, Carlos and Roberto Manabeira Unger (1999), 'The Market Turn Without Neoliberalism' *Challenge: The Magazine of Economic Affairs*, January/February

Sally, Razeen (1998), *Classical Liberalism and International Economic Order: Studies in Theory and Intellectual History* (London: Routledge)

Samuels, Warren J. (1994), 'Smith, Adam' in Hodgson, Samuels and Tool (eds.), *The Elgar Companian to Institutional and Evolutionary Economics: L–Z* (Aloleshot: Edward Elgar)

——(1994), 'Law and Economics' in Hodgson *et al.*, *The Elgar Companion to Institutional and Evolutionary Economics, L–Z* (Aldershot: Edward Elgar).

Sarfati, Hedva (1998), 'Negotiating Trade-offs Between Jobs and Labour Market Flexibility in the European Union' 14:4 *The International Journal of Comparative Labour Law and Industrial Relations*, 307–24

——(1999), 'Labour Market Flexibility vs. Jobs: A Challenge for Social Dialogue in Europe', IAE de Paris, Université Paris 1, Panthéon-Sorbonne, GREGOR Working Paper 1999–07

Sauter, Wolf (1998), 'The Economic Constitution of the European Union' 4 *Columbia Journal of European Law*, 27–68

Scharpf, Fritz W. (1996), 'Negative and Positive Integration in the Political Economy of European Welfare States' in Marks, Scharpf, Schmitter and Streeck (eds.), *Governance in the European Union* (London: Sage)

——(1997), 'Combating Unemployment in Continental Europe: Policy Options Under Internationalization' European University Institute Robert Schumann Centre Policy Papers, RSC No 97/3

——(1997), 'Balancing Positive and Negative Integration: The Regulatory Options for Europe' EUI/RSC Policy Papers, RSC No 97/4

——(1999), *Governing in Europe: Effective and Democratic?* (Oxford: OUP)

——(2001), European Governance: Common Concerns vs the Challenge of Diversity' Jean Monnet Working Paper No 6/01, New York University Law School, Symposium: Responses to the European Commission's White Paper on Governance

Scheurman, William (1999), 'Free Market Anti-Formalism: The Case of Richard Posner' 12:1 *Ratio Juris*, 80–95

Schmid, Günther (1997), 'The Dutch Employment Miracle? A Comparison of Employment Systems in the Netherlands and Germany', Wißenschaftszentrum Berlin, Discussion Paper FS 1 97–202

Schmitt John, Lawrence Mishel and Jared Bernstein (1998), 'Dangers for European Workers in the US Economic Model' *WorkingUSA*, May/June 1998, 73–85

Schmitter, Philippe C. and Michael W. Bauer (2001), 'A (modest) proposal for expanding social citizenship in the European Union' 11:1 *Journal of European Social Policy*, 55–65

Schömann Klaus, Ralf Rogowski and Thomas Kruppe (1998), *Labour Market Efficiency in the European Union: Employment Protection and Fixed-Term Contracts* (London/ New York: Routledge)

Schotter, Andrew (1985), *Free Market Economics: A Critical Appraisal* (New York: St Martin's Press)

Schütz, Holger, Stefan Speckesser and Günther Schmid (1998), 'Benchmarking Labour Market Performance and Labour Market Policies: Theoretical Foundations and Applications' Wißenschaftszentrum Berlin Working Paper FS I 98–205

Schwab, Stewart J. (1987), 'Collective Bargaining and the Coase Theorem' 72 *Cornell Law Review*, 245–87

Sciarra, Silvana (1999), 'The Employment Title in the Amsterdam Treaty: A Multi-Language Legal Discourse' in O'Keefe and Twomey (eds.), *Legal Issues of the Amsterdam Treaty* (Oxford: Hart Publishing) 157–70

——(2000), 'Integration Through Coordination: The Employment Title in the Amsterdam Treaty' 6:2 *Columbia Journal of European Law*, 209–29

——(2001a), (ed.), *Labour Law in the Courts: National Judges and the European Court of Justice* (Oxford: Hart Publishing)

——(2001b), '*Job Centre*: An Illustrative Example of Strategic Litigation' in Sciarra (ed.), *Labour Law in the Courts: National Judges and the European Court of Justice* (Oxford: Hart Publishing)

——(2002), 'Market Freedom and Fundamental Social Rights' in Hepple (ed.), *Social and Labour Rights in a Global Context: International and Comparative Perspectives* (Cambridge: CUP)

Sciarra, Silvana, Paul Davies and Mark Freedland (2004), (eds.), *Employment Policy and the Regulation of Part-Time Work in the European Union: A Comparative Analysis* (Cambridge: CUP)

Scott, Joanne (1998), 'Law, Legitimacy and EC Governance: Prospects for "Partnership"' 36:2 *Journal of Common Market Studies*, 175–94

——(1999), 'Regional Policy: An Evolutionary Perspective' in Craig and de Búrca (eds.), *The Evolution of EU Law* (Oxford: OUP)

Scott, Joanne and David M. Trubek (2002), 'Mind the Gap: Law and New Approaches to Governance in the European Union', 8:1 *European Law Journal*, 1–18

Shaw, Jo (1997), 'Socio-Legal Studies and the European Union' in Thomas (ed.), *Socio-Legal Studies* (Aldershot: Dartmouth)

——(2000), (ed.), *Social Law and Policy in an Evolving European Union* (Oxford: Hart Publishing)

Siebert Horst (1997a), 'Labor Market Rigidities: At the Root of Unemployment in Europe' 11:3 *Journal of Economic Perspectives*, 37–54

——(1997b), (ed.), *Structural Change and Labor Market Flexibility: Experience in Selected OECD Countries*, Institut für Weltwirtschaft an der Universität Kiel (Tübingen: Mohr/Paul Siebeck)

——(1999), 'How Can Europe Solve Its Unemployment Problem?' Kiel Discussion Paper No 342, Kiel: Institute for World Economics

Sengenberger, Werner (1992), 'Future Prospects for the European Labour Market: Visions and Nightmares' in Castro, Méhaut and Rubery (eds.) *International Integration and Labour Market Organisation* (London: Academic Press)

Simitis, Spiros (1987), 'Juridification of Labor Relations' in Teubner (ed.) *Juridification of Social Spheres* (Berlin: Waltes de Gruyter)

Simon, Herbert (1957), *Models of Man* (New York: John Wiley & Sons)

Simonazzi, Annamaria (2002), 'Innovation and growth: supply and demand factors in the US expansion' Università degli Studi di Roma 'La Sapienza' Dipartimento di Economia Pubblica, Working Paper No. 53

Simonazzi, Annamaria and Paola Villa (1999), 'Flexibility and Growth' 13:3 *International Review of Applied Economics*, 281–313

Simpson, A. W. Brian (1996), 'Coase v. Pigou Reexamined' 25 *Journal of Legal Studies*, 53–97

Sisson, Keith, James Arrowsmith and Paul Marginson (2003), 'All benchmarkers now? Benchmarking and the "Europeanisation" of industrial relations' 34:1 *Industrial Relations Journal*, 5–31

Sisson, Keith and Paul Marginson (2000), 'Co-ordinated Bargaining: A Process for our Times?', ESRC *One Europe or Several*? Programme Working Paper 14/00

——(2001a), 'Benchmarking and the "Europeanisation" of Social and Employment Policy', ESRC *One Europe or Several*? Programme, Briefing Note 3/01, April 2001

——(2001b), '"Soft Regulation"–Travesty of the Real Thing or New Dimension?', ESRC *One Europe or Several*? Programme Working Paper 32/01

Smismans, Stijn (2005), 'Reflexive Law in Support of Directly Deliberative Polyarchy: Reflexive-Deliberative Polyarchy as a Normative Frame for the OMC' in de Schutter and Deakin (eds.), *Social Rights and Maket Forces: Is the Open Coordination of Employment and Social Policies the Future of Social Europe?* (Brussels: Bruylant)

Smith, Andrew (1998), 'New Figures Reveal that New Deal is Tough on Shirkers', Press Notice 1998/0513 (previously 513/98) 4 November 1998

Smith, David (2005), 'Sad to say, Europe's big boys are stuck in the mire', *The Sunday Times: Economic Outlook*, 27 March 2005

Smith, Rodney (2000), 'Full employment for Europe', *BBC News Online: Business*, Friday, 11 February 2000

Snower, Dennis J. (1997), 'Evaluating Unemployment Policies: What do the underlying Theories Tell Us"', in J. Snower and de la Dehesa (eds.), *Unemployment Policy: Government Options for the Labour Market* (Cambridge: CUP)

Snower, Dennis J. and de la Dehesa, Guillermo (1997a) (eds.), *Unemployment Policy: Government Options for the Labour Market* (Cambridge: CUP)

——(1997b), 'Preface' in Snower and de la Dehesa (eds.) *Unemployment Policy: Government Options for the Labour Market* (Cambridge: CUP)

Snyder, Francis (1993), 'Soft Law and Institutional Practice in the European Community', European University Institute, Working Papers in Law No 93/5

——(1999), 'EMU Revisited: Are We Making a Constitution? What Constitution Are We Making?' in Craig and de Búrca (eds.), *The Evolution of EU Law* (Oxford: OUP)

Solow, Robert M. (1998), 'What is Labour-Market Flexibility? What is it Good For?' (Keynes Lecture in Economics) 97 *Proceedings of the British Academy*, 189–211

Soltwedel Rüdiger, Dirk Dohse, and Christiane Krieger-Boden (1999), 'EMU Challenges European Labor Markets' IMF Working Paper WP/99/131

Sorrentino, Constance (2000), 'International Unemployment Rates: How Comparable Are They?' 123:6 *Monthly Labour Review*, 3–20

Sorrentino, Constance and Joyanna Moy (2002), 'US Labor Market Performance in International Perspective' *Monthly Labor Review*, 15–35

Soskice, David (1990), 'Wage Determination: The Changing Role of Institutions in Advanced Industrialized Countries' 6 *Oxford Review of Economic Policy*, 31–61

Spineux, Armand, Bernard Francq, Evelyne Leonard, Philippe Barre, Xavier Leloup, Pierre Walthery and Marie Gilot (1999), *Comparative Analysis: Developments in Social Concertation and Collective Bargaining on Employment and the Labour Market in Europe* (Louvain: Université Catholique de Louvain, Institut des Science du Travail)

Spithoven, A. H. G. M. (2002), 'The Third Way: the Dutch Experience' 31:3 *Economy and Society*, 333–68

Standing, Guy (1993), 'Labor Regulation in an Era of Fragmented Flexibility' in Büchtemann (ed.), *Employment Security and Labor Market Behavior: Interdisciplinary Approaches and International Evidence* (Ithaca, NY: ILR Press)

——(1997), 'Globalization, Labour Flexibility and Insecurity: The Era of Market Regulation' 3:1 *European Journal of Industrial Relations*, 7–37

Stigler, George J. (1964), 'The Economist and the State' Presidential Address delivered at the Seventy-Seventh Annual Meeting of the American Economic Association, Chicago, 29 December 1964; reprinted in George J. Stigler, *The Citizen and the State: Essays on Regulation* (Chicago: University of Chicago Press, 1975)

——(1966), *The Theory of Price*, 3rd edition (New York: Macmillan)

Stråth, Bo (2000a), 'After Full Employment and the Breakdown of Conventions of Social Responsibility' in Stråth (ed.), *After Full Employment: European Discourses on Work and Flexibility* (Brussels: PIE–Peter Lang)

——(2000b), 'The Concept of Work in the Construction of Community' in Stråth (ed.), *After Full Employment: European Discourses on Work and Flexibility* (Brussels: PIE–Peter Lang)

——(2000c), (ed.), *After Full Employment: European Discourses on Work and Flexibility* (Brussels: PIE–Peter Lang)

Streeck, Wolfgang (1994), 'European Social Policy after Maastricht: The "Social Dialogue" and "Subsidiarity"' 15:1 *Economic and Industrial Democracy*, 151–77

——(1995) 'Neo-Voluntarism: A New European Social Policy Regime?' 1:1 *European Law Journal*, 31–59

——(1995), 'From Market-Making to State-Building? Some Reflections on the Political Economy of European Social Policy', in Leibfried and Pierson (eds.), *European Social Policy: Between Fragmentation and Integration* (Washington DC: The Brookings Institute)

——(1996), 'Public Power Beyond the Nation-State: The Case of the European Community' in Boyer and Drache (eds.), *States against Markets: The Limits of Globalization* (London: Routledge)

——(1999), 'Competitive Solidarity: Rethinking the "European Social Model"' Max Planck Institute for the Study of Societies (MPIfG) Working Paper 99/8

Summers, Clyde W. (2000), 'Employment At Will in the United States: The Divine Right of Employers' 3 *University of Pennsylvania Journal of Labor & Employment Law*, 65–86

Sun, Jeanne-Mey and Jacques Pelkmans (1995), 'Regulatory Competition in the Single Market' 33:1 *Journal of Common Market Studies*, 67–89

Sunstein, Cass R. (1984), 'Rights, Minimal Terms and Solidarity: A Comment' 51 *University of Chicago Law Review*, 1041–60

Supiot Alain *et al.* (1998), *Transformation of Labour and the Future of Labour Law in Europe*, Final Report of the Expert Group established by the European Commission V/98/776 (Luxembourg: OOPEC)

Supiot, Alain (with Pamela Meadows) (2001), *Beyond Employment: Changes in Work and the Future of Labour Law in Europe* (Oxford: OUP)

Swedish Ministry of Industry, Employment and Communications/Ministry of Health and Social Affairs (2001), *A Europe for Full Employment and Social Cohesion: Swedish Presidency Priorities* (Stockholm: Ministry of Industry)

Swygert, Michael and Katherine Earle Yanes (1998), 'A Primer on the Coase Theorem: Making Law in a World of Zero Transaction Costs' 11 *DePaul Business Law Journal*, 1–42

Symes, Valerie (1995), *Unemployment in Europe: Problems and Policies* (London: Routledge)

——(1998), *Unemployment and Employment Policies in the EU* (London: Kogan Page)

Syrpis, Phil (2001), 'Smoke Without Fire: The Social Policy Agenda and the Internal Market', 30:3 *Industrial Law Journal*, 271–88

Szyszczak, Erika (1995), 'Future Directions in European Union Social Policy Law' 24:1 *Industrial Law Journal*, 19–32

——(2000), 'The Evolving European Employment Strategy' in Shaw (ed.), *Social Law and Policy in an Evolving European Union* (Oxford: Hart Publishing)

——(2001), 'The New Paradigm for Social Policy: A Virtuous Circle?' 38 *Common Market Law Review*, 1125–70

Talley, Eric (1997), 'Interdisciplinary Gap Filling: Game Theory and the Law' 22 *Law and Social Inquiry* 1055–86

Tanzi, Vito (2000), 'Globalization and the Future of Social Protection' IMF Working Paper WP/00/12, Washington DC

Teague, Paul (1998), 'Monetary Union and Social Europe' 8:2 *Journal of European Social Policy*, 117–38

——(1999a), 'Reshaping Employment Regimes in Europe: Policy Shifts Alongside Boundary Change' 19:1 *Journal of Public Policy*, 33–62

——(1999b), *Economic Citizenship in the European Union: Employment Relations in the New Europe* (London: Routledge)

——(2000), 'Macroeconomic Constraints, Social Learning and Pay Bargaining in Europe' 38:3 *British Journal of Industrial Relations*, 429–52

——(2001), 'Deliberative Governance and EU Social Policy', 7:1 *European Journal of Industrial Relations*, 7–26

Teague, Paul and John Grahl (1998), 'Institutions and Labour Market Performance in Western Europe' 46:1 *Political Studies*, 1–18

Terry, Michael and Brian Towers (2000), 'Editorial: Developing Social Policy in the EU: Prospects and Obstacles' 31:4 *Industrial Relations Journal*, 242–6

Teubner, Gunther (1983), 'Substantive and Reflexive Elements in Modern Law' 17:2 *Law and Society Review*, 239–85

——(1987a), (ed.), *Juridification of Social Spheres: A Comparative Analysis in the Areas of Labor, Corporate, Antitrust and Social Welfare Law* (Berlin/New York: Walter de Gruyter)

——(1987b), 'Juridification: Concepts, Aspects, Limits, Solutions' in Teubner (ed.), *Juridification of Social Spheres: A Comparative Analysis in the Areas of Labor, Corporate, Antitrust and Social Welfare Law* (Berlin/New York: Walter de Gruyter)

——(1993), *Law as an Autopoietic System* (Oxford: Blackwell)

Thomas, Philip A. (1996), (ed.), *Legal Frontiers* (Aldershot: Dartmouth)

——(1997), (ed.), *Socio-Legal Studies* (Aldershot: Dartmouth)

Tilly, Chris (1997), 'Arresting the Decline of Good Jobs in the USA?' 28:4 *Industrial Relations Journal*, 269–74

Towers, Brian (1993), 'Employee Protection Policy, the Labor Market, and Employment: The UK Experience' in Büchtemann (ed.), *Employment Security and Labor Market Behavior: Interdisciplinary Approaches and International Evidence* (Ithaca, NY: ILR Press)

Towers, Brian and Michael Terry (1999), 'Editorial: Unemployment and Social Dialogue' 30:4 *Industrial Relations Journal: European Annual Review 1998*, 272–6

Trade Union Advisory Committee to the OECD (TUAC) (2004), *OECD Employment Outlook July 2004: TUAC Evaluation* (Paris: TUAC–OECD)

Tran, Mark (2005), 'EU scales down economic ambitions', *The Guardian*, 2 February 2005

Traxler, Franz (1995), 'Farewell to Labour Market Associations? Organized versus Disorganized Decentralization as a Map for Industrial Relations', in Crouch and Traxler (eds.), *Organized Industrial Relations in Europe: What Future?* (Aldershot: Avebury)

——(2003), 'Bargaining (De)centralization, Macroeconomic Performance and Control over the Employment Relationship', 41:1 *British Journal of Industrial Relations*, 1–27

Tronti, Leonello (1999), 'Benchmarking Employment Performance and Labour Market Policies: The Results of the Research Project' 4 *Transfer: European Review of Labour and Research*, 542–62

Trubek, David M. and James S. Mosher (2003), 'Alternative Approaches to Governance in the EU: EU Social Policy and the European Employment Strategy' 41:1 *Journal of Common Market Studies*, 63–88

Tucker, Clive (2000), 'The Luxembourg Process: The UK View' 16:1 *International Journal of Comparative Labour Law and Industrial Relations*, 71–83

UNICE (Union des Industries de la Communauté européenne) (2000), Press Release, 24 March 2000 (Brussels: UNICE)

——(2002), *European Business says: Barcelona Must Revitalise the Lisbon Process* (Brussels: UNICE)

US Department of Labor, Bureau of Labor Statistics (2005a), *Labor Force Statistics from the Current Population Survey* (Washington DC: BLS)

——(2005b), *News—The Employment Situation: March 2005* (Washington DC: BLS)

Valdés Dal-Ré, Fernando (1996), 'Economic and Social Cohesion and the European Social Fund' in Davies, Lyon-Caen, Sciarra and Simitis (eds.), *European Community Labour Law: Principles and Perspectives. Liber Amicorum Lord Wedderburn* (Oxford: Clarendon Press)

Van den Bergh, Roger (1996), 'The Growth of Law and Economics in Europe' 40:3–5 *European Economic Review*, 969–77

Vandenbroucke, Frank (2002), 'The EU and Social Protection: What Should the European Convention Propose?' Max Planck Institute for the Study of Societies (MPIfG) Working Paper 02/6

van Ours, Jan C. (2003), 'Has the Dutch Miracle Come to an End?' CESifo (Munich Society for the Promotion of Economic Research) Working Paper No 917 Category 4: Labour Markets

Van Reenen, John (2001), 'No More Skivvy Schemes? Active Labour Market Policies and the British New Deal for the Young Unemployed in Context', The Institute for Fiscal Studies, Working Paper 01/09

Viskovatoff, Alex (1999), 'Foundations of Niklas Luhmann's Theory of Social Systems' 29:4 *Philosophy of the Social Sciences*, 481–516

Visser, Jelle (2000a), 'From Keynesianism to the Third Way: Labour Relations and Social Policy in Postwar Western Europe', 21:4 *Economic and Industrial Democracy*, 421–56

—— (2000b), 'The First Part-Time Economy in the World: Does it Work?' Amsterdam Institute for Advanced Labour Studies (AIAS) University of Amsterdam, Working Paper 00–01

Visser, Jelle and Anton Hemerijck (1997), *'A Dutch Miracle': Job Growth, Welfare Reform, and Corporatism in the Netherlands* (Amsterdam: Amsterdam University Press)

Vos, Ellen (1997), 'The Rise of Committees' 3:3 *European Law Journal*, 210–29

Vousden, Stephen (2000), 'Albany, Market Law and Social Exclusion', 29:2 *Industrial Law Journal*, 181–91

Ward, Ian (1998), *An Introduction to Critical Legal Theory* (London: Cavendish Publishing)

Weiss, Manfred (1998), 'The Future Role of the European Union in Social Policy' in Engels and Weiss (eds.), *Labour Law and Industrial Relations at the Turn of the Century: Liber Amicorum in Honor of Roger Blainpain* (The Hague: Kluwer)

Wellens, K. C. and G. M. Borchardt (1989), 'Soft Law in European Community Law' 14 *European Law Review*, 267–321

Wendon, Bryan (1998), 'The Commission as Image-Venue Entrepreneur in EU Social Policy' 5:2 *Journal of European Public Policy*, 339–53

Western, Bruce and Beckett, Katherine (1999), 'How Unregulated is the US Labor Market? The Penal System as a Labor Market Institution' 104:4 *American Journal of Sociology*, 1030–60

Western, Bruce and Josh Guetzkow (2002), 'Punitive Policy and Neoliberalism in the U.S. Labor Market', unpublished paper, prepared for the American Sociological Association, Chicago (Chicago, 2002) available at *http://www.princeton.edu/~western/*

Western, Bruce, Meredith Kleykamp and Jake Rosenfeld (2005), 'Did Falling Wages and Employment Increase U.S. Imprisonment?' Russell Sage Foundation Working Paper Series (New York: RSF)

Wilkinson, Frank (2000), 'Inflation and Employment: Is There a Third Way?' 24 *Cambridge Journal of Economics*, 643–70

Williamson, Oliver E. (1975), *Markets and Hierarchies* (New York: The Free Press)

—— (1983), 'Credible Commitments: Using Hostages to Support Exchange' 73 *American Economic Review*, 519–40

—— (1985), *The Economic Institutions of Capitalism: Firms, Markets and Relational Contracting* (London: Macmillan)

—— (1993), 'Transaction Cost Economics Meets Posnerian Law and Economics' 149:1 *Journal of Institutional and Theoretical Economics*, 99–118

—— (1996), *The Mechanisms of Governance* (Oxford: OUP)

—— (2000), 'The New Institutional Economics: Taking Stock, Looking Ahead' 38 *Journal of Economic Literature*, 595–613

Williamson, Oliver E., Michael L. Wachter and Jeffrey E. Harris (1975), 'Understanding the Employment Relation: The Analysis of Idiosyncratic Exchange' 6:1 *Bell Journal of Economics and Management Science*, 250–78

Wolfson, Michael C. and Brian B. Murphy (1998), 'New Views on Inequality Trends in Canada and the United States' 121:4 *Monthly Labour Review*, 3–23

Wonnell Christopher T. (1998), 'Compulsory Job Security and Unemployment' Social Science Research Network (SSRN) Working Paper Series, May 1998

Wynn, Michael (2000), 'European Social Dialogue: Harmonisation or New Diversity?' in Collins, Davies and Rideout (eds.), *Legal Regulation of the Employment Relation*, W G Hart Legal Workshop Series (London/The Hague: Kluwer)

Zagelmeyer, Stefan (2000), *Innovative Agreements on Employment and Competitiveness in the European Union and Norway*, report compiled for the European Foundation for the Improvement of Living and Working Conditions (Luxembourg: OOPEC)

Zeitlin, Jonathan (2005), 'Introduction: The Open Method of Coordination in Question' in Zeitlin and Pochet with Magnusson (eds.), *The Open Method of Coordination in Action: The European Employment and Social Inclusion Strategies* (Brussels: PIE–Peter Lang)

Zeitlin, Jonathan and Philippe Pochet with Lars Magnusson (eds.) (2005), *The Open Method of Coordination in Action: The European Employment and Social Inclusion Strategies* (Brussels: PIE–Peter Lang)

Zeitlin, Jonathan and David Trubek (eds.), (2003), *Governing Work and Welfare in a New Economy: European and American Experiments* (Oxford: OUP)

# Index